Money

MAGAZINE'S

100 Steps to Wealth

Vol.3

Money

MAGAZINE'S

100 Steps to Wealth

A COMPLETE SYSTEM FOR

ACHIEVING YOUR PERSONAL

FINANCIAL FREEDOM

Published by JMJHI
Libertyville, IL

Under license with **Money**

For Barbara,
Joey, Danny,
Tommy and Genny

PUBLISHED BY
JMJHI
28140 North Bradley Road
Libertyville, IL 60048
under licensing arrangement with
MONEY Magazine
1271 Avenue of the Americas
New York, NY 10020

First Edition
Copyright ©1997

Library of Congress Card Number: In Process
ISBN: 1-890188-00-X
Printed and bound in the United States of America.

Money Magazine's 100 Steps to Wealth and its associated materials were created for educational purposes only. It is not a professional investment service and does not recommend any specific investment, security, instrument or trade. The material in this publication, and in its associated materials, should not be relied upon as the sole basis for any investment decision. Any misinterpretation of the material is not the responsibility of the publisher or of Money.

The individual and corporate tax information in these volumes was written for tax year 1996, that is for individual taxes due April 15, 1997. Although most information in this publication transcends the particulars of any specific tax year, e.g., the fact that the individual exemption may be of a certain value in one year and not the next, the reader should always refer to the most recent allowable numbers found in the IRS publications made available just prior to tax time each year.

Senior Editor: David Nield
Franchise Director: Caryn Feinberg
Franchise Manager: Sharon Madison
Senior Contributor: Larry D. Spears
Contributors: Scott McMurray, Brooke Stoddard, Mike Harris, Richard Sherer, Benjamin Baldwin, Peter Adam, Martin Shenkman, Ronald Creten, Donald Mitchell, Gary Chappell, David Dwek
Design and Layout: Zev Remba, Joe Tarbell & Laurie Painter of Utopia Publishing Group, Washington, DC
Printed by: Malloy Lithographic, Ann Arbor, MI

10 9 8 7 6 5 4 3 2

CONTENTS

VOLUME 1

The 100 Steps...ix

Introduction xiii

Wealth building can be safe, rewarding, and fun ...1-1

The structure of this wealth building program. Determining your goals. The importance of starting as soon as possible. Compounded interest and the Rule of 72. Historic annual returns of various investment options. Available investments by liquidity and risk. Why saving too much can be imprudent when factoring inflation and taxes. Types and sources of risk.

The secret to 'finding' extra money to invest: Controlling cash flow.....................................2-1

Determining your net worth and your spending patterns. Credit card management, insurance premium cuts, home mortgage and tax strategies. Increasing your returns on liquid assets. The basics of the Asset Allocation Framework—how much to allocate to each broad class of investments at different life-stages.

How to invest in bonds: The bond alternative........3-1

Why invest in debt rather than equity? Types of bonds and how to select, buy and sell them. The relationship between bonds and interest rates. Understanding credit ratings. Calculating yields. Reinvestment rates. The secrets of bond investing: callables, retractables and extendibles. Should you buy premium/discount bonds and the exciting $7,000 Eurobond? Keeping commissions under control.

How to invest in mutual funds: Finding the brightest and the best..4-1

Pure vanilla versus more flavorful investments. How to earn the highest returns possible with minimal increased risk. Minimizing transaction costs. Types of investment companies: their asset allocation and diversification. Nominal versus real rates. Tables of alternative safe investments. Beginning an equity mutual fund purchase plan.

Tax-motivated wealth accumulation strategies 5-1

Three tax strategies to use now. Finding deductions and income accumulation vehicles. Tax-deferred plans. Marginal and average tax brackets. Tax savings devices. Finding tax deferred investments. After-tax yields. Tax-sheltered growth tables. Saving $1,000 to $10,000 annually on tax-deferred plans. Strategies for homeowners.

How to use Asset Allocation to create a diversified portfolio: Starting up the pyramid — investment opportunities 6-1

Portfolio construction with safety first. The meaning of a portfolio to include real, financial and intangible assets. Hard worth v. net worth. Expected income streams and future prospects as components of a portfolio. Term structure of interest rates. Comprehensive discussion of Asset Allocation. Gambling, speculating and investing—how to distinguish. Quiz illustrating that you gamble on your financial future without knowing it. Switch fees. Understanding the universe of available investments and assessing their attributes.

How to get more from your bank: Winning the banking game 7-1

How interest rates are determined in the U.S. Understanding banks and how they disguise true yields. How to borrow at the lowest rates; assessing your debt capacity. Selecting the two best and avoiding the two worst sources of money. Reducing credit costs. Tax motivated actions. Credit management and personal lines of credit. Evaluating credit costs including tax effects. Tips to use when preparing loan applications. Consumer protection legislation, debt consolidation, consumer credit, collateral demand loans and installment purchases.

CONTENTS

How to invest in equity funds: The equity fund approach 8-1

How to select profitable equity funds. Types of equity funds: closed-end, open-end, index funds and specialty funds. How to evaluate fund performance. Mutual fund management companies. Timing strategies for mutual funds. Exotic alternatives. Program trading and does it matter? The deep-discount approach to closed-end fund selection.

The profit approach to real estate 9-1

Finding and financing the right property for you using evaluation methods. Understanding the financial calculations of income properties – cap. rate, income statements, depreciation. Cutting the costs of personal and investment ownership financing by thousands. Squeezing profits from your home. Equity appreciation. Chart indicating comparable interest rate and point combinations. Borrowing against equity. What real estate leverage is and calculating its costs. Characteristics of residential, industrial and commercial real estate. Five absolute do's; three absolute do nots.

Dealing with the financial world 10-1

Recognizing and dealing with the industry-wide gray areas. What is negotiable and what is not. The new world of global de-regulation. What you wanted to know about dealing with brokers but didn't know who to ask. Pitfalls, barriers and transaction costs of the different markets from pork bellies to blue-chips. Principles of transaction costs. Principles of domestic and foreign investment protection. Where and how to seek arbitration.

How to invest in preferred shares: Shifting risk/reward—preferreds and convertibles............11-1

The special feature approach to buying preferreds: retractable, non-callable, cumulative. How corporate treasurers decide between issuing equity or debt and how their markets work. Legal distinctions to the investor. Preferred share features and preferred share selection techniques. Calculating yields, evaluating special features, credit ratings and why floating rates could be ideal.

Glossary G-1
Index I-1

VOLUME 2

Climbing the pyramid: finding the uncommon common share 12-1

How to select common shares using the best selection techniques. The whys and wherefors of fundamental analysis. Economic and industry analysis. Financial statement analysis. Top-down versus bottom-up approaches. Sector investments and defensive stocks. Asset allocation implications. Do dividends matter? Does beta matter? Selecting your stock broker and how to work with him or her. Discount versus full service brokers.

Looking through the clouds: how to pick stocks like a professional................................13-1

Finding undervalued securities. Growth stocks and valuation models. Dividend discount, multi-growth models, the contrarian approach, and value versus growth stocks. Assessing technological developments. Market indexes and sub indexes. How to find small capitalization companies with exciting potential.

Timing your trades 14-1

Does timing really work? How to implement a timing strategy should you so choose. Dow Theory and technical indicators including odd lot indexes, confidence indexes, short ratios, random walks and anomalies. Filters, trading orders, and how short selling works. When to enter and when to sell.

International investing 15-1

Portfolio theory and diversification in action: how to diversify internationally. How foreign markets work. Do different markets move together? Why barriers to investment are actually a boon. How to find global hot spots. Comparative markets and bourses. Bubbles, cascades, and melt-downs. Depository receipts, closed-end funds, emerging market funds.

CONTENTS

High-yield mortgage investment strategies 16-1

The FAIT-way to success: frequency, amortization, interest rate, and term mortgage selection strategies. How to find high quality mortgage investment instruments. Some mortgage "legalese". Are deep discount mortgages for you? Mortgage investment funds and investment company fees. Loads and trailers—do they matter? Mortgage-backed securities: GNMA's and others.

Work, employment and investment.........................17-1

Company pension and employee benefit plans: money purchase, defined benefit and others. The relationship between income and your investments. Naive versus efficient diversification. Extending diversification to include portfolio and job correlation.

Entrepreneurism: for those who already are, and for the 'wannabes' 18-1

The assumption of success. Analyzing and identifying a business opportunity in detail. Finding diamonds in your own backyard. Market research on a budget, for as little as $1,000. Proprietorship, partnership or corporation. Evaluating franchises. How to network for cash. How to buy an existing business. Why a sapling can be a safer investment than a seed. How to combine commercial real estate with your business. The principles of negotiating, including if you don't ask, you don't get. Real life case studies.

Advanced tax strategies: Thwarting the tax gatherer.......................................19-1

Tax-loss creation and tax deferment strategies. Managing both principal residences and investment properties for tax purposes. Ensuring active income. Rolling over passive income situations. Does domicile matter? World-wide income tax havens and investment corporations. Taxation of foreign income.

How to invest in convertibles: The best-of-everything investment.........................20-1

Selecting the best convertible around today. Option identification and call options. American, European and Asian options. Option valuation models and how to analyze and select convertibles.

How to invest in options: Lots of options with options..21-1

The nature of exchange-traded options and how trading is conducted. Contract standardization. How to use calls to increase your returns. How to use puts against short-sales. Spreads and straddles. The huge profit potential in warrants. Commodity warrants.

How to invest in commodity and financial futures..22-2

The nature of futures contracts, performance bonds, marking to market, and open interest. Fundamental and technical analysis of commodity and financial futures. Spread trading, combined futures and options strategies. Evaluating managed futures funds. Derivative securities and insurance principles. Principles of hedging and mini-contracts.

Glossary..G-1

Index..I-1

VOLUME 3

Insuring the now and future family.........................23-1

Types and amounts of insurance coverage: life insurance protection, disability insurance, medical expense insurance, property and liability insurance. Who should be insured? When to start? What type is appropriate? Evaluating life insurance products: term, whole-life, universal life. Using variable universal life as a tax-free investment vehicle.

How to invest in currency: Greenback alternatives 24-1

How to profit from the fluctuating U.S. dollar. The mechanics of foreign exchange rates. Futures and forward distinctions including the interbank forward market. How to select foreign currencies. Where does gold fit in? Is silver still a precious metal? Investing in instruments denominated in foreign currencies. Are collectibles, art and jewelry true investments?

CONTENTS

Venture investing — enjoying the fruits of entrepreneurial success..........................25-1

Two ways to invest in venture capital situations: mutual funds and do-it-yourself. Evaluating a venture opportunity. The three biggest mistakes even the pros make. Asset allocation implications. Seed, bridge and interim financing—what is right for you? Creating a boutique fund: share the risk and the fun. Brokers and listing services.

Advanced strategies for property investing 26-1

Analytic techniques for finding the ideal property. Litmus tests for overpriced properties. Mixed use developments: why never to go them alone. How to diversify property holdings by continually rolling equity. How brokers can be valuable at any time for any use. Sunbelt properties. Time sharing condos and offshore real estate.

The top of the pyramid: aggressive risk strategies.......................................27-1

Four favorite aggressive high yield strategies. The nature of risk and how to contain it. How to calculate risk/reward ratios. How to use scenario analysis.

Super aggressive, super high-yield strategies.....28-1

Identifying and evaluating speculations. How to identify, categorize and play the odds. Use trading orders to efficiently enter and exit positions. How to read the charts, or, how to read the footprints on the ceiling to enhance returns.

How to profit from the changing times 29-1

Economic cycles: the meaning of inflation, recession and depression. How to forecast economic change. Economic cycles and leading indicators. How the changing geo-political structure of Europe will affect your investment opportunities. Effects of the ever-emerging Pacific Rim. Financial plan revision strategies in changing times. Economic cycles graphs. Inflation-proofing your portfolio. How to make asset allocation timing switches.

Coming down the pyramid: liquidating your investments...................................30-1

How to minimize liquidation costs. How to liquidate a stock portfolio. Bargaining on commissions. Systematic mutual fund withdrawal plans. Selling your principal residence and tax planning. How to protect instruments that will be most vulnerable to inflation. Is there still a need for insurance and annuities? Adjusting bonds from fixed to floating.

Retirement planning 31-1

How much cash will you need? Lifestyle decisions. Your maturing IRA's, 401(k)'s and pension alternatives. When and why should you annuitize. Adverse selection. Personal issues of estate inheritance.

Estate planning: your golden years 32-1

Selecting executors. Gift and estate taxes. Generation skipping transfer tax, unified transfer credit. Residence, citizenship and domicile. Types of trusts. The gross estate: exclusions and valuation. Share switches to children. Estate freezing techniques. Wills, trusts, intestacy and the probate process. Lifetime transfers.

Electronic investing 33-1

What the electronic investor needs to get started — hardware, software. Where to find investing information on the big three on-line services. The best web sites for investing information. Yahoo, Edgar, FinanceNet, Motley Fool, Wall Street Net, InvestorWeb, MarketPlex. All about investment software: technical and fundamental analysis, downloading market data, trend lines, flags and signals. On-line trading and electronic brokerage.

Glossary...G-1

Appendix — Investment Industry Contact information and Bond Ratings A-1

Index...I-1

THE STEPS

Personal tips culled from the advice of some of America's top financial advisors and successful investors

1. Switch into money market funds with fee waivers 1-10

2. Take advantage of opportunities created by NAFTA 1-11

3. Buy floating rate bonds 1-19

4. History says for the long term: S&P Index Funds or Protected Index Notes (PINS) 1-27

5. Set up an Automatic Cash Allocation Program (ACAP) 2-9

6. Use Dollar Cost Averaging 2-24

7. Diversify with international bond funds 2-29

8. Boost your portfolio returns with the exciting new Eurobond 3-18

9. How to protect yourself against the hidden losses built into every bond there is 3-20

10. The best bond to buy in a time of fluctuating interest 3-29

11. How to select a family of funds 4-9

12. Understand roller coaster returns and benefit from them 4-22

13. Buy a global, deep-discount, closed-end, equity fund 4-27

14. Use your 401(k), IRA or Keogh as a wealth accumulation vehicle 5-12

15. Use your children for more than just an exemption 5-19

16. Use bond swaps for year-end tax boosts 5-21

17. Boost your portfolio with short term U.S. Government Notes 6-18

18. Augment returns with an international money market fund 6-21

19. Make real estate liquid by using REITs 6-23

20. Buy adjustable CD's 7-11

21. Buy municipal bonds: how to select the best ones 7-21

22. Buy German Mark/Swiss Franc Term Deposits 7-29

23. The 7 step method to selecting the best equity mutual fund 8-13

24. Possibly augment your mutual fund portfolio with L.E.A.P.S. and B.O.U.N.D.S 8-22

25. How to build a portfolio that will keep pace with the Dow year in and year out 8-26

26. How to spot closed-end investment funds that can turn into a mutual fund coup 8-29

27. Make leverage work for you with real estate 9-14

28. Create your own mortgage for maximum benefit 9-18

29. Three ways to find and buy a home or rental property below market value 9-33

30. The 3-prong approach to avoiding financial scams and sharp practices 10-9

31. The little-known arbitration process available to all investors 10-16

32. Strategies for slashing transaction costs 10-25

33. Customize your stock investments with dual-purpose fund shares 11-7

34. Playing it safe with "eternal" preferreds: retractable, non-callable, cumulative 11-14

35. Implement a DRIP plan 11-27

36. The techniques to use for building a properly diversified portfolio 12-11

THE STEPS

37. Make money and change the world at the same time **12-14**

38. How to look for the next hot industry before stocks are overvalued **12-20**

39. Dual exercise warrants: the best of both worlds **12-30**

40. Select three under-valued stocks **13-9**

41. How to pick the next super growth stock while minimizing risk **13-17**

42. Stock index bonds can pay off under nearly most conditions **13-21**

43. How to use "Super Shares": the most flexible investment vehicle developed **13-25**

44. The three most reliable technical indicators and how to use them **14-7**

45. The best day of the week and time of the year to buy and sell **14-18**

46. Improve returns by using limit orders instead of market orders **14-22**

47. Make money when the market is dropping with short selling **14-25**

48. How to buy puts and write calls **14-33**

49. How to identify the best emerging market opportunities and how to actually invest in them **15-7**

50. Act on hidden overseas investment opportunities in restricted markets **15-13**

51. Investment vehicles that could pay off big: "bubble" or "cascade" **15-21**

52. The 2 best ways to buy and sell foreign securities **15-26**

53. Gear-up mortgage investment yields with GNMAs **16-13**

54. Find a high quality mortgage investment fund **16-21**

55. Determine if your company's pension plan will meet your goals **17-13**

56. How to use investing as a hedge against job loss **17-27**

57. The most important factors of how to start from scratch successfully **18-6**

58. The best and fastest sources of cash **18-13**

59. Use this proven method for finding the successful bandwagon company **18-26**

60. The essential skills of deal making and negotiating **18-34**

61. Three easy-to-implement tax reduction strategies **19-7**

62. Three not-so-easy-to-implement but powerful tax strategies **19-23**

63. When you should buy convertible bonds **20-6**

64. L.Y.O.N.S.: the most exciting convertible in years **20-8**

65. Spot the signals for buying commodity bonds .. **20-28**

66. Use covered options contracts **21-13**

67. Insure your stock portfolio's value **21-17**

68. Implement the low-risk, potential-high-return expiring warrant gambit **21-26**

69. How to select an option fund **21-32**

70. When to trade futures **22-9**

THE STEPS

71. Two contained-risk strategies for futures trading **22-17**

72. Trade small futures **22-27**

73. Where futures can be used to hedge your portfolio risk **22-34**

74. How to evaluate life insurance products **23-11**

75. Use "named perils" and other sufficient product extensions **23-29**

76. How to evaluate and possibly use one of the new innovations such as 100-pay-life **23-35**

77. How to pick the ideal foreign currency denominated investments **24-11**

78. Three little-known ways to trade in precious metals **24-29**

79. Boutique first, bounty later, or "How pigs get fat, but hogs can get slaughtered." **25-8**

80. Employ protection-based tax moves for venture capitalists **25-12**

81. Avoid the liquidity effects of restrictive stock ownership **25-18**

82. Four questions to ask of an opportunity that no one does **25-31**

83. Techniques to spot the best commercial property at the best prices **26-13**

84. Conversion properties: when to convert, when to pass **26-18**

85. Strategies to negotiate commercial real estate transactions **26-23**

86. How to make money in an over-developed environment **26-31**

87. Employ the four best high-yield, limited-risk commodity trades: corn, gold, coffee, soybean . . **27-8**

88. The three best, highly favorable option spreads: German Mark butterfly, soybean straddles, S&P straddles **27-19**

89. Use commodity/option combos and why they are favored **28-7**

90. Start currency speculation with these three historically highest-returning currencies **28-21**

91. Monitor key indicators for knowing when to change your portfolio mix **29-11**

92. Establish an asset re-allocation alarm formula . . **29-21**

93. How to minimize your costs when liquidating . . . **30-12**

94. Two mutual fund withdrawal options **30-18**

95. Three defensive strategies against inflation **30-28**

96. How to select the appropriate withdrawal options for your maturing IRA's, 401(k)'s, etc . . . **31-10**

97. Calculate the timing needs of your estate and act early when necessary **31-22**

98. Choose between variable or fixed annuities **31-28**

99. Implement estate freezing techniques **32-24**

100. The method for determining the proper trusts for your desires **32-28**

Bonus 101. The essential electronic investor's toolbox **33-32**

Insuring the now and future family

100 Steps to Wealth

Insuring the now and future family

I detest life insurance agents. They always argue that I shall someday die, which is not so. — Stephen Leacock (1869-1944), *English-born Canadian economist and humorist.* Literary Lapses.

INTRODUCTION

Like the purchase of a security or real estate, insurance too is an investment. Few households view it as such though. Insurance is too easily considered simply an expense in the family's budget — one for which there will be, hopefully, no benefit. All too often, the focus is on the premium costs and not on the potential benefit. However, lack of protection against loss — whether from a repair shop's bill, as in the case of an automobile accident, or from the loss of family income, as in the case of death — can have as negative a financial impact as a poor investment in a security or real estate. What asset allocation and its associated diversification are to portfolio construction, insurance is to the household finances. Both are forms of risk management.

Nearly every household faces decisions on insurance investments. For example, lenders require that the vast majority of mortgagees have homeowner's insurance, some landlords require renter's insurance, many states require automobile insurance and nearly everyone faces decisions on health insurance. In addition, there are insurance products that have guaranteed investment returns attached to them, as in the case of many life insurance products. We have included, in the course, this lesson on insurance because no investment decision confronts more wealth-builders so routinely as does insurance.

Among many things, this lesson contains a valuable tool to assist you in your personal risk-management program — your insurance inventory, found on pages 9 and 22.

The inventory helps you gather the important information from your existing insurances so you can evaluate the benefits you presently have and what they are costing.

This inventory will also help you deal with people who sell insurance. The majority of people who sell insurance are fine people with valuable benefits to offer. It's just that they often have to, let's say, *oversell* in order to get people to realize that insurance really is an investment — one that can prove a wise decision in the long run. However, some *do* deserve the reputation that insurance peddlers create. We will try to help you distinguish the peddler from the pro, and the good advice from the sales talk.

This lesson is divided into sections — one each for health and disability, vehicle, homeowners and life insurance. The material is designed to assist you in comparing the insurance coverage you need with the coverage you have. We will help you to buy insurance when you should, not buy when you shouldn't, and have cost-effective benefits in force when you need them. Now for the first of your insurance investments: health — and it's relative, disability insurance.

HEALTH INSURANCE

There is no better place to begin than with the area of insurance investment that everyone evaluates, and evaluates often: medical insurance. As with nearly every commodity or service in the market, there are as many choices as there are tastes and budgets to purchase them. Often you may not be in a position to choose your coverage. The majority of Americans are covered by an employer provided program and, although more and more employers are offering cafeteria benefits, the flexibility of individually purchased plans is not present. But let's start with employer plans since they cover most readers.

Employer-Provided Plans

Almost always, the employer-provided plan is most cost beneficial to you and your family. Although some employer plans contain nothing but bare bones — requiring some to augment them with their own purchases — these bones are still better than nothing. If nothing else, these bare basics come to you with pre-tax dollars since employers get the tax deductibility of the insurance premiums. (Premiums are the insurance industry's word for the payments you make to them to pay for your insurance.) Employed individuals do not.

Medical insurance plans, regardless of whether individually purchased or employer provided, have some common elements. Although you're no doubt familiar with them, let's review quickly. All plans have maximums — i.e., the ceiling in payments for which the insured will have to pay on his or her own. Some plans have, for example, "out-of-pocket" maximums of $5,000 per year per individual — ensuring that, regardless of the severity of illnesses in a year, you will never be out of pocket for more than the $5,000.

Plans have limits on services covered, otherwise called eligible services. Some plans may cover only one heart bypass surgery every few years, or may exclude experimental treatments or in-hospital, overnight chemo therapy treatments. All plans vary extensively here.

Plans also have deductibles and co-payments. The deductible is the amount of the first dollars spent on eligible services that you must pay. This is usually expressed as a dollar figure per person or per family — e.g., you must be out of pocket for the first $250 in annual expenditures on health care per person. The co-payment, or co-insurance amount, is the percentage of subsequent expenditures above the deductible. The insurance provider will pick up a percentage, with you making up the difference — e.g., an 80/20 split is often seen.

Medical insurance plans usually are one of four types. Ranked by level of flexibility to the individual, most to least, they are: Indemnity Plans, Preferred Provider Plans, Service Provider Plans and Health Maintenance Organizations. Let's examine each.

■ *Indemnity Plans* — These are the most flexible to you. They essentially allow you to freely choose where and when you want to use a health care provider: what hospital, what doctor and what course of treatments — if there are options. Subject only to prudent constraints on overcharges or excessive testing, for example, an indemnity plan allows you to fully chose your care.

After experiencing a loss, indemnity plans reimburse you for that particular loss in accordance with the policy provisions. Indemnity plans offer you the advantage of selecting your own physician and/or hospital. You may choose the best, even though the best may also be the most expensive—which has been the problem with the indemnity plan. The giver of care and the receiver of care have no personal incentive to keep costs reasonable. More recent medical insurance plan designs involve both you and the care-giver in providing cost-efficient medical care.

■ *Preferred Provider Plans* — Preferred Provider Organizations (PPOs) are arrangements established by commercial insurance companies following a Blue Cross/Blue Shield example (more on that in a moment). Coalitions of insurance companies negotiate with providers — doctors, diagnostic clinics, hospitals — to obtain discounted rates for the insureds and then guarantee patients to that provider. You will be encouraged to use these providers by means of lower deductibles, lower co-insurance and, in some cases, less paperwork than if you went to a provider outside of the PPO network. The preferred providers agree to charge less so they can get the "business." You generally cannot go outside of this plan for treatment except, say, for emergencies.

■ *Service Provider Plans* — Blue Cross/Blue Shield, the first service provider plan in the U.S., offered the first "fee for service" plans in which the insurance organization itself actually engaged in being the provider of care. Blue Cross/Blue Shield provides their participants with the facilities of the member hospitals and physicians for monthly subscriber fees. If the insurance company and the provider are one and the same, the insurance company can try to maintain cost control. Theoretically, this makes them better able to estimate the charge to subscribers. Many Blue Cross organizations contract with a provider to supply the benefits required by its plan. Since it is sending that provider a substantial amount of business, it will negotiate discounted rates whether that provider is a doctor or a hospital.

■ *Health Maintenance Organizations* — A health maintenance organization (HMO) is an assemblage of physicians and hospitals joined together in one business arrangement. In effect, they state to their members that they will "maintain their health" for a stipulated amount of money per month. HMO's are generally the most restrictive in options of all the plans, but do provide routine services such as doctor's visits, prescriptions, eyeware, etc., for low fees

Health maintenance arrangements can work well if they are economically sound and have strong finances and good facilities. However, if either of these factors deteriorate, the whole system may deteriorate. In 1989, for example, a major health maintenance organization in Chicago went into Chapter 11, leaving hundreds of thousands of people in doubt about their coverage.

In health maintenance organizations, the management is primarily conducted through what is called a "gatekeeper" physician. All of your physician services will be delivered through this physician. If you need a specialist, this gatekeeper will assign that specialist; and if that specialist wants to take an X-ray, he will ask permission of your gatekeeper to do so. If the organization providing your care works properly, and all participants are confident in each other's fairness, permission will be granted for your X-ray. However, don't be surprised if the gatekeeper doctor demands that the request for the X-ray be in writing and insists on responding to that request in writing, a process that could delay your X-ray 10 days or more.

- **Point of Service Plan** — This is a hybrid plan, and many commercial insurance companies offer it as a combination of the indemnity plan and the PPO option. Under this arrangement, you do not commit to the indemnity or the PPO plan in advance. You decide which to use at the time care is needed, just as with the point of service plan. The employer will attempt to "steer" you toward the PPO by means of lower deductibles and lower co-insurance payments than are available under the indemnity plan, but it is ultimately your choice. If you feel the care is needed for something that can be handled well by the PPO, the PPO would be the choice. It's cheaper and often easier for you. The PPO often delivers benefits without annoying paperwork and with low, or no, deductibles and/or co-insurance.

We've just described the various employer plans available. Regardless of the plan you may have available to you — if you are employed by an employer that offers plans — there may be gaps in the plan that you will want to shore-up. If so, you, like those who do not have employer-provided plans, will most likely want to shop in the open market for individual plans. Let's therefore move on to individually purchased plans, but first as a chronological transition, let's assume you've lost your job and your employer-provided health insurance and will be looking for an individual plan. You will, however, before buying an individual plan, have the opportunity to take advantage of the COBRA option — and then, after that, possibly convert to become part of the employer's plan.

- **COBRA** — On April 7, 1986, the Consolidated Omnibus Budget Reconciliation Act (COBRA) was enacted. It is a federal law applicable to employers providing health benefits to groups of 20 or more employees. It allows you to continue your group insurance, even after your employment has terminated. You pay the full cost of what the employer was paying for the plan and possibly up to 2 percent more for administrative expenses. The continuation of your coverage may extend up to 18 months. Your spouse and children may have up to 36 months of continued health insurance. As a rule of thumb, if you qualify, sign up. Don't ever go even one day without health insurance! The exception might be younger single employees who sometimes can find comparable coverage for less cost through individual policies.

  The COBRA provisions are a boon to terminating employees and dependents since the provisions make health insurance available regardless of physical condition. You must, however, make premium payments promptly to continue the coverage. The insurance industry estimates that an employee or dependent covered under COBRA receives $2 in benefits for each dollar of premium paid. As a result, employers have been advised to terminate employees' COBRA coverage if they don't pay their premiums on time. So don't be late!

  If you work for an employer with less than 20 employees that does not have to comply with the Federal COBRA regulations, check with your state. Many states have passed laws similar to COBRA for these smaller groups.

- **Conversion** — In many states, your final chance to continue your health insurance, without having to requalify medically, would come at the end of your COBRA benefits. This is when you can actually join the former employer's plan — i.e., convert to the plan. Typically, these conversion policies are relatively expensive and the benefits are very restrictive. The conversion privileges are of value only to those who cannot obtain health insurance in any other way.

Individual Medical Insurance

If employer-provided health insurance is not a viable alternative, you can apply directly to an insurance company for an individually issued policy. The advantage of this procedure is that you can more or less dictate the type of benefits you want. The disadvantage is that you have no employer to help you pay for the insurance. Unfortunately, individual insurance is most readily available if you are healthy.

In applying for an individual health insurance policy, the insurance company will ask you a dizzying array of medical questions. They will want to know your personal health history and that of everyone in your family. It is in your best interest to divulge everything because, even if you have a particular health condition that the insurance company might not wish to cover, they may be able to issue the policy with an exclusion rider. The policy would cover everything but that particular condition, certainly a better alternative than no health insurance at all.

Another advantage of an individual policy is the availability of a guaranteed renewable contract that allows the insurance company to adjust the costs for the insurance as long as it does so on a class basis. It cannot single you out for an increase. If you are turned down for individual health insurance, immediately contact your state insurance department. Many states have set up health insurance arrangements for their citizens who have been turned down for health insurance. When applying for medical insurance, you will want to use your version of the action letter we've provided below.

Individual Medical Insurance Action Letter

Dear Sir:

I am in need of private medical insurance. I am male/female born _____. I am a smoker/non-smoker in excellent / good / fair health.

My spouse is a male / female born _____ and is a smoker / non-smoker in excellent / good / fair health.

We have / do not have children. Their names, dates of birth, sex and basic health condition are listed on the back of this letter.

I would like a comprehensive major medical policy that is Lifetime Guaranteed Renewable and has an Unlimited Lifetime Maximum.

Other plan features are:

1. Individual deductible $100 / $200 / $500 / $1,000 / $2,000/ $ _____.

2. Co-Insurance Provision 80/20 (Insurance company pays 80%, I pay 20%)

3. STOP-Loss Provision — What is my maximum out-of-pocket requirement?
For the family _____
For how long _____

4. A PPO and/or HMO option.
Please send me quotes from a number of companies including any descriptive material you have on the plans along with enrollment forms and instructions.

I would appreciate your evaluation of the coverages regarding which one you feel is fairly priced and sufficiently comprehensive to provide for my family.

Sincerely,

The Action Letter requests quotes for private health insurance. It lists the specifics regarding those members of the family who need health insurance (dates of birth, smoker or non-smoker, health conditions). It then requests a comprehensive major medical policy that is guaranteed-renewable throughout your lifetime and has an unlimited lifetime maximum. You then select an appropriate deductible. You can ask for quotes at various deductibles so that you may choose the one that is most cost-effective for you.

It states your requested co-insurance provision — that is, how much of the initial billing you would pay and how much the insurance company would pay, stipulating the most typical split, 80%/20%. The letter next asks for your maximum out-of-pocket exposure so that you would know what medical bills could be under a worst-case scenario. You should consider all of these when choosing services that fit your family's needs from among the menu's options. All of these are important considerations. There is, however, one that you will have to consider that is not faced by those with the luxury of employer provided plans — making sure the insurance company you're buying from is financially stable. Be sure to see the sidebar below.

Let's examine the remaining considerations you'll face with "How much should you buy?"

■ *How Much to Buy* — Everyone seeks different levels of protection based on perceptions of their potential exposure. All people's choices have a common denominator though: to make sure they and their family are never exposed to medical bankruptcy. With this objective in mind, the first specification you want to shop for is a policy that has as high of a maximum as you can obtain. Ideally you'll want an unlimited maximum — that is, you will never have a cap on the money your insurer is willing to incur on your behalf. This option is not always possible and, in fact, it used to be more readily available than it is now. Many insurance companies have reduced their maximums to one million dollars per family. Although the million-dollar maximum sounds like a significant amount, it is not necessarily enough. A severe accident involving your whole family, leaving them with a lifelong condition, could easily exhaust one million dollars. Your strategy will be to go for the best, request the unlimited, and compromise only if you find that the best is unavailable or impractical.

■ *What Expenses Should the Plan Cover?* — Optimally, the policy should cover all physician-prescribed treatments to diagnose and correct a medical condition. The insurance company should pay those bills after an acceptable deductible; and you will participate in the payment of the bills up to some relatively small percentage called "co-insurance amount," such as 20 percent, while the insurance company pays the 80 percent of those bills. It is entirely possible that you could go medically bankrupt paying 20 percent of unlimited bills. As a result, you will want a "stop-loss provision" in order to obligate the insurance company to pay 100 percent of the bills for the balance of the calendar year, after some stipulated limit on your out-of-pocket costs.

Rating the Financial Integrity of Insurance Companies

Rank Number	Standard & Poors (S&P)	Moody's	Weiss	A.M. Best
1	AAA	Aaa	A+	A++
2	AA+	Aa1	A	A+
3	AA	Aa2	A-	A
4	AA-	Aa3	B+	B++
5	A+	A1	B	B+
6	A	A2	B-	B
7	A-	A3	C+	B-
8	BBB+	Baa1	C	C++
9	BBB	Baa2	C-	C+
10	BBB-	Baa3	D+	C
11	BB+	Ba1	D	C-
12	BB	Ba2	D-	D
13	BB-	Ba3	E+	
14	B+	B1	E	
15	B	B2	E-	
16	B-	B3		
17	CCC			

Several services rate the financial integrity of insurance companies. For convenience, we've listed the four that are used most frequently. Although heavily regulated by federal and more extensively by state governments, insurance companies are not all equal in financial stability. You will want to be sure they'll be able to pay for your claim after having just paid several hundreds of millions in hurricane damages in Florida, or be around with your money when it comes time to cash in some universal life insurance money 30 years from now. Maintaining the highest ranking is not always easy. We recommend sticking to companies rated in the A's, regardless of which ranking service your insurance company quotes. Always ask for the current rating of the company to which you're thinking of giving money.

It is important that you know how much you would have to pay of your own money in the way of deductibles and co-insurance if you and others in your family suffered a number of severe illnesses in one year. Once you have determined the maximum "out-of-pocket" amount, you can make sure that your emergency fund is able to provide for this worst-case scenario.

MEDICAL & DENTAL INSURANCE INVENTORY

	Insured	Company	Policy Number	Policy Maximum	Deductible	Co-Insurance	Stop-Loss	Annual Premium
1	_____	_____	_____	_____	_____	_____	_____	_____
2	_____	_____	_____	_____	_____	_____	_____	_____
3	_____	_____	_____	_____	_____	_____	_____	_____
4	_____	_____	_____	_____	_____	_____	_____	_____
5	_____	_____	_____	_____	_____	_____	_____	_____

Total Annual Family Premium: _____

Our specifications call for an unlimited maximum, comprehensive coverage, reasonable deductibles and an acceptable stop-loss. Complete your Medical Insurance Inventory above to see how you are doing on meeting the specifications.

■ *Pre-Existing Conditions* — You may have to face the problem of pre-existing conditions. When applying for insurance coverage you will have to answer questions regarding your medical history. This will reveal anything that has happened in your past that would affect the insurance company's ability to provide health insurance for you profitably. With employer provided group medical insurance, you may not have to complete medical questions, but the policy may state that it will not pay benefits for conditions that manifested themselves before the policy was put in force.

Pre-existing conditions may be excluded entirely, or they may be excluded only for a certain period of time. In some cases, insurance companies will pay some benefits for pre-existing conditions but limit the amount of the total payments. It does not pay to turn in fraudulent applications to insurance companies. When you file a claim for a pre-existing condition that was not revealed, the insurance company will, and must, refuse to pay. You are much better off being candid with the insurance company. That way, if and when they do issue a policy, you have reasonable assurance they will pay the promised benefits and they will not rescind the policy because of any erroneous or misleading statements on the application.

■ *Guaranteed Renewable* — Health insurance policies may be guaranteed renewable, meaning the insurance company cannot cancel or change the policy benefits once it is issued. However, the insurance company does reserve the right to change *the cost* of the policy on what they refer to as a *class basis*. This means that all people with similar policies would be exposed to the same cost increase at the same time. In effect, the insurance company would not select you individually for a rate increase.

Association Medical Insurance

Another alternative for obtaining medical insurance may be through an association to which you belong or could easily become a member. Some organizations sell insurance just to provide an extra benefit for their membership; others in order to make a profit for their organization. You obviously would prefer the former. Some of the less savory fare offered up by associations are policies that pay you a stipulated amount of money each day you are in the hospital. Keep in mind that the average stay in the hospital is less than 10 days, and a $50 per day indemnity policy paying you $500 is not going to be much help. Also, beware of policies that will pay benefits only if your medical condition is caused by an accident or some specific illness. They are cheap policies, but not as cheap as they ought to be. These are high-profit items to the insurance companies issuing them. Avoid them — obtain high-quality comprehensive coverage instead.

Regardless of the options you secure for you and your family, and regardless of the insurer, the bottom line on medical insurance is don't go a day without it. A lack of medical insurance can be hazardous to your economic health. . . and to that of those around you.

DISABILITY INSURANCE

Although not as popular as medical coverage, we will cover disability next since it is actually a form of medical coverage. Unlike automobile or homeowner's coverage, disability insurance is an issue when — but only if — you incur a major medical catastrophe.

**Odds of a Disability Occurring
Versus a Death at Various Ages**

Age	Chances of a 90-day or more disability vs. death
22	3.6 to 1
32	3.5 to 1
42	3.0 to 1
52	2.3 to 1
62	1.8 to 1

Source: Insurance Commissioners' Disability Table

Contrary to perception, you are indeed more likely to become disabled than to die. See the table at left. People, while in their wealth-building years at least, are generally rather safe from dying. They are not as safe though from a disabling auto accident or disease. The risk of a disability lasting 90 days or more exceeds the risk of death by three and one-half times for a 32 year old, three times for a 42 year old and almost twice for a 62 year old. And the only thing worse than being permanently disabled is to be permanently disabled without wages.

That is why you should give disability insurance serious consideration. We have given it a very serious place in the course of studies. Disability, especially permanent disability, is the one thing that can wipe out even the most successful wealth-building regimen. It is so important that we've given it it's own step. See wealth-building Step 74, Protect Against Disability Now and Until Age 100, found on page 11.

The insurance industry finds that fewer than one in six individuals owns enough disability income insurance protection to provide for a disability lasting more than 90 days. The industry claims the average duration of a disability lasting longer than 90 days is at least five years. The unfortunate aspect of disability, other than of course the disability itself, is that it will not only terminate income, but also increase costs for medicines, medical care and associated care expenses. And, if you're dependent on two incomes for the lifestyle you want to maintain, then you should have disability insurance on both bread winners.

Government and Employer-Provided Disability

Let's first determine the various sources of government and employer-provided disability income and then ascertain what shortfall might exist for you.

■ *Government Disability Plans* — Although it is true that Social Security will provide benefits for disabled workers, they deny 75 percent of all individual disability claims! If you are able to do any daily work activities, your claim for disability benefits probably will be declined. Social Security defines disability as " ... an inability to engage in any substantial gainful activity by reason of any medically determinable physical or mental impairment that can be expected to result in death, or which has lasted or can be expected to last for a continuous period of not less than 12 months." This is a tough standard to pass. The high rate of application denials, combined with the tough definition of disability and the fact that many government programs are going through severe cutbacks, indicates that you should not depend on the government to provide for your disability income needs.

■ *State Programs* — There are state mandated worker's compensation laws that impose absolute liability on an employer for certain injuries suffered by employees in the course of their work. These do not pay, however, if you are not disabled on the job! And the amount of compensation for those who do incur the disability on the job are vastly inadequate in amount and are payable for too short a time to provide for real needs. Plus, many states are cracking down on disability claims as well.

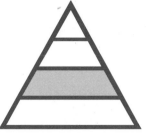

100 Steps to Wealth

STEP 74

Protect Against Disability...
Now and Until Age 100

What: Invest in disability insurance coverage to avoid losing the wealth you've accumulated.

Why: Disability can be the worst hazard to both income and wealth-building since it cuts off further earnings potential and places a severe financial drain on the resources you already have.

Risk: None. Rather than risk, investing in a full-coverage disability policy carries only the expense of the premiums as a downside consideration.

Safety: High. The only safety consideration is that your insurance company, despite heavy government regulation, can go under. Be sure to invest with a quality company as explained in the sidebar on page 8.

Liquidity: Oddly enough, a disability policy can affect your liquidity. If you are providing for the losses associated with disability by keeping liquid assets at bay, those funds can be freed up for investment.

Why not: If other, more essential expenses are not being met in your household, you may not be able to afford this investment.

Buy from: A quality insurance salesperson from a quality company.

Background: As discussed in the body of this lesson, disability is perhaps the single most important, yet most overlooked, insurance there is. Although the body of this lesson stresses and discusses disability, we've given it priority by singling it out in a step.

Most people see the benefits of maintaining some level of life insurance. However, since there is a higher probability that someone in their wealth-building years will become disabled than die, it makes more sense to also invest in a disability policy.

Modern medicine actually plays a hand in this. Where people used to die from, say, a debilitating injury, they now may live — but with significantly decreased capabilities. A disabling event may result in not only a loss of your income-producing ability, but also an increase in your costs. Disability, and the special care required (such as home modifications, expensive medications, etc.) can be costly — especially while you've lost your wage earning ability.

Should total disability strike, you may need an expensive special care facility. For example, in Florida, the cost of such a facility is over $50,000 annually.

If you are dependent on two incomes in your home, cover both wage earners. Don't risk having to try getting by on only one income. Even worse, you both could be disabled in an accident while out for dinner some Saturday night and end up with no source of income.

If you want to get started today protecting against disability, here's what you need to do:

Begin by making phone calls. Call your insurance agent; call around in the phone book; call Quotesmith, described on page 13, at 1-800-556-9393. Compile a record of the best prices for the most benefits you can purchase. Remember, as this lesson teaches, don't necessarily go for the least expensive policy. It may have no flexibility, be cancelable by the insurance company when you take up bungie jumping, or actually have declining coverage over time. Be sure to read the entire section on disability in this lesson. ▲

Continued from p. 10

If you live in California, Hawaii, New Jersey, New York, Rhode Island or Puerto Rico, you probably have access to a state-sponsored compulsory temporary disability plan that is designed to provide income to disabled workers from "non-occupational" causes. These programs provide only a base of benefits on which you can build, and are generally insufficient as a total provider for your personal disability income needs. Don't expect any state to pay more than 40 percent of income.

- ***Association Disability Insurance*** — You may be a member of an organization or association that offers group disability income benefits to its membership. Some of these plans are very enticing because of their low cost, but beware! These plans are sometimes inadequate. They may have very constrictive definitions of disability — e.g., rendered incapable of performing any occupational duty! You would not be considered disabled even if the only thing you could possibly do was sell pencils on the street corner. Many offer benefits only in the event of accident and/or only for a very limited period of time.

You do not control what happens with an association plan, and it can be canceled! If the insurance provider decides to terminate the plan, you may find yourself trying to replace the benefits at what could be a very inopportune time. You may actually be disabled or in ill health so that no one else will insure you, and you cannot replace the benefits. Try not to depend on association group insurance for your primary disability insurance needs.

- ***Employer-Provided Disability Insurance*** — Employers also often offer group disability income insurance plans. Just as in the association plans, it will be important for you to check the benefits provided by the plan both for duration and quality. The advantages of employer-provided, group disability income insurance are both its low cost and the fact that you have the employer as an advocate in dealing with the insurance company. However, neither you nor your employer control the continuation of the coverage. If the insurance company finds that providing benefits for your employer has become economically unfeasible, that insurance carrier may decide to cancel that coverage. This lack of personal control is the primary disadvantage of employer-provided group disability income insurance. But, because of its relatively low cost — 20 percent to 30 percent cheaper than any plan you can buy now — take it if you can get it.

Employer coverage usually has restrictions regarding the amounts and durations of benefits, the definition of disability, the integration of the benefits provided by the plan with those provided by social security and/or any other sources of disability income benefits, and restrictions on your ability to continue the coverage should you terminate employment.

Despite the various sources of disability income protection, these government, association and employer-sponsored coverages do not give you control over your benefits like an individually owned policy.

Individually Owned Disability Insurance

If you can afford it, buy an individually owned disability income policy. Buy a policy that may not be canceled during your entire working life and one that will never charge you more than the amount you pay on the date the policy is issued. This is referred to as non-cancelable and guaranteed-renewable coverage. If you want non-cancelable and guaranteed-renewable disability insurance, this plan is for you. Act now though. Many major disability companies are ceasing to offer this type of coverage.

- ***What To Look For*** — The policy should define disability as you being unable to perform the duties required by your own occupation. That definition of disability should insure you within your own occupation for as long as possible (preferably

A 1-800 Quote Service!!

If you dislike dealing with salespeople directly, there is a 1-800 service that can help you for free. Quotesmith monitors current coverages and market rates of over 400 insurance companies. You can request quotations on health and life insurance, as well as annuities. They'll ask you for the basic information on you and your family — birthdates, and whether you're a smoker for example — and mail you a free market comparison showing which companies offer the most competitive rates in your area. Be careful when shopping this way though; often the cheapest rates offer the least coverages. Be sure to ask all the questions you're learning in this lesson before buying. You can reach Quotesmith at 1-800-556-9393.

for life) — or, at least, until retirement, when pensions and Social Security can kick in. Remember though, neither pensions nor Social Security will have as much in their kitties if you do not work for several years as a result of a disability.

It is to your advantage to get today's insurance prices locked in for a lifetime. Prices are increasing because claims have been going up faster than expected. The risk of disability is increasing substantially today because the killer diseases no longer kill quickly...they disable. AIDS-related claims are up, and disability claims by women are higher than the insurance industry had anticipated. As a result of the AIDS claims, men may pay 5 to 45 percent more in premiums. Claims for mental, nervous and drug and alcohol disorders are up. The medical profession is increasingly capable of extending the dying process. All of this will continue to increase prices and restrict supply. No one knows the importance of disability insurance as well as someone who cannot buy it at any price.

■ *How Much Disability Insurance Should You Have?* As a general rule, use 60 to 80 percent of the wages you are dependent on now for your current lifestyle as a measure of how much coverage to buy. That is only a rough estimate. We could get very scientific about *"how much"* by dissecting your budget to determine what expenses would terminate, what expenses would remain, and what expenses would increase if you were disabled. Believe it or not though, if you want to get more scientific about the estimate, the easiest way to determine appropriate coverage is to simply ask the insurer.

Disability is the one insurance for which the insurance companies try very hard not to over- nor under-insure you. As you recall, we have asked the insurance company to pay these benefits for as long as possible — preferably for the rest of your life — if you should be disabled that long. What would encourage you to go back to work? Insurance companies feel you will be encouraged to go back to work — relieving them of their obligation to pay benefits — if you have an economic incentive to do so. That's why they will offer a package in which you can make more money going back to work than by continuing to receive the benefits.

The insurance company will not offer you 100 percent of your regular earnings because you would have no incentive to go back to work. Instead they will only offer you up to about 60 percent (only rarely the full 80 percent) of your income. The clue to purchasing insurance to replace your wages is to ask for as much as they will give you, and buy as much as you can afford. If you are ever disabled, you probably won't ever feel that you have too much income.

■ *Disability Income Without Taxation* — Uncle Sam encourages you to buy and pay for your own disability income insurance through a tax law that excludes from personal taxation the benefits paid to you from policy premiums paid for by after-tax dollars. That is, if you purchased and paid the premiums for your own disability income insurance policies, then the benefits paid to you as the result of a disability are to be delivered without being taxed. Suppose your policy states that, in the event of your disability, your benefits will be $1,000 per month. If you paid for that policy with your after-tax earnings, that $1,000 is delivered month after month without any income tax due whatsoever.

However, if you have paid that premium with pre-tax dollars through some employer plan, or if your employer had paid those premiums for you and did not add the cost of those benefits to your W-2 compensation, then those benefits would be subject to ordinary income taxation. It is highly likely that 30 percent or more of your disability benefit, depending on your state and federal income-tax bracket, would have to go to Uncle Sam. Paying part of your benefits to the government when you are disabled is not a pleasant experience.

The only thing worse than being permanently disabled is to be permanently disabled without wages.

■ *Employers Can Help* — Employers also can help you buy individually owned non-cancelable, guaranteed-renewable disability income insurance policies (the kind recommended) that are entirely portable — that is, you can continue the policy as private after you leave your employer. In spite of the fact that, in most cases, you would pay the entire premium and have to qualify medically, it still would be less expensive than if you were to buy the identical contract on your own. Insurance companies frequently will discount rates up to 15 or 20 percent for policies that they can bill through employers. In some cases, an employer sponsor will even make it a little easier for you to qualify medically for coverage. This is a great way for your employer to help you without having it cost the employer very much.

■ *Back to 'What to Look for'* — The following benefits are what to secure in your policy:

Accident and/or Sickness Benefits — Have the policy stipulate that benefits will be payable for life not only as a result of accident, but also, unlike many policies, if disability is caused by sickness. Your policy should stipulate that benefits will be payable for as long as possible, regardless of whether illness or accident has caused your disability.

When Benefits Begin — Policies that begin disability benefits the moment you are disabled are very expensive. If you want to reduce the cost of your policy, defer benefit payment until a period of time after your disability occurs. If you can wait 30, 60 or 90 days, referred to as an elimination or a waiting period, you'll gain a substantial reduction in premium. The 90-day wait is often the most cost-effective choice. *Note: insurance companies pay the benefit at the end of the month in which it is due, so with a 90-day waiting period, you would receive your first benefit payment 120 days after the start of the disability.*

Definition of Disability — Disability may be defined as the inability of the insured, due to injury or sickness, to engage in the substantial and material duties of his or her regular occupation. Try to avoid a definition of disability as the inability of the insured to engage in any occupation. A compromise, if needed, between these two would be the inability of the insured to engage in any occupation for which he or she is reasonably qualified by reason of training, education and experience.

CPI Cost-of-Living Adjustments — Try to secure a policy that gives annual increases in benefits due to increases in the cost of living. This will generally add 20 to 30 percent to the premium cost. This option is sometimes referred to as an inflation rider. Watch for significant differences in this rider among companies. Check if the increases are calculated on a simple-interest basis or compounded — it makes a big difference! Also, check for limits on how high the increases can go.

Guaranteed Insurability — This allows you to purchase additional monthly income periodically without having to provide evidence of medical insurability, (i.e., take a physical examination each time you want to increase your coverage). We strongly recommended this so that you can increase your protection as your earnings and lifestyle improve while you are not disabled.

Return of Premium Rider — This is an interesting option but comes at a significant cost. This option appeals to those who can't conceive of themselves as being disabled — the "I'm as healthy as a horse" group. They never expect to make a claim, so they like the feature that promises to return a portion of their premium, less claims paid, at some future dates, such as every five years. These riders are not cheap, carrying extra premiums as high as $100 per month for a guaranteed 60 percent return of premiums paid if no claims are made for five years. In most cases, you probably would be better off putting the extra $100 per month in a good stock mutual fund.

Take Action — In order to put an individual disability income policy in force, you may have to contact an agent licensed to sell disability income policies in your state. A professional salesperson should be able to help you find quality coverage from a quality company. The agent may earn up to half your first year's premium, so make sure to ask questions to determine if they are seeking what is best for you, or merely working for the highest commission.

The disability income marketplace is constantly changing, but it has not been improving for the consumer. The costs of this type of coverage have been increasing. As mentioned earlier, recently companies have increased men's rates by 5 to 45 percent and women's rates as much as 35 percent. The majority of companies charging the same rates for men and women, however, have experienced more moderate increases. If you lock in today's rates with a quality contract in a quality company, you will be extremely happy that you had the foresight to do so. The ability to "lock in" rates to age 65 from your current age is disappearing, so act as soon as you've decided the course of coverage that is best.

VEHICLE INSURANCE

Second only to medical insurance in level of widespread interest and need is automobile insurance. Industry statistics show that quite nearly every automobile policy incurs a claim, and the odds are 1 in 2 that a person will be actively involved, some way, in a major automobile accident during his or her lifetime. With these facts, and the possibility of incurring damage at the hands of someone who is uninsured and unable to pay damages, it makes little sense to be uninsured in vehicle coverage. Let's begin by examining who should be covered in your policy.

The Terminology of Vehicle Insurance

Just when you were becoming used to insurance terms like co-payment, we have to throw more terms at you that only vehicle insurance would be capable of serving up. Here are the most important terms. Vehicle insurance is actually divided into three categories of coverage: collision, liability and comprehensive. Collision coverage insures you against damages to your car should someone hit you. Liability protects you from having to pay someone else if you do damage to them — that is, should you hit them, their car or their property.

Comprehensive, unlike the other two, has virtually nothing to do with motor accidents. Instead, it protects you from non-transport related damages such as vandalism or those caused by a hail storm. We'll deal with each of these three in a moment, but first let's establish some of the ground rules for vehicle insurance, such as who should be covered.

Not only should you cover yourself, of course, but make sure you've covered everyone who is reasonably expected to drive your vehicle. *Note: For practical purposes, we'll refer to vehicle as car even though all the vehicles you may use — motorcycles, planes, trains and automobiles — should be covered.* The name(s) of the covered will be listed on the declarations page of your policy. Cover your spouse, who is a resident in your house, and all other family members, including a ward or foster child who is in your house.

The term "resident" has a special legal connotation and may extend beyond the confines of the insured's dwelling. A son or daughter away at school or in the military may still be considered a resident of the household as long as the household is considered "home" and there is an intent to return to the household.

Although the industry's covered-person definition does not make reference to a requirement of permission on your part, the policy normally will exclude coverage of anyone operating a vehicle without a reasonable belief that he or she was entitled to do so. Damage to stolen cars will not be covered by insurance companies. The coverage applies to the operation of both the covered vehicle and non-owned (borrowed or rented) vehicles.

The Potential Loss Is Large

If any of these covered people should happen to injure a bright, young medical student, preventing her from practicing medicine for the rest of her life, you could find yourself the object of a judgment that could force you into personal bankruptcy. However, even personal bankruptcy would not relieve you of the obligation of paying the judgment as a result of the injuries to that young student. Such a judgment could follow you the rest of your life. Substantial coverage is thus essential for your economic health.

We recommend that you increase your liability coverage to the maximum practical limit, coordinated with your umbrella or comprehensive personal liability policy (more on this later). You will find hundreds of examples of automobile accidents and injuries that have resulted in judgments against car owners for one million dollars and more. However, you will not find many insurance companies that will issue an automobile policy with more than a million-dollar liability section. As a result, we recommend you purchase a personal umbrella liability policy, which will be discussed in the homeowners section to come. For now, let's dive into the big three: collision, comprehensive and liability.

Collision Coverage

Collision coverage is to pay for losses caused by the rollover or collision of your covered auto. This coverage is provided regardless of who is at fault in the accident and will apply when you cannot recover damages from another party whose negligence was the cause of your loss. Generally you want to carry insurance equal to the amount at which your car is valued in what is commonly referred to as the blue book. This is the used car industry's standard and is used not only by used car salespeople, but also by lenders and insurance companies. Simply ask your insurance agent for your auto's value.

Collision coverage basically makes sure you can get your vehicle back in operation as quickly as possible. If you are not at fault in an accident, you generally won't have to pay for the damages. Your insurance company will make a claim against the negligent party's insurance company and seek reimbursement from that company.

Comprehensive Coverage

If you sustain a loss other than as a result of the rollover of your vehicle or its collision with another object, you will be reimbursed under the comprehensive section of your policy.

You would make a claim under the comprehensive section of your policy for such occurrences as broken glass, losses caused by flying objects, fire, theft, larceny, explosion, earthquake, windstorm, hail, water, flood, malicious mischief or vandalism, a riot or civil commotion, or contact with a bird or animal.

There are, however, a number of exclusions under comprehensive coverage that you should be aware of. If you have special radio, sound or video equipment in your car, you may want to request additional riders, costing around $10 to $50 annually, to make sure they are covered if stolen or destroyed.

The amount you can expect your insurer to pay for physical damage to your vehicle will be either the actual cash value of the damaged or stolen property — meaning its replacement value less an allowance for depreciation — or the amount required to repair the property. You would prefer the latter.

Generally you want to cancel comprehensive coverage when the value of the vehicle has dropped so low the premium payments just aren't worthwhile, say $2,500 in value. You, of course, won't like this advice if you cancel your comprehensive and, the next day, suffer auto damage covered by comprehensive.

Uninsured/ Underinsured Motorist Coverage

People still drive motor vehicles without insurance despite the mandatory laws and financial-responsibility regulations in force in practically all states. Nearly every state insists you have either adequate insurance or adequate resources to satisfy judgments against you before driving an automobile. For example, in Cook County, Illinois, which includes the city of Chicago, a study showed that half the drivers on the road do not have insurance. In California, it is estimated that two million of the eleven million vehicles registered in that state are uninsured. It is typically people without resources that drive motor vehicles without insurance.

> *For example, in Cook County, Illinois, which includes the city of Chicago, a study showed that half the drivers on the road do not have insurance. In California, it is estimated that two million of the eleven million vehicles registered in that state are uninsured. Remember, underinsured motorist coverage is to protect you, not others.*

If you were to have an accident in either Chicago or California under those circumstances, the odds are pretty high that the other party involved would be one of those people without insurance and without resources. How then, and from whom, are you going to be reimbursed for your losses? Look at your inventory of vehicle insurance. Have you filled in the section under uninsured/underinsured motorist coverage? If you have recorded $15,000/$30,000, which is the amount we see much too often, you are severely underinsured.

In most states, this coverage is not optional. Rather, the state mandates individuals to carry uninsured motorist coverage. Regardless of whether it's mandated in your state or not, it will typically add $20 to $40 to an annual policy depending on where you live.

Remember, underinsured motorist coverage is to protect you, not others. The declarations page in your policy will state how much you are paying for that coverage at the present time. You probably can increase the reimbursement to $100,000/$300,000 for a relatively insignificant increase in premium. If someone uninsured hits you or someone you love, you will know the extra cost was insignificant.

The underinsured provision in your coverage exists because some people have insurance with limits that are too low to protect you adequately. If you or your family sustain losses exceeding the other driver's coverage, you may find yourself making a claim under your own coverage.

No-Fault

No-fault insurance has received a great deal of attention. Many states require no-fault coverage to some degree. The personal auto policies issued in such states will be in compliance with the state regulations — which, by the way, vary considerably.

A few states, Massachusetts for one, have a total no-fault policy. Regardless of who causes the accident, the respective parties' insurance companies pay the damages. The costs of this are automatically borne by the policy holders in their annual premium payments.

The concept of no-fault insurance is to save money by not having to go through the process of determining who is at fault. The conventional means of indemnification, which necessitates determining who is at fault and who pays, takes time and also may involve substantial legal fees. No-fault, in its pure form, means that it does not matter who caused the accident that resulted in bodily injury. The insured party suffering the loss would seek recovery for medical expenses, loss of income and other costs from his or her own insurer, and there would be no claim for general damages or suffering.

Modified no-fault, however, provides limited immunity from the requirement to establish blame in the event of an automobile accident. Under modified no-fault, a certain amount of expense will be reimbursed by your own policy, regardless of fault. Beyond that limit amount — usually $2,000 to $5,000 — liability would be determined and you would seek recovery from the party at fault. Treatment of claims for pain and suffering vary from state to state under the modified plans.

The Top Ten Things to Do After an Accident (Advice from the Home Office)

An automobile accident is normally a traumatic experience, and most of us do not think clearly when we are involved. Therefore, it is wise to know what you have to do in the event of an accident.

1. Promptly notify the police and obtain care for the injured.
2. Cooperate with the authorities on the scene.
3. Take reasonable steps to protect the vehicle and equipment from another loss.
4. Acquire a copy of all police reports.
5. Have the insurance company inspect and appraise the damage before any steps have been taken to repair it.
6. Cooperate with the insurer in the investigation, defense or settlement.
7. Promptly send the insurer copies of any notice or legal papers received in connection with a loss.
8. Submit to physical examinations by physicians selected by the insurer as often as the insurer reasonably requires. The insurer pays the cost of examinations.
9. Authorize the insurer to obtain medical reports and other pertinent records.
10. Submit proof of loss as required by the insurer.

The pure form of no-fault coverage has not been a very popular concept. The dilemma in no-fault coverage is that, although we all would like to eliminate the expense of lawyers and the legal process necessary to obtain just compensation, no one wishes to give up the right to sue people who cause them general damage and suffering.

Which Vehicles to Cover

Any vehicle contained on the declarations page is covered. Check your inventory page to be sure that all vehicles you own are listed on that page and are included in the declarations pages in your policies as covered vehicles under all applicable conditions. You may be surprised.

In addition to the vehicles you have indicated on the declarations page, you will automatically be insured for any vehicle you acquire during the policy period — providing you ask the insurance company to insure it within 30 days of becoming the owner. This will apply to private passenger cars and, as long as you do not use them in business, also to pick-ups, panel trucks and vans. Also covered is any trailer that you might own and any non-owned auto or trailer being used as a temporary substitute for any vehicle described above that is out of normal use because of breakdown, repair, service, loss or destruction.

Rental cars are an issue, too. When you rent a car, the rental company encourages you to purchase a collision-damage waiver that eliminates both your liability for the deductible and any uninsured losses to which the rental car agency is exposed. The typical charge of nine dollars per day totals up to $3,285 per year, which is a rather significant premium to have to pay for a potential loss of $500 to $3,000. In most cases, your personal auto policy or family auto policy will provide coverage to indemnify you for the payment of any of these deductibles. However, problems can occur when you return to the rental agency on a Sunday night with a damaged vehicle. You may have difficulty proving you have coverage to pay the bill because you can't reach your insurance company by phone. The rental agency could demand immediate damage payment.

In order to avoid such problems, credit card agencies have included in their package of benefits — and in some cases have later withdrawn — automatic coverage if you rent a car using their credit card. This will only be a secondary coverage though, should your other policies fail to cover all your liability. Though they will assume the immediate liability, they will then seek reimbursement from your insurance company. In most cases, the rental car agencies have accepted this type of coverage and no longer hassle renters for immediate payments. This appears to be a very satisfactory solution to the problem. Check with your credit card company for the availability of this benefit, and check with your insurance company regarding how your policy protects you when you rent a car.

Additionally, make sure your policy covers all motorcycles, mopeds, all-terrain vehicles, snowmobiles and other miscellaneous vehicles you own. Or, if it doesn't, secure an endorsement referred to as a miscellaneous vehicle endorsement. There is no coverage under the endorsement for rented or borrowed vehicles of this type. We recommend caution whenever you rent a recreational vehicle. Read the waivers you are asked to sign and consider the risks you may be taking. For instance, don't sign for your neighbor's children — their own parents should be there to do it for them.

Medical Payments

This is a special form of accident insurance that provides coverage for medical expenses incurred by insured persons in automobile accidents. The standard limit for most policies is $1,000 per person; however, this limit can be raised by the payment of a small additional premium, usually only $10 to $20 annually. A health insurance policy may cover most injuries incurred in an automobile accident, but not always all. Always check your health policy. Basically, the medical payments provision is designed to pay reasonable expenses incurred for necessary medical and funeral expenses because of bodily injury caused by accident and sustained by a covered person. It usually limits the payment of these expenses to within three years of the date of the accident.

Vehicle insurance medical payments, unlike many other policies like homeowner's, apply to the named insured only — you and your family members who suffer bodily injury caused by an accident while occupying a covered automobile. The coverage will also apply to you and your family members if, while pedestrians, you are struck by either a motor vehicle designed for use on the public roads or by a trailer of any type. Additionally, people other than you and your family members are covered for medical payments while occupying your covered auto even if they're just a passenger.

There are a number of circumstances under which you will not be covered by this provision. You will not be covered for vehicles with less than four wheels. Get rid of that three-wheeled all-terrain vehicle. You will not be covered in autos that are used for carrying people or property for a fee, or if you are injured in your employer provided vehicle. Business vehicles need business policies. Additionally, you will not be covered if you were operating an auto that you weren't entitled to operate.

It could be argued that since most people are covered under some form of individual health insurance, medical payments coverage is redundant. However, there are too many circumstances where you, your family members or the passengers in your vehicle may be temporarily without medical coverage. For example, your dependent child may be a recent graduate who no longer fits the definition of "dependent and in school" and may, therefore, not be covered under your employer-provided group medical insurance. As mentioned earlier, for only about $20 you can increase this coverage above the $1,000 to an amount that would provide reasonable benefits in the event of an injury — perhaps $5,000 to $10,000. If Murphy's Law prevails, that is when an accident will occur. The general rule applies, "Don't risk a lot for a little."

Summary   All vehicle insurance is costly, but to upgrade from minimal coverage to the best coverage is really not that much more expensive and represents a wise purchase — one you will appreciate at claim time. And, as was said at the beginning of this section, if the insurance industry statistics are right, you hold a near 100 percent chance of someday having to make a claim.

RESIDENTIAL AND REAL ESTATE MEDICAL LIABILITY INSURANCE

Both a man's and a woman's home is their castle, and today the castle is insured not by moats and draw bridges but by the much more practical homeowners insurance policy. This section explains both residential coverage and a close relative — the medical real estate coverage.

Residential coverage is an often considered and often purchased insurance investment. It is third in number of policies in force behind only medical and automobile insurance. Residential coverage is divided into two areas: personal property loss — often referred to as homeowner's or property insurance — and medical coverage, which protects the policy holder from damages resulting from injuries on their property. Let's first examine property insurance.

Real Property Loss   The goal of residential property loss insurance, or homeowner's insurance, is to protect yourself from the costs of having to replace all or a portion of your dwelling and your possessions that are on your property.

The starting place for analyzing this coverage is with the big picture. The insurance company relates property coverage to the replacement cost of your property. Check your policy's coverage to see that the maximum the insurance company will pay, in the event of total destruction of your property, is sufficient to cover 100 percent of its full replacement cost. Do not consider the "fair market value" of your home to be the replacement cost of your home. This is a common error.

With the exceptions of very depressed, local real estate markets, the replacement cost of your dwelling is always less than the market value of your property for several reasons. First your market value often includes the value of the land the dwelling sits on. This is true of apartment dwellers too! Unless a meteor eliminates your land, you won't need to insure it. (The exceptions are, of course, beach property loss due to storm or wave erosion and total loss due to flood, which is covered in flood insurance — two things that are so relatively rare we do not discuss them here.) If the total coverage is not sufficient, and your home is totally destroyed, the insurance company will not pay more than the fixed amount stipulated in your policy under what is usually referred to as Coverage A.

To solve this problem, your policy should include a valuable rider called an inflation-guard endorsement. The rider automatically adjusts the benefits of your policy to the replacement value of your property. As the value of the property goes up, so does the coverage. This rider typically adds no more than 2 percent to your premium.

To determine replacement costs, the insurance company will ask about the construction of your home and its location. Typically they will inspect the home and/or request pictures. They will use this information, along with their data on construction costs in your area, to estimate a replacement cost figure for you. They will recommend you insure your home for that amount, and add an inflation-guard endorsement to your policy. If you're still uncomfortable, you can always hire an independent appraiser. Keep in mind insurance companies are so highly regulated that there are very few problems with companies not honoring the intent of an inflation rider.

To solve this problem, your policy should include a valuable rider called an inflation-guard endorsement. The rider automatically adjusts the benefits of your policy to the replacement value of your property.

If their estimate of the replacement cost of your home proves inaccurate at the time of your loss, it will be the insurance company's responsibility to make up the difference, not yours. If you have the proper coverage in the event of a total loss, you are more likely to have the proper coverage in the event of a partial loss. For example, a fire that causes a $20,000 loss to a home that has a replacement value of $100,000 — and is fully insured for the $100,000 — would result in a payment of the full $20,000 in loss (less the policy deductible, of course).

There is an 80 percent rule that applies to partial losses, however. This rule states that a $20,000 claim would still be fully paid even if a $100,000 home was insured for only $80,000, or 80 percent of its true replacement cost. However, if the owner, or owners, of this home were risking a lot to save a little and had the home insured for only $40,000, the insurance company would not pay the entire loss but would share the loss with the insured. The amount the insurance company would pay would relate the amount carried, in this case $40,000, to the amount of insurance required to receive full reimbursement — $80,000 on the $100,000 replacement value of the house. Since the insured was carrying only half the amount of insurance required, the insurance company would reimburse for only half the loss — in this case, only $10,000 rather than the $20,000 loss. Of course, any applicable policy deductible would come off first.

Note: It may not be that easy for California and Florida residents though. State mandates have caused insurers to restrict coverage availability in some areas. In your case, as in some other states, you will need to contact your governor's office and the state insurance department and put pressure on the companies when needed insurance is unavailable.

Real Estate Medical-Payments Coverage

A medical payment provision to a homeowner's policy covers your losses for such things as medical expenses, and even funeral fees, incurred by persons injured on your premises — but only those given permission to be on your premises by someone covered by your policy.

This coverage is so unique that its nature warrants explanation. You should have this liability insurance because you, or a member of your family, may make a mistake that injures someone else. The law requires that people behave as reasonable and prudent individuals — and if you do not, this can constitute negligence. If that negligence leads to another's injury, or damage to the property of another, the negligent party may be held liable for damages. More importantly, not only will you be held liable for your own actions, but also for the actions of your relatives who are residents in your household, those under age 21 and in your care, or someone else who is a resident of your home. You may also be held liable for the animals for which you are legally responsible, and also for the negligent operation of your insured, unlicensed vehicles that are used with your consent. If you own an unlicensed all-terrain vehicle that the neighborhood kids use, you are exposing yourself to a big lawsuit!

You should write the policy to also pay when someone is injured away from your premises but their injury results from the activity of both you and those insured under your policy. The medical-payments provision will not pay benefits to you or your other insureds. It is to reimburse others for injuries related to the real estate. You will find the additional cost to go from minimal coverage to maximum coverage is not significant.

CASUALTY INSURANCE INVENTORY

RESIDENCE/REAL ESTATE INSURANCE: DATE: _____

	Insurance Company/ Real Estate	Policy Number	Policy Type	Liability Maximum	Property Maximum	Medical Maximum	Special Riders	Annual Premium
1								
2								
3								
4								
5								

Estimated Replacement Value of Your Home _____

VEHICLE INSURANCE:

	Vehicle	Insurance Policy Number	Liability Maximum	Medical Maximum	Collision Deductible/ Premium	Comp. Deductible/ Preimum	Un/Under Insured Motorist	Annual Premmium
1								
2								
3								
4								
5								

Blue Book Value of Your Autos   1)_____   4)_____
2)_____   5)_____
3)_____

COMPREHENSIVE PERSONAL LIABILITY INSURANCE — UMBRELLA LIABILITY POLICY:

	Insurance Company/Insured	Policy Number	Liability Maximum	Deductible	Special Features	Remarks	Annual Premium
1							
2							
3							
4							
5							

PERSONAL UMBRELLA LIABILITY INSURANCE:
The insurance needed by successful, high-net-worth wealth-builders

This is an add-on to your other policies that essentially extends your coverage to fill in any gaps not covered by your homeowner's and vehicle policies. If you've read or heard about large liability suits, you've probably thought what would happen if you were the subject of such a suit. If a judgment was won against you, the claimant could take everything you own in addition to whatever insurance you might have. If you have deep pockets, the probability of such a suit happening against you increases.

Unfortunately, the hard work you've done to achieve a high net worth increases the willingness of people to pursue a lawsuit when they might otherwise have simply shrugged off an occurrence as a case of bad fortune rather than negligence on your part. That innocent paper boy can often be talked into becoming a plaintiff if he breaks his ankle on your property. And since most homeowner's policies have maximum coverages, usually one million dollars, you could become vulnerable. Courts have been known to award damages not so much on the degree of negligence as on the degree of the defendant's ability to pay the damages. The recourse is to have a comprehensive personal umbrella liability policy. This may typically cost, say $400 to $500 annually for $2,000,000 in coverage

You can purchase a comprehensive personal umbrella liability policy as either a separate comprehensive liability policy or, sometimes, by purchasing a rider on your homeowner policy. You should consult with your property casualty insurance professional to find which is more appropriate for you. This policy expands the liability coverage that a home and automobile policy normally cover — paying costs that become the insured's legal obligations due to bodily injury or property damage not covered by the other two policies.

In addition, the policy will pay the legal expenses and attorney's fees for the insurance company's chosen counsel. The insurance company has the right to settle a claim or suit against you that it decides is appropriate. In addition to the expense, the contract will pay the interest on judgments plus certain other legal costs.

The insureds under your comprehensive liability policy are you, your relatives who are residents of your household, and any other person under age 21 who is in the care of a resident of the household.

You may also want your umbrella liability policy to encompass the areas of slander, defamation of character and invasion of privacy. You may also want it to cover damages caused by non-owned property in your care and control, such as a borrowed snowblower on which a neighbor's child gets hurt. There are circumstances in which you would be liable for that injury yet your homeowner's policy would not provide coverage. Your umbrella liability policy should provide the protection.

As mentioned above, you may also want to include coverage for libel, slander and invasion of privacy. Libel is written defamation of character; slander is spoken defamation of character. Invasion of privacy may be claimed by anyone who feels their piece of mind has been invaded. People have a right to privacy in personal matters and feel they should not be commented upon or scrutinized in public without their consent. Additionally, if you are exposed to claims of plagiarism or violation of copyright laws, your comprehensive personal liability or umbrella liability policy could provide proper protection.

Don't take a chance by thinking everyone has medical coverage. Take a mental inventory of your household. How many people are you responsible for? Do any of them do things that you would not describe as reasonable and prudent, or more importantly, that your neighbor would not describe as reasonable and prudent? Do you have any animals that could cause someone injury? What about toys, bikes, boats, all-terrain vehicles, snowmobiles and so on? What about equipment such as the lawnmower and the snowblower? Do you allow others to use any of your possessions, on your own insured property — or, more hazardous still, off your own insured property? You need to know how your policy protects you from economic loss in all circumstances where you may be held responsible.

We feel your liability maximum should be increased to the maximum amount practical when coordinated with your umbrella or comprehensive liability policy. We recommend you obtain an umbrella liability policy (see sidebar above) or a comprehensive personal liability policy coordinated with your other property casualty insurances. The cost of such a policy is frequently related to the quantity and quality of your underlying property/casualty insurances. Your agent can evaluate the increases in costs resulting from increasing your underlying policy and compare those increased costs with the resulting decreased cost of the umbrella policy. The coordination of the two should provide the most cost-effective package for you. There is more on a personal umbrella liability policy above.

Over 40 million people in the United States do not have property medical insurance, and the number is increasing rather than decreasing. If the person making a claim against you is uninsured, they will look to you for reimbursement. And if you are a truly successful wealth-builder, you are risking even greater exposure without it. (See the sidebar on page 23.) Ask your property liability insurance professional about liability where homeowner's policies are not effective in providing this protection.

LIFE INSURANCE

Life insurance is the one investment in which you are guaranteed to never see the results. It is for the benefit of the survivors. (Some newer policies though are allowing the terminally ill to reap their investments when it will still do some good — immediately before their impending death. Look for more on this in an upcoming lesson.) Life insurance benefits can range from merely covering the costs of a modest funeral to full lifelong financial security for all family members and for your favorite charities to boot. Life insurance guarantees that the person who will suffer an economic loss in the event of your death will be indemnified for that loss. Replacing the economic work value of human life is the primary purpose of life insurance.

Determining the amount of life insurance you want for your beneficiary(ies) is a very personal decision. We can assist you in determining the amount that will satisfy your objectives, but the final decision will be a value judgment of your own.

Do an Inventory and Determine Your Needs The first task is to inventory all your life insurance policies and record them on one document — recording the beneficiaries, annual premiums, death benefits, asset values and any outstanding loans on the policies. Be sure to include any employer provided coverages. Look closely at each policy. Usually you will find a short statement of exactly what type of policy it is, such as whole life, term insurance, universal life, fixed premium variable life, or a universal variable life. (We'll discuss these in a few pages.)

Look for the asset value of the policy. It is the amount that the insurance company would pay you if you cashed it in for its cash surrender value. If you have borrowed against the policy, record the amount of the policy loan in the next column. If your policy is other than term insurance, and increases in cash value annually, record the latest annual increase in cash value. Next, record the annual dividend if the policy provides for one. Record the gross annual premium — not the annual premium reduced by the dividend.

Record the primary beneficiary, the secondary beneficiary, and the policy features such as waiver of premium, accidental death benefit, the existence of any surrender charges or contingent withdrawal charges, and so on. Carefully check those beneficiary provisions—you would be surprised how often they turn out to be inappropriate. Finally, record the interest rate that the insurance company would charge if you wanted to take a policy loan. *Note: Death benefits to beneficiaries and wills have nothing to do with one another. Probate courts treat the two as blind from one another so you do not need to represent beneficiaries of life insurance policies in your will.*

Once you have completed the inventory, total up your present life insurance. If you are in doubt about the beneficiary provision on your existing life insurance, ask for a change of beneficiary form and complete it as it should be.

Determining Your Life Insurance Requirements

Now that you have inventoried your policies and made the logical corrections, determine if they are sufficient. Let's start with an objective form that will assist in considering your individual needs for life insurance explaining the more difficult items.

Although most of the line items on this form explain themselves or depend on your unique circumstances, we'll still explain the more esoteric ones. Item 1: The legal process to clear an estate from any legal and tax obligations is called probate. The costs usually consume around 5 percent of the deceased's estate. Other administrative costs, such as appraisals, filing fees, etc., should be provided for with, say, another 2 percent. Add a little more if you're leaving behind a particularly complex estate.

Items 2 through 5 are really up to you. You should complete them based on the pledges, debts, tastes in funerals and any tax liabilities, etc., you may have.

Items 6 and 7, however, are not common or individually specific. Here's a quick lesson in federal and state estate tax laws for the common wealth-builder. (There's more to come in the estate planning lesson!) There are no federal and almost never any state taxes on estates of $600,000 or less left to designated heirs. There are no taxes at all on 100 percent of the estate if it is left to a surviving spouse. If you give property (money is property) in excess of $600,000 to any heirs other than a spouse, taxes start at 37 percent of the excess above $600,000 and climb to 55 percent. If you expect to be in this taxable group, of course, seek competent counsel, and seek it before death. Once you have died there is no way to then "put the toothpaste back in the tube," as they say.

Life Insurance Needs Analyzer

Funds Required for Cash Expenses & Sinking Funds

1. Probate and Administration Expenses:
   a. 5% of Probate Property _____
   b. 2% of Non-Probate _____
   c. ?% for Complexity _____
2. Funeral Expenses _____
3. Special Obligations
   Pledges _____
   Contracts _____
   Divorce _____
   Business _____
4. Debts/Insurance Loans/Current Bills _____
5. Income Tax Liabilities:
   a. Year of death return _____
   b. Retirement plan payout _____
   c. IRA/KEOGH/TSA payouts _____
   d. Deferred annuity payouts _____
   e. Tax Shelter - Liability exceeds:
      1. Basis _____
      2. Fair Market Value _____
6. Federal Estate Taxes _____
7. State Inheritance Taxes _____
8. Education Fund
   (Calculated or today's cost estimate) _____
9. Mortgage(s) _____
10. Extra Fund for Error,
    Family Emergency Fund _____

Funds Required For Cash Expenses & Sinking Funds _____

The Quick Method for Determining Desired Coverage

There is no better way to determine your desired death benefits than using the chart above. There is, however, a short "rule of thumb" method. This is shown on page 26.

The quick method for determining the death benefit you should leave behind in order to meet your survivors' needs assumes you will have the survivors live off the interest earnings of your death benefit. And it further assumes they will never dip into the principal, or *corpus,* as many financial advisors and insurance salespeople may call it.

To do this simply determine the annual income needed in the most expensive year of your survivors' lives and divide that by .06. Then gross that amount up to pay for the funeral, taxes, probate and other special obligations. (We'll walk through an example in a moment). *Note: If, in your death benefit, you leave money to pay off your mortgage for the sake of your survivors, remember not to include a mortgage payment in their annual expenses.* The model basically assumes you will earn an average of 6 percent annually on the money. Not an unreasonable rate when averaged over, say, 20 years.

Quick Method Calculation

$$\frac{\text{Maximum single year expenses your survivors might need}}{\text{Divided by .06}} = \begin{array}{l}\text{Amount of net death benefit}\\\text{needed in the bank after}\\\text{funeral, probate, tax and}\\\text{special obligation expenses}\\\text{are paid after death.}\end{array}$$

You are to do the calculation in today's dollars despite increases in the cost of living. All the years in which the survivors will not need to draw the maximum will accumulate the funds that are eaten by inflation. The non-peak years will both accumulate annual surpluses and will increase due to compounded interest earnings.

Let's take an example. If the highest income required from supplemental funds in any of the years you want your survivors looked after is $2,000 per month ($24,000 per year), then divide $24,000 by .06. Doing this you will find that you need $400,000 in capital to generate $24,000 a year in income at a 6 percent interest rate. Then add to the $400,000, say, $10,000 for a funeral and any amount of outstanding income tax due in the year you die. (This shouldn't be much if you or your employer have been keeping up with the withholdings.) Let's say $2,000 to be very conservative. Now we're at $412,000 as a death benefit required for your survivors.

Now gross-up the $412,000 by, say, a 10 percent factor for probate and other related death expenses. This is done by taking 1 minus the gross-up factor: in this case, 1.00 - .10 to equal .90. Dividing $412,000 by .90, we get about $458,000 (or $46,000 in probate costs). Thus we are left with $458,000 to pay probate ($46,000), outstanding taxes ($2,000), and funeral expenses ($10,000), leaving us $400,000 worth of capital to generate the income needed by your survivors.

For quick calculation purposes, you can assume that for every $500 per month you want for your survivors, it is going to take at least $100,000 of capital to provide it.

Comparing What You Need to What You Have

Now that you have determined the total amount of capital your family needs in the event of your death, you may start subtracting what you already have accumulated for their benefit, such as your present invested capital, the net benefits of your life insurance and the cash generated by your retirement funds. The difference between what you decided was required and what you have accumulated is your shortage or surplus. The most immediate way to provide for that shortage is to purchase a life insurance policy with a face amount — or death benefit — equal to what you are lacking in capital.

For example, in the case examined above, the $458,000 needed may be partially offset by a nest-egg in various banks and securities of $158,000. The remaining unfunded portion, $300,000, is the value of the life insurance you would purchase.

Once the insurance company has accepted you as an insured and issued your policy, that total amount of capital is immediately available at your death for your family's benefit. There is no other economic tool that can do this for you. Sorry though, your research and decisions are not over.

Now you must decide what kind of life insurance!

Life Insurance Costs

All forms of life insurance, (and we're going to discuss the many forms in a moment) cause an insurance company to incur costs. Unlike other forms of insurance, such as homeowners, life insurance is one area in which insurance companies often actually share their costs with you when making a proposal for your business. Let's explore this first since an understanding of these costs will help to understand the various forms of life insurance.

The most obvious cost is what the industry calls mortality cost — funds issued to pay the death claims. The second is expenses. Expense costs are incurred in issuing and managing the policy to include commissions to salespeople.

The insurance company calculates mortality costs to cover the amount of death benefit they promised to pay you under your policy. To do this, the insurance company, in effect, has pooled you with others of your same age, sex, smoking habits and physical make-up. You and I don't know if we are going to die next year, but if there are enough of us, the number of people who will die in any one year from among this large group can be predicted with great statistical accuracy. The insurance company has taken an uncertainty on our part, and turned it into a certainty on their part. Therefore, if we all contribute a mortality charge to the fund held by the insurance company, there will be sufficient dollars in the fund to pay the death benefits to those who will die in the coming year. That's the mortality cost, the cost of the life insurance.

The expenses, or administrative costs, cover the monthly, quarterly or annual billing, having a customer support staff available to answer questions, prove to a lender you have life insurance, etc. As mentioned, it also covers the commissions to the salespeople. The rate and timing of when one company pays its salespeople over another company are as varied as the number of life insurance companies. Some pay a fixed amount, broken up and paid out over many years, while others pay it all up front within a month after you make out your first check.

These two costs, mortality and expenses, are in every life insurance policy quotation and in every premium you pay. They cannot be avoided or the insurance company would go out of business. You do not want your insurance company going out of business before you do.

Now let's go on to review the various forms of life insurance available.

Types of Life Insurance: Term and Term-Plus

There are two categories of life insurance: term, and term plus an investment program. We'll call this second one term-plus for short. Note the chart on page 28.

In this chart, term insurance is further subdivided into term that has virtually no flexibility and few guarantees — other than to provide the death benefit promised — and term that has much more flexibility. We'll discuss this in more detail shortly.

The chart also shows term-plus life insurance options, which are whole, variable, universal and variable universal life insurance. The total of six options are then compared across six key variables for which many options may be extended by the insuring company — the insurer. Let's now discuss each. For a concise discussion, however, of the life insurance products found in the table, turn to wealth-building Step 75, How to Evaluate Life Insurance Products, found on page 29.

■ *Term Life Insurance* — With term insurance, you will pay for only the mortality and expense charges, and no more. There is no additional collection to pay for a savings plan — insurance is all you get. Term itself has a few variations; let's explore them.

Menu of Life Insurance Products

Term

	General Description	Investment Vehicle	Flexibility of Investment	Flexibility of Premium	Flexibility of Face Amount	Appropriate For
Non-Guaranteed Term	Lowest cost. No control.	None	None	None, but premiums do increase.	None	Very limited situations.
Yearly Renewable Convertible Term	Higher cost. Greater control.	None	None	None, but premiums do increase.	None	Limited cash flow. Meets temporary needs. Offers protection now.

Term-Plus

	General Description	Investment Vehicle	Flexibility of Investment	Flexibility of Premium	Flexibility of Face Amount	Appropriate For
Whole Life	Dividends provide investment return.	Insurance company's bond & mortgage general account.	None. You can borrow.	None. Loans or dividends can reduce premium.	None. You must buy another policy to expand.	Conservative savers, older persons, and substandard insureds.
Variable Life	You direct the Investments.	Money market, stock & bond, all in separate accounts.	High. You split it. You move it. No withdrawals.	None. Loans can reduce premiums.	None. You must buy another policy to expand.	Investors. Alternative to "Buy term & invest the difference."
Universal Life	Returns float with current interest rates.	Short-term guaranteed interest.	None. You can borrow and withdraw.	Maximum. Enough for mortality & expenses up to maximum the law allows.	Maximum. You may increase or decrease it, but stay healthy for increases.	For those who like only short-term earnings rates.
Variable Universal Life	You get control, disclosure and flexibility of Investment options.	Money market, stock & bond, all in separate accounts, plus guaranteed interest.	Maximum. You split it. You move it. You withdraw it or borrow it.	Maximum. Enough for mortality & expenses up to maximum the law allows.	Maximum. You may increase or decrease it, but stay healthy for increases.	Investors. Alternative to "Buy term & invest the difference." I want it MY way!

Term Only or Non-Guaranteed Term — Typically, the most efficient and least expensive form of term insurance is yearly renewable and convertible term. With this policy, you pay the mortality and expense charges for the current year only, and you accept the fact that as you get older, your mortality costs will go up — after all the probability you'll die is increasing. In each succeeding year, you can expect the premium to increase. It is efficient because you won't need to contact the company to make changes and the company won't be contacting you except to receive payments.

It is the least expensive of all also, especially if you don't ask the insurance company to do anything more than pay the death benefit. Beware though, the absolute, "stripped down" version of term insurance does not promise to renew you automatically year after year. The company can cancel or make you take another physical to keep down the cost. This no-frills term insurance is very cheap and is often the type quoted in ads or by quotation services in order to get your attention. Similarly, if the company does not promise

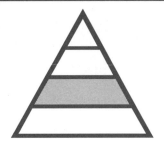

How to Evaluate Life Insurance Products

What: Evaluate your life insurance options: both term and term-plus.

Why: Life insurance is an investment purchased to provide for the deleterious financial effects on your dependents caused by your death — whether they be simply the costs of your funeral or the loss of income and the change in lifestyle it produces. Many people, although they may believe in this insurance's benefits, do not understand it, nor know how to optimally employ its full potential.

Risk: Like all insurances, the only risk, other than investing with a bad company (see next line), is the cost of the premium payments that could go toward other investments.

Safety: High. But be sure to invest with a quality company as explained in the sidebar on page 8.

Liquidity: Like other insurance, such as disability, if you are providing for the potential losses associated with losing your life by keeping liquid assets at bay, those funds can be freed up for investment.

Why not: In the case of term insurance, if you already have enough funds secured to cover all the expenses you want taken care of upon death, you may have no need for term. In the case of term-plus insurance, if your household's spending priorities do not allow for more funds to be spent on long-term or retirement-oriented investments, then term-plus and its ability to grow wealth tax-free holds little importance. For example, your spending horizon may require active, available income for such expenses as an elderly parent.

Buy/invest from: A quality insurance salesperson from a quality company.

Background: We've provided a discussion of how to evaluate life insurance in the body of this lesson, but we'll cover more of it here. Term insurance buys you a death-benefit payment payable, usually in a lump sum, shortly after death. Term-plus not only buys the death-benefit payment, but also has a financial investment program attached, usually structured as tax-free investing.

First let's cover term. As you can see in the Menu of Life Insurance Products found on page 28, there is non-guaranteed term and term that is renewable and convertible. Non-guaranteed term means the cost of insurance will go up with your age and you may have to continue to prove medically, usually with a physical exam, that you are insurable. Also you will not be able to increase the amount of your death-benefit payment without disproportionate increases in costs.

Renewable term allows you to continue to be insurable year after year without either proving you're insurable or, possibly, increases in premium costs. Convertible term allows you to convert the term life insurance product into a term-plus product and take advantage of some cost savings in the process.

Term-plus products include whole life, the granddad of term-plus policies; universal, which allows tax-free investing as a component of the policy package; and variable, which gives you greater flexibility to direct the tax-free investments that are attached to the policy. And then there is variable universal — which, as you've guessed, is a hybrid of both universal and whole life. It is discussed in greater detail in the next wealth-building step.

Step 75: *How to Evaluate Life Insurance Products*

> ▶ ▶ ▶ **If you want to want to get started today, here's how to begin evaluating life insurance:**

You must first decide if your spending priorities allow for you to spend more money than you currently are on tax-free investing that cannot be accessed very quickly. Some households have already given the maximum they can afford to employment-related programs such as 401(k)s and SEPs (see the lesson Work, Employment and Investment). Some households have a priority on short- or medium-term requirements, such as college tuition for children or nursing home expenses for parents. If there is essentially little or no room for additional funds to be socked away for longer term purposes in your household, then term insurance may be best for you.

If you decide that term is all your investment horizon and priorities allow for, then evaluate the options offered by the companies that offer term. Give heavy consideration, though, to paying the extra required for renewable policies. You want to place the control of the options in your hands for such things as guarantee of renewability.

If you decide you have more cash to stow away in longer-term investments, and you have reached your allowable maximums in IRAs and work related plans such as 401(k)s, then move into term-plus policies as the next tax-advantaged place for funds.

Call your insurance agent; call around using the phone book; call Quotesmith, mentioned earlier, at 1-800-556-9393. Compile a record of the best prices for the most benefits you can purchase. Remember, as this lesson teaches, don't necessarily go for the least expensive policy. It may have little or no flexibility. And, be sure to read this entire section on life insurance, as well as the next wealth-building step, where we expressly talk about variable universal life insurance. ▲

Continued from p.28

you the right to renew, the company is not likely to have to pay a death claim. As a result of not having to make any of these extra promises, the insurance company will be able to minimize your cost. However, you will have little control over your policy.

Renewable Term Insurance — If you want more from the insurance company, such as the promise to accept your premium in the coming years and to allow your insurance to continue — i.e., renewable term insurance — you will have to pay a little bit extra for the promise of renewability. Most people willingly pay extra for this renewable privilege because you never know when you may go from insurable to uninsurable. Uninsurability may result from the deterioration of your health, your latest avocation or your current occupation. An insurance company may not wish to provide life insurance for you at any cost. At that time, that renewable privilege on your existing policies will become particularly important to you. You are in control, not the insurance company.

Convertible Term Insurance — You also may want to pay for the convertibility feature in a life insurance policy. This allows you to change your term insurance policy into any of the other types of contracts that are issued by the same life insurance company, such as universal life. If you are dealing with an insurance company that has an incomplete portfolio of products, or does not have the product you need, then replace your term insurance. The convertibility feature is not of any value. You will want to deal with an insurance company that has a complete portfolio of products and/or at least the type of product that you may wish to use in the future.

Level-Premium Term Insurance — There are also term insurance policies that charge the same premium for five years, ten years, even as long as twenty years. The insurance company has taken a look at the yearly renewable and convertible term rate required each year and has averaged it out over the period of time. They then charge you a level premium for the five-, ten- or twenty-year period. They will take more than is required in the early years of the policy so they can afford to take less in the later years. This way, starting out, you pay more into the policy than you do toward the end.

If you keep the term insurance policy for the total period of time, it might be a fair arrangement. However, since many people adjust their term insurance policies from year to year, paying this additional premium in the beginning of the period — when you may not own the policy at the end of the period — can be a waste of money.

Also, when you come to the end of the level-premium period, you might run into some policy brick walls. For example, you may be confronted with substantial increases in costs or requirements for new physicals. Watch it! Those brick walls can make level-term insurance look deceptively cheap. The insurance company knows it has a chance to get rid of you as an insured before you die. The solution is to secure a policy that is automatically convertible and renewable.

Decreasing Term Insurance/Mortgage Term Insurance — You can also buy a term insurance policy with a level premium but with a reducing death benefit so that the same premium is sufficient to cover the mortality and expense charges during all years. This is commonly referred to as decreasing term insurance. The insurance companies like to market it as mortgage insurance to make you feel as if you need to buy it. This type of insurance reduces the amount of your death benefit over the life of the policy. The insurance company automatically reduces your death benefit as you get older and your statistical chances of dying increase. Although it does serve a viable purpose for some individuals who are in the market for this, it is often deceptively attractive to those who truly do not want this continually reducing benefit but who do want the benefits of life insurance. You may be better off paying more for a better package.

■ ***Term-Plus Life Insurances — a.k.a., The Investment Types of Life Insurance*** — We have described the various forms of term-only life insurances. Term-plus continues to contain the two basic elements of term insurance — mortality and expense charges — but adds a tax-advantaged investment element, hence the plus designation. Term-plus life insurance includes whole life, universal life, fixed premium variable and universal variable life insurance.

It is our opinion that the only reason you would put additional money with an insurance company would be to earn a tax-advantaged return. What is unique about the investment return inside term-plus life insurance is it can be used to pay the mortality and expense charges without the imposition of income taxes. Excess earnings on your investment, after the mortality and expense charge have been paid, are not subject to current taxes. The fact that you may purchase a consumable commodity — the mortality and expense charges of a life insurance policy — with pre-tax earnings to protect your beneficiaries, is unique to the investment types of life insurance. It is a frequently overlooked and underutilized tax advantage, especially if you can find good investments inside of life insurance contracts. So, let's examine the options available that have investments attached to them.

Whole Life...A General Account Policy — Diminishing in popularity, but still available today, is whole life. If you bought this, probably prior to 1976, your "whole life" policy may have been called a family policy, a life paid-up at 65 policy, an endowment policy, a ten- or twenty-pay life policy, or even a single-pay life policy. The names described how long you were to pay the fixed premium required by, and unique to, your whole life insurance. Each policy was issued with a fixed face amount — that is, the death benefit, say, $200,000 — and a fixed annual premium. Whole life insurance policies pass investment results through to the policy owner by way of dividends and guaranteed cash values. Dividends are considered to be a return of premium. They are free of income taxation as long as the total dividends paid you do not exceed the total premiums you paid into the policy.

Note: Once the money you withdraw from your policy exceeds the money you put in (less mortality and expense costs), you will have to pay taxes on the withdrawals at ordinary income tax rates. Nonetheless, the gains have grown tax-free. This is true of all forms of term-plus insurance.

Variable Life Insurance — In 1976, the industry introduced the first variable life insurance policy. Essentially, the insurance company created this policy by changing the investment available within the contract. In those first policies, they removed the bond and mortgage account and replaced it with two accounts, a common stock account and a money market account. They gave the policy owner the option of using either one or both, and the ability to change back and forth between the two. This was the first-generation variable life policy. This policy, just like its predecessor, whole life insurance, had a fixed premium and a fixed face amount.

If you wanted more life insurance, you had to buy another contract. If you couldn't pay the premiums when due, the policy would lapse. Relative to the investment performance of whole life, variable whole life has performed admirably, assuming that the policy owner had the assets invested in the common stock account. Ironically, one reason it did so well was because the stock market did so poorly. The stock market languished below the 1000 point of the Dow Jones Industrial Average from 1976 until late 1982 — six full years while people were putting in the money and building up their number of shares very cheaply. They were able to purchase many shares to enjoy the ride up (and occasionally down) in the Dow since that time. It, of course, has essentially quintupled since then.

Universal Life Insurance — This product, introduced around 1980, changed the industry. Universal life was the industry's response to the demands for the high interest rates of the time. Insurance companies decided to use relatively short-term investments and to promise policy owners a stipulated rate of interest for a one-year period commencing on the date they purchased their policy. The interest rates of the early 1980s were high, money market funds were popular, and these policies immediately became popular as well.

Since the insurance company promised policy owners a stipulated rate of return for a year, the policy owner naturally wanted to be able to verify he or she actually was receiving the promised rate of return — and so did the regulators. As a result, for the first time, it was necessary for the insurance company to reveal to the policy owner the expenses and the mortality charges required by the contract.

The day this happened, all life insurance changed. For the first time, a life insurance policy was transparent. You could now see interest earnings and mortality costs. Prior to that time, all anyone had ever seen were the end results, without a breakdown of exactly what was going on inside of the policy each month and each year. Universal life brought disclosure to life insurance. Now you could see the mortality costs and the administrative expenses the consumer bears on his or her existing policy. The impact of this ability to see costs is continuously improving the quality of life insurance products for the consumer. Both consumers and salespeople have yet to realize its full impact since it fundamentally continues to bring down costs.

> *It [life insurance] is a frequently overlooked and underutilized tax advantage, especially if you can find good investments inside of life insurance contracts.*

Not only did universal life bring cost disclosure to life insurance, it also brought flexibility to life insurance policies. Whole life dictated a fixed face amount — that is, death benefit — a fixed annual premium and a fixed investment vehicle to the policy owner. Variable life had the fixed minimum face amount and fixed premium; however, it gave the policy owner the flexibility of an investment vehicle. Universal life eliminated the fixed premium and fixed face amount but, for the moment, offered no flexibility in investment. (More on this in a moment.)

When you shop for a universal life policy, the agent presents you with an illustration, or annual report, with three columns — the expense, mortality and interest columns. If you want to increase or decrease your death benefit and see the impact on both your premium payment and your potential interest earnings, you can simply look up and down the illustration to see the increasing or decreasing charges in the mortality column and/or the expense column. Thus, universal life offers flexibility of death benefit, so that you can use one policy and increase it or decrease it as your life situation dictates.

Note: Caveat emptore! These illustrations, or tables, presented by companies have historically been quite unreliable. A study done by the American Society of Insurance Professionals found no company's illustration to be indicative of actual results. We encourage you to call the Society at 1-800-392-6900 and ask for an Illustration Questionnaire. Give a copy of the questionnaire to each company vying for your universal life dollars. The questionnaire asks the right questions to reveal just how probable the company's rosy prognostications may be.

Universal life can be a valuable insurance instrument. However, don't let overzealous salespeople sour your interest. The competition in life insurance is intense. Universal life offers flexibility of premium payment that other products don't offer. You can add to the investment in the policy by increasing premium payments. At a minimum, the policy must have sufficient moneys in it to cover simply the mortality and expense charges. On occasion, if prevailing earnings rates drop wildly, you may be asked to add additional funds to cover mortality costs. And your insurance can lapse if you do not respond to the insurance company's notices.

Since term-plus policies allow for savings to accumulate tax-free, much like an IRA, in 1988 Uncle Sam set a maximum amount on the funds you can hide away in these policies. A change to the Internal Revenue Code in 1988 limited the tax benefits of life insurance by reducing the maximum you could put into a policy. Check with your sales representative on the maximums.

Variable Universal Life — The next inevitable step in the evolution of the life insurance policy came in 1985. The industry introduced a policy that combined the flexibility of premium payment and face amount offered by universal life with the flexibility of investment offered by variable life. In these new variable universal policies, insurance companies give you personal control over the life insurance policy's face amount, amount of premium and types of investment. You now control all three basic features of your life insurance!

Such control makes these policies very unlike the whole life policy that you tend to put in the safety deposit box and forget. Variable universal life insurance gives you a great deal of control. Your own financial management can make these policies perform extremely well, or poorly. You can make decisions not only on death benefit but also on levels of funding within the policy. Funding level refers to how much you choose to pay into the contract. You choose where the moneys you pay in are invested. The market share of this type of policy is increasing rapidly at the expense of the other types. New policies and new investment options are added daily. The advantage of investing in separate accounts similar to some of your favorite mutual funds, but without taxation, is the most attractive aspect of this product. For more on this optimal form of term-plus insurance, see wealth-building Step 76, How to Evaluate and Possibly Use One of the New Innovations Such as Variable Universal Life, found on page 35.

Second-to-Die Life Insurance

A strategy now being used with greater frequency is for the estate owner and spouse to minimize estate taxes at the first death as much as possible. This involves using the marital deduction and the $600,000 exemption to eliminate estate taxes entirely on up to $1,200,000 in assets. (Congress is on the prowl, getting ready to change this soon, though.) Estates larger than this, or unplanned estates, probably face estate taxes. In order to make sure that cash is available at the second death, you may purchase a second-to-die policy (also called survivorship life). Such a policy will not pay off at the death of the first of the two to die, but rather at the second death. As a result, this type of life insurance requires lower mortality costs than a regular life insurance policy. It also allows a couple, one of whom may not be in the best of health, to obtain life insurance that will pay off at the second death. These policies come in whole life, universal life and variable universal life designs.

Is Life Insurance a Good Investment?

Insurance companies are essentially forbidden from marketing a term-plus policy as an investment vehicle — constructed for purposes of increasing your net worth with tax-free investments. Instead, life insurance is to protect your survivors from a loss of income.

This does not, however, change the fact that if a comfortable retirement or, at least, long-term yield are primary goals of yours, then recommendations need to be consistent. You should always, using your household's discretionary dollars, fill up the tax-advantaged instruments that exist, starting with IRAs, 401(k)s and SEPs. Term-plus insurance policies, since they build tax-free but hold a few more restrictions than say 401(k)s, could be filled up next. Then, turn to annually taxable instruments, such as mutual funds, and securities like stocks.

If, however, your household's spending priorities are not as heavily weighted toward long-term yield or retirement as toward other concerns, then term-plus holds less importance. You may have a higher emphasis on active, available income, whether for plain old fun or for planned impending expenses such as college tuition.

Separate from the tax-free, retirement-income aspects of term-plus, term insurance holds its own kind of worthiness concern. The key fact is, if you want and need the protection of term life insurance, it can be a wonderful investment. If you don't want life insurance, then the loss of part or all of your investment return to pay mortality and expense charges is an unnecessary expense. This is a fundamental concern that only you can ponder. You are no doubt investing a lot of your time, talents and treasure trying to build financial security — otherwise you would not be in this course. Life insurance offers the opportunity to hedge against losing much of what you've worked for.

Wrapping it Up

Insurance coverage can be a vitally important tool to manage your wealth by containing risk. In the case of some life insurance products, it can actually contribute to the growth in net worth rather than simply protect from loss, as with, say, homeowner, or vehicle insurance. As you learned in a previous lesson, many write covered call options to both pick up some additional income on their assets and to purchase insurance on their gains in net worth. Insurance is much like writing a covered call option. As you progress through this course and apply its information properly, your net worth is sure to grow. Insurance will help you prevent loss on that worth and protect your gains. Remember, don't risk a lot to save a little! ▲

STEP 76

How to Evaluate and Possibly Use One of the New Innovations Such as Variable Universal Life

What: Determine if variable universal life insurance — a relatively recent invention of the insurance industry — is right for you.

Why: If you have determined that term-plus life insurance is right for your long-term wealth-building plans, variable universal may be the best option since it offers the greatest degree of freedoms, such as investment direction and changes to the death benefits, of all the life insurance products.

Risk: Same as the risks for the other insurance instruments highlighted in this lesson's steps: the expense of the premiums and investing with a bad insurance company (see next line).

Safety: High. But be sure to invest with a quality company as explained in the sidebar on page 8.

Liquidity: Like other insurance, such as disability, if you are providing for the potential losses associated with losing your life by keeping liquid assets at bay, those funds can be freed up for investment.

Why not: If your household's spending priorities do not allow for additional funds to be committed to long-term or retirement-oriented, tax-advantaged investments, then variable universal will not be right for you. For example, your spending horizon may require all cash to be available for that move out of your three-room apartment and finally into the home your growing family needs.

Buy/invest from: A quality insurance salesperson with a quality company.

Background: Variable universal life insurance gives you the flexibility of premium payment and death benefit offered by universal life, along with the flexibility of investments offered by variable life. In these relatively new variable universal policies, insurance companies give you personal control over the life insurance policy's death benefit (face amount), amount of premium payment and the investment direction. You now control all three basic features of your life insurance!

Most of the more established companies selling variable life insurance give you a broad array of investment options (allowing you to divide your money among several instruments). This essentially allows the money to be a kind of self-directed IRA (tax sheltered until you take more money out than you put in).

If you want to get started today, here's what you need to do to invest in variable universal life insurance:

Just like investing in securities, you can and should request from your insurance professional a prospectus for any variable universal life policy. You will find the prospectus rather revealing.

First look for items that are specific to life insurance. Make sure to check that the expense and mortality costs are reasonable and competitive. Then look for the same things you would with mutual funds (quality of the company, the investment directions, diversification, managers, etc.).

Also just as with mutual funds, look in the prospectus for both expenses and investment alternatives. Look for expenses that are competitive with those of mutual funds, say from 0.5 percent to 3.5 percent. For investment alternatives, look for families of funds to include not only bonds but broad options across equities, to include value, income, growth and international equities. This will enable you to start off with a well-diversified investment program that you can set into place and not have to bother with tactically reallocating. Variable universal life should be viewed as a long-term investment, so allocate and diversify accordingly. Remember though, still consider it to be part of your total wealth-building program. Don't allocate its money in the same places you've placed all of your other long-term or retirement funds. Diversify it away from, say, the direction of your 401(k). ▲

How to invest in currency:

Greenback alternatives

LESSON 24

How to invest in currency:
Greenback alternatives

"Money speaks sense in a language all nations understand."
— Aphra Behn, The Rover, Part II, 1680

THE WORLD'S MOST RESPECTED CURRENCY

American investors are among the most fortunate in the world — for a variety of reasons. Their domestic markets are well established and well regulated, with ample rules in place to protect their interests. The capitalistic system in which those markets operate generates a broad variety of investment vehicles and a multitude of wealth-building opportunities. The trading systems for those vehicles are generally uniform, providing both efficiency and liquidity. And last, but certainly not least, virtually all of the investments are denominated in U.S. dollars — without question, the world's most respected currency.

The dollar — though at times besieged as a result of both internal and external economic events, such as in 1995 — remains the worldwide symbol of monetary stability. Americans traveling abroad find that their dollars are welcomed — in many cases, even preferred — in virtually any country they visit. Foreign governments sell precious native resources simply to raise dollars for use in international trade, substituting the U.S. currency for their own weaker monetary units in dealing with other countries. Many major commodities — most notably gold and crude oil — are priced in dollars throughout the world, regardless of the markets on which they are trading. Some countries, like Argentina, even peg the values of their own currencies directly to that of the U.S. dollar.

It's a Trap for U.S. Investors
In spite of this worldwide love affair with the greenback, far too many American investors make the mistake — and it is, indeed, a potentially grave mistake — of keeping all their money in dollar-denominated investments. By so doing, they hamstring their wealth-building efforts — putting all their hopes for the future at the mercy of domestic inflation, internal economic and market upheavals and often-capricious U.S. government spending, taxing and regulatory policies. They also risk diminishing their international purchasing power — making it harder for them to buy imported goods, to travel overseas in style or (the dream of many individuals) to consider retiring abroad.

Finally, and perhaps most damaging, they exclude themselves from roughly 70 percent of the world's investment opportunities, many of which will undoubtedly produce far higher returns than those available on U.S. markets as the global economy continues to mature, forging ahead into the 21st century. It's almost as if the long-time strength and popularity of the U.S. dollar has turned it into a trap for modern-day American investors and consumers.

Learning How To Avoid the Trap

In this lesson, however, you'll learn how to sidestep that trap as you proceed along your road to wealth. We'll explain how the currencies of the world are interlinked, the mechanics of the foreign-exchange markets, how currency exchange rates change, how those changes affect you and how you can profit from them.

We'll also discuss how to select the best foreign currencies, the distinctions between the futures and forward markets with respect to currencies and we'll review some of the things you learned in "The global approach" lesson regarding foreign currency-denominated investments.

Lastly, we'll touch on some other alternatives to dollar-based investments, including gold, and briefly examine whether collectibles have a viable role in your investment plans. First, however, let's take a quick look at the history of the "greenback" — and just how it got where it is today.

A BRIEF HISTORY OF THE U.S. DOLLAR

The term "dollar" comes from the old German "thaler," which was originally a contraction of the word "Joachimsthaler," the name given a coin first minted in 1519 in Joachimstal, Bohemia. The term "thal" or "tal" is also the root word for the Dutch taler, and actually means "valley" — which, given the performance of the dollar the past few years (especially in early 1995), seems almost eerily prophetic.

"Dollar" was adopted as the name for the new U.S. currency when it was first authorized by Congress in 1792. Prior to then, the fledgling nation had used a variety of foreign monies, including the Spanish "pieces of eight." At the same time, the Congress adopted the so-called "bimetallic monetary system" in use in most of the European countries, linking the value of the dollar to the values of gold and silver.

That system was maintained until 1900, when the U.S. adopted a strict gold standard — abandoning silver because the value of the metal had fallen sharply due to a surge in supplies coming from the vast lodes of Nevada and newly opened mines in Peru.

The next change in the dollar situation came in 1944 at Bretton Woods, New Hampshire, where 44 nations from around the world met for a joint monetary conference. At that meeting, the countries agreed to a system of fixed exchange rates, with all currencies pegged to the value of the dollar, which was simultaneously pegged to a gold price of $35 per ounce. Under the agreement, currency values were allowed to fluctuate against the dollar by a maximum of plus or minus 1 percent, and the International Monetary Fund (IMF) was established to oversee the system.

The Death of the Gold Standard

The Bretton Woods Agreement held for more than 25 years despite mounting pressure on the dollar due to ballooning post-war U.S. trade deficits. Finally, however, in 1971, the pressure became too great and a new meeting was held. That resulted in the Smithsonian agreement, which basically kept the fixed exchange rates in place, but increased the allowable fluctuation amount to 2.25 percent. Unfortunately, the new system collapsed almost immediately when the dollar came under massive pressure after the U.S. implemented wage and price controls.

As a result, the government was forced to demonetize the dollar — withdrawing its fixed link to gold — which helped spark the wave of hyperinflation that carried into the 1980s. (At the same time, U.S. citizens were allowed to physically own the yellow metal, something they'd been barred from doing for more than half a century.)

The Smithsonian agreement was officially abandoned in 1973 when the currency markets were completely deregulated and a system of floating exchange rates went into place — essentially meaning that currency values would be set by free-market forces, subject only to intervention by the central banks of the countries whose currencies were being devalued.

Erosion of the Dollar's Value — 1985 to 1996

Country	Currency	Currency Per U.S. Dollar In Jan. '85	U.S. Dollar Per Foreign Currency In Jan. '85	Currency Per U.S. Dollar In March '96	U.S. Dollar Per Foreign Currency In March '96
Japan	Yen	254.777	0.004	105.720	0.009
Britain	Pound	0.884	1.131	0.656	1.524
France	Franc	9.671	0.103	5.095	0.196
Germany	D-mark	3.162	0.316	1.484	0.674
Switzerland	Franc	2.674	0.374	1.201	0.833
Canada	Dollar	1.327	0.753	1.368	0.731

That system continues in force today, and is the mechanism that allowed the dollar to drop so dramatically against the Japanese yen, the German mark and numerous other currencies in the early '90s (the Canadian dollar and Mexican peso being two notable exceptions). This deterioration in the dollar's value is shown in more detail in the table at left.

HOW CURRENCY VALUES ARE DETERMINED

Determining what currencies are worth can be somewhat problematic because, in actuality, paper money has value only in relation to the value of other things. As noted earlier, for many years, the dollar was backed by gold — its value pegged at $35 per ounce — with the values of 40 odd other currencies pegged to that of the dollar. Since the gold standard was abandoned, however, most of the world's currencies — including the dollar — have been backed only by the "good faith and credit" of the countries issuing them. This makes it more difficult to "value" a given currency — but there are two commonly accepted methods of doing it.

The first determines what is known as a currency's "internal value" — which measures how much the citizens of a country can buy with their country's money. For example, if an American shopper has to pay $100 to buy a new dress, then the internal value of the dollar could be said to be 1/100th of a dress. It could also be 1/300th of a new TV set, 1/2,000th of a new computer, etc. — the product is irrelevant, it's the concept that's important. The internal value of a currency is subject to many influences, but the most common is inflation. If, for example, the inflation rate is 5 percent this year, then the shopper's dress will likely cost about $105 next year. Thus, the internal value of the dollar will have fallen to 1/105th of a dress.

The second means of determining what a currency is worth involves calculating its "external value" — in other words, its value relative to other currencies. The external values of two currencies can be estimated by comparing their internal values. For example, if the same dress that cost an American $100 would cost a London shopper 50 British pounds, then the pound would obviously have a value roughly twice that of the dollar.

However, a more precise method of determining external values is to see exactly how much of a foreign currency you can "buy" with a single unit of your own currency. Assume, for example, you were planning a trip to Berlin and went to the bank to convert $1,000 into German marks.

If the bank gave you 1,484 D-marks (Deutschemarks), then the external value of the dollar relative to the mark would be 1.484 — meaning each of your dollars would "buy" 1.484 marks. For a German coming to New York, the scenario would be reversed — he'd have to give his Berlin bank 1,484 D-marks to get $1,000 in U.S. currency. That would make the external value of the mark relative to the dollar roughly 0.674.

Obviously, because each country is different, the external value of that country's currency relative to the U.S. dollar is also different. For example, if you were off to England instead of Germany, you would need to convert your dollars into British pounds. At early 1996 exchange rates, you would get just 656 pounds for your $1,000 (meaning the pound is obviously worth more relative to the dollar than is the D-mark) — i.e., one dollar would "buy" 0.656 British pounds. Conversely, a Londoner heading to Los Angeles would get 1.524 dollars for each pound he converted, and that would be the external value of the pound versus the dollar.

External Value or Exchange Rate?

Most people use the term "exchange rate" when talking about the dollar's worth against other currencies — but, in general, it is the external value of the dollar that they are really expressing. The exchange rate, rather than being the number of foreign currency units one U.S. dollar will buy, is actually the reciprocal — i.e., the number of dollars it takes to buy one unit of a given foreign currency. To clarify:

- External value means: 1 dollar = X units of foreign currency.

- Exchange rate means: 1 foreign currency unit = X dollars.

Foreign Exchange Rates

Currency	Fgn. Currency In Dollars 3/2	3/1	Dollar In Fgn.Currency 3/2	3/1
Prices as of 3:00 p.m. Eastern Time.				
Rates for trades of $1 million minimum.				
f-Argentina	1.0000	1.0000	1.0000	1.0000
Australia	.7358	.7363	1.3591	1.3581
Austria	.0989	.0970	10.110	10.305
c-Belgium	.0332	.0332	30.10	30.15
Brazil	1.1765	1.1765	.8500	.8500
Britain	1.6130	1.5839	.6200	.6314
30-day fwd	1.6126	1.5834	.6201	.6316
60-day fwd	1.6120	1.5827	.6203	.6318
90-day fwd	1.6117	1.5820	.6205	.6321
Canada	.7116	.7172	1.4052	1.3944
30-day fwd	.7103	.7160	1.4078	1.3966
60-day fwd	.7092	.7151	1.4101	1.3985
90-day fwd	.7082	.7143	1.4120	1.3999
y-Chile	.002439	.002436	409.95	410.45
China	.1186	.1186	8.4308	8.4311
Colombia	.001162	.001166	860.50	857.95
c-CzechRep	.0372	.0372	26.90	26.86
Denmark	.1722	.1718	5.8060	5.8208
ECU	1.27270	1.27200	.7857	.7862
z-Ecuador	.000414	.000413	2415.00	2421.50
d-Egypt	.2948	.2948	3.3920	3.3920
Finland	.2272	.2232	4.4015	4.4805
France	.1972	.1946	5.0720	5.1390
Germany	.6925	.6832	1.4440	1.4638
30-day fwd	.6932	.6838	1.4426	1.4624
60-day fwd	.6939	.6844	1.4411	1.4611

Currency	Fgn. Currency In Dollars 3/2	3/1	Dollar In Fgn.Currency 3/2	3/1
90-day fwd	.6945	.6851	1.4398	1.4597
Greece	.004371	.004290	228.80	233.10
Hong Kong	.1293	.1293	7.7312	7.7312
Hungary	.0090	.0089	111.66	111.74
y-India	.0322	.0319	31.044	31.380
Indonesia	.000451	.000451	2218.00	2216.50
Ireland	1.5947	1.5787	.6271	.6334
Israel	.3351	.3347	2.9839	2.9874
Italy	.000607	.000611	1647.66	1638.00
Japan	.010465	.010336	95.56	96.75
30-day fwd	.010499	.010369	95.25	96.44
60-day fwd	.010536	.010409	94.91	96.07
90-day fwd	.010571	.010441	94.60	95.78
Jordan	1.4409	1.4388	.69401	.69502
Lebanon	.000610	.000610	1638.50	1639.00
Malaysia	.3920	.3918	2.5513	2.5520
z-Mexico	.168634	.168919	5.9300	5.9200
Netherland	.6101	.6088	1.6391	1.6425
N. Zealand	.6360	.6329	1.5723	1.5800
Norway	.1548	.1546	6.4585	6.4698
Pakistan	.0324	.0324	30.85	30.85
y-Peru	.4464	.4464	2.240	2.240
z-Philippines	.0385	.0387	25.96	25.83
Poland	.4115	.4132	2.43	2.42
Portugal	.006612	.006583	151.25	151.90
a-Russia	.000227	.000227	4407.00	4407.00
Saudi Arabia	.2667	.2667	3.7500	3.7500
Singapore	.6911	.6902	1.4470	1.4488

Currency	Fgn. Currency In Dollars 3/2	3/1	Dollar In Fgn.Currency 3/2	3/1
SlovakRep	.0333	.0333	30.02	30.02
So. Africa	.2780	.2783	3.5975	3.5935
f-So.Africa	.3236	.2564	3.0905	3.9000
So. Korea	.001266	.001267	789.70	789.40
Spain	.007871	.007819	127.05	127.90
Sweden	.1384	.1369	7.2255	7.3050
Switzerland	.8190	.8068	1.2210	1.2395
30-day fwd	.8207	.8085	1.2184	1.2369
60-day fwd	.8225	.8102	1.2158	1.2343
90-day fwd	.8239	.8118	1.2137	1.2319
Taiwan	.0380	.0379	26.35	26.36
Thailand	.04016	.04010	24.94	24.94
Turkey	.000024	.000024	41475.00	41373.50
U.A.E.	.2724	.2724	3.6710	3.6710
f-Uruguay	.170940	.170940	5.85	5.85
y-Venezuela	.0059	.0059	169.8700	169.9700

ECU: European Currency Unit, a basket of European currencies. The Federal Reserve Board's index of the value of the dollar against 10 other currencies weighted on the basis of trade was 85.05 Thursday , off 0.99 points or 1.15 percent from Wednesday 86.04. A year ago the index was 94.55.

a-fixing, Moscow Interbank Currency Exchange, c-commercial rate. d-free market rate. f-financial rate, y-official rate, z-floating rate.

This is a subtle distinction, but it is an important one for many investment and currency-trading transactions. Futures prices, for example, are quoted in terms of the dollar's "exchange rate" relative to the specific currency represented by the contract, whereas "spot" market trades (actual "physical" currency transactions) are generally reported based on the dollar's "external value."

To help alleviate some of the possible confusion, most currency tables featured in the financial press, such as the sample shown at left from *Investor's Business Daily,* list both the exchange rate (the columns headed "Fgn. Currency in Dollars") and the external value (the columns headed "Dollar in Fgn. Currency").

Market Action Determines Currency Values

As with most securities, commodities and financial instruments traded in a free-market system, the actual day-to-day values for the world's currencies are determined by supply and demand factors that develop as billions of dollars in currencies change hands among large international banks, global investment companies and multinational corporations. More so than with virtually any other market, however, currency values are also impacted by government actions. These actions can be either indirect (involving such things as the setting of interest-rate levels) or direct (e.g., stepping into the open market and buying a given currency to increase demand and thus support its value).

We will discuss the role of governments in influencing currency values in more detail in just a few pages. First, however, let's briefly look at how currencies are actually traded.

Three Trading Alternatives

There are essentially three primary arenas for the trading of currencies — the spot market, the forward markets and the futures markets. (The IMF and the World Bank also facilitate a number of direct government-to-government transactions. These transfers — while monetary in nature — don't involve the exchange of actual currencies and are thus considered to be "off market" since they seldom have any impact on exchange rates or currency values.) Here's a quick look at the basics of each:

- The spot market involves currencies bought and sold for immediate delivery — e.g., the instant exchange of, say, 10 million U.S. dollars for 14,630,000 German marks. The trades made there generally establish the external values and exchange rates for the world's major currencies at any given time — the exceptions being the currencies with fixed values or values pegged to other currencies. *Note: Some countries maintain two different currency values — a fixed rate applied to the currency's use in internal commerce, and a floating rate that applies when the currency is used in international trade or banking activity.*

    The rates and values established in the spot market are the ones you will typically see reported in newspaper price tables such as the one just shown from *Investor's Business Daily* (although those tables also include some quotes from the forward markets, usually designated by a time reference, such as "30-day" and the letters "fwd"). However, you should be aware that the quoted rates are based on transactions involving minimum lots of U.S.$1 million.

    Thus, if you take $1,000 to your local bank, or one in a foreign country you are visiting, you'll likely get a slightly less favorable rate. And if you try to exchange your money "on the street," say to pay for a purchase or get change for a taxi, you will certainly get a less favorable rate. *Note: There are exceptions to this latter statement. If you happen to be in a country, such as Russia, where certain goods can only be purchased with so-called "hard" currencies, you may find your dollars in such demand that local citizens will pay a premium in their local currencies just to get them. Be aware, however, that some governments consider such "unauthorized currency exchanges" illegal — meaning you should check the local regulations before attempting to spend your dollars abroad.*

- The forward markets involve the purchase or sale of currencies for delivery at a future date — typically in 30, 60 or 90 days, but sometimes up to a year or longer. Forward contracts are primarily used by hedgers — financial institutions or corporations that know they'll have to make payments denominated in a foreign currency in the near future and want to lock in an exchange rate to protect against market fluctuations and facilitate budgeting operations.

    For example, a company that manufactures chrome bumpers for U.S. automakers might purchase a freighter load of chromium ore from a foreign mining operation, with payment due when the ship makes delivery to a port on Lake Erie in roughly 30 days. The company and the mine have agreed on a price for the ore, but the price is denominated in

British pounds — meaning the actual cost to the company could rise significantly should the dollar fall in value relative to the pound in the ensuing 30 days.

To guard against this possibility, the company goes into the forward market and buys a contract for the exact number of pounds it needs to pay for the raw ore, with the currency deliverable in 30 days — at the same time the ship is due to arrive. The company thus ensures that the ore purchase price it agreed to — based on present exchange rates — will be the same price (in dollars) it has to pay when the freighter eventually ties up at the Lake Erie dock.

Currency forward contracts function very much like futures contracts (which you learned about in the lesson "Commodity and financial futures"), but they have several key differences. For one, they represent an actual purchase or sale of currency for future delivery, rather than just the "right" to buy or sell a currency at a specific future date.

For another, they can also be "custom tailored" with respect to the underlying currency, size of contract and desired delivery date, whereas sizes and delivery dates are standardized for futures contracts, which are available on only a limited number of currencies. In addition, whereas all futures contracts traded in the United States are valued relative to the U.S. dollar, forward contracts can be structured involving any two currencies — say, the British pound and the German mark. *Note: Standardized forward contracts in U.S.$1 million lots with 30-, 60- and 90-day delivery dates are also available on certain key currencies, including the British pound, Canadian dollar, German mark, Japanese yen and Swiss franc.*

Finally, unlike futures prices, which are set in a free-wheeling auction-style market, prices of forward contracts tend to be more carefully negotiated, based on the relative interest rates and inflation rates in the two countries whose currencies are involved in the trade. As a result, forward contracts can trade at either a premium or a discount to spot-market rates, whereas currency futures nearly always trade at a premium.

■ Currency futures, as you already learned in an earlier lesson, represent the "right" to buy or sell a set amount of foreign currency at a specific price at a set date in the future. Currency futures contracts are standardized in terms of size and delivery date, and are traded on organized futures exchanges. In the U.S., the leading currency futures trade on the International Monetary Market (IMM), a part of the Chicago Mercantile Exchange (CME).

While futures are also used by hedgers, much like forward contracts, the vast majority are bought and sold by speculators, hoping to profit from changing currency values relative to the U.S. dollar. As such, fewer than 5 percent of currency futures are ever converted into actual currencies. Rather they are "offset" by traders, who sell (or buy) identical contracts (except in price) before the scheduled delivery date, thus canceling out the ones they originally bought (or sold short).

Even traders who use futures to hedge their actual currency needs usually don't make or take delivery of the currencies themselves. Rather, they use the profits from their futures trades to offset any losses they might suffer as a result of exchange-rate adjustments during the period leading up to the time when they'll need the actual currencies.

Of course, the biggest reason traders choose futures over forward contracts is the leverage they offer. Currency futures can be purchased for only a small margin deposit — perhaps 5 to 10 percent of the value of the underlying currencies involved. By contrast, forward contracts, being actual currency purchases or sales for future delivery, cannot be leveraged — meaning they must be paid for in full at the time of the transaction.

Note: Limited currency hedges can also be structured employing option contracts on either futures or the actual physical currencies. Options on currency futures also trade on the Chicago Mercantile Exchange, while options on the actual currencies are traded on a special division of the Philadelphia Stock Exchange. For more information on using options, refer back to the lesson, "Lots of options with options."

THE IMPACT OF EXCHANGE-RATE FLUCTUATIONS

Now it's time to see how this background information affects you — both as an American consumer and an American investor.

Most people never give much thought to exchange rates and currency values unless they plan a vacation or business trip to a foreign country. After all, the events in the currency markets — even dramatic ones like those in early 1995 — don't seem to have much immediate impact at the neighborhood grocery store, area shopping mall or local bank. In fact, even your stocks and bonds probably seem fairly steady in the short term.

However, when viewed from a longer-term perspective, changing world currency values can have a truly insidious effect on your purchasing power, the performance of your investments and, in the end, your overall wealth-building strategy. In addition, if you are in business — even one that seemingly has no international connections — shifting exchange rates can still influence your sales and profits. First let's see what changes in currency values can do to your purchasing power.

Exchange Rates and Purchasing Power

As we've mentioned in prior lessons, the world economy is becoming more and more intertwined with each passing year. Markets are linked in 24-hour global trading networks, communications systems reach instantly to the farthest corners of the world and the manufacture of many products includes parts made or assembled in several different countries. Payments for all of these international functions — and thousands of other goods and services — involve the transfer of funds, and frequently the exchange of currencies.

This loss of dollar purchasing power is the primary reason why you must keep at least some of your assets denominated in foreign currencies.

When the values of the currencies used for these international transactions change, so do the prices of the goods and services involved. If the currency of the purchasing country increases in value, the prices effectively fall — and if the currency of the importer declines in value, the prices effectively rise. As the world's premier consuming nation, America — and its citizens — have been profoundly affected by this principle over the past decade.

For example, since January 1985, the Japanese yen — the currency of America's second largest trading partner — has more than doubled in value relative to the U.S. dollar. As a result, a Japanese-made product that could have been purchased for $1,000 in 1985 costs roughly $2,470 today. *Note: This actually understates the increased price for American consumers since it is based on currency differentials alone and does not factor in any internal Japanese inflation, which could have increased production costs.*

And, unfortunately this situation has been little different with many of the world's other leading currencies. Over the past decade, the dollar has slipped against every other Group of Seven (G-7) nation currency except that of Canada, the third largest U.S. trading partner. (The dollar has also gained against the peso, the currency of Mexico, America's biggest trade partner.) That means goods manufactured in any of those countries now cost American consumers significantly more than they did 10 years ago, although Canadian (and Mexican) products now cost less, as illustrated in the table on the following page.

This loss of dollar purchasing power — and the possibility it could continue in the future — is the primary reason you must keep at least some of your assets denominated in foreign currencies if you hope to preserve the personal wealth this course helps you to build.

Otherwise, you could wind up with lots of dollars, yet still not be able to buy the foreign products you want, travel to the overseas destinations you hope to visit or retire to that tropical paradise of your dreams.

For some tips on how to begin adding such assets to your portfolio, refer to Wealth-Building Step No. 77, How To Pick the Ideal Foreign Currency-Denominated Investments, found on page 11.

The Dollar's Declining Purchasing Power

This table shows what a foreign-made item that cost $1,000 in January 1985 would have cost an American buyer at the beginning of 1996, based on changes in currency values alone (not including any internal inflation in the foreign country):

Product's country of origin	Dollars Per 1,000 foreign currency-1985	Dollars Per 1,000 foreign currency-1/1/96	Deval-uation factor	1996 cost
Japan	3.93	9.69	2.47	$2,465.65
Britain	1,131.09	1,553.00	1.37	$1,373.01
France	103.40	203.90	1.97	$1,971.95
Germany	316.31	696.10	2.20	$2,200.69
Switzerland	374.00	866.90	2.32	$2,317.91
Canada	753.41	732.90	0.97	$ 972.78

There Can Be Benefits, Too

Of course, as with most statistics, the situation is not really as simple as the raw numbers may make them seem. While a weak currency may hurt a country's citizens in one respect, it can be beneficial in many others. For example, by making imported products more expensive, a weak currency tends to raise demand for domestic goods, improving business conditions at home, creating more jobs and generally helping the economy. It also makes the prices of those goods more attractive to foreign buyers, thus increasing exports, which provides a further economic boost, as well as improving the country's balance of trade. In turn, these events may lead to higher business profits, which can translate into higher stock prices and better investment returns (although a weak currency is typically accompanied by low relative interest rates, which can make it harder to sustain such returns).

However, by making imported products more expensive, a weak currency tends to raise demand for domestic goods.

Such macro-economic benefits were quite apparent in the period from 1985 through mid-1987, when the U.S. economy surged ahead and the stock market reached then-record heights — in spite of the fact that the dollar lost roughly one-third of its value versus the Japanese yen and most of the major European currencies.

And, when all the statistics are in, the same may well prove to be true for the mid-1990s period of U.S. currency instability. At the same time the dollar was losing more than 12 percent of its value — falling to post-World War II lows against the yen, the German mark and the Swiss franc — the U.S. economy was maintaining a steady (though moderate) growth, domestic inflation was holding below 3 percent, unemployment was tumbling to five-year lows and the stock market was surging to new all-time highs, with the Dow Jones Industrials climbing well above 5000 for the first time in history.

In addition, in the case of the United States, there are several of other factors that tend to mute the impact of a declining currency. For example:

■ Because America *is* such a strong consumer market, with a broad array of available products, retail competition tends to be quite fierce. As a result, Japanese, German and other foreign manufacturers often take lower profit margins rather than passing on 100 percent of currency-related price increases. That's why, for instance, that while our earlier table showed the cost of a Japanese product rising from $1,000 to $2,465 between 1985 and 1996, the prices of very few (if any) Japanese-made cars soared from $10,000 to $24,650 during the same period. Competition from the U.S. auto industry simply wouldn't allow it.

How to Pick the Ideal Foreign Currency-Denominated Investments

What: Select foreign bonds denominated in currencies other than the U.S. dollar.

Why: Interest rates are frequently higher on foreign debt securities than on similar instruments in the United States, and picking bonds denominated in currencies expected to be stronger than the dollar will provide an extra measure of protection against inflation.

Risk: Medium. A loss in value by the currency in which the bonds are denominated could cancel out any advantages of higher interest rates.

Safety: High to medium. Although some foreign debt markets aren't as closely regulated as those in North America, you should have few problems if you stick to securities offered by major overseas companies or backed by established foreign governments.

Liquidity: Medium. There are active markets for foreign bonds in Europe, Asia and the United States, and most major U.S. brokerage firms have trading departments dealing in these securities. However, bid/ask spreads (which translate into sales charges) may be higher than for domestic bonds, and it could take several days to complete purchases or sales of more obscure foreign issues.

Why not: Investing in foreign securities can be more complicated than investing in domestic markets. Government supervision of investment and banking activities is generally less stringent than in the United States, financial disclosure laws may be more lax (or non-existent), accounting standards may be different and foreigners may have little legal recourse in the event of default or even outright fraud by security issuers. In addition, changes in currency values and exchange rates can negatively impact the performance of your investments.

Buy/Invest from: Most major full-service brokerage firms, some leading discounters with bond-trading departments and many large banks with international branches or correspondent relationships with foreign institutions.

Background: From the perspective of Americans, "foreign" bonds are those denominated in currencies other than U.S. dollars. They are issued by governments, government agencies and multinational corporations in foreign countries (and, occasionally, in the United States) for one of three reasons — to raise money at the lowest possible interest rate, to profit from a yield-differential between interest rates at home and those in a foreign country or to gain exposure to a specific currency to reduce trade risks. These bonds are valued by investors because they provide exchange-rate exposure and typically offer higher yields than term deposits, bank accounts and other similar instruments.

There are three types of foreign currency-denominated bonds:

■ *Straight domestic bonds,* which are issued by domestic entities and denominated in the domestic currency — for example, a Japanese government bond denominated in Japanese yen and sold in Japan.

■ *Eurobonds,* which are bonds that are sold outside the country of the issuer and denominated in a currency other than that of the issuer — for example, a Swiss franc-denominated bond issued by the government of Japan and sold in Germany.

■ *Foreign bonds,* which are sold outside the country of the issuer but in the same country as the currency denomination — for example, a Swiss franc-denominated bond issued by a German corporation and sold in Switzerland.

Step 77: *How To Pick The Ideal Foreign Currency-Denominated Investments*

Like all bonds, foreign currency-denominated bonds pay interest at periodic intervals and mature at their par, or face, value. In other words, the only difference between them and conventional bonds is that they are denominated in the foreign currency. Most are issued in a fixed-rate format and pay interest annually at a pre-set rate. However, floating-rate, zero-coupon and convertible issues can also be found. Typical maturities are 10 to 30 years. Trading is conducted primarily in the over-the-counter market, both in the United States and abroad.

These bonds are highly attractive because they give U.S. investors a chance to earn higher rates than those at home, and also benefit from exchange-rate fluctuations that favor the foreign currency in which they are issued. For example, in January 1985, U.S. investors were offered a 10-year Swiss bond denominated in German marks and carrying a 4.50 percent coupon. That translated to $142.34 on a DM10,000 bond in the first year following issue. However, because the German mark rose from 3.1615 per U.S. dollar in 1985 to 1.5307 per U.S. dollar in January 1995, it translated to an annual payment of $293.98 in the tenth year. In addition, the value of the bond in dollars rose from $3,163.06 in 1985 (DM10,000/3.1615 = $3,163.06) to $6,532.96 at maturity (DM10,000/ 1.5307 = $6,532.96) — a gain of $3,369.90, or 10.65 percent annualized on the exchange-rate fluctuation alone. Add in the stated coupon yield of 4.50 percent, plus the exchange-related gain on the annual interest payments, and American investors wound up with an annualized yield on the bond of nearly 16 percent — far more than they could have gotten on any fixed-income investment at home.

The same result would have applied to bonds denominated in most of the major foreign currencies over the past 25 years, with the average annualized yield in D-marks, Swiss francs and Japanese yen rising from 7.71 percent, 5.07 percent and 6.71 percent, respectively, to annualized respective yields in U.S. dollars of 11.30 percent, 10.72 percent and 12.54 percent. By contrast, annualized yields on bonds denominated in currencies that fell in value against the dollar would have fallen by similar amounts — an example being Italian lira-denominated bonds, which produced an internal annualized yield of 12.74 percent, but an annualized yield of only 7.81 percent when converted to dollars.

The danger, of course, is that these yield patterns are far from stable. For example, a study by Paul Burik and Richard Ennis, published under the title "Foreign Bonds in Diversified Portfolios: A Limited Advantage," in the March-April 1990 issue of *Financial Analysts Journal,* found that:

■ From 1979 through 1984, when the U.S. dollar was extremely strong, a mixed portfolio of international bonds would have yielded an average annual rate of return of 14.0 percent in their own currencies, but just 4.8 percent in dollars.

■ From 1985 through 1987, when the U.S. dollar was quite weak, an identically weighted portfolio of international bonds would have yielded an average annual return of 10.4 percent in their own currencies, but a whopping 31.2 percent in dollars.

▶ ▶ ▶ ▶ **If you want to get started today, here's what you need to do to begin investing in foreign-currency denominated bonds:**

The key factors in selecting quality international bonds are the type of issue, the coupon rate, the frequency of interest payments, the term to maturity, the security of principal, the type (corporate, government, etc.) and credit rating of the issuer, the presence of any call features and the currency in which the bond is denominated. In general, you want to seek out bonds:

- Issued by entities that have a solid credit rating.

- That have protection against an early call (which could force you to liquidate and reinvest at lower rates).

- That offer an attractive stated coupon rate.

- That are denominated in a "hard" currency (the German mark, say, as opposed to the Russian ruble).

And, you want to avoid bonds:

- Issued by or denominated in the currencies of countries where the inflation rate is higher than the yield.

- Denominated in currencies of countries where there are rising interest rates.

- With early call features that create substantial reinvestment risk.

- Issued by entities that represent a high credit risk — i.e., that may have trouble making interest payments or could default entirely (Mexico being a good current example).

- Issued by or denominated in the currencies of countries where there are indications of a change from democracy to a more repressive style of government, or where there is instability in central bank monetary policies.

You can buy and sell these bonds through most leading U.S. brokerage firms, but you should definitely shop around as quotes can vary widely. If you are quoted a net price (i.e., no commission), the maximum bid/ask spread you should have to pay is 1 percent (e.g., $10 per $1,000 equivalent value). Also be sure to ask about any maintenance or safekeeping fees or other hidden charges sometimes associated with these issues. (This is important because taking physical delivery of these bonds can be a problem; it's better and safer to simply leave them on deposit with the broker, where they'll be held in the firm's Eurodollar account.) Whatever you do, don't use a "market" order to buy. Liquidity can be low with many of these issues, which pushes up the prices substantially. Instead, give your broker a "limit" — the maximum amount you are willing to pay for the bond — and if you can't make the purchase at that price, wait for a better opportunity. The interest payments and gains on these bonds are generally not taxed in the country of issue; you merely list your returns on your U.S. tax forms and pay the appropriate taxes here.

Note: If you want to avoid the hassle of trying to pick a good foreign country or currency, you might consider bonds denominated in the ECU, or European Currency Unit. This is a weighted composite "basket" of the 12 currencies of the members of the European Economic Community — Belgium, Denmark, France, Germany, Greece, Ireland, Italy, Luxembourg, the Netherlands, Portugal, Spain and the United Kingdom. ▲

Continued from p. 10

■ Although you may well know several people who drive German cars, sport Seville Row suits and wear Italian shoes, America is not nearly as dependent on imports as the media make it seem. In fact, according to the U.S. Department of Commerce, nearly 90 percent of products purchased in America are also made in America — and a drop in the value of the dollar generally won't make those goods cost more (unless U.S. manufacturers use higher import prices as an excuse to boost their own profit margins).

Still, the specter of widely fluctuating exchange rates can be unnerving, simply because the potential impact on any given worker, business owner or investor can be so hard to predict. That's why you need to clearly understand the various types of exchange-rate exposure you might face.

The Three Types of Currency Risk

Essentially, there are three primary types of currency exchange-related risk — economic exposure, transaction exposure and translation exposure. Here's a brief explanation of each:

Economic exposure — This involves the direct impact of foreign exchange rates on company cash flows before conversion to dollars. It encompasses many of the potential broad ramifications already mentioned — e.g., a stronger dollar makes your company's products more expensive overseas, its export sales drop, profits dip and you get laid off. However, there are also numerous more indirect possibilities.

> *According to the U.S. Department of Commerce, nearly 90 percent of products purchased in America are also made in America — and a drop in the value of the dollar generally won't make those goods cost more.*

For instance, assume you work for a New York company that markets ski vacations to Stowe in Vermont, charging $1,000 a week for a typical package including lodging, lift tickets, etc. The firm does no business overseas and has only an occasional foreign customer, so the chances of getting hurt by shifting exchange rates seem remote. Right? Wrong! The government of France, trying to boost its economy, cuts interest rates — and, as a result, the French franc plummets against the U.S. dollar. Suddenly, because the dollar is so much stronger, the cost of ski packages to the French Alps falls from $1,500 a week to only $900. What happens? Your New York customers — given a choice between paying $1,000 for Stowe and $900 for the Alps — opt for France instead of Vermont, and your business goes quickly downhill (no skis needed)! That's a prime example of "indirect" economic exchange-rate risk.

It's even possible for U.S. companies to suffer when the dollar doesn't change at all. For example, assume you work for a U.S. company that manufactures ski equipment, 40 percent of which is sold in Switzerland for retail to Alpine skiers. The dollar/Swiss franc exchange rate is stable, so there's little threat to your company's export business. Right? Wrong again! Because of internal political conflicts, the German mark falls in value relative to the Swiss franc. As a result, German products — including ski equipment — become cheaper in Switzerland than U.S. goods, and Swiss orders for your company's products melt away, cutting its profits almost in half. Another victim of indirect economic exchange-rate exposure.

Of course, as already noted, this works both ways. For example, following the big drop in the dollar in early 1995, German automaker Mercedes-Benz estimated it had lost 3 million marks in U.S. sales for every penny the mark gained against the dollar — sales that most likely went to General Motors, Ford and Chrysler.

Transaction exposure — This risk category is generally much more direct than the economic exposure we've just discussed. It is simply the danger that money denominated in a foreign currency will be worth less than it is now when you eventually convert it back to your domestic currency — or vice versa (i.e., that your domestic currency will be worth less in the future when you have to convert it into a foreign currency).

This type of risk applies primarily to business transactions such as those we discussed earlier when talking about how forward contracts and futures contracts are used for hedging purposes. However, it can also have significant implications for Americans who travel overseas, live abroad or invest in foreign markets.

For example, if you were to retire abroad on the income you receive from your U.S. pension, paid in dollars, your standard of living could fall drastically if the dollar were to start falling in value against the currency of your new home country. Each time your pension check arrived and you had to convert it, you'd get less of the local currency with which to pay your bills. If the value of the dollar fell too much, you might even be forced to move back to the U.S. — just to restore the purchasing power of your pension dollars. The same scenario applies to Americans who travel overseas, although the risks are generally more limited and short-lived.

For Americans who invest abroad, the risk is reversed — i.e., they suffer when the dollar rises in value against the currency in which their investments are denominated. For example, if the dollar/D-mark exchange rate is 0.6666 or 66.66 cents, an investment of $1,000 will buy 100 shares of a German stock priced at 15 marks per share, for a total value of 1,500 marks ($1.00/0.6666 = 1.50 x $1,000 = 1,500 marks/15 = 100 shares). If the German stock market does well, and the price of the stock climbs to 30 marks a share, the value of the stock will increase to 3,000 marks — and the American investor will double his money. Right? Not necessarily. If, in the interim, the dollar/D-mark exchange rate slides to 0.5000, the 3,000 marks the investor receives for his stock will be convertible into just $1,500 (30 marks x 100 = 3,000 marks x 0.5000 = $1,500). Thus, the American investor's 100 percent gain on the German stock, in D-marks, will be cut to just 50 percent, in dollars, because of the exchange-rate loss.

Likewise, when the dollar falls in value, the profit on a foreign stock will equate to a higher percentage return when converted back to dollars. In fact, the dollar could actually fall by such a substantial amount that a loss on a foreign stock could even turn into a gain once the conversion back to dollars was made.

Once again, the perspective is exactly the opposite for foreigners buying stocks or other investments denominated in dollars. If the dollar increases in value during their holding period, their gains will be larger when converted back to their native currency. And, if the dollar falls, their gains will be smaller — perhaps even becoming losses. Both German and Japanese investors in American stocks suffered this fate in the first 10 weeks of 1995. The Dow Jones Industrial Average rose by 3.34 percent during that time — but, because the dollar fell so sharply against both the D-mark and the yen during the same period, the stock gains turned into losses of 8.46 percent and 6.18 percent, respectively!

The worst of all possible worlds, of course, would involve losing money on your investment abroad *and* having your currency rise against that of the foreign country. You take both an investment loss and a transaction loss on the currency conversion — essentially doubling your woes.

Translation exposure — This risk category relates primarily to corporate accounting functions as they apply to the valuation of foreign assets or the calculation of foreign debts and other liabilities. For example, if a U.S. company has a subsidiary based in France, a drop in the value of the French franc relative to the dollar will force the parent firm to devalue the subsidiary when it calculates its assets in the preparation of its balance sheets. As a result, the U.S. company may have to show a loss on its French operation, even though it has experienced no drop in either franc-denominated sales or subsidiary profit margins — and even if it fails to repatriate any of the French earnings.

Typically, translation risk applies only to foreign-held equity or foreign operations financed by U.S.-issued debt. If, for example, the French subsidiary was financed 100 percent with French debt (e.g., franc-denominated bonds or bank loans), the translation exposure would be reduced to zero since any currency-related drop in asset value would be offset by a corresponding decline in foreign liabilities (e.g., interest or mortgage payments).

WHAT AFFECTS EXCHANGE RATES?

As we noted earlier, there is really only one overriding cause for exchange-rate fluctuations — and it's the same thing that causes prices changes for virtually every security or commodity. That's right — supply and demand. However, there are a number of things that can impact the demand for and the supply of currencies, so let's briefly discuss those.

The primary supply and demand factors fall into two categories — those related to the "real" sector and those linked to the financial sector. The "real" sector considerations are fairly straightforward, arising from the actual demand for currencies to pay for imported and exported goods and services.

With respect to inflation, the basic rule is: "A foreign currency depreciates or appreciates at a rate equal to the amount by which the country's inflation rate exceeds or lags that of the U.S. — all else being equal."

In simplest terms, when the U.S. exports goods, foreign countries must get dollars to pay for those goods — and, when the U.S. imports goods, it has to exchange dollars to get the foreign currencies needed to make its payments. Thus, the demand for dollars — and, on a relative basis, for other world currencies — rises and falls with the ebb and flow of international trade. And, when a nation has a consistently negative trade balance — as has been the case in the United States in recent years — it tends to depress the value of its currency.

The financial sector influences are considerably more complex, being linked to such things as international interest-rate differentials and relative inflation rates. Essentially, however, there are three primary supply factors and three main demand factors.

On the supply side, you have:

■ The growth in the domestic money supply through increased private savings, the lowering of bank reserves and other internal monetary adjustments.

■ The adjustment of government exchange controls, if any exist.

■ The quantity of currency in circulation as a result of government economic policies (such as issuance of unfunded debt, the lowering of interest rates, the excess printing of new money, etc.)

On the demand side, you have:

■ *Interest-rate differentials.* The currencies of countries that offer high real (after inflation) rates of return frequently rise in value as international traders attempt to boost their investment yields by buying those currencies and selling those of countries offering lower real returns.

■ *Inflation-rate differentials.* The same situation as above applies with respect to inflation, which erodes the purchasing power of a currency. As a result, currencies of countries with low current and expected inflation are in high demand by investors, while those of countries with rapidly rising prices are dumped.

■ *Central bank intervention.* When countries feel their currencies are under unwarranted pressure, they often step into the market and buy those currencies. This action, reflecting economic policy rather than actual trading conditions, creates an artificial demand that serves to slow or even stop the market-driven devaluation.

Note: The central banks of most of the world's major countries, including the United States, maintain special reserve funds for the purpose of intervening in the currency markets when needed. However, the use of such funds can sometimes backfire. When the Mexican economy collapsed in late 1994, dragging down the value of the peso, President Clinton pledged $20 billion from the U.S. currency reserve fund to help prop up the peso and bail out Mexico. That move left the dollar unprotected and speculators stepped in and began selling the American currency — which, according to many analysts, triggered the dollar's early 1995 skid to post-World War II lows.

The degree to which inflation and interest-rate differentials affect the values of currencies can be calculated fairly accurately and is generally factored into the relative exchange rates of the currencies involved, particularly with respect to the pricing of futures and forward contracts.

With respect to inflation, the basic rule is: "A foreign currency depreciates or appreciates at a rate equal to the amount by which the country's inflation rate exceeds or lags that of the U.S. — all else being equal."

For example, if Canada's annualized inflation rate was projected to be 8 percent and the U.S. yearly inflation rate was projected to be 5 percent, the Canadian dollar could be expected to *depreciate* by roughly 3 percent versus the U.S. dollar over the coming 12 months. And, if Japan's inflation rate was expected to be just 2 percent annually, then the yen could be expected to *appreciate* by about 3 percent against the U.S. dollar over the same period. (The actual calculations are a bit more complicated and subject to adjustment for other factors, but you get the general idea.)

This explains why the currencies of many Latin American nations, with high relative inflation rates, have historically fallen versus the dollar, whereas the currencies of Japan, German and Switzerland, with low relative inflation rates, have risen against the dollar in recent decades.

With respect to interest rates, a similar rule applies: "The expected rate of currency depreciation or appreciation should offset the current interest-rate differential."

For example, if the interest rate on one-year U.S. Treasury bills was 8 percent, while the interest rate on one-year Swiss Treasury bills was 6 percent, then the dollar could be expected to lose roughly 2 percent of its value versus the Swiss franc over the coming year. This can be more clearly illustrated by comparing two identical loans, one taken out in the U.S. and one taken out in Switzerland, as detailed at left.

Obviously, in the real world, there are lots of things that can happen over the course of a year (or even a few days) to upset expectations — meaning inflation and interest-rate differentials rarely translate quite as precisely as explained in our examples.

How Changing Currency Values Offset Interest-rate Differences

The difference between the interest rates in two countries should be reflected in changes in their respective currency values over any set period of time. For example, assume the current U.S. dollar/Swiss franc exchange rate is 1.4180 in the spot market (meaning 1 U.S. dollar will buy 1.4180 francs), and the one-year forward rate (i.e., the expected spot rate one year in the future) is 1.3917. Now assume a borrower wanted to take out a $1 million loan, and had the choice of doing so in the U.S. at a rate of 8 percent — or in Switzerland at a rate of 6 percent. At first, it would appear the Swiss loan would be a better deal — but, as the following figures show, the impact of the expected exchange-rate adjustment would essentially equalize the cost of the two loans:

Borrow in the United States:

Loan amount:	$1,000,000
Interest expense at 8% ($1,000,000 x 0.08):	$ 80,000
Payback amount in one year:	$1,080,000

Borrow in Switzerland:

Loan amount ($1,000,000 x 1.4180):	SF1,418,000
Interest expense at 6% (1,418,000 x 0.06):	SF 85,080
Payback amount in one year:	SF1,503,080
Payback in U.S. dollars (1,503,080/1.3917)	$1,080,031

And that, of course, is why we have currency markets — so investors can protect themselves against the consequences of unfulfilled economic expectations or derive profits from their impact on worldwide exchange rates.

WHY INVEST IN FOREIGN CURRENCIES?

As you've probably surmised by now, there are really only two primary motives for investing in foreign currencies themselves or in foreign currency-denominated securities. The first is speculation — preferably reasoned, rather than rampant — in search of higher overall portfolio returns, and the second is to "purchase insurance" or, more accurately, to hedge other investments or business activities against potential losses due to fluctuating currency values.

Reasoned speculators attempt to generate higher than normal investment returns by exploiting any of a variety of opportunities that can arise when the U.S. dollar becomes over- or under-valued relative to other currencies as a result of the factors just discussed. (More rampant speculators generally try to profit by outguessing the market or playing the emotional reactions of other less-informed traders, who tend to buy too eagerly or sell too frantically in response to government actions, key economic reports or unexpected price moves.)

Hedgers, on the other hand, are not so much concerned with generating excess returns as they are with protecting their existing assets or business prospects against declines in the external value of the U.S. dollar. Hedging can be a vital function for those who travel extensively abroad, buy substantial amounts of imported goods, rely on foreign markets or customers for business profits or, for any other reason, anticipate having current or future needs for foreign currencies.

Profiting From a Fluctuating U.S. Dollar

As explained earlier, there are several ways in which to trade in foreign currencies. However, the spot and forward markets — with their high cash requirements and multimillion-dollar trading lots — are outside the realm of all but the wealthiest and most sophisticated individuals. As a result, when individual investors try the currency markets, they usually pursue one of two directions:

- Those seeking to hedge against declining U.S. dollar values tend to take a longer-term approach, investing in foreign equity or debt securities, international mutual funds or other vehicles that offer opportunities for both growth and protection against an eroding dollar. *Note: Most of these vehicles were discussed in the lesson, "The global approach," so we won't repeat that information here. If you have questions regarding a particular type of investment or strategy, refer to the explanations there.*

- Those having a more speculative bent tend to set shorter-term objectives, turning to the currency futures or options markets as a means of generating highly leveraged gains in a minimum amount of time. As with the hedging vehicles, we've discussed the mechanics of both futures and options in other lessons ("Commodity and financial futures" and "Lots of options with options"), so we won't repeat the information here. However, we will offer an example of a currency futures trade, just so you can see the potential attraction — and the risks — of speculating in these often volatile markets.

A Sample Currency Futures Trade

Assume, for example, that it's late February of 1995, and you are concerned about the potential impact the escalating Mexican economic crisis might have on both the U.S. economy and the U.S. dollar. The dollar has already to begun to skid against the leading European currencies. Given this situation, you decide that a speculative venture in currency futures might prove highly profitable. So, you look at the futures price tables in the newspaper (we've provided a sample from *Investor's Business Daily* below) and see that the current price of the June German Mark futures contract is .6864 — meaning 1 mark is worth 0.6864 dollars, or 68.64 cents.

BRITISH POUND (IMM) – $ per pound – 1 point equals $0.0001
Est. Vol. 18,794 Vol. 11,690 open int 47,617 – 821

1.6440	1.4640 Mar	45,676	1.5950	1.5950	1.5798	1.5874	–70
1.6380	1.5348 Jun	1,923	1.5958	1.5960	1.5770	1.5850	–72
1.5940	1.5600 Sep	12	1.5800	1.5800	1.5730	1.5814	–72
1.5820	1.5660 Dec	6				1.5770	–76

CANADIAN DOLLAR (IMM) – $ per dlr – 1 point equals $0.0001
Est. Vol. 4,867 Vol. 6,160 open int 42,460 – 399

.7605	.6983 Mar	35,527	.7164	.7183	.7156	.7181	+12
.7522	.6948 Jun	4,027	.7144	.7152	.7126	.7151	+12
.7438	.6920 Sep	1,635	.7128	.7132	.7113	.7131	+12
.7400	.6895 Dec	941	.7115	.7120	.7105	.7119	+12
.7335	.6900 Mar	255	.7090	.7100	.7088	.7106	+12
.7085	.6935 Jun	75				.7093	+12

GERMAN MARK (IMM) – $ per mark – 1 point equals $0.0001
Est. Vol. 48,247 Vol. 31,791 open int 104,621 + 1,706

.6833	.5810 Mar	94,324	.6817	.6854	.6773	.6844	+25
.6855	.5980 Jun	9,261	.6830	.6873	.6792	.6864	+24
.6862	.6347 Sep	831	.6888	.6888	.6820	.6882	+25
.6875	.6700 Dec	171	.6850	.6890	.6842	.6898	+25
.6890	.6525 Mar	34				.6914	+25

JAPANESE YEN (IMM) – $ per yen – 1 point equals $0.000001
Est. Vol. 29,453 Vol. 19,367 open int 91,563 + 738

.010560	.009680 Mar	79,654	.010352	.010386	.010282	.010326	–29
.010670	.009776 Jun	10,639	.010472	.010490	.010395	.010437	–29
.010775	.010175 Sep	744	.010540	.010545	.010540	.010548	–29
.010760	.010300 Dec	391				.010663	–29
.010930	.010485 Mar	104	.010780	.010780	.010780	.010783	–29
.010910	.010780 Jun	31	.010880	.010900	.010870	.010901	–29

SWISS FRANC (IMM) – $ per franc – 1 point equals $0.0001
Est. Vol. 28,053 Vol. 21,589 open int 49,380 + 252

.8136	.7287 Mar	44,874	.8019	.8055	.7967	.8042	+24
.8165	.7193 Jun	4,254	.8069	.8100	.8017	.8091	+24
.8155	.7618 Sep	147	.8140	.8140	.8075	.8137	+25
.8190	.7835 Dec	105				.8180	+25

You then call your futures broker and place an order to buy one June D-mark futures contract — putting up a margin deposit of just $3,000 to secure your new position, which is actually worth $85,800 (0.6864 cents x 125,000 marks/contract = $85,800). The market holds steady for the next few days, trading in a very narrow range as traders watch the events unfolding in Washington and Mexico City. In fact, you're actually showing a small loss (under $100) after the first three days.

Then, however, the president announces he'll authorize use of $20 billion from the Federal Reserve's emergency U.S. dollar support fund to help prop up the peso. Fearful the Mexican problems will spill across the Rio Grande, traders and speculators begin unloading their U.S. dollar holdings — in the stock and bond markets, as well as the currency markets — and the German mark, Japanese yen, Swiss franc and other leading currencies begin to rally.

The first day's move in the D-mark price isn't huge — less than a penny per mark — but the dollar drop rapidly accelerates. The second day, the mark gains almost a cent, the next day it moves up by a cent and a quarter — and the fourth day it shoots up by nearly 2 full cents. The closing price for the June D-mark future that day is .7340, or 73.40 cents — meaning it has gained 4.76 cents (or 6.93 percent) since your purchase just 10 days earlier.

Anticipating that either the Fed will intervene to halt the dollar's slide or that short-term profit taking will force a correction, you decide to go ahead and grab your gain. Even though the market opens higher the next morning, you call and close out your position, getting a final price of .7364, exactly 500 points (or 5.00 cents) more than you paid. Your profit on the 125,000-mark contract is thus a whopping $6,250 (0.0500 x 125,000 = $6,250), minus a commission of around $50. That leaves you with a net gain of $6,200, or a return of 206.67 percent on your original $3,000 margin deposit! In just 11 days!

That kind of return seems totally unbelievable to most investors who've never played the futures markets, but such gains are entirely possible — especially when currency trading heats up. In fact, the scenario you've just read describes the actual events — and the actual progression of D-mark futures prices — that occurred between Feb. 24 and March 8, 1995!

The Risks Are Just as High

Of course, taking about the potential profits in currency futures isn't the whole story — the potential risks are just as high. Unlike the stock market, where all shareholders profit when prices move higher, the futures market is essentially a "zero-sum" game (discounting commissions and fees). In other words, for every winner, there must be a loser of equal magnitude. Thus, had you been wrong in assessing the U.S./Mexico/currency market outlook in early 1995, your losses could have been equally large, as illustrated in the table on the following page.

D-Mark Futures Speculation — A Scenario

The following table gives several possible outcomes for the German mark futures speculation described in the text, assuming the standard IMM contract size of 125,000 marks, a margin deposit of $3,000, no commissions and an initial June futures price of .6864 (68.64 cents), which equals a full position value of $85,800:

Ending D-mark futures price	Value of position	Profit, (loss)	Return on $3,000 margin
.7500	$93,750.00	$7,950.00	265.00%
.7364*	$92,050.00	$6,250.00	208.83%
.7250	$90,625.00	$4,825.00	160.83%
.7000	$87,500.00	$1,700.00	67.67%
.6864*	$85,800.00	0	0
.6750	$84,375.00	($1,425.00)	(47.50%)
.6500	$81,250.00	($4,550.00)	(151.67%)
.6250	$78,125.00	($7,675.00)	(255.83%)

*Actual 1995 prices.

Which is why we recommend only "reasoned" speculation!

Note: Some of the risk can be eliminated while retaining much of the profit potential if you use options on currency futures — or on the actual currencies themselves. However, the chances of loss remain quite high, so be absolutely sure you understand what you are doing before you venture into these markets.

Hedging Your Business Currency Risks

Given the rapidly expanding global nature of business, the odds are high that many individuals — especially those who own their own companies or work in a financial capacity for a sizable corporation — are likely to encounter foreign-exchange risks in the course of their professional activities. As such, we'd be remiss if we didn't offer at least one example of a hedging scenario involving a business situation.

Assume, for example, that you are a top officer of the Global Traveler Inns, a major East Coast and Caribbean hotel chain that derives roughly 40 percent of its revenues from business travelers and tourists residing in Great Britain. As such, your profits — which are denominated and reported in U.S. dollars — are highly susceptible to fluctuations in the U.S. dollar/British pound exchange rate. In other words, if the dollar rises in value, the money your British customers have is worth less, so they cut back on travel to the United States and your sales fall. In addition, you have some direct currency exposure in that a number of your Caribbean locations actually do business in pounds.

The company's projected sales for the coming year are U.S.$450 million, but your analysis of the economic climate indicates the likelihood is high that the dollar could rise in value, reducing those revenues. You'd like to hedge against such risks — but how do you do it?

The simplest approach would be to go into the cash interbank market and sell a one-year British pound forward contract for $180 million — representing the 40 percent of your projected $450 million in annual sales generated by British customers ($450,000,000 x 0.40 = $180,000,000). However, that would require making either a large cash payment to secure the contract or heavily tapping into your bank credit line to finance the deal. You'd also have pay a sizable spread (equivalent to a commission) on the trade, which would reduce your profit margins. And, finally, the one-year contract, while hedging your annual performance, would do nothing to offset cash-flow problems that might result from both the seasonal nature of your business and any interim currency fluctuations.

A better approach would be to go into the futures market and sell enough British pound futures to offset the likely currency risk to your expected revenues in each of the coming four quarters — i.e., sell March, June, September and December contracts in an amount equal to your British sales projections for each period. That would lock in the current exchange rate for the full year, while still allowing you to compensate for your seasonal revenue variations. For example, assume your seasonal sales pattern looked like this, with the British pound exposure based on 40 percent of total revenues coming from Great Britain customers:

Sales period	Percentage of annual sales	Value in dollars	Br. pound exposure
1ST QUARTER	19%	$ 85,500,000	$ 34,200,000
2ND QUARTER	27%	$121,500,000	$ 48,600,000
3RD QUARTER	32%	$144,000,000	$ 57,600,000
4TH QUARTER	22%	$ 99,000,000	$ 39,600,000
TOTAL	**100%**	**$450,000,000**	**$180,000,000**

Based on the current British pound/U.S. dollar exchange rate of BP2.10 = U.S.$1.00 and the standard IMM currency futures contract size of 62,500 pounds, you'd need to sell futures contracts in the following quantities:

1st Quarter/March Futures: $34,200,000/2.10 = BP16,285,714

16,285,714/62,500 = 260.57 CONTRACTS

2nd Quarter/June Futures: $48,600,000/2.10 = BP22,857,143

22,857,143/62,500 = 365.71 CONTRACTS

3rd Quarter/Sept. Futures: $57,600,000/2.10 = BP27,428,571

27,428,571/62,500 = 438.85 CONTRACTS

4th Quarter/Dec. Futures: $39,600,000/2.10 = BP18,857,143

18,857,143/62,500 = 301.71 CONTRACTS

Rounding off, then, you would sell 261 March futures contracts, 366 June contracts, 439 September contracts and 302 December contracts, for a total of 1,368, covering a total of $180 million in sales (even though you'd have to put up a margin deposit of just $4.104 million at $3,000 per contract.

Now assume the U.S. dollar did rally in the first quarter, with the British pound/dollar exchange rate falling to 1.9417 by the time the March futures came due for delivery. Suppose, as well, that your hotels suffered a 6 percent drop in British-based business as a result of the dollar's higher value. What would be the outcome of your hedge?

Well, since you anticipated $34,200,000 in first-quarter British pound-related revenues, the 6 percent drop in business would have cost you $2,052,000 ($34,200,000 x 0.06 = $2,052,000). However, you would have made $2,582,073 on your 261 short March futures contracts, calculated as follows:

2.1000 - 1.9417 = 0.1583 X 62,500 = $9,893 X 261 = $2,582,073

Obviously, then, your hedge would have worked beautifully — covering your $2.052 million loss in revenues, with a $530,073 profit as a bonus (less expenses). But, what would have happened had the dollar fallen in value relative to the pound? Let's assume that did happen in the second quarter, with the British pound/ dollar exchange rate rising to 2.2075 and your business increasing by 4 percent as a result (remember, the weaker dollar makes travel to the U.S. cheaper for British citizens).

Since you expected $48,600,000 in second-quarter British-based business, the 4 percent increase would have generated an additional $1,944,000 ($48,600,000 x 1.04 = $50,544,000 - $48,600,000 = $1,944,000). However, this time you would have lost money on your hedging June futures position — $2,459,062, to be exact, calculated as follows:

$$2.2075 - 2.1000 = 0.1075 \times 62,500 = \$6,718 \times 366 = \$2,459,062.50$$

Perhaps the simplest way to gain some foreign-exchange exposure for your portfolio is to maintain a portion of your liquid assets in a foreign currency-denominated bank account.

Your net loss (not including commissions) would have thus been $515,062.50 — roughly equal to the excess profit you made in the first quarter. Thus, even though this wasn't a perfect hedge (you would prefer discrepancies a bit smaller than half a million dollars), it still worked out nicely. Your net revenues (after hedging) for the first half of the year were almost exactly as originally projected — meaning you successfully adjusted for both your seasonal business swings and the currency-related risk associated with your large British clientele.

We could go ahead and work through the third and fourth quarters as well, but you should already have a fairly clear idea of how the whole process works, so we won't waste your time. Instead, we will now move ahead and review the basic ways you — as an individual investor — can protect yourself against an eroding U.S. dollar and thus keep your overall wealth-building plan on track.

THE BASIC FOREIGN-CURRENCY INVESTMENT VEHICLES

Although the methods of directly playing the foreign-currency markets are limited for individuals — being restricted primarily to currency futures, currency options or options on currency futures — there are any number of ways to gain foreign-currency exposure through investment. These include, but are not limited to:

- Foreign currency-denominated bank accounts.

- Foreign bonds, either government or corporate.

- Direct ownership of foreign stocks — either listed on foreign bourses or traded on U.S. exchanges through interlisting agreements.

- Foreign-equity ownership through the purchase of American Depositary Receipts (ADRs), which trade on U.S. stock exchanges.

- Investment in diversified foreign bond or stock portfolios (or a combination of both) through the purchase of shares in international or global mutual funds.

- Investment in the foreign bonds and/or stocks of a single foreign country or international region through the purchase of shares in closed-end investment funds, which trade on the U.S. stock exchanges.

- Direct ownership of foreign real estate or business interests. *Note: Opportunities in these areas are quite limited — and, in some cases, even restricted by foreign governments. The intricacies of such investments mandate use of professional advisors. As a result, we won't offer any additional discussion of this area, although we did feel compelled to mention it.*

As we noted earlier, the basics regarding most of these investments are detailed in other segments of this program — either those on mutual funds or in the lesson, "The global approach." As such, the comments here should be considered primarily a review — focusing on the merits of these vehicles in terms of providing foreign-currency exposure — rather than a complete explanation of the mechanics, risks and rewards of these instruments. If you want more information or need to refresh your memory about how something works, refer to the other lessons mentioned above.

Foreign Currency-Denominated Bank Accounts

Perhaps the simplest way to gain some foreign-exchange exposure for your portfolio is to maintain a portion of your liquid assets in a foreign currency-denominated bank account. These accounts are offered by many leading U.S. banks or are available to Americans through larger international banks in most foreign countries. Most of them pay interest (although some Swiss accounts do not) — and, as you saw earlier, the interest-rate differentials should offset any exchange-rate fluctuations arising from changes in the dollar's value relative to the account's host country.

The drawbacks of these accounts include high minimum balances (in many cases, $25,000 or more); difficulty of access to your funds (although checking accounts are available for most of the major foreign currencies — albeit without interest); and poor translation of exchange rates by the host banking institution. However, the biggest drawback is that you get protection from dollar fluctuations against only a single currency. Still, if you travel extensively to a particular nation, have relatives living there who depend on you for financial assistance or have hopes of retiring to that country, such an account can give you needed protection against erosion of your dollar-denominated assets.

Investing in Foreign Debt

Corporate bonds and government securities from many major foreign countries are available to American investors, either through the U.S. over-the-counter debt market or via the Eurobond market. Purchases can be made through most leading U.S. brokerage firms with international bond departments, as well as through accounts with foreign brokerage firms. As with foreign currency bank accounts, the interest-rate differentials on these bonds should compensate you for risks related to dollar erosion.

Again, however, there are drawbacks, including potentially high transaction costs (if your U.S. broker has to buy through a foreign broker, you get a double commission hit) or, alternatively, hefty spreads between "bid" and "asked" quotes on less actively traded issues. Cash requirements are also high — with a typical minimum being the equivalent of U.S.$10,000 — which makes it difficult for most individuals to build a diversified foreign debt portfolio — meaning you'll again have difficulty getting protection against fluctuations in more than one or two of the leading foreign currencies.

Investing in Foreign Equities

The same concerns related to transaction costs apply to direct investment in foreign equities — and, if you try to trade via a foreign brokerage firm, you'll also likely face high minimum account requirements. There's also a heavy "analytical risk" (as there is with foreign bonds) due to a shortage of quality information and different accounting and reporting standards in various countries.

Some of these problems go away when you trade in foreign stocks listed on U.S. exchanges or buy ADRs. However, the availability of both is limited (only the largest and best-known of the foreign corporations have shares traded on domestic markets, though the number is steadily growing). As a result, you can expect the issues to have fairly high prices, with the markets heavily dominated by institutional traders. This again makes it difficult to build a diversified portfolio — and also excludes you from many of the better foreign growth companies that are just beginning to gain international prominence.

Funds Remain the Best Alternative

For most individual investors, that leaves U.S.-based investment funds — either open-ended (i.e., mutual funds) or closed-end — as the best method for gaining foreign-currency exposure. Both offer convenience and the safety of U.S. regulation, as well as reasonably low (or non-existent) commissions and management fees and extremely high liquidity. You also gain the benefits of wide diversification, professional management and effortless conversion of foreign currency-denominated interest payments, dividends and capital gains (or losses, let's not forget).

The assortment of open-ended mutual funds is extensive, meaning you can tailor your foreign exposure to meet your specific needs — investing entirely in debt, entirely in equities or a combination of both. Within the debt class, you can also choose strictly government securities, opt for corporate bonds or get a mixture of both. With both debt and equities, you can select international funds (those investing only in foreign securities) or global funds (those investing in both foreign and U.S. securities). You can also choose regional funds — focusing on such areas as the Pacific Rim and Latin America — or emerging-markets funds.

For most individual investors, U.S.-based investment funds are the best method for gaining foreign-currency exposure.

The selection of closed-end funds is more limited, particularly within the debt sector — and most are highly specialized, focusing on the securities of a single country, a particular region or a particular class (such as precious metals or emerging markets). As such, they can be extremely useful for hedging against specific as opposed to general currency-related risks. In addition, because closed-end fund shares frequently trade at a discount to the actual value of their net underlying assets, you can get added downside price protection or increased potential for capital gains if you buy at the right time.

The ultimate choice regarding which method to use in gaining foreign-currency exposure must be left up to you — based on your individual needs and objectives, as related to both your lifestyle and your investment goals. However, unless you are an extremely rare person — buying only 100 percent U.S.-made goods, working for a firm dealing only with local suppliers and customers, investing only in companies doing strictly domestic business and traveling only within America's borders — you must have at least some of your wealth in assets that can increase in value independent of the fate of the dollar.

If you don't — and the U.S. currency continues its downward progression of recent years — you can't help but suffer financially as a result.

A LOOK AT OTHER GREENBACK ALTERNATIVES

There are, of course, a few other investments you can make to hedge against declining dollar values — both internal and external.

For example, through the years, real estate has held its own with respect to inflation (although the economic slowdown of the early 1990s, coupled with overbuilding and slower demand, has resulted in some recent price erosion). Likewise, a basket of basic commodities, representing essential goods needed within the economy, should maintain price parity with the dollar. However, the most commonly recognized hedges against erosion in paper currency values — both here and abroad — are the precious metals.

The Eternal Appeal of Gold

Since the earliest days of civilized man, gold has been prized for its beauty, its rarity and its utility. As such, it has been a favored medium of exchange throughout history (as, to a lesser degree, have been silver and certain other metals). In fact, as you learned earlier, it was the "security" behind the U.S. dollar and most of the world's other currencies well into the 20th century. And, even though it no longer serves that role, it is still considered a valuable "diversifying element" for investors.

That's because gold has traditionally proven to be a "safe haven" in times of political or monetary crisis, military conflict or even unusual stock market volatility. As these events diminish the value and safety of paper currencies, gold's price typically rises — thus making it an ideal long-term hedge against severe inflation.

It should be noted, however, that gold today is not as sensitive to world events as it once was. It now seems as if it works as an effective hedge only in times of extremes — i.e., during violent political turbulence or periods of hyper-inflation. There is no longer a day-to-day, or even year-to-year correlation between inflation rates and gold prices — and gold doesn't always respond to limited political turmoil or minor military conflicts.

In addition, because bullion yields no dividends or interest payments — and may in fact entail extra costs for storage and safekeeping — it is probably unwise to view it as a true investment. A better perspective would be to think of it as a long-term "insurance policy" against unwelcome events, much as your homeowner's insurance is a hedge against unexpected household disasters. If you adopt that attitude, you won't be disappointed should your gold holdings fail to produce large profits — and may actually be pleased that the world around you is humming along in reasonably stable fashion.

Alternative Ways of Holding Gold

What's the best way to add a gold component to your portfolio? Actually, there are nearly a dozen different alternatives, with products available for everyone from the conservative investor with $500 to spend up to the aggressive speculator with $25,000 or more to put at risk. Some of these represent true investment value, with the potential for outstanding profits, while others have little if any investment merit. However, in the spirit of fairness, we'll list the full range, including:

- Gold bullion.
- Bullion coins.
- Bullion certificates.
- Shares in gold-mining companies.
- Options on gold futures or gold-mining stocks.
- Gold mutual funds (both open-ended and closed-end).
- Gold futures.
- Commemorative gold coins.
- Numismatic coins.
- Jewelry.

The Merits and Drawbacks of Bullion

The most direct method of holding gold is to buy the bullion itself. This is considered the ultimate hedge against extreme turmoil — a fact any good survivalist will confirm. That's because, "once our decaying political and financial systems collapse, leaving all paper assets worthless," gold will undoubtedly regain its former role as the world's primary medium of exchange. While we certainly don't take such a dismal view of our planet's future, we do agree that man will continue to be fascinated by the yellow metal, hoarding it in times of crisis.

That persistent demand will push prices higher, providing protection against the declining value of currencies resulting from the turmoil or related inflation. In the meantime, however, bullion just sits there, providing no income and accruing costs for storage and security.

In addition, unless you leave your metal in a certified depository from time of purchase to time of sale, it usually has to be "assayed" (i.e., verified for weight and purity) before you can sell. Spreads (the difference between the price you pay to buy and the price you receive when you sell) can be quite high relative to other investment commissions — and many states charge sales taxes on the purchase of bullion. (The IRS is even considering whether to exclude profits on bullion sales from the capital gains preference.)

Gold bullion comes in sizes ranging from 1/10th of an ounce up to 100-ounce bars, though you'll usually be subject to a minimum of $1,000 to $2,000 on purchases. (An exception is Merrill Lynch's "Blueprint" metals program, which has a minimum initial purchase of $100, with $50 minimums thereafter. Call 1-800-637-3766 for more information.) Bullion can be purchased through most major banks and brokerage houses, as well as through specialized dealers. There are even some "discount" dealers — an example being Benham Certified Metals (1-800-447-4653).

The Coin Alternative

If you like gold for its beauty as well as its hedging value, you may prefer bullion coins to bullion bars. These coins, minted by governments (or government-authorized mints), were designed with beauty in mind, and some are quite stunning — making them popular with people who like to hold and/or display their coins. Most are available in sizes ranging from 1/10th of an ounce up to one ounce, with some having five-ounce versions. (The one-ounce size is the most commonly used metals trading unit, making pricing simple and boosting liquidity.)

A Note About Silver

Once considered "the poor man's precious metal," silver has become even less responsive than gold to world events. It is now considered primarily an "industrial" metal — with prices subject more to manufacturing-related supply-and-demand fluctuations than to purely political or economic events. As evidence of this, consider that the ratio of gold prices to silver prices has risen sharply in recent years — climbing from as low as 19-to-1 20 years ago to as high as 95-to-1 in the early 1990s. Although this ratio has recently retreated into a range between 65-to-1 and 75-to-1, it now seems likely that silver's changing role has permanently altered its fundamental relationship with gold.

Bullion coins can be purchased from the same sources as bullion bars, as well as directly from some of the issuing governments or authorized mints. Prices are slightly higher than bullion, and usually run at a premium of 3 to 5 percent over the pure metal value. (Most of the other disadvantages associated with bullion also apply to bullion coins.) The leading gold bullion coins include the American Gold Eagle, the Canadian Maple Leaf, the Mexican 50 Peso piece, the South African Krugerrand, the Australian Nugget, the Austrian Corona and the Chinese Panda.

Note: Bullion coins should not be confused with "numismatic" or collectible gold coins — which are priced based on their rarity, beauty and condition, as well as their metal content — and thus trade at large premiums over their gold value. While anyone can enjoy coin collecting, numismatic coins should be viewed as investments only by experienced individuals qualified to judge the many subtleties that go into their pricing.

Certificates Make More Sense

Unless you truly are concerned about the ultimate demise of our economic system, there's really very little reason to own actual gold bullion or bullion coins given the problems, costs and risks involved. A better alternative is to hold gold certificates (also sold by banks, brokerage firms and metals dealers).

These certificates represent ownership of a specified quantity of gold (usually 5 or 10 ounces), which is actually held in a depository by the selling institution, providing extreme safety. You'll generally have to pay a small annual storage fee, but this is offset by the fact you don't have to pay for a home safe or bank deposit box. Certificates are also secure from loss or theft since your ownership is registered. And, you get one other bonus — unlike bullion, there's no sales tax on certificates. Bullion certificates can usually be converted into actual metal on demand, but you'll be assessed a "bar charge" when you pick up the gold. Some coins — e.g., the Canadian Maple Leaf — can also be purchased in certificate form, with the same sort of conversion charge applied if you later decide you want the actual coins.

Warning: Deal only with reputable, well-known institutions when buying certificates. There have been numerous cases in the past where fraudulent dealers or outright scam artists have sold certificates for bullion or coins that didn't actually exist.

Mining Shares and Gold Mutual Funds

For more liquidity — as well as more excitement and a chance to earn some dividends on your gold holdings — you may want to consider either the stocks of leading gold-mining companies or the shares of gold mutual funds. Either choice is generally cheaper — in terms of both total price and commissions — than buying the metal, and you get more opportunities for profits.

Coins Are Not What You Think

Many people buy numismatic coins, commemorative coins and fancy gold jewelry thinking they're making an investment in precious metals — but they're wrong.

While numismatic coins may prove to be good investments for those who really know and understand the rare-coin markets, they can't be considered an investment based solely on the fact they're made of gold. If you buy a collectible coin at its numismatic price, then have to sell it for its metal value, we can absolutely guarantee that you'll lose money.

As commemorative coins, simply forget about them. These coins sell at a huge premium to the actual price of the gold they contain — and that premium is almost entirely sentimental value (plus sales commissions). As a result, the only way you'll ever get a higher price if you need to sell them is to find someone more sentimental than you. If you like them because they're pretty, or want one as a keepsake, fine — but don't think of them as investments.

Jewelry is even worse. As much as 75 percent of the price of any piece of gold jewelry is attributable to the craftsmanship and the seller's profit margin. The gold value is thus fractional — and you're unlikely to get even that if you have to sell since the piece will have to be melted down to get at the metal. If you enjoy wearing jewelry, by all means buy it and wear it — but if you need to sell, you'd best head for a pawn shop, not an investment broker.

The North American gold-mining companies are among the most efficient in the world, so rising gold prices tend to translate into higher profits for the companies — which, in turn, lead to higher stock prices and larger dividends (if the stock has one). The excitement factor comes in because gold stocks also have a record of being somewhat more volatile than gold itself. Thus, percentage gains (and losses) on the stock price moves are often larger than on the price moves in the underlying gold itself. You also stand to benefit from stock price increases associated with general market rallies or economic upturns.

For die-hard metals advocates, the major problem with gold stocks is that they are still "paper securities" — meaning they could end up being worthless following a major economic collapse. You'd have no way to sell them or exchange them for real gold. By contrast, bullion bars or coins represent "metal in your hands" — metal that would likely skyrocket in value during the crisis.

Mining stocks should be carefully evaluated before purchase, with close attention paid to operating margins, production figures and reserves — as well as to the financial facts you'd review with any other type of company. The most promising choices are companies that have steadily reduced production costs while maintaining or expanding ore reserves. Some stocks to consider include:

- *American Barrick,* traded on both the New York Stock Exchange (NYSE) and the Toronto Stock Exchange (TSE) under the symbol ABX.

- *Agnico-Eagle,* traded on the TSE (symbol: AGE) and on the over-the-counter market in the United States (symbol: AEAGF).

- *Echo Bay Mines,* traded on the American Stock Exchange (Amex) and the TSE (symbol: ECO).

- *Euro-Nevada Mining Corp.,* TSE (symbol: EN).

- *Homestake Mining,* NYSE (symbol: HM), which also produces lead and zinc.

- *LAC Minerals,* NYSE (symbol: LAC).

Note: Shares of most foreign gold-mining companies should be avoided as they tend to be less efficient than North American producers and are also frequently subject to labor unrest and political instability.

If you'd prefer to have someone else select your mining stocks, there are a number of mutual funds that specialize in precious metals. These funds offer the same advantages as individual mining stocks, with the added benefits of diversification and professional money management. Share prices also generally tend to be somewhat less volatile than individual mining stocks, although fund performance can vary dramatically from year to year.

Most funds invest primarily in North American gold-mining stocks, although some also invest directly in gold, silver and platinum bullion. There are also several funds that invest in the shares of foreign gold-mining companies — most notably those based in South Africa — as well as a few that specialize in hedging strategies involving options and futures. At left are several funds that have historically kept pace with gold price movements.

Gold Funds that have Kept Pace with the Price of Gold

- Dynamic Precious Metals Fund (Canadian).
- Excel Midas Gold.
- FCMI Precious Metals (Canadian).
- Fidelity Select American Gold.
- Vanguard Specialty Gold & Precious Metals.
- IDS Precious Metals.
- Keystone Precious Metals Holdings.
- United Services World Gold.
- United Services Gold Shares.
- Franklin Gold.
- Bull & Bear Gold Investors.
- Scudder Gold.

As with all other types of mutual funds, you can buy gold funds either through your broker or directly from the company at the net asset value per share, plus any applicable "loads" or commissions. When you cash in, you redeem the shares at the current net asset value per share, less any deferred or back-end fees. To get current prices and recent annualized return figures for the funds at left, check the weekly tables in *Barron's*. For daily quotes and year-to-date percentage changes, check the tables in *Investor's Business Daily,* which also gives phone numbers for the management companies in case you want additional information.

Gold Futures and Options

Futures and options are the vehicles of choice for gold speculators, as well as those seeking short-term "paper" profits to help defray the cost of their longer-term bullion holdings. Since both futures and options are covered in other lessons of this program ("Commodity and financial futures" and "Lots of options with options"), we won't go into further detail on their use here.

However, we will refer you to Wealth-Building Step No. 78, Three Little-Known Ways to Trade in Precious Metals, found on page 29. It covers two strategies involving futures and options as they relate specifically to gold, as well as one other highly unusual gold-linked investment vehicle.

ARE COLLECTIBLES TRUE INVESTMENTS

Many people view their collectible items as investments or as a hedge against inflation. And, some collectors do make large profits on sales of specific items. However, as you should have surmised from our comments on numismatic coins, commemorative coins and jewelry, very few collectibles ever pan out as investments — and their illiquidity and volatile price swings make them unsuitable as hedges.

Whether your passion is art, coins, antiques, rare books, guns, rare documents, baseball cards, old toys or something we haven't thought of, your best approach is to view collecting strictly as a hobby. Buy items because you like them and would be proud to own them. Trade because you enjoy the challenge of adding new items to your collection or improving its quality. If you wind up making a profit when you sell, that's great — but if you don't, you shouldn't be disappointed.

That doesn't mean, however, that you should ignore the financial considerations in your collecting efforts. The reason it's so hard to make money with collectibles is that it's typically a "retail/wholesale" market — i.e., you buy at retail, but sell at wholesale. As a result, your transaction costs — the spread between the two prices — often run from 50 to 100 percent, which makes it really hard to turn a profit unless you're dealing with true rarities (pieces that sell for $50,000 and up).

Another problem is that quality — and prices — are extremely subjective. Is that uncirculated silver dollar an MS-63 grade or an MS-65 grade? Ninety-nine people out of a hundred can't tell, but the price difference can be $400 or $500. The same types of questions apply to nearly all fields. To us, one kind of clay looks pretty much like another, but pottery made of one can be worthless, while another similar piece can be priceless.

Three Little-Known Ways to Trade in Precious Metals

What: Generate income from your gold bullion holdings or other gold-linked investments or added profits from gold-price movements by:

- Employing covered option-writing strategies.
- Trading gold futures.
- Buying the unusual "gold/yen bonds."

Why: Gold bullion pays no interest or dividends and many other gold-linked investments produce profits only in times of turmoil or hyperinflation. In spite of that, most high-net-worth investors should have at least some gold in their portfolios as "insurance" against just such turbulent times. With these strategies, you can get the insurance — and some profits besides. Also, futures and options offer substantial leverage, which can greatly boost your returns.

Risk: Medium (for covered option writing) to speculative (for futures trading).

Safety: Medium. With the exception of the gold/yen bonds, these are well-known vehicles and the mechanics of trading are widely understood. Clearing houses also guarantee performance. The gold/ yen bonds are unusual, but they are backed by the government of Denmark so there's little risk of outright default.

Liquidity: High for options and futures, low for gold/yen bonds.

Why not: Risk of losing your hedging insurance is the biggest reason not to write covered options — i.e., if gold rises in price by too much, the option you sold could be exercised, forcing you to surrender (or sell) the underlying asset, be it your gold, your mining stocks or a futures contract. High volatility and unlimited risk is the main argument against futures trading, which is really suitable only for sophisticated, well-financed investors. The gold/yen bonds are a unique product, with unproven performance and risks that may not be clearly understood. Liquidity is also poor.

Buy/Invest from: Any full-service or discount futures broker in the case of futures and options on futures; any full-service or discount stock broker for gold-mining stocks and related stock options; or any major full-service brokerage or bond dealer for gold/yen bonds.

Background: Here's some basic information you'll need to do each of these strategies, in order:

- **Covered call writing.** This is one of the fundamental strategies in the option trader's arsenal — designed to produce or increase cash flows and/or returns from portfolio holdings, or to reduce the effective cost basis of those assets. It was thoroughly explained in Wealth-Building Step No. 66 in the lesson "Lots of options with options," so we won't repeat the mechanics here. The strategy can be used successfully in any type of market environment — except when prices are crashing downward — but it works best when conditions are stable or mildly bullish. To apply it with respect to gold, there are three basic alternatives:

  - Buy shares in the common stock of a leading North American gold-mining company and then write one out-of-the-money call option for each 100 shares you own.

  - Buy a gold futures contract and write a corresponding gold call with a striking price above the current futures price. The ratio here is one option for each futures contract. (You can also do a bearish version of the strategy, selling a futures contract short and selling a corresponding out-of-the-money put option.)

  - Deposit your gold bullion or gold coins with a major futures or stock brokerage and then use part of its value as margin to cover the otherwise "naked" sale of an out-of-the-money futures call or a similarly positioned call on a gold-mining stock. Gains on the underlying physical gold should cover any losses incurred if the call moves into the money, although you could be forced to sell the gold to cover your losses if they grow too large. *Note: This is a little-known and rarely used way to generate income from your bullion or coin holdings. In fact, many brokers don't even know that their firms will accept gold in lieu of cash margins. Be aware, however, that you are borrowing money from the brokerage firm, meaning interest charges and transaction fees could severely reduce the effectiveness of the strategy.*

■ **Gold futures.** Gold futures are mainly speculative vehicles designed to produce highly leveraged gains on even modest changes in the price of the underlying metal. (Again, the mechanics of futures trading were covered in the lesson, "Commodity and financial futures," so we won't repeat them.) However, they can also be useful in hedging against adverse short-term price moves in other gold-linked portfolio holdings — perhaps as a result of inflation reports or other economic events. For instance, if you own a large amount of gold bullion or several gold-mining stocks, you could be subject to a sizable short-term loss if the government's monthly report on inflation showed prices rising at a slower-than-expected rate. To protect yourself, you could sell a gold futures contract — representing control of 100 ounces of gold — shortly before the report's release date. This would lock in your right to sell gold at the current price, regardless of what happened as a result of the report. If the inflation numbers did come in low, and gold dropped, you would buy another gold futures contract to offset the one you earlier sold. The profit on the futures transaction would offset some or all of the loss in value you might have on your bullion or stocks.

If purely speculative profits are your goal, simply find out the release dates of similar reports, analyze the markets so you can make a reasoned estimate of the potential impact, then buy or sell short a futures contract that would profit from any resulting move in the price of gold. Remember, it only takes a small change in gold prices to produce big profits on futures — e.g., a $10 move by gold will translate to a $1,000 change in the value of a standard Comex gold futures contract.

■ **Gold/Yen bonds.** The Kingdom of Denmark "gold/yen" bond is a joint speculation on the price of gold and the Japanese yen/U.S. dollar exchange rate. The bond matures on March 20, 1997, and pays interest each March and September at a variable rate equal to the six-month London Interbank Offering Rate (LIBOR), minus 55 basis points, but adjusted by a factor that reflects the differential between U.S. and Japanese interest rates. The minimum coupon is 0.00 percent. At maturity, you receive $1,000 face value, adjusted for the combined price of gold and the yen/dollar exchange rate. If gold falls to $200 an ounce or less at maturity and the yen rises to the point that 73.72 yen will buy 1 U.S. dollar, you'll receive nothing. (To put that risk in perspective, gold was priced about $400 an ounce and it took around 105.00 yen to buy 1 U.S. dollar in early 1996, roughly a year ahead of maturity.) If, on the other hand, gold rises to $500 an ounce and the yen's value falls to the point that it takes 180.00 yen to buy 1 dollar, you would get back $1,562.50 rather than the $1,000 face value. At the recent actual prices listed above, the bond would pay off roughly $836.70 for each $1,000 in face value. If those same prices remained stable, your interest payments in the interim would run about 70 basis points below those on a straight bond with otherwise similar features.

In essence, then, this bond is a bet that gold prices will rise and yen values will fall relative to the dollar in the period remaining until the bond's 1997 maturity. If you think that's likely to happen, then this bond would offer you a chance for rising interest payments and a substantial capital gain — making it a good choice. If you think the odds of gold climbing and the yen falling are slim, then you should steer clear.

▶ ▶ ▶ ▶ **If you want to get started today, here's what you need to do to use these three little-known gold-trading methods:**

First, analyze your current portfolio of gold-linked holdings or review your investment objectives to see which of these plays might be applicable to your situation. If you opt for the gold/yen bonds, call your regular full-service broker (if you have one) or a bond dealer, get price quotes and, if you like them, place an order. (The broker or dealer will help you quickly set up an account if you need one.) If you choose one of the other strategies, make sure the appropriate brokerage account is in order, and then begin monitoring the markets and the news, looking for signs of developing conditions or upcoming events that could signal a trading opportunity. When you find one, call the proper broker and place your order. As always, use strict limit orders and attempt to quantify your expenses, potential risks and possible rewards before initiating the trade (i.e., work out a scenario as explained in the lessons on options and futures). ▲

Continued from p. 28

Not only quality but even authenticity is a major issue. If you read the newspapers regularly, you've no doubt seen stories about major art museums being duped with forgeries — and they have the world's top experts available as advisors. So, what's the answer?

The prime rule for any collector is to learn as much as you possibly can about the area in which you're interested. Read journals, reference books, newsletters and price sheets. Talk to other collectors and interview experts. Visit collecting shows and attend meetings of collecting clubs. Ask questions; take notes; learn.

The next rule is to specialize. Don't just collect coins; collect U.S. silver dollars minted between 1865 and 1900. Don't just collect stamps; collect 19th century British colonial issues. Nearly every collecting field is far broader than one person can hope to master on a spare-time basis, and someone who tries to be a "generalist" in collecting will "generally" get taken.

Another rule is one we've already mentioned: Buy things because you like them and want to own them — not because you think they will go up in value. This is particular true with art, antiquities and other pieces with values based on "beauty, style and/or aesthetic appeal," rather than on rarity or novelty. There's nothing worse than having to daily look at a painting you don't like and can't sell for even half of what you paid.

Finally, if you have any doubts, don't buy — or, at least don't buy without getting an objective appraisal or opinion first. Even if the seller is considered an expert in the field, remember that he or she is still trying to sell. Find out why an item is being sold — and what justifies the price being asked. If you don't like the answers, walk away. This may be a field where the investment potential is limited, but it's one where the monetary risk is great!

You've now had a thorough briefing on how the world of currencies works, how currency price fluctuations can affect both your investments and your daily life, and how the prospect of future erosion in the value of the U.S. dollar can impact your wealth-building plans. You've also learned several of the things you can do about it — from investing in foreign currency-denominated securities to reduce your portfolio's exchange-rate exposure to holding gold as a hedge against both turmoil and inflation.

In your next lesson, we'll get back to business — the business of venture investing, that is. You'll learn how venture capitalists work, how to get in on the action yourself, how to analyze prospective opportunities and the various pitfalls you may encounter. Following that, we'll return to the real estate arena, offering some advanced strategies for investing in property — from apartment buildings and condo conversions to commercial buildings.

These two lessons are filled with information, tips and vital warnings for those who want to expand their investment horizons beyond the realm of stocks, bonds, mutual funds and other market "basics." ▲

Riding to Collectible Profits

There is one type of collectible that you can literally take to the bank — assuming you have a driver's license, that is. Cars — from antiques to classics to exotic sports models — have been among the most popular and profitable of collectibles over the past three decades, driven by America's undying love affair with the automobile. However, because of the relatively high values of the vehicles involved — from $10,000 to $500,000 — the recent economic slowdown has forced many collectors to liquidate some of their holdings. As a result, prices have fallen and it's now a buyer's market.

Cars are almost unique as far as collectibles go, simply because they are also utilitarian. In other words, you don't have to just look at them — you can also drive them to the store if you need a quart of milk. There's also a major social culture revolving around auto collecting, ranging from the fancy "Concours de' Elegance" events for owners of high-priced antique models through rallyes for sports-car enthusiasts to "car hop nights" at local drive-ins for collectors of '30s through '60s American hot rods.

Autos also offer a rare opportunity for hands-on collectors with mechanical skills. With very few other collectibles can you take what is essentially a piece of junk and turn it into something both beautiful and worth thousands of dollars. As with other collectible fields, however, there are cautionary notes. David Stewart, a California stockbroker who has collected both Jaguars and classic American pick-up trucks, warns that restoring an old car will almost always

cost more than you expect and will only rarely prove profitable. "The only cars I ever made big money on," Stewart says, "are those I bought fully restored and later resold."

Stewart also notes that the field is not without it's scam artists. "The 1963 split-window Corvette is a prime example. Sellers claim there are nearly twice as many of these machines today as were originally produced." How can that be? The answer is easy, Stewart explains: "The '63 Corvette is very valuable, and the '62 'Vette can easily be modified to split-window specifications."

So, if collecting cars strikes your fancy, what's a good buy? "The best values today are in the classic British sports cars," says Reed Nichols, owner of Reed's Mountain British of Lake Elsinore, Calif. "MGA's are great for low-budget, backyard mechanics, and the 1967 MGB roadster with wire wheels and overdrive is a good choice for more sophisticated buyers. This was the last MG made with a steel dash and no smog equipment." He also suggests the Austin-Healey "bug-eye" Sprites and the 1979 and 1980 LE (Limited Edition) MG's, which "are all black with silver trim, very affordable, very collectible."

Stewart's personal recommendation is the 1974 V-12 Jaguar, which can be bought today for as little as $30,000 (down from $50,000 a few years ago). "It's the only front-mounted V-12 machine in the world today for less than $200,000. The lines are priceless; but the price tag isn't — yet."

Venture investing — enjoying the fruits of entrepreneurial success

Venture investing — enjoying the fruits of entrepreneurial success

"Anyone who desires to achieve success and wealth in business must have imagination and be farsighted. He must also be willing to spend — and risk — money, but only when the expenditure is justified and the risk is calculated to be worth it." — J. Paul Getty

WHAT IS VENTURE INVESTING?

This lesson covers "venture investing" — a proven approach to wealth building involving financial participation in new, fairly new or newly purchased businesses. Venture investing covers a broad spectrum of financial involvement in various types of enterprises. It is not, however, synonymous with venture capital — an industry that has, in recent years, become a formalized network of individuals and institutions active in providing equity capital to fledgling enterprises.

Venture investors may or may not be venture capitalists. In addition to financing new enterprises, venture investors also often buy into established companies or firms serving limited or strictly local markets. In other words, rather than being entrepreneurs themselves, venture investors instead team up with entrepreneurs to create wealth.

Most millionaires (at least in the United States) earned their fortunes through entrepreneurism — that is by building up their own companies or businesses in which they had a direct stake. Venture investing is for people who want to become involved in entrepreneurial activity as backers, rather than as direct participants.

Put another way, venture investing gives you the chance to realize ambitious financial aspirations and enjoy the fruits of entrepreneurial success, without having to become a hands-on entrepreneur yourself.

Risks Are High — But So Are Rewards Venture investing is not easy. It takes a great deal of effort. And, it's also risky. By its very nature, involvement in venture investing means possibly losing all that you put in. You must also have patience since venture investing often means committing your capital for several years — to someone else's venture.

As a venture investor, you will be backing entrepreneurs who have already decided what opportunities to exploit and how to proceed. You will, at least initially, review business plans and strategies rather than formulate them. This sounds fairly basic, but it is no easy task — the volume, type and accuracy of information entrepreneurs provide can vary as extensively as the activities of the ventures themselves. But, then, so can the nature of your involvement.

At the very least, you will have to decide whether:

- The information entrepreneurs provide is sufficient to assess the venture's viability.

- The business concepts they present are sound.

- The conditions they offer concerning your participation are consistent with your investment goals — and worth the risks as you perceive them.

These issues are extremely important because, as a venture investor, your ability to influence or exit the venture once you have committed to it may be limited.

From Treasury Secretary to Venture Investor

In 1981, a group led by William E. Simon, former secretary of the Treasury, took a small company, Gibson Greeting Cards Co., private in a leveraged buyout (or LBO) — a transaction in which an investor group takes control of a public company and recapitalizes it, borrowing money to purchase all its shares on the open market. Prior to Simon's deal, LBOs had been limited to companies with less than $1,000,000 in assets. The Gibson deal set off a wave of ever-larger LBOs — culminating in the buyout of RJR Nabisco. Although subsequent LBOs gained more notoriety, few were as profitable. The annualized return to the original investors in the Gibson deal was 1,320 percent.

In exchange, however, you can get potentially enormous payoffs — earning exceptional multiples of your initial investment. For example, in 1981 an investor group headed by former Treasury Secretary William E. Simon purchased the Gibson Greeting Card Co. in a leveraged buyout (LBO).

Just 18 months later, the new owners issued shares to the public — earning $200 for each dollar originally invested!

Be advised, though, that such returns are exceptionally rare. As a typical venture investor, you are unlikely to do as well as William Simon and his partners — particularly starting out. It is also improbable that your association with a new venture will make you as wealthy as Bill Gates, entrepreneur and founder of software giant Microsoft — although you may be able to do as well as some of his original backers (who have indeed done very nicely).

Venture investing can enhance overall returns on a diversified investment portfolio that includes stocks, bonds, mutual funds, real estate holdings, etc. Many of the same techniques you must master to do well in those areas will apply equally as well in venture investing. That's why much of the information in this lesson, rather than being totally new, will build on what you learned in other sections of the course.

Hard work, discipline, persistence and patience will also serve you well.

What Is a Venture Investor?

A venture investor is a financial participant in one of the following:

- A business start-up.

- The expansion of a relatively small, but potentially fast-growing enterprise (growth-phase financing).

- A transaction involving financing for a transfer of business ownership.

Start-ups include enterprises that are not yet operating, but that need seed capital — i.e., financing either for business planning, product research and development or to set up initial operations. Start-ups also include businesses that have been operational for a while (from a few

Can the Venture Investor Be Categorized?
Academics Think So. Do You Fit the Profile?

Professors Jeffrey E. Sohl and William Wetzel Jr. of the Center for Venture Research at the University of New Hampshire have studied participants in "angel networks" — part of the informal capital investment market that exists in the United States. These networks are made up of venture investors looking for opportunities and entrepreneurs seeking capital. Publishing their findings in a report titled, "The Private Investor Market for Venture Capital," Sohl and Wetzel said the typical venture investor is:

■ Well educated, with at least a college degree.

■ Middle-aged (typically 45 to 50).

■ Male more often than female.

■ Reasonably well off, having built up a substantial net worth.

■ Accomplished in business, frequently with entrepreneurial experience as a business owner or manager.

They also found that venture investors tend to favor start-up businesses — usually stepping in during the very early stages — and prefer that their ventures be located relatively close to home. Their exit horizons are similar to those investing in later-stage venture capital funds — i.e., five to seven years. The majority take an active role in ventures in which they become involved, usually by taking seats on boards of directors or serving in an active consulting capacity to an area of the company's operations — e.g. finance or marketing.

While this is the profile of the "average" venture investor, they do run the gamut — from successful, "cashed-out" investors in earlier ventures to total novices taking their first tentative steps into the entrepreneurial arena.

months to as long as a few years), but that have not yet become sufficiently established to rely completely on banks, other financial institutions or the capital markets (e.g., stock and bond exchanges) for the additional financing they require.

Growth-phase enterprises have reached a point where they may have some access to conventional sources of capital — banks, finance companies and/or the capital markets — but must still rely, at least in part, on equity capital for expansion. In many cases, successful businesses continue for many years to require private capital before approaching banks and institutional lenders or issuing shares to the public. Some enterprises also choose to remain privately held throughout their entire existence — i.e., they may seek loans from banks and other financial institutions, but never issue shares to the public.

Financial involvement in the outright purchase of an established enterprise (an ownership transfer) typically doesn't have the profit potential of an investment in a start-up or growth-phase venture — at least initially. However, established businesses can offer more predictable profits — and, depending on the price, earn investors generous rates of return. At the same time, a certain type of business transfer — known as a "turnaround" — can be exceptionally profitable.

A turnaround involves buying a money-losing or bankrupt business at a distressed price. The new owners — particularly if they have good capital resources — then take charge of the enterprise (or its assets) and realize gains either by selling when the market for the assets turns or by streamlining the business so it starts to operate profitably.

What Does a Venture Investor Expect?

Generally, a venture investor expects to earn a greater (and sometimes far greater) return than is possible through normal equity (stocks) or fixed-income (bonds) investing. How much is that precisely? Well, in a typical deal, you should shoot for a return of at least 25 percent annually — and, in some cases, hope to earn 50 percent or more. However, the pay-off may not come until:

■ Someone buys the venture investor(s) out.

■ The company is sold to a larger entity.

■ The company goes public through issuing shares that are traded on an exchange or in the over-the-counter market.

These are milestones in a venture's development that can take years — and a great deal of hard work — to reach. Thus, the venture investor gives up liquidity — the ability to sell his or her participation on the open market at any time — and perhaps endures some sleepless nights in exchange for the chance to earn a greater reward than he or she could through other, presumably less-risky types of investing.

How Do You Become a Venture Investor?

To become a venture investor, you must first have capital — and it must be capital you can afford to lose! Thus, the funds you invest should be your own, not borrowed. And they should not represent a significant portion of money you plan to eventually retire on — or money you might need to live on in the immediate (or even somewhat distant) future. Even if the venture is successful, you'll likely have to commit your money for several years — and, even then, you may not have total control over when you can "cash out."

Although there is no precisely defined minimum for getting started in venture investing, it's unlikely to be worth your while if you commit anything less than $10,000. On the other hand, even if you have hundreds of thousands of dollars (or more) to commit, you should probably refrain from doing so until you've built some experience in the venture arena.

Often venture investors get started when someone such as a CPA, investment advisor, stock broker, attorney, business broker, banker, associate, relative or friend recommends a venture investment. Perhaps a business is up for sale. Perhaps there is an attractively priced commercial property, a franchise opportunity or a restaurant on the market. A developer may intend to put up a strip mall and need financing partners. Or a fraternity brother or relative who is a computer whiz may have a great idea for a software company.

If you have not been approached as a potential venture investor, but want to become involved in venture investing, you may already know people who can help you. A CPA, investment advisor, banker or attorney you know may be aware of a prospective investment or refer you to someone who is. As an alternative, you can contact one or more of the following organizations:

- *The National Association of Small Business Investment Companies* (SBICs), 1199 N. Fairfax St. Suite 200, Alexandria, VA 22314, Tel. (703) 683-1601, Fax (703) 683-1605, for a Small Business Investment Company in your area. These federally supported financial entities are always looking for investors.

- *The Center for Venture Research at the University of New Hampshire,* Durham, NH 03824-3593, Tel. (603) 862-1981, Fax (603) 862-4468. This organization can steer you to "angel networks." These are groups whose members are venture investors looking for investment ideas, as well as entrepreneurs seeking financing.

- *The Western Association of Venture Capitalists,* 3000 Sand Hill Road, Building 2, Suite 260, Menlo Park, CA 94025, Tel. (415) 854-1322, which publishes a directory of its members.

- *The Business Brokerage Press,* P.O. Box 247, Concord, MA 01724, Tel. (508) 369-5254, Fax (508) 371-1156, will refer you to a business broker in your area.

You can also contact firms listed in Pratt's Guide to Venture Capital Sources, available in most libraries, published by Venture Economics Inc., 75 Second Ave., Needham, MA 02192. You will find that representatives of most firms listed in this guide will assist you if you are seriously interested in venture investing.

Be forewarned, however, even though these organizations represent reputable entities, the word may get out that you are looking to invest. A novice venture investor is a target for unscrupulous business brokers, disreputable wheeler dealers who call themselves money managers, etc., who may try to contact you. Check everyone you deal with very carefully, and get references — particularly if you get unsolicited calls. Remember, it is always better to deal with people you have known for a long time and have grown to trust.

Aristotle Onassis, Venture Investor Nonpareil, and the Societe de Bains de Mere et Cercle des Etrangers

Aristotle Onassis, the legendary shipping magnate, was an exceptionally shrewd venture investor. He demonstrated early on in his business career how to take advantage of a good investment opportunity. In the 1930s, Onassis, then in his 30s, got his start as a fleet owner/operator when he was able to pick up half a dozen vessels for little more than their scrap value. At the time, Onassis owned only one small freighter, which he operated along the eastern coast of Latin America. While on a visit to London, he learned through a business contact that a distressed shipping concern, the Canadian National Steamship Co., had ten freighters for sale laid up along the St. Lawrence River. With a marine engineer in tow, Onassis flew to Montreal to have a look. Together they scrutinized the vessels carefully, checking engine rooms, boilers and bulkheads. On their hands and knees, they crawled through ventilation ducts and inspected every store. Onassis took extensive notes and made detailed calculations. He submitted an offer. The Canadians accepted, and Onassis picked up six vessels for a song. He was off.

Onassis was able to operate these and other vessels profitably, which gave him the wherewithal to make venture investments later on. Twenty years after acquiring the Canadian vessels, he spied the turnaround opportunity of a lifetime — a company known as the Societe de Bains de Mere et Cercle des Etrangers (Sea Bathing Society and Foreigners' Club, or SBM). SBM, whose shares traded on the Paris Bourse, owned 375 acres of land in Monaco (approximately one third of the Principality). Following World War II, before Europe had recovered, Monaco had fallen on hard times. Tourism was off and property values had declined. All this was reflected in SBM's share price. Nonetheless, the company's assets included the principality's casino, yacht club and the Hotel de Paris.

Through a Byzantine maze of Panamanian companies that he owned, Onassis snapped up SBM's shares. He then refurbished the properties and restored to Monaco a climate of grandeur. To give the principality a new aura of excitement he held extravagant, highly publicized parties on his yacht, the Christina, docked in the Monte Carlo Yacht Club's premier berth. And, to crown it all off, Onassis helped arrange the marriage between American movie star Grace Kelly and Monaco's Prince Rainier, which added to the principality' glamour. All this brought the wealthy of Europe back to Monaco and into its casinos. As prosperity returned to the Continent, the principality began, once again, to thrive. At the roulette wheels, the croupiers raked it in for Onassis — a venture investor par excellence.

Though brilliant, there was actually nothing new in Onassis' approach to venture investing. He was using principles laid down more than 2,500 years earlier — principles you'll learn more about in wealth-building Step 79, found on page 8.

BACKGROUND: PREPARING TO INVEST IN VENTURES

Once you have taken the course outlined in wealth-building Step 79, and are satisfied that a venture's management passes muster and will give you access to all the material you need, you can prepare to analyze a venture investment.

This is a lengthy process in which you will have to sift through and verify a great deal of information — as well as assess projections and assumptions others make. You will have to verify information, do a fair amount of independent research, and draw up your own plans to augment those entrepreneurs present to you. You should practice extreme care — "due diligence" — throughout your analysis.

Validity of the Books

In the case of an ownership transfer, entrepreneurs should provide you with balance sheets and income and cash-flow statements from prior years. These financial statements will be one of three types — audited, reviewed or compiled — defined as follows:

■ *Audited Statements* — These are highly reliable. A CPA firm has performed a complete audit and attests to the fact that the statements are presented in accordance with generally accepted accounting principals (GAAP).

STEP 79

Study First, Prosper Later — How Pigs Get Fat, But Hogs Can Get Slaughtered

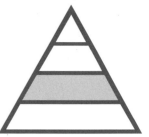

What: Apply principles laid down 2,500 years ago to analyze potential risks and rewards — and avoid slaughter as a venture investor on today's business battlefields.

Why: The perils of financial involvement in a major business venture are high, and you can't afford to ignore what the ancients had to say about risk and reward trade-offs.

Risk: Modest. There is the slight risk that despite learning the principals we've laid out, without in-depth consideration, they could be misapplied.

Safety: High. The more you study existing ventures — and what makes them tick — the greater your odds of success.

Liquidity: Not applicable.

Why Not: There's no good reason not to apply the fundamentals of risk/reward analysis to any new venture you undertake.

Buy/Invest From: Not applicable.

Background: Writing in the 5th century BC, the Chinese military strategist Sun Tzu pioneered what would today be called risk/reward analysis.* No one since has surpassed the clarity and perceptiveness of his discourse.

While Sun Tzu formulated a rational basis for the planning and conduct of military operations, much of his thinking is germane to investors today — particularly venture investors. Military commanders who have studied his thought (among them Mao Tse-tung) have been victorious in battle. Sun Tzu's approach can help you avoid being slaughtered — and achieve victory in business.

There are two basic aspects to Sun Tzu's approach — analysis and leadership — explained as follows:

- *Analysis* — Sun Tzu defined the superior commander as one "who takes correct actions, based on correct decisions, based on a thorough and indispensable review of the facts."

- *Leadership* — Sun Tzu held that the superior commander should not appraise risks and rewards in isolation, but in terms of various fundamental factors. The first of these is "moral influence." This Sun Tzu defined as "that which causes the people to be in harmony with their leaders, so that they will accompany them in life and unto death without fear of mortal peril."

In identifying leadership as the primary factor of military engagement, Sun Tzu was on the money. The same quality management is always the real key to success in any commercial enterprise. While managers may not have to inspire employees to face the possibility of death in business combat, they'd better know how to rally the troops.

If you want to start today, here are some keys to conducting a proper risk/reward analysis:

1. At the outset, learn all you possibly can not only about the specific business venture, which is obvious, but the entire industry it's a part of. You should be willing to keep learning as much, if not more, than the entrepreneur(s) or management team involved — not to mention the enemy (your competitors and potential competitors). If you aren't annoying someone by your phone calls and snooping around you had better not invest. You don't know enough.

2. You must analyze the venture in terms of the enterprise's managers. After all, the fate of your investment rests in their hands. You, the venture investor, must make sure that entrepreneurs running any commercial enterprise must, of course, have appropriate skills and experience. They must be able to manage effectively, seize opportunities, solve problems, and make profits. If they can't, you as a venture investor are not likely to realize any gain. Put another way, never give money to an A quality idea being managed by a B quality team. Make sure they include resumes of all those involved, as well as references (which you should check before starting on the business plan itself).

3. In order to make a complete and indispensable review of the facts, you have to make sure the managers, and other backers, will grant you access to all the information you will need before proceeding. In a transfer of ownership you will (or should) be allowed to examine all historical records (which you will have to authenticate). Don't even think about investing in any going concern unless you have complete access to the books. In a start-up, or the expansion of a recently started venture, the entrepreneur is likely to have put together a detailed, formal business plan.

4. If the entrepreneurs have not prepared such a document, you should insist that they draw one up. Participating in its production would serve you well. Ask yourself, though: If the entrepreneurs have not put together a "battle plan," how is the venture going to conquer the market?

5. Get hold of any previous business plans or documents that the entrepreneur has distributed in past efforts to raise capital for his venture. Information such plans contain could provide vital clues concerning the probable performance of the enterprise — and the individuals involved. Don't stop there, either; dig further. Do your own research on the industry, and the companies in it — they may soon be competitors. Make sure your assessment is consistent with what the principals in the venture are telling you — either about a going operation or in the business plan.

6. Keep in mind that business plans for new ventures are "best guesses." Much of the financial information they contain is not subject to verification. You won't be able to audit proforma numbers. You can, however, insist on knowing how the team arrived at the fact such-and-such a widget will cost the business $1.26.

7. Use the plan as a departure point to ask the principals pointed questions. After all, few businesses evolve according to plan, and even the most carefully drawn business forecasts can really just be "dream sheets." Treat them as such.

8. Never venture more than you can afford to lose.

George Soros, known as the Wizard of Wall Street, is a venture investor as well as a speculator. In his book, The Alchemy of Finance*, he puts forth a general approach to investments that is consistent with Sun Tzu's. Soros will get an investment idea (in his words "investment thesis"), research it thoroughly and commit some capital. If it starts to work, it emboldens him — and he increases his exposure. If not, he will cut his losses while they are still small.

So, be like Soros and do as Sun Tzu advised: Slowly and methodically review all the facts in order to take correct actions, based on correct decisions, based on a complete and indispensable review of the facts. Consider the venture in the context of the managers and others involved and never commit more capital than justified by the potential reward — and never commit more than you can afford to lose. ▲

* Sun Tzu, *The Art of War,* translated by Samuel Griffith, Oxford University Press, 1971.
* Soros, George, *The Alchemy of Finance,* Simon and Shuster, 1987.

Continued from p. 7

■ *Reviewed Statements* — These are less reliable. A CPA affirms that there appear to be no material discrepancies between the statements and the finances of the business.

■ *Compiled Statements* — An accountant affirms that he has compiled information provided by the owner in standard formats. Although the least reliable of the three formats, those compiled by an outside, independent CPA firm are more reliable than those compiled internally by the entrepreneur.

Most small business do not audit or review their financial statements. As a result, you may have to conduct your own audit, checking a random sample of invoices and bills and verifying transactions involving customers, and suppliers — preferably going back several years.

Putting Together Your Own Plan

Once you have checked the information presented concerning an established business, you should — if the entrepreneurs have not presented you with a business plan — draw one up yourself. *Tip: Multi-billionaire investor Warren Buffett, the "Wizard of Omaha," who invests in stocks as if he were buying the businesses they represent, always writes his analysis down before committing any capital. He finds this clarifies his thinking on the investment. Better to outline your thoughts as a business plan, particularly in the case of an ownership transfer, before investing — rather than later on as a post mortem.*

Keep detailed notes of meetings, discussions, phone conversations, etc. — everything you do as part of the review process. And, with regard to any unwritten representations, remember the saying attributed to Louis B. Mayer, the great Hollywood producer concerning verbal contracts: "They're not worth the paper they're printed on."

Demand to get as much information as you can concerning the investment in writing. This is a part of practicing what is known as due diligence.

Due Diligence

Experienced venture investors — as well as others involved in capitalizing new or existing businesses — use the term due diligence on a day-to-day basis. Those starting out in venture investing should be aware of what this is.

In the United States Securities Act of 1933, due diligence refers specifically to the requirement that securities dealers provide "full and fair disclosure" of all pertinent data regarding stocks and bonds they sell that are subject to federal regulation. State laws make similar requirements.

In terms of investing generally — and venture investing in particular — due diligence has a broader meaning. It refers to the thoroughness with which investors, lenders and/or business purchasers must make certain that representations concerning the enterprise are accurate, comprehensive and timely.

If someone approaches you concerning a venture investment, find out whether the entrepreneurs have registered the offering of shares, certificates of participation, partnership interests, etc., with federal or state authorities. If so, the issuer or underwriter of the securities will have completed a due diligence review of all pertinent material.

Caveat Investor: If no formal due diligence review has been performed, you should take it upon yourself to do so. The process should involve a comprehensive review of all legal, financial and commercial aspects of the venture. Your investigation is unlikely to carry the legal weight of a formal document lawyers draw up attesting to due diligence, but it will protect you in case of any dispute concerning your investment.

A competent due diligence review will help you answer the following questions:

- Should I participate or buy into the venture?

- How much should I invest, and what are the risks?

- How am I going to pay for it?

- How will the investment perform?

- Will the potential rewards be worth the risk?

- What is the worst case scenario that I may get stuck with?

FINANCIAL CONFIGURATION AND LEGAL STRUCTURE: LEVERAGE, RISKS, AND LIABILITIES

A venture's structure, both in terms of legal form and financial configuration, is of particular importance to venture investors. The legal basis of an enterprise determines the extent to which authorities can hold participants responsible should anything go wrong. Because different types of business organizations are taxed at different rates — some at the rates of the individuals involved and others at the corporate tax rate — a venture's legal form also has a strong impact on profitability. (For more information on the tax impact of venture investing, refer to wealth-building Step 80, found on page 12.)

A company finances its operations with either debt (loans) or equity (giving up stock ownership for cash). The financial structure of a company is its mix of debt/equity. This impacts profitability and is a major determinant of a venture's risk. Generally, the more debt an enterprise carries, the greater its interest expense and the more difficult it is to reach break-even. At the same time, a company with extensive debt (said to be highly leveraged) can dramatically increase investor returns — when (and if) it operates profitably. Let's examine legal and financial structures beginning with leverage and an understanding of leverage.

Leverage   Leverage is defined as the impact that changes in a company's revenues will have on its profits. There are two types of leverage: financial and operational. The extent to which debt obligations can magnify return to a venture's owners is known as financial leverage. A venture with a high degree of debt may generate a much higher return per dollar of invested capital. Operational leverage is the extent to which fixed costs magnify operating profits when revenues increase. This is how leverage works:

Equity Inc. is the same size as Leverage Inc., but Leverage Inc. has a much greater debt obligation. A comparison of the balance sheets is shown in the table below.

Summary Balance Sheets of Equity Inc. and Leverage Inc.

	Equity Inc.	Leverage Inc.
ASSETS:	$100	$100
LIABILITIES:		
DEBT (INTEREST 10%)	$ 10	$ 90
EQUITY	$ 90	$ 10
TOTAL	$100	$100

An investor puts $90 into Equity Inc. (Equity). It is successful and generates operating profits of $10 dollars. It pays $1.00 in interest, is taxed at a 30 percent rate and therefore makes an after-tax profit of $6.30, earning the venture investor a 7 percent return ($6.30/$90). If however, Equity earns an additional $1.00 in operating profit, Equity's net income to rises $7.00, earning the venture investor a 7.8 percent rate of return ($7.00/$90), an 11 percent improvement.

STEP 80

Reduce Tax Liabilities Through Venture Investing

What: Consider seriously the tax benefits of venture investing.

Why: Venture investing can allow you to save money on your taxes.

Risk: High. Taking advantage of tax benefits improves a venture's potential returns and improves the risk/reward trade-off in venture investments. It does not, however, eliminate the risk associated with the investments.

Safety: Not applicable.

Liquidity: Lowest of all investments. You usually forgo liquidity when you make a venture investment.

Why Not: Not applicable — the tax benefits come with the territory.

Buy/Invest From: Not applicable.

Background: Venture investors generally enjoy attractive tax benefits. Venture investments are, by nature, long-term and thus subject to long-term capital gains rates — which, at 28 percent, are lower for most investors than the taxes on dividend and interest income or profits from short-term investments. The maximum tax rate on earned income is currently 39.5 percent, and that rate is also applied to interest, dividends and gains on investments held less than a year.

Suggested modifications to the tax code may even make venture investing more favorable. Certain members of Congress are calling for a flat income tax. The rate most often quoted is 17 percent. There is also support for doing away entirely with capital gains taxes. If these proposals are enacted into law, the tax advantage enjoyed by venture investments relative to dividend and interest income would nearly double.

In addition, if you are an investor whose income varies significantly from one year to the next, you may be able to influence the payment of dividends from your venture investments so that you incur greater income in years when you expect your marginal rate to be lower. But most important is the fact that losses — which nearly every new venture has — can be used to reduce your taxable income. For example, a $100,000 passive investment entitles you to use up to — but no more than — $100,000 in losses to offset passive income (income from sources such as dividends, interest or some partnership investments). If you're in the 39.5 percent tax bracket, your venture investment just got 39.5 percent cheaper than you thought. Those tax losses are as good as cash since they directly reduce the tax you pay Uncle Sam on April 15. (You should always check with your tax advisor first though to verify if you can better yet, qualify for active losses.)

If you want to start today, here's how to calculate the potential effects of a venture investment on your taxes:

First project your income tax liability throughout the period of time you expect to participate. Then calculate the real marginal rate on your income (after all deductions, adjustments, etc.).

If the venture is structured as a Subchapter S Corporation or a limited-liability company, you may be able to deduct your pro-rated share of depreciation expenses and venture losses from your income tax. Remember, losses too are deductible: subject, of course, to the usual active/passive loss tests. Now, adjust the cash flows (as discussed in the main text sections on NPV and IRR analysis) to reflect any favorable tax impacts, and discount accordingly.

Adjust the expected value of your portion of the venture at an estimated "cash out" date to reflect capital gains taxes. Recalculate NPV and IRR to get a more accurate picture of the real, after-tax net present value and rate of return on your investment. Finally, check with a tax attorney, investment advisor or CPA to verify the validity of your analysis, as well as to see whether there is any benefit to considering involvement in specific venture investments, such as research and development partnerships.

Continued from p. 11

At the same time, another venture investor puts $10 in Leverage Inc. (Leverage). With the same revenues and operating expenses, Leverage Inc. pays $9.00 in interest, earns $0.70 after tax and generates the same rate of return. However, when Leverage generates an additional $1.00 in operating profit, net income after tax doubles to $1.40 — and the return on equity increases from 7 percent to 14 percent, doubling the rate of return to the investor. The income statement in the table below details a comparison between the two ventures:

Summary Income Statements of Equity Inc. and Leverage Inc.

	Equity Inc.		CHANGE	Leverage Inc.		CHANGE
REVENUES	$100	$110	+10%	$100	$110	+ 10%
OPERATING EXPENSES	($ 90)	($ 99)		($ 90)	($ 99)	
OPERATING PROFIT	$ 10	$ 11	+10%	$ 10	$ 11	+ 10%
INTEREST CHARGE	($ 1)	($ 1)		($ 9)	($ 9)	
NET INCOME (PRE-TAX)	$ 9	$ 10		$ 1	$ 2	
TAX (30%)	($2.70)	($3.00)		($.30)	($.60)	
NET INCOME AFTER TAX	$6.30	$7.00	+11%	$ .70	$1.40	+100%
RETURN ON EQUITY/INVESTMENT	7.0%	7.8%		7.0%	14.0%	

Leverage is, however, a much riskier enterprise — break even is harder to reach. As operating profits start to slip for Leverage, net income drops at a much faster rate than would be the case for Equity Inc. If Leverage slips from $10 to $9 in operating income, the company could go bankrupt.

Operational Leverage

Operational leverage works basically the same way as financial leverage. Higher fixed costs (such as rent and administration costs) amplify the percentage rate at which increased revenues improve operating profits, as shown in the table below, which compares two similar companies — HiFix Enterprises and LoFix Inc. Prices ($2/unit of sales) and variable costs ($0.90 per unit of output for direct labor and materials) are the same for both companies. Of the two, however, HiFix has much higher fixed costs — $10.00 vs. $5.00 for LoFix. HiFix enjoys greater economies of scale in production, and profits jump when sales go up. HiFix has a more difficult time reaching break even, however and therefore has greater operational leverage.

Summary Income Statements of LowFix and HiFix

	LoFix Incorporated		CHANGE	HiFix Enterprises		CHANGE
UNIT SALES	100	120	+20%	100	120	+20%
REVENUES	$200	$240	+20%	$200	$240	+20%
FIXED COSTS	($ 5)	($ 5)		($ 10)	($ 10)	
VARIABLE COSTS	($ 90)	($108)		($ 90)	($108)	
TOTAL COSTS	($ 95)	($113)		($100)	($118)	
OPERATING PROFITS	$105	$127	+21%	$100	$122	+22%
FIXED/TOTAL COST RATIO	5.3%	4.4%		10.0%	8.5%	
BREAK EVEN POINT:						
IN UNITS	5	5		10	10	
IN DOLLARS	$ 10	$ 10		$ 20	$ 20	

Legal Structure

With respect to the legal basis of an enterprise, the owners of a venture can structure it in various ways:

- *Sole Proprietorship* — Most small businesses and many start-up ventures, at least initially, structure themselves as sole proprietorships. This is the most basic business structure. A single individual is owner of the entire enterprise. The Internal Revenue Service considers the proprietor and his business to be essentially the same. Setting one up entails little more than filing simple documents with state and local authorities.

The principal drawback of a sole proprietorship is that the proprietor is personally liable for all legal claims against the business. With regard to venture investments, financial backers cannot become formal co-owners of a proprietorship without transforming it into a partnership.

Shareholders in S Corporations can take personal tax deductions for depreciation of business assets and losses, which are expected in the initial years of a start-up.

A venture investor's involvement in a proprietorship is limited to making personal or business loans to the owner. In such cases, whenever possible, insist on a secured loan. This involves holding title to an asset until the proprietor pays you back in full. You should, of course, require that the proprietor provide a satisfactory explanation for seeking capital from a private individual instead of a bank or other conventional lending institution.

The rate of interest you receive should reflect the riskiness of the loan and is likely to be significantly higher than what a formal financial institution would charge. Anywhere from prime plus two to prime plus eight percent can be expected. Since there are legal limitations on interest charges, however, it would be prudent to consult an attorney knowledgeable about such matters before entering into any loan arrangement.

- *Partnership* — This is essentially the same as a proprietorship but involves more than one person. A partnership is fairly simple to establish legally.

Involvement of a number of individuals increases the financial and other resources available to a business venture. At the same time, the greater the number of people involved, the more complex an enterprise becomes. Apart from the increasing potential unwieldiness, the main drawback to a partnership is that each member, individually, can be held responsible for all the obligations of the entire partnership. As a backer, you could be liable for the entire amount of any partnership obligation — regardless of the relative size of your interest.

- *Corporation* — This is the most formal type of business organization. In a corporation, the owners hold shares of stock in an entity that has legal independence in its own right. Incorporation limits liability, insulating shareholders from legal risk.

If a corporation goes out of business or runs afoul of the law, investors stand to lose only the value of their investment — unless, of course, it can be shown the shareholders themselves were involved in some sort of criminal activity.

Corporations enjoy greater access to capital than do other business structures. They can issue shares to the public and offer venture investors potential liquidity — i.e., the ability to buy or sell shares at any time on an organized market (such as the New York Stock Exchange, Nasdaq's National Market System or in "over-the-counter" trading).

Incorporation does not necessarily mean a company will eventually go public, however. Shares of a privately held corporation can remain in the hands of a limited group of individuals and/or institutions indefinitely.

Corporations have their drawbacks. They can be far more complex than other types of business organizations. State and federal filing requirements are extensive when raising capital through public stock offerings. And shareholder dividend income is taxed twice — once through the corporate tax and again as income to shareholders.

- *Subchapter S Corporation* — This attractive alternative for structuring ventures is often used in start-ups and small businesses. A Subchapter S Corporation (also known as an S Corporation) offers the liability features of a corporation while allowing shareholders certain financial advantages over a conventional or Chapter C Corporation. Shareholders in S Corporations can take personal tax deductions for depreciation of business assets and losses, which are expected in the initial years of a start-up. They can also treat corporate earnings as personal income, and thus avoid double taxation.

  An S Corporation can, however, change itself into a conventional corporation when it is advantageous for shareholders. Once it does so, however, it is almost impossible to change back.

  There are also restrictions on the number of individuals and the types of institutions that can hold stock in an S Corporation, and limitations as well on S Corporation's holding stock in other corporations.

- *Limited Liability Company* — A limited liability company, or LLC, is essentially a partnership that has some of the attributes of a corporation. Except for issuing stock, a limited liability company can engage in practically all of the activities of a corporation. The ownership configuration is set out in articles of organization filed with state authorities.

  Although the characteristics of LLCs vary from state to state, they shield the owners — together, as well as individually — from liability. Those involved in LLCs are liable for their pro-rated portion of any liability only, not for the aggregate liabilities of the enterprise.

  With regard to taxes, an LLC provides an alternative to an S Corporation. Participants avoid paying a tax on corporate profits, instead paying only personal taxes on income they derive from their investment in the company. LLCs are more cumbersome to set up and manage than S Corporations. At the same time, they are less limited with respect to the number of individuals and institutions that can become shareholders and to their ability to own shares in other companies.

- *Limited Partnership* — Somewhat similar to S Corporations, Limited Partnerships (LPs) combine the structure of a partnership with the liability features of a corporation. Many venture investors become involved in start-up businesses initially as limited (financing) partners in such arrangements, which are widely used to develop real estate and natural resources (oil and gas, timber lands, etc.), as well as in financing films. With regard to government registration and public disclosure requirements, limited partnerships can be easier to set up than many corporations.

  As in the case of a corporation, the liabilities incurred by participants in an LP are limited. In contrast to a simple partnership, however, there are two distinct types of partners in an LP — limited and general. Limited partners usually provide most of the capital, while the general partners manage or oversee the venture's administration and are, as a rule, the only ones liable for the partnership's debt.

  General partners are not likely to share in any profits until the limited partners have recouped at least part of their investment. They do, however, receive management fees — and, in some cases, earn commissions on sales of limited partnership interests.

  A note of caution: Be wary of "tax-shelter deals," which in many cases are structured as limited partnerships. The federal Tax Code is far more circumscribed than it used to be. Also, make sure the general partners have experience in the type of business involved, and that they are not earning excessive commissions on sales of limited partnership interests or paying themselves too generously if it is a start-up venture. As in the case of any venture investment, you should consult an experienced attorney and/or financial advisor in reviewing all aspects of any limited partnership.

Environmental Liabilities

A sometimes hidden risk in venture investing arises in the area of environmental liabilities — which can beset almost any business, even one apparently far removed from an involvement with nature.

The Comprehensive Environmental Response, Compensation and Liability Act (CERCLA) of 1990 — sometimes called the "Superfund Act" — coupled with recent court decisions and state legislation, has changed the whole issue of environmental liability. Drastically!

A building your business owns may have asbestos that gets in the air or paint with lead in it that you may have to remove. Some land you've bought for development may have been used as a dump site, meaning you'll have to clean it up. Or, your land might have old storage tanks that are leaking chemicals into a river, forcing you to excavate the debris and purify the land.

CERCLA mandates that businesses pay the cost of cleaning up environmental contamination they cause. The law — and subsequent rulings — often hold that owners and operators of a business venture, both past and *present,* can be held jointly responsible for the removal of waste, hazardous substances and remediation. This can cost real money and possibly lead to a venture's insolvency.

In every transaction regarding the sale of property or a business, the seller has the obligation of full disclosure of any environmental problems. However, the buyer or investor — who can inherit the problem and the expense that goes with it — also has the responsibility of investigating the possibility of environmental liability. Venture investors usually can avoid any environmental liability arising from the actions of former property owners and business managers by requiring that indemnification from environmental damages be written into purchase contracts.

While CERCLA is the major piece of environmental legislation with which investment venturers should be concerned, other regulations that impose environmental responsibilities or liabilities should be reviewed as well. These include the Clean Air Act (CAA), the Clean Water Act and National Ambient Air Quality Standards.

Financial and Capital Structure

The finances of most enterprises seeking venture investors tend to be straightforward, and include both equity capital (representing ownership interest) and debt capital (representing mandatory obligations).

The simplest capital structure for any venture to have is pure equity. This means the enterprise has no fixed obligations to banks, other financial institutions or individuals (other than commercial credit owed to suppliers).

Although it's less risky, a venture financed with pure equity does not have leverage. Net income and operating revenues increase at the same rate. At the same time, it is easier for an equity-financed enterprise to break even.

Alternatively, a venture may be financed purely with debt — which is rare except in the case of a highly leveraged buyout, such as the Gibson Greeting Cards LBO. In a venture where the

With regard to the debt obligations of small enterprises, an experienced banker can help you determine if a venture has debt in excess of what is considered normal for a particular type of business.

equity investment is minimal, financial institutions or individuals (bond or note holders) put up all or almost all the money to purchase the enterprise. The owners, in many cases shareholders, have to convince creditors, however, that the enterprise can handle the debt. After paying costs and interest charges, the owners receive all profits. Because the venture is leveraged, when income goes up, net income soars. Thus, if the equity holders can improve operating efficiencies and/or sell shares to the public, they stand to benefit handsomely. If their efforts do not work, however, the debt holders can seize the venture's assets as specified in the terms of the lending arrangements.

Most businesses are financed with a combination of debt and equity — and enterprises in various industries follow certain norms with respect to the levels of debt they carry. Generally, an industrial company with a debt-to-total-capital ratio of more than 40 percent — such as an automobile manufacturer or mainframe computer company — is considered risky. Exceptions include firms with a long histories of dependable earnings and stable, predictable cash flows — utilities, for example. Companies whose earnings are not stable run into trouble when they pile on too much debt — particularly if their industries are competitive (as evidenced by the number of recent bankruptcy filings of deregulated airlines in the United States).

With regard to the debt obligations of small enterprises, an experienced banker can help you determine if a venture has debt in excess of what is considered normal for a particular type of business. As for larger, publicly held enterprises, you can get an idea of the debt levels of companies in most industries by looking at Standard & Poor's Corporate Directories or the Value Line Investment Survey, both of which are available in most libraries.

In order to determine whether a start-up or growth-phase venture can withstand the degree of risk a particular debt level gives it, you should check not only industry practice, but also carefully examine the degree of certainty inherent in profit projections. If the earnings performance of a venture seems likely to be erratic and unpredictable — or the forecasts too optimistic — be careful. Overstated profit potential, coupled with high degrees of operating and financial leverage, can lead to disaster.

Complex Financial Structures

As enterprises grow, their finances evolve and can become complex — in certain cases extremely so. With respect to equity, a corporation can issue various types of common stock. Some of the shareholders of these stocks will vote and some will have no voting rights.

Along with stock, companies can issue preferred stock, a form of equity in which shareholders generally cannot vote, but whose holders receive dividends. Should an enterprise fail to pay preferred dividends, however, the obligation becomes cumulative. An enterprise has to pay off all previous preferred dividend obligations before it can make distributions to its common stock holders. *Note: For more information on preferred shares, refer to the lesson titled "Shifting Risk/Reward: Preferred Shares," found earlier in the course.*

Be aware, too, that certain types of stocks may restrict voting rights and impose other constraints that could impact your right to sell your shares, thus limiting your liquidity (as explained in wealth-building Step 81, found on page 18).

As for debt, an enterprise can incur several types of secured and unsecured financial obligations. These include loans from banks and other financial institutions, notes, bonds and/or debentures issued to individual or institutional investors via private placements (limited offerings) or through public issues traded on an exchange.

100 Steps to Wealth

Avoid the Constraints of Restrictive Stock Ownership

What: Make sure your stake in an investment venture won't be diluted and that others in the company can't impose restrictions on what you can do with your stock.

Why: Restrictions on stock that affect transferability, liquidity or diminution of your interest alter the risk profile of a venture considerably, and have the potential of turning what appears on the surface to be a good venture investment into a poor one.

Risk: Low. Accepting restricted stock poses a far greater risk in that you may not be able to get your money out as you expected — i.e., you may not be able to transfer shares freely and could have to sell them to other shareholders on their terms. If your stock is restricted, the company can also reduce the percentage of your holdings by issuing new non-restricted shares.

Safety: High. Confirming the lack of restrictions on any stock received increases the safety of a venture investment.

Liquidity: Moderate. Confirming the lack of restrictions on stock can enhance liquidity.

Why Not: No reason. You should always investigate all aspects of your shareholder rights when considering a venture investment.

Buy/Invest From: Not applicable.

Background: Corporate charters and bylaws can impose restrictions that benefit some shareholders at the expense of others — particularly harming those who want to protect the percentage of their stake, transfer shares or get out of a deal earlier than initially planned. Such restrictions are perfectly legal, but they can diminish or negate the value of even the best performing venture investment.

If you want to get started today, here are some steps you should take to avoid being unexpectedly trapped in a venture investment by stock restrictions:

1. Review carefully the corporate charter to ensure you will have unencumbered stock-ownership rights.

2. In a privately held enterprise, insist on a share-pricing mechanism that suits your interests — and get the entrepreneurs to agree to it in writing.

3. Make sure privately held stock is re-valued regularly — e.g., annually at a shareholder meeting, or perhaps even quarterly.

4. Get in writing any commitments pertaining to share transferability to third parties or sales to other investors. You'll want to be able to give your shares to immediate family members, trusts and estates. You won't want others to be able to give their shares away to someone outside the deal that could cause problems.

5. Insist on rights issues that protect you against dilution and could enhance the return on your investment. If you hold less than 51 percent of the deal you will have to be subject to some minority shareholder constraints such as a devaluation of share price should the majority of shares vote for such. You don't have to settle for other constraints though, such as not being able to hold consecutive seats on the board.

6. Review the matter with a competent attorney. ▲

Continued from p. 17

Doing the Deal: Offering Investors Convertible Debt — The Best for All

When Michael Troy, a Petaluma, California-based entrepreneur, founded KnowledgePoint Inc., an interactive computer software company, in 1987, he knew securing finance would not be easy. But Troy had plenty of experience, having already successfully launched one company, Native Sun Energy Systems Inc., a solar-engineering firm. Troy invested $24,000 of his own savings, borrowed $20,000 on his credit cards and took out a $40,000 home equity loan — but he still needed an additional $80,000 to start KnowledgePoint. Reviewing the company's needs from an investor's perspective, he designed a five-year convertible debenture (debt instrument) that guaranteed investors an attractive rate of return — 5 percentage points above prime, capped at 15 percent.

The debenture holders had the right to convert to common stock a year after issuance, but not later than six months before final payment was due. The company could also trigger an early conversion opportunity by paying off 10 percent or more of the principal amount of its obligation to the debenture holders. The deal worked, and Troy raised $76,000 through the issue — enough to start KnowledgePoint. After two years, the company called the debenture; holders had to convert to stock or lose their right to do so for the remainder of the term. Two thirds chose to convert. And, when cash was tight, KnowledgePoint issued additional debentures in lieu of interest.

While the debenture deal was instrumental in getting KnowledgePoint off to a good start, it did have one drawback. Because the venture's balance sheet looked debt heavy, it complicated bank financing. This did not slow Troy's venture down, however. In 1993 KnowledgePoint made 364 on INC. Magazine's list of the 500 fastest growing privately owned corporations in America.

Convertible Securities

In addition to conventional equity and debt, a corporation can issue convertible securities. These are bonds, notes or preferred shares that can be converted into shares of common stock based on a specified formula. Convertible instruments have something to offer both issuers and investors. They allow entrepreneurs to lower their costs of capital. At the same time, they offer venture investors the security available to bond or preferred stockholders, while giving them the right to participate as a full common shareholder should they chose to do so. An example of convertible financing is featured in the box above, and additional information on convertibles can be found in the earlier lesson titled The Best of Everything Investment.

A Final Word on Structure and Liabilities

With regard to the structure of ventures generally, you may decide that a business concept is sound, its management capable and its operational approach sensible, but decline to participate based on the risks inherent in the structure of the venture. Don't hesitate to make your feelings known to the principals, or suggest modifying the structure. Depending on the nature of the venture, the extent of your involvement and the point at which you choose to invest, your co-venturers may be willing and able to accommodate you — especially early on in the venture's formation. This cannot hurt — and is well worth trying — but be cautious (especially in partnerships) of taking on excess risks.

Regardless of the scope of your participation, however, always insist on formal agreements — clear and comprehensive documents, prepared or reviewed by a competent attorney — before participating in any venture investment as a debt or equity holder, and especially before entering into a partnership. Speaking with an insurance broker concerning general business liability insurance could also be well worth your while.

DOING THE DEAL: GETTING IN, GETTING OUT, INCREASING YOUR PARTICIPATION

After considering structure and liability, the next factors you should consider are:

- What is your investment going to be used for?
- What precisely are you getting for your money?
- Exiting — how are you going to get out?
- Increasing your participation.

Use of Proceeds

As you enter a venture, you should have a precise idea what the entrepreneurs will use your funds for. They can use them for "general purposes," which gives them wide latitude, or put them to some specific use (e.g., to retire debt, purchase new equipment, research and develop new products, fund expansion, etc.). If the venture will use your investment to acquire a tangible asset, you should require that it serve as collateral so you can take possession in the case of default.

Tip: There is a fraudulent type of scheme, known as a Ponzi operation, in which promoters promise investors high rates of return (such as a doubling of their money in six months — guaranteed). Like a chain letter, a Ponzi operation works only as long as the number of participants grows rapidly. Initially, the principals pay the backers (and themselves) out of funds collected from subsequent investors. The word spreads concerning the great investment opportunity. Interest eventually drops off and the operators can no longer pay the returns investors expect. The operation then collapses, and the perpetrators abscond, leaving many investors broke. Be sure the business in which you are investing is a valid one — not a Ponzi scheme.

Evaluating Your Participation

Determine carefully the potential value of your participation in any venture. Look at what you are paying for in terms of what earlier investors and principals paid for when they invested. Find out if you are getting a better deal. You can come up with a "quick-and-dirty" estimate by dividing projected cash flows and, separately, expected profits by the number of shares (or percentage of participation offered) for your involvement.

Compare these figures with similar calculations based on representations made to previous investors (if any). If you are getting a much better deal, perhaps things did not turn out as well as planned for the earlier entrants and the entrepreneurs have to offer more this time. If you are not getting as good a deal as previous backers, perhaps the venture's prospects have improved. In any case, find out the reason for any discrepancies between the value of former and current offerings. And, if you find that the venture warrants closer scrutiny, closely examine any discounted cash flow analyses — or derive one of your own (as explained later in this lesson).

How to Get Out

Getting into many ventures is easy; getting out can be difficult. In many cases, a venture's entrepreneurs, its operating owners or its managers plan to buy out the backers at a specific juncture in the venture's growth. Some common exit points include:

■ When the enterprise is sold to another entity.

■ When it reaches a point where conventional financial institutions can provide the necessary capital and are willing to refinance the enterprise.

■ When the venture issues shares to the public.

Specifics governing buying out investors vary widely from one enterprise to the next. However, a venture investor does not have to wait for one of these events in order to "cash out." Before you get in, give thought to getting out. You can try to negotiate a predetermined buyout mechanism. Often entrepreneurs will commit to buying you out at a multiple of revenues, profits, cash flow or asset values — after a certain period of time, or at certain intervals (every year, say) or when the venture meets certain revenue or profit targets.

Be careful, however, of getting out too early — and completely. Warren Buffett's strategy of holding on to a stock "forever" has made him the richest man in the United States. Both in start-ups and growth-phase venture investments, the value of a company's shares often soars in the years after a public offering. Patient investors can reap fortunes. And, you can have it both ways — negotiate to get a portion of your investment out early, while retaining at least a small residual benefit.

Increasing Your Participation and Role

You can also increase your participation in profits or your role in making decisions in other ways, such as:

■ *Options and warrants* — Sometimes when entrepreneurs capitalize a corporation, they will "sweeten the deal" by combining options or warrants with the stock. Investors buy units consisting of common shares, with options or warrants "attached." Options and warrants give you the right to buy shares in the future, priced at a favorable discount to market, thus giving you the right to expand your involvement on favorable terms.

■ *Board representation* — Major shareholders often expect to sit on or appoint members to corporate boards. If your stake in any corporate enterprise is sizable, you should have this right — which will enable you to set venture policy. Be aware, however, that the responsibility can be time consuming and board members have greater legal responsibility vis a vis companies' activities than do investors generally. You should review the enterprise's bylaws and check with an attorney before considering becoming a board member. Once again, it pays to protect yourself.

EVALUATING A VENTURE'S STRATEGY

According to Dr. Wendell E. Dunn III of the University of Pennsylvania's Wharton School and academic director of the university's Sol C. Snide Entrepreneurial Center, the most common mistake entrepreneurs make is failing to plan. And, planning is a continuing process that doesn't end with the model building that goes into generation of a formal document. Carefully analyzing or assembling a business plan will give you the opportunity to learn the essence of the enterprise, invest successfully and assist the entrepreneurs in achieving their goals.

The Business Plan: Strategic Statement

A business plan should be a flexible guide to venture action as well as a "sales" document. It should start with a summary one or two pages long covering three primary matters:

■ The market (i.e., clients and customers).

■ The purpose and structure of the enterprise.

■ The capabilities the enterprise will use to exploit opportunities in the market.

The summary should preface all the material included in the body of the plan, which should cover the following subjects:

■ Venture structure (organization/ownership, legal implications and financial configuration).

■ Management.

■ Market(s), customers, products and competition.

■ Industry dynamics, including production processes and cost issues.

■ Profit margins.

■ Operational leverage and break-even projections.

■ Patents and franchises.

■ Suppliers and vendors.

■ Promotion and advertising.

■ Research and development.

■ Salaries and overhead.

- Future growth prospects.

- Conversion of start-ups and growth-phase ventures to mature enterprises.

- Flexibility (scenario analyses).

- Personnel.

- Comparables.

- Accounting, environmental and legal issues.

- Financial control.

- Financial performance projections.

Note: For more details on the exact content of a good business plan, refer back to the lesson titled Entrepreneurism: For Those Who Already Are and for the Wanna Be's, which describes how to prepare your own comprehensive plan.

Management — Taking a Closer Look

As noted earlier, you should always consider managers of a venture before analyzing any other aspect of the proposed enterprise. However, because proper management is such an important issue, you should review the matter again as you go over any business plan. Even if the central idea of an enterprise is sound and things seem likely to work well, friction among managers can doom any venture.

Individual potential is one thing; teamwork, which is essential to effective management, is another. A gathering of business "super stars" will not work out if they cannot function well together. You should consider this at the outset.

Beware of managers who have become too "corporatized." Often employees whose experience has been limited to large, successful corporations — no matter how well qualified — do not do well in small ventures or start-ups. In some cases they have grown too accustomed to expense-account living and plush offices to be able to function well in the "bare-bones" environments many ventures require.

Some types of administrative experiences are also of dubious value to smaller ventures — e.g., supervising two or three people can be more difficult than overseeing hundreds. And, if the venture's managers have major stock holdings from their former employers, or are earning too much in salary (even in a start-up), they may not be "hungry" enough to put shoulder to the wheel and make a smaller, newer outfit work.

"Corporatized" managers with marketing and sales backgrounds can be particularly detrimental to start-up or growth-phase ventures. Experience selling well-known brand-name goods or services that, to a large extent, "sell themselves" may work against someone who is unaccustomed to the rejection that can come with trying to introduce something new

Management Guru Peter Drucker's Theory of the Business

According to management guru Peter Drucker, every business operation rests on sets of assumptions that shape its behavior, dictate its decisions and define what it considers meaningful results. This is an enterprise's theory of the business. A theory of the business has three types of assumptions:

- Those concerning environment in which it exists: society and its structure, the market, the customer, technology, etc.

- Those that concern the specific mission of the enterprise.

- Those concerning the core competencies needed to accomplish the mission.

In order for an enterprises' theory to be valid, it must meet four criteria:

1. Its assumptions about environment, mission, and core competencies must fit reality.

2. Its assumptions in all three areas must be internally consistent and complementary.

3. The theory must be known and understood throughout the organization.

4. It must be tested constantly.

A theory that is valid, clear, consistent and focused is extraordinarily powerful and can lead any venture to success. An invalid or weak theory will do just the opposite. Does your venture have a clearly stated business theory?

Personal Qualities That Lead to Business Failure

According to Tanya Korkosz, a psychologist and management consultant with Leadership Consulting Group in Belmont, Mass., there are three personality qualities that will significantly hinder anyone directing an entrepreneurial undertaking:

- *Arrogance* — Thinking that the venture's ideas, products or services are so good they will sell themselves.
- *Impulsiveness* — Acting rashly without careful consideration and planning.
- *Pessimism* — The inability to stay motivated continually and take adversity in stride.

Watch for these characteristics. Do the entrepreneurs in your venture display these qualities? If so, you should invest elsewhere.

from an unknown enterprise to a skeptical customer in a competitive market. A successful advertising manager for Sports Illustrated, say, might not fare well working for a specialized business publication start-up that has limited capital resources. By contrast, a simple salesperson who earlier participated in a similar publishing new venture might be a far better person to have on board.

Look again for strong personal characteristics — such as independence and, for lack of a better term, grit — that show the managers will carry the venture. Appropriate experience and technical and managerial expertise are essential — but sometimes sheer drive will keep a struggling young venture afloat.

The Market: Characteristics, Identity and Differentiation

Underestimating the difficulty of penetrating, finding or holding on to markets is a common business mistake — across the board. In the decade from the mid-1970s to the mid-1980s, U.S. automobile makers misjudged the mood of the nation and watched their market shares shrink as consumers bought Japanese imports by the boatload. More recently, high-tech computer outfits such as Lotus Systems spent millions developing hand-held, pen-operated computers no one bought. Complacency — a "build-it-(or produce-it) and-they-will-come" attitude — is a quick way to business failure.

Analyzing the market for any venture with specificity and precision is one of the most difficult — and important — things entrepreneurs and those who back them must do. An effective marketing strategy must address:

- Size, expanse and characteristics of the market's customer base — i.e., is it local, national or international; general vs. specialized; mass vs. niche; consumer, industrial or governmental; uniform vs. fragmented, etc.?

- Numbers of competitors and their strengths and weaknesses (in terms of products and services offered, and of operations and finances of the entities involved).

- Differentiation of product(s) or service(s) the venture will offer in terms of price, quality, innovation, packaging, promotion, customer service, etc.

- Costs — what are the unit economics of production, distribution, marketing, etc.?

- Pricing and demand characteristics of the goods/services to be offered: Are they luxuries or necessities? And is demand sensitive to price? Will prices cover them? And who sets prices?

- Dynamics of the market: Is it new and expanding; mature; shrinking; stable or volatile? Does industry performance track cycles of the economy? What determines demand?

Although it seems obvious, many entrepreneurs' plans overlook the basic fact that, in order to grow faster than the overall market, a venture either has to take business away from competitors or acquire them outright. A plan has to assess each alternative.

If market growth is slow, competitive pricing and control of production costs are likely to determine success. If the market is expanding, however, the venture that stays on top of the changing customer preferences and gets to market the fastest — not necessarily with the state-of-the-art products — has an advantage. This is particularly true with high-tech companies in such areas as computers and software.

Does the business plan include provisions for further product development and market research sufficient to sustain an enterprise beyond start-up?

Tip: Always be wary of ventures that are trying to "buy market share." An enterprise should either produce (and promote and market) more economically than its competitors, or offer something unique. A new entrant into any market — a one-trick pony — may do all right for a while if promoted and priced properly. But ask yourself: Can the venture go the distance? Unless there is some unique and projectable value to the new product or service, others may be able to outspend or sustain greater losses longer, thus forcing the venture out of business — meaning you lose.

Industry Analysis: Product Cycles and Cost Structure

Entrepreneurs must demonstrate a firm grasp of operating and financing fundamentals that characterize their industry and the precise qualities that make for success or failure. (This can be presented as part of the market analysis section of a business plan.) Their analysis should include a precise number of competitors, and assessments of their general characteristics, covering areas such as start-up costs, the degrees of capital and labor intensity. It should also cover the product cycle — how long it takes to develop, manufacture and market products; the time frame governing obsolescence; and whether price, customer service, quality, convenience, promotion, etc., determines success in the industry.

Profit Margins: A Key to Successful Operations

What ensures favorable rates of return for a business? In production ventures, it's high margins per unit; in service ventures, high margins per employee. The higher — and more secure — the profitability, the more room a venture has to maneuver. Even if prices or sales volumes are disappointing, a venture with high margins can perform well. If margins are slim to begin with, the enterprise is vulnerable — and any error in planning or operations may well be fatal. It is extremely important to assess how carefully the entrepreneurs determine all costs and all revenues in projecting profitability.

Operational Leverage and Break-Even Points

A business plan should make it easy to determine the sensitivity of a firm's profits to changes in sales volumes. It should delineate clearly all fixed costs (rent, insurance, salaries), as well as those that are variable (materials, energy and direct labor). High fixed costs can give a firm leverage and amplify returns. However, they also make the firm vulnerable should revenues and operating profits decline.

Patents and Franchises

If the venture's success depends on exploiting a patent or some other sort of franchise (a well defined area of business operation representing some type of "lock" on the market), you must determine how secure it is. Any type of a monopoly gives businesses protection from competition and enhances profitability prospects.

At the same time, however, excessive profits attract competitors, who may be able to offer products or services the market will consider as a substitute. With respect to a formal franchise, you can often participate as an investing partner. You should be careful, however, to avoid some of the recent pitfalls — such as market saturation — that different "fast food" franchisors have experienced in the past few years.

Promotion and Advertising

Developing a market often depends on successful promotion and advertising. This can, however, be costly and drag down profits — and the venture is vulnerable if the competition has the wherewithal to outspend it. By the same token, building up a clientele or customer base by word of mouth — often the most effective marketing approach — may take time. Be certain that the entrepreneurs have thought this through and developed a plan for getting their product or service to consumers.

Research and Development (R&D)
Does the business plan include provisions for further product development and market research sufficient to sustain an enterprise beyond start-up? If a venture plans to grow, the owners must specify how they intend to expand — with new products, variations of established products, expanding into new territories, etc. Make sure that R&D plans are consistent with expansion.

Salaries and Overhead
Are your co-venturers using your funds to finance a lavish lifestyle? Or are the principals taking pay cuts as they help build up a business by paying themselves less than other executives of similar, established companies?

If they are making the same or more than their old jobs, they may not have the psychological investment required to make the venture succeed. You can find out what similar publicly held companies pay their people by requesting 10-K forms (annual filings with the Securities and Exchange Commission) from publicly held competitors.

According to Dun & Bradstreet figures, over the last ten years, the fewer employees a company had to start with, the greater the survival rate of the companies.

Future Growth Prospects
Any venture should spell out its growth path carefully, particularly in a mature industry. Will growth depend on continually introducing new products, modifying existing product lines, changing the cost structure through acquisition of similar operations and achieving economies of scale or developing new technologies? Remember, your money may be tied up for five to seven years — and a firm has to generate quite a consistent growth record over that interval to offer a good return.

Suppliers and Vendors
If the venture depends on a certain source of supply for raw or intermediate materials, make certain that source is dependable, competitive and capable of delivering the required quantities. If suppliers can't keep up with the venture's expansion, it will constrain growth.

Conversion to a Mature Enterprise
Strategic plans for start-up and growth-phase ventures should address a leveling off of growth in the market or the enterprise's reaching an optimal state. Does the strategy specify the optimal size of the company in terms of employees, facilities, marketing techniques and capabilities, etc.? Will it then grow through acquisition? Will there be enhanced returns due to economies of scale in production and research and development and marketing? And, once established, will the company agree to buy venture investors out by going public, seeking other sources of financing or offering itself for sale?

Flexibility: Utilizing Scenario Analysis
In order for a strategy to be comprehensive, it must address a variety of contingencies. The entrepreneurs must assess the impact of different developments on operations, cash flow and profits, as well as operational finance and capital investment. What happens if a venture's sales are disappointing? What happens if prices are lower than expected? If competition is stiffer than planned? Or if interest rates go up? What happens if it takes longer than planned to achieve objectives? Where will the entrepreneurs cut spending? Will dividends be affected? Plans should be laid out for dealing with each of these scenarios.

By the same token, entrepreneurs often fail to plan for success. What if business is better then expected? How will production keep up? Operations that grow unexpectedly fast can quickly outrun their cash resources? Failure to plan adequately may well lead to cash squeezes.

Is management ready to exploit opportunities rapidly? Or recover from disappointments? Scenario analysis can provide venture investors with information concerning how safe the venture is, as well as how comprehensive the entrepreneurs can plan. If small changes in sales volumes and revenues can have a major impact on profitability, the venture is highly leveraged — and risky — but could also generate superior returns.

Personnel

Small is beautiful! According to Dun & Bradstreet figures, over a recent 10-year period, the fewer employees a company had to start with, the greater the survival rate of the companies.

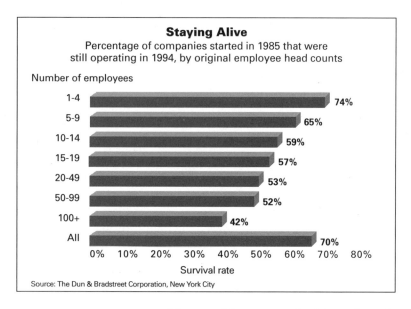

Staying Alive
Percentage of companies started in 1985 that were still operating in 1994, by original employee head counts

Source: The Dun & Bradstreet Corporation, New York City

An effective strategy should spell out personnel policies and ensure that they are consistent with the overall strategy. Will per-unit labor costs go up — or will there be declining costs as output increases? Can personnel be added quickly as the business grows, or will there be production constraints? Again, scenario analysis can answer these questions.

Comparables

There is a wealth of business information at your disposal in any library that you can check to verify the financial and operational characteristics of a business and use for checking assumptions and projects in business plans. You can also find information to guide you with respect to the fair market prices of established, start-up or growth-phase ventures. All are priced according to industry formula — a multiple of profits, cash flow or revenues (actual or expected), etc. By checking comparable values and past sales prices, you can find out if the business or venture you are buying into is being offered at a reasonable price based on established industry norms. A check with any of the organizations cited on page six or other venture-related trade associations can also provide valuable comparative data.

Accounting, Legal and Environmental Issues

Although smaller ventures are unlikely to have extensive off-balance sheet liabilities, they may. In reviewing any transfer of ownership, you should include lease obligations when assessing debt and risk levels. The same applies to pensions; they may be under funded or even unfunded — meaning pension assets are insufficient to meet liabilities and must be paid out of the enterprise's profits. Accounting conventions often allow enterprises to "bury" such commitments in the notes to their financial statements and thus understate the true liabilities of the firm. Read the small print! Be sure to take such factors into consideration when assessing the riskiness of a venture. Also check to make sure the enterprise is not involved in any legal disputes that could have an adverse impact, nor liable for any environmental problems.

Control Issues

Although smaller ventures don't generally have to set up complex systems of management and financial controls, there are exceptions. Enterprises that grant patents and licenses, or that sell through distributors and agents dispersed nationally or worldwide, may have to establish extensive financial control systems. Make sure the entrepreneurs have planned for this.

Seller Financing — Getting Rich on Other People's Money

As a venture investor, you may be able to leverage your participation in an ownership transfer if the seller finances a portion of the transaction. There are compelling reasons for him to do so. According to the small business information service BIZCOMPS, business sellers who require cash payment receive only 70 percent of the asking price vs. 86 percent for those who offer financing. In addition to increasing the likelihood that the deal will go through at a favorable price, sellers can usually obtain higher interest on the notes they receive from buyers than they can elsewhere, thus increasing their returns and providing, in certain cases, tax advantages by deferring income. They may even be able to receive cash themselves, offering the buyers' note as collateral. Provision of credit may demonstrate to a buyer the seller's faith that the business can support itself.

Seller-financing arrangements involve a promissory note signed by the purchasers agreeing to pay for the business (or that portion of it greater than the down payment) in the future — usually in installments. These come in a variety of types, as follows:

- Adjustable-rate notes, whose interest rate varies, keying off of some widely reported, market-set rate such as the prime rate, a cost-of-funds index (COFI) for a Federal Home Loan Bank District, or T-bills.
- Graduated-payment notes, which offer lower payments to a buyer at the beginning of the repayment term and increase gradually — presumably as the business becomes more profitable.
- Periodic-reduction payment notes, which are for

businesses that are seasonal in nature, such as toy stores, liquor stores or resorts. Here major payments can correspond to those times when business is good.

- Balloon-payment notes, in which all payments made for the duration of the instrument, except for the last, represent interest, and the entire principal is due at the end of the note's term.
- Shared-appreciation notes, which — in a rising market — give the seller a residual interest in appreciation of the business.

In all such arrangements, the seller is likely to insist that the purchasers demonstrate credit worthiness and have verifiable experience in the type of operation involved. The seller may, however, agree to stay on in the business for a certain period of time or act as a consultant to facilitate transition to the new ownership and management. Before participating into any seller-financing arrangement, you should discuss the specific details of the various options with knowledgeable bankers, accountants and attorneys.

For further information on seller financing, contact:

- *The International Business Brokerage Association,* P.O. Box 704 Concord, MA 01742, Tel. (508) 369-2490.
- *The Institute of Certified Business Councilors,* P.O. Box 70326, Eugene, OR 97401, Tel. (503) 345-8064.
- *BIZCOMPS,* P.O. Box 711777, San Diego, CA 92171, Tel. (619) 457-0366.

FINANCIAL EVALUATION OF A VENTURE

A sound financial plan is the cornerstone of any successful business strategy. Representations to potential investors should be sufficiently detailed to serve as an operating blueprint for a venture. A representative financial plan should include:

- Estimates of the overall financial potential of the venture.
- Capital (investment) and operating (expense) budgets.
- Profit forecasts, cash-flow projections and balance sheets for several years.

Financial Liability Review

You should personally check all credit information supplied. Review any mortgages, loans and other liabilities. Often lenders will write covenants into agreements restricting the business's operations under various financial conditions. These can have a decided impact on the enterprise's activity, particularly if the firm's financial position deteriorates. And various credit-rating services — TRW, Dun & Bradstreet, etc. — will provide credit histories of the business and individuals involved. You do not want to back dishonest and unreliable people! Also review any disclaimers or warranties presented. If the principals will not stand by what they provide you and put everything in writing, consider it a warning.

Net Present Value, Discounted Cash Flows and Internal Rates of Return

Many financial plans include precise estimates of an enterprise's ability to generate cash, known as net present value (NPV), and internal rate of return (IRR) calculations.

Both NPV and IRR take into consideration the time value of money. A dollar today — a relatively sure thing — is worth more than a dollar tomorrow and after; the future is, after all, uncertain. Interest rates indicate the return those who have capital expect, given the uncertainties they accept when making loans. Thus the future value of a debt (principal plus interest) is higher than the face value of the loan. More precisely, the future value of the transaction equals the present (face amount) augmented by the interest rate — face value multiplied by 1 plus the applicable interest rate. Mathematically, this is expressed as:

$$FV = PV \times [1 + R(N)]$$

where "FV" is the future value, "PV" is the nominal amount of the loan (i.e., the principal), "r" is the interest rate and "n" is the number of time intervals — usually expressed in years.)

According to this formula, the value today of estimated future payments can be calculated by "discounting" — multiplying the payment by the inverse of an applicable interest rate — known as a discount rate. Mathematically, this is accomplished with this formula:

$$PV = \frac{FV}{[1 + R(N)]}$$

where "r" is the interest rate and "n" is the number of time intervals in the future. The lower the discount rate, the greater the uncertainty surrounding the likelihood (and value) of the payment.

When deciding how to allocate capital, venture capitalists, bankers, financial analysts and corporate planners frequently calculate the NPV of different investment alternatives. Following is the way in which you determine an investment's NPV:

1. For each year you plan to participate in the venture, derive your pro-rated portion of cash flow (after-tax profit plus non-cash charges such as depreciation). Discount each cash flow using the discount rate — the inverse of an interest rate that factors in the risk implicit in a venture. (If you plan to be involved indefinitely, estimate a pro-rated salvage or residual value of your participation at the end of 15 years.)

2. Add together the discounted cash flows from each year of the estimated life of your involvement.

3. Subtract the initial, as well as any subsequent investment (subsequent investments should be discounted too, using the factor for the year the venture expects to make them).

Mathematically this is expressed as:

$$NPV = \frac{CF1}{[1+R(1)]} + \ldots \frac{CFN}{[1+R(N)]} + \frac{SV}{[1+R(N)]}$$

where

CF = CASH FLOW IN PERIOD 1 THROUGH N

SV = SALVAGE VALUE OF ASSETS OR RESIDUAL VALUE OF PROJECT/VENTURE (ASSUMED FOR ANALYSIS TO BE 15 YEARS).

NPV gives you a standard for measuring various investment alternatives. When choosing among various investments, the one with the highest NPV gives you the most bang for your buck.

Note: Any finance textbook should have a detailed explanation of discounting, as well as a table of discount factors. A discount rate should take into consideration the riskiness of any venture. For most venture investors (assuming that the project is located in the U.S.) a good rule of thumb would be to use 20 percent — roughly double the long-term estimate for return on stocks, and appreciably higher than equity returns over the last several years (S&P 500 total annualized returns for the past 10 years has been approximately 12.6 percent). If the venture has high operating and financial leverage, 25 or even 30 percent might give a more accurate assessment. In finance theory, short-term U.S. Treasury bills are considered risk free, and the rate of interest they pay is the risk-free rate. Corporations and financial institutions use the discount factor implicit in the risk-free rate as a starting point and use complex processes to derive discount rates for calculating NPV in various investments. They take into consideration market rates over the term of the investment, expected corporate returns on assets and equity, as well as risk factors inherent in different markets, industries, and countries.

Another way to analyze venture investments involves calculating internal rates of return, or IRR (sometimes also referred to as rate of return, or ROR). This can be done by using the same basic framework for calculating NPV:

$$NPV = \frac{CF1}{[1+R(1)]} + \ldots \frac{CFN}{[1+R(N)]} + \frac{SV}{[1+R(N)]}$$

To calculate IRR, set the NPV equal to zero and solve for "r." This involves complex mathematical calculations, but most business calculators and spread sheet PC programs have an IRR function. The higher the internal rate of return, the better an asset will — in theory — perform. Remember, though, NPV indicates the present value of discounted returns, while IRR indicates the rate at which capital will appreciate.

Working Capital Requirements

A full financial analysis of any venture or project should augment discounted cash-flow and internal rate of return computations with calculations of how various favorable and unfavorable developments, or scenarios, can impact the investment. Such an approach will give an indication of the impact of disappointing sales volumes or increased production or finance costs on the cash-generating value of your investment. If such calculations are not included in a business plan, you should derive them yourself — preferably with professional assistance.

NPV and IRR calculations can give any investor an idea of the potential of a venture — in the long run. But, as the great British economist John Maynard Keynes observed, "In the long run, we are all dead." A venture can die prematurely if it does not have enough funds on hand to meet routine expenses, suppliers' charges, payrolls, taxes, etc.

A rapidly growing venture can quickly outrun its cash resources, particularly if customers take longer to pay than anticipated. Disappointing performance can, of course, also lead to cash deficits — as can seasonal merchandise requirements. Many retail operations do most of their business over the Christmas season. Many restaurants and hotels are seasonal as well.

The entrepreneurs should ensure adequacy of working capital (current assets minus current liabilities) in their plans. If cash shortfalls appear likely, you should check to make sure that the entrepreneurs have lined up credit arrangements with a bank, or have a factor ready to finance receivables.

Estimating General Capital Adequacy

General capital adequacy is a more comprehensive measure of a venture's financial resources. Any enterprise must be able to fund long-term growth in addition to its day-to-day operations. If the financial portion of a business plan does not address this, it could spell trouble. Ascertain whether it will be necessary to secure term loans and estimate the "bankability" of the company in the future, based on debt-to-equity ratios. Check Standard & Poor's Corporate Directories for industry debt/equity ratios, but keep in mind that most publicly traded companies are far larger and probably have greater financial resources. High debt levels for an enterprise that needs capital to fund future growth can make profitability difficult to achieve.

J. Paul Getty — Venture Investor

In addition to being an entrepreneur industrialist, J. Paul Getty was a venture investor. Although he built a fortune finding oil in the ground, Getty was also good at prospecting for it on Wall Street — and was just as skilled in his non-oil venture investments. In 1938, he bought the Hotel Pierre on Manhattan's Fifth Avenue for $2.35 million. Writing about it in 1965, long before inflation in the U.S. picked up steam, he calculated it would then have cost ten times that to replicate the building. His reasons for the purchase were straightforward: "The country was rapidly emerging from the Depression; business conditions were improving steadily. Business and personal travel were bound to increase greatly. There had been very little hotel construction in New York for several years, and none was planned for the immediate future. The Pierre was a bargain — and a hotel with great potential."

In buying the Pierre, Getty employed the same type of analysis he had developed for stock purchases, asking these questions:

1. What is the enterprise's history? Is it a solid and reputable firm — and does it have able, efficient and seasoned management?

2. Is the enterprise producing or dealing in goods or services for which there will be a continuing demand in the future?

3. Is the enterprise in a field that is not dangerously overcrowded, and is it in a good competitive position?

4. Are its policies and operations farsighted and aggressive without calling for dangerous over-expansion?

5. Will the balance sheet stand up under the close scrutiny of a critical and impartial auditor?

6. Does it have a satisfactory earnings record? Will it?

7. Has it paid reasonable returns regularly to investors? Or, is it capable of doing so? If not, why?

8. Is the enterprise well within safe limits insofar as both long- and short-term borrowing are concerned?

9. Has its value varied considerably without explanations?

10. Does the value of its net realizable assets exceed the sales price?

Other Considerations

Apart from effective management, promising products, good profit margins, capital adequacy, profitability and cash flow, there are other very important factors that can make a venture a worthwhile investment. These include the value of any property (including an established brand name), undeveloped real estate, business reputation, equipment, leasehold, etc., which could be sold off.

The value of assets stated on the balance sheet of an enterprise is based on historical cost, not on current market value. The salvage value of the enterprise (now and in the future) should reflect any difference between the stated value of assets on the balance sheet and their true market price. The company's assets may have a salvage value greater than the price you are paying for the business, although this is unusual. However, it does happen from time to time and is worth looking into. Given that, even a venture with questionable financial prospects may be a good investment.

Don't Forget the Final Questions

J. Paul Getty developed an approach for analyzing investments — both in the markets and in the business world — based on asking a series of questions about the proposed venture. Those questions are detailed in the box above. Review them, and you too can employ J. Paul Getty's approach for analyzing a business venture — or any other type of investment.

However, don't stop there — as too many people do. There are at least four other final questions you should ask yourself at the very end — just to make sure you know what you are letting yourself in for and whether you will be able to handle it. Those questions are detailed in wealth-building Step 82, Four Final Questions to Ask Yourself About Any Venture Investment Opportunity, found on page 31.

Review them — and, when you can answer them to your satisfaction, consider yourself ready to enter the potentially high-profit world of venture investing. ▲

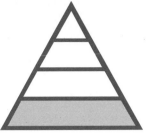

Four Final Questions to Ask Yourself About Any Venture Investment Opportunity

What: As a final step of your venture investment analysis, ask four key questions to ensure that this is the right opportunity for you.

Why: If you aren't totally satisfied that the venture is for you, you increase the likelihood of conflict — or even total failure.

Risk: Low. The real risk lies in rushing into a venture without analyzing both the structure of the investment and your own attitudes toward it.

Safety: High. It costs nothing to give the entire deal one last careful consideration.

Liquidity: Not applicable.

Why Not: No reason. Failure to ask these key final questions increases your risk of disappointment with the investment.

Buy/Invest From: Not applicable.

Background: Venture investment is, without question, risky — and there are no set rules. You have only your smarts to guide you, based on the extensive work you've done analyzing the basics of the specific venture. As such, it only makes sense to conduct one final review of the potential rewards, the possible risks — and your feelings about the entire deal — before handing over your money.

If you're considering a venture investment today, here are the four final questions you should ask yourself before committing your funds:

1. Is the theory of the business solid? Does it have all the attributes specified by Peter Drucker (as detailed in the main text of this lesson)?

2. Do the profit margins — based on all applied, overhead, capital and finance costs — justify the risks involved? When successful venture investor and multimillionaire Ron Creten — who owns several businesses and has financed a score of others — first considers an investment, he looks at the profit margins. If they are ample or hold the potential to easily be ample, he looks further; if not, he's unlikely to spend much time analyzing it.

3. Is the price fair? Creten is also careful to pay only for what a business is now doing, or capable of doing in the immediate future and with little work, such as realizing greater cash from no longer having overpaid relatives of the previous owner on the books. Never pay today for earnings a company could make two years from now because you've done loads of work to make it profitable.

In a start-up or growth-phase investment, this means a careful, conservative assessment of potential profitability. In a transfer of ownership, it means paying for what a business shows on its books — not for what it could do (regardless of what the owner claims). And, Creten warns, don't ever get involved in a business where the owner explains how much you can make "off the books" (to avoid taxes). Not only will you pay too much, but you could be headed for a federal indictment.

4. Does the venture represent my investment interests? Only you can answer this question. Give the matter careful thought; do you want to be committed to a venture — and, if so, to this particular venture? Be honest with yourself, but remember as well — "no guts, no glory." ▲

Advanced strategies for property investing

100 Steps to Wealth

LESSON 26

Advanced strategies for property investing

"Good things come to those who wait. But only what's left from those who hustled." — *Abraham Lincoln*

INTRODUCTION

Many investors' impression of commercial real estate was formed by the boom and bust 1980s, when developers went on a binge and nearly one-half of the existing commercial office space in the country was built. Many of those projects were financed by out of control savings and loans or other super-aggressive lenders, and billions subsequently were lost when deal after deal went sour. When the holders of the $1.3 billion mortgage on Rockefeller Center filed for bankruptcy in the spring of 1995 it may have been the final '80s mega-deal, the Manhattan office complex was bought in 1989 only to collapse under the weight of excessive leverage, closing one of the sorriest chapters in the history of commercial real estate. *Note: The center was sold in 1996 for less than half its original cost.* Properties within reach of the smaller investor were never as depressed as the institutional market in most cases. But the spillover effect hit the little guy too, especially in terms of financing all but drying up by the early 1990s in many markets. It is still being felt today in terms of lenders requiring down payments of 20% to 30% for most commercial real estate transactions, or often times twice what would have been required when the market was booming in the 1980s.

The good news is that, at mid-decade, commercial real estate markets around the country appear to be in the early stages of a seven to 10 year cycle of appreciating prices. While commercial real estate vacancies are still above normal in many central business districts across the country, and will remain so for years to come, smaller retail and industrial properties and multi-unit apartment buildings are appreciating in many markets thanks to the extended economic recovery. Individual investors in some commercial real estate markets may see yearly returns of 10% or more on their investments, and much of that in certain instances may be effectively tax sheltered by depreciating the property.

Bolstered by a continued surge in the commercial real estate market in 1995, investors nationwide were predicting steady growth across a diverse mix of property types, according to a nationwide survey conducted by CB Commercial Real Estate Group, a leading diversified commercial real estate services firm. "Now appears to be a good time to buy, because the market has definitely hit bottom and is continuing to recover," said Doug Haney, executive vice president of appraisal services at CB Commercial.

Emerging Trends in Commercial Real Estate Markets

Office
- Slower office job growth and continuing corporate consolidations result in declining demand for office space.
- Upgrading of space slows due to declining vacancy rates and increasing rents in higher quality space.
- New construction limited to build-to-suits and substantially pre-leased projects. Suburban properties remain the focus of investment and construction activity.

Industrial
- Declining vacancy rates and strong absorption result in sharp increases in rental rates.
- NAFTA stimulates demand in southern border states for warehouse/distribution space.
- Highly specialized needs of tenants drive new construction as many existing buildings are obsolete.
- Most new construction is build-to-suit although some speculative warehouses are being constructed.

Retail
- Soft goods sales rebound fueling rising demand and rent increases as construction remains below historic levels.
- Product specialization and trend towards "bigger is better" continues. However, some consolidation occurs among selected big-box retailers.
- Power center and outlet mall construction declines; renewed investment focus on regional malls and neighborhood centers.

Apartment
- Continued strengthening occupancies and rental rates due to strong demand, especially as interest rate hikes dampen new home purchases.
- Construction heaviest in markets with significant population and household growth resulting from employment gains (e.g., sunbelt cities).
- Upper tier projects with home-like features and substantial amenities dominate new construction.
- Capitalization rates stabilize after declining for the past three years due to strong demand from REITs and pension funds. Existing Class A investment product remains in short supply.

Source: Arthur Andersen, 1995.

Commercial real estate opportunities aren't limited to only a few geographic regions either, although they are likely to be more prevalent in the south and west, in line with long-term population shifts. Surveying the investment outlook for commercial real estate through 1999, for instance, the Arthur Andersen real estate consulting group recently rated Washington, D.C., Atlanta and Dallas four out of a possible five, where a five is the strongest rating and a one the weakest. Chicago and Boston each rated a three.

COMMERCIAL REAL ESTATE RETURNS ON THE REBOUND

Period ending 1st Qtr.	Total return 1 year	Income 1 year	Appreciation 1 year
1985	11.86	7.40	4.23
1986	9.75	7.56	2.07
1987	6.42	7.22	-0.76
1988	5.50	6.99	-1.42
1989	7.03	7.02	0.00
1990	5.99	6.63	-0.61
1991	0.13	6.74	-6.29
1992	-6.09	7.06	-12.48
1993	-3.52	8.04	-10.90
1994	1.55	8.71	-6.73
1995	7.14	9.27	-2.00

Source: National Council of Real Estate Investment Fiduciaries, Chicago, IL.

The fact that many commercial real estate investors showed positive returns in 1994 compared to the losses suffered by many stock and bond holders highlights real estate's ability to help you diversify your investment portfolio. The percentage of your total portfolio that might be devoted to real estate investments depends on your particular financial situation. Since real estate is a relatively illiquid investment, most experts recommend holding a property at least 10 years before selling or exchanging it for another investment property. Real estate probably shouldn't make up a sizeable chunk of an investor's portfolio if he is nearing retirement or faces significant near-term demands on his savings, such as funding a college education.

Signs that most commercial real estate markets are on the rebound doesn't mean that buyers can afford to forget about their investments and go fishing. Several variables could help or hurt the real estate investor for the balance of the decade. Any reduction in capital gains taxes would most likely encourage property holders to sell and take advantage of the lower rate, thereby freeing up choice investment properties around the country. On the other hand, a flood of properties hitting the market would increase supply beyond what could be expected to be absorbed by average demand, depressing prices as a result. A sharp upward spike in interest rates could send real estate lenders pulling back from the market for fear of rising default rates. Or the lenders might make terms so onerous that credit could be choked off, especially for smaller buyers without a track record in real estate.

Research, Research, Research

Making money in commercial real estate in the 1990s puts a premium on doing your homework, scouting out which types of real estate investments offer the best return for your situation, and how to work different financing options into your personal financial picture. This lesson focuses on the main sectors of the commercial real estate market and what characteristics you should focus on to find the best values in each area. A separate section on financing is applicable to most types of commercial real estate investment. When it comes to making money in the second half of the 1990s in commercial real estate, the old real estate cliche, "location, location, location" ought to be supplemented with a new motto: "research, research, research."

OFFICE BUILDINGS

In the downtown of nearly every major American city, a handful of towering office buildings are tombstones marking the spot where institutional investors' and developers' dreams of making a killing in real estate died in the 1980s. Some so-called vulture investors have already swooped into central business districts and snatched up properties that were turned over to lenders or taken over by the government-owned Resolution Trust Corp., or RTC. By buying such properties for a few dimes on the dollar, they can turn them around and lease them out at below market rates and still make a handsome return. That's a high-risk business even for the deep-pocketed professionals, and it's more than likely much too risky, and expensive, for many individual investors, even on a much smaller scale. That doesn't mean that you aren't going to be able to spot signs of life in the commercial office market. It does mean, however, you have to head for the suburbs in most major urban areas.

Existing national trends bode well for suburban class A office space for the remainder of the decade.

The Suburbs Beckon

Most suburban office markets bottomed out a year or two before prices in the central business districts hit bottom. That has created a two-tiered market, with the suburbs leading the cities in terms of investment opportunities. This is expected to prevail for the balance of the decade, if not into the next. Desirable properties in the suburbs tend to range from 5,000 to 100,000 square feet. This effect is referred to in the real estate business as the "hole in the donut," with the hole being the depressed central business district market. In Atlanta, for instance, the downtown office vacancy rate at year-end 1995 was about 21%, while Buckhead, Perimeter and other northern suburban areas had vacancies in the 10-11% range. Houston and Dallas suffer from similar downtown-suburban disparities.

"Existing national trends bode well for suburban class A office space for the remainder of the decade," said Richard Pogue, CB Commercial senior executive vice president and Eastern Division manager.

The suburban trend in commercial real estate fits with other societal trends favoring the suburbs. Smaller companies and start-ups tend to locate in the suburbs with easy access to major transportation routes. And it is these companies that have been the engines of job creation in the U.S. over the past several years, and that trend is likely to continue for the foreseeable future. Indeed, many major corporations continue to shed layer after layer of their white collar ranks as they struggle to remain competitive in global markets. Many of these corporate cast-offs have gone into business for themselves, with suburban locations the obvious choice for quality office space and labor at reasonable rates. In fact, business owners buy their own office buildings in the suburbs and lease out unused space to other entrepreneurs, thereby sharply cutting their own operating costs with the help of the lease income and investing in an asset that's likely to appreciate in price for the foreseeable future.

Regions whose diversified economic base and strong growth among conventional suburbs and newly formed distant suburbs — so-called edge cities — are likely to support rising commercial real estate values include the suburbs of cities such as Atlanta, Dallas, Detroit, Chicago, Los Angeles, New York and Washington, D.C. That said, with so much commercial office space built in the 80s that is still overhanging the market and acting as a drag on price increases in many areas — office properties in many areas are still selling below their replacement costs — it is important to stick with quality properties when delving into commercial office space, even in suburban areas where economic growth is robust.

Trends Favoring Commercial Real Estate Investment

Demographic and economic trends tend to favor commercial real estate investments in the south and west for office and other types of properties, although local market conditions will at times more than offset positive or negative population trends.

The U.S. economy generated roughly 1.7 million office jobs from 1993 through 1995. Even as job growth slows from over 2% annually to 1.5% as many predict for the balance of the decade, demand for office space is expected to remain strong. Even though many major markets such as New York and

U.S. POPULATION TRENDS BY REGION: 1993 TO 2020

Region	1993	%Total	2000	%Total	2010	%Total	2020	%Total	% Change
NORTHEAST	51,227	19.9	51,884	18.8	53,301	17.7	55,352	17.0	-2.9
MIDWEST	61,149	23.7	63,836	23.1	66,333	22.1	68,983	21.2	-2.5
SOUTH	89,362	34.6	97,244	35.2	107,385	35.7	117,498	36.0	1.4
WEST	56,190	21.8	63,278	22.9	73,411	24.4	84,106	25.8	4.0
UNITED STATES	257,928		276,242		300,430		325,939		

Source: U.S. Commerce Dept.; Bureau of the Census.

LARGEST STATES BY POPULATION: 1993 TO 2020

1993	2000	2020
CALIFORNIA	CALIFORNIA	CALIFORNIA
NEW YORK	TEXAS	TEXAS
TEXAS	NEW YORK	FLORIDA
FLORIDA	FLORIDA	NEW YORK
PENNSYLVANIA	PENNSYLVANIA	ILLINOIS

Source: U.S. Commerce Dept.; Bureau of the Census

Philadelphia will remain weak due to high vacancy rates and slow job growth — 0.9% annually is projected for New York — nationwide the office market is shifting from a tenants to a landlord's market by the end of the decade. Fully 85% of the urban areas with employment bases of more than 500,000 are gaining jobs. At the state level, job growth was strongest in the intermountain states in the mid-1990s, with Nevada posting 6% annual growth, followed by Utah (5.9%), Idaho (5.7%), and Arizona (4.0%). The southeastern states of Georgia, with 4.8% growth, and Florida (3.3%) were also strong.

Top Office Real Estate Markets: 1995 to 2000

Based on a composite "momentum index" of supply and demand trends for each market, developed by Landauer Associates, Inc., New York. The higher the index number, the stronger the market for office space. Median = 100.

Salt Lake City, UT	184	Milwaukee, WI	116	Norfolk-Virginia Beach, VA	85
Columbus, OH	176	Phoenix, AR	115	Dallas, TX	84
Portland, OR	173	Seattle-Everett, WA	114	Riverside-San Bernardino, CA	84
Charlotte-Gastonia, NC	161	Oakland, CA	112	New Orleans, LA	79
Austin, TX	154	Atlanta, GA	109	St. Louis, MO	78
Minneapolis-St. Paul, MN	153	Memphis, TN	108	Los Angeles-Long Beach, CA	76
Nashville-Davidson, TN	141	Boston, MA	108	Pittsburgh, PA	75
Birmingham, AL	135	Cincinnati, OH	108	Chicago, IL	73
Sacramento, CA	135	Indianapolis, IN	107	San Jose, CA	72
Greensboro, NC	133	San Francisco, CA	101	Cleveland, OH	66
Tampa-St. Petersburg, FL	132	Ft. Worth, TX	100	Detroit, MI	63
Ft. Lauderdale, FL	131	San Diego, CA	100	Greenville-Spartanburg, SC	60
Jacksonville, FL	129	Miami, FL	97	Honolulu, HI	56
Kansas City, MO	128	Richmond-Petersburg, VA	96	Philadelphia, PA	55
Washington, D.C.	127	Houston, TX	94	Newark, NJ	54
San Antonio, TX	125	W. Palm Beach, FL	94	Hartford, CT	52
Denver, CO	118	Baltimore, MD	93	Middlesex-Somerset-Hunterdon, NJ	47
Orlando, FL	117	Tulsa, OK	92	Nassau-Suffolk, NY	47
Monmouth-Ocean, NJ	116	Anaheim, CA	89	Oklahoma City, OK	45
				New York, NY	40
				Bergen-Passaic, NJ	38
				Bridgeport, CT	37

Source: Landauer Associates, Inc.

What makes for a booming market for office space when so many large corporations are selling plants and corporate headquarters in an attempt to become lean and mean competitors? Strong technology and business services sectors are driving the strength of the Salt Lake City real estate market, which tops the preceding Landauer index. Both the central business district and suburbs have occupancy rates of greater than 90%, and Landauer projects office employment growth of 2.5% annually. Similar factors are fueling growth in the rest of the top five metropolitan areas for office space. *The risk in these and other hot real estate markets is that lenders will start to lower their standards and a flood of easy money will finance an overbuilding boom, possibly to be followed by a late decade bust.*

Investment Returns

What sort of a return could an investor expect to receive from commercial office space, or for any commercial space for that matter? At this point it is worthwhile to review some of the financial aspects of real estate investing that you were introduced to in the lesson, The profit approach to real estate.

The *capitalization (or cap) rate* is to real estate what the price/earnings ratio is to investing in stocks — the single most widely used yardstick to gauge whether an investment makes economic sense. The higher the risk that a property investment might go sour, if it's in a marginal neighborhood, for instance, the higher the buyer should demand that the cap rate be. The cap rate is computed by taking the property's net operating income and dividing it by the total purchase price. If a property generates $50,000 in net operating income (NOI), which in real estate is the cash flow from rents and other sources of income before mortgage expenses and taxes, and its purchase price is $500,000, then its cap rate is 10%. Mortgage and tax-related expenses are excluded from the NOI calculation because the borrowing terms for different properties, and different investors, vary so widely that it isn't practical to try and include mortgage costs in a generic formula that can be applied to a multitude of property types. The same argument applies to taxes.

Capitalization Rate

NET OPERATING INCOME	$50,000	= 10%
PURCHASE PRICE	$500,000	

Cap rates of from 9-11% are typical in many suburban areas for office buildings. The best situated, Class A properties, which by definition are relatively low-risk investments compared to other office space, generate cap rates of closer to 8%. Investors tend to demand higher cap rates to compensate for the greater amount of risk associated with a property.

Cap rates are often used by buyers and sellers of commercial real estate to calculate what the asking price should be for a property. If an office building generates $50,000 in net operating income, and similar office buildings or retail centers in an area have sold for cap rates of 10 percent to 11 percent, then the seller reasons that he should ask $500,000 to $550,000 for the property. Since no two buildings are exactly alike, differing in location, state of repair, amenities, etc., cap rates should be taken as a widely used guide, but not the final arbiter, of price for a property.

NET OPERATING INCOME	$50,000
COMPARABLE CAP RATES	10-11 %
ASKING PRICE	$500,000-$550,000

The *cash on cash return* is a way to express the percentage return you are earning on the cash you have tied up in the property — typically your down payment. If the net operating income on your property is $50,000, and principal and interest payments on your mortgage and taxes (after depreciating the property and deducting interest expenses on your mortgage) came to $35,800, your after-tax cash flow would equal $14,200. Divide that amount by the down payment on the property of, for example, $75,000, and you have a cash on cash return of 18.9%

Cash On Cash Return

AFTER-TAX CASH FLOW	$14,200	=18.9%
CASH INVESTED	$75,000	

To get to net operating income, it is first important to lay out what is included in calculating income, and the expenses that are deducted from income to get to the NOI. Income and expense statements can range from a few figures scratched on the back of an envelope to reams of data included in state-of-the-art computerized spreadsheets, depending on the level of sophistication of the parties involved in the transaction. Bigger isn't always better, however. It's important to remember that it is the assumptions behind the numbers, not just the numbers themselves, that determine whether an investment is worthwhile. Rest assured that nearly every one of the phenomenal real estate failures of the 1980s was promoted using documents that contained column after column of figures that were intended to add up to a good investment.

There are a few standard lists of income and expenses that illustrate what is involved in calculating office real estate returns. With a few modifications the income statement can be applied to other commercial real estate as well. The National Association of Realtors' Institute of Real Estate Management, or IREM, chart of income and expenses includes the following:

Office Building Income Statement

Income

GROSS SPENDABLE INCOME
LESS: VACANCIES AND DELINQUENT RENT
TOTAL RENT

Expenses

All utilities
Janitorial payroll/contract
Maintenance and repair
Management fee
Administrative payroll
Insurance
Net operating costs
Real estate taxes
Total operating costs

Experience suggests that annual expenses for office space in the suburbs can easily approach 50 percent of gross scheduled income. An IREM survey of suburban office buildings came up with the following breakdown of expenses:

Suburban office building expenses

Type of expense	Percent of gross income
Utilities	15.8
Janitorial, maintenance, repair	14.6
Real estate taxes	10.2
Insurance and services	3.5
Administration and payroll	5.5
Total	**49.6**

> *It's important to remember that it is the assumptions behind the numbers, not just the numbers themselves, that determine whether an investment is worthwhile.*

Key to successful commercial real estate investing is a willingness to roll up your shirt sleeves and pore over every income and expense item for your building and comparable buildings before you buy. Brokers and related real estate industry professionals can be a big help in suggesting what expense or income items typically run in your area, based on their experience. (Obviously, you should ask for references and professional affiliations from your broker to check on his experience.) But you can't take anything for granted. If maintenance figures for a building are well below normal, for instance, it doesn't necessarily follow that the building is well maintained. It may mean that the current owner is deferring maintenance to keep his expenses down during tough times, or while he is developing or trying to lease another project. If so, that becomes a bargaining point for you when it comes time to sit down and negotiate — subtract the cost of a new boiler from the offering price, for instance. If you do install new and more efficient heating and air conditioning equipment, you can also assume that your fuel costs wills be lower. That means you could shave 10% off the utilities expense line, for instance, which gives you more flexibility when it comes to negotiating a deal.

Checking Out the Competition

The same attention to detail that you apply to your target purchase also needs to be trained on competitive buildings in your area in making what's known as a competitive market analysis. The definition of a building's market area can vary widely. It's usually better to keep the area relatively small. Office buildings rarely draw tenants from a wide area or from out of the region altogether. What a building owner is able to charge on the other side of a major metropolitan area with different growth characteristics, transportation access and nearby amenities isn't likely to tell you much about your property beyond providing very broad guidelines. Again, brokers can be very helpful is compiling this type of information. Following is some of the information that needs to be gathered when analyzing the competitive market:

- Address and comments on quality of the location

- Building size — gross and net rentable

- Current occupancy level and list of tenants including square feet occupied, rent paid and lease expiration date

- Age and condition of building

- Building site, lobby and other amenities

- Parking and parking pricing policy

- Asking rent and effective rent

- Concession package

- Tenant improvement policy

- Off-site support facilities such as restaurants, shopping

- On-site support facilities such as shopping, food, secretarial services

- Parking bay depths, column spacing

- Building efficiency

- Any special advantages of this property from the tenant's viewpoint

- Disadvantages such as poor access or visibility, inconvenient or too little parking, poor outdoor lighting, poor heating, venting and air conditioning, hazardous materials problems, mediocre elevator service, poor maintenance or management.

Source: Grubb & Ellis.

Good management and a strong local and regional market in real estate can produce impressive results, even when national trends in real estate are weak.

Good management and a strong local and regional market in real estate can produce impressive results, even when national trends in real estate are weak. An example is Duke Realty Investments, a real estate investment trust whose shares trade on the New York Stock Exchange. In 1994, they posted a 4.8% increase in NOI on its "core portfolio" of office and industrial properties that it had held for more than a year. Occupancy rates for the Indianapolis-based company's properties also were well above average at 92.9% to 94.4%, compared to occupancy rates of between 85% to 90% in many parts of the country. Key to Duke's success is the fact that most of its money is invested in commercial real estate in the Indianapolis, Cincinnati and Columbus, Ohio, areas. This region wasn't as overbuilt as many in the late '80s, and the recession that began in 1991 didn't do much damage to the local economies, either.

Leases: Triple Net to Gross

Leases are the lifeblood of commercial real estate. Much of a lease may appear in fine print, and every word needs to be read. Any investor who settles for what is presented as a "standard" lease is guaranteeing himself substandard investment returns — if any. Leases typically range from what's known as a triple net lease, where the tenant pays the taxes, insurance and maintenance costs of the space he leases, to a gross lease which is based on a single non-itemized figure. The fine print becomes critical when owner and tenant negotiate a lease that falls somewhere between these two extremes, which is fairly common. A tenant may be willing to pay taxes and insurance, for instance, since they are fairly easy to gauge in advance, but balk at paying maintenance. From the owner/investor's point of view, the triple net lease, where, for example, unforeseen maintenance cost increases can be passed on to the tenant, is usually the simplest and most advantageous to use.

Business owners or professionals in the suburbs who are leasing space should look at their own operations when considering investing in office space. They can build or buy a building and then execute a triple net lease — meeting arm's-length requirements that the terms meet those for comparable properties — with their company. The property is owned by the business owners, and the company holds the triple net lease, the costs of which are a business expense. The depreciation for tax purposes and any appreciation in the value of the property goes to the business owners.

Depreciation and Taxes

In addition to hoping to realize some appreciation on their real estate, a major reason many investors buy office or other commercial real estate is to depreciate the value of the property for tax purposes, which reduces the investor's overall tax burden. Depreciation is a non-cash expense for the wear and tear of certain assets. Unlike residential property, which is depreciated on a straight-line basis over years, office and other non-residential properties are depreciated over 39 years. The value of the land under any property isn't depreciable. (The land doesn't wear out.) The annual straight-line depreciation on a $400,000 office building, for instance, would be $10,256.41 ($400,000 divided by 39 = $10,256.41.). Landscaping and other improvements, as well as furniture, are also depreciable, although over much shorter time periods, usually seven to 10 years.

A major reason many investors buy office or other commercial real estate is to depreciate the value of the property for tax purposes.

The fact that an investor borrowed, for instance, 75% of the value of the property to buy it doesn't affect his ability to depreciate the property based on 100% of the purchase price. On the other hand, depreciating a property reduces its cost basis, which is used in determining the taxes due on a property at sale. The more depreciation taken on a property, the lower the cost basis and the greater the amount of a taxable gain at sale time, all other things being equal. Remember that while depreciation is a "paper" expense that doesn't require a cash outlay, it does reflect real wear and tear on your property over time. Owners need to create a reserve fund that will eventually pay the cost of a new boiler, roof, windows, etc., or else they will eventually be hit by some nasty one-time maintenance expenses.

Rental income losses are considered to be passive losses by the IRS. These losses can't be deducted from your wages, interest or dividends unless you spend at least 750 hours per year in the real estate business. Losses must be used to offset gains only from other passive investments, such as other real estate ventures. An exception to this rule applies to taxpayers whose adjusted gross incomes are less than $100,000. They are able to write off up to $25,000 of passive losses in one year. This $25,000 exception is phased out by the time an investor's adjusted gross income hits $150,000. Any allowable unused losses can be carried forward to use in future tax years.

There are two main techniques an investor should consider to reduce his income tax burden when it comes time to sell a property:

Installment sale — An installment sale is a method used to defer payment on the taxes on the profits of a sale. An investor, for instance, finds a buyer who agrees to purchase his property and make payment in equal annual installments over 10 years, as well as interest due on the unpaid amount. The total taxes paid at the end of the decade by the seller will be the same as if they had been paid in a lump sum, but the burden on the seller will have been spread out over 10 years. Buyers will often be willing to agree to a higher asking price for a property under these conditions, since they don't have to come up with the entire purchase price at the time of the sale.

Tax-Deferred Exchanges — A tax-deferred exchange allows an investor to trade property without paying any current taxes on the gains. Taxes are postponed until the replacement property is sold. The IRS has said that, in effect, real or personal property that is used in the trade or business, or held for investment purposes, of the taxpayer qualifies for this sort of postponement if it's exchanged for *like kind* of property. Such exchanges are occasionally referred to as "1031" exchanges after the specific IRS rule covering their treatment for tax purposes. Commercial real estate investors considering their first exchange are often confused by the phrase "like kind." The properties to be exchanged don't have to be office buildings. One can be a warehouse, or for that matter, one could be a farm. And they don't have to be of the same investment quality. The important element they have in common is that they are investment properties. Exchanges should be the preferred means of sale if the investor plans to sell for a profit and make another purchase within a short period, generally within 180 days after closing on the first property.

For example, say you bought a suburban office complex several years ago for $200,000, and have depreciated it down to $120,000. Assume that while you held the property it doubled in value to $400,000. If you sold the building, you would be subject to long-term capital gains taxes on $280,000 ($400,000 - $120,000 = $280,000.) If you traded this property for another worth $400,000 you would still have a gain, but it wouldn't be taxable at the time of the exchange. You also would also be able to depreciate the new property. Any consideration received as part of an exchange that isn't "like kind" investment property, cash or bonds to make up for the different in prices between two properties being exchanged, for instance, is a taxable gain at the time of the exchange and is referred to as "boot."

As when making other major investments, you will want to consult a tax specialist to review the specific impact of such a transaction on your overall tax liability.

Rolling or Pyramiding Equity in Commercial Real Estate

The five-to-one (and sometimes better) leverage you can achieve in commercial real estate investing — that is, you only need to put up 20% equity as a down payment to own 100% of a property — affords the investor the opportunity to rapidly increase his equity in a property, and to use that increase to buy other properties and diversify his commercial real estate holdings. For instance, you put up $40,000 to buy a $200,000 property when you estimate that prices in the local market are just starting to bounce off the bottom. Five years later the property has appreciated by 30%, or $60,000. Your investment has actually increased by 150%, since you only put up $40,000 to buy the property. You could then sell the property for a gain, but taxes would eat up a substantial part of the return on your investment.

A better strategy may be to borrow against your increased equity in the first property to make a down payment on a second income-producing property. You could do this by offering a second mortgage on the first property as a down payment to the owner of the new property you want to buy. Say you borrowed $50,000 of the $60,000 gain on the first property as a down payment for the new property. Increases in rental income would help make the payments on the second mortgage on the property. Since $50,000 is 20% of $250,000, you could use the equity built up in the first property to buy a property worth $250,000. That means that within just five years, your initial $40,000 investment in commercial real estate would be controlling two properties with a combined value — $260,000 for the appreciated value of the first property and $250,000 for the second — of $510,000! By buying the second property you also capture the cash flow from that property, assuming the lease income more than covers the new mortgage you take out to buy the property, as well as the ability to depreciate its value to offset taxable gains.

INDUSTRIAL

Industrial real estate is the Rodney Dangerfield of the commercial real estate market — it doesn't get any respect from many investors. Attractive apartment complexes and well-designed retail malls are guaranteed eye-catchers by comparison. But industrial properties can produce industrial-strength yields.

Trends in Industrial Property

The Commerce Dept. publishes a certain amount of information covering the supply of new industrial property on a nationwide basis. Some of the reports, such as one on the "Value of New Construction Put in Place," is published monthly. 1995 new construction ran nearly 8.3% ahead of 1994's pace for industrial real estate, but still was well below the recent peak of $21.4

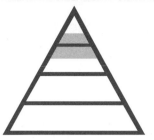

STEP 83

Techniques to Spot the Best Commercial Property at the Best Price

What: Finding the particular commercial real estate investment that best fits your needs involves examining your financial and personal strengths at the same time that you are evaluating properties. Finding a property with attractive net operating income is a starting point, it isn't the final information you need to make an investment decision.

Why: Most investors who fail to make money, or lose money, when buying commercial real estate do so more often because they have failed to evaluate their own resources and abilities rather than because they have poorly evaluated a particular property, although the latter happens, too. No matter how thoroughly you evaluate a property, expect the unexpected to happen, especially as a beginner, and be prepared to deal with it.

Risk: Moderate to high. You can't always know that you have made the right investment decision, since so many variables, some you control, some, such as economic growth trends, you don't. The more advance planning you put into the purchase of commercial real estate, including analyzing your own goals and abilities, the better chance you'll be able to moderate your overall risk.

Safety: Moderate. The odds that if you have done your homework you will grossly overpay for a property, or that prices in your area will crash, are relatively limited, given the widespread decline in real estate prices in the late 1980s and early 1990s.

Liquidity/ Flexibility: Low. There is no centralized market like a stock exchange for trading real estate. Even highly desirable properties can remain on the market for months. Most commercial real estate purchases ought to be approached as 10-year investments. If you are likely to need the money you have earmarked for commercial properties sooner, reconsider your investment priorities.

Why Not: The allure of owning real property compared to "paper" stock and bond investments has tempted many people to make poor investment decisions in real estate over the years. If you can't make a level-headed analysis of the return on a real estate investment the same way you would on a bond or stock, keep your checkbook in your pocket.

Buy/Invest From: Individual/corporate sellers, with the advice of a seasoned broker and real estate tax attorney.

Background: If you have accumulated enough capital in other investments so that you can make a sizeable down payment, but your after-tax income is limited, you should consider properties that are more likely to produce a steady stream of current income, such as warehouses, suburban office space, small retail centers or apartment buildings. Buying undeveloped land, on the other hand, is much more likely to be a drain on your income unless you can sell quickly for a profit.

If you are a handyman or you have experience dealing with customers or managing the books of a small business, you could use your abilities to perform some or all of the management duties of a particular property and pay yourself what you would pay a property manager. In this way many investors buy a property and "buy" a job. You should also honestly evaluate yourself as a risk-taker to determine how comfortable you are with highly leveraged purchases that involve more than one source of financing, such as seller-financed deals. If that makes you uneasy, stick with larger down payments and more conventional financing.

The key to successful investing in commercial real estate is to have planned ahead for unexpected contingencies, such as temporarily greater than expected vacancies, and be able to cope. You need to be able to afford to have a cash cushion left over after you invest to handle such emergencies. You also need to be willing to increase your borrowing, meaning you will be further in debt, if need be to hang on to or improve a property. More importantly, you need to be able to

Step 83: *Techniques to Spot the Best Commercial Property at the Best Price*

approach an investment in commercial real estate as a business proposition. Too many property investors who fail and are forced to sell at a loss were seduced into investing with tales of spectacular price appreciation and sharply escalating rental income. They didn't taking a hard look at whether they would be able to handle the inevitable ups and downs of property investing.

▷ ▷ ▶ **If you want to get started today here is what you need to do to spot the best commercial property at the best prices:**

■ Work with a reputable broker. Clearly state your financial limitations and goals to the broker, and contact banks and other lenders about financing while you are in the early stages of your search. They may make suggestions on the type of property that would suit your ability to borrow, and in many cases they may be able to direct you to available properties, given their knowledge of the local real estate market.

■ Limit your search, especially if you are a neophyte investor, to properties that produce a positive cash flow after all expenses, including debt service and taxes — this is known as your "cash on cash" return. If that return doesn't exceed returns from more conventional investments, such as stocks or bonds, don't buy the property, or try to negotiate better terms with the seller.

■ Make slight adjustments in the amount of down payment, or try convincing a seller to take back a mortgage on the property you want to buy, in order to tip the after-tax return in your favor. Hold out until you find a property that delivers a return that justifies taking the added risk that is inherent in commercial real estate investing. ▲

Continued from p. 12 billion in new construction set in 1990, before the Gulf War and recession that followed. Local and regional data on industrial property is available from the assessor or planning department in the cities or counties in which you are considering investing.

COMMERCIAL REAL ESTATE RETURNS BY PROPERTY TYPE *(First Quarter 1978 Through First Quarter 1995)*			
Property	**Total return**	**Income**	**Appreciation**
WAREHOUSE	9.07	8.09	0.92
RETAIL	8.95	7.95	1.20
R&D/OFFICE	8.42	8.39	0.02
APARTMENT*	6.34	7.89	-1.47
OFFICE	6.33	7.47	-1.08

Source: NCREIF, based on appraised values.
**The inception date for Apartments is first quarter 1988.*

A revitalized manufacturing base is the engine driving the U.S. economy, and that's obviously good news when it comes to continuing demand for industrial real estate in much of the country. The trend toward just-in-time manufacturing has also led many companies to build regional warehouses and distribution centers where parts are kept and then sent to area factories so the factories themselves can maintain lean inventories.

On the other hand, industrial space is probably the most sensitive to fluctuations in the business cycle among the major commercial real estate categories. There is plenty of appropriately zoned property in most parts of the country, and so-called "tilt up" construction is a very quick building technique. If construction continues at a relatively brisk pace for the next few years and then economic growth slows significantly, returns from industrial real estate could "tilt down" sharply.

Warehouses

Warehouses account for about 60% of the industrial real estate in the country and can be a very good investment opportunity for smaller investors. Indeed, smaller warehouses starting at 5,000 to 10,000 square feet that might be within your price range as you near the peak of the investing pyramid are precisely the properties that are likely to benefit the most from the demographic trends discussed earlier. That is, smaller companies building in farther out suburbs from central business districts are going to be building and demanding smaller warehouse space, even while the total demand for warehouse space may be flat at best, based on industrial employment trends. Your warehouse investment may get an added boost if suburban expansion continues in your direction and the land value of the property escalates as development surrounds the site. Capitalization rates of 10% are standard for suburban warehouse properties in many parts of the country. Investors should demand 15% to 20% for higher risk inner city industrial sites.

Warehouse vacancy rates are in single digits throughout the U.S.

In certain cases warehouse properties can also be less management intensive than other commercial real estate properties. A smaller warehouse with one to two tenants with 10- to 15-year, triple-net leases can be managed well by many "ma and pa" investors who are willing to devote a portion of their time to property management. The more tenants, the more need for hands on management, which adds to costs in terms of your time as owner, or paying a property manager.

An investment in a typical suburban warehouse property might look something like this:

- Triple net market rents range from $2 to $5 a square foot

- A 10,000-square-foot warehouse in a well-located industrial park rents for $4 a square foot

- The warehouse produces annual income of $40,000

- With a cap rate of 10% the warehouse is valued at $400,000

On average, buyers are required to make down payments of about 20% for 15- to 20-year mortgages on warehouse properties. Lenders not only look at the financial strength of the owner, they also look at the financial strength of the major tenant or tenants to assure themselves that the tenants are going to be able to make rent payments required.

Top Ten Markets for Warehouse/Distribution Center Growth

Based on several factors, including vacancy, employment trends, wage rates, rents, local infrastructure and proximity to end markets.

1. Dallas	6. Salt Lake City
2. Seattle	7. Houston
3. Miami	8. Atlanta
4. Portland, OR	9. Charlotte
5. Tampa	10. Minneapolis

Source: Landauer Associates

Despite the glut of office space plaguing Dallas, at least in the central business district, warehouse vacancy rates are in single digits throughout the U.S. The rash of building following the passage of the North American Free Trade Agreement, or NAFTA, was a major factor propelling the growth of warehouse construction in Dallas and Houston as well as San Antonio, which ranked 11th. Mexico's economic crisis that was triggered in late 1994 by the collapse of the value of the peso has cooled any demand for additional construction to service NAFTA-related trade for the near future in many markets. Port cities provide an obvious stimulus for warehouse construction tied to international trade. Industrial occupancy rates in Seattle and Portland, for instance, topped 96%. And Salt Lake City, home to thriving manufacturing growth, doesn't face competition from another industrial hub for 350 miles in any direction.

Industrial Lenders

Many lenders are making what amounts to a vote of confidence in the future prospects for warehouse total returns by traveling out of state to try and make loans to such projects. Developers in Milwaukee noted in mid-1995, for instance, that a handful of Boston banks were offering to finance warehouse investments in Milwaukee. In one sense this activity suggests that the regional economy in New England wasn't growing fast enough at the time to absorb the banks' surplus cash. But it also indicates that as the banks scouted far afield for lending opportunities, they chose warehouses as likely to outperform other real estate investments.

As with office space, business owners should consider buying warehouse or other manufacturing space and leasing it to their companies. They also can lease unused space to other businesses and bring in income to offset their operating costs. For instance, a business owner paid $600,000 for a 67,000-square-foot building and had 30,000 square feet of unused space. He leased the space for seven years on a triple-net basis for $2 a square foot. The $60,000 in income represented a 10% return on the cost of the building. But considering the fact that he was occupying slightly more than half of the building (37,000 square feet) himself, the return was actually more than 20% based on the space that was leased out. The income came close to covering his mortgage payment, allowing him to occupy his building practically "rent free."

Multi-Tenant and Mixed Use Properties

The key to multi-tenant properties is compatibility. One developer had a food production company operating in a building with a prime location and wanted to lease the unused space in the building to other tenants. "We got a lot of requests to become co-tenants from other manufacturers and even a day care center, but from a cleanliness and safety point of view, they weren't compatible," he said. And if one tenant in a property is spray painting parts, for instance, the adjacent tenant can't have workers standing on an assembly line who might be exposed to fumes from the paint operation.

Mixed use properties, which combine office and industrial space, for instance, or office, hotel and retail space, are a growing segment of the commercial real estate market in many parts of the country. The different property types can function much as a diversified portfolio of securities — total return from one segment may be robust during a certain period, helping to offset a slump in one of the other segments. But the different properties often have very different management requirements. Industrial space is rented to a small number of tenants for relatively long lease periods, while smaller office and retail properties tend to turn over leases more frequently. Triple-net leases are also more common in industrial space than in smaller retail operations, for instance. *Note: For these reasons it makes the most sense to find a partner or partners when considering a mixed use investment. Ideally, one investor or group of like-minded investors would have control of each type of commercial real estate in a mixed use development.*

Environmental Issues

Environmental issues can have an impact on all types of commercial real estate, but they are most likely to be felt in the industrial market. Whoever buys a property with an environmental hazard associated with it inherits the problem legally even if the previous owner was the one who caused the hazard. Investors in industrial properties are rolling the dice if they turn a blind eye to environmental problems. Many potential investors in industrial real estate have an environmental assessment of the property they are interested in carried out. In some situations sellers who are motivated to unload a particular property for whatever reasons may be the ones to hire an expert who will literally dig in to their property and see if they have a problem. Environmental studies are typically divided into two types: Phase I and Phase II assessments.

Phase I

A Phase I assessment entails a physical inspection of the property and historical research to detect whether hazardous materials were likely to have been used on site by previous owners going back 50 years or more. A check is made of surrounding properties as well to determine if hazardous materials might have been able to migrate onto the target property. This study only tries to determine the possibility of environmental contamination, it doesn't determine whether in fact the contamination exists.

Phase II

In this step, actual soil and water samples are gathered and tested for contaminants. If contamination is confirmed and reported as required by law with state regulatory authorities in most cases, it triggers a clean up order by the state Department of Natural Resources or similar authority. Brokers and specialized consultants can recommend companies to perform the work required in both phases and the specifics of the property site investigation.

RETAIL

Once again, trends in this commercial real estate sector favor you as the smaller investor. Super regional malls and slightly smaller "power centers" are overbuilt across much of the country. Smaller retail properties, from neighborhood centers to local convenience store strip projects, are where the best investments are likely to be found in the retail arm of commercial real estate, depending on local market conditions. The threat of superstores being built around the country by K-mart and Wal-Mart, however, is a trend that any potential investor in retail space has to closely monitor for the next several years.

Any retail space being bought or sold for the next several years will be done so in the context of a retail market that is overbuilt on a national basis. In 1990 there was about 13 square feet of retail space per capita in the U.S. By 1993 that figure had jumped to 17.7 square feet, and is forecasted at about 16.4 square feet by the year 2000. Market balance in any average region is typically estimated at about 15 square feet of retail space per regional consumer.

Not only will there be an above average amount of retail space available for the balance of the decade, compared to the optimum balance of 15 square feet per capita, but forecasts for retail sales growth appear to be suspiciously optimistic. Household income is widely expected to grow at about 2% annually for the next several years. Retail sales, on the other hand, are forecast by some industry experts to grow by about 25% from the mid-1990s to the year 2000. *Note: Buyers of retail real estate should be especially critical of any such overly optimistic forecasts that are used by sellers to justify projected rent increases or other factors.*

Before getting into the details of the smaller retail investments within your reach at this stage in your investing career, it's worthwhile to take a look at the competition that you may face in many parts of the country. The table below gives a good summary of factors involved with the major retail development categories. Many of these retail developments are accomplished through conversions of non-retail property into retail property. For advice on this see wealth-building Step 84, found beginning on page 18.

SHOPPING CENTER TYPES

Item	Neighborhood	Community	Power	Regional and Super-regional
SIZE	30,000 SQ. FT. TO 150,000 SQ. FT.	100,000 SQ. FT TO 350,000 SQ.FT	250,000 SQ. FT. TO 1,000,000 SQ. FT.	400,000 SQ. FT TO 2,000,000 SQ. FT
MERCHANDISE	FOOD, CONVENIENCE GOODS AND SERVICES	GENERAL MERCHANDISE	HUGE SELECTION, NARROW MERCHANDISE GROUP, LOW PRICES	CURRENT FASHIONS
ANCHORS	SUPERMARKET, DRUG	DISCOUNT DEPARTMENT STORE	1 TO 4, OR MORE BIG-BOX RETAILERS	3-7 FULL-LINE DEPARTMENT STORES
SATELLITE STORES	LOCAL SERVICE MERCHANTS, 50% TO 60% OF SPACE	SPECIALTY SHOPS	SMALLER CATEGORY KILLERS, 10-15% SPACE	50-100 MALL SHOPS
SITE SIZE	3-15 ACRES	10-35 ACRES	25-100+ ACRES	40-200+ ACRES

Source: Grubb & Ellis.

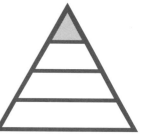

STEP 84

Conversion Properties: When to Convert, When to Pass

What: Convert commercial real estate to a different use to increase its value.

Why: Converting real estate to a different use is one of the fastest and usually most economical ways to boost the value of a property. A relatively modest investment (compared to the cost of new construction) to convert a vintage warehouse in a central city area into retail space for trendy shops and office space for professional groups such as attorneys and architects, for instance, can boost the value of the property much faster than can finding new warehouse tenants.

Risk: High. Unlike in the movie Field of Dreams, just because you build it doesn't mean that "they" will come. Not every tenant wants to rent space in a converted warehouse or similar property. Many prefer new construction that may have more amenities that appeal to a particular type of renter, even if the cost per square foot is higher in new construction. Modern construction may allow more flexibility in locating such equipment as computer terminals and cash registers, for instance, and be more accessible to the handicapped.

Safety: Moderate to Low. A well-planned conversion that offers the maximum flexibility that is feasible for tenants based on pre-conversion surveys of trends in commercial leasing in the immediate area has a good chance of success.

Liquidity/ Flexibility: Low to Medium. Converting a property typically involves taking a single-use property and converting it to multi-use, as in the above example of combining retail and office space. Switching to multi-use should increase the owner's flexibility in trying to boost the income from the property and possibly make it more liquid as well by making it more attractive to a broader range of buyers. That said, it's still commercial real estate, which tends to be illiquid.

Why Not: Existing zoning rules may prohibit you from converting to the use that you determine makes the most economic sense for the property. Check zoning restrictions before you buy if you have the slightest inclination that you may want to convert the property at a future date. It it possible to get a zoning variance to allow a different use for the property, or to get the zoning rules changed by appealing to the local city council or other governmental body. But that can be a time-consuming process with the end result often depending on local politics. You may also find that not enough tenants appear interested in working in a converted structure in the area, or that enough conversions have preceded yours that the market appears glutted.

Buy/Invest From: Private or corporate sellers, utilizing a broker with experience in commercial properties that have been converted to multi-use properties.

Background: Conversions have been occurring for decades, typically in areas where it is too congested or too expensive to put up new construction. The trend toward the gentrification of "red brick" inner city commercial areas in the 1970s and 1980s fueled a boom in economic conversions across the country. Overbuilding in many cities in the late 1980s and early 1990s, however, created a glut of office space with relatively cheap lease terms, slowing the pace of conversions in some areas. At the same time the glut of new office space has led to some creative conversions in certain areas. One developer in the Upper Midwest bought a medium-sized office building and converted it into medical offices on the ground floor and hotel suites on the upper floors, and expects a return of 15% to 20% a year from the property .

If you want to get started today here is what you need to do to convert properties to increase their economic value:

Research the market for tenant interest in converted properties before you commit to buy.

Step 84: *Conversion Properties: When to Convert, When to Pass*

Be careful not to tip your hand completely or too soon to the seller or to lenders — someone may take your idea or suddenly decide that the property is worth much more than they thought. Line-up long-term commitments from a half-dozen tenants, perhaps at discounted rates, in order to attract other tenants and financiers. Doing this will also give you a sense if the market is overdeveloped. Don't fall in love with the idea of conversion for conversion's sake. If the numbers and occupancy rates don't work — that is, a potential meager increase in returns doesn't justify the increased expense to convert — then don't do it. ▲

Continued from p. 17

Strip Centers   Smaller, speciality or convenience strip centers in suburbs, and increasingly in urban areas, are attractive niche markets for you to consider when surveying retail investment opportunities. A 6,000-square-foot auto repair-oriented strip center in suburban Chicago that generated about $68,000 in net operating income sold for $750,000 in early 1995, giving the investment a capitalization rate of about 11%. Leases charging $10 to $15 a square foot are typical for this type of rental investment. Down payments of 20% to 30% of the purchase price, in this example at least $150,000, are required for most strip center investments.

Lease Terms   Negotiating retail leases is crucial to an investor making a positive return on her investment. Leases are important to all real estate investments, or course, but they are especially crucial in small retail investments. Here's why:

INVESTMENT: AUTOMOTIVE ORIENTED STRIP CENTER

SIZE	6,000 SQ. FT.
TYPE	AUTO REPAIR THEME
NOI	$68,000
CAP RATE	11%
SALE PRICE	$750,000
DOWN PAY	$150,000+
RENT	$10 - $15 SQ. FT., TRIPLE-NET LEASES

In the above example, the anchor tenant leases 4,000 square feet, or two-thirds of the center, and had 13 years left on a 20-year lease when the investor bought the property. To make the investment work, the anchor tenant needs to be paying as much of the investor's cost of owning the center as possible. That's because the remaining space was leased out on a three-year lease. The risk is that the smaller tenant, who probably isn't as strong financially as the anchor tenant, although this isn't always the case, will move out when his lease is out rather than exercising his option to renew. Or he could go out of business. That means that one-third of the center is vacant and the investor is only receiving income on two-thirds of her property.

This isn't a crisis if the anchor tenant's lease is structured so that he effectively pays 85-90% of the cost of the property, including debt service. Working with a broker, banker, or both prior to buying a specific property, you can determine if the lease income from the anchor tenant gives you enough of a financial cushion. Since investors' financial situations vary so greatly, and the amount that you might need to borrow to finance such a purchase is likely to differ from another buyer, it's hard to generalize further.

In any case, your banker will want to examine the creditworthiness of the anchor tenant, if not the smaller tenants as well, before setting a down payment and approving the loan. If the lease only covers two-thirds of the cost of the property, however, the investor may be in trouble. Unlike apartment vacancies, which typically are filled within 60 to 90 days in relatively strong markets, retail vacancies often persist for six to months to a year before a tenant is found for the space.

To fill vacancies as quickly as possible with the right kind of tenant, and to provide tenant services that are aimed at getting tenants to renew leases at terms favorable to the owner, brokerage firms or other property management companies are often brought in to manage a property. In this example the brokerage company that sold the property also managed it, collecting a management fee of 7% of the first year of lease income, and 3% a year thereafter.

MULTI-UNIT APARTMENTS

Although we've already covered residential real estate in an earlier lesson, we thought we'd highlight some important advanced understandings in this lesson, especially since multi-unit apartment investing is associated with commercial real estate.

Suburban markets tend to offer more attractive investments given their lower vacancy rates on average.

Despite the fact vacancy rates have tightened in many markets a warning light is flashing in the apartment sector of the commercial real estate market. Since the apartment market tended to start bouncing back before other sectors, it attracted a tremendous amount of investment capital from roughly 1991 through 1994. The amount of money pouring in from institutional investors and raised from public investors via real estate investment trust, or REIT, offerings have raised concerns that too much "easy money" is already chasing too few legitimate investment opportunities. As a result, some contrarian investors who got into the apartment market early when others wouldn't touch it were already taking profits in 1995 and early 1996, according to industry experts. Other savvy investors were migrating toward higher-risk, lower-priced properties in search of higher returns.

To succeed in commercial real estate you have to develop a clear sense of where supply and demand trends are heading in your hometown or area market for real estate. Suburban markets tend to offer more attractive investments given their lower vacancy rates on average. The impact of local trends, such as the opening of large suburban developments or the gentrification of an urban neighborhood, tend to far outweigh any influence nationwide demographic trends may have on local real estate prices at any given moment. (On the other hand, don't forget that the longer-term national trends are likely to have more of an impact on your market in a decade or so, which is when you may be considering selling a property you buy today or borrowing against it to make another purchase.) Thomas P. "Tip" O'Neil, the famous former Speaker of the U.S. House of Representatives, used to be fond of reminding his Boston constituents and others that "all politics is local." When it comes to investing in commercial properties, investors would do well to remember that "all real estate is local."

Top Ten Apartment Markets

Based on market occupancy trends, rental pricing patterns, demand indicators and construction volumes.

1. Las Vegas
2. Honolulu
3. Austin
4. Raleigh-Durham
5. Oakland
6. San Jose
7. Charlotte
8. Seattle
9. Tampa
10. Sacramento

Source: Landauer Associates, 1995.

How does an investor take the pulse of the local real estate market? A first step is to visit or contact local municipal, county or state authorities who are involved in recording real estate transactions or have a say in zoning or other land use provisions. The county assessor's office in many communities keeps detailed records of real estate transactions. Depending on how busy the staff is in the office, they should be willing to guide you in your effort to scout out recent real estate transactions in the areas where you are considering investing. Some real estate sections of local newspapers also publish real estate transactions, although the lists may be several months out of date by the time they are gathered and printed in the paper. Reading the real estate classified ads in the local paper is also a must to help you determine what level of rents are being charged for which types of buildings in your area.

Using Brokers

Brokers are also an obvious source of information on recent transactions, as well as market gossip as to which types of properties are "hot" at the moment. As insiders in the business, brokers also may have a much better idea than you do regarding what is motivating a particular seller to want to unload a property. Has he been deferring maintenance while waiting for the right time to sell his building, or does he have his hands full with another property he is trying to upgrade and needs the cash from the sale of the building you're interested in buying?

Brokers traditionally have worked for the seller of a property, although many buyers have assumed that the friendly agent always had their best interests at heart when showing them specific properties. An increasing number of states allow for the designation of a "buyer's broker" who does work specifically for the buyer of a property. The buyer's broker splits the commission on the sale of a property with the seller's broker, although the split doesn't have to be 50-50 in most cases. In some states, Illinois for instance, brokers can act as *both* the buyer's and seller's broker. You should ask yourself whether you really think it is possible for a broker not to favor one party's interest over the other's in the sale and purchase of a property before agreeing to this type of arrangement.

Investors in certain situations may prefer to try and work without a broker and deal directly with the seller of a property. This approach can have certain advantages. The biggest potential advantage is that the buyer can try and negotiate a lower price or more favorable terms based on the fact that the seller won't have to pay a broker's fee on the sale of his property, which is typically 6% or more of the sales price. Most first time buyers, however, are likely to find that the advice they get from a broker more than pays for itself in terms of educating them.

Apartment Income and Expenses

Calculating the true income and expenses for an apartment investment is crucial for determining whether a particular investment is right for you. Prospective buyers will be given an income statement from the seller that will also include a breakdown of expenses. But as an investor you should consider this information to be the starting point for your investigation of the property's ability to generate cash, not the final word on the subject. Generally speaking, the newer the building the lower the operating expenses compared to a comparable older property.

For instance, a seller wanting to showcase his property in the most favorable light might list rental income projected forward for the next 12 months based on the current month's rent. Then he would list trailing 12-month expenses. While there is nothing fraudulent about such a practice, it does tend to overstate income by understating expenses. Projecting expenses forward 12 months would necessitate adding an increase for inflation if nothing else that in some cases could equal or exceed any projected increases in rents. Professional management companies and other industry experts may have elaborate computerized spreadsheets that can be very useful in giving you a breakdown of income and expenses for the type of property you are considering. You should ask to see the monthly rent income statements from which the annual statement was drawn.

While we're on the subject, what do the expense records of the past few years indicate about the upkeep of the property? Is money being spent regularly to maintain the property? If not, that could be a sign that maintenance has been deferred and that you as the new owner will be left paying the bill. A fresh coat of paint and a few other cosmetic touches can cover a multitude of maintenance sins unless you look beyond a property's superficial appeal to see if it's supported by a foundation of regular spending on upkeep and maintenance. Big ticket items, boilers, air conditioners, roofs, have finite lives and all eventually need to be replaced. Has any

EXAMPLES OF INCOME AND OPERATING COSTS FOR THREE TYPES OF APARTMENT COMPLEXES

	Garden type	Low-rise 12-24 units	Low-rise 25+ units
ADMINISTRATIVE EXPENSES	10.2%	9.4%	11.2%
OPERATING EXPENSES	8.5%	8.3%	11.5%
MAINTENANCE EXPENSES	7.6%	14.8%	10.3%
TAXES AND INSURANCE	7.7%	11.0%	7.2%
OTHER PAYROLL AND AMENITIES	7.2%	7.4%	6.1%
VACANCIES AND RENT LOSS	7.6%	5.5%	5.5%
NET OPERATING INCOME	51.2%	43.6%	48.2%

Source: National Association of Realtors, Institute of Real Estate Management, Chicago.

such work been done in the past five to 10 years? If not, has the owner created a reserve to fund the future cost of such replacement and repair expenses? Again, these issues don't have to force you to walk away from a property you like, but they are all negotiating points. And speaking of negotiating, you'll want to read more on this in wealth-building Step 85, found beginning on page 23

LAND

Unlike developed commercial real estate, raw land doesn't generate income in most cases for the investor, and its value can't be depreciated, since it doesn't "wear out," at least not in the opinion of the Internal Revenue Service. But, of course, you still have to pay taxes on it. These details shouldn't necessarily deter you from investing in land, but they do highlight the fact that raw land is a different animal compared to other commercial real estate properties.

The timing of an investment in land is usually more important than for other commercial real estate. Land doesn't generate a significant amount of income until it is developed or otherwise converted for different, income-producing use. You may be absolutely right in anticipating the growth of a region and the path of development. But if you buy land that lies in that path and for some reason development doesn't reach you particular parcel for another 10 years, you probably will have bailed out in the interim and sold for little if any after-tax gain. Or you will have tied up capital that most likely could have been earning a much higher rate of return during the decade-long wait.

Researching local and area growth patterns and understanding zoning regulations that apply to the area you are interested in are two of the most important steps you can take en route to making money investing in land. Your local zoning department will be able to provide you with maps of the region that lay out which uses are approved for each parcel of land. Zoning officials are also obvious sources of historical data on zoning changes in the region, and of growth patterns. Historical maps on file at the zoning office are likely to give you a year-by-year or decade-by-decade series of "snapshots" of growth for the area you are interested in.

Slower Growth Ahead?

Investors shouldn't count on suburban growth, some would call it sprawl, to keep driving up land prices near far suburban locations or "edge cities" indefinitely. Rising rates of traffic jams, pollution and crime are alerting many suburban dwellers and planning officials that there is a price to pay for nearly unrestricted growth. The trend over the next few decades in many areas, especially in the Northeast and Midwest, is most likely to be toward slower and much more planning-intensive growth.

An emerging trend in suburban development that also will slow growth is the spread of planned communities that place houses much closer together than in a typical suburb, using less total space, and then include open "common" spaces for residents to congregate. The goal is to create a sense of community akin to an early 20th century small town where people sat on front porches and walked to local markets and parks. Such developments have already cropped up on the Florida Gulf Coast, in Maryland and in Indiana on the shore of Lake Michigan, among other locales. As they become more popular they are likely to spread to most parts of the country.

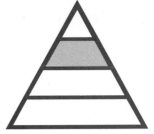

Strategies to Negotiate Commercial Real Estate Transactions

What: Following the best negotiating techniques for buying or selling commercial real estate can mean the difference between making or losing money for the investor.

Why: Negotiating price and terms of a real estate transaction in your favor can allow you to buy a property with the right combination of financing and down payment to get the best return.

Risk: Medium. You risk alienating the other party to a transaction and killing the deal if you are too aggressive or abrasive in making bids and counter offers.

Safety: Medium. A well thought out negotiation strategy should increase your chances of success. Use a broker to increase the odds of success and avoiding letting your ego dictate the terms of the negotiation.

Liquidity/ Flexibility: High. Part of being a successful negotiator is being able to keep your options open in the process of trying to agree on a transaction. You also want to offer your counter-party options that will lead him or her to agree with you, not say no and walk away.

Why Not: You may get pulled into continued negotiations when it is in your own best interests to walk away from a deal.

Buy/Invest From: Be willing to negotiate with anyone seriously interested in making a deal. Use a broker in most cases, especially if the other party appears to be more experienced in buying and selling commercial real estate.

Background: Successful negotiating strategies can be applied to many different kinds of transactions, including real estate:

- Learn as much about the property and its owner as possible before you start negotiating. Knowledge is power.

- Learn what is motivating the seller to sell. (Or buyer to buy.) Is it a personal financial issue or is there some defect in the property? If the latter, this doesn't have to kill the deal, but it is a detail you can use to give you leverage negotiating. Counter parties tend to reveal more about their motivations as negotiations progress and you get more comfortable with each other. Draw him out, emphasize that you both want to make this deal work, and keep your antenna up to gauge his motivation, while keeping your guard at least partially up to avoid revealing too much of your motivation. A negotiation is the last place you should confess your fears or anxieties.

- Set deadlines for the acceptance of offers. Let the other party know you're serious.

- Avoid saying no when it's in your best interests not to. Don't reject an offer flat out as too low or too high, make modifications and say you would accept it on those conditions.

- Use a broker, especially if you are new to investing in commercial real estate. A broker can more than earn his or her commission by acting as the go-between on whom the negotiating parties can vent their emotions or frustrations without alienating each other. A professional broker also encourages the negotiating parties to act professionally and get beyond petty concerns. Remember, however, that unless it is agreed to otherwise, the broker represents the seller.

- Look for "win-win" situations. Get the best deal you can by making the counter party feel as if he has also won some concessions. To accomplish this goal, don't put all the concessions you would be willing to make on the table at one time. Keep one or two in reserve — be willing to alter your asking or offering price by a percent or two, or make minor changes to the amount of down payment or terms of seller financing, if any, so you can demonstrate flexibility and good faith on your part to close a deal.

■ But don't compromise just for the sake of compromise. Your goal isn't to build a continuing relationship as you would with a co-worker in an office, your goal is to get the best price and terms possible.

■ Don't be pressured into accepting a serious counter offer without taking the time to analyze it. If the other party insists on an immediate answer, it is most likely in your best interest to walk away, saying you would be happy to consider the new terms if given adequate time.

■ If your spouse or partner participates in a negotiation, agree ahead of time not to debate the merits of the deal in front of the counter party or broker. Your spouse should emphasize any negatives about a property you are considering buying during a tour, for instance, but avoid effusive praise that could weaken your bargaining position.

▶ ▶ ▶ **If you want to get started today here is what you need to do to negotiate commercial real estate transactions:**

■ Write down your goals that you need to accomplish to make the purchase of a particular property worthwhile, such as positive after-tax cash flow of $1,000 a month.

■ Don't be afraid to discuss with a banker or broker how you would structure financing to accomplish that goal. They are service providers, they aren't doing you a favor.

■ Determine the maximum you would be willing or arrange in financing to make the purchase work. Remain open during negotiations to alternatives that you might not have thought of. Again, don't be afraid to run the alternative past your banker and broker.

■ Always start the negotiation process off with several factors in addition to price. You'll want as many issues on the table as possible.

■ Assume that the asking price of most properties is inflated 10% to 20% beyond what the seller reasonably expects to receive. In extremely tight markets this inflation factor may be less, and in weak markets it may be greater. Always start the price offer at about 80-85% of asking price. Don't be embarrassed either. It doesn't hurt to ask and you'll already start the seller thinking low. On occasion when you start very low, you'll detect softening early and it could reveal a reason on their part. ▲

Continued from p. 22

**Planning
and the
Environment**

If the area you are interested in has a planning or land-use department that is separate from the zoning department, then that is your next stop. Many areas have developed master plans for balanced or restricted growth around their communities. It is important that you make officials of this and other regulatory or governmental bodies your allies, not your enemies. Few such officials are anti-development. They want to ensure that the area is developed with an eye toward accomplishing broader goals of managing land use and preserving special natural features of the area such as streams or woods. Knowing these sorts of restrictions going into a proposed purchase of a piece of property can allow you to tailor your plans to fit the broader goals of the community. Showing local officials that you are willing to work with them from the get-go to accomplish these goals also is a good way to get them on your side. Allies like this are invaluable of your proposed purchase becomes the subject of a public hearing, for instance.

Environmental regulations are obviously a prime concern of any investor in raw land. Check with environmental regulators at the local and state level if necessary to see if there are any records of any sort of contamination on the property you are considering buying. Remember, contamination doesn't have to be visible to be a problem, and the property could have changed hands several times in the past when owners were much less sensitive to issues such as contamination and the proper burial or disposal of hazardous wastes. Even innocuous-looking rural fields may have once been a dumping ground for farm wastes such as pesticides, formaldehyde and other widely used products.

Just as importantly, make contact with local, citizen-run environmental and land-use groups. Know what the hot button issues are in your area — fights over condo developments along waterways, or development encroaching on a woodland or nature preserve area, for instance. If these groups don't know you they may naturally think of you as the enemy. Introduce yourself at a meeting, say you are interested in buying property and talk about development ideas. A few zealots may never be won over, but you can at least make a good faith effort to show the majority of members that you are sincere about buying property for environmentally responsible uses. Countless hours and thousands of dollars can be saved if you spend the time and effort up front to scope out the local situation, and become aware of past and present controversies over development. You may decide that the property you are interested in isn't worth the fight that will most likely ensue if you or a buyer wants to develop it.

Once you own a piece of property, there are a few interim steps you can take to generate income while you are holding the land in anticipation of selling or developing it in the future. If surrounding areas are still in agricultural use, the simplest step is to rent out the property to a farmer for cultivation or to use as a pasture for livestock. Only slightly more preparation is needed to use the property as a temporary parking lot for trucks, heavy equipment or the like. Adding a few improvements such as a driveway and asphalt pavement on at least a portion of the lot gives you the possibility of renting out the space as a parking lot or used car or equipment sales lot.

REMOTE CONTROL REAL ESTATE

Most real estate experts advise that you invest in commercial real estate in your immediate area, or at least in cities or areas you regularly visit. The aim is to keep on top of changes in the market for your property, as well as ensure that your investment is being properly maintained and managed if you're not performing either of those functions yourself. Some investors make exceptions to this rule when it comes to investing in Sunbelt properties, certain time shares or offshore real estate. The exceptions are usually justified by noting these are popular investments that often tend to appreciate in value in good economic times and bad, and that compared to other forms of real estate, they are relatively liquid investments if well maintained. That means it is probably easier to get your money out faster from a Florida Gulf Coast condo than a warehouse outside Des Moines.

Sunbelt properties is an admittedly broad category that can cover a multitude of real estate investments across much of the southern tier of states. For our purposes let's assume that these are resort-area properties, usually condominium developments, that attract seasonal renters from the North willing to pay top dollar during the winter months, but are also rented out for as much of the rest of the year as possible at lower rent levels.

Much of the earlier discussion of multi-unit apartment buildings applies to Sunbelt properties as well. Figuring rental income includes the added step of calculating varying rental rates depending on the time of year. Vacancy rates also vary, being lower in the "high" season and treading higher for the rest of the year. Coping with these fluctuations also should alert the potential buyer that management costs are likely to be higher compared to a building with a more stable year-round rental pattern. Exposure to salty sea air can also raise maintenance costs due to rapid corrosion of many metal parts and fixtures, for instance. Insurance costs are also likely to be higher if you buy in an area that's considered a hurricane zone.

If you decide to try and sell your time share while the developer is still placing new units on the market its highly unlikely you will be able to get anything approaching the price you paid for your used unit.

All of the above considerations should underscore the importance of finding a good broker to aid your search for a sunbelt property. Don't be tempted to buy something based on a classified ad in the back of a travel magazine and a long weekend visit. If you deal with a broker locally who is affiliated with a nationwide company, ask him or her to recommend a broker from the same group in the area you are considering. And since you will visit the area at least once before buying, check local papers for real estate listings for names of brokers, or contact the local chamber of commerce or other business group in the area for recommendations.

Time-share vacation properties are an extremely popular form of vacation property ownership. Typically the owner buys a one- or two-week interval at a particular resort comprised of villas or apartments. The interval is either for a specific period of the year, or it is for floating time. In some cases buyers may acquire what's called a lease-hold interest for a specific number of years, as opposed to outright ownership of real estate.

Buyers tend to be sold on the time-share concept in part for the opportunity to return to a specific vacation spot every year, as well as the added enticement that they can swap their time share interval with that of another time share owner at another resort in an area they want to visit. A handful of organizations have sprung up to facilitate time-share swapping, and any reputable resort property you consider making a time share investment in should be associated with one of them.

The trouble with time shares is that they may not be as easy to swap as the resort representative made it sound as he handed you a complimentary pina colada as you sat at poolside. The number of time shares available for swapping in the resort you want to go to may be relatively limited, and your time share may not be as easily swapped as you thought. It is important to shop around for time shares just as you would for any other investment property, purchase prices and annual fees for swapping privileges can vary widely.

Resort promoters are counting on most buyers succumbing to their pitch after the first drink and "free" lunch. It is also important to do some research on the resort developer. How many units is he offering, and how many more areas is he planning to develop for time-share purposes. If you decide to try and sell your time share while the developer is still placing new units on the market its highly unlikely you will be able to get anything approaching the price you paid for your used unit.

An alternative is a do-it-yourself time share. You and a group of friends or associates pool your money and buy a resort property. You then each claim a certain number of weeks out of the year as your time to use the property, depending, for instance, on the amount of your investment or services you might render the group, including record keeping or lining up financing. Such joint ventures can be structured a number of different ways, including a limited or general partnership, for financing and tax reasons. For that reason it's best to hire an experienced real estate tax attorney before attempting such a move.

Offshore investing can be as romantic as commercial real estate gets. Imagine your own property on stilts overlooking a placid blue bay with white-foam breakers tracing the path of the coral reef: a place for a quick snorkeling trip offshore. If you've found a place in an area that is just starting to be frequented by North Americans as a vacation destination, you should be able to buy at a relative bargain price and expect rapid appreciation as others discover the charm of the area. Travel agents specializing in off-beat locations in Central America, for instance, are a good initial contact when it comes to searching out such locales.

It can work, and it has for thousands of Americans who made the leap overseas. But it's not for everybody, and there are several potential pitfalls that investors aren't nearly as likely to encounter stateside. As anyone who has invested in Mexico prior to the roughly 50% devaluation of the peso that began in December 1994 can tell you, currency fluctuations heighten the risk of foreign property investment. Other currency controls implemented by local governments, such as periodic attempts to "fix" the value of the local currency at an official exchange rate, can also greatly complicate doing business in the host country. Some developers in tropical resort areas will buy and sell properties valued in dollars, which eliminates your direct exposure to fluctuating rates of exchange for the local currency, although that will continue to be a problem for maintenance and labor and management expenses on-site.

Currency fluctuations heighten the risk of foreign property investment.

Finding a local insider, usually an attorney or banker, in the area you want to invest is crucial to investing overseas. Local real estate customs and tax laws are likely to be drastically different than those you are familiar dealing with — formal title searches or title insurance may be alien concepts in certain countries — so it is important to be willing to pay for the services of someone who knows the ropes. Ask for references of other North Americans this particular broker has done business with to get added insights into the workings of the local market. Also, check with the embassy or nearest consulate from the country where you want to invest for information on investing, taxes and the treatment of bank accounts held by foreigners. But don't count on an unbiased view, they almost always tend to describe their countries in the most favorable light possible — a commercial attache from a foreign country, after all, is over here to drum up business, not drive it away.

The U.S. embassy in the country's capital, or better yet, a U.S. consulate in the city nearest your proposed investment, can be an excellent source of insider insight on the investment climate. Most travel guides to the country or area you're interested in will carry these addresses. In addition to the official rules for currency transactions and banking and taxes, the local officials from your country are seeing the country from your point of view. They will usually be willing to tell you what it is *really* like to invest in the country, despite what the official regulations may say.

Offshore investment horror stories abound in Central and Latin America. In many instances North Americans bought property, only to have their ownership rights contested in local courts that may be under the control of the local political elite. Even if they are not, judges may be prone to rule in favor of locals against *gringos* who may consider themselves middle class, but are wealthy by local standards. Recently, more than 60 cases were on file with the U.S. embassy in Tegucigalpa, the capital of Honduras, in which Americans claimed to have been defrauded in real estate investments with local sellers.

FINANCING

Banks are the most likely lenders for smaller and first-time investors in commercial real estate, and so they should be your first stop. (For a review of the basics of mortgage loans, refer to the lesson, The profit approach to real estate.) Bankers and other lenders are primarily looking at two financial ratios when considering whether to finance your commercial real estate investment: the loan-to-value ratio and the debt-coverage ratio.

Loan-to-Value Ratio. This the amount of money you borrow expressed as a percentage of the total value of the property. For instance, if you want to buy a $200,000 property and the bank agrees to lend you $150,000 to make the purchase, the loan-to-value ratio is 75%. Looked at from the borrower's point of view, the bank is requiring you to make a down payment of 25% of the purchase price to receive the loan on the property. Most banks in the mid-1990s are requiring commercial real estate buyers to make down payments of 20% to 30% of the proper-ty — roughly twice the amount required prior to the "credit crunch" that rocked the banking and thrift industries in the late 1980s and early 1990s as overbuilding and poor lending prac-tices led to plunging commercial real estate prices across the country.

Debt-coverage ratio. Lenders will require that the projected gross rental income from the com-mercial property you purchase exceed by a certain amount the debt payments you make to them. Banks typically require that the gross rental income equal from 1.15 to 1.25 the debt payments before they will make a loan. In other words, your gross rents may have to be as much as 125% of your mortgage payments for you to qualify for a loan. Lenders build in this "fudge factor" so that if all doesn't go exactly according to plan, and it often doesn't when it comes to investing in commercial real estate, there is a built-in cushion that will allow you to make your mortgage payments. The quality of the property you are buying is a factor in set-ting the debt-coverage ratio as well. A first class property in a prime neighborhood will most likely qualify for the 1.15 end of the debt coverage range.

As mentioned earlier, lenders will also look at the financial health of major tenants in cer-tain commercial real estate properties such as retail strip centers and warehouses. If your anchor tenant's parent company has had its corporate debt downgraded to junk-bond status recently your lender may not be too anxious to fund your purchase of the property. For that matter, you should pre-screen the credit histories of major tenants yourself, there are compa-nies that provide such services, or you can request this sort of information from the seller, so that you don't buy into a situation where your biggest source of rental income is about to go out of business.

The more aggressive the lending institution, the lower the required debt-coverage ratio. A national or regional mortgage banker that is trying to expand its market share in your area may be pricing loans very aggressively, for instance, and come in at the low end of the debt-cover-age scale. All things being equal, take the loan with the lowest required debt-coverage ratio, since that will allow you to borrow more money if necessary to purchase a particular property. As with most things in life, it pays to shop around for real estate financing.

Conventional bank financing doesn't come just in plain vanilla, like fixed or adjustable rate mortgages of from 15 to 30 years that many investors are familiar with from buying and selling their own homes. Some loans, known as *graduated payment mortgages*, may be structured so that for the first five years or so monthly payments are at a lower level, then jump to a higher level for the remainder of the mortgage. The difference between the initial lower rate and the higher rate is added to the loan principal. Other so-called *balloon payment* loans are structured with a fixed monthly payment, usually for five to seven years, followed by a balloon payment due for the balance of the mortgage. That forces the borrower to come up with the funds or, as is typically the case, refinance at the prevailing interest rates. In both cases, the loans are structured to make it easier for the borrower to qualify initially. In return the costs of the loan effectively increase at a future date when, presumably, the borrower will be in a stronger financial position due to an increase in income or the value of the property (asset) he holds, or both.

Beyond Bank Loans

A host of financing alternatives exist in addition to traditional bank financing. Some are used more widely when interest and mortgage rates are high and credit scarce, and others may or may not be available in your state. For this and other reasons, including to help ensure that you're borrowing money at the lowest price for the best possible terms, it's crucial that you get the advice of a good real estate attorney. If he is working frequently with lenders in your area, then he also will be aware of who is being the most aggressive, and may be aware of properties that are on the market, or about to be put on the market, that you should take a look at.

Seller financing. Sellers of real estate often provide financing in one form or another to help a sale go through. This is especially true in times when interest rates are high and credit is tight, although seller financing can be a viable source of credit, especially for speculative purchases of undeveloped land, even when banks are flush with cash and interest rates are low. Banks typically shy away from financing raw land purchases since the property isn't producing any current income.

A variation on the seller financing theme is referred to as a purchase-money mortgage.

A loan from the seller is often referred to as a *contract of sale* or *contract of deed*. The buyer makes an agreed-to down payment, which can often be less than the amount required under most banks' loan-to-value formulas, and then makes regular monthly payments to the seller. The seller retains the title to the property until the loan is paid off. A plus of seller financing is that the parties structure the terms to meet their specific requirements, and there aren't any loan fees, beyond legal fees to cover review of the agreement.

It is vital that the buyer ensure that the contract is written in recordable form and is signed by all parties in the presence of a notary public. It then should be recorded in the county clerk' office or the office of the recorder of deeds, which ever is appropriate for your area. The purpose of recording the contract is so that there is a public record. This protects the buyer's interest in case an unscrupulous seller tries to sell the same property twice, or thrice.

A variation on the seller financing theme is referred to as a *purchase-money mortgage*. Here the seller gives the buyer the deed to the property and takes back a mortgage secured by the property, often times the difference between an agreed-to down payment and the total purchase price. This is also used when the buyer assumes an existing mortgage on the property held by the seller. An advantage to the buyer is that sellers will often accept a smaller down payment than would a bank. An advantage to the seller is that the rate he charges the buyer on the mortgage is almost sure to be greater than the interest he could earn on his money if he placed it in bank CDs or other fixed income investments.

Purchase-money mortgages are also often used as second mortgages to close a transaction, since lenders often won't finance a real estate deal if a second mortgage is involved. A second mortgage is a junior lien on a property behind the first mortgage, and typically carries a higher interest rate and shorter term, reflecting the increased risk of being second in line to try and recover the value of the mortgage in case of a default.

The major advantage to the buyer in a purchase money mortgage is that if the buyer can't make the payments, the seller forecloses and puts the property up for sale. Any amount received at sale beyond the loan value due the seller reverts to the buyer. With a contract of sale, the seller in certain situations has the right to the property free and clear if the buyer defaults. In most states the seller has to give the buyer notice of forfeiture, and the buyer has 60 to 90 days to come up with the balance due.

Another type of second mortgage is called a *wraparound mortgage*. Here, the buyer makes a 10% down payment of $20,000, for example, on a $200,000 property and finances the balance with a note to the seller, which includes the unpaid balance of an existing mortgage of, say, $150,000. Typically the buyer pays the seller the full mortgage payment on the second mortgage, while the seller continues to make payments on the first mortgage. Since the interest rate on the second mortgage is usually higher than on the first, the seller gains on the difference between the two. For the buyer the advantage is once again the ability to make a lower down payment than would be allowed by a bank lender, and to get more favorable interest rates on the loan than would usually be available from a bank.

Another variation on seller financing is for a buyer to give a seller a second mortgage on other real estate owned by the buyer. This money is then used as the down payment, and creates the opportunity to have the balance financed by a bank, since there is no second mortgage on the property being purchased that typically would cause a bank to reject financing the property. It is also possible to go to third parties to raise the funds for a down payment if the seller, for instance, needs cash on the sale and doesn't want to take a second mortgage.

All of these creative financing methods are really the core of how to invest in, and actually make money during, an overdeveloped market. For more information on this, see wealth-building Step 86 beginning on page 31.

> *Another variation on seller financing is for a buyer to give a seller a second mortgage on other real estate owned by the buyer. This creates the opportunity to have the balance financed by a bank.*

Using financing strategies such as this, it is possible to buy income producing properties for "no money down" or little money down, just as in the ads that appear on cable TV for seminars touting real estate as the no-money-down road to wealth. Genuine no-money-down deals are the exception, not the rule, however, requiring among other things a seller who, for whatever reason, is willing to be extremely accommodating toward the buyer's financial needs.

Another type of loan, which typically is in vogue when interest rates are high and traditional real estate financing scarce, is a *participating loan*. As the name implies, this form of a loan gives the lender an interest rate, often set below prevailing rates, and a participation in cash-flow improvement from a property, or an "equity kicker" in the form of a set percentage of the value of the property on a future sale.

Options Options, while not a form of financing per se, are used by buyers to effectively tie up a property for a given time period, usually to give the buyer time to arrange financing. An option is the payment of an amount to the seller in exchange for the right to buy his property within a certain time period at an agreed-to price. For example, you find a warehouse for sale for $500,000 that you are confident is underpriced based on comparable sales in the area and the number of manufacturers building distribution hubs in your region. But you won't be able to secure financing until you sell another property. Instead of walking away, you offer the seller $5,000 for an option to buy the property within six months for the $500,000 asking price. You effectively are willing to bet 1% of the asking price that the property will appreciate in value during the life of the option by

100 Steps to Wealth

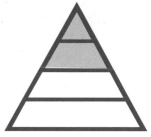

How to Make Money in an Overdeveloped Environment

What: Be able to profit from investing in commercial real estate when the markets you are interested in are overbuilt and prices are weak.

Why: Some of the savviest investors in commercial real estate buy when the markets are at their most depressed as a result of overdevelopment. The profits that can be realized from buying properties at below market rates are multiples of typical profit projections.

Risk: Medium to High. You may buy before markets have bottomed out and be stuck with a property that is depreciating in value while at the same time your tenants want to renegotiate their leases downward. Or the market once it hits bottom may trend sideways before showing any sign of a rebound.

Safety: Low to Medium. The potential for above-average returns are accompanied by the potential for above average risks. One way to try and limit your risks is to wait and determine that your market has stabilized, if it has not already started to rebound, before buying. You'll miss some gain by not buying at the bottom, but you'll also eliminate some of the risk from trying to time the bottom in the market. Commercial real estate markets in much of the country, in fact, appear to have already started to bounce off their early '90s price bottoms, improving the odds that the markets won't move against you.

Liquidity/ flexibility: Low. Markets are at their most illiquid at price extremes. Being willing to step in and buy a property when there are few other buyers is what gives you the negotiating leverage to get a superior price and terms. You may face a similar dearth of buyers if you find that you are forced to sell the property in the near future if the market hasn't started to rebound.

Why Not: There is a real risk that you may lose money in commercial real estate when markets are overdeveloped, or at least that you won't earn a return to justify the risk you are taking on in this market.

Buy/Invest From: Private or corporate sellers.

Background: Commercial real estate tends to go through boom and bust, or overbuilt cycles, on a seven- to 10-year basis. As we've said, markets in most parts of the country appear to be in the first few years of a sustained rebound — whether or not this rebound will end up being called a "boom" is too early to tell. Some of the distressed properties with the best values may have already been snatched up in your area, but it is always worth checking local listings for foreclosure and public and private auction sales. A listing of government sources for foreclosed properties was included in the lesson, The profit approach to real estate. The body that is likely to have the most commercial properties for sale is the Resolution Trust Corporation. Its general number is (800)-RTC-3006. In any case, it is the characteristics of the particular property you buy, not the broader market trend, that will have the biggest impact on the total return on your commercial real estate investment over the next several years.

If you want to get started today here is what you have to do to make money in an overdeveloped market:

- Talk to your broker and banker. Using a broker is especially important for most investors when the market is overdeveloped. The temptation to buy a property at what seems to be a bargain basement price is very strong, you need a broker to give you a sense of perspective on what you might expect to be able to resell the property for, and when. Your banker may have recently foreclosed on a property that could be of interest to you, or know of other bankers in the area with properties that fit the bill.

- Be creative. You will never have more negotiating leverage in commercial real estate than when you are a buyer in an overbuilt market. Insist on a lower-than-specified down payment and seller financing, in which the seller takes back a mortgage on the property and receives payments from you, if it fits your overall financial plan.

- Use your head. When markets are overdeveloped, there is no shortage of properties being offered for sale, often at distressed prices. What's in short supply is the market judgment needed to determine which property is the best investment to fit your goals. ▲

Continued from p. 30
at least as much as the option's price. An added plus is that you didn't pay any management fees or taxes while your option was locking in the appreciation on the property. Even if the property doesn't appreciate in value during the six months, you have only paid an additional 1% (or sometimes 2%) to buy a property that you are confident will appreciate in the future.

Conclusion

Investing in commercial real estate can be a rewarding step toward building your personal wealth. The variety of investment categories, from offices to warehouses and convenience store strip centers, make commercial real estate an asset class that appeals to an especially wide range of investors. The unusual flexibility in financing terms available for real estate, encompassing everything from traditional fixed-rate mortgages offered by a bank to seller financing and tax-deferred "like kind" exchanges of properties, compared to the typical cash purchase of stocks and bonds also can help broaden commercial real estate's appeal.

Successful commercial real estate investing, however, demands that the investor devote a considerable amount of time to researching properties and local, regional and national market trends. If you're not willing to roll up your sleeves and do some serious number crunching and comparisons of income and expense statements for properties before you buy, commercial real estate may not be for you. On the other hand, the fact that commercial real estate isn't included in many financial planners' traditional client portfolios, which tend to focus on paper assets such as stocks, bonds and cash, also suggests that undiscovered values may be found by the astute investor who has done his research. Lastly, there is the sense of pride in owning a real asset that can provide you and your family with both income and the capital appreciation for years to come! ▲

The top of the pyramid: aggressive risk strategies

LESSON 27

The top of the pyramid: aggressive risk strategies

"If you play it totally safe in life, you've decided you don't want to grow anymore."
— ©*Shirley Hufstedler, quoted in All About Success, 1988*

THE VALUE OF PRUDENT SPECULATION

To this point, the information contained in *100 Steps to Wealth* has been devoted largely to helping you learn about the investment vehicles and strategies needed to construct the bottom three levels of a solid wealth-building pyramid. You've learned how to find money to begin investing, how to wisely allocate that money to provide both growth and safety, and how to avoid some of the pitfalls that can undermine even the best of financial plans.

You have also been introduced to a variety of related subjects and peripheral products — covering such topics as banking, insurance, taxes, inflation, entrepreneurism, real estate, currencies and precious metals. This information is essential for anyone who hopes to accumulate — and then preserve — real wealth in the modern global economy.

In the two lessons you've just received, however, we will shift our focus somewhat — turning from the investment basics to the more esoteric tools and techniques you will need to complete the very top of your wealth-building pyramid. This area is reserved exclusively for the most aggressive investment strategies — ones that offer the potential for exceptional returns, but that also carry significant risks. In other words, speculations.

Why Bother To Speculate? Many traditional financial advisers and more conservative investors shun such strategies like the plague. "With the potentially high risks and uncertain prospects for success, why even bother to speculate?" they ask — adding the oft-cited admonition that, in investing, "Slow and steady wins the race."

To a degree, such a cautious stance is legitimate, especially for smaller or beginning investors. If you are working with an asset base of only a few thousand dollars, or don't yet fully grasp the mechanics of the markets, the speculative arena is definitely the wrong place to be. In such cases, one failed venture can wipe out a significant portion of your capital, thus cutting off access to areas far more important to long-term financial success. A severe loss early in your investing career can also seriously undermine your confidence — both in your own analytical abilities and, far more damaging, in the investment process as a whole.

However, for better financed and more experienced investors, we feel many of the expressed concerns about speculation are a bit too all-inclusive — and in fact, somewhat shortsighted. Indeed, for those who have already established a strong, well-diversified financial base, some speculation is not only prudent, it's literally essential to building truly substantial wealth.

That's because successful speculation — the taking of at least some extra risk with a modest portion of your assets in certain calculated situations — is the best (if not the only) means to significantly enhance your overall returns and rapidly increase the pace of your portfolio's growth. To prove this point, let's look at a quick (and admittedly over-simplified) example:

The Power of Successful Speculation

Assume you have a $200,000 investment portfolio (over and above your home equity) that consists of money market funds, stocks, bonds, an international equity fund, a global bond fund and 10 Canadian Maple Leaf gold coins. You've been earning an overall return of 10 percent, which most investors would consider quite good given the fact that the money funds have been yielding just 4.5 percent, and you've had no gains at all on the gold coins.

It's likely the majority of your individual speculative endeavors may result in losses — the key is to cut losses quickly but let profits ride.

However, as good as that performance might be, you would like to increase your overall return to 12 percent in order to speed your wealth-building efforts. But, what do you do? Shifting from the money market funds to stocks would improve your growth potential, but reduce your liquidity and wipe out your safety net. Switching from dividend-paying stocks to growth issues would increase your risk and reduce your income. Exchanging your AA+ bonds for lower-rated issues would increase your income, but also boost your default risk. Cashing in the gold coins and buying something else might generate more income or growth, but you'd lose your inflation protection.

The list of possibilities could go on and on, but all would have both advantages and drawbacks and all would impact your strategic asset allocation — with no guarantee the changes would generate the added return you wanted. Let's face it, it's simply not that easy to boost your overall return 2 percent by merely juggling the basic investment vehicles or trying to pick better individual stocks, bonds or mutual funds.

But, throw a little speculation into the mix and you could readily achieve your goal (although, again, there are no guarantees) while maintaining your present asset mix (and quality levels). Here's an example of how you might go about it:

How Speculative Success Can Boost Portfolio Returns

Without Speculative Investments:

$200,000 Portfolio Earns 10%	= $ 20,000 Return
$200,000 Portfolio Grows To:	$220,000

With Speculative Investments:

$190,000 Portfolio Earns 10%	= $ 19,000 Gain
$10,000 Speculations Make 50%	= $ 5,000 Gain
Total Return on $200,000 Portfolio	= $ 24,000
New Return on $200,000 Portfolio	= 12.0%
$200,000 Portfolio Grows To:	$224,000

Sell 200 shares of a $20 stock, one bond and a few of the money market and mutual fund shares and you should be able to easily raise $10,000 without disturbing the overall integrity of your portfolio. Then apply that $10,000 to no more than two of the speculative strategies you'll learn about in these two lessons. All of these strategies are quite capable of producing returns of 100 percent or more, but you don't even need that much. A 50 percent return on this one small speculative portion will suffice to generate the 2 percent increase you desire on your overall portfolio (assuming you continue to earn the same 10 percent on your other investments) — as demonstrated by the table at left.

Avoid the two biggest threats to speculative success — fear and greed.

We chose an example using a $200,000 portfolio and $10,000 in speculative money for two reasons:

- First, the return numbers are simple to calculate and the impact on portfolio growth is easy to comprehend.

- More importantly, however, we recommend you consider using the strategies discussed in these two lessons *only* after you have established a strong, well-diversified portfolio worth *a minimum of $200,000,* and that you devote only a small portion of your assets — *no more than 5 to 10 percent* — to such speculations.

In addition, we also recommend spreading your speculative money around, *never risking more than half on a single strategy* — and reducing that percentage further as your pool of speculative capital increases over time. For example, if your portfolio value grows to $400,000 and you want to devote $40,000 (10 percent) to aggressive-risk investments, you should plan to make a minimum of five speculative plays, risking no more than $4,000 on any one strategy.

Mitigating the Impact of Failure

If you follow these guidelines, a speculative failure may slightly diminish your overall returns — in our opening example, for instance, losing the entire $10,000 would have cut your 10 percent return to 9.5 percent. However, it won't cause irreparable damage to your portfolio, or destroy your fundamental asset-allocation mix. In addition, a single failure will never prove so disheartening you'll swear off speculation forever — thus forgoing the opportunities such plays offer for enhanced wealth generation.

This second point is extremely important because, as we earlier said, speculation is the best way to improve overall investment returns and speed portfolio growth. However, you must recognize two things right up front:

- First, not all speculations work; if they did, they wouldn't be speculations. In fact, it's likely the majority of your individual speculative endeavors may result in losses — or, at best, only marginal gains. The key is to cut losses quickly but let profits ride.

- Second, the losses on unsuccessful speculative plays tend to be far larger — on a percentage basis, at least — than losses on other failed investments, be they Blue Chip stocks, bonds or mutual funds. Indeed, many of the speculative vehicles that offer the greatest potential for gain also entail the possibility that you might lose your entire investment — or even more (e.g., futures or other securities purchased on margin).

Given those risk factors, a rigid overall limit like that imposed by our "$200,000/10 percent" rules is essential in developing the proper speculative perspective — one that lets you operate with objectivity regarding the potential impact, both positive and negative, that speculation can have on your overall financial plan.

Beating a Speculator's Worst Enemies

In addition, as you progress through the remainder of this lesson and the one that follows, you will learn a number of other guidelines for employing individual speculative vehicles and evaluating the possible outcomes of specific aggressive-risk strategies. These tips will help you realistically assess every speculation you consider, and thereby avoid the two biggest threats to speculative success — fear and greed.

We've already touched on fear — noting how a few early failures will often scare novices out of the speculative arena entirely. That type of fearful reaction is unfortunate, but it's seldom devastating since it really represents only lost opportunities. Far more dangerous is "trade-specific" fear — an unrealistic concern that you will suffer a loss on any given strategy, or that you'll let a small early profit get away. Such fear can lead to "micro-managing" of your speculative plays, something that rarely works — and can wind up costing you a small fortune in trading fees. Even worse, it will likely guarantee that you'll never score any of the really major gains you were speculating for in the first place — simply because you'll bail out in panic each time prices move even slightly against you.

However, the information you'll learn in the pages ahead — including how to use a technique known as "scenario analysis" to determine the possible outcomes of a given speculation — will help you avoid succumbing to such fears. It will also ensure that you never go overboard in the other direction — losing your perspective out of greed.

Greed Is Even More Costly

Greed, you see, probably costs speculators even more money than fear. They run up a quick profit, develop unreasonable expectations about making more, hold on too long — and wind up losing the gains they had in the first place. Or, they use early profits on a winning trade to add to their position, thus raising their overall cost basis, then lose their entire profit — and often more — when prices suddenly reverse by even a modest amount.

Or, worst of all, they run up a string of successful trades, decide they have the market figured out, risk an ever-larger percentage of their assets on speculation — and then lose much more than they can afford when a trade goes sour.

Whatever the exact pattern, the effect of greed in speculation is clear: lost objectivity about the true potential of an investment— usually resulting in lost profits (or outright losses) as well.

Thus, given the negative impact of fear and greed, it is extremely important that you strive to resist both in your own speculative trading activity. And, the best way to do that is to religiously adhere to our overall guidelines — i.e., shunning speculation altogether until you've built a diversified portfolio worth at least $200,000, and then devoting no more than 5 to 10 percent of your assets to a minimum of two different aggressive-risk strategies.

Respecting those limits will ensure that no loss on a single speculation can threaten your overall financial well-being — which should go a long way toward eliminating the fear factor. Likewise, limiting the amount of money you can devote to any one speculation should force you to develop realistic expectations about potential profits, thus damping any fires of greed that might be sparked by early successes.

UNDERSTANDING THE NATURE OF RISK

If you're just getting started in investing and eager to see your portfolio grow, you may think these restrictions on the use of aggressive-risk strategies are overly severe. After all, American investment lore is filled with stories of men and women who risked everything — frequently losing it all (sometimes more than once) — before going on to build great fortunes. Why shouldn't you do the same — and hope for the same results?

We don't dispute that such a path to wealth might be possible — but all the studies of investment theory we've seen indicate it's highly unlikely. The reason most of the financial legends who took this route to great wealth eventually succeeded is that they had some form of specialized knowledge or ability the rest of us don't possess — some unique skill or talent that enabled them to safely convert excessive risk into unlimited opportunity.

Given time, it's possible you might be able to learn a comparable skill or hone a similar talent, but that would still be no guarantee of success with a strategy of full-blown speculation. That's because virtually all the great market wizards also had two other things that are impossible to either teach or learn — nerves of steel and an exceptional amount of luck.

Thus, unless you are absolutely sure you already possess this rare combination of attributes (in which case you probably wouldn't be reading this in the first place), your best course is almost certainly to take a more prudent approach to investing in general — and speculation in particular.

And, that means learning as much as possible about the nature of risk — which is the defining element underlying all speculative investment strategies.

Volatility Determines the Degree of Risk

By now, you're certainly aware of the axiom, "The greater the reward, the greater the risk" — in fact, it's already been cited several times in earlier lessons. But, do you really understand the full implications of the adage?

In simplest terms, it means that, in order for an investment to be capable of making a large move in your favor, it *must* likewise be capable of making *an equally large move against you*. In other words, an investment vehicle capable of producing a large profit in a short period of time must, by nature, be volatile — subject to wide price swings in both up and down directions.

For more conservative investors, so-called "mini" corn contracts — calling for delivery of just 1,000 bushels — are traded on the Mid-America Commodity Exchange.

And, the wider those potential price swings — i.e., the greater the degree of volatility — the greater the risk that you could have to sell the investment at an inopportune time, thus losing some (or even all) of your original principal.

Given this inalterable financial law, you must make some hard decisions about the course you want to take as an investor. If your primary goal in investing is to preserve your principal and build wealth slowly, you must stick to investment strategies involving securities or other assets with low volatility — e.g., Blue Chip or high-dividend stocks, investment-grade bonds, U.S. Treasury securities, money market mutual funds, etc.

On the other hand, if your objective is to make as much profit as possible as quickly as possible, you can venture into strategies employing securities or other investment vehicles with high volatility — e.g., "junk" bonds, "low-cap" stocks, options, and commodity or financial futures. In so doing, however, you must recognize — and emotionally accept — the extreme likelihood that you may, at some point, lose a substantial portion of your original capital in just a short period of time. *Note: Even if you can accept this possibility, you should — as we have said a couple of times already — refrain from engaging in speculation with aggressive-risk strategies until such time as you have built a sizable and well-diversified base portfolio. We also advise committing no more than 5 to 10 percent of your assets to speculative plays at any one time.*

The Primary Measures of Risk

You must also learn how to evaluate the true risk factors in the vehicles you choose to employ in your speculative endeavors — as well as how to use those vehicles in specialized strategies designed to either contain or strictly limit the risk normally associated with such volatile assets. *Note: Four such strategies are detailed in Wealth-Building Step No. 88, "The Four Best High-Yield, Limited-Risk Commodity Trades," which begins on page 8.*

There are two commonly used quantitative measures of investment risk. They are the "standard deviation," and the "beta." (A third measure, the "semi-variance," gauges only downside variations from an investment's expected return. This would seem to be an appealing means to evaluate risk, but the semi-variance has confusing mathematical properties that actually make it less effective as a risk indicator.)

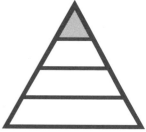

STEP 87

The Four Best High-Yield, Limited-Risk Commodity Trades

What: Sharpen your speculative skills with four potentially high-yielding, contained-risk commodity trades.

Why: Commodity-related trades, while offering the potential for enormous returns, are notorious for their volatility, which can produce equally large losses. Thus, until you develop a sizable asset base and a greater familiarity with the commodity markets, it's best to restrict your trading activities to situations or strategies with features that act to contain — or even limit — potential losses.

Risk: High. Even though these strategies have loss-containment features, all commodity-related plays must be considered high risk because of the volatility of the markets involved.

Safety: Medium to high. These strategies employ well-known and widely used vehicles listed on recognized exchanges. Thus, there is little chance of losses due to defaults or technical problems.

Liquidity: High. Each of the vehicles used in these strategies represent popular underlying commodities with large trading volumes. Thus, you should be able to easily buy and sell whenever you want at prices close to those you desire.

Why not: Commodity speculation is inherently dangerous, with fast-moving markets and the possibility of large losses. As a result, these markets are not suitable for small or beginning investors, nor for larger or more experienced investors with a low emotional tolerance for risk (i.e., if concern over possible trading losses keeps you awake at night, you shouldn't trade commodities regardless of how much money or experience you have). Unless you have a portfolio worth a minimum of $200,000 (exclusive of the equity in your home), you should not do these trades. And, even if you do, you should limit the amount of money you devote to the strategies to 10 percent of your total assets — and split your funds among two or more speculative plays.

Buy/Invest from: Any discount or full-service futures broker — or the futures division of any of the leading stock brokerage firms. *Note: You must have a separate account to trade futures and options on futures; these strategies cannot be done through your regular stockbroker.*

Background: For the sake of clarity, the basis for each of the four strategies featured in this Step will be included in the trading descriptions that follow.

If you want to get started today, here's what you need to do to begin employing these four potentially high-yielding, contained-risk commodity strategies...

Strategy No. 1 — The Seasonal Corn Speculation: Corn, being an essential worldwide food product, is one of the most popular and actively traded commodities. In addition, the leading corn futures contract, which is listed on the Chicago Board of Trade, is fairly small in size, calling for delivery of just 5,000 bushels. These factors make it an ideal vehicle for the small retail speculator. *Note: For more conservative investors, so-called "mini" corn contracts — calling for delivery of just 1,000 bushels — are traded on the Mid-America Commodity Exchange. However, there is less liquidity on the mini contracts, so you may have difficulty executing trades at the prices you want if you use the smaller futures.*

Corn also has one other feature that makes it perfect for those seeking commodity trades with limited or contained risk: At certain times of the year, prices for futures contracts representing corn that will be produced by the current year's crop generally follow historically consistent price patterns dictated by weather conditions in the major U.S. corn-growing regions.

To be more specific, if extreme weather conditions — perhaps a drought, a late freeze, widespread hail or even flooding from too much rain (as was the case in 1993) — delay planting or damage the growing crop, the prices of futures contracts related to the new crop will rise sharply in price. In addition, the risk tends to be limited because, even if no weather problems develop, the possibility that they might — at any time prior to the harvest — tends to provide a support level for prices.

The best way to take advantage of this seasonal speculation is to purchase the December CBT futures contract in the month of April — just at the start of the normal corn-planting period. If any weather-related problems develop before late July (when the corn plants are generally mature enough to resist further damage), the price of the December future should rise, producing a nice — and sometimes spectacular — profit. For example, in 1988, during the worst drought in more than a decade, the December future rose by $1.40 per bushel from mid-April through late July — representing a possible profit of $7,000 per contract.

As already noted, the fear of bad weather sets a support level for prices, which should help to limit your risk on this play. However, we would also apply two other risk-containment rules:

- Do not pay more than $2.50 per bushel for the December future. Usually, if the price is that high at that time of the year, it means some other factor, such as extremely strong export demand or sharply reduced planting plans by farmers, has already influenced the market — meaning the normal seasonal pattern is less likely to repeat itself. In addition, corn rarely falls below $2.00 per bushel (its low during the past five years has been about $2.10), so the closer you can enter to that price, the less likely your chance of suffering a large loss.

  Note: As you learned in the lesson "Commodity and financial futures," when we say you "pay" $2.50 per bushel for a corn futures contract, we do not mean that you have to put up the full value — in this case $2.50 x 5,000 bushels, or $12,500. As with all futures contracts, corn futures are purchased "on margin" — meaning you put up only a small deposit of "earnest money," recently around $1,200 for corn, as a guarantee that you will live up to the terms specified in the contract. The size of this deposit is set by the Chicago Board of Trade, based on the recent volatility of the market, and may be adjusted at any time.

- Impose a loss limit of $800 per contract by placing a "stop-loss" order at a level 16 cents per bushel below your entry price ($0.16 x 5,000 bushels = $800). For example, if you buy the December future at $2.32 per bushel, place a stop order at $2.16. (Note: When you use a stop-loss order, there is no guarantee that you will actually get the specified price. However, in an active market such as corn, you'll usually get a fill within a penny of your stop price — meaning your maximum loss would rise to $850, plus commissions. In extreme cases, the losses could be larger.)

  Unless prices have already risen sharply and the rally appears likely to continue based on widespread crop failures, plan to close your position by Aug. 1 as the final harvest prospects are fairly well established by that point. In the interim, protect your profits by raising your stop price by 8 cents per bushel for each 10-cent rise in the price of the

December future. (As prices rise, the market tends to become more volatile, so you need to allow a little more downside room to avoid being stopped out on a temporary pullback.) However, as you near your planned exit date — say, during the last two weeks of July — tighten the stop up to a level about 10 cents below the current futures price. That way, you shouldn't normally give back more than $500 of your profits.

Note: A potentially lower-cost and lower-risk way to make this seasonal play is to buy a "call option" on the corn. As explained in the lesson, "Lots of options with options," a call gives you the right to buy the underlying security — in this case, a corn futures contract — at a set price for a set period of time. The implied volatility of corn options is often very low, particularly at the start of the planting season, meaning an at-the-money call can sometimes be purchased for 10 to 15 cents per bushel — which would give you both a lower potential loss and a higher potential percentage return than the direct purchase of the futures contract. However, options also have certain drawbacks compared to futures — such as the loss of your entire purchase premium should prices fall slightly or even remain stable — so be sure to review the basics of options in the earlier lesson before trying this alternative.

Strategy No. 2 — The Platinum/Gold Spread: Even more popular than corn among futures traders are the leading metals — gold, silver, platinum, copper and palladium. Unfortunately, with the exception of copper — which is primarily an industrial commodity used heavily in the construction industry — there are no proven seasonal patterns you can take advantage of in trading metals. However, there are established "inter-commodity" relationships that can, at times, be the basis for reasonably limited-risk futures speculations. The platinum/gold spread is such a strategy.

Gold, silver and platinum are so-called precious metals, meaning they are valued not only for their actual uses as commodities, but also for their beauty and for their roles as "havens" in times of political turmoil, economic uncertainty or inflation. As such, their prices tend to move in the same direction, either all rising at the same time or all falling at the same time. However, they hardly ever move by comparable amounts. Savvy speculators — those who are aware of the historical price relationships — can take advantage of this fact by playing one metal against another. This approach offers substantial profit potential, but significantly lowers the risk associated with an outright metal futures purchase.

For example, in the period since 1980, platinum and gold have traced out essentially the same directional patterns, but platinum has shown more volatility than gold — rising farther than the yellow metal during rallies and falling more during market declines. Throughout that period, however, platinum has nearly always traded at a higher price than gold. In fact, there were only two periods — from mid-1982 through mid-1983 and during the middle eight months of 1985 — when gold prices were higher than platinum prices for any extended length of time. (Both of those periods followed major metals market declines in which platinum prices fell farther and faster than gold prices.) During the rest of the 15-year period, platinum prices were never lower than gold prices for more than a couple of weeks at a time.

Given that historic pattern, our recommendation is to buy platinum futures and sell gold futures any time the price of platinum falls to a level $5 an ounce or less above the gold price, based on contracts with the same delivery month. For example, if October gold futures were trading at $380 per ounce, you would initiate a trade if October platinum futures fell to a price of $385 an ounce or less. Your goal following entry is to have the spread widen — i.e., for the price of platinum to move to a larger premium over the price of gold.

Step 87: *The Four Best High-Yield, Limited-Risk Commodity Trades*

There are really only four key rules for this spread trade:

- As just stated, enter only when platinum futures prices are $5 an ounce or less above gold futures prices.

- Always use matching futures — i.e., those having the same delivery months. This means you will always use either the April or October futures, the only two sets of matching contracts.

- Always buy two platinum futures contracts and sell one gold futures contract short. This is necessary to establish a balanced spread since platinum trades on the NYMEX division of the New York Mercantile Exchange in 50-ounce contract sizes, while gold trades on the New York Merc's COMEX division in 100-ounce contracts.

- Always place your order as a "spread order" rather than specifying prices for the individual contracts involved. For example, say, "I want to buy two NYMEX platinum contracts and sell one COMEX gold contract at a spread of $5 or less, favor platinum" — not "I want to buy two platinum contracts at $385 an ounce and sell one gold contract at $380 per ounce." The latter order is too restrictive and may prevent you from getting an orderly execution, whereas the former allows the broker to fill your order at any set of prices, so long as they are no more than $5 apart.

The profit potential in this strategy is enormous since platinum has traded as much as $150 an ounce higher than gold on numerous occasions (it was about $35 higher in August 1995). However, the risk has historically been limited to around $25 an ounce since gold has rarely risen to a price more than $20 higher than platinum (it's happened only four times in the past 15 years — twice during the 1982-83 period and twice for brief periods in 1985). That means your potential gain on the entire strategy could be as high as $14,500 ($150 - $5 = $145 x 100 ounces = $14,500), while your potential loss should be $2,500 or less ($25 x 100 ounces = $2,500).

You will normally get an entry opportunity for this spread at a time when metals prices have suffered a sharp decline, and you'll score your largest gains when the metals are rallying strongly. Stable or trading-range markets — such as the one in the first half of 1995 — are unlikely to produce chances for entry. Once you enter a platinum/gold spread, you should normally plan to hold it until the first notice day for the platinum futures contracts — or until metals prices begin to move downward and the spread starts to narrow. (Note: If you need a refresher on the workings of futures contracts and the definition of such terms as "first notice day," refer back to the lesson, "Commodity and financial futures.")

If metals prices are still in a strong upward trend when it comes time to close your initial position, you may want to "roll over" your spread to the next set of matching futures contracts — even if the spread is no longer within the $5-an-ounce entry limit. For instance, if you were holding a profitable April 1996 spread and metals prices were still rising in late March 1996, you could close your April positions and simultaneously open a new October 1996 spread in order to keep riding the rally. This will have the effect of locking in much of your initial profit, while allowing you to continue riding the rally to the maximum possible profit. For example, a speculator who entered the April platinum/gold spread in late December 1985 and rolled over three times during the ensuing two-year metals rally would have seen the spread widen from just $4.75 to $157.20 — a gain of $152.45 an ounce, or $15,245 per spread (less commissions, of course).

Note: This can be a fairly volatile spread, with $20-an-ounce swings not uncommon. However, the initial margin requirement for the trade is fairly high — typically $5,000 to $7,500 — which should give you room to weather these swings without having to worry about a "margin call." Still, you should always watch your trades closely as it is not possible to enter an official stop-loss order on a metals spread position.

Strategy No. 3 — The Silver Call Speculation: As we just explained, the metals can be highly volatile because their prices respond to fears of economic uncertainty and political turmoil as well as normal industrial-based supply/demand factors. And, silver is the most volatile of all, with futures prices capable of spiking or sagging by $1 an ounce or more in a very short period. On the standard 5,000-ounce COMEX silver futures contract, this equates to a potential profit — or loss — of $5,000 or more.

Potential losses of that size make silver futures trades unsuitable speculative vehicles for most typical investors. However, there is a safer alternative — the silver call speculation. This maneuver involves watching for a sizable pullback — at least 50 cents an ounce — in the price of silver futures, and then buying a silver call option.

Silver call options, which also trade on the COMEX division of the New York Mercantile Exchange, give the holder the right to purchase one COMEX silver futures contract at a set price (the "strike" price) for a set period of time (until the expiration date). Thus, a July $4.50 silver call would give you the right to purchase one July COMEX silver futures contract at a price of $4.50 per ounce any time prior to the second Friday of June.

Note: Although silver options are identified according to the deliver month of the underlying futures contract, they actually expire on the second Friday of the prior month — e.g., the March options would expire on the second Friday of February.

Our recommended entry conditions for this speculation are quite simple:

- Buy a silver call only after silver futures prices have fallen sharply — at least 50 cents per ounce — and the implied volatility of silver options is low.

- Buy the nearest out-of-the-money call (i.e., the one with the strike price closest to, but still above, the current silver futures price) that still has at least three months remaining prior to expiration.

- Don't pay more than $800 — or 16 cents per ounce — plus commissions (which will usually run around $35) for each option you buy.

If you follow these entry guidelines, you will capture a large portion of the profit generated by any sharp spike in the price of silver, but your loss will be strictly limited to the premium you initially pay for the option. For example, if silver prices do indeed move up by more than a dollar an ounce, your gain could be as much as $4,200 (the $5,000 move in the silver future, minus the $800 premium you paid) — while your loss will never exceed the original $800 you put up to purchase the option. (Note: We say "as much as $4,200" because you must also deduct the amount by which the call you buy is out of the money.)

A perfect example of how this speculation works played out in the spring of 1995. On March 6, 1995, the July silver future was trading at $4.556 per ounce, having fallen from well above $5.00 per ounce in late December 1994. The July $4.75 silver call (the nearest out-of-the-money call with at least three months of life remaining) was priced at 13.2 cents per ounce, or $660. Thus, the potential gain on this play, assuming a $1 rise in silver prices, was $3,370 ($5.556 - $4.75 - $0.132 = $0.674 x 5,000 = $3,370).

What actually happened? Well, the spike did indeed come as the Fed's failure to hike interest rates and the concern over fighting in Bosnia conspired to spark a metals rally. By April 24, 1995, the price of the July silver future had jumped almost $1.20 an ounce (to $5.731) and the price of the July $4.75 call (now deep in the money) had soared to 99.2 cents per ounce. Had you chosen to sell then, your profit would have been 86 cents per ounce, or $4,300 ($0.992 - $0.132) x 5,000 = $0.86 x 5,000 = $4,300), less commissions.

The main problem with this speculation is deciding when to exit. Unless the metals rally is still going on when your calls expire, forcing you to cash in your gains, you will have to "guess" — based on your analysis of the market or the silver price charts — when to sell your call. The simplest approach is to set a target profit — say, $4,000 — and close out when it is reached, or just prior to expiration, whichever happens first.

If you're more conservative, you can set a lower target, but you should probably go for a gain of at least $2,500. That's because this speculation will probably work only one out of every three tries, so you need at least a 3-to-1 risk/reward ratio in order to generate an overall profit.

Warning: This is indeed a pure speculation, meaning that if silver prices fall or remain stable, you will probably forfeit the full premium you paid for the call — or, at best, have to sell it prior to expiration at a sizable loss.

Strategy No. 4 — The New Crop/Old Crop Wheat Spread: In strategy No. 1, using corn, we introduced you to grain futures and explained the weather-related factors that affect prices during the period between the planting of the crop and its harvest. The same factors also play a role in the pricing of wheat futures, and the weather-related crop risks create the opportunity for a potentially profitable "intra-commodity" spread strategy that play the contracts calling for delivery of the "new crop" wheat against the contracts calling for delivery of "old crop" wheat.

To clarify, wheat futures that call for delivery in May of each year must be fulfilled using wheat from the previous fall's harvest — the so-called "old crop." That means the quality and quantity of the wheat available for delivery is already widely known, and that futures prices reflect those factors. By contrast, wheat futures that call for delivery in July of each year will typically be fulfilled partly or entirely using wheat from the just-completed spring harvest — the "new crop." Thus, the condition and size of that new spring crop will be in doubt throughout much of the winter (planting) and spring (growing) seasons.

As such, the price could be subject to sharp spikes if weather conditions or other problems develop that might hurt the crop.

The best way to take advantage of this situation is to buy the new-crop July Chicago Board of Trade wheat futures contract in November of the prior year, and simultaneously sell the old-crop May CBT futures contract. *Note: This trade can also be done with the smaller, 1,000-bushel Mid-America Commodity Exchange wheat futures, although the lower trading volume may affect your ability to position the spread at the prices you want.*

Step 87: *The Four Best High-Yield, Limited-Risk Commodity Trades*

Based on the historical price charts, we recommend that you:

- Buy the July (new crop) CBT wheat future and sell the May (old crop) CBT wheat future at a spread of "minus 50 cents" a bushel — meaning the May future is priced 50 cents per bushel higher than the July contract.

- Look to close your position — selling the July future and buying back the short May future — in April at a spread of "plus 30 cents" a bushel (i.e., the July future is priced 30 cents a bushel higher than the May future).

- Use actual spread orders — rather than specifying prices for the individual contracts — to both open and close your position.

What you are hoping for are weather problems or reduced planting intentions that will result in a smaller projected spring crop — which should drive up the price of the July future while leaving the May future's price essentially unchanged. Historically, when this has happened the spread has moved from around -50 cents per bushel to above +30 cents a bushel. This 80-cent swing on the 5,000-bushel CBT contracts represents a potential gain of $4,000 per spread ($0.80 x 5,000 = $4,000).

The risk factor should be considerably smaller, coming into play under two different sets of circumstances. First, if nothing bad happens, prices for both contracts will remain in a narrow range. You'll then suffer a modest loss — say, 10 to 15 cents a bushel — because the risk premium built into the early July price will bleed away as the growing season progresses uneventfully. Second, if something really bad happens, raising fears of a major wheat shortage, the prices of all wheat futures — including the old-crop May contracts — will skyrocket. You could then score either a small profit or a modest loss, depending on how the price relationships line up after the rally. However, a large profit will be unlikely since the broad market concern will have overwhelmed the normal seasonal considerations.

As noted earlier, your goal should be to exit sometime in April at a spread of +30 cents, favor July. However, you can close out earlier if your $4,000 target is reached, or if you are more conservative and wish to shoot for a smaller gain. We would advise, however, that you look for a gain of at least $2,500 (50 cents a bushel) as this trade won't work every year — meaning you need to maximize your profits when it does. ▲

Continued from p. 7

The "standard deviation" — This is the most widely used method of evaluating risk. It involves calculating the average return of an investment over an extended period, based on a series of independent observations of price movement for specified time periods (ranging from a single day's activity to a full year of trading, depending on the holding period in which you are interested).

Once that average is obtained, the actual return for each of the individual time periods is subtracted from the expected average return to determine the deviation for that single trading period. The deviations in return for the single trading periods — both positive (gains) and negative (losses) — are then squared, then totaled, and the sum is divided by the number of observations. The result is the standard deviation for that particular investment over the specific time period being measured.

27-14   **100 STEPS TO WEALTH VOL. 3**

Note: The actual mathematical formula for determining the standard deviation of an investment is relatively complex, so we won't present it here. If you are interested, however, any good book on investment finance will feature it, along with a thorough explanation, so check with your local library. From a practical standpoint, you shouldn't have to actually calculate the standard deviation on your own. Most major brokerage firms have already calculated the standard deviations for the leading types of investment vehicles and can give them to you on request. And, if they don't have it for a particular vehicle, their computer can calculate it readily enough since most financial software has the formula built in.

What the Standard Deviation Tells You

Innumerable theoretical studies have shown that, under normal conditions, an investment will trade within the range of its standard deviation roughly two-thirds of the time, and within a range of two standard deviations about 95 percent of the time.

For example, if a given stock had an annual average return of 9.0 percent (its "expected" return for one year) and a standard deviation of 4.9 percent, then it would be statistically likely to produce an actual annual return of between 4.1 percent and 13.9 percent (the expected 9 percent return, plus or minus the 4.9 percent deviation) 66 percent of the time. In addition, it would be statistically apt to produce an actual annual return of between -0.8 percent and 18.8 percent (the expected 9 percent return, plus or minus double the 4.9 percent deviation) approximately 95 percent of the time. Only 5 percent of the time would it be expected to produce a return of less than -0.8 percent or greater than +18.8 percent.

Most major brokerage firms have already calculated the standard deviations for the leading types of investment vehicles and can give them to you

Thus, while this particular stock would be considered fairly volatile — with returns expected to vary by as much as 9.8 percent roughly two-thirds of the time — the actual chances of suffering a loss greater than 0.8 percent would be less than 5 percent in any given year. Not exactly suitable for widows and orphans, but not highly speculative either.

By contrast, a silver futures contract might have an expected monthly return of 3.5 percent with a standard deviation of 5.7 percent, meaning it would have a 5 percent chance of posting a monthly loss greater than -7.9 percent or a monthly gain of more than +14.9 percent. That would represent both extreme volatility and a high probability of suffering an actual capital loss — the benchmarks of a speculative investment vehicle.

The "beta" — This popular indicator — widely used with bonds, stocks and mutual funds — measures the degree to which an investment fluctuates relative to a benchmark index. For example, betas for most individual stocks are calculated relative to the S&P 500 Stock Index.

A high-beta security (one with a beta greater than 1.00) tends to be more volatile than the related market index — i.e., it rises more than its benchmark average when the market rallies, and it falls more when the market declines. Likewise, a low-beta security (one with a beta of less than 1.00) is usually less volatile than the index, gaining a smaller percentage in rallies and falling by less in market slumps.

Unfortunately, there are no widely recognized market indexes that can be appropriately compared to many of the more common speculative vehicles — including low-priced stocks, commodity futures and options on futures. Thus, beta is of only limited use in evaluating the true risk of most speculations.

However, there are numerous ways aggressive investors can offset the lack of risk-evaluation tools when speculating — and we'll cover the best of those methods next.

DISCIPLINE AND KNOWLEDGE — VITAL RISK-CONTROL TOOLS

No one — no matter how smart, how well-trained, how unemotional they are, or how much money they have to work with — can eliminate the risk from every investment. In fact, the only thing we can absolutely guarantee you in this course is that, if you invest, you *will* — sooner or later — have a losing trade. And, if you make the move into aggressive-risk investing, the odds are it will be sooner rather than later.

However, there are a variety of things you can do to control or fully limit your risks — even when making the most speculative of plays. The two most important are:

- Develop a strong level of discipline, and rigidly stick to it in all your speculative activities. Know what you expect from every trade, what you're willing to accept and what your loss limits are — before you ever place your orders.

- Work constantly to improve your knowledge of the markets in which you participate and the mechanics of the vehicles you use, as well as the fundamentals that underlie the situations from which you are trying to profit.

What follows is a brief discussion of 10 specific actions you can take to both improve your investing discipline and increase your knowledge of the areas in which you'll be dealing. Follow these guidelines, and you should easily be able to contain your risks to a degree that your speculative activities will never impair the safety, income or growth potential of your overall wealth-building portfolio.

Start With Our Overall Guidelines

1. Limit Your Speculative Activity — The very first thing you should do when you start to contemplate aggressive-risk investing is decide how much you can comfortably afford to lose. This may seem like a really negative outlook with which to begin, but it is essential. Otherwise, if your first few attempts go sour, you may not recognize that it's time to quit — at least until you can rebuild your capital base from other sources and also evaluate what you might have done wrong. People who fail to set overall loss limits are at risk of falling victim to "gambler's ruin" — betting more and more money on the assumption they are eventually bound to win and recover their losses. That does sometimes happen — but you're more likely to go broke first!

Having said that, we should now emphasize that, just because you set an overall loss limit, it doesn't mean you actually have to lose that much — or anything at all, for that matter. If you follow the other risk-containment guidelines you're about to learn, and employ controlled-risk strategies like those featured in Wealth-Building Steps No. 88 and 89, there's no reason you can't start off as a winner. The overall loss limit is just a fundamental safety measure — much like the fire insurance on your house.

If your portfolio is worth a total of:	You can devote this much to speculation:
$200,000	$10,000 to $20,000
$300,000	$15,000 to $30,000
$400,000	$20,000 to $40,000
$500,000	$25,000 to $50,000
$500,000-plus	$50,000 maximum*

Given the risk-containment guidelines for individual speculative strategies found in this lesson, this $50,000 limit is probably sufficient for anyone. Otherwise, you'll have to start looking for lower-quality trades just to keep all your money in play.

As we've said several times before, we feel a suitable allocation to high-risk speculations is 5 to 10 percent of your portfolio's total value. And, we recommend against even starting the speculative game until your portfolio has grown to at least $200,000 — not including the equity in your primary home. The table at left provides a guide regarding how much to devote to speculation.

2. Know Your Trades — Before you do any kind of speculative trade, take the time to learn about it. Study the fundamentals, review the mechanics of the vehicles, make sure you understand why it's likely to work —

and why it may not. You may even want to practice a strategy — doing a trade on paper — before you actually put your money on the line.

Study the Fundamentals Involved When considering commodity or financial futures trades, be sure that you understand the key characteristics of the underlying asset — whether it is Treasury bonds, currencies or corn. Learn to recognize key technical and fundamental details, such as:

- Whether the commodity is trading near life-of-contract or historic lows.

- Whether it's trading just above government support levels.

- Whether it's at historic (and probably unsustainable) highs.

- If it's out of line with important benchmark ratios (such as the gold/silver ratio, the gold/oil ratio, corn/hogs ratio, etc.) or other historic market relationships.

- Whether it's at a critical two-way stage — e.g., soybeans at planting time, when weather can produce big rallies or sharp declines (making strategies such as straddles attractive).

- Whether important government or regulatory reports or events are pending that might impact prices (e.g., trade talks often result in major shifts in currency trends — once again creating opportunities for two-way trades such as straddles).

You may also want to observe or chart the trading pattern of a commodity, financial future or stock over a couple of seasons or a couple of years before actually trading it. At the very least, you should look at and evaluate a chart prepared by one of the charting services to see if you can recognize any key patterns. This will help you develop the perspective needed to make accurate risk/reward assessments (which we'll discuss later in Point No. 8).

3. Start Small — Restrict your first high-risk trades to single futures positions, less-volatile commodities (such as corn), smaller full-size contracts (such as oats), or the "mini" contracts (usually one-fifth to one-third the regular size) available on certain contracts (e.g., gold, silver, soybeans). Avoid the large contracts and/or super volatile commodities (such as copper, soybeans and stock index futures). Other alternatives for beginning speculators include contained-risk futures spread strategies, limited-risk option contracts, small-dollar-risk option combination strategies or small-capitalization stocks.

Don't Over-Extend Yourself **4. Don't Over-Extend Yourself** — Even if you have just $5,000 to $10,000, you should plan to split your speculative money among several trades — but don't try to do them all at the same time. When you're just getting started, limit yourself to one or two positions at a time — following the news on two markets will be more than enough to keep you busy.

In addition, don't over-commit your capital. As a general rule, you should have $3 in reserve for every $1 committed to a position (either as a margin deposit or in outright cost). The broker should keep the excess cash in a money market account for you (if not, consider another brokerage firm). When you close a trade, factor in the gain or loss to maintain the $3-to-$1 reserve ratio on your next trade. This will keep you from taking positions that are "too expensive" for accounts the size of yours.

5. Limit the Risk *Within* Each Position You Take — Avoid positions — such as the outright purchase or short sale of futures or the naked sale of options — that carry unlimited risk. Instead, focus on options (which have limited risk as set by the premium you pay) or option spreads (which have both limited risk and maximum profits); limited-risk combination strategies involving both options and futures; or futures or futures spreads whose volatility and historical records imply contained risk levels.

If you do trade futures alone, use stop-loss orders. However, make sure there is a technical or fundamental reason for positioning the stop where you do; don't just arbitrarily place it at a level that represents a specific dollar loss. If putting the stop where it should go would translate into too large a loss for comfort then you shouldn't be doing that trade in the first place.

*Set a maximum loss
on every position —
and stick with it*

And, remember, there's no guarantee you'll get the price specified in your stop order. In a market collapse, your order might get filled at a price several hundred dollars below what you expected.

6. If You're Not Absolutely Sure, Take a Pass — You don't have to be "in the market" all the time. Have the patience to wait for a good opportunity — and then don't enter the position until it "feels just right." If you have any doubts, don't do the trade.

*Note: Although a well-structured asset-allocation program should normally contain some securities in **every** asset class, maintaining a "zero" position in the aggressive high-risk category is quite acceptable much of the time. Choosing not to make a speculative play is just as much an asset-allocation decision as making one — especially if no good opportunities are available.*

7. Set a Maximum Loss on Every Position — and Stick With It — When establishing a new position, the first thing you have to do is set a loss limit for the individual play. This could be the premium on an option purchase, the maximum possible loss for an option spread or futures/option combination, or a pre-set dollar amount for an outright futures position or spread.

For example, if you were trading a corn futures contract, you might set a loss limit of $700 — or 14 cents per bushel on the 5,000-bushel contract. Then, if that level were hit, you would sell immediately. Better yet, use a stop-loss order as discussed in Point No. 5. Automatic controls often make for better discipline than manual ones, but only if they make good market sense.

Sticking with your loss limit is just as important. To be a successful speculator, you must be able to take losses without hesitation. Never "hang on" waiting for a reversal; when your loss limit is hit, get out! Likewise, never add to a losing position; opening added positions may "average down" the purchase price, but it will also expand your risk — probably well beyond your limit. As noted earlier, taking speculative losses is inevitable — and if you find you are psychologically unable to do so, then speculation is not for you!

If you develop the discipline to keep your losses small, you will also remove some of the pressure to be right on every trade. With small losses and large profits, you can be wrong well more than half the time — and still make money!

Note: If you have real difficulty sticking to your loss limits, revert back to the types of limited- or contained-risk strategies discussed in Point No. 5. Three such plays are explained in detail in Wealth-Building Step 89, "The Three Best Highly Favorable Option Spreads," which begins on page 19.

8. Look for Trades With Positive Reward/Risk Ratios — Even the most flagrant speculation should have a positive reward-to-risk ratio. In other words, the expected profit should always exceed the possible loss — otherwise it's not worth doing.

With some plays, such as option spreads, the reward/risk ratio is easy to determine since both maximum profit and maximum loss are set by the opening prices. With other strategies, like outright futures or option purchases, accurately assessing the reward/risk ratio may be more difficult. However, there are cues you can look to for help. For instance, if a commodity is trading near its historic or life-of-contract lows, it could represent a favorable — and easily quantifiable — opportunity.

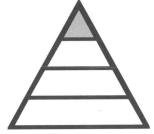

100 Steps to Wealth

The Three Best Highly Favorable Option Spreads

What: Try out the high-reward, limited-risk world of options trading using three of the most favorable option spread strategies.

Why: The outright purchase of options is generally considered to be an "all-or-nothing" speculation, meaning you're likely to lose your entire investment. However, by creating option spreads and other combination positions, you can more precisely define your potential profits and losses, as well as create positions capable of producing smaller, more consistent gains.

Risk: Medium to high. Although these strategies are more conservative than outright option purchases or short sales, they must still be considered to have above-average risks because of the volatility of the underlying markets.

Safety: Medium to high. These strategies employ widely used and standardized options listed on major exchanges, so there is little chance of losses due to defaults or technical problems.

Liquidity: High. All of the options used in these plays are extremely popular and actively traded.

Why not: Because the options involved in these trades call for delivery of underlying futures contracts, they are subject to the same volatility-related risk factors as the futures themselves. In addition, options have other unique risk features — such as the erosion of the "time value" contained in every option purchase premium — that make these strategies dangerous for novice or undercapitalized speculators. As such, you should also refrain from considering these plays until you have a well-diversified portfolio worth at least $200,000 — and, even then, devote no more than 5 to 10 percent of your assets to all your speculative endeavors.

Buy/Invest from: Any discount or full-service futures broker, or any major stock brokerage firm with its own futures division. These trades do require a separate trading account; they cannot be done through your regular stock brokerage account.

Background: For the sake of clarity, the basis for each of the four strategies featured in this Step will be included in the trading descriptions that follow.

If you want to get started today, here's what you need to do to begin using the three best highly favorable option spreads...

Spread No. 1 — The Bullish or Bearish T-Bond Option Spread: As any student of the economy (or anyone with an adjustable-rate mortgage) knows, interest rates tend to move in prolonged trends — either rising steadily for long periods or moving downward for months (or even years) on end. And, prices of long-term Treasury bond futures generally follow the same pattern (though they move inversely with interest rates). This trending tendency makes options on T-bond futures ideal vehicles for doing either bullish (using calls) or bearish (using puts) spreads.

The most popular form of bull or bear option spread — whether on T-bonds, other futures or even stocks — involves buying the in-the-money option with a strike price closest to the actual price of the underlying security and simultaneously selling an out-of-the-money option of the same type and expiration date. The choice of strike prices for the option you sell depends on the frequency of strike prices available, but in most cases involving options on futures you want two strike prices between the option you buy and the option you sell.

For example, if June T-bond futures were trading at 104-18/32nds and you expected bond prices to rise (meaning you thought interest rates would fall), you would buy the June 104 T-bond call option (the nearest in-the-money call) and simultaneously sell the June 106 T-bond call (the out-of-the-money call of the same type, but two strike prices higher).

Your risk in this speculative spread would be your net debit on the two transactions — i.e., the premium you paid for the call you bought, minus the premium you received for the call you sold (plus commissions, of course). And, your maximum potential reward on the play would be the difference between the two call strike prices — in this case, 2-00 points, or $2,000 — minus your cost in establishing the position (and, once again, commissions).

If you were right, and bond prices rose — moving above 106-00 by the expiration date for the June options — you would make the maximum profit. If you were wrong, and bond prices fell — moving below 104-00 at expiration — you would suffer a maximum loss, losing the entire amount you paid to open your position. If bond prices remained stable — ending up somewhere between 104-00 and 106-00 — you'd suffer either a partial loss or a partial profit, depending on the exact bond closing price at expiration. To illustrate, let's look at an example using real numbers.

The situation described above represented the actual conditions on April 3, 1995. After repeatedly raising interest rates for more than a year, the Federal Reserve Board had failed to take action at either its February or March meetings. The market perceived this as a sign an interest-rate cut might be in the offing, and bond futures prices had been rising steadily for more than three weeks with more gains expected. The June futures contract closed that day at 104-18, the perfect alignment for a bullish T-bond option spread. The June 104 call was priced at 1-41/64 (or $1,640.625), while the June 106 call was trading at 45/64 (or $703.125). Buying the 104 call and selling the 106 call created a bullish spread with a net cost (and maximum risk) of $937.50 ($1,640.625 - $703.125 = $937.50) and a maximum potential profit of $1,062.50 ($2,000.00 - $937.50 = $1,062.50).

Note: Normally, in doing a bull or bear option spread, you would prefer to get a better reward/risk ratio than this — preferably at least a 3-to-2 ratio. However, with strongly trending markets, such as T-bonds and currencies, anything above a 1-to-1 ratio is acceptable — so long as you are going with the trend.

As it turned out, the Federal Reserve didn't cut interest rates prior to the June option expiration on May 19, 1995 (that didn't happen until early July). However, T-bond futures prices continued to rise anyway, closing on May 19 at 110-09, well above the 106 strike price at the top of the spread — meaning the position would have produced the maximum profit of $1,062.50 if held until the expiration date.

Note: Most option spread traders don't hold their positions until expiration, preferring instead to close out early if they get a nice profit — say 80 percent of their potential maximum. This eliminates the possibility that a last-minute reversal might turn a winning trade into a loser — something that's always a danger with option spreads, which have a relatively narrow price range between maximum loss and maximum profit.

Option spreads have several major advantages over outright option purchases, including:

- It takes only a modest move to produce the maximum profit. In our example, June T-bond futures need to rise only 1-14/32nds — from 104-18 to 106-00 — to achieve the maximum profit.

- The initial cost — and risk — is far lower than merely buying the nearest in-the-money option. In our case, the risk in just buying the 104 call would have been $1,640.625 — and you would have suffered it at any futures price below 104-00, the same as with the option spread. Even buying the out-of-the-money 106 call would have had a risk of $703.125 — only slightly less than our spread — and the speculator would have suffered a total loss at any bond price below 106 (the price at which we made our maximum profit).

- The break-even point is far lower than with an outright option purchase. With our 104/106 bull spread, bond futures prices had to rise just 12/32nds — from 104-18 to 104-30 — by expiration for us to break even (i.e., at that level, we could have exercised the 104 call and received 30/32nds, or $937.50, which was our original cost, (not counting commissions). By contrast, with the outright purchase of a 104 call for $1,640.625, June bonds would have had to rise to 105-21 at expiration for the buyer to break even — and to 106-23 to match the profit earned on the option spread.

The major drawback with an option spread, of course, is that you cut off all additional profit potential once the price of the underlying security moves beyond the out-of-the-money option's strike price. In our example, for instance, with bonds rising to 110-09, a speculator who simply purchased the 104 call would have made a profit of $4,616.625 (110-09 - 104-00 = 6-09, or $6,281.25 - $1,640.625 = $4,616.625), but our gain was limited to $1,037.50 — no matter how high bond prices went. That limited reward potential is the price you pay for the reduced risk you take.

We offer five suggested rules for entering T-bond option spreads:

- Open a position only when a T-bond futures price trend has been firmly established, or shortly after some action has been taken by the Federal Reserve that signals a shift in the direction of interest-rate policy.

- Always have two strike prices between the option you buy and the option you sell — e.g., with bond prices at 104-18, do the 104/106 spread, not the 104/105 spread. A bond point is worth just $1,000, so a one-point spread doesn't offer enough profit potential to be worthwhile.

- Enter a spread only when you can get a reward/risk ratio better than 1-to-1 — i.e., only when your maximum potential profit is higher than your maximum possible loss.

- Always use options having at least a month remaining prior to expiration. (T-bond options expire the second Friday before the final business day of the expiration month.)

- Always initiate your trades with an actual spread order rather than specifying prices for the individual options.

Spread No. 2 — **The Seasonal Wheat Option Spread:** This strategy works exactly the same way as the bullish T-bond option spread, but it is done only at a specific time of the year to take advantage of seasonal factors that often affect the wheat market.

Step 88: *The Three Best Highly Favorable Option Spreads*

As you learned in wealth-building Step No. 87, found on page 8, the grain markets — including both corn and wheat — are subject to sharp price movements when weather-related problems develop during the planting and growing seasons. In 1995, for example, prices of wheat futures soared more than $1.10 a bushel between mid-April and mid-July when late freezes and severe flooding in key Midwestern growing regions combined with rising export demand to spark fears of a possible shortage.

This recognized pattern offers a reasonably high-reward/limited-risk futures play (similar to the Seasonal Corn Speculation). However, a safer, yet still quite lucrative alternative is to structure a bullish wheat option spread that will also profit in such a seasonal price move.

The exact strategy — which should be implemented only in March, April or May of each year — involves buying an at-the-money Chicago Board of Trade wheat call option and simultaneously selling the out-of-the-money CBT wheat call with the same expiration date and a strike price 40 cents a bushel higher. The July, September or December options can be used (all represent futures calling for delivery of new-crop wheat), though July options should not be used for trades opened in May as they expire in mid-June.

This trade has an extremely attractive reward/risk ratio — often as high as 3-to-1 — since it is initiated at a time when the wheat market is typically fairly stable, meaning the options have a low implied volatility. That's because the fall harvest is long over, with the results well known, the winter crop has not yet progressed to the point where it is subject to huge weather risks and the spring planting has not yet begun.

However, as you already know, that changes by late May or June, with bad weather posing a possible threat to both the late spring harvest and the planting and early growth of the fall crop. And, that results in greatly increased volatility in the wheat futures market, with the resulting potential for large gains on the call options — and on bullish seasonal wheat spreads. To prove it, here's an example from 1995:

Through most of February and March of 1995, wheat futures prices had been quite stable, trading in a fairly narrow 15- to 20-cent range. However, in early April a series of late freezes hit the Midwest and forecasts were issued calling for heavy spring rains, which posed a threat to wheat planting. Prices began to rise and, by April 18, the September wheat future was trading at $3.5950 a bushel. The at-the-money September $3.60 wheat call was priced at 15-7/8 cents ($0.15875) and the September $4.00 wheat call (the one with a 40-cent higher strike price) was priced at 5-1/2 cents ($0.0550).

Thus, a bullish September $3.60/$4.00 wheat spread could have been opened on that day for just 10-3/8 cents ($0.10375), or $518.75 for the full 5,000-bushel contracts — which would have also been the maximum risk on the trade. However, the maximum profit would have been 29-5/8 cents, or $1,481.25 (the 40-cent strike price difference x 5,000 = $2,000 - $518.75 = $1,481.50) — a very attractive reward/risk ratio of almost 3-to-1.

Since we've already told you that wheat rose more than $1.10 a bushel in the early summer of 1995, the outcome of this sample trade should be obvious. By the option expiration date in mid-August, September wheat futures were trading above $4.25 a bushel, having been even higher earlier in the month. Since that was far above the $4.00 strike price of the short call in the spread, the trade resulted in a maximum profit of $1,481.50 (though most traders would have again cashed out early, avoiding the risk of a late reversal).

Once again, our suggested rules for this spread are quite simple:

- Open your spreads only in the months of March, April or May.

- Use only the July, September or December options — but do not do a July trade if you are opening a position in May.

- Buy the at-the-money call option and sell the out-of-the-money call with a strike price 40 cents a bushel higher.

- Pay no more than 15 cents per bushel for your spread, which will give you a maximum loss of $750 and a maximum potential profit of $1,250 (not including commission costs).

- Initiate your position using a spread order.

- Look to close just prior to the option expiration date, or when you achieve 80 percent of your maximum profit if you want to avoid the risk of a late reversal. (Note: An early close is strongly recommended when using the December options as most of the seasonal wheat price gain is likely to come during the summer, leaving you with a long and potentially risky wait for the mid-November expiration date.)

Spread No. 3 — The Soybean Straddle: This strategy isn't really a spread in the conventional sense, more accurately being defined as a defined-risk option combination play. However, because it offers unlimited profit potential in both rising and falling markets, we decided to include it in this section anyway.

Unlike a conventional spread, which involves buying one option and simultaneously selling another of the same type but with a different strike price, a straddle involves simultaneously buying two options of different types (i.e., one call and one put), both having the same strike price and expiration month. (A straddle should always be positioned with at-the-money options — i.e., those having strike prices closest to the actual future price.)

To clarify, if the May soybean futures contract was priced at $5.74 per bushel, a straddle would involve buying a May $5.75 soybean call option and simultaneously buying a May $5.75 put option.

As noted above, straddles can work whether the price of the underlying futures contract rises or falls. However, in order for the strategy to be profitable, the price change must be fairly large. That's because any time you score a gain on one option, you'll also suffer a loss on the other. Thus, the only way you can make an overall profit is if one option makes more money than the other loses.

Obviously, then, straddles are suitable only for highly volatile markets — which is why we've applied this strategy to soybeans, among the most volatile of the agricultural commodities. That's because soybeans are always in great demand, a function of their many uses

in both food and non-food products. In addition, soybeans require very specific weather conditions during the growing season. Otherwise, the plants may be damaged, sharply cutting the crop yields and leading to supply shortages.

As a result, soybean futures prices are subject to sharp price moves — either up or down — in response to even minor shifts in demand patterns or slight changes in the weather during the growing season. Soybean futures also have the largest daily trading limit in the grain complex, 30 cents per bushel, which means the 5,000-bushel soybean contract can rise or fall in value by as much as $1,500 in a single day. (Note: This liberal limit is expanded even further for trading days following a session in which the market closed "limit up" or "limit down.")

Given these factors, price moves of 50 cents a bushel or more in a matter of days occur fairly regularly in the soybean futures market. In fact, moves of $1.00 a bushel are not all that uncommon — and that's more than enough to produce a hefty profit on a soybean option straddle.

For example, if you open a soybean straddle using options with a $6.50 strike price and pay a total of 50 cents per bushel for the two options, your initial cost (not including commissions) will be $2,500 ($0.50 x 5,000 = $2,500). If soybean prices subsequently fall a dollar a bushel to $5.50, the $6.50 call will be virtually worthless, but the $6.50 put will be worth at least $1.00 a bushel (or $5,000) — meaning you will have doubled your money.

Note: It may seem like $2,500 is a lot to risk on a speculative option strategy such as this — and it is. However, it's highly unlikely that you'll ever suffer a total loss on a straddle. That would happen only if the futures price closed on expiration day at exactly the strike price of the two options. More often, even in a very flat market, one of the options will expire worthless, while the other will have an exercise value of 10 to 25 cents — thus allowing you to recover a portion of your original cost.

Straddles also have another advantage in highly volatile markets such as that for soybean futures: If you watch the market closely (which you absolutely should if you're going to speculate), you can often make a nice profit even if you don't get a major price move by doing what is referred to as "legging out" of your position. For example, on June 28, 1995, the September soybean future was priced at $5.9725 per bushel, and a September $6.00 straddle could have been purchased for a total cost of $2,525 (the $6.00 call was priced at 24.5 cents and the $6.00 put was quoted at 26 cents, for a total of 50.5 cents).

Soybean prices subsequently rallied on a fierce heat wave in the Midwest, with the September future climbing to $6.4925 a bushel by July 17. However, export demand had been slack throughout the period, keeping a lid on the rally, and many traders felt prices would fall back when the weather broke. A savvy straddle trader, recognizing this danger, would have taken advantage of the run up to sell his September $6.00 call, which was priced at 53.5 cents on July 17. By doing so, he would have received $2,675 — enough to recover his original stake and pay commissions, with a few dollars left over.

Had he expected prices to remain stable at that level, he could have also sold his $6.00 put, which was priced at 5.25 cents — bringing in another $262.50 in profits. Although small in dollar terms, that would have represented a 10 percent-plus return — not bad for a 19-day investment. However, he had a better idea; instead of selling the put, he held in anticipation of a price pullback — and it paid off.

By Aug. 2, just 16 days later, the September soybean future had plunged back to $5.9925 — almost exactly where it had been back on June 30 — and his $6.00 put had risen in price to 11 cents. Selling then brought in $550 — which, added to the $2,675 he received earlier for the call, gave him a total of $3,225, good for a profit of $700. Even after paying commissions of around $100, his $600 net gain would have represented a return of 23.76 percent on his original investment of $2,525 — quite nice considering the underlying soybean future wound up essentially unchanged. *Note: If soybean prices reverse by a substantial amount in only a few days, it's often possible to sell both the call and the put at a profit — which could generate an overall gain comparable to what you'd make on a large single-direction price move.*

The biggest drawback in doing a straddle is that you have to beat not only the market, but time as well. Virtually all of the premium in at-the-money options is composed of time value, and that value steadily erodes as time passes. That's why the $6.00 put in our example, which was worth 26 cents on June 28 with the future at $5.9725, was worth just 11 cents on Aug. 2 with the future at $5.9925. In slightly over a month, it lost just 2 cents in real value — but 13 cents in time value.

Here are our suggested guidelines for doing a soybean straddle:

- Buy both an at-the-money soybean call and an at-the-money soybean put.

- Use options that give you as much time as possible — at least six weeks until expiration. Otherwise, you won't have time to try for two smaller profits if you decide to leg out.

- Don't pay more than 50 cents total ($2,500) to open a soybean straddle. (We fudged by $25 on our example because it was the best recent illustration of successfully legging out.)

- Do a straddle only if the price of the underlying soybean future is trading between $5.50 and $7.00 per bushel. As noted, it takes a price move of roughly $1.00 to double your money with a straddle. Since up moves of that magnitude are rare above $7.00 (there have been two in the past decade) and down moves of that size are even rarer below $5.50 (none in recent memory), it makes little sense to use a two-way strategy at those price levels. Instead, use bear spreads at prices above $7.00 a bushel and bull spreads at prices below $5.50.

- Use a combination order when you buy, specifying the total price you want to pay rather than exact prices for the individual options.

- As a general rule, play for the big move ($1.00 per bushel or more) during the growing season, and for smaller moves the rest of the year — unless your observations of the soybean market give you a reason to do otherwise.

Trading Tip: Soybean futures prices tend to make their biggest moves on Mondays as traders respond to weekend weather events — and this volatility drives up option premiums. Prices then settle down at mid-week — and option premiums shrink again. Thus, you will likely get better prices — perhaps 5 or 6 cents lower — for straddles positioned on Wednesday or Thursday than for those opened on Mondays. ▲

Continued from p. 18

Restrict your first high-risk trades to single futures positions, less-volatile commodities (such as corn), smaller full-size contracts (such as oats), or the "mini" contracts (usually one-fifth to one-third the regular size) available on certain contracts (e.g., gold, silver, soybeans).

For example, in mid-1995, December silver futures were trading at about $5.27 an ounce, very near their low for the year, while the at-the-money December $5.25 silver call option was priced at 32 cents an ounce. Based on the economic conditions at the time, the past performance of the specific contract and the historic silver price patterns, a reasonable upside price target for the December silver future was $6.35 an ounce (it had been there earlier in the year), and a reasonable downside limit was $4.40 (the historic low for silver in recent years).

Given those numbers, the potential return on the $5.25 silver call would have been $3,900 ($6.35 - $5.25 - $0.32) x 5,000 = $0.78 x 5,000 = $3,900), excluding commissions and assuming no remaining time value. And, the potential loss would have been just $1,600 (the original 32-cent premium paid for the call x 5,000 = $1,600), again excluding commissions. Thus, the reward/risk ratio on the silver option speculation would have been 2.43 to 1 ($3,900/$1,600 = 2.4375).

Any ratio over 2-to-1 is quite good for a speculation involving an outright futures or option purchase, so look for situations such as this when you start seeking out your own speculative opportunities.

9. Use Scenario Analysis To Examine Reward/Risk Possibilities — One of the most useful tools in determining reward/risk ratios for virtually any speculative play is a technique known as "scenario analysis." This involves constructing a grid showing the potential outcomes of a particular trade at various closing price levels. With such a grid, you can tell at a glance what the maximum probable profit and maximum possible loss will be, as well as the exact break-even point for the trade.

Scenario analysis for purchase of $5.25 silver call option

Possible silver futures price	Exercise value of $5.25 call	Profit (loss) on $5.25 call*	Return on Investment
$4.50	$0.00	($1,600)	(100.0%)
$4.75	$0.00	($1,600)	(100.0%)
$5.00	$0.00	($1,600)	(100.0%)
$5.25	$0.00	($1,600)	(100.0%)
$5.30	$0.05	($1,350)	(84.4%)
$5.40	$0.15	($ 850)	(53.1%)
$5.50	$0.25	($ 350)	(21.9%)
$5.57	$0.32	$ 0	0.0%
$5.60	$0.35	$ 150	9.4%
$5.70	$0.45	$ 650	40.6%
$5.75	$0.50	$ 900	56.3%
$6.00	$0.75	$2,150	134.4%
$6.25	$1.00	$3,400	212.5%
$6.40	$1.25	$4,650	290.6%

Based on initial purchase price of 32 cents, or $1,600.

Note: Virtually all scenario analyses involving options assume that the position is held until the option expiration date, when the options have only real value left. The only alternative would be to estimate the time value portion of the option premium at various price levels — and such estimates would essentially render the analysis meaningless.

To illustrate how a scenario analysis might work out, the table below presents a sample based on the silver call option purchase detailed in Point No. 8. *Note: If commissions are significant on a given trade, as is the case with some multiple-option plays, they should also be factored into the scenario analysis as they can significantly impact the overall return.*

10. Control Your Emotions When Trading — An article published in one of the leading financial journals in the late 1980s reported on a study showing that investors have an overwhelming tendency to sell winners early and hold losing positions too long. This — at least in part — reflects an emotional and misguided attitude regarding the nature of profits and losses.

The prevailing notion is that, if you sell your winner, you establish — for real and for all time — the fact that you did indeed make a profit. This provides both emotional satisfaction and bragging rights — i.e., most investors relish peer approval, and a profit generates respect (and, presumably, envy) among associates who haven't done as well.

The same erroneous logic prevails with losing trades. In other words, if you sell your losing position, you establish yourself as a real loser — a psychologically damaging notion for some.

If your trading motivation reflects either of these two notions, you won't be able to make objective decisions regarding your investments — in which case, speculative trading, with its ultra high risks, is definitely not for you.

There you have it — 10 tips on developing the proper discipline and learning the necessary information you need to be a successful speculative trader. Take them to heart, and you'll be well on your way to becoming at ease in virtually any high-risk investment situation.

A COMFORTABLE WAY TO START YOUR SPECULATIVE CAREER

As should be apparent by now, we advise extreme caution before entering the world of speculative investing. However, we also firmly believe that at least limited speculation is essential if you hope to move beyond the mere financial-comfort level and into the realm of the true wealth builder.

Unfortunately, many people hear the word "speculation" and immediately think "commodities, futures and options," believing those are the only vehicles available for such aggressive investing. Frightened by the many horror stories they've heard (the bulk of which, if not outright false, are greatly exaggerated), and hesitant to go through the hassle of opening up the required secondary trading accounts, they decide to not even try — thereby forgoing the many opportunities available for using speculations to enhance returns and speed portfolio growth.

The lower the share price, the greater the stock's price swings are likely to be.

What these people don't realize is that there are a variety of other speculative arenas besides futures and options — including an often-overlooked area that's easy to understand, requires no special trading account, takes only a modest investment, offers tremendous potential for both percentage and dollar gains, and has risk levels that can be both small and easily managed. We're talking about the world of low-priced stocks.

Small Stocks Produce Big Profits

Of all the high-reward/high-risk vehicles speculative investors might consider, these low-priced equity issues — more commonly known as "penny" stocks — offer some of the best profit characteristics available in any market. This is particularly true in today's low-inflation/low-interest-rate environment, which has kept many traditional speculative vehicles, such as agricultural commodities and precious metals, locked in narrow trading ranges.

There is no recognized market index for penny stocks; however, since they are the quintessential examples of emerging-growth stocks, performance comparisons with that sector should be valid. One recent appraisal was performed by stock analyst Ron Cram, publisher of *Ron Cram's Emerging Profit Newsletter,* in March 1995. He found that, if you had invested $1,000 in 1940 in stocks making up the S&P 500, your investment would be worth more than $400,000 today. But, had you invested the same $1,000 in smaller, emerging-growth stocks, it would now be worth over $2.5 million!

Other comparisons have found similar results, painting a superior performance picture of America's "market midgets." Indeed, regardless of the yardstick used — be it statistical, mathematical or historical — developmental and emerging-growth stocks have consistently outperformed virtually all other investment vehicles.

More Than a Penny's Worth of Potential

The financial world's number crunchers have also demonstrated the "inverse curvilinear" relationship that exists between the price of a stock and its probable percentage move. Simply put, the axiom states, "the lower the share price, the greater the stock's price swings are likely to be."

Writing in the February 1995 issue of *The Stewart Report* newsletter, growth-stock analyst J. David Stewart explained the phenomenon quite succinctly, saying: "The sheer mechanics of money suggest that it's a lot easier to quadruple $10 million than to double $400 million. The financial rules of nature also make it easier for a young company to grow faster than an older one. For example, I have seen many stocks go from $2 a share to $20, but *rarely* have I seen one go from $27 to $270 — and *never* in as short a period of time."

Thus, based on these studies and statements, it's apparent that volatility — the key factor in determining speculative potential — is an inherent feature of penny stocks.

Just What Are 'Penny' Stocks?

It used to be that a "penny" stock, by definition, was one trading for less than a dollar per share. Lately, however, a trend has developed in which corporate directors "reverse split" their company's penny-denominated shares into dollar stocks. As a result, penny stocks are now more commonly defined in terms of market value than price, with the cutoff point usually considered to be $5 million or less. *Note: The market value is determined by multiplying the price per share times the number of shares outstanding. Thus, a $2.50 stock would still be considered a penny stock if it had only 2 million shares outstanding.*

The typical penny stock (if there is such a thing) represents an ownership share in a firm in its developmental or emerging-growth stage. These embryonic companies usually have a very specialized product line or service, and they are often on the cutting edge of the newest technologies — the potential of which, if any, is difficult to value because there are only apples to compare to their oranges.

Pennies Defy Traditional Analysis

The vast majority of these companies are so young they have yet to achieve profitability — and those that are operating in the black pay no dividends, choosing instead to plow 100 percent of earnings back into the business to fuel additional growth. Most also have limited financial resources and produce operating results that are almost entirely immune to standard textbook, trend or fundamental securities-analysis techniques.

As such, successfully investing in penny stocks is as much of an art as it is a science. Fortunately, it also happens to be an art form where common sense and good instincts can earn you more than an M.B.A. from Harvard. That's why some of Wall Street's most noted investment managers are often outperformed by rank amateurs in the penny stock field.

One evaluation technique that does work extremely well in finding big winners in the penny stock market is so-called "open-air analysis." Essentially, open-air analysis simply means paying attention to what's going on in the world around you. In other words, if you come across a new or unusual product or service in the day-to-day course of consumer life, buy it and like it — invest in the company that makes it or provides it.

You Can Beat the Crowd

The product or service can be anything — perhaps a new line of herbal cosmetics or a software program that's light years ahead of anything you've ever run. Whatever it is, look at the package — and, if it's made by someone other than a recognized name like Revlon or Microsoft, write to the manufacturer and ask whether it is a publicly traded company. Chances are it is — and you'll own the stock, based on a trip to the grocery store, months before the analysts sitting at their desks on Wall Street discover it.

Open-air analysis also involves keeping a keen eye out for any new socio-economic consumer trends you find you or your family partaking in. Whether it's your kid's new-found interest in roller blades or the fact that you find yourself frequenting a new chain of coffee house, always ask yourself: "Would I like a piece of the action?" If the company behind the new trend is new itself, but already publicly traded, you can get that piece — and, most likely, at a ground-floor price. You must, however, be cautious about mistaking something that is merely trendy for something that represent a full-on new trend.

When selecting companies based on "open-air" analysis, give preference to those that offer a "pure play." By that we mean make certain that the company you're investing in benefits primarily from the product or service that caught your interest and doesn't have a lot of unwanted businesses mixed in, thus diluting the focal purpose of your investment.

Finally, try to objectively measure the size of the fish relative to the scope of the pond. The bigger the pond (industry group), the more room your fish (company) will have to grow before it rules the pond — or, more likely, before it gets eaten by a bigger fish (i.e., bought out at a substantial profit to you, the shareholder).

To augment your search for potential penny stock purchase candidates, you may also want to:

1. Find a stockbroker at one of the lesser-known regional brokerage firms that specializes in these stocks. The table at left lists a number of such companies, with names of brokers you can contact personally at each firm.

2. Buy a subscription to a financial newsletter that specializes in penny stocks and developmental-stage companies.

The brokers and the newsletter will give you exposure to far more potentially good stocks than you'd ever be able to find on your own, as well as providing analytical information you might otherwise be unable to find about any companies that might seem interesting to you.

Some brokers who specialize in small stocks

If you're interested in trading "penny" stocks, the following brokers and brokerage firms are active in this field and would welcome your inquiries about opening new accounts:

Charles Fedy
Russo Securities, Inc.
128 Sand Lane555
Staten Island, NY 10314
1-800-451-7877

David Ganz
Meyers, Pollack, Robbins, Inc.
Broad Hollow Road, Ste. 426
Melville, NY 11747
1-800-601-1151

Jay Harris
Interstate/Johnson
101 E. Bay Street
Savannah, GA 31401
1-800-929-0838

Fred Hogg
LaneKemper Securities
121 S.W. Salmon, Ste. 1515
Portland, OR 97204
1-800-547-8575

H. Glen Leason
Torrey Pines Securities
78060 Calle Estrado
La Quinta, CA 92253
1-800-867-7390

Pat Sheedy
Toluca Pacific Securities
3500 W. Olive Ave., Ste. 1190
Burbank, CA 91505
1-800-284-8772

Leonard Siegal
Janney, Montgomery, Scott
1801 Market Street
Philadelphia, PA 19033
1-800-526-6397

Andrew Snett
Kemper Securities
6400 Canoga Ave., Ste. 1
Woodland Hills, CA 91505
1-818-226-2275

Larry Turel
Baron Chase
2255 Glades Road, Ste. 212-E
Boca Raton, FL 33431
1-800-937-4466

Bob Zimmerman
Westport Resources
1110 W. Valley Road, Ste. 10
Wayne, PA 19087
1-610-964-8693

That can be important because, as we've already noted, most of the stocks in this sector have very little to offer, or analyze, in the traditional financial sense. After all, how can you compare P/E (price/earnings) ratios when there's no "E" with which to work?

In spite of this, there are a couple of financial yardsticks you can use in virtually every case to determine if a penny stock is reasonably priced. They don't provide a lot of quantitative information but they should at least keep you from making a stupid mistake. They are:

The Current Ratio — Even an innovative company with a hot new product in an exploding growth industry is likely to fail if it doesn't have enough cash to meet next week's payroll. That's why a small company's current ratio is an important consideration. It shows a company's ability to cover its short-term debts — and is also one of the few widely recognized analytical measures you can apply to companies in the developmental stage.

To determine the current ratio, check the company's balance sheet and compare "total current assets" to "total current liabilities." It's difficult to generalize about what constitutes a high or low current ratio in the penny sector — but, as a rule, it's encouraging to see current assets at least twice as large as current liabilities.

... stocks jumping from the Pink Sheets, or EBB system, to NASDAQ average a 15 to 25 percent rise in price within a month of being listed.

The MV/R Ratio — This measure can serve as a substitute for the P/E ratio in analyzing companies with no record of earnings. You determine it by comparing a company's total market value (MV) to its total revenues (R). *Note: The market value of a company is determined by multiplying the total number of shares outstanding, which can be found in the balance sheet, by the current bid price of the stock. The total revenues figure is found in the "Statement of Operations" section of the company's annual or quarterly report.*

If the company's total market value is less than its total revenues — i.e., if its MV/R ratio is 1-to-1 or less — then it's highly unlikely the stock is overpriced. The logic behind this assessment is simple. The average U.S. corporation nets 5 percent after taxes — or, put another way, its profit margin is 1/20th of its total revenues. Therefore, if the company's total market value is equal to its total revenues — and the total revenues are theoretically 20 times greater than its probable earnings — then the stock is statistically selling at 20 times earnings. In other words, it has a theoretical P/E ratio of 20.

The significance of this ratio in selecting penny stocks cannot be overemphasized — simply because, once you start using it on a lot of penny stocks, you'll be amazed at how many companies you'll find with theoretical P/E's of 100, 150 or even 200. Consider how well a company with real earnings would have to perform to justify a P/E ratio of 200 (you probably can't even think of one), and it should be instantly obvious why you shouldn't pay that for a company that has only projected future earnings. Any slowing of growth at all, and the stock price will almost certainly tumble. Thus, you should avoid a penny stock with an excessive MV/R ratio.

**Penny Stock
Trading Tips**

The smallest penny stocks trade on the over-the-counter (OTC) market via the so-called "Pink Sheets" or NASDAQ's Electronic Bulletin Board System. Quotes on these stocks can only be obtained by calling your broker, so they are a little harder to get. The penny shares of relatively larger companies that can meet more stringent criteria for net worth, number of shareholders, etc., are listed on NASDAQ, so quotes can sometimes be found in the newspaper. However, since there are thousands of stocks on NASDAQ, even a world-class financial paper like *The Wall Street Journal* can list only a fraction of them — and they tend to choose the largest issues. So, once again, you'll probably have to call your broker for a quote on smaller issues.

The quote you get will have two parts — a "bid" price and an "ask" price. Typically, you'll buy at the higher of the two (the ask price) and sell at the lower (the bid price). The difference between the two is known as the "spread" (not to be confused with option or commodity spreads) — and represents the trading department's profit and/or cushion against loss in making a market in the stock.

Actively traded pennies will usually have a fairly narrow spread, based on the share price — i.e., 1/32nd ($0.03125) for stocks priced under 50 cents; 1/16th ($0.0625) for those under a dollar; 1/8th ($0.125) for those under $3 and no more than 1/4 ($0.25) for those in the $3 to $5 range.

It's acceptable to pay these spreads, but you have to be careful if you're quoted a higher one (and you almost certainly will be) since a high spread can wipe out months of profits. For example, if a stock was quoted at "1/2 bid, $1 ask," buying 1,000 shares would cost you $1,000 — but, if you were to turn around and sell five minutes later, you'd get only $500! That's obviously ridiculous — but some of the best penny stocks have the worst spreads.

Fortunately, you don't have to let that stop you from owning the shares. Simply refuse to play the spread game by placing a limit, good-till-canceled (GTC) order at a price somewhere between the bid and the ask — say, at 5/8ths in the above example, or maybe even 3/4ths if you really want the stock.

Find Out Why the Spread is High

Having said that, you should still know what the spread is — and, if it's extremely high, find out why before you buy. For example, if the spread is high because it's a pharmaceutical company with only 2 million shares in the float, because physicians and others "in the know" have bought most of it over the past few months and because the FDA trials for its new drug are scheduled for completion, then the spread may be justified. But, if it's just another potential turkey, someone in the brokerage industry may be trying to take advantage of you.

A couple of other important tips:

■ Make sure you know when the company went public and the dates any stock from private placements was issued. Both types of stock offerings involve "restricted" shares (which can't be sold for two years), usually issued at prices well below the current market. When the restriction is lifted — regardless of how rosy the company prospects may be — the appearance on the market of a couple of hundred thousand shares bought at 25 cents will almost certainly depress a current $1.00 stock price as the owners rush to cash in their gains.

■ Look for companies that may have recently announced application for listing on NASDAQ proper. By virtue of the fact the company is now in a position to apply, it's axiomatic that it has made certain strides and is financially positioned to attain a higher rating within the market system. Moreover, the simple signed approval of the NASD for listing on the Automated Quotation (the "AQ" in NASDAQ) system will give the stock added exposure and more respect within the financial community — which invariably leads to higher share prices.

In fact, several brokerage house surveys have found that stocks jumping from the Pink Sheets, or EBB system, to NASDAQ average a 15 to 25 percent rise in price within a month of being listed.

A Recommended Trading Strategy

Given their low cost (and thus limited risk) and their enormous potential, penny stocks are an ideal starting place for beginning speculators — particularly those still nervous about venturing into the futures or options markets. They also offer substantial ongoing profit opportunities for more experienced speculators seeking diversification for the growing aggressive-risk segment of their portfolios.

Still, that doesn't mean you shouldn't adopt a trading strategy designed to further boost your potential and contain your risks. J. David Stewart, the analyst for *The Stewart Report* we mentioned earlier, advises a three-step approach:

- First, limit the amount of capital you put in penny stocks to no more than 2 to 5 percent of your total portfolio value (again assuming that value is at least our recommend $200,000).

- Second, use those funds to buy six different stocks. *Note: You don't need to buy all six at once or hold them all at the same time.*

- Third, buy stocks in very different industries. For example, don't buy six different bio-tech stocks; otherwise, you'll simply own a diversified bio-tech portfolio. This should be obvious, but Stewart says many people make the mistake — particularly "gold bugs," who pump their whole stake into penny mining stocks.

Stewart believes a reasonable expectation for such a portfolio, if well selected, would be:

- For one of the stock certificates to become an expensive piece of wallpaper.

- For four of the other five issues to perform well enough to cover the total loss on the first one.

- For the final stock to be a very big winner — perhaps rising to 5 or 10 times its initial value — that represents virtually all of the portfolio's profit.

Obviously, it would be nice to have more than one big winner; in fact, it would be nice to have all six be big winners. However, Stewart says that hardly ever happens. And, if it does, he adds, you should probably sell all your stocks immediately — not just your pennies — because the overall market is almost certainly overheated and very close to a major crash.

So, view your penny stock portfolio the same way you should view your other speculations — with a highly positive attitude, but realistic expectations.

A Final Word You've now had your first significant exposure to the world of aggressive-risk investing. You've learned why speculation can be important in building wealth, the factors that define a speculative investment, how to measure risk and some ways you can manage your trading activities — and your emotions — to contain that risk. You've also been introduced to seven good speculative plays — all with small, strictly limited or easily controlled loss possibilities, but really strong profit potential.

That should be enough to at least spark an ongoing interest in aggressive-risk investing — even if you're still not quite financially ready to actually begin speculating. In the next lesson, we'll continue with the topic of speculation — this time looking at a number of super aggressive strategies, explaining exactly how they work, and detailing methods for ensuring that the odds are in your favor, so start reading now! ▲

Super aggressive, super high-yield strategies

100 Steps to Wealth

Super aggressive, super high-yield strategies

"One great speculation is worth a lifetime of prudent investing.
The problem comes in finding that great speculation."
— *Michael Reilly, President, Global Financial Traders, Long Island, N.Y.*

THE WEALTH-BUILDING POWER OF SPECULATION

In the last lesson, we introduced the concept of aggressive-risk investment — or speculation. We also noted that, in spite of the high degree of risk, a certain amount of speculation is vital to most truly effective wealth-building plans — simply because speculation provides the means to greatly enhance the overall rate of return on your investments, as well as speed the rate at which your portfolio grows. In addition, we detailed a variety of different speculative strategies and provided examples illustrating just how powerful many of them can be on an individual basis.

However, except for one example showing how successful speculation with only a small portion of total assets could increase a portfolio's overall return from 10 to 12 percent, we didn't really quantify the impact using such strategies can have on your wealth-building success. For that reason, you may have a little trouble buying into our opening quote for this lesson — but, we can assure you it's true!

10 Years Versus 10 Days
One great speculation can, indeed, prove just as powerful in building wealth as years of prudent investing. For example, assume you invest $1,000 in an equity mutual fund that earns 11.9 percent per annum — roughly the rate of return on the S&P 500 over the past 50 years. If you leave your money in place for 10 years, letting your gains compound, your $1,000 stake will grow to $3,078.22 — a profit of $2,078.22.

Now, assume you take the same $1,000 and use it as a margin deposit to purchase a single wheat features contract. You make your speculative play in early May, when you know that a spell of bad weather could potentially damage the new crop, causing the price of wheat to soar. A period of searing temperatures and dry skies ensues, and wheat prices begin to rise — climbing 42 cents per bushel in just 10 days. *Note: Lest you think we're "stacking" this example, there were three separate moves of 42 cents or more by wheat prices — each in just 10 to 15 trading days — during May, June and July of 1995 alone.*

You decide to cash in your gains, so you sell your futures contract — which, as you learned in the last lesson, represents 5,000 bushels of wheat. Your profit is $2,100 ($0.42 per bushel x 5,000 bushels = $2,100) — meaning your original $1,000 stake has grown to $3,100. That's right — essentially the same amount (with some minor difference due to commissions) you would have had after your 10-year investment in the mutual fund!

That's certainly an amazing comparison. However, before you go rushing off to cash in your mutual funds and buy wheat futures, remember that our example compared only one possible outcome of speculation versus prudent investing — the winning side. Besides, as we indicated at the beginning of the lesson, The Top of the Pyramid, speculation should be contained so as to not interrupt your long-term investment portfolio. To get the true picture, you need to look at several other possibilities as well.

Reviewing the Other Possibilities

Returning to our wheat speculation, for example, had the hot, dry weather not developed, it's doubtful prices would have risen by 42 cents a bushel. More likely, absent any other factor, they'd have held steady — or fallen a bit as the spring weather fears abated. In the first case, you would have earned nothing on your $1,000 stake; in the second, you'd have taken a small loss.

And, had some negative price factor come into play — perhaps a U.S. Department of Agriculture prediction of larger-than-expected crop yields — wheat could have fallen substantially. That could have been disastrous since even a 20 cent-per-bushel drop would have wiped out your entire $1,000 stake ($0.20 x 5,000 = $1,000) — leaving you not just with a negative return, but with no cash to try again. *Note: Harkening again to the real world, it should be noted that in May, June and July of 1995 — even during what was essentially a very strong wheat market — there were two pullbacks of 20 cents per bushel or more.*

That's the primary reason we so strongly advise speculating with only a small portion of your assets — no more than 5 to 10 percent of your portfolio value. Risk — and lose — more, and you simply make it too difficult to recoup your losses with other, safer investments. That's particularly true if you have limited capital to begin with — which is why we also recommend not speculating at all until your portfolio reaches at least $200,000 in value (exclusive of your primary residence).

Repeating Successes Is Also Difficult

There's also another reason for not cashing in your more prudent investments in favor of active speculation: Even if you do wind up on the winning side of an aggressive-risk strategy such as our seasonal wheat play, what are you going to do next?

History has shown that the equities underlying the equity mutual fund in our initial example are likely to continue chugging along at something close to that 11.9 percent average annual return over time. However, the odds any type of speculation will repeatedly triple your money are long indeed. For example, our wheat strategy was a good speculation only because it was the right time of the year — a time when the grains have historically shown strong upward potential due to the weather-sensitive nature of the market during the crucial early stages of the growing season. Had you made the same $1,000 investment in wheat in September or October, you might have waited six or seven months without seeing a 42-cent price increase — or any increase at all.

Thus, it's plainly foolish to think you will be able to roll up one huge speculative success after another. That's why our opening quote featured a second part: "The problem comes in finding that great speculation."

Michael Reilly, the author of the quote, runs an advisory service dedicated to actively seeking out great speculative opportunities (as well as quality investments of other types), and he has an exceptional track record. However, he frankly admits ferreting out successful speculations is tough — even when it's your full-time job. And, finding four or five major winners in a row is virtually impossible — especially if, like most people, you can devote only a few hours a week to your investments.

It's equally unlikely you will be able to find several stellar speculative opportunities at the same time — which is why you should limit the amount of capital you devote to speculation. If you have too many dollars chasing too few opportunities, you'll either wind up risking more than you should on a single play, or you'll start getting into less attractive situations just so you can keep all your money working. Either way, you're setting yourself up for a major set-back when something goes wrong — as it inevitably will.

Teamwork Is the Best Approach

The real solution to the speculation versus prudent investment puzzle is, of course, to combine the two. Together, your prudent investments and your selective speculations can create a powerful and efficient wealth-building team — helping you to reach your financial objectives more quickly without a significant increase in risks.

> *If you have too many dollars chasing too few opportunities, you'll either wind up risking more than you should, or you'll start getting into less attractive situations just so you can keep all your money working.*

Going back to our original $1,000 equity fund investment versus the $1,000 wheat speculation should give you an idea of how this teamwork concept can work on even a small scale. As noted, if you invested $1,000 in the equity mutual fund and made 11.9 percent a year, you'd have $3,078.22 after 10 years. However, if you made the speculative investment and it worked the way we described it, you'd have $3,100 after 10 days. *Note: You should be aware that, even if you wanted to risk only $1,000 on a speculation such as this, you'd have to put up at least $2,500 — and more likely $5,000 — to open a futures trading account. However, the excess money, over and above the required margin deposit should earn interest, just as in a regular money market account.*

You could then put that entire $3,100 into the equity fund, earning the same 11.9 percent rate, and your total assets would grow to $9,542.50. That's a difference of nearly $6,500 in 10 years (plus the 10 days for your speculation) — produced by just this one tiny bit of teamwork.

You could also keep the $1,000 for future speculations, hopefully scoring similar profits, and put $2,100 into the equity fund. If your future speculations worked, your total assets would increase dramatically. However, even if you lost the entire $1,000 on your next speculation, the $2,100 in the equity fund would still grow to $6,464.28 in 10 years — more than double what you would have made on the fund investment alone. Another strong testimonial for the teamwork approach.

Of course, as we've repeatedly said, you shouldn't even be thinking of speculating unless you have a much larger total asset base than $1,000 — i.e., a minimum of $200,000.

It should be obvious that even a modest improvement in your portfolio returns as a result of using speculative strategies will pay huge dividends. As our opening quote stated, however, the problem is finding just the right strategies — ones that offer opportunities for large profits without forcing you to take unacceptable risks.

However, the remainder of this lesson will help you do just that — providing details on several additional types of speculative investments, as well as outlining exactly how some of the more popular contained and/or defined-risk speculative plays work.

THE BASIC RULES OF SPECULATION

The fundamental rules of speculation are really quite simple. As alluded to earlier, the problem comes in finding the best vehicles and strategies through which to apply those rules.

As you learned in the last lesson — and in earlier sections of the course devoted to them — futures and options are among the most powerful, and most popular, of the speculative vehicles. Used independently, they offer tremendous leverage — i.e., the ability to generate major profits with only a small investment — as well as numerous other advantages. However, they also carry some severe disadvantages — not the least of which is the severe emotional trauma attached to the notions of extreme volatility, large and potentially unlimited losses and the possibility of having several tons of soybeans or pork bellies dumped on your front lawn.

While much of this is pure myth — especially the part about having to unexpectedly take delivery of 5,000 bushels of soybeans or 40,000 pounds of pork bellies (contract provisions and exchange rules *specifically* prohibit such unwanted deliveries) — the fact that such fears persist explains part of the reasoning for the most basic of the speculative rules, which is:

All speculations — regardless of the type — must make sense relative to your own personal goals, financial objectives and risk tolerances, both economic and emotional.

In other words, regardless of how big a profit a particular vehicle or strategy might offer, if a speculation doesn't fit in with your overall financial plan — or if it keeps you awake at nights — then it's not a *good* speculation. For example, if you cannot tolerate the possibility of unlimited losses, for whatever reason, then you must refrain from trading futures contracts, even though they offer enormous profit potential. To do otherwise would undermine the integrity of your entire wealth-building plan, as well as creating severe emotional stress — neither of which represent acceptable risk factors.

Your only alternative is to utilize futures in such a way as to contain or absolutely limit the risks involved — either by trading them only in ways that alter their risk parameters, such as in spreads, or by combining them with other types of investment vehicles, such as options, in ways that more precisely meet your defined objectives. *Note: A number of such combined futures/options strategies, along with explanations of how and when they work best, are detailed in Wealth-Building Step 89, "Using Commodity/Option Combinations — a Favored Strategy," which begins on page 7.*

The Second Basic Rule

The second fundamental rule of responsible speculating is equally simple:

The potential reward in any given speculation must justify the potential risk.

While this would seem obvious, many people have trouble quantifying it in practice. A comic strip we saw recently clearly illustrates this perceptual problem:

A man, seeing his friend buying a lottery ticket says, "Don't you realize what the odds are on those things?" To which the friend replies, "Sure, they're 50-50 — either I win $2 million or I don't!"

We don't know whether the man was truly oblivious to the fact the odds were really something like 14 million to one, or whether he was simply saying that the potential reward of $2 million justified the potential risk of $1 — regardless of the odds. However, we do know that you'll repeatedly be called on to make such risk/reward evaluations in the course of your speculative investment career — and you must have some guidelines.

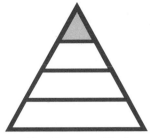

Using Commodity/Option Combinations — A Favored Strategy

What: Expand your speculative opportunities by employing strategies that combine the use of both futures and options on futures.

Why: By themselves, futures and options offer the potential for large speculative profits — but both also have major drawbacks that limit the manner in which they can be used. By combining the two vehicles, however, you can greatly increase their versatility — retaining the features you need to achieve specific objectives while reducing or strictly controlling the risks.

Risk: Medium to high. Although the risk in using combination strategies is generally lower than with individual futures or option trades, the potential losses can still be large on a percentage basis, if not in pure dollar terms.

Safety: Medium to high. Futures and options on futures are listed on recognized exchanges and most are clearly understood and widely traded. Thus, there is little chance of losses due to defaults or technical problems.

Liquidity: High. The futures and options discussed in this Step represent popular underlying commodities with large trading volumes. Thus, you should be able to buy and sell whenever you want at prices quite close to those you desire.

Why not: Trading in commodity or financial futures and their related options is highly speculative, featuring fast-moving markets and the risk of large losses. As a result, strategies involving these vehicles are not suitable for small or beginning investors, nor for larger or more experienced investors with a low emotional tolerance for risk. In other words, if worrying about possible trading losses will keep you awake at night, you shouldn't trade futures or options, no matter how much money or experience you have. At a minimum, you should have an investment portfolio worth at least $200,000 (exclusive of the equity in your primary residence) before doing these trades — and, even then, it's best to limit the amount of money you devote to the strategies to no more than five to 10 percent of your total assets.

Buy/Invest from: Any discount or full-service futures broker — or the futures division of any of the leading stock brokerage firms. *Note: You must have a separate account to trade futures and options on futures; these strategies cannot be done through your regular stockbroker.*

Background: Futures contracts in varying sizes are available on more than 70 well-known commodities, financial instruments, currencies and market indexes — and options are traded on most of the full-size futures. Each futures contract also has anywhere from four to 12 delivery months per year, and each option typically has three to 4 expiration months and eight to 20 different striking prices in play at any given time. Thus, there is an almost unlimited number of choices for investors desiring to structure combination strategies involving the two vehicles.

In spite of this, there are really only six basic combinations that involve an individual futures contract and a single option — and only four of these are commonly used. The six one-on-one combinations are:

1. *Buy the futures contract and buy a call option*: This would be an extremely bullish combination since both the future and the call would profit on rising prices. However, because the future and the call option essentially provide duplicate opportunities and risks, this combination is seldom used — with investors more likely to either buy two futures contracts or buy two call options. *Note: If you need a refresher on exactly how futures or options work — or on any of the related terminology — refer back to the lessons "Lots of options with options" and "Commodity and financial futures," both found earlier in the* 100 Steps to Wealth *program.*

2. ***Buy the futures contract and buy a put option***: This is also an aggressively bullish combination since it profits only when futures prices rise substantially. This combination is commonly referred to as a "synthetic call" because it offers unlimited profit potential in a rising market, but precisely defined and limited risk in the event prices fall — essentially the same benefits enjoyed by the purchaser of a call option. The advantages it has over a plain call purchase are the possibility of a "two-way" profit in a highly volatile market environment and the fact that it is sometimes less risky (lower maximum exposure) than a call option. The principal disadvantage is that the break-even point is usually (although not always) higher than with an outright call purchase. The strictly limited risk is the obvious advantage over an outright futures purchase, while the main disadvantage is a higher break-even point. *Note: A variation on this strategy involves purchasing a put option only after you have achieved a substantial profit on a long futures position. This "locks in" a large part of the profit since any loss on a subsequent drop in the futures price below the striking price of the put will be offset by gains on the put side of the combination, reduced only by the premium paid for the option.*

3. ***Buy the futures contract and write (or sell) a call option***: This combination strategy, known as "covered call writing," is a neutral to mildly bullish play designed to generate income and/or provide limited downside risk protection. If the price of the futures contract rises, the investor's profit will rise until it reaches a maximum when the future passes the striking price of the short call option. If the futures price remains stable, the investor will break-even on the future, but profit by the amount received for the sale of the call, which will expire worthless. If the futures price falls, the investor will lose money on the future, but some or all of that loss will be offset by the premium received for the call, which will again expire worthless. The principal disadvantage is the lost opportunity the investor suffers if the future rallies strongly — i.e., no additional profit can be made once the future moves above the striking price of the call. A secondary disadvantage is the unlimited risk should the futures price fall sharply — though, as stated before, part of this loss will be offset by the retained call premium.

4. ***Sell the futures contract and buy a put option***: This would be an extremely bearish combination since both the future and the call would profit on falling prices. However, because the future and the put option effectively provide duplicate opportunities and risks, this combination is seldom used — with investors more likely to just sell two futures contracts or buy two put options.

5. ***Sell the futures contract and buy a call option***: This is an aggressively bearish combination since it profits only when futures prices fall substantially. This combo is commonly referred to as a "synthetic put" because it has unlimited profit potential in a falling market, but precisely defined and limited risk should prices rise — essentially the same benefits enjoyed by the purchaser of a put option. The advantages it has over an outright put purchase are a lower level of risk (always limited to the call's time value) and the possibility of a "two-way" profit in a highly volatile market environment. The main disadvantage is that the break-even point is usually (though not always) higher than with a straight put purchase. The strictly limited risk is the main advantage over the outright sale of a futures contract, while the key disadvantage is a more remote break-even point. *Note: As in strategy No. 2 above, this combination can also be established to lock in most of a profit achieved on an earlier futures short sale.*

6. ***Sell the futures contract and write (or sell) a put option:*** This strategy, known as "covered put writing", is neutral to mildly bearish play designed to generate income and/or provide limited upside risk protection on a short futures position. If the price of the futures contract falls, the investor's profit will increase until it reaches a maximum when the future drops below the striking price of the short put option. Should the futures price remain stable, the investor will break-even on the future, but profit by the amount received for the sale of the put, which will expire worthless. If the future rises in price, the investor will lose money on the short future, but some or all of the loss will be offset by the premium received for the put, which will again expire worthless. The principal disadvantage is the lost opportunity the investor suffers if the future falls sharply, since no added profit can be made once the future falls below the striking price of the put. A secondary disadvantage is unlimited risk should the futures price rally strongly — though, once again, part of this loss will be offset by the retained put premium.

The risk/reward parameters and the break-even points on any of these combinations can be adjusted by selecting varying option strike prices — i.e., by buying or selling in-the-money, at-the-money or out-of-the-money options. Construction of a scenario-analysis grid, as discussed below, will define the possible outcomes for any play you are considering, allowing you to pick the option/futures combination that offers the risk/reward parameters best suited to your objective.

There are also several combination strategies that involve the purchase or sale of a futures contract and the simultaneous purchase or sale of more than one option. The most common strategy of this type is known as a "fence" and has risk/reward characteristics similar to an option spread in that there is both a maximum possible loss and a maximum potential profit — both defined by the option prices received when the trade is opened and the range between the striking prices of those options.

The strategy has two versions:

- The bullish combination involves the purchase of a futures contract, the purchase of an out-of-the-money put option and the sale of an out-of-the-money call option.

- The bearish version involves the sale of a futures contract, the purchase of an out-of-the-money call option and the sale of an out-of-the-money put option.

Note: To be successful, these strategies usually require a striking-price range between the two options that equates to at least $2,000 to $2,500 — e.g., on a 5,000-bushel wheat contract, there should be at least 40 cents between the striking prices of the two options used, and 50 cents might be even better.

▷ ▶ ▶ ▶ **If you want to get started today, here's what you need to do to add futures and options combinations to your arsenal of speculative trading strategies:**

As noted, the key to success with any strategy involving a combination of futures and options is analyzing the risk/reward characteristics of the trade. This will help you determine three key things:

- Whether the risk is an amount you are comfortable with.

- Whether the potential reward is worth the risk and the effort.

- Whether the moves required to both break even and achieve a satisfactory profit are reasonable given the time frame allowed by the option.

So you can see exactly how each of the four leading combination strategies work and compare the risk/reward characteristics of each — as well as gauge the impact striking-price selection can have — we are going to present six scenario-analysis grids based on actual conditions and prices in the wheat futures and options markets on May 30, 1995.

The first three scenarios will cover the most common speculative combination strategy — buying a futures contract and buying a put option (No. 2 above) — as done with three different puts (the at-the-money, the in-the-money and the out-of-the-money).

We'll then do three additional scenarios for strategies No. 3, 5 and 6 above so you can compare their risk/reward characteristics with strategy No. 2. *Note: We won't bother with scenarios for combinations No. 1 and 4 since, as we said, they offer no strategic advantage over the outright purchase of two futures contracts or two options and are thus rarely used.*

We will then show exactly how each of the six strategies would have actually performed through late July 1995 — a point at which the 1995 wheat crop was firmly in place, with few remaining uncertainties as to weather or crop conditions. All scenarios and results are based on a May 30, 1995, entry — when December wheat futures were priced at 392.75 cents per bushel ($3.9275) and December wheat options were quoted as shown in the following table:

DATE: May 30, 1995 — December wheat at 392.75 cents

December calls		December puts	
380	29	420	40-3/4
390	24-1/2	410	33-3/4
400	21	400	27-1/4
410	17-1/2	390	21-1/4
420	15	380	16-1/2

All prices in cents per bushel.

Strategy No. 1 — As we said, this offers little strategic advantage and is therefore not worth explaining.

Strategy No. 2, Scenario No. 1 — Buy the December wheat future at 392.75 cents per bushel and simultaneously buy the out-of-the-money December 380 put option at 16-1/2 cents ($0.1650) a bushel. This is considered an aggressive speculation. As the following scenario grid shows, it has a limited, but relatively high level of risk; large and unlimited profit potential; and a fairly high break-even point — nearly 17 cents a bushel above the starting wheat futures price. See the grid on the following page:

Step 89: *Using Commodity/Option Combinations — A Favored Strategy*

Buy December future at 392.75 cents and buy 380 put at 16.50

Ending Futures Price	Futures Entry Price	Profit/ (Loss) On Futures	Ending Option Value	Option Entry Value	Option Profit (Loss)	Total Profit/ (Loss)
360.00	392.75	($1,637.50)	$1,000	($825)	$175	($1,462.50)
370.00	392.75	($1,137.50)	$ 500	($825)	($325)	($1,462.50)
380.00	392.75	($ 637.50)	0	($825)	($825)	($1,462.50)
390.00	392.75	($ 137.50)	0	($825)	($825)	($ 962.50)
400.00	392.75	$ 362.50	0	($825)	($825)	($ 462.50)
409.25	392.75	$ 825.00	0	($825)	($825)	0
410.00	392.75	$ 862.50	0	($825)	($825)	$ 37.50
420.00	392.75	$ 1,362.50	0	($825)	($825)	$ 537.50
430.00	392.75	$ 1,862.50	0	($825)	($825)	$ 1,037.50
440.00	392.75	$ 2,362.50	0	($825)	($825)	$ 1,537.50
450.00	392.75	$ 2,862.50	0	($825)	($825)	$ 2,037.50
460.00	392.75	$ 3,362.50	0	($825)	($825)	$ 2,537.50
470.00	392.75	$ 3,862.50	0	($825)	($825)	$ 3,037.50
480.00	392.75	$ 4,362.50	0	($825)	($825)	$ 3,537.50

Strategy No. 2, Scenario No. 2 — Buy the December wheat future at 392.75 cents a bushel and simultaneously buy the at-the-money December 390 put option at 21-1/4 cents ($0.2125) a bushel. This is considered a less aggressive speculation. The risk is limited and slightly smaller than in play No. 1, and the profit potential is still large and unlimited. However, the break-even point is a bit higher — the trade-off you make for the reduced risk. Nevertheless, this is probably the best play, balancing moderate risk with a good probability of success. Here's the grid:

Buy December future at 392.75 cents and buy 390 put at 21.25

Ending Futures Price	Futures Entry Price	Profit/ (Loss) On Futures	Ending Option Value	Option Entry Value*	Option Profit (Loss)*	Total Profit/ (Loss)
360.00	392.75	($1,637.50)	$1,500	($1,063)	$ 437	($1,200)
370.00	392.75	($1,137.50)	$1,000	($1,063)	($ 63)	($1,200)
380.00	392.75	($ 637.50)	$ 500	($1,063)	($ 563)	($1,200)
390.00	392.75	($ 137.50)	0	($1,063)	($1,063)	($1,200)
400.00	392.75	$ 362.50	0	($1,063)	($1,063)	($ 700)
410.00	392.75	$ 862.50	0	($1,063)	($1,063)	($ 200)
414.00	392.75	$1,062.00	0	($1,063)	($1,063)	0
420.00	392.75	$1,362.50	0	($1,063)	($1,063)	$ 300
430.00	392.75	$1,862.50	0	($1,063)	($1,063)	$ 800
440.00	392.75	$2,362.50	0	($1,063)	($1,063)	$1,300
450.00	392.75	$2,862.50	0	($1,063)	($1,063)	$1,800
460.00	392.75	$3,362.50	0	($1,063)	($1,063)	$2,300
470.00	392.75	$3,862.50	0	($1,063)	($1,063)	$2,800
480.00	392.75	$4,362.50	0	($1,063)	($1,063)	$3,300
490.00	392.75	$4,862.50	0	($1,063)	($1,063)	$3,800

Numbers are rounded.

Step 89: *Using Commodity/Option Combinations — A Favored Strategy*

Strategy No. 2, Scenario No. 3 — Buy the December wheat future at 392.75 cents a bushel and simultaneously buy the in-the-money December 400 put option at 27-1/4 cents ($0.2725) a bushel. This is considered the least aggressive speculation because it has the lowest level of risk. However, it has a much higher break-even point and, as a result, the potential profit is lower — although it remains unlimited should wheat make a major up move. In spite of the reduced risk, this version of the strategy has the lowest probability of success and is thus less desirable than the more aggressive speculations in Scenarios 1 and 2. Here's the grid:

Buy December future at 392.75 cents and buy 400 put at 27.25

Ending Futures Price	Futures Entry Price	Profit/ (Loss) On Futures	Ending Option Value	Option Entry Value*	Option Profit (Loss)*	Total Profit/ (Loss)
360.00	392.75	($1,637.50)	$1,000	($ 825)	$ 175	($1,462.50)
360.00	392.75	($1,637.50)	$2,000	($1,363)	$ 638	($1,000.00)
370.00	392.75	($1,137.50)	$1,500	($1,363)	$ 138	($1,000.00)
380.00	392.75	($ 637.50)	$1,000	($1,363)	($ 363)	($1,000.00)
390.00	392.75	($ 137.50)	$ 500	($1,363)	($ 863)	($1,000.00)
400.00	392.75	$ 362.50	$ 500	($1,363)	($1,363)	($1,000.00)
409.25	392.75	$ 825.00	0	($1,363)	($1,363)	($ 537.50)
410.00	392.75	$ 862.50	0	($1,363)	($1,363)	($ 500.00)
420.00	392.75	$1,362.50	0	($1,363)	($1,363)	0
430.00	392.75	$1,862.50	0	($1,363)	($1,363)	$ 500.00
440.00	392.75	$2,362.50	0	($1,363)	($1,363)	$1,000.00
450.00	392.75	$2,862.50	0	($1,363)	($1,363)	$1,500.00
460.00	392.75	$3,362.50	0	($1,363)	($1,363)	$2,000.00
470.00	392.75	$3,862.50	0	($1,363)	($1,363)	$2,500.00
480.00	392.75	$4,362.50	0	($1,363)	($1,363)	$3,000.00

Numbers are rounded.

Strategy No. 3 — Buy the December wheat future at 392.75 cents a bushel and simultaneously write (sell) an at-the-money December 390 call option at 24.50 cents per bushel. This is a classic example of a covered-writing play — to be used in a stable or mildly bullish market. It has a limited profit potential if prices hold steady or move higher, although the maximum profit will be achieved even if prices fail to rise at all. The possible loss is unlimited if prices should drop sharply, but the play has a very favorable break-even point — with no loss incurred until the futures price drops more than 24 cents per bushel. Here's the grid:

Buy December future at 392.75 cents and sell 390 call at 24.50

Ending Futures Price	Futures Entry Price	Profit/ (Loss) On Futures	Ending Option Value	Option Entry Value	Option Profit (Loss)	Total Profit/ (Loss)
300.00	392.75	($4,637.50)	0	$1,225	$1,225	($3,412.50)
310.00	392.75	($4,137.50)	0	$1,225	$1,225	($2,912.50)
320.00	392.75	($3,637.50)	0	$1,225	$1,225	($2,412.50)
330.00	392.75	($3,137.50)	0	$1,225	$1,225	($1,912.50)
340.00	392.75	($2,637.50)	0	$1,225	$1,225	($1,412.50)
350.00	392.75	($2,137.50)	0	$1,225	$1,225	($ 912.50)
360.00	392.75	($1,637.50)	0	$1,225	$1,225	($ 412.50)

(Chart continued from page 13)

Buy December future at 392.75 cents and sell 390 call at 24.50

Ending Futures Price	Futures Entry Price	Profit/ (Loss) On Futures	Ending Option Value	Option Entry Value	Option Profit (Loss)	Total Profit/ (Loss)
368.25	392.75	($1,225.00)	0	$1,225	$ 1,225	0
370.00	392.75	($1,137.50)	0	$1,225	$ 1,225	$ 87.50
380.00	392.75	($ 637.50)	0	$1,225	$ 1,225	$ 587.50
390.00	392.75	($ 137.50)	0	$1,225	$ 1,225	$1,087.50
400.00	392.75	$ 362.50	($ 500)	$1,225	$ 725	$1,087.50
410.00	392.75	$ 862.50	($1,000)	$1,225	$ 225	$1,087.50
420.00	392.75	$1,362.50	($1,500)	$1,225	($ 275)	$1,087.50
430.00	392.75	$1,862.50	($2,000)	$1,225	($ 775)	$1,087.50
440.00	392.75	$2,362.50	($2,500)	$1,225	($1,275)	$1,087.50

Strategy No. 4 — Like strategy one, it bears little benefit in explaining.

Strategy No. 5 — Sell the December wheat futures contract at 392.75 cents a bushel and buy the at-the-money December 390 call option at 24.50 cents per bushel. As should be obvious, this play is simply the bearish equivalent of Strategy No. 2, as detailed in Scenario 2. It has strictly defined and limited risk that's considered moderate, and pays off big, with potentially unlimited gains if prices fall sharply. It does, however, have a reasonably low break-even point, requiring a drop in the futures price of more than 24 cents before you make a profit (a reflection of the higher premium generally afforded calls over puts). In addition, it will suffer the maximum loss if prices merely stay where they are. Even so, this is considered the most prudent combination play for highly bearish speculators. Here's the grid:

Sell December future at 392.75 cents and buy 390 call at 24.50

Ending Futures Price	Futures Entry Price	Profit/ (Loss) On Futures	Ending Option Value	Option Entry Value	Option Profit (Loss)	Total Profit/ (Loss)
300.00	392.75	$4,637.50	0	($1,225)	($1,225)	$3,412.50
310.00	392.75	$4,137.50	0	($1,225)	($1,225)	$2,912.50
320.00	392.75	$3,637.50	0	($1,225)	($1,225)	$2,412.50
330.00	392.75	$3,137.50	0	($1,225)	($1,225)	$1,912.50
340.00	392.75	$2,637.50	0	($1,225)	($1,225)	$1,412.50
350.00	392.75	$2,137.50	0	($1,225)	($1,225)	$ 912.50
360.00	392.75	$1,637.50	0	($1,225)	($1,225)	$ 412.50
368.25	392.75	$1,225.00	0	($1,225)	($1,225)	0
370.00	392.75	$1,137.50	0	($1,225)	($1,225)	($ 87.50)
380.00	392.75	$ 637.50	0	($1,225)	($1,225)	($ 587.50)
390.00	392.75	$ 137.50	0	($1,225)	($1,225)	($1,087.50)
400.00	392.75	($ 362.50)	$ 500	($1,225)	($ 725)	($1,087.50)
410.00	392.75	($ 862.50)	$1,000	($1,225)	($ 225)	($1,087.50)
420.00	392.75	($1,362.50)	$1,500	($1,225)	$ 275	($1,087.50)
430.00	392.75	($1,862.50)	$2,000	($1,225)	$ 775	($1,087.50)
440.00	392.75	($2,362.50)	$2,500	($1,225)	$1,275	($1,087.50)

Step 89: *Using Commodity/Option Combinations — A Favored Strategy*

Strategy No. 6 — Sell the December wheat futures contract at 392.75 cents a bushel and sell the at-the-money December 390 put option at 21.25 cents per bushel. This is the bearish equivalent of strategy No. 3, designed to produce income and loss protection in stable to mildly bearish markets. It has a limited, but still quite nice profit potential if prices hold steady or move lower. The possible loss is unlimited if prices rally strongly, but the strategy has a very favorable break-even point, with no loss incurred until the futures price climbs more than 21 cents a bushel. In addition, the price needs to fall less than 3 cents a bushel — and stay down — to produce the maximum profit. Here's the grid:

Sell December future at 392.75 and sell 390 put at 21.25

Ending Futures Price	Futures Entry Price	Profit/ (Loss) On Futures	Ending Option Value	Option Entry Value	Option Profit (Loss)	Total Profit/ (Loss)
340.00	392.75	$2,637.50	($2,500)	$1,063	($1,438)	$1,200
350.00	392.75	$2,137.50	($2,000)	$1,063	($ 938)	$1,200
360.00	392.75	$1,637.50	($1,500)	$1,063	($ 438)	$1,200
370.00	392.75	$1,137.50	($1,000)	$1,063	$ 63	$1,200
376.25	392.75	$ 825.00	($ 688)	$1,063	$ 375	$1,200
380.00	392.75	$ 637.50	($ 500)	$1,063	$ 563	$1,200
390.00	392.75	$ 137.50	0	$1,063	$1,063	$1,200
400.00	392.75	($ 362.50)	0	$1,063	$1,063	$ 700
410.00	392.75	($ 862.50)	0	$1,063	$1,063	$ 200
414.00	392.75	($1,062.50)	0	$1,063	$1,063	0
420.00	392.75	($1,362.50)	0	$1,063	$1,063	($ 300)
430.00	392.75	($1,862.50)	0	$1,063	$1,063	($ 800)
440.00	392.75	($2,362.50)	0	$1,063	$1,063	($1,300)
450.00	392.75	($2,862.50)	0	$1,063	$1,063	($1,800)
460.00	392.75	($3,362.50)	0	$1,063	$1,063	($2,300)
470.00	392.75	($3,862.50)	0	$1,063	$1,063	($2,800)
480.00	392.75	($4,362.50)	0	$1,063	$1,063	($3,300)
490.00	392.75	($4,862.50)	0	$1,063	$1,063	($3,800)
500.00	392.75	($5,362.50)	0	$1,063	$1,063	($4,300)

Now, let's see what actually happened. As noted in the main text of this lesson, May, June and July of 1995 saw a very strong market for wheat, based first on flooding in the Midwest and later on rapidly developing hot, dry weather. Export demand was also strong, particularly from China. As a result, by July 21, 1995, the price of December wheat futures contracts had risen to 479.50 cents per bushel ($4.7950) — a gain of almost 90 cents a bushel ($4,500 on a 5,000-bushel contract) from May 30 levels. Option prices had also changed dramatically, as shown in the following table:

DATE: July 21, 1995 — December wheat at 479.50 cents

December calls		December puts	
3809	9-1/2	420	6-1/2
390	90	410	4-1/2
400	81	400	3-1/4
410	72-1/2	390	2-1/4
420	64-3/4	380	1-5/8

All prices in cents per bushel.

Step 89: *Using Commodity/Option Combinations — A Favored Strategy*

Given those prices, here's how each of the six plays shown in our scenarios stood on July 21, 1995:

Strategy No. 2, Scenario No. 1 — Buy the December wheat future at 392.75 cents per bushel and simultaneously buy the out-of-the-money December 380 put option at 16-1/2 cents ($0.1650) a bushel.

Ending Futures Price	Futures Entry Price	Profit/ (Loss) On Futures	Ending Option Value	Option Entry Value	Option Profit (Loss)	Total Profit/ (Loss)
479.50	392.75	$4,337.50	$81.25	($825)	($743.75)	$3,593.75

Strategy No. 2, Scenario No. 2 — Buy the December wheat future at 392.75 cents a bushel and simultaneously buy the at-the-money December 390 put option at 21-1/4 cents ($0.2125) per bushel.

Ending Futures Price	Futures Entry Price	Profit/ (Loss) On Futures	Ending Option Value	Option Entry Value	Option Profit (Loss)	Total Profit/ (Loss)
479.50	392.75	$4,337.50	$112.50	($825)	($712.50)	$3,625.00

Strategy No. 2, Scenario No. 3 — Buy the December wheat future at 392.75 cents a bushel and simultaneously buy the in-the-money December 400 put option at 27-1/4 cents ($0.2725) a bushel.

Ending Futures Price	Futures Entry Price	Profit/ (Loss) On Futures	Ending Option Value	Option Entry Value	Option Profit (Loss)	Total Profit/ (Loss)
479.50	392.75	$4,337.50	$ 175	($1,363)	($1,188)	$3,150.00

Strategy No. 3 — Buy the December wheat future at 392.75 cents a bushel and simultaneously write (sell) an at-the-money December 390 call option at 24.50 cents per bushel.

Ending Futures Price	Futures Entry Price	Profit/ (Loss) On Futures	Ending Option Value	Option Entry Value	Option Profit (Loss)	Total Profit/ (Loss)
479.50	392.75	$4,337.50	($4,500)	$1,225	($3,275)	$1,062.50

Strategy No. 5 — Sell the December wheat futures contract at 392.75 cents a bushel and buy the at-the-money December 390 call option at 24.50 cents per bushel.

Ending Futures Price	Futures Entry Price	Profit/ (Loss) On Futures	Ending Option Value	Option Entry Value	Option Profit (Loss)	Total Profit/ (Loss)
479.50	392.75	($4,337.50)	$4,500	($1,225)	$3,250	($1,062.50)

Strategy No. 6 — Sell the December wheat futures contract at 392.75 cents a bushel and sell the at-the-money December 390 put option at 21.25 cents per bushel.

Ending Futures Price	Futures Entry Price	Profit/ (Loss) On Futures	Ending Option Value	Option Entry Value	Option Profit (Loss)	Total Profit/ (Loss)
479.50	392.75	($4,337.50)	0	$1,063	$1,063	($3,275)

If you are strongly bullish, you'll want to use Strategy No. 2; mildly bullish, Strategy No. 3; strongly bearish, Strategy No. 5; mildly bearish, Strategy No. 6

Obviously, given what happened in the wheat market in the early summer of 1995, the strategies with a bullish orientation worked to perfection, while those dependent on a stable or falling market fared the worst — i.e, Strategy No. 5 suffered the maximum loss, and Strategy No. 6, the bearish covered-writing play took a huge $3,275 hit (the perfect example of what happens to a covered option writer when prices move too much).

It should be noted, however, that — as with all speculative strategies — timing can be extremely important in combination plays. By mid-August of 1995, December wheat had pulled back substantially, and the profit/loss pictures looked significantly different on many of these trades.

There are no specific rules for doing any of the combination strategies. You have to determine the proper entry points, based both on your expectations for the market and on the risk/reward scenarios you can create given the current futures and option prices. If you are strongly bullish, you'll want to use Strategy No. 2; mildly bullish, Strategy No. 3; strongly bearish, Strategy No. 5; mildly bearish, Strategy No. 6 — but only if the prices produce favorable risk/reward balances with reasonable break-even points.

*Note: There is one iron-clad rule for doing futures/option combination trades — **always** make sure you use **matching** futures and options. In other words, make absolutely sure the options you are buying or selling call for delivery of the futures contract you are buying or selling. With most futures, this won't be a problem since both will be identified by the same month — i.e., the delivery month for the future and the expiration month for the option will be the same. However, some futures, such as the currencies, have so-called "serial" options, meaning each futures contract has three sets of related options — e.g., the April, May and June German mark options all call for delivery of the June D-mark futures contract. Be aware too that, while some options are identified by the futures contract delivery month, they actually expire in the prior month — e.g., the December wheat options we used in our scenarios actually expire the third Friday of November.*

Some advice on placing your orders: Unlike the option spreads you learned about in the wealth-building step: The Three Best, Highly Favorable Option Spreads, found in the previous lesson, you cannot position a combination strategy with a single order. Although futures and their related options typically trade on the same exchange, they generally trade in different "pits" — meaning one floor broker will have to execute your futures trade and another will have to do your option trade.

In most instances, this shouldn't be a problem since you'll be dealing in fairly active markets and should have little difficulty getting the prices you want — assuming you verify their availability with your broker at the time you place your order. Still, if you want to avoid the possibility of getting only half a combination, you should probably allow a little extra leeway on the price of the option you want to buy or sell since the options are less actively traded than the futures.

We advise against using market orders for options simply because the bid/ask spreads can be quite large, resulting in bad fills that will upset the risk/reward balance of your trade. However, if you're concerned about safety (i.e., you don't want to be left holding just an unlimited-risk futures position), you may want to place your option order first, instructing the broker to enter your futures order only after the option purchase or sale is confirmed.

When closing a combination position involving a "long" option — i.e., one you've bought — always close the futures portion of your combination first, then sell the option. That way, you'll never have to worry about holding just a long or short futures contract. However, when you exit a combination position with a "short" option (one you've sold), you need to take a different approach. The safest strategy is probably to place a limit order on both the future and the option, with instructions to convert the remaining order to a market order as soon as one is executed. This may occasionally result in a bad fill on an option — but that's less of a danger than holding either an outright futures position or a "naked" short option.

Note: If you are interested in trying a "fence" — one of the combinations using multiple options — you can construct a scenario grid in exactly the same fashion shown in this Step. All you have to do is add another column for the extra option, and then total all three values, rather than just two. Such a scenario will quickly define both the maximum potential profit and the maximum possible loss for such combinations, as well as giving you the exact break-even point. In addition, the grid doesn't have to be too extensive. A bullish fence will always show the maximum profit any time the ending futures price is above the strike price of the call you sell, and the maximum loss any time the futures price is below the strike price of the put you buy. Likewise, a bearish fence will always show the maximum profit when the ending futures price is below the strike price of the put you sell, and the maximum loss when the ending futures price is above the strike price of the call you buy. ▲

Continued from p. 6

Unfortunately, there are no hard and fast rules that we can give you — you're pretty much on your own, depending on your individual situation and your specific goals, as well as the characteristics of each individual trade. We do, however, want to warn you against trying to come up with some "universal law" that will apply to all your speculations.

For example, it's not enough to say "I'll only do a speculation when I can get a 5-to-1 reward/risk advantage." Why? Simply because that single rule doesn't give you enough information.

For example, most people would probably find it quite acceptable to risk $200 on a speculation with a potential reward of $1,000 — even if it offered a fairly low probability of success. However, given an equally low chance of success, very few people would feel comfortable risking $200,000 on a speculation offering a reward of $1 million — despite the fact that it had an identical 5-to-1 ratio.

The difference is clear. The loss of $200 would have a minimal impact on the overall portfolio of most speculators — particularly those following our primary rule requiring a minimum portfolio of $100,000 before engaging in speculation. However, even the most seasoned of speculators would likely shudder at the prospect of a $200,000 loss — and it would literally wipe out the majority of newer or less experienced traders (which is why we also suggest limiting your speculative capital to no more than 5 to 10 percent of your total asset base).

Scenario Analysis Is The Answer

So, what do you do? The answer is to religiously practice a technique known as scenario analysis, which takes the conditions and prices available at the time a speculative trade is being considered and uses them to project all the possible outcomes for the play, based on likely movements in the prices of the vehicles involved. *Note: You've already seen a number of examples of this technique in previous lessons, and many more are featured in the wealth-building steps included in this lesson. Study these and you should easily be able to determine how to do your own.*

Depending on the type of strategy being evaluated, scenario analysis can tell you many things:

- It can define the maximum potential profit and the maximum possible loss — essential in determining exact reward/risk ratios for option spreads and other types of combination strategies.

- It can tell you the break-even points, maximum-profit points and maximum-loss points — and how far the prices of the securities involved need to move to reach those levels — all extremely helpful in determining the probability of success on any given trade.

- It can provide insight into the best levels at which to set profit targets or place stop-loss orders, as well as helping you set loss limits on trades that don't have strictly defined or limited losses.

- It can provide a basis for timing your trade entries — i.e., helping you determine the most favorable entry prices and conditions and providing the incentive to wait for those circumstances to develop.

- Most importantly, it can assist you in comparing various types of trades and identifying the best internal alternatives (such as the choice of striking prices in option trades) so that you select the strategies or vehicles best suited to achieving your objective at any particular time.

Scenario analysis can be used with almost any type of speculative investment situation — from the simple purchase of a penny stock to the most complicated option strategy (such as a "butterfly") or combination futures/options play (such as a "fence"). The only difference will lie in the number of columns you have to use in your grid and the number of values you have to add or subtract to project the possible outcomes. However, whether it involves writing down a single column of projected stock prices or constructing a four-column grid representing long and short futures and/or option positions, scenario analysis is always worth your while.

Fundamental Rule No. 3

The third basic rule for successful speculation is also simple:

Always learn as much as possible about the markets in which you plan to speculate.

Again, this should be obvious — but many people still fail to do their homework. They see a market or a particular stock or commodity moving, and decide to jump on board without adequately investigating why the moves are occurring — or what might cause them to stop (or reverse). Then, they're totally surprised when things don't work out as expected and they suffer a loss.

Even scenario analysis won't help offset the impact of failing to learn about the market in which you're speculating. In fact, that is the major failing of scenario analysis. It will tell you quite precisely all the possible things that can happen — but it won't give you a clue as to "why" or "how soon" they might occur.

Only a fundamental knowledge of the specific market or individual commodity can do that. *Note: To refresh your knowledge regarding fundamental analysis and what to look for in eval-*

uating a given market or security, refer back to the lessons titled "Climbing the pyramid: finding the uncommon common share;" "Looking through the clouds: be a professional stock picker" and "Commodity and financial futures."

These people feel that, since they've gone to the trouble of learning the fundamentals of the market, checking out the technical situation and doing a scenario analysis, their efforts will be wasted if they don't do some kind of trade. The speculative sector [however] is the one asset-allocation category where it's perfectly alright to have a "zero" commitment of assets.

Likewise, while scenario analysis can give you a good idea about when to enter or exit a trade based on the most favorable reward/risk parameters, it can't tell you "when" the market will reach the point that those conditions exist — or if, for some reason, it might never reach such a point. Fundamental analysis will help with that, but technical analysis — reviewing past trading and price patterns, and looking for similar current conditions — may be more beneficial.

Make it a practice to at least look at a chart for any commodity you trade (*Investor's Business Daily* runs charts for all the major commodity markets over the course of each week's papers) before making entry or exit decisions (unless the exit decisions are based on having achieved your target profit). That should help you identify any shifting market trends, as well as avert the possibility that you might open a trade dependent on a move counter to an existing trend — always a bad idea when speculating in futures and options. *Note: For a refresher on the basics of technical analysis, refer back to the lessons titled "Timing your trades" and "Commodity and financial futures."*

By combining a fundamental knowledge of the market and the individual commodity or security with an awareness of the technical patterns in play at any given time — and then doing a good scenario analysis of the particular situation in which you're interested — you should greatly improve your odds of success with any speculation you choose to undertake. In addition, you should also improve your chances of avoiding unfavorable speculations in the first place — which brings us to fundamental rule No. 4

Patience — The Fourth Speculative Requirement

Many people consider successful speculation as being the art of making a large profit in a short period of time. However, that doesn't mean you have to rush to get your money in play.

As we noted in the prior lesson, the speculative sector is the one asset-allocation category where it's perfectly alright to have a "zero" commitment of assets. In fact, in many cases — your long-term wealth-building efforts may be impacted more by the speculations you choose not to undertake than by those you actually do. That's because a failed speculative play not only results in a current loss, it also reduces the amount of capital that will be working for you in the future — robbing you of the power of compounding on the lost assets for years to come.

Thus, it's extremely important for you to follow the fourth fundamental rule of speculation, which is:

Be patient. Don't undertake any speculative trade until the conditions are highly favorable and the odds of success are clearly on your side.

Again, this would seem to be an obvious guideline — but it's one an amazing number of people have trouble following. These people feel that, since they've gone to the trouble of learning the fundamentals of the market, checking out the technical situation and doing a scenario analysis, their efforts will be wasted if they don't do some kind of trade. So, they ignore everything they've just discovered (or, at least, some key part of it), and go ahead with a speculation — even though it has a weak fundamental basis, a poor technical outlook, a less-than-optimum reward/risk ratio or a low probability of success.

There is one iron-clad rule for doing futures/option combination trades — always make sure you use matching futures and options. In other words, make absolutely sure the options you are buying or selling call for delivery of the futures contract you are buying or selling.

And, lo and behold, they're surprised when the thing doesn't work. "How could I lose money," they cry. "Look how much time I spent checking things out."

Unfortunately, time and effort expended don't automatically equate to profits — but, if you read the results right, they can nearly always equate to the prevention of losses. In other words, if you do your research and find anything you don't like — anything at all — *don't do the trade!*

Instead, simply use the knowledge you've gained as the basis for further study and examination of the market and the technical situation. Wait for conditions to improve — and for subsequent scenario analyses to show more favorable reward/risk parameters. If those things never happen, you'll have lost nothing but a little more time — but, if they do, you'll be ready to enter a speculative position with a much higher probability of success.

Don't Jump on the Bandwagon

The application of patience to your speculative trading also applies to so-called "bandwagon" situations, which we've described before. People see a market moving, and — fearful that they'll miss out on an opportunity that others have already discovered — they rush to enter a trade without properly evaluating why the move is occurring.

This is an almost guaranteed prescription for disaster — simply because you're operating from a position of ignorance (and everyone knows that "a fool and his money are fun to be with..." oops, rather... "are soon parted"). Besides, in many volatile markets, the fact that a move large enough for you to notice it has already taken place typically means prices are more apt to reverse than to continue in the same direction.

So, always ignore bandwagon situations — and patiently wait for a trading opportunity based on reasons you understand and reward/risk scenarios that are strongly in your favor.

Note: Don't make the mistake of confusing a bandwagon situation with the beginning or continuation of a significant trend. As you will learn in your ongoing study of investment, many markets tend to move in prolonged trends — and the astute speculator takes advantage of this tendency at every opportunity. For example, two of the plays featured in Wealth-Building Step 90, "Start Currency Speculation With Three Historically High-Return Strategies" — which begins on page 21 — are designed to take advantage of the fact that currencies have a strong tendency to move in trends. Learn which markets are "trending markets" and which are more volatile, and you'll not only avoid bandwagon mistakes, but also improve your chances of profiting with many speculative trades.

The Final Fundamental Trading Rule

There's only one other basic rule that applies to all speculative trading situations — and it can be stated even more simply than the others:

Always pay attention to the details — especially regarding trading costs.

This rule covers a lot of ground, much of it mentioned at various other points in this course, so we won't devote a lot of time to it here. However, there are a few key points that need to be emphasized:

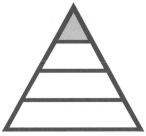

STEP 90

Start Currency Speculation With Three Historically High-Return Strategies

What: Turn your speculative eye to the foreign currency futures markets with these three historically high-return strategies.

Why: The currencies are among the most popular of the financial futures — and they offer some of the most dramatic profit opportunities for speculators. This potential results from the tendency of currencies to move in sustained long-term trends, punctuated by significant short-term volatility. Currency speculation can also provide profits to offset any purchasing-power losses you may suffer on your other assets when the U.S. dollar is falling in value.

Risk: Medium to high. All strategies using futures and options on futures are inherently risky. However, the techniques discussed in this Step all feature strictly limited risk, with the potential loss precisely defined at the time the position is opened. Thus, these plays represent a relatively low-risk way to play the currency futures market.

Safety: Medium to high. These strategies use well-known and highly popular vehicles listed on recognized exchanges. Thus, the chance of losses due to defaults or technical problems must be considered minimal.

Liquidity: Medium to high. Each of the vehicles used in these strategies is actively traded, with high daily volumes. Thus, you should be able to buy and sell fairly quickly at prices close to those you desire. You may, however, have some difficulty getting exactly the combination of prices you want since each trade involves the purchase or sale of multiple options, which will frequently require separate orders.

Why not: Even though each of the strategies featured in this Step has strictly defined and limited risk, all carry the danger that you may lose your entire capital commitment. In addition, the currency futures markets can, at times, be highly volatile. This can result in wide single-day swings in the value of your positions, which may cause emotional stress for less-experienced traders or those operating with limited capital. As a result, you should refrain from using these speculative plays until you have built an overall portfolio worth at least $200,000 (exclusive of your primary residence). In addition, you should limit the amount of money devoted to such strategies to no more than 10 percent of your total asset base.

Buy/Invest from: Any discount or full-service futures broker — or the futures division of any of the leading stock brokerage firms. *Note: You must have a separate account to trade futures and options on futures; these strategies cannot be done through your regular stockbroker.*

Background: For the sake of clarity, the basis for each of the three strategies featured in this Step will be included in the trading descriptions that follow.

If you want to get started today, here's what you need to do to begin using these three historically high-return currency strategies...

Strategy No. 1 — **The Deutschemark Butterfly:** Butterflies are among the most unusual creatures in the world of investing. Why? Because they are designed to make the very most money when prices are absolutely stable — in other words, when prices neither rise nor fall.

For many people, that's a hard concept to understand. Everyone knows you'll make money if you buy something and prices subsequently rise — and more sophisticated investors understand that you'll also profit if you sell something short and prices subsequently fall. But, how can you make money if prices don't move at all?

The answer lies in the unique way a butterfly combines the purchase and sale of four different options — a deep-in-the-money call, two at-the-money calls and a deep-out-of-the-money call. In fact, it is this unusual configuration that gives the butterfly its name — you buy the deep-in-the-money call, which serves as one wing; sell the two at-the-money calls, which combine to make up the body; and buy the deep-out-of-the-money call, which acts as the other wing. If you visualize the long call positions as horizontal lines and the short call positions as vertical lines, it looks sort of like this: —||—. See the resemblance to a butterfly?

The striking prices of the options establish the risk/reward parameters for the trade. If the price of the underlying future falls below the striking price of the deep-in-the-money call, or rises above the striking price of the deep-out-of-the-money call, you suffer the maximum loss possible on the trade — which is often quite small. However, if the futures price stays at or near the striking price of the two calls you sold, you will make close to the maximum profit on the position. *Don't worry if this isn't clear just yet; we'll do a scenario in a second that should show exactly why the strategy works this way.*

Given this requirement, it's obvious that the butterfly is suitable only for extremely quiet markets or relatively stable underlying securities. And, that's why we've applied it to the German mark. As the leading currency in Europe, backed by the strongest economy and the most powerful central bank on the continent, the D-mark is where European investors (and many Americans) run when trouble is brewing elsewhere in the world — especially when the trouble involves the U.S. dollar (which also tends to serve as a "haven" currency in normal times).

It thus tends to be less volatile than the other leading currencies on which futures and options are traded in the United States (these include the Japanese yen, British pound, French franc and Swiss franc). It's also very actively traded, which makes it relatively easy to buy and sell the options you need to structure the butterfly. So you can see just how the strategy works, let's look at a couple of actual cases from mid-1995.

On April 5, 1995, the June D-mark future was trading at 73.18 — meaning it would take 73.18 U.S. cents ($0.7318) to buy one German mark — and the scenario for a May D-mark butterfly was highly favorable, based on the following set of option prices:

■ The at-the-money May 73.00 calls were priced at 1.57 cents.

■ The deep-in-the-money May 72 call was priced at 2.12 cents.

■ The deep-out-of-the-money May 74 call was priced at 1.12 cents.

Step 90: *Start Currency Speculation With Three Historically High-Return Strategies*

Given that, the following transactions could have been used to structure a May D-mark butterfly:

Opening a German Mark Butterfly
April 5, 1995 — June D-mark Future at 73.18

Option Transaction	Price Per Contract	Total Price	Dollar Value*
BUY 1 MAY 72 CALL	(2.12)	(2.12)	($2,650)
SELL 2 MAY 73 CALLS	1.57	3.14	$3,925
BUY 1 MAY 74 CALL	(1.12)	(1.12)	($1,400)
TOTAL POSITION VALUE		(0.10)	($ 125)

Based on a 125,000-mark contract.

As the following scenario analysis will show, the "Total Position Value," or initial cost, of $125 was also the maximum possible loss on this particular trade (exclusive of commissions), while the maximum potential profit was $1,125 (again minus commissions) — which makes for a very attractive reward/risk ratio of 9-to-1. Here's the grid that shows the possible outcomes for the trade at different June German mark futures prices, assuming the options will be held until the expiration date (in this case, the first Friday in May 1995):

A D-Mark Butterfly Scenario Analysis

Futures Price	Premium for Calls 72	73	74	Total Credit	Dollar Credit*	Less Cost	Profit (Loss)*
70.00	0	0	0	0	0	($125)	($ 125)
71.00	0	0	0	0	0	($125)	($ 125)
71.50	0	0	0	0	0	($125)	($ 125)
72.00	0	0	0	0	0	($125)	($ 125)
72.25	0.25	0	0	0.25	$ 312	($125)	$ 187
72.50	0.50	0	0	0.50	$ 625	($125)	$ 500
72.75	0.75	0	0	0.75	$ 937	($125)	$ 812
73.00	1.00	0	0	1.00	$1,250	($125)	$1,125
73.25	1.25	(0.25)	0	0.75	$ 937	($125)	$ 812
73.50	1.50	(0.50)	0	0.50	$ 625	($125)	$ 500
73.75	1.75	(0.75)	0	0.25	$ 312	($125)	$ 187
74.00	2.00	(1.00)	0	0	0	($125)	($ 125)
74.50	2.50	(1.50)	0.50	0	0	($125)	($ 125)
75.00	3.00	(2.00)	1.00	0	0	($125)	($ 125)
76.00	4.00	(3.00)	2.00	0	0	($125)	($ 125)

Numbers are rounded.

So, what happened? Well, as it turned out, this D-mark butterfly worked almost perfectly. In spite of considerable volatility in the currency markets as a whole — sparked by the surging Japanese yen — the June D-mark futures price had changed a mere 26 points by the time the May options expired on May 5, 1995, falling to 72.92 cents. Thus, this trade produced a profit of $1,025 (minus commissions) — a return of 820 percent on the $125 at risk! In only a month!

Note: Even though we have excluded commissions in this example for the sake of clarity, you must pay close attention to commission rates when doing butterflies. That's because, at a minimum, a butterfly will require four transactions — the two opening purchases and the two opening sales. That's assuming the price of the futures contract falls and all four of the options expire worthless — which would give you a maximum loss. And a butterfly could require up to eight transactions if the futures price rises above the highest striking price — forcing you to sell or buy back all four calls and again take the maximum loss. In the optimum situation, such as the one in the above example, you will incur five commissions — the four opening ones, plus one to sell your long deep-in-the-money call. Thus, depending on who you do your trades with, your commission costs could run as little as $50 to as much as $200 — although $125 would probably be typical.

One of the best features of the D-mark butterfly is that it can be done quite frequently, perhaps as often as every five to six weeks — just so long as the market remains stable and the option premiums continue to combine to give you a favorable scenario. For example, another good opportunity arose in June 1995, just seven weeks after our first sample trade was closed. This was the situation:

**A Second German Mark Butterfly
June 26, 1995 — September D-mark Future at 72.23**

Option Transaction	Price Per Contract	Total Price	Dollar Value*
BUY 1 AUGUST 71 CALL	(2.09)(	2.09	($2,612.50)
SELL 2 AUGUST 72 CALLS	1.37	2.74	$3,425.00
BUY 1 AUGUST 73 CALL	(0.95)	(0.95)	($1,187.50)
TOTAL POSITION VALUE		(0.30)	($ 375.00)

Based on a 125,000-mark contract.

The New D-Mark Butterfly Scenario

Futures Price	Premium for Calls			Total Credit	Dollar Credit*	Less Cost	Profit (Loss)*
	72	73	74				
70.00	0	0	0	0	0	($125)	($ 125)
70.00	0	0	0	0	0	$375)	($ 375)
70.50	0	0	0	0	0	($375)	($ 375)
71.00	0	0	0	0	0	($375)	($ 375)
71.25	0.25	0	0	0.25	$ 312	($375)	($ 63)
71.50	0.50	0	0	0.50	$ 625	($375)	$ 250
71.75	0.75	0	0	0.75	$ 937	($375)	$ 562
72.00	1.00	0	0	1.00	$1,250	($375)	$ 875
72.25	1.25	(0.25)	0	0.75	$ 937	($375)	$ 562
72.50	1.50	(0.50)	0	0.50	$ 625	($375)	$ 250
72.75	1.75	(0.75)	0	0.25	$ 312	($375)	($ 63)
73.00	2.00	(1.00)	0	0	0	($375)	($ 375)
73.50	2.50	(1.50)	0.50	0	0	($375)	($ 375)
74.00	3.00	(2.00)	1.00	0	0	($375)	($ 375)

Numbers are rounded.

So what happened this time? Well, the September German mark future moved as high as 72.89 and as low as 71.26 — but, by Aug. 4, when the August D-mark options expired, the future was at 71.72, just 51 points from where it started (but on the other side of the at-the-money call). Thus, the 72 and 73 calls expired worthless, and the 71 call was worth 0.72 cents — or $900. Subtract the $375 initial cost, and you had a profit of $525 — not as good as in our first example, but still a return of 140 percent. Even after subtracting commissions of around $125, the gain would have been $400 — a return of more than 106 percent in only about five weeks!

There are only four key rules for the D-mark butterfly (assuming you're already observing the rule to always use matching futures and options). They are:

- Always use D-mark call options rather than D-mark put options. Calls traditionally have higher premiums than puts, and this generally means smaller opening butterfly spreads.

- Always buy and sell D-mark calls with strike prices at least a full cent apart — i.e., 72.50-73.50-74.50 or 68-69-70. Do not do butterflies with either 50-point or 150-point ranges between the option strike prices.

- Always use options with at least a month remaining prior to the expiration date. However, avoid butterflies with more than two months of life left as this allows too much time for the underlying futures price to change.

- Never pay more than $400 to initiate a D-mark butterfly — and $200 is an even better maximum. Given the $1,250 value of the 1-cent strike price range, the former will give you a reward/risk ratio of 2-to-1 (with a small allowance for commissions), while the latter will offer a 5-to-1 advantage. *Note: On very rare occasions, it is actually possible to position a butterfly spread at a small credit — meaning the worst you can do is make a small profit, less commissions. However, such situations usually occur only when the market has been volatile, sending option premiums higher, so you may not want to do a butterfly under such conditions.*

Since you will be dealing strictly with German mark calls, which trade in the same pit, you may be able to use a combination order to position your butterflies. Try telling your broker you want to "buy one June 71 D-mark call, buy one June 73 D-mark call and sell two June 72 D-mark calls at a net debit of 10 points or better" and see what happens. If your broker can execute such orders, you will have a lot better luck getting attractive butterflies than if you have to specify prices for the individual options involved.

Strategy No. 2 — The Canadian Dollar Strangle: A "strangle" is very similar to a "straddle" and works exactly the opposite of a butterfly. In other words, it depends on highly volatile markets rather than stable situations to generate profits. In addition, longer-term strangles (and straddles) also work extremely well in markets showing a defined trend that's likely to continue. As such, they are particularly well suited to currencies since, as we've already noted, currencies tend to move in prolonged trends punctuated by short-term volatility.

To refresh your memory, a straddle simply involves simultaneously buying two options on the same underlying futures contract — the at-the-money call and the at-the-money put with the same striking price. A standard strangle works the same way, except you buy an *out-of-the-money* call and an *out-of-the-money* put with striking prices one cent apart. *Note: The name "strangle" derives from the fact that the option strike prices "wrap around" the price of the underlying futures contract — much as your hands would wrap around the throat of someone you were strangling.*

Step 90: *Start Currency Speculation With Three Historically High-Return Strategies*

For example, if the June Canadian dollar future were at 69.25 cents, you might buy the June 70-cent call and simultaneously buy the June 69-cent put — or buy the June 69.50-cent call and simultaneously buy the June 68.50 put. Either would work — with the choice based on which set of options offered the most attractive scenario.

Our preferred version of the strangle is slightly different, however. We advise using a *two-cent strike price range* rather than buying options with strikes one cent apart. This results in lower costs — and risks — though it extends the break-even points by a modest amount. We also prefer using *only full-cent strike prices* as half-cent strikes are less-actively traded, meaning it may be harder to get good prices.

For example, with the June Canadian dollar future still at 69.25 cents, we would either buy the 72-cent call and the 70-cent put or buy the 71-cent call and the 69-cent put. Again, the choice would be based on which set of options offered the lowest risk.

Note: Some more experienced traders may want to try "biasing" their strangles to take advantage of the existing trend. For example, with the Canadian dollar future priced at 69.25 cents and trending upward, a trader doing this would choose the 68-70 combination over the 69-71 combination, even if it costs a bit more. The reasoning is that, if the trend continues in the same direction — as trends tend to do — the position will move into the money and reach the break-even point that much more quickly.

What you are hoping for when you speculate with either a straddle or a strangle is that the underlying currency will make a major move in one direction or the other, producing large enough gains on one of the two options to offset the loss on the other — and still provide an overall profit. The risk on a strangle is fairly high (although it's lower than on a straddle), but it is strictly limited to the total premium paid for the two options — and, in most cases, you won't suffer a total loss as at least one of the options will usually have some residual value at expiration.

The biggest drawback with a strangle is the distance to the break-even points, but this is off-set somewhat by the fact that profits are potentially unlimited in a major currency move. (For example, in 1995's major Japanese yen rally, some yen strangles could have produced profits in excess of $20,000 on initial investments of $1,500 or less.) As with a straddle, strangles also offer an added advantage in that it is sometimes possible to score a profit on both sides of a position if the market makes a sharp move in one direction, then just as quickly reverses.

Virtually any currency would be suitable for use in a strangle — simply because all show the same trending tendency, with intermittent short-term volatility. However, we have chosen the Canadian dollar because the contract size is smaller — 100,000 Canadian dollars as opposed to 125,000 units with most other currencies — which means both the cost and the risk in a strangle will usually be lower. To see just how the Canadian dollar strangle might work, let's look at an actual example from early 1995. The following table illustrates the situation:

Step 90: *Start Currency Speculation With*
Three Historically High-Return Strategies

Opening a Canadian Dollar Strangle
Feb. 1, 1995 — June Canadian Dollar Future at 70.65

Option Transaction	Price Of Option	Dollar Value*
BUY 1 APRIL 72 CALL:	(0.26)	($260)
BUY 1 APRIL 70 PUT:	(0.47)	($470)
TOTAL POSITION COST:	(0.73)	($730)

*Based on a 100,000-Canadian dollar contract.

As the following scenario analysis will show, the "Total Position Cost" of $730 was also the maximum possible loss on this strangle (exclusive of commissions), while the maximum potential profit was unlimited — a very attractive risk/reward situation. The break-even points were also fairly close, given the volatility of the market. Here's the grid that shows the possible outcomes for the trade at different June Canadian dollar futures prices, assuming the options are held until the expiration date (in this case, the first Friday in April 1995):

A Canadian Dollar Strangle Scenario Analysis

Futures Price	April 72 Call	April 70 Put	Strangle Value	Entry Cost	Profit (Loss)	ROI
67.00	0.00	3.00	$3,000	($730)	$2,270	310.96%
68.00	0.00	2.00	$2,000	($730)	$1,270	173.97%
68.50	0.00	1.50	$1,500	($730)	$ 770	105.48%
69.00	0.00	1.00	$1,000	($730)	$ 270	36.99%
69.27	0.00	0.73	$ 730	($730)	0	0%
69.50	0.00	0.50	$ 500	($730)	($ 230)	(31.51%)
70.00	0.00	0.00	0	$730	($ 730)	(100.00%)
70.50	0.00	0.00	0	($730)	($ 730)	(100.00%)
71.00	0.00	0.00	0	($730)	($ 730)	(100.00%)
71.50	0.00	0.00	0	($730)	($ 730)	(100.00%)
72.00	0.00	0.00	0	($730)	($ 730)	(100.00%)
72.50	0.50	0.00	$ 500	($730)	($ 230)	(31.51%)
72.73	0.73	0.00	$ 730	($730)	0	0%
73.00	1.00	0.00	$1,000	($730)	$ 270	36.99%
73.50	1.50	0.00	$1,500	($730)	$ 770	105.48%
74.00	2.00	0.00	$2,000	($730)	$1,270	173.97%
75.00	3.00	0.00	$3,000	($730)	$2,270	310.96%

And, how did the trade turn out? Well, in this case, it didn't work out well at all. In fact, it suffered the maximum loss of $730 (plus commissions of $50 to $75) as the June Canadian dollar future traded in a fairly narrow range, ending up at 71.62 cents on April 7, 1995, when the April options expired.

But, then, as we've been telling you all along, that's the nature of speculation. You can't possibly expect to score a winner every time — even when you're just looking at sample trades. And, we'd be totally dishonest about your speculative prospects if we showed you nothing but winning examples.

Step 90: *Start Currency Speculation With Three Historically High-Return Strategies*

Still, you can rest assured that this strategy will work often enough to make your effort in learning it worthwhile. For example, had you turned around on April 7, 1995 — the day our first sample strangle expired — and opened a new position, the situation would have penciled out as shown in the following table:

A Second Canadian Dollar Strangle Example
April 7, 1995 — June Canadian Dollar Future at 71.62

Option Transaction	Price Of Option	Dollar Value*
BUY 1 JUNE 72 CALL:	(0.47)	($470)
BUY 1 JUNE 70 PUT:	(0.14)	($140)
TOTAL POSITION COST:	(0.61)	($610)

Based on a 100,000-Canadian dollar contract.

We won't bother showing a full scenario analysis on this strangle — you can do your own if you like; the practice will be good for you. Instead, we'll just note that the maximum risk on the trade was $610 (plus commissions), and that the break-even points were 69.39 cents on the downside and 72.61 on the upside.

And, what happened in this instance? Well, the Canadian dollar showed a bit more volatility while also continuing gradually along its established upward path. By June 8, 1995, expiration date for the options, the June future was priced at 72.82 cents — 21 points above the upside break-even point. Since the Canadian dollar futures contract represents 100,000 Canadian dollars, that translated into a profit of $210, less commissions of about $75, for a net gain of around $135.

That may not seem like much — and it really isn't for a speculator — but it still represented a return of 22.13 percent on the initial investment in just two months, which is nothing to sneer at. And, with patience and careful monitoring of trends in the currency markets in general and the Canadian dollar in particular, larger profits will almost certainly come your way.

As with most of our recommended strategies, the suggested entry rules for the Canadian dollar strangle are quite simple:

- Initiate a Canadian dollar strangle only when the currency is in a prolonged trend or showing considerable short-term volatility.

- Simultaneously buy an out-of-the-money Canadian dollar call and an out-of-the-money Canadian dollar put with the same expiration month and strike prices two cents apart.

- Never pay more than $800, plus commissions, to open a Canadian dollar strangle.

- Try to buy options with as much time remaining as possible until expiration, imposing a minimum time frame of two months. Since a fairly large move is required to produce a profit with this strategy, the added time gives the underlying future more of an opportunity to move in your favor.

Note: Getting extra time also sets the stage for a potential two-sided play. If you get a large move in one direction shortly after opening, you can take profits on your winning option and hold your loser, which will have very little value anyway. If the market then reverses sharply, that option will regain some or all of its lost value, enabling you to add to your gains by selling it at or before expiration.

Step 90: *Start Currency Speculation With*
Three Historically High-Return Strategies

■ If the Canadian dollar futures market has been volatile, you may want to try for a two-sided play, closing out one side of your position as soon as you have a gain large enough to cover all costs and provide a small overall profit, then hoping for a reversal. However, if the market is trending strongly in one direction or the other, plan on holding until expiration to maximize the potential impact of the trend.

As with the D-mark butterfly, you should be able to enter your Canadian dollar strangles with a combination order. Simply tell the broker you want to "buy one June 70 Canadian dollar put and buy one June 72 Canadian dollar call at a debit of 60 points or better." That way the broker can fill your order at any combination of prices totaling 60 points ($600) or less, rather than having to work to get specific prices for the individual options.

Strategy No. 3 — Japanese Yen Vertical Spreads: Since we fully explained the concept of vertical option spreads — both bullish and bearish — in the lesson, The Top of the Pyramid (see the step, "The Three Best Highly Favorable Option Spreads"), we won't provide a lot of additional background here. Suffice it to say that such trades work exactly the same with currencies — and are generally highly successful when done with the prevailing trend.

As a refresher, we will note that the standard vertical spread has two versions:

■ The bullish trade involves buying the in-the-money call option with a strike price closest to the actual futures price and simultaneously selling the out-of-the-money call option with the same expiration month and a strike price one cent higher (in the case of currencies).

■ The bearish trade involves buying the in-the-money put option with a strike price closest to the actual futures price and simultaneously selling the out-of-the-money put option with the same expiration month and a strike price one cent lower.

However, vertical currency option spreads can also be positioned either completely in the money (less aggressive) or completely out of the money (more aggressive). For example, with the Japanese yen future at 105.25, you would have these bullish choices:

■ The standard vertical spread would involve buying the 105 call and selling the 106 call.

■ The in-the-money spread would involve buying the 104 call and selling the 105 call.

■ The out-of-the-money spread would involve buying the 106 call and selling the 107 call.

Similarly, with the yen future still at 105.25, you would have these bearish choices:

■ The standard vertical spread would involve buying the 106 put and selling the 105 put.

■ The in-the-money spread would involve buying the 107 put and selling the 106 put.

■ The out-of-the-money spread would involve buying the 105 put and selling the 104 put.

In either case:

■ The in-the-money vertical spread would feature the worst risk/reward scenario — i.e., the highest risk and lowest potential gain — but would have the highest probability of success since it would produce the maximum possible profit even if the future failed to move in your favor (so long as it didn't move against you either).

Step 90: *Start Currency Speculation With Three Historically High-Return Strategies*

- ■ The out-of-the-money vertical spread would offer the best risk/reward scenario — i.e., the lowest risk and highest potential gain — but would have the lowest probability of success since it would require a large move in your favor just to break even and a move of nearly 2 cents to produce the maximum profit.

- ■ The standard vertical spread would offer the best balance — with a favorable risk/reward scenario and a better than average chance of success (especially if done with the trend) since it would need a move of less than a cent to produce the maximum possible profit.

So you can see the exact numerical comparisons, the following three tables recreate actual bullish opportunities available in April 1995 using Japanese yen call options:

Three Sample Yen Vertical Bull Spread Possibilities
April 24, 1995 — June Yen Future at 121.10

In-the-Money Spread		Out-of-the-Money Spread	
BUY JUNE 120 CALL:	3.56	BUY JUNE 122 CALL:	2.62
SELL JUNE 121 CALL:	3.07	SELL JUNE 123 CALL:	2.23
SPREAD:	0.49	SPREAD:	0.39
MAXIMUM RISK:	$612.50	MAXIMUM RISK:	$487.50
MAXIMUM REWARD:	$637.50	MAXIMUM REWARD:	$762.50
MOVE REQUIRED FOR		MOVE REQUIRED FOR	
MAXIMUM PROFIT:	-0.10	MAXIMUM PROFIT:	+1.90

Standard Vertical Spread	
BUY JUNE 121 CALL:	3.07
SELL JUNE 122 CALL:	2.62
SPREAD:	0.45
MAXIMUM RISK	$562.50
MAXIMUM REWARD	$687.50
MOVE REQUIRED FOR	
MAXIMUM PROFIT	+0.90

To further clarify the potential of each of the three vertical yen bull spreads, the following scenario analysis grids show the possible outcomes for each spread at various futures prices:

In-the-Money June 120/121 Yen Vertical Bull Spread

Futures Price	April 72 Call	April 70 Put	Strangle Value	Entry Cost	Profit (Loss)	ROI
118.00	0.00	0.00	0	($612.50)	($612.50)	(100.00%)
119.00	0.00	0.00	0	($612.50)	($612.50)	(100.00%)
120.00	0.00	0.00	0	($612.50)	($612.50)	(100.00%)
120.25	0.25	0.00	$ 312.50	($612.50)	($300.00)	(48.98%)
120.49	0.49	0.00	$ 612.50	($612.50)	0	0%
120.50	0.50	0.00	$ 625.00	($612.50)	$ 12.50	1.04%
120.75	0.75	0.00	$ 937.50	($612.50)	$325.00	53.06%
121.00	1.00	0.00	$1,250.00	($612.50)	$637.50	104.08%
121.50	1.50	0.50	$1,250.00	($612.50)	$637.50	104.08%
122.00	2.00	1.00	$1,250.00	($612.50)	$637.50	104.08%

Step 90: *Start Currency Speculation With Three Historically High-Return Strategies*

Standard June 121/122 Yen Vertical Bull Spread

Futures Price	April 72 Call	April 70 Put	Strangle Value	Entry Cost	Profit (Loss)	ROI
119.00	0.00	0.00	0	($562.50)	($562.50)	(100.00%)
120.00	0.00	0.00	0	($562.50)	($562.50)	(100.00%)
121.00	0.00	0.00	0	($562.50)	($562.50)	(100.00%)
121.25	0.25	0.00	$ 312.50	($562.50)	($250.00)	(44.44%)
121.45	0.45	0.00	$ 562.50	($562.50)	0	0%
121.50	0.50	0.00	$ 625.00	($562.50)	$ 62.50	11.11%
121.75	0.75	0.00	$ 937.50	($562.50)	$375.00	66.67%
122.00	1.00	0.00	$1,250.00	($562.50)	$687.50	122.22%
122.50	1.50	0.50	$1,250.50	($562.50)	$687.50	122.22%
123.00	2.00	1.00	$1,250.50	($562.50)	$687.50	122.22%

Out-of-the-Money June 122/123 Yen Vertical Bull Spread

Futures Price	April 72 Call	April 70 Put	Strangle Value	Entry Cost	Profit (Loss)	ROI
120.00	0.00	0.00	0	($487.50)	($487.50)	(100.00%)
121.00	0.00	0.00	0	($487.50)	($487.50)	(100.00%)
122.00	0.00	0.00	0	($487.50)	($487.50)	(100.00%)
122.25	0.25	0.00	$ 312.50	($487.50)	($175.00)	(35.90%)
122.39	0.45	0.00	$ 487.50	($487.50)	0	0%
122.50	0.50	0.00	$ 625.00	($487.50)	$137.50	28.21%
122.75	0.75	0.00	$ 937.50	($487.50)	$450.00	92.31%
123.00	1.00	0.00	$1,250.00	($487.50)	$762.50	156.41%
123.50	1.50	0.50	$1,250.00	($487.50)	$762.50	156.41%
124.00	2.00	1.00	$1,250.00	($487.50)	$762.50	156.41%

As it turned out, none of these vertical bull spreads wound up being the right choice in April of 1995. After rising nearly 25 percent versus the U.S. dollar in just under three months, the yen peaked a week before these trades were positioned. By June 8, when the June 1995 options expired, the yen had dropped back below the 120 level — meaning each of these spreads would have resulted in a maximum loss.

However, a similar set of June yen vertical bear spreads — which could have been positioned at the same time with virtually the same risk/reward parameters — would have proven universally successful, each producing the maximum possible profit.

Obviously, we can't tell you whether you should do bullish or bearish yen vertical spreads since we have no way of knowing what the conditions will be in the currency futures markets at the time you read this. However, if you plan to speculate in any arena, it goes without saying that you should closely monitor the markets you're interested in — try to identify trends in progress, recognize fundamental events that could prompt volatility or market reversals and utilize technical analysis to spot important trading patterns.

If you are willing to do these things, you should be able to make bullish or bearish decisions with a fair degree of ease and enjoy a reasonably consistent pattern of winning trades. If you're not willing to devote the time and effort needed to understand the markets, then you shouldn't be speculating in the first place!

Step 90: *Start Currency Speculation With Three Historically High-Return Strategies*

We have five suggested rules for entering vertical yen option spreads, either bullish or bearish:

■ Open a position only when a Japanese yen futures price trend has been firmly established — or shortly after some action has been taken by the U.S. or Japanese governments that might cause a reversal in the direction of currency prices (or, at a minimum, a period of increased volatility). Be aware, as well, of important trade meetings, such as GATT, or other conferences, such as G-7 meetings, that might influence currency prices.

■ Always have one full cent between the strike prices of the option you buy and the option you sell — e.g., with the yen at 115.20, do a 115/116 bull spread, not a 115/115.50 or 115/117 spread. A cent on a yen futures contract is worth $1,250, so a spread with a range less than that isn't worthwhile and one with a range larger than that requires too big a move to reach maximum profit. *Note: The yen futures contract actually represents 12,500,000 yen and the yen futures prices should technically be 1.1520 cents rather than 115.20 cents, with the same differential applying to option strike prices and premiums. However, the standard practice is to move the decimal point two places and quote the yen futures and options as if the contract was really 125,000 yen and the prices were really in cents — just as with the German mark and Swiss franc.*

■ Enter a spread only when you can get a reward/risk ratio enough better than 1-to-1 to cover your trading costs — i.e., only when your maximum potential profit is higher than your maximum possible loss by enough to pay all commissions and leave you with a 100 percent profit on a successful trade.

■ Always use options having at least a month remaining prior to expiration. (Currency options usually expire the first Friday of the stated expiration month, though they may occasionally expire the second Friday if the month starts on a Thursday or Friday.)

■ Always initiate your trades with an actual spread order rather than specifying prices for the individual yen options.

With regard to closing your trades, you should generally plan on taking your profits any time you achieve 80 percent of the maximum with more than two weeks remaining until expiration. The extra few dollars you might gain by hanging on aren't worth the risk that a reversal might wipe out your early gains. If you haven't achieved an 80 percent profit by the final two weeks before expiration, hold until expiration unless you see signs that the market may be ready to change directions or fear the impact of some interim event. ▲

Continued from p. 20

■ Although we have excluded them from many of our examples and from most of our scenario-analysis grids, commission costs are of major importance in many speculative strategies — especially those dealing with multiple-option positions, spreads or combination trades. For example, a butterfly that produces a $300 profit on a $400 investment might seem like a highly successful trade — unless you've failed to factor in $200 in commissions. That converts a 75 percent gain into a 25 percent net return — which isn't too bad, but it's not exactly the path to the speculative hall of fame either. Thus, you should always shop around for the best commissions — regardless of the type of speculation you plan to undertake — and you should also factor them into each scenario analysis you do, changing your entry parameters if necessary to compensate for the costs. *Note: It's not necessary to actually put them in the grid, which greatly complicates all your calculations. Instead, just do the calculations and then adjust the projected results by the amount of the expected commissions.*

Commission costs are of major importance in many speculative strategies. . . always shop around for the best commissions — regardless of the type of speculation.

■ Learn which trading orders you can use in which markets — and which work best for various types of strategies. Using the wrong type of order can hurt you in two ways — by keeping you out of a position altogether, or by changing the risk/reward parameters that prompted your entry decision. Try never to use a market order with either futures or options unless you are desperate to get out of a position or need to complete the other side of a combination position or spread so you won't be left holding a "naked" contract. Likewise, never use individual limit orders when opening a spread or combination position unless the exchange on which you're trading won't take such orders.

■ Learn the mechanics of the vehicles you're using and the markets in which you're trading. Before even considering a speculative trade, make sure you know as much as possible about the securities you'll be using. With futures, that means contract sizes, minimum price changes ("ticks"), daily limits, expanded limits, delivery dates and notice dates. With options, it means contract sizes, underlying securities, strike-price levels, expiration dates, pricing structure (which is frequently different from that for the underlying security), etc. Be aware, as well, that many commodity options are identified by the delivery month of the underlying futures contract — even though they may actually expire in the prior month.

■ Pay attention to margin requirements and maintenance margin levels (i.e., how much leeway you have before you receive a margin call). Even if a trade appears to have a high probability of success, it may not be worth doing if your projected profit is just $600 and you have to put up a $6,000 margin deposit to do it. The opportunity loss on the idle margin money would negate most of the advantage of the speculation, even if it worked to perfection. Likewise, a potentially profitable combination play might turn into a loser if a margin call on the future forced you to act at an inopportune time.

■ Be aware of other factors that can affect your ability to enter and exit trades — particularly open interest. If very few of the contracts you want to trade are outstanding, you'll have a harder time getting your speculations positions — and you'll likely get prices much worse than you'd really like. The same applies to outside factors — such as government crop reports, Federal Reserve Board meetings, year-end or quarterly financial reports, anything that might impact a position you already hold or one you are considering.

■ If you have questions or uncertainties, don't be afraid to ask. So long as you don't make a perpetual pest of yourself, most good brokers — even those at discount houses — will be happy to help you out. And don't be afraid to go to the source. The addresses and phone numbers of most of the leading U.S. stock, option and futures exchanges are listed in other lessons in this course — and all have customer service departments that can answer questions or send out free or low-cost reference materials. A little time spent getting information now can save — or make — you a lot of money later. (After all, getting good financial information is the main reason you're taking the *100 Steps to Wealth* course, isn't it?)

Wrapping Up the Speculative Rules

In summary, then, the fundamental rules for speculative investing really aren't that complex. In fact, speculation itself — or any other type of investing, for that matter — isn't really all that complicated. All you're doing is identifying a promising situation, categorizing the risks and playing the odds in the expectation of reaping an appropriate reward.

However, as we said earlier, finding the right speculation is a bit more difficult. That's one reason this lesson and the one just before it have focused so heavily on the Wealth-Building Steps — which outline more than a dozen specific speculative trading strategies, explaining how they're structured, the background of the markets and vehicles involved and why they work the way they do (as well as some reasons why they may not work).

Study those Steps, practice the strategies on paper, do your own scenario analyses based on current market conditions and prices at the time you read this, and try some "practice" trades on paper. That's the only way you'll continue improving your knowledge about the markets and grow more comfortable with the concept of speculation.

It's More Than Futures and Options

Remember, too, that speculative investing isn't just limited to the futures and options markets. There are all kinds of speculations involving other investment vehicles and other markets. These include buying penny stocks, which we covered in detail at the end of the last lesson, as well as junk bonds, "fallen angels" (the buying of stocks in companies that have declared bankruptcy or fallen on hard times), and many others. Even many aspects of real estate investing, such as the purchase of raw land in anticipation of future development, can be considered speculation. It all depends on the risk/reward scenarios and the probabilities of success.

Whatever your speculative choice, however, you'll greatly improve your chances of success if you follow our two overall rules and our five fundamental trading rules.

Again, the two overall rules are:

■ Don't even consider speculating until you have built a portfolio worth at least $200,000, not including the equity in your home.

■ Even then, don't allocate more than 5 to 10 percent of your total assets to speculation — and commit no more than half of that at any one time.

And, the five fundamental trading rules are:

■ All speculations, regardless of the type, must make good sense relative to your own personal goals, financial objectives and risk tolerances — both economic and emotional.

■ The potential reward in any given speculation must justify the potential risk. In other words, regardless of how much money you might make, you shouldn't do the trade if it would involve the possibility of losing more than you feel you can afford.

- Always learn as much as possible about the markets in which you plan to speculate. As is said of so many aspects of life, knowledge is power — and speculation is certainly no exception. In any type of speculative investing, the more you know, the more likely you are to make the right decisions — and the hoped-for profits.

- Be patient. Don't undertake any speculative trade until the conditions are highly favorable and the odds of success are clearly on your side. Also refrain from letting your emotions rule your trading decisions. Any time you get worried, remember why you did the trade in the first place. If those reasons are no longer valid, then forget it. Otherwise, stay with your original plan.

- Never forget the details — especially the trading costs. They can mean the difference between a successful speculation and just another mediocre — or even losing — trade.

Follow these overall rules and basic trading guidelines, and you can make speculation a valuable part of your financial life — using the profits to both top off your wealth-building pyramid and speed the pace at which it gets built.

A Final Word   You've now learned the basic rules for speculating both wisely and successfully — and you've been introduced to a variety of strategies and investment vehicles you can use to put those rules into practice. As we just said, speculation is an essential part of any truly dynamic wealth-building program, simply because it has the unique power to both enhance your overall investment returns and greatly speed the growth of your assets.

The speculative strategies you've learned will also increase your versatility as an investor, giving you more alternatives in dealing with changing financial times and the vagaries of the rapidly emerging global economy, as well as market and business cycles here at home — which we'll cover in considerably more detail in your next lesson.

It's all a part of the complete financial toolbox we've attempted to help you put together throughout this course — a toolbox containing everything you need to start a foundation, erect a structure and then add the finishing touches to a wealth-building pyramid of your own personal design. However, building that pyramid is just the beginning. You also need to consider how you want to use the wealth you amass, how to access it in the most efficient and cost-effective manner, how to make sure it lasts as long as you do and how best to pass what's left on to your heirs. Those are the topics covered in the final phase of the course. ▲

How to profit from the changing times

LESSON 29

How to profit from the changing times

"Success is more a function of consistent common sense than it is of genius." — An Wang

DEALING WITH A WORLD OF UNCERTAINTY

It's said that the only real constant in the field of economics is that things are always changing. It's also said that, if you put any three economists in a room for an hour, they'll come out with six different opinions on what those changes will likely be.

While both those sayings are unquestionably exaggerations, there is little doubt that the world of economics is indeed a world of uncertainty. Will interest rates come down? Will inflation remain under control? Will the government lower tax rates or bring runaway budgets into balance? Will the economy continue to grow, or are we due for a recession? Will corporate earnings — and stock prices — keep going up?

Obviously, we could fill the rest of this page, and several more, with similar questions — none of which can be answered with absolute certainty. So, with the wealth you've already built on the line and your financial future potentially at stake, how do you deal with the situation?

Unfortunately, there are no magic answers — simply because we're no more able to precisely predict the future than you (or those three fictional economists). However, based on research and experience, we can assure you of one thing:

If you stick to the same principles and methods you have learned in the first 28 lessons of *100 Steps to Wealth,* you should be able to minimize the negative impact of all but the most disastrous economic shifts — and actually profit from many of them.

Your Personal Pyramid Is the Key

After all, based on the information we've provided, you should already be developing one of the most important tools for dealing with changing economic times — a well-diversified wealth-building pyramid constructed using sound asset-allocation principles. That pyramid, when completed, will be solid — able to withstand the swirling forces of economic change much as the original pyramids in Egypt have survived the swirling desert winds.

And, unlike the original pyramids, your wealth-building plan will also be flexible. You'll be able to move even the largest stones around — responding to the achievement of interim goals, changes in your lifestyle situation or fluctuations in the overall economy — without worry about toppling the entire structure.

The key questions, of course, will be exactly when (or even if) you should move those stones around — and where you should move them to — in order to continue strengthening your pyramid. And, that's what this lesson is all about. In the pages that follow, you'll learn how to identify changing economic and market conditions — and how to respond to them. The exact focus will be on two different approaches:

- Timing the market in response to changing economic conditions.

- Adjusting your asset mix for financial planning purposes.

UNDERSTANDING THE ECONOMIC CYCLE

Before you can hope to begin planning for economic changes, you have to understand the basic forces underlying those changes — and that means understanding the primary economic cycle.

Although there are innumerable internal distinctions — and the time parameters are highly variable — the economic cycle generally follows essentially the same four-phase pattern. These four phases are:
1. Trough.
2. Expansion.
3. Peak.
4. Recession (or depression).

So you can gain an overall picture of how the typical economic cycle unfolds, let's walk through the phases one by one.

Tracing the Economic Cycle

As just noted, the first phase of each new cycle is the trough. During this phase, the economy is still sluggish coming out of the previous recession. Business sales are slow, inventories are at reduced levels, manufacturers are utilizing only small portions of their capacity, unemployment is still at or near peak levels, stock market volume is down, trading and price action is lackluster and there's generally excessive media speculation that further bad times remain ahead.

Then, however, something happens. Perhaps it's the latest in a series of interest-rate reductions; the one that finally proves just enough to inspire a few more people to begin borrowing — and using the money to buy. Perhaps it's the latest round of retail price cuts; the one that makes certain items too much of a bargain to resist. Perhaps it's simply a change in people's attitudes; one that leads them to decide buying a few new things will make them feel better about what's going on.

Whatever the cause, or combination of causes, consumers slowly begin making new purchases — and a chain reaction begins. As sales figures improve, corporate profit expectations begin to rise and managers start to plan increased production. As this production comes on line, new jobs are created, still more consumer spending results and the expansion phase moves into full swing. See the graph on the following page.

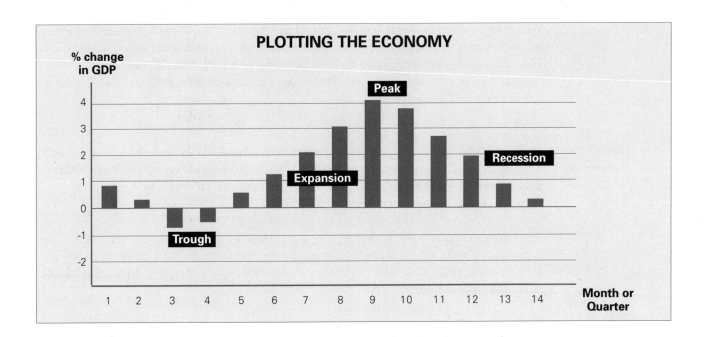

PLOTTING THE ECONOMY

% change in GDP

Peak

Recession

Expansion

Trough

Month or Quarter

The Expansion Phase Intensifies

As this phase intensifies, often with the help of further interest-rate reductions, working hours expand, formerly laid-off workers are recalled, new laborers are hired, wages rise as companies compete within a shrinking labor pool, growth in personal incomes escalates and personal spending kicks up another notch.

This is usually accompanied by a steady increase in personal savings and investing, which enlarges the nation's capital pool and helps fuel new plant construction and new product development. It also reduces the competition for new funding sources, which keeps interest rates on the decline, and typically heats up the modest stock market rally that began earlier when corporate profit expectations first started to rise.

This process feeds on itself in a series of internal cycles (within the primary phase) as the consumer sector continues to accelerate, capital-goods manufacturing expands, other cyclical industry groups start to join in, corporate sales and profits continue to rise and the equity markets respond with further advances in both price and volume.

The Cycle Approaches Its Peak

Eventually, however, the growth rate begins to slow as the pool of qualified labor is depleted, supplies of raw materials become more scarce and manufacturing plants and equipment reach full capacity. With consumer product demand still high, both prices and wages start to come under pressure and inflation begins to inch steadily upward.

This puts added financial stress on companies, which are already carrying the costs of expanded inventories, higher receivables and the extra fixed assets added earlier to meet the demands of the expansion. They respond by stepping up the use of corporate debt — and interest rates typically start to rise.

At the same time capital expenses, carrying costs and fixed-asset charges are moving higher, prices start to become static, weighed down by increasing competition — and corporate profit margins begin to erode.

With orders starting to slump, inventories continuing to expand and capacity exceeding potential sales, corporate managers begin to cut back and plans for new capital projects are shelved. The capital-goods sector begins to stagnate and earnings disappointments (and other factors) slow the pace of stock market buying. Profit taking forces a major correction — or, worst case, sparks a panic sell-off and market crash.

Enter the Recession

As current conditions continue to worsen, retail-sector managers reduce orders for goods and services, cut back on inventory purchases, repay loans and begin to lay off personnel. Other workers, fearing for their own jobs, cut back on spending, the consumer sector begins to shrink — and the economic cycle moves into recession.

The length and depth of the recession — or depression, if conditions become too severe — are dependent on many variables (we'll have more about recessions in just a couple of pages). However, in a typical downturn, corporate cutbacks will accelerate, unemployment will keep rising and consumer spending will continue to decline.

Eventually, with everyone hanging on to their money, the credit markets will go flat and interest rates will begin to fall. This will translate into lower mortgage rates, and housing activity — even in a recession — will start to pick up. Government spending will also increase, filling in some of the gap left by collapse of the consumer sector. *Note: The exact nature and amount of government spending will depend somewhat on the policies of the political party in power, but most of the expenditures will be tied to "safety net" programs put in place following the Great Depression of the 1930s and can thus be counted on as a relative constant in the cyclical equation.*

These factors (and others) will slow the avalanche of corporate cutbacks and stem the ebbing tide of consumer confidence, and the economy will flatten out into a new trough phase — awaiting just the right set of circumstances or specific action needed to trigger the next expansion phase.

No Two Cycles Are Identical

Obviously, everything we've just outlined is fairly general in nature. The specifics of each economic cycle are different — and no two cycles are identical in every respect (or even a majority of them). Some phases may be extremely prolonged and some may be quite short — or non-existent. For example, the economy can fall directly from expansion into recession with virtually no peak at all — or it can bounce from recession into expansion without a prolonged trough (or stagnant) period.

Likewise, the so-called "soft landing" so sought after by government economists and Federal Reserve Board officials is an attempt to go from an expansion, through a downward-sloping peak and back into a moderate expansion without slipping into a recession and a trough in between.

This lack of uniformity makes it extremely difficult to precisely identify which part of the cycle we're in much of the time — and even harder to predict exactly when we'll move from one phase to the next.

With the trough and the expansion phases, this is not so much of a concern — simply because a well-diversified wealth-building pyramid based on sound asset-allocation principles will almost always have you positioned to profit from the associated economic growth. However, the risks are higher — and the missed opportunities greater — in failing to anticipate and/or quickly identify peaks and ensuing recessionary periods.

That's because an unforeseen recession — while never fatal to a well-diversified portfolio — can greatly slow your expected rate of financial growth, affecting your ability to achieve goals within the desired time frame. An ill-timed economic slowdown — coming just when you need to sell certain assets or purchase others to accommodate changing lifestyle needs — can also disrupt carefully laid plans, forcing adjustments you'd rather not make. And, finally, for advocates of market timing, an unexpected recession represents lost opportunity — a missed chance to reallocate your assets and reap profits while the rest of the pack is struggling just to stay afloat.

For those reasons, we'll now take a closer look at the nature — and varying types — of recessions, and then examine some of the indicators you can use in an effort to predict them.

THE NATURE — AND TYPES — OF RECESSIONS

As noted, the normal course of the economic cycle features an expansionary period of growth that peaks out and then slips — or, occasionally, free-falls — into a recessionary phase in which manufacturing output, employment, income levels, commerce and trade all decline.

A forecast of inflation rising to or above the 4 percent level can generally be considered a warning sign that it is time to make adjustments to your portfolio.

Recessions are often, though not always, signaled by two consecutive calendar quarters of declining — not just decelerating — gross domestic product (GDP). They generally extend from six to eighteen months and result in moderate to severe contractions in all sectors of the national economy. *Note: An extremely severe contraction is designated a depression. Although there is no universally accepted definition of a depression, they are typically marked by massive unemployment, huge inventories and so much excess capacity that plant and equipment shutdowns are widespread. Officially, no economic contraction since the 1929-39 "Great Depression" has been labeled as a depression, though this is again a matter of perspective. Harry Truman's definition may be best: "A recession is when your neighbor is out of work. A depression is when you are out of work."*

Even the National Bureau of Economic Research (NBER) — widely accepted as the ultimate judge of business conditions — doesn't always adhere to the classical definition of a recession as "two straight quarters of declining seasonally adjusted real output;" in 1980, it declared a recession after only one quarter's drop in real output. However, the NBER's definitions are generally cited in classifying the type of recession — mild, moderate or severe.

Here are those definitions — as well as an explanation of how the recession generally impacts on the performance of the stock market:

A mild recession — An economic downturn with an average duration of 14 months and an average decline in business activity of about 8 percent. A peak in the stock market usually occurs about five months in advance of the peak for the economy as a whole. The bear market usually lasts about 12 months and prices tend to decline about 22 percent overall.

A moderate (or average) recession — An economic downturn with an average duration of roughly 17 months and an average overall decline in business activity of about 16 percent. The peak in the equity markets occurs about seven months in advance of the economy's peak. The bear market tends to last about 15 months, with an overall price decline of around 26 percent.

A severe recession — An economic downturn with an average duration of around 27 months and an average decline in business activity of about 27 percent. The stock market peak normally occurs about five months in advance of the economic peak. The ensuing bear market lasts about 25 months and prices tend to fall about 42 percent (although there hasn't been a bear market of this magnitude and duration since the 1930s).

Since the Great Depression, the United States has experienced a recessionary period roughly twice per decade — in 1947, 1953-54, 1957, 1960-61, 1969-70, 1974-75, 1980, 1982 and 1990-91. Each of these recessions has culminated with a fairly extreme drop in interest rates.

THE ART OF PREDICTING RECESSIONS

As you saw when we walked through the four phases of a typical business cycle, a change in the direction of the economy is very rarely the result of any single event. Rather, a tremendous number of factors conspire to ignite an expansion or trigger a recession. In other words, the typical cycle reflects a broad sequence of events — the cumulative effect of which is an ultimate turn in the economy.

Thus, if you hope to predict the next recession (or the next expansion, for that matter), you need to identify a set of indicators that have traditionally moved a certain way prior to past periods of recession (or expansion). These key economic readings are known as "leading indicators," and they are closely watched by economists, corporate managers and market analysts around the country.

Note: There are two other sets of key indicators that are also closely watched for confirmation of the advance signals provided by the leading indicators. These are the "coincident indicators," which tend to turn in tandem with changes in the overall economic cycle, and "lagging indicators," which usually change directions after the economy as a whole has already turned.

A Closer Look at the Leading Indicators

The National Bureau of Economic Research and the U.S. Commerce Department track 12 different statistical factors that are currently considered to be "leading" indicators of economic change — reporting their status on a monthly basis. *Note: The exact list of leading indicators is revised from time to time as some statistics are deemed less reliable predictors than others. The current status of various indicators is published regularly in the Business Conditions Digest — which is prepared by the Commerce Department.*

The individual leading economic indicators (LEI) are chosen because their readings normally reach a transitional point — i.e., either a peak or a trough — well in advance of the economy as a whole. Although the numbers vary from indicator to indicator, the group as a whole generally signals a transitional change 10 to 12 months ahead of the eventual turn in the full economy. *Note: Each of the individual indicators is generally reported separately, and the readings are then analyzed carefully before being combined and distributed by the Commerce Department in a special LEI report.*

The current leading economic indicators, in no particular order of importance, are:

- The average number of hours in the work week in the manufacturing sector.

- The average monthly level of new claims for unemployment benefits.

- The volume of new orders for consumer products.

- Net new-business formation (i.e., the number of new businesses being started, minus the number of older companies ceasing operations.)

- The number and trend of permits for new housing construction being sought.

- The number and trend of new contracts being signed for the purchase of manufacturing plants and equipment.

- Month-to-month changes in business inventories on hand and on order.

- Changes in the wholesale prices of raw materials used in key industrial and manufacturing sectors.

- The nation's money supply (i.e., personal and corporate money on deposit in relatively liquid form, as well as funds available for lending by the nation's financial institutions).

- Changes in the level of total liquid assets.

- The direction and intensity of stock price movements.

Are Market Crashes Really Good Leading Indictors?

Declining stock prices are generally considered to be one of the key leading indicators when it comes to predicting economic downturns. However, a study by Forbes magazine casts some doubt on the reliability of stock market crashes in forecasting recession or depression.

Forbes examined nine periods between 1929 and 1987 when the stock market crashed by 25 percent or more as measured by the Dow Jones Industrial Average — but it found some surprising results when it looked at the course of later economic activity. Just one of the crashes — the 89 percent Dow plunge from 1929 to 1932 — led to a true depression, and only three were followed by sharp economic downturns (all fairly short). The other five were followed by periods of continued economic advance.

Here's a brief summary of the nine crash periods studied by Forbes and the ensuing action by the nation's economy:

- **Sept. 3, 1929, to July 8, 1932** — The Dow went from a high of 381 to a low of 41, falling 89 percent in a 34-month period. The Great Depression of the 1930s followed.

- **March 10, 1937, to March 31, 1938** — The Dow slipped from a high of 194 to a low of 99, losing 49 percent in 13 months. A slowdown did follow as the economy slipped back into recession for about a year before beginning to expand again.

- **Jan. 3, 1940, to April 28, 1942** — The Dow went from a high of 153 to a low of 93, a 39 percent decline in 28 months. However, the economy kept steadily growing, with GNP nearly doubling from 1940 to 1943 as the nation mobilized for war.

- **Dec. 13, 1961, to June 26, 1962** — The Dow retreated from a high of 735 to a low of 536, losing 27 percent in six months. However, the economy — already on the mend from the 1960-61 recession — kept right on growing for seven more years.

- **Feb. 9, 1966, to Oct. 7, 1966** — The Dow slipped from a high of 995 to a low of 744, a loss of 25 percent in eight months. However, the pullback had no more impact in halting the '60s expansion than had the 1961-62 market correction.

- **Dec. 3, 1968, to May 26, 1970** — The Dow fell from 985 to 631, a loss of 36 percent in 18 months, and the pullback did indeed foreshadow the economic downturn of 1969-70.

- **Jan. 11, 1973, to Dec. 6, 1974** — The Dow slumped from a high of 1052 to a low of 578, losing 45 percent of its value over a 23-month period. The start of this decline did precede the 1974-75 recession, but the steepest drop in the market didn't come until late 1974, when the economic pullback was already well under way.

- **Sept. 21, 1976, to Feb. 28, 1978** — The Dow lost 27 percent in 17 months, falling from a high of 1015 to a low of 742. However, the economy kept growing steadily until mid-1980 (some say until 1982, disputing whether the brief 1980 downturn was really a recession).

- **Aug. 25, 1987, to Oct. 20, 1987** — Although it stands in most people's minds as the greatest crash because of the one-day, 508-point Dow nosedive on Oct. 19, this move from a Dow high of 2722 to a low of 1739 amounted to just 36 percent and had virtually no impact on the overall economy, which expanded strongly for well over two more years. It wasn't until several months after the mini-crash of October 1989 (not covered in the Forbes study) that the economy finally slipped into the 1990-91 recession.

THE IMPLICATIONS OF THE ECONOMIC CYCLE

Obviously, from the standpoint of applying the economic cycle to your wealth-building efforts, the last of the 12 leading indicators — stock prices — carries the most importance. That's because once you've established a well-diversified portfolio of investments, shifting into and out of equities (i.e., changing your asset-allocation mix) is essentially the only way you have of responding to turns in the economic cycle.

Although there is some doubt about just how reliable stock market crashes are as a true leading economic indicator, as discussed in the box below and evidenced by the October 1987 crash, there is little or no question that stocks do tend to decline — or at least turn listless — shortly before and during the early stages of a recession. In fact, in 1989, the NBER proclaimed that stock prices may indeed be the best of the leading indicators of U.S. economic activity.

Why? Because, as noted in our earlier description of the economic cycle, corporate profit levels tend drop before — and to a greater degree — than the actual level of business activity. And, as you know well from earlier lessons, profit levels — and expectations — are the primary driving factors behind stock price movements.

Thus, when corporate profit margins begin to decline — even if overall business activity remains strong — stock prices quickly follow suit. By the accepted definitions for the three types of recessions (as outlined earlier), this usually occurs from five to seven months before the economy as a whole actually begins to slow. Given that, the best time to consider shifting assets out of equities is probably two to three months prior to the official beginning of a recession.

Act much sooner than that and you risk getting whipsawed by a temporary slowing in the rate of continued expansion; act much later and the bulk of the market decline may already be behind you — a distinct problem in these days of triple-digit, single-day drops and 5 percent price corrections that last only four or five days.

Don't Get Overwhelmed By Numbers

Once again, of course, this begs the question of exactly how to predict when an official recession will begin. The federal government spews out hundreds of economic numbers every month, and the major states add even more in an effort to regionalize conditions. Try to analyze them all and you'll quickly wind up pulling out your hair — not to mention slumping into a prolonged state of inertia-breeding confusion.

That's one of the reasons we chose the opening quote featured at the start of this lesson. For the typical investor attempting to forecast the prospects for the economy, success is indeed more a function of consistent common sense than of analytical genius. Follow just a few key indicators, learn to understand how they work and what changes in them mean — and you should be able to make fairly solid judgments about what the economy is likely to do.

And, that in turn should help you in making key decisions regarding when — or if — you should adjust your asset mix to take advantage of economic fluctuations.

So, which of the many indicators do you use? There are a number of different approaches, but common sense is once again the key. For example, two of the most dominant factors in determining the health of the U.S. economy are interest rates and inflation. An individual who understands these powerful forces — and how they interact with virtually every segment of the economy, including the stock and bond markets — can become fairly proficient in predicting changes just by following them.

Note: This approach is outlined in wealth-building Step 91, Monitor Key Indicators for Clues on When to Change Your Portfolio Mix, which begins on page 11.

Monitor Key Indicators For Clues on When To Change Your Portfolio Mix

What: Monitor inflation rates and interest rates for changes that could signal it's time to adjust the allocation of assets within your investment portfolio, shifting money out of equities and into either debt securities or cash.

Why: Increasing inflation and rising interest rates have traditionally coincided with falling stock prices.

Risk: Low to medium. The major risk you face in making an asset reallocation is opportunity loss if you are wrong — i.e., stock prices could continue to rise, with you missing out on the resulting gains and thus slowing your overall rate of asset growth.

Safety: Medium to high. Generally, any asset reallocation you undertake based on these indicators will be defensive in nature — meaning you act to preserve your capital rather than placing it at greater risk.

Liquidity: Not applicable — so long as you conduct your asset reallocation in an orderly and well-planned fashion. The only time liquidity might be a factor would be if you wrongly attempted a "panic" reallocation, trying to unload large quantities of stock or buy large numbers of bonds in a very short period of time.

Why not: As you have learned in earlier lessons, numerous studies have shown that accurate market timing is extremely difficult. Most investors who try it actually fail to beat those who take a simple buy-and-hold approach. Similar studies have also shown investors usually miss out on market rallies because they're out of the market due to their faulty timing efforts. In addition, any time you undertake even a modest asset reallocation, you incur excess transaction costs and also face immediate tax liability for any accumulated gains you may be cashing in. These expenses can offset most (if not all) of the benefit you might gain by even a perfect timing decision.

Buy/Invest from: Not applicable.

Background: Although there are no ironclad rules with respect to the linkage between key economic indicators and the future performance of the stock market, stock prices have traditionally tended to fall in response to rising inflation or increases in interest rates. The problem for asset allocators, of course, is identifying the potential for these events before they actually happen in order to reposition assets in time to benefit from the shifts.

With respect to inflation, there are a number of factors that are generally considered to be portents of higher prices ahead. Among these are reported shortages of key raw materials used in manufacturing, high (and rising) levels of employment and a steady drop in unused factory capacity (both domestic and overseas). Each of these factors reflect rising demand and shrinking supply in the manufacturing sector, a combination that can only lead to higher prices at the consumer level. As for specific numbers, a forecast of inflation rising to or above the 4 percent level can generally be considered a warning sign that it is time to make adjustments to your portfolio, closing out some profitable equity positions (or those that have failed to live up to expectations) and moving the money to either bonds or cash. *Note: Some guidelines on how to reallocate your portfolio assets during various phases of the economic cycle are featured in wealth-building Step 92, found on page 21.*

Potential increases in interest rates can also be identified by watching for certain changes in business and economic conditions. As a rule, interest rates tend to rise during the later stages of the economic cycle as business activity begins to top out. Among the signals of a potential rise in overall interest rates are:

- Increasing demand for business credit.

- Rising demand for mortgage credit.

- Growing demand for consumer credit.

- Increasing expectations of higher inflation and a corresponding rise in the required inflation premium in investment yields.

Short-term rates are more heavily driven by business and consumer credit and thus tend to turn higher before long-term rates, which respond more to government, mortgage and high-dollar corporate debt demand. Among the leading indicators of rising short-term interest rates are:

- Falling unemployment.

- Rising industrial production.

- Rising producer prices.

- Accelerating growth in the nation's money supply.

- Rising business demand for short-term credit.

- A sharp upturn in the index of leading economic indicators (LEI), which includes the above items, as well as numerous other measures of business and commercial activity (all of which are widely reported in the financial media).

Once again, though it's not universally true, rising short-term interest rates tend to be associated with a falling stock market — and expectations of such an upturn should be considered a signal to start thinking about reallocation of portfolio assets.

▶ ▶ ▶ **If you want to get started today, here's what you need to do to begin monitoring inflation and interest rates for signals on when to adjust your portfolio asset allocation:**

Start maintaining a log — either in your computer or in the notebook where you keep your investment records — showing both monthly inflation rates and leading interest rates. The two leading measures of inflation are the consumer price index (CPI), which tracks inflation at the retail level, and the producer price index (PPI), which monitors price increases at the wholesale (or manufacturing) level. Both indexes are reported monthly by the U.S. government, with rates announced the first week of each new month for the prior month.

There are numerous interest-rate measures, but the two most popular are the Federal Reserve Board's discount rate (short term) and the "prime" rate (long term) charged by banks to their best customers. These rates are listed daily in the financial press and changes in either will usually be widely reported (although they generally don't change that often). For a more precise picture of day-to-day interest-rate activity, you may also want to monitor the yields for U.S. Treasury bills (short term), Treasury notes (intermediate term) and Treasury bonds

Step 91: *Monitor Key Indicators For Clues on When To Change Your Portfolio Mix*

(long term) as established in regular government auctions of new debt securities and through daily trading in the secondary markets.

Also note, on the same tracking sheet, the current figures and trends for the key indicators listed above that tend to foretell rising inflation or interest rates. (The purpose here is to get familiar with how all of these indicators are moving so that you will, in the future, be able to identify the correlation between changes in the key indicators and what eventually happens with inflation and interest rates.)

Your primary objective in tracking both inflation and interest rates is not to notice any little blip or change in direction, but rather to identify and track any trends in progress — and then spot any significant slowing or potential reversals in those trends. Sometimes these reversals can come quite quickly, such as when the Federal Reserve Board announces an increase or a cut in the discount rate. Generally, however, what you will see is a slowing of a trend — or perhaps a period of relative stability — followed by a move in the opposite direction (which may, in fact, reflect market pressures building up that will lead the Fed or the major banks to take "official" action in hiking or cutting the benchmark rates).

Once you have been through a couple of cycles, noting the changes in interest and inflation rates — and the changes in economic indicators that led up to them — you should be able to fairly accurately recognize the signals warning you it may be time to change the allocation of assets in your personal portfolio. ▲

Continued from p. 10

Common Sense Paints a Clear Picture

Another common-sense approach — particularly for those who want to try timing their asset shifts based on the movements of the economy and the stock market — evolves from the fact that, ultimately, all business activity depends on sales. An investor could select and track five or six key indicators that reflect on the public's future desire and ability to buy products and services. For example, if you wanted to take this approach, you might monitor:

- The current level of and trends in interest rates, as measured by some benchmark such as the prime rate.

- The current level and trend of wholesale inflation as reported monthly by the government with its Producer Price Index. (The PPI is a better indicator of future spending potential than the retail-based Consumer Price Index because price increases being felt now by manufacturers will eventually be passed on to shoppers.)

- Personal disposable income, which is reported monthly by the government and measures trends in the amount of income people have left over for discretionary purchases after covering their day-to-day expenses.

- The installment credit ratio, which gauges the amount of short-term debt (including credit-card debt) consumers are carrying relative to their personal incomes.

- Unemployment and new-job creation rates. Reported monthly by the U.S. Department of Labor, these numbers track the number of people currently seeking employment and the number of new non-farm jobs being created for them to fill.

- Consumer sentiment, which is a measure of how the public feels about prospects for the economy — and, by association, whether consumers are more or less likely to make new purchases. There are several sources for consumer-confidence data, including the Conference Board and the University of Michigan, both of which issue monthly reports based on their proprietary indexes.

With these six indicators and a bit of common-sense analysis, you should be able to make fairly accurate projections about the prospects for future business activity — and, by extension, expected corporate profits and stock-price reactions.

If the indicators on which you focus are too narrow, you'll likely get a lot of contradictory readings that will leave you more confused than enlightened.

For example, if interest rates are low, inflation is in check, unemployment is low, new jobs are being created, personal incomes are rising, the installment credit burden isn't too high and consumers are reasonably optimistic, then the economy is likely to keep growing, with higher corporate profits — and higher stock prices.

On the other hand, if inflation, interest rates, unemployment and consumer debt are rising, while job creation, personal incomes and public optimism are falling, the odds of an economic downturn increase substantially — and a downturn in corporate profits and stock prices could be the early signal that it's time to adjust your asset mix.

Obviously, these are broad generalities and offer very little aid with respect to precise timing. However, once you choose which indicators to follow and begin tracking them, you will learn how they perform under varying conditions, how they interact with one another and how they relate to other events in the economy. And, after you've followed them through a couple of complete economic cycles, you should be able begin recognizing key readings that will signal future turns in the economy — and the market.

A Couple of Important Tips

Whichever approach you choose, there are several important points to keep in mind, among them:

- Select broad-based indicators and view them only as they relate to the overall economic picture. If the indicators on which you focus are too narrow, you'll likely get a lot of contradictory readings that will leave you more confused than enlightened.

- Be aware that indicators rarely move as neatly in tandem as we just described them, particularly at or near key economic turning points. More often, if you're following six indicators, you will get three pointing one way, two pointing another and one not pointing anywhere.

- Focus on long-term patterns and trends, not on short-term blips or reversals. The economy is a complex and often cumbersome machine and its almost impossible for it to stop on a dime or make quick U-turns.

- Don't pay too much attention to the general media. Newspapers have to have headlines every day and each TV newscast has to have a sensational sound bite or two, but that doesn't mean all the news is important (or even accurate).

- Don't worry too much about Washington. The same caution we just made about the news media also applies to politicians. These folks need to attract attention in order to attract votes — and bemoaning the state of the economy is one way to do it. As a result, politicians may say almost anything about the economy or introduce frightful sounding pieces of economic legislation. However, while their words and actions may appeal to a vocal or disgruntled minority, it's generally unlikely that the legislation will ever become law — at least without substantial modifications to ensure the true impact on the economy is minimal.

- Don't fall in love with your own predictions. If you read your indicators one way for a couple of months, then see a shift in the other direction, never assume that the numbers are lying to you and that you're really right. That's the quickest way to ruin in the financial world, as evidenced by the huge number of investors steadfastly holding $10 stocks — for which they originally paid $25 or $30.

APPLYING ECONOMIC CYCLES TO YOUR INVESTING

Once you've gotten relatively comfortable with your understanding of the economic cycle, your choice of indicators for monitoring it and your ability to forecast its future course, what do you do with your newfound expertise?

As we said at the start of this lesson, once you've structured a carefully diversified wealth-building pyramid, there are really only two reasons to tinker with your asset mix in anticipation of changing economic conditions. They are:

- Market timing, in which you shift funds from one asset class to another in hopes of avoiding market pullbacks or capturing market advances, thereby increasing your rate of asset growth and improving your long-term portfolio returns.

- Financial planning, in which you assume an essentially defensive posture in the face of predicted economic fluctuations, thereby preserving earlier gains and ensuring that you meet specific personal or lifestyle goals as originally scheduled.

Since adoption of a market-timing approach requires a more immediate decision — and involves a far more complex process — we'll examine it first.

The Merits of Market Timing

As you learned earlier in the *100 Steps to Wealth* course, most specifically in the lesson titled Timing Your Trades, there is considerable debate regarding both the validity of market timing as an investment strategy and the ability of most individuals to successfully undertake it.

Also known as "tactical asset allocation," market timing involves actively changing the mix of assets in your portfolio in anticipation of major turns in economic, business or market cycles. Put another way, it is an ongoing process of portfolio management involving three primary steps:

- The identification of specific assets (or asset classes) that have reached the peak of their current short-term growth cycle and have thus become overpriced (i.e., the anticipated risk in continuing to hold exceeds the potential reward).

- The sale of those assets to permanently lock in profits and avoid an ensuing cyclical downturn.

- The replacement of those assets (or asset classes) with others that are just entering cyclical upswings — and are thus still underpriced (i.e., the potential reward in assuming a position exceeds the anticipated risk).

As should be obvious, the key to successful timing lies in correctly evaluating the cycles for the particular assets involved, and for the economy in general. The shift must also improve overall returns enough to cover all related transaction costs and offset any incremental tax liabilities incurred as a result of the trade.

Market timing stands in contrast to so-called "strategic asset allocation," in which you construct a diversified portfolio spanning all the key asset classes, fill it with quality securities and other investment vehicles and then hold for the long term — trusting that the broad asset mix will even out the interim market and economic cycles and provide steady growth over time.

A Threat to Diversification? It's also exceedingly difficult — and, according to many experts (including Nobel Prize-winning economist Paul Samuelson), potentially hazardous to your financial health. The difficulty aside, these critics say tactical asset shifts can disrupt the strategic balance originally built into a portfolio, and that an ill-timed tactical shift can expose investors to risks normally offset by effective diversification. *Note: Some market timers counter this potential risk by restricting their activities to shifts within the same asset class, as discussed in the box at left.*

This criticism was validated by many of the early studies of both actual and hypothetical market-timing performance. For example, a study by William G. Droms (published in the January/February 1989 edition of the *Financial Analysts Journal*) found that, over a 60-year period, a frequent market timer would have to be correct almost two thirds of the time in order to beat a simple buy-and-hold approach — a performance record most experts felt is beyond the scope of even professional portfolio managers.

Even more damaging was a historical study conducted by the American Funds Group and reported in *Money*'s April 1994 issue. It found that, even if your timing had been absolutely perfect over the 40-year period ending Dec. 31, 1993, the actual difference in returns was so small as to make the risk unacceptable.

Market Timing Within Asset Classes

One way to potentially improve investment returns on a well-diversified portfolio without upsetting the strategic balance is to practice market timing within a given asset class. This approach — known as sector investing — attempts to take advantage of the fact that all groups within a given market rarely move in unison. Rather, one group will move strongly higher, carrying the overall market with it. Then, as that group starts to peak, a new market leader will emerge, bolstering the overall rally until it too begins to weaken, at which point still another sector will move to the forefront. It's sort of like a horse race, where one thoroughbred breaks fast out of the gate and sets the early pace, then is overtaken at the mid-point by another steed, which leads the way until the final turn, when still another horse emerges from the pack and heads up the charge for the wire.

With respect to stocks, this so-called "sector rotation" occurs for a couple of reasons. The first is that different industries respond at different rates to economic cycles, with some showing increases in sales and profits while the overall economy is still in a trough, and others not entering a full-fledged growth period until the overall economy is near a peak. The second is that different industries have different growth rates, with some spurting to almost instant large profit gains in the first months of an expansion, and others building momentum slowly over a more extended portion of the upswing. Still another reason has to do with the emotions of investors, who get caught up in the excitement of a rally and, fearing missed opportunities, scurry to buy more and more speculative issues as a market advance progresses. *Note: Sector rotation can also occur in the debt market, with strength starting in long-term bonds, then extending to intermediate-term issues and finally expanding to the short-term sector.*

In most recent U.S. stock market rallies, the sector rotation has followed a fairly consistent pattern. Financial companies, which are the first to profit from falling interest rates and increased borrowing activity, begin the upturn. Leadership is then picked up by the growth-stock sector as the rally builds up steam, passes to the industrial (or cyclical) group as the advance matures and dashes the final distance to the peak in a flurry of activity among speculative issues (a phase typically marked by lots of buyouts, mergers and new public offerings). A quality rotation also prevails in most rallies, with Blue Chips assuming the leadership in the early stages, secondary issues joining in next and tertiary (or speculative) issues carrying the advance to its peak.

Recognizing these patterns, a timer can improve overall performance by concentrating equity holdings in financial stocks during economic troughs, then switching to growth stocks, cyclicals and speculative issues as the expansion progresses — all the while preserving essentially the same strategic asset balance.

The study compared the returns achieved by an investor buying at the market's absolute low point each year and one buying at its absolute high. It found that investing on the day the market hit its yearly low would have netted a return of 11.5 percent a year, including dividends, while investing on the day the market hit its annual high would have still earned a healthy 10.7 percent — a mere 0.8 percent difference in compounded return.

Conditions May Be Different Now

From a strategic standpoint, that sounds fairly discouraging. However, before you completely reject market timing based on those studies, be aware that conditions may well have changed in recent years. Chaos theory, a relatively new approach to financial analysis, suggests the present-day nature of the markets — driven as they now are by program trading, derivative vehicles and institutional investors (fund managers) — may be considerably more conducive to market-timing success.

The shift must improve overall returns enough to cover all related transaction costs and offset any incremental tax liabilities incurred as a result of the trade.

There is also evidence that the changing differential between returns provided by various asset classes may have positive implications for market timing. For example, during the period from 1934 to 1972 — when much of the data for the early studies on timing was recorded — stocks provided an excess return of 8.9 percent over U.S. Treasury bills (the standard for so-called "risk-free" investment returns).

Given that extreme differential, it made it almost possible for an investor to come out ahead by shifting from "risky" stocks to "risk-free" T-bills. With transaction costs and tax liabilities factored in, the market would have had to correct by roughly 15 percent before the investor broke even on the basis of cost-adjusted long-term returns. And, there simply weren't enough market pullbacks of that magnitude to make the timing effort worthwhile.

During the 1970s and '80s, however, the excess yield of stocks over T-bills dwindled to just over 3 percent — which means investors would not have lost that much when shifting from stocks to T-bills (and have lost even less when shifting to some of the higher-yielding, but still fairly low-risk cash-equivalent investments available today that weren't around from 1934 through 1970).

Thus, with tactical asset shifts paying off on smaller market downturns, newer studies have found a higher rate of success for market timers during the past 25 years — and that advantage is likely to continue for investors who work diligently at honing their skills in predicting economic cycles and key market turning points.

To illustrate the potential benefits of successful market timing, look at the chart below, which shows the performance results calculated for good and bad market years in a study by Wilson Sy (published in "Market Timing: Is It Folly?" Journal of Portfolio Management, Summer 1990, p. 13).

STOCKS vs. RISK-FREE RETURNS — 1970-1988	S&P 500 Index	Treasury Bills	Differ-ential
OVERALL AVERAGE ANNUAL RETURNS	10.59%	7.52%	+ 3.07%
GOOD-YEAR RETURNS (11 YEARS)	23.32%	7.31%	+16.01%
POOR-YEAR RETURNS (8 YEARS)	- 3.89%	7.88%	- 11.77%

During the good years (defined as a year in which the S&P 500 closed higher on a year-over-year basis), an investor who held stocks would have enjoyed a return advantage of more than 16 percent over someone who just held T-bills. However, during the poor years (defined as a year in which the S&P 500 closed lower on a year-over-year basis), T-bills would have produced a yield advantage over stocks of nearly 12 percent — more than enough to justify switching, even on a cost- and tax-adjusted basis.

Overall, the reward in switching out of stocks during the bad years would have been substantial. While the buy-and-hold stock investor would have earned 10.59 percent per annum from 1970 through 1988, the market timer who successfully avoided each of the eight bad years would have had an average annual return of 23.31 percent — a difference of roughly 12.7 percent per year!

Don't Overlook the Risk Factors

That certainly sounds exciting — but it fails to reflect two major problems. First, no one could possibly achieve 100 percent accuracy in timing the market on a year-to-year basis over a 19-year span. Second, assuming you do make a few mistakes, the cost of missing some of the good years is substantial. Give up that 16 percent performance edge in just three of the good years, and you knock over 3 percent off your performance for the total period.

International Implications for Market Timers

The American economy isn't the only one that moves in cycles, nor is the U.S. stock market the only potential focal point for tactical asset allocators. As you learned in the earlier lesson, "The Global Approach," the economies of most major foreign countries and many entire regions also tend to move in well-defined cycles — cycles that are frequently in different phases from the U.S. economic cycle. For example, recoveries in Latin America typically lag those in the United States, with economies often being jolted out of the trough phase by increasing American demands for imported goods as the U.S. expansion matures.

Recognizing these disparities, an American market timer may be able to maintain a proportional portfolio commitment to equities while extending his or her superior performance by shifting from U.S. stocks to foreign securities in the later stages of a U.S. market rally. As in the case of sector rotation, discussed earlier, this type of switch maintains the strategic balance of a diversified portfolio while still allowing a longer and more aggressive pursuit of high equity returns. It does, however, impose an additional risk since potential currency-exchange losses must be factored into the total-return equation (see the earlier lesson titled Greenback Alternatives). Higher transaction costs for trading in some foreign securities must also be considered in determining the true yield advantage of such a strategy.

Add in a few years when you took a loss by holding stocks in a down market, throw in your switching costs and incremental taxes — and you're right back where you started, with only aggravation to show for your timing efforts.

That's why market timing strategies should *only* be undertaken if you have a very strong belief in your ability to correctly assess the importance of key indicators and accurately predict economic cycles based on what you see.

A Final Word on Market Timing

The final verdict on the true benefits of market-timing strategies may not be in until well after the turn of the century, if then. The nature of the markets will no doubt continue to change as more new trading vehicles are introduced and technological innovations improve both the flow of information and the mechanics of the trading systems. The "globalization" of the financial markets and the increasing interdependence of worldwide economies will also affect both returns and timing opportunities here and abroad.

In the meantime, we have tried to present as clear a picture as possible of both the risks and rewards of market timing. For most individual investors, we suspect the task will be too daunting to be worthwhile. However, the choice is yours. If you feel highly confident in your abilities as an economic analyst and want to give it a try, go for it!

Don't, however, hesitate to back away if the effort begins to negatively impact the success of your personal wealth-building program.

Whether you try your hand at market timing or choose to stick to the more conservative approach of structuring a well-balanced portfolio and then letting time level out the ups and downs, we have no doubt that — using what you've learned in this course — you will eventually be successful in your wealth-building effort.

Add in a few years when you took a loss by holding stocks in a down market, throw in your switching costs and incremental taxes — and you're right back where you started, with only aggravation to show for your timing efforts.

That's why market timing strategies should only be undertaken if you have a very strong belief in your ability to correctly assess the importance of key indicators and accurately predict economic cycles based on what you see.

We also feel certain that you are making this effort for reasons other than the mere accumulation of wealth. Obviously, you are striving to achieve financial control in order to meet any number of specific goals — ranging from purchase of a first (or second) home and funding of your children's educations to a more enjoyable overall lifestyle and a secure retirement.

And that, of course, brings us to the second key purpose behind learning to analyze economic conditions and forecast (at least in broad terms) the future course of the economy and the markets in which you've invested your hard-won wealth — financial planning.

Whatever your personal objectives — even if they are far less noble than those we've just listed — you don't want to work for years building to the brink of achievement and then have success snatched away at the last minute by an adverse economic turn. Unfortunately, the risk of that happening grows larger and larger as you get nearer each goal — particularly if the objective is time-specific.

The reason for this is simple. If you make a mistake or suffer a major setback early in your financial quest, you can generally correct your errors or recoup your losses and still achieve your goal within the allotted time. However, if calamity comes just as you are about to reach your final target, the objective may be lost forever.

For example, if you are investing in order to fund a college education for your 3-year-old daughter and have most of your assets in stocks, a 25 percent market correction won't prove too worrisome. You'll have plenty of time to ride out the downturn, profit from the eventual recovery and still be ready to send her off to the halls of academia, full tuition in hand.

However, if you are just getting ready to sell $40,000 worth of stocks to finance your June grad's fall enrollment at Stanford when the same 25 percent market correction hits, you'll most likely be in serious trouble — $10,000 short with only two months to go! What do you do? If the money for next year's tuition was also in stocks, stealing from that fund probably won't be an option. Because it will also have lost 25 percent of its value, meaning taking out $10,000 would reduce the capital base by a full 50 percent — making recovery almost impossible, even if the market rebounded sharply.

By the same reasoning, other alternatives — such as robbing from a retirement fund — prove equally unattractive. You're essentially left with nothing to do but pray for a quick (and massive) summer rally — or, failing that, sacrifice one of your goals. That is a potentially devastating prospect — particularly if the goal is one, such as retirement, that comes later in life. Then, you may have no remaining goals to sacrifice (with the possible exception of leaving a large estate for your heirs), which could force you to delay retirement or accept a much less lavish lifestyle than you had planned for.

Shifting to a Defensive Stance

Fortunately, the examples just presented represent worst-case scenarios. In most cases, such risks can be greatly reduced, or even eliminated, through a combination of economic analysis and defensive adjustments in your basic asset-allocation mix. Here's how it works:

A good rule would be to begin watching key indicators about three to four years before you're due to reach a time-specific goal.

Even if you don't constantly monitor the economic cycle, a good rule would be to begin watching key indicators about three to four years before you're due to reach a time-specific goal. What you're trying to do is pinpoint an identifiable economic phase that you can use as a base for future projections.

Once you have one, as verified by government economists and analytical reports in the financial media, apply the same time frame that played out in the most recent previous cycles to the current one. Based on that, project where in the cycle the economy — and the markets — will likely be when you reach your goal date, as well as what is likely to happen in the interim.

Depending on what your projections suggest, there are two basic defensive strategies you should take:

- If the probability of a recession occurring shortly before, or right when, you are due to achieve your goal appears high, begin gradually reducing your equity holdings. If your intent is merely to preserve your current asset base in anticipation of, say, retirement, then you can shift into a mix of shorter-term bonds, Treasury notes and money-market funds. If, on the other hand, your goal will require full liquidation of some assets in order to make a purchase or some type of payment, move the bulk of the money into low-risk, cash-equivalent investments such as money-market funds or even T-bills.

- If the probability is high that your goal date will come during an expansion or peak period, begin gradually reducing your bond and other intermediate-term debt holdings. If the start of the expansion period appears imminent, your initial shifts can be into Blue Chip stocks and then growth issues in order to capture one last surge in appreciation, with a later move to more defensive sectors or cash. However, if you know you'll need to liquidate to meet a specific expense, you may want to go ahead and start moving to cash equivalents.

Obviously, the precise timing of your shifts will depend on the nature of the goal you're approaching, as well as your assessment of where in the projected cycle you currently are and when you anticipate key turning points to occur. You may also want to adjust your switch points as time passes if events don't unfold the way you expected or the indicators you're following start to contradict your earlier projections.

Retirement Requires Special Care

If the goal you are approaching is retirement, it's also a good idea to carry your projections a couple of years beyond the actual effective date. That's because retirement generally involves a significant asset shift — perhaps involving liquidation, freezing of some income-producing classes or the annuitization of some assets. As a defensive measure, you'll also want to switch out of sectors that carry substantial interest-rate or inflation exposure. Extending your projections will help alert you to any difficulties you might face in making these shifts because of where in a cycle the economy will likely be.

Some suggested portfolio guidelines for various phases of the economic cycle are featured in wealth-building Step 92, Establish an Asset Reallocation Alarm Formula, which begins on page 21.

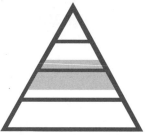

Establish An Asset Reallocation Alarm Formula

What: Select an "alarm" system to actually trigger reallocation of your portfolio asset mix in anticipation of a move into the next phase of a typical economic cycle.

Why: The indicators you'll be tracking as a result of following wealth-building Step 91 are valuable in helping paint a picture of where the economy and the stock market are likely to go, but they can also provide confusing and contradictory signals that could cause you to delay taking action. As a result, you need to decide on one or two definitive "alarms" that will definitively trigger your reallocation moves.

Risk: Low to medium. Once again, your major risk in making an asset reallocation is one of opportunity. If you are wrong and move too many assets from one class to another too soon, you could miss out on substantial additional appreciation.

Safety: Medium to high. As a rule, it's better to have a set plan for dealing with specific situations than to merely react. By setting up a pre-determined alarm system — and following it — you eliminate the risk that you will misread certain signals, or read them correctly but over-react.

Liquidity: Not applicable.

Why not: As noted earlier, studies have found that accurate market timing is beyond the scope of most individual investors, who generally fail to outperform a simple "buy-and-hold" approach on a cost-adjusted basis. These same studies have shown that the opportunity risk in missing a major market upmove due to faulty timing can be far more significant than the actual risk involved in riding out a typical market slump.

Buy/Invest from: Not applicable.

Background: While no single "trigger mechanism" has a 100 percent record of historical accuracy, there are three commonly accepted approaches that have proven reasonably effective in signaling the time to make shifts in asset allocation. Two of them are relatively simple, while the third is a bit more complex. However, all are worth a quick review.

The first, and perhaps most commonly used approach involves maintaining a moving average of market performance. A moving average can be calculated for virtually any length of time — from a few hours to 20 years. However, for timing purposes, we feel the most reliable is the 53-week moving average — calculated using either the Dow Jones Industrial Average, the S&P 500 Index or (if you invest primarily in secondary issues) a broader-based index such as the Wilshire 2000.

To construct a moving average, you simply total the Friday closing numbers for the index you're tracking over the past 53 weeks and then divide by 53. The result will be the average closing price for the index over the past year — a number that should be plotted on your chart for the index directly under (or over) the most recent closing price. The following week, you do exactly the same thing — dropping the oldest price, adding the most recent close to the remaining 52 and again dividing the total by 53. You once again plot that number on the chart, and then connect it to the point showing the previous week's average close.

After you've done this for several weeks in a row, you will have a clearly observable "moving-average line" showing the direction of the market in recent weeks, the strength of the recent trend (based on the steepness of the moving-average line) and the market's current position relative to that trend. The latter point is the most important since it provides your trigger. So long as the market's most recent closing level remains above the 53-week moving-average line, it can be assumed that a current upward market trend is still intact.

The indicators you'll be tracking... are valuable... but they can also provide confusing and contradictory signals.... As a result, you need to decide on one or two definitive "alarms" that will definitively trigger your reallocation moves.

However, if the market closes below the moving-average line, it's generally considered a signal that the trend is broken — meaning it could be time to sell stocks and either hold more cash or re-allocate the assets into other investment classes. (Note: The same approach can be used to trigger a stock-buying decision. If the market has been trending downward based on the 53-week moving-average line and the index then makes a weekly close above that line, it could signal an impending rally — meaning it would be time to buy stocks.)

A second approach involves gearing your alarm to the previously discussed relationships among stock prices, interest rates and inflation rates. Normally, a rise in either interest rates or inflation rates will result in a drop in corporate price/earnings (P/E) ratios — which will, in turn, lead to lower stock prices. Thus, an upward surge in either inflation or interest rates can be considered a viable alarm regarding the rising peril in holding stocks.

As noted before, however, changes in inflation and interest rates are both hard to predict and easy to misinterpret. One solution is to employ the so-called "Rule of 20," which has been successfully used by the investment firm Donaldson Lufkin & Jenrette as an indicator of changing economic times. The "Rule of 20" simply states that the composite P/E ratio of the Dow Jones Industrial stocks, plus the current rate of inflation, normally runs around 20. When the total of the two gets too far below that mark, stock prices are viewed as undervalued relative to earnings and tend to rally. And, when the total gets too far above that mark, stocks are considered overvalued relative to earnings, and prices tend to fall.

Thus, a sharp surge by the combined Dow P/E and inflation rate to a level well above the 20 mark could signal an impending market decline — which would alert you to sell stocks (or at least tilt your asset mix in favor of bonds). As clearly shown in the table below, this rule would have gotten you out of the stock market in early 1987 — and kept you out till well after the October crash.

	DJIA	DJIA P/E	Inflation Rate	Inflation Plus P/E
SEPTEMBER 30, 1986	1767	14.9	3.6%	18.5
DECEMBER 31, 1986	1895	16.4	3.7%	20.1
MARCH 31, 1987	2305	18.2	3.8%	22.0
JUNE 30, 1987	2418	19.2	3.9%	23.1
SEPTEMBER 30, 1987	2596	18.8	3.8%	22.6
DECEMBER 31, 1987	1938	14.6	4.0%	18.6

A third, more detailed approach involves tracking average market P/E ratios, dividend-payout ratios and/or market-to-book-value ratios and using a deviation from historical norms by any two of them as an asset reallocation alarm. Although subject to some debate, the suggested trigger points for each of these indicators are as follows:

■ The average P/E ratio for the market as a whole has rarely been above 20 — and when it has, it's almost always been concurrent with a market top.

Step 92: *Establish An Asset Reallocation Alarm Formula*

■ The average stock dividend-payout ratio (i.e., the percentage of corporate earnings paid out to shareholders as dividends) has rarely been above 33 percent — and when it has, it's almost always coincided with a market top.

■ The market-to-book-value ratio (i.e., the current market value of stocks divided by the actual book value of the underlying companies) has been above 2.50 only 5 percent of the time since 1926, usually just before market reversals.

Thus, if at least two of these indicators is above the historical norms, it could be an alarm warning you it's time to adjust your portfolio asset mix — moving money out of stocks and into bonds, cash or other asset classes. Low readings on these three indicators can also signal good stock buying opportunities. For example, the following table shows where the indicators stood at the end of each U.S. recession during the past 50 years — as well as the average growth in corporate earnings the following year. In almost every instance, low readings across the board were followed by higher earnings — and higher stock prices — in the ensuing year (the exception being 1980, when the economy really only blipped higher before settling back into the 1981-82 recession). The table also illustrates that even the best indicators aren't infallible — i.e., in 1992, all three indicators were above the levels that have historically signaled a market top, yet earnings growth surged 41 percent in 1993, and stocks continued to rally.

Year	Avg. P/E	Div. Ratio	Market Value/ Book	Short-Term Interest Rates	Earnings Growth Next Year
1949	7	15	1.10	1.3%	22%
1954	11	20	1.42	1.4%	31%
1958	14	25	1.53	1.5%	17%
1961	21	34	1.99	1.6%	15%
1970	18	29	1.82	2.4%	11%
1975	10	24	1.32	3.2%	24%
1980	8	22	1.23	4.6%	3%
1982	11	20	1.25	5.8%	10%
1992	26	34	2.51	3.6%	41%

▷ ▷ ▶ ▶ **If you want to get started today, here's what you need to do to establish an asset reallocation alarm formula:**

Select one or more of the approaches outlined above and begin tracking the appropriate indicators, recording the data on a weekly basis and building a long-term log so you can become familiar with trading patterns and learn to see trends developing. *Note: If you want to use a moving average — which we readily endorse even if you are also using another approach — we advise purchasing one of the leading stock market charting software packages. For example TeleChart can be reached by calling 1-800-776-4940 and Dow Jones Market Analyzer Plus is at 1-800-815-5100, ext. 511. Constructing moving averages by hand can be quite a cumbersome process, whereas the software programs will do them automatically in a matter of seconds.)*

Step 92: *Establish An Asset Reallocation Alarm Formula*

Based on our suggested norms, plus your own observations (and further study, if you so desire), decide exactly what you want your trigger points to be — and then stick with them. Be aware, however, that it's seldom wise to take a major action based on just one indicator. Our recommendation is to have at least two, and preferably three different alarms — taking action only when two of them sound at the same time. Also pay close attention to where we are in the economic cycle at any given time so you will know where to put your assets once you begin reallocating them. The following table offers some suitable asset mixes for each of the four major phases of the economic cycle:

Asset Class	Overall Economic Outlook			
	Recession	**Neutral**	**Expansion**	**Inflation**
MONEY MARKET FUNDS	50%	20%	10%	40%
SHORT-TERM BONDS	20%	10%	10%	20%
LONG-TERM BONDS	10%	20%	10%	—
BLUE CHIP STOCKS	20%	30%	30%	—
GROWTH STOCKS	—	20%	40%	20%
GOLD/GOLD FUNDS	—	—	—	20%
TOTALS	100%	100%	100%	100%

Continued from p. 20

INFLATION PROOFING YOUR PORTFOLIO

In any review of economic cycles — or of effective portfolio asset allocation — inflation is a bit of a wild card. Although the onset of excessive inflation is usually associated with the later stages of the expansion phase, it can also persist throughout a cyclical peak and well into a recession. In fact, at least a modest degree of inflation is present nearly all the time.

Most economists don't view moderate inflation as a major concern (although you couldn't prove it by watching Federal Reserve Board Chairman Greenspan), with many even arguing that it is essential to a healthy economy. The alternative, these theorists contend, is price "deflation" — which normally translates into either a severe recession or a full-blown depression.

Still, for investors, inflation — which, on the off chance someone doesn't know, simply means rising prices — is a potentially deadly enemy. In fact, for someone who puts in the intense care and planning required to build a portfolio based on the principles outlined in this course, getting caught in an inflationary spiral is perhaps the worst thing that can happen.

That's because extreme inflation hits directly at virtually all asset classes (with the exception of precious metals and other basic commodities). It wipes out the purchasing power of assets you've already accumulated, devalues the income you have coming in and cripples your ability to create new wealth.

During periods of high inflation, cash becomes a liability because it buys less and less with each passing day. Fixed-income investments such as bonds also take a beating because "real" interest rates (coupon yield minus inflation) move to extremely low levels — or even go negative (as happened during the inflationary spirals of the 1940s and the 1970s). In addition, high inflation is frequently accompanied by little or no economic growth — a condition known as "stagflation" — which creates a terrible environment for traditional equity investments.

As a result, one of the keys to successful wealth-building is developing a plan to protect against this peril.

Quantifying Inflation

While there is no universally accepted definition of what constitutes an inflationary period, the general view is that inflation in the area of 3.0 percent per year or less is acceptable, while overall price increases of 4.0 percent or higher are potentially damaging.

A Low-Inflation Tip

While fixed-income investments are at considerable risk during periods of high inflation, bonds and Treasury bills can be extremely attractive when inflation is very low — such as in the 1960s, mid-1980s and early 1990s. That's because real rates of interest climb sharply, and the purchasing power represented by the regular interest payments is substantially higher on a risk-adjusted basis than that of cash flows generated by other, more volatile investments (such as dividend-paying stocks).

As noted earlier, periods of high inflation typically begin in the later stages of an economic expansion cycle, when demand becomes excessive and/or shortages of goods or services develop — either one of which can trigger price increases. For this reason, the federal government (and most private economists and financial analysts) keep a steady eye on price trends.

The two most closely watched measures of inflation are:

■ *The Producer Price Index (PPI),* which (as noted earlier) tracks the cost of raw materials, plant and equipment used by manufacturers and other businesses operating at the wholesale level.

■ *The Consumer Price Index (CPI),* which measures the cost of a representative basket of consumer goods — e.g., foods, clothing, rents, gasoline, health-care products — routinely purchased by the average urban household.

Both indexes are compiled and reported monthly by the U.S. Department of Labor, with price increases quoted on both a per-month and an annualized basis. For example, if the monthly quote was 0.6 percent (six-tenths of one percent), the annual rate of price growth would be 7.20 percent (0.6 x 12 mos. = 0.72%).

Where to Look for Inflation Protection

The traditional view is that equities provide a fairly effective hedge against inflation — and over the long run that is true. In the short term, however, that isn't always the case. If both inflation rates and interest rates are rising, and corporate profit margins are rising more slowly (or holding steady or shrinking), then your purchasing power in holding stocks will be eroded relative to inflation and relative to yields on other investments offering the real rate of interest.

In other words, in order for stocks to be an effective hedge against inflation, earnings per share must rise by at least the current (or, more accurately, the expected) rate of inflation in order for the share price to increase enough to offset your loss of purchasing power in holding stocks, assuming a constant price/ earnings (P/E) multiple. This is illustrated by the following equations:

$$P1 = Po \times (1+IN)$$
$$\text{Or:} \quad Pi = P/E \times eps \times IN$$

Where:

P1 = Required future share price to hedge expected inflation.

Pi = Required share price increase to hedge expected inflation.

Po = Current share price.

P/E = Price/earnings multiple.

eps = Earnings per share.

IN = Inflation rate.

Putting numbers to the equations, if inflation were expected to be 6 percent over the coming year, a $20 stock with current earnings per share of $1.00 — meaning a P/E multiple of 20 — would have to see earnings rise to $1.06 per share next year in order to produce a price of roughly $21.20 per share, which would be needed to match the loss of purchasing power due to inflation. In other words:

$$P1 = Po \times (1+IN)$$
$$P1 = \$20 \times (1+0.06)$$
$$P1 = \$21.20$$
$$\text{Or:} \quad Pi = 20 \times \$1.00 \times 0.06$$
$$Pi = \$1.20$$

Thus, on a short-term basis — i.e., in an inflationary phase of any given economic cycle — stocks probably won't provide an adequate hedge against the effects of inflation on the rest of your portfolio or on your overall purchasing power.

The short-term hedge value of stocks grows even more dubious if you consider that average P/E multiples may fall, which frequently happens in an inflationary environment. If that occurs, then stocks will provide a hedge only if earnings per share rise by enough to offset the lower P/E valuation and more — which becomes increasingly difficult as economic conditions deteriorate.

That's because there are only a few variables in the calculation of corporate earnings — i.e., "earnings" equal sales revenues, minus cost of sales, minus operating expenses, minus non-operating expenses, minus taxes. Thus, for earnings to increase, there are only three possible scenarios:

■ Sales revenues must rise while expenses and/or taxes remain constant.

■ Sales revenues must remain constant while expenses and/or taxes fall.

■ Some combination of changes in sales revenues and expenses must develop in proportion so that profit margins remain constant or improve.

Typically, companies attempt to raise prices in order to try and keep sales revenues growing at a rate equal to the rate of inflation. However, since all the company's suppliers are doing the same thing, costs fairly well keep pace and profit margins soon begin to erode. That results in lower reported earnings — and that almost always translates into a lower stock price, with the decline being compounded if average P/E multiples are also falling.

Thus, on a short-term basis — i.e., in an inflationary phase of any given economic cycle — stocks probably won't provide an adequate hedge against the effects of inflation on the rest of your portfolio or on your overall purchasing power.

Another Bit of Traditional Wisdom Revised

Because they no longer have earned income with which to offset investment losses, retirees have to remain particularly vigilant against inflation. However, in times like these, when inflation is not a significant threat, most must also be concerned about continued capital growth — especially with average lifespans increasing at a steady pace. Otherwise, their asset base may expire before they do.

Traditional financial-planning wisdom dealt with this concern by advising retirees to keep a percentage of equities in their portfolios equal to 100 minus their age. Thus, a 70-year-old would devote 30 percent of his or her portfolio to stocks, and 70 percent to a mix of fixed-income securities, cash equivalents and inflation hedges. With increasing lifespans, however, this technique has now become too conservative — i.e., retirees now need to focus on growth in addition to capital preservation until they are well into their 70s.

To accomplish this, seniors should multiply their current age by 80 percent (0.80) and put all but that amount of their assets in equities. For example, a 70-year-old would multiply 70 times 0.80 and get 56. Subtracting that from 100 percent, the retiree would determine that 44 percent of his or her assets should be devoted to stocks.

Look Overseas for Protection

So, if you can't count on stocks to provide an adequate hedge against the dangers of high inflation, what can you use? Surprisingly, one answer for at least a portion of your assets may be stocks — just not domestic ones.

As noted earlier, the economies of the world's major nations and leading regions are rarely in perfect synch — and neither are their inflation rates or their stock markets. Thus, maintaining a reasonable portion of your assets in foreign equities (or, depending on the economic climate, debt securities) can provide a hedge against both domestic market reversals and rising internal U.S. inflation.

If, for example, the U.S. economy goes into a recessionary phase, but growth continues in Scandinavia or the Far East, gains recorded on your securities from those regions can offset much of your loss at home. (The economies of Great Britain, Germany and Japan, although not perfectly in step with the U.S., will tend to move with ours.)

The same is true with inflation. If higher prices here start to sharply erode the power of the dollar to purchase basic goods, the greenback will also likely lose value relative to key foreign currencies in regions where inflation is not yet a problem. Thus, any investments you have that are denominated in those currencies will hedge your purchasing power loss here at home, even if your foreign securities don't actually rise in price (i.e., the same number of foreign currency units will return a greater number of dollars when the security is sold and the proceeds repatriated). The domestic purchasing power of income from foreign debt securities will also be enhanced as the foreign-currency denominated interest payments translate into larger numbers of dollars.

Focus on Europe and the Far East

Even if your primary concern isn't currently inflation or an end to the long U.S. bull market in equities, you should still take a close look at Europe and the Far East as these two regions offer substantial opportunity for future asset growth.

In fact, we strongly feel inclusion of securities (or funds) from both areas is essential to any well-balanced present day investment portfolio — on the basis of both opportunity and protection through international diversification.

Numerous studies have also shown that commodity prices tend to move inversely with stocks — particularly in periods of very rapid inflation.

The 14 members of the European Community — including new 1995 members Austria, Finland and Sweden — are continuing to move toward implementation of the terms set out in the 1992 Maastricht Treaty for the eventual monetary union of Europe and the adoption of a common currency. As a result, the overall economic numbers show a healthy picture — relatively low interest rates, low inflation rates by historic standards and an above-average rate of economic growth. As such, Europe, as an increasingly growing common market, represents a strong potential source of excess investment returns.

The Far East represents a similar, but longer-term opportunity. The leading countries in this region demonstrate high economic efficiency and firm business discipline — which, when coupled with the enormous and still largely untapped consumer spending potential of the native populations, creates a very attractive picture for foreign investors. As a result, we recommend securities (or funds) representing investment in Korea and Taiwan as the minimum acceptable exposure in this region — and holders of larger portfolios should consider other countries as well. Be sure and look back to the lesson, The Global Approach.

Other Potential Inflation Hedges

Once you move beyond the realm of domestic and foreign equities, the list of potential inflation hedges is relatively short. Here is a brief summary of the leading options:

Gold (and, to a lesser extent, silver and platinum) are the traditional inflation hedges. However, gold prices have become far less responsive to inflation in recent years than they once were. (The same is true of gold's role as a turmoil hedge.) As a result, though we still recommend holding gold certificates or bullion bars in expectation of really severe economic times, we no longer feel it's likely to provide complete protection.

Commodities. Perhaps the perfect inflation hedge is a broad basket of industrial and agricultural commodities — or, as a proxy, a portfolio of commodity futures. Numerous studies have also shown that commodity prices tend to move inversely with stocks — particularly in periods of very rapid inflation. Unfortunately, it is extremely difficult — and risky — to build and maintain a diversified portfolio of commodity futures. Pooled commodity funds, though available, really aren't suitable for most typical investors either since they have very high investment minimums — and, quite frankly, their track records are more than a little spotty.

Inflation futures. Although relatively new and still lacking a proven track record, it may well be that these instruments — which trade on New York's Coffee, Sugar and Cocoa Exchange — offer the best hedge against inflation. You can purchase them for a fairly low margin requirement any time your indicators point to a coming period of rising prices. If you're right and the inflation rate does indeed rise, you can cash in, collecting a cash differential representative of the change between the inflation rate at the time you purchased the contract and the higher rate at the time you sell.

Real estate. Like gold, property prices have become less responsive to inflation over the past decade or so than they were in earlier times. And, in fact, real estate in many economically slow regions of the country has lost a substantial portion of its value (as much as 40 percent in some areas) in recent years. The other drawback, of course, is that property is highly illiquid. Thus, if you're not planning on living in it, real estate is probably not the best inflation hedge these days.

Collectibles. Though price appreciation in some of these has far outstripped even the worst inflation, they are not recommended because of the expertise needed to successfully invest and the high mark-ups charged at the time of purchase.

So, given those alternatives, it turns out to be most likely that you'll find the best inflation hedge right back where you started — with a well-balanced, globally diversified portfolio structured according to the proven asset-allocation principles we have outlined throughout this course!

Simply monitor the indicators and the markets closely — and make appropriate adjustments to your asset mix as you foresee turns in the economic cycle or near your specific wealth-building goals. That's a more appropriate response to changing times than taking a purely passive approach — and it carries far less risk (and aggravation) than attempting to actively time the markets. ▲

Coming down the pyramid: liquidating your investments

100 Steps to Wealth

LESSON 30

Coming down the pyramid: liquidating your investments

"The key to everything is patience. You get the chicken by hatching the egg, not by smashing it." — *Arnold Glasow*

BEWARE THE VIEW FROM THE TOP

Congratulations! You've made it. Following the principals and the strategies you've learned in this course, you've now reached the top of your personal wealth-building pyramid (or certainly will in the not so distant future). Many of your interim objectives — such as the purchase of your own home and a college education for your children — have now been met. You're positioned to achieve your ultimate goal — a secure retirement built around a comfortable lifestyle, free of financial worries.

So, what do you do next?

Obviously, while you could just sit there, enjoying the view from the top, that really wouldn't be the most prudent course — and it could be downright dangerous. Just as your personal lifestyle situation has changed, so too have your financial needs. Growth is less of a priority than it was in earlier years (although it certainly can't be overlooked entirely). Income from your investments is more important. Preservation of capital — or, at least, the careful management of its consumption and eventual distribution to heirs — is essential.

Nurturing Your Nest Egg

However, as our opening quote indicates, while some changes are obviously necessary, you shouldn't try to do everything at once. A lot of time, effort and planning went into the creation of your nest egg, so you don't want to carelessly break it now.

Rather, you want it to hatch into a healthy financial future — one that will carry you comfortably through the rest of your life — and that takes some additional nurturing. In other words, you need a plan.

Before you get confused, we're not just talking about a retirement plan or an estate plan. Obviously, you do need each of those — and both are covered in detail in other lessons of this course. What we're talking about is a "transition" plan, a strategy to help you shift your focus from wealth building to wealth utilization — without excess expense, aggravation or risk.

Lesson 30: *Coming down the pyramid: liquidating your investments*

The need for such a plan is often overlooked, simply because the transition phase — although one of the most important periods in anyone's financial life — is also frequently overlooked. All too often, an individual will work furiously at building wealth right up until the day he or she retires, then do one of two things — either of which can be extremely dangerous:

■ They say, "I've worked hard all my life, and built up lots of money, so I don't have to worry about finances any more." Based on this attitude, they fail to make essential portfolio adjustments or appropriately reallocate their assets — and wind up exposing themselves to far too much risk or holding unsuitable investments (e.g., those that produce too little income, are too illiquid or that have negative tax consequences).

■ They say, "I'm retired now, so I've got to change everything immediately." They sit down the first morning they don't have to go into the office and start buying and selling — swapping stocks for bonds, cashing in mutual funds, converting cash into annuities, etc. They feel they're now retired, so they have to have all elements of their retirement plan in place instantly. And, they suffer the predictable consequences in terms of poor trading prices, high transaction costs and ill-timed shifts in assets relative to current economic conditions.

A Simple, But Important Truth

Obviously, neither approach is particularly prudent — and both ignore one simple truth that you must recognize:

Even though retirement may represent an immediate and substantial change in your personal and financial life, the rest of the world isn't likely to notice — and it certainly isn't going to change along with you.

When you retire, the economic cycle will keep chugging along, investment markets will open and close on schedule each day, prices will continue to rise and fall, brokers will keep charging commissions, and salesmen will continue pitching their products to you. Thus, it will be up to you to adapt your new financial situation to the rest of the world — the financial world won't automatically act to accommodate you.

And, that's where your transition plan comes in. When properly developed, it will:

■ Cover a period extending from 12 to 24 months before you retire until 24 to 36 months afterward — giving you the time to make reasoned choices rather than rush decisions.

■ Include a schedule of things you must do, but also allow you ample flexibility regarding when to do them.

■ Extend over several phases of the economic cycle, giving you the chance to time transactions so as to maximize returns on current holdings and get the best prices on new investments — while also reducing trading costs.

■ Help you coordinate adjustments in your both your investment holdings and your lifestyle patterns so that changes in spending requirements are matched with changes in income levels.

Obviously, no two people will have exactly the same investment holdings, nor will they have identical goals for retirement living. Thus, it's impossible for us to lay down a precise transition plan to fit your particular situation.

The fact that you begin to liquidate doesn't turn what was a good investment last week into a bad investment now.

However, in this lesson, we'll offer a number of guidelines for you to consider in devising your own plan, as well as tips on which of your holdings to eliminate first, what to replace them with, different approaches for structuring cash withdrawals from investment plans, ways of reducing transaction costs, etc. We'll also review a few relevant topics discussed in more detail elsewhere in this course, provide some pointers on the best retirement use of a couple of key investment vehicles and offer several suggestions that relate to specific lifestyle situations.

Start With An Asset Inventory

Before you can do anything with respect to liquidating assets or converting holdings from one asset class to another, you have to know exactly what you have.

That means conducting a thorough inventory of your investment holdings, listing specific securities by asset class and assigning current values to each based either on exact prices, where available (e.g., stocks, bonds, funds), or estimates, where necessary (e.g., real estate, collectibles). Be sure, as well, to note any other important details, such as dividend amounts for stocks and mutual funds, coupon payments and maturity dates for bonds, interest rates and maturity dates for CD's, etc.

If you've followed a strict asset-allocation plan and diligently stayed on top of your record keeping, that may not be too much of a chore. But, if you're like most people in today's busy world, you probably do an exact accounting only once or twice a year (if then), and have only a general idea of your precise asset mix and the value of all your holdings. In that case, you could have several days of work ahead of you. *Author's note: As I sit here busily writing this good advice, for example, I'm roughly six months behind in entering my own reinvested stock dividends and mutual fund distributions in my computer's portfolio management program. And, in a market like we've been having, payouts over such a period can translate into a considerable sum of unrecognized assets.*

Either way, take as much time as is needed to do a thorough and complete job. The shift from wealth building to wealth consumption represents one of the most important turning points in your life — and you don't want to base your future on guesswork. Besides, the more information you have at hand about each individual investment, the easier it will be to make decisions about what to keep, what to convert into other asset types and what to sell outright.

Look for Hidden Assets, Too

If you've accumulated as many possessions as most Americans these days, it will probably also pay to take a little extra time and look for "hidden assets" — non-investment items you may no longer need after retirement that can be converted into cash.

At first, this suggestion may seem trivial, prompting visions of a weekend yard sale — but it really isn't. For example:

- If you have two cars because you commute to work daily, you may need only one after retirement. Sell the second car for $5,000, add in $2,500 in savings for maintenance, insurance and gasoline, and you'll likely be able to defer liquidation of $7,500 in mutual fund holdings for a year. If that year happens to be a repeat of 1995 and your fund merely matches the market performance, you will start the next year with $10,000 in extra fund shares — as opposed to no fund shares and a used car that's a year older! *Note: Don't forget to consider the reverse situation, as well. If you take the train to work and have only one car, you may feel the need for a second vehicle once you're retired and both of you are free to roam around all day. Fail to plan for such a purchase and you could face an early cash-flow complication.*

Buy funds with the longest average maturity near the beginning of bond market upswings, and hold funds with the shortest average maturity as the bond rally nears a top.

■ If you live in a cold climate and are planning to retire to a warm one, you probably have $10,000 or $15,000 worth of "winter" gear that can be converted to cash. Used snowmobiles, snow blowers, snow tires, tire chains, skis, sleds, leftover fireplace wood, even quality coats and boots can all be sold for surprising amounts if you plan ahead rather than just waiting till you're ready to move and trying to unload the stuff as fast as you can. Don't forget such items as handcrafted quilts, either; they may be just bed warmers to you, but they're art to lots of people.

■ If you're moving to a resort area, the same strategy can be applied to vacation gear you won't be needing anymore — ranging from motor homes and campers to tents and sleeping bags. Likewise, if you're moving into a smaller place — either elsewhere or in the same location — set a plan for selling off furnishings you won't need or be able to take with you. The more time you allow yourself to find the right buyer, the better price you'll get.

Turn a Picture Into a Profit

Paintings and other signed artworks by popular local artists can often be hidden assets for those planning to move after retirement. Most of us don't collect Old Masters, but rather buy works we like without much thought to eventually selling them. Then, if we move to a smaller place in a different locale, we don't have room to display them, and we can't sell them because the artist's name has no value in the new market. They wind up crated in a garage or storage locker someplace. However, if you identify any such works you own before you move, and offer them to galleries that handle the artists — or go through a local art auction — and you might actually make a profit on a picture you bought for pure enjoyment.

Depending on your current lifestyle and the circumstances of your planned retirement, such hidden assets might total up to $20,000, $30,000, even $50,000 in "found" cash that you can add into your planning equation. It's essentially tax free, unless you make a capital gain on a painting or something (though you may be liable for vehicle sales taxes in some states). It isn't income, so it doesn't have to be reported and thus won't affect your pension or Social Security payments. And, it could allow you to keep more of your growth or income-producing assets working for another year or two, rather than having to convert them to cash.

Thus, while it may sound mundane, the potential results are far from trivial. (P.S. — A plain old yard sale isn't really a bad idea either; lots of them can cover a month's expenses or more! And who wouldn't work just three days for a month's income.)

MOVING AHEAD WITH YOUR TRANSITION PLAN

Once you know what you have, where it is and what it's worth, you are ready to begin planning your actual transition. As we noted earlier, the general design and timing of your personal plan will depend on a number of factors, including (but not limited to) the present value of your assets, your projected cash flow needs, how long you want your assets to last and whether you want to leave a sizable estate for your heirs.

Review The Long-Term Picture Next

As such, your next step should be a careful review of both your longer-term retirement plan and your estate plan. Since both of those are covered in detail in their own complete lessons (titled Retirement planning and Estate planning: your golden years), we won't go into a lot of discussion of them here. What we will do is note several key relationships that can serve as guides in developing your transition plan. They are:

■ If your current asset base is limited, you may have to opt for either a lower periodic cash flow or a shorter period of retirement. The former choice may require significant lifestyle adjustments; the latter, delay of your projected retirement date to give you more time to accumulate additional assets — and your current assets more time to grow.

- If you want a high cash flow, you may have to pursue a faster rate of growth for your assets — accepting a higher degree of capital risk — or, once again, shorten the projected time line for your retirement.

- If you want a longer life for your retirement plan, you may have to accept a reduced cash flow or put more emphasis on growth during the early stages of your retirement.

- If you want to leave a large estate, you may have to both lower your cash-flow requirements and reduce your risk exposure, choosing investments that stress capital preservation over income or growth.

If you can reduce your total transaction costs by just 1 percent on a $300,000 portfolio, you're talking about saving $3,000!

Ideally, of course, none of these trade-offs will be necessary. Based on what you have learned in *100 Steps to Wealth,* you will have been highly successful in your wealth-building efforts — and will have ample assets to provide the cash flow you desire for as long as you need, while still leaving a hefty estate for your heirs.

That would indeed be nice — and, as you now know, it's entirely possible. Unfortunately, it's also possible that the future could turn out far differently than we anticipate. There could be a return of hyperinflation, or a change in the political climate that would negatively impact your personal situation. Or, on a more positive note, you could simply live longer than expected — in essence, outlasting your assets.

In any event, regardless of your current asset base, it's best to at least consider the possibility of such negative happenings in the future — and factor them into your transition plan. For example, you may choose to start retirement with a higher percentage of your assets in stocks than originally planned, forgoing a few dollars in current income in exchange for enhanced growth potential. Or, you might select a periodic withdrawal plan from a mutual fund rather than a lump-sum liquidation — again allowing added time for growth. Likewise, you may choose to delay tapping into an IRA account for a couple of years to ensure that it will last longer — or to defer the purchase of an annuity a while so that the same capital outlay will buy larger monthly payments.

Scores of variations are possible, all affecting your long-term plans, and most requiring near-term action — or, at least, consideration in your transition planning.

There Are 'Micro' Issues, Too

Those are the "macro" considerations, however, the transition plan must also deal with many "micro" issues — ones related to specific investments.

Earlier, we advised you of a simple, but important truth — i.e., "the financial world isn't likely to notice your retirement, and it certainly isn't going to change because you do." As an extension of that, here's another basic truth you need to recognize:

The fact that you begin to liquidate doesn't turn what was a good investment last week into a bad investment now.

That's a simple way of summarizing an often troublesome conflict between the realities of actual investing and the theories (however sound) underlying asset allocation. While the advocates of asset allocation tell you what percentage of your assets should be devoted to equities and what percentage to debt securities at various stages of your life, they rarely tell you exactly what to sell or precisely what to buy.

They also make little distinction regarding what's going on in the markets when you reach recommended reallocation points. For example, a suggested asset allocation formula might call for an equity-debt split of 75-25 at age 30, 60-40 at age 45, 50-50 at age 55, 35-65 at age 65 and 20-80 at age 75. That sounds good in principle, but do you really want to move another 15 percent of your assets into bonds if, when you turn 65, interest rates are at 4 percent, inflation's showing signs of picking up and the Fed's due to meet in two weeks? *Note: Before you get too critical here, we know that asset allocation is designed to alleviate the need for market timing and that reallocation is supposed to take place gradually, not all at once. However, we're trying to make a point — and exaggeration usually does that better than plain old fact.*

Stick With Your Investment Analysis

Our point is simply this: If you followed the advice you received in this course, you had very good reasons for buying every individual security, mutual fund or other asset in your portfolio. And, you also had an objective you expected each of those investments to achieve. Thus, if the investment is still on track and the objective has not yet been reached, there's no good reason to bail out just because you're turning 65 — or whatever age you plan to shift into retirement mode.

Likewise, you should never switch into a specific investment simply because it's in a particular asset class. Any security, mutual fund, bond or other investment vehicle must represent a good value at the time of purchase; otherwise, you shouldn't buy it — no matter how badly you need to fill out a given asset class. Instead, just keep your money in cash (i.e., a money-market fund or other cash equivalent) until a real opportunity comes along.

It is in fulfilling these two mandates that much of your actual transition-period planning, evaluation and trading will occur. That's why we advise starting the transition process at least 12 months (and preferably 24) before your retirement date, and extending until well after you actually retire. You need time for your existing investments to achieve their objectives, and for good buying opportunities to arise for new ones (if appropriate in your longer-term plan).

Note: We are discussing transitional planning in terms of retirement because that is typically the most important transition in people's lives. However, many of the same ideas, planning tips and trading guidelines can be applied to other transitional periods, whether they involve liquidating assets to buy a home, raising money to start a business or some other goal. Plan your transitions carefully, and you'll almost always improve your overall wealth-building results.

A Sample Transitional Scenario

You also need the flexibility to make incremental sales and purchases that capture shifts in the continuing economic cycle, and thereby maximize your returns. For example, assume you hold four different equity mutual funds, each worth about $100,000. You're six months away from retirement, at which time you'll need about $100,000 to finance your move to a condo in Scottsdale. What do you do? Liquidate a quarter of each? Half of two? All of one — and, if so, which one?

Based on what you learned in the last lesson (How to profit from the changing times), you recognize that the economy is several months into an expansionary phase, and that stocks are marching higher, led by issues in the financial sector. You know that the typical market rally moves in rotation, with financials going first, growth issues following, and cyclical and speculative issues bringing up the rear.

So, you examine the latest quarterly reports for all four funds, picking out the one with the highest percentage of financial stocks — and, secondarily, the one with the strongest weighting in growth issues. You then have a choice of two strategies, based on the continuing pace of the market rally before you're ready to sell:

The Fine Art of Selling

As you well know, the financial world is full of people willing to tell you when to buy a stock. However, finding someone who'll tell you when to sell is a different matter. That's why it's important to set an objective any time you buy an individual issue — based on its growth and earnings projections (or on its chart patterns, if you're a technician). However, you should never fall into the trap of viewing that objective as an absolute — meaning there will be times when you should sell before the target price is reached, and times you should hold after the objective is met.

So, if you're in a transitional period, what's the key to making your sell decision? The answer is performance. As long as the stock keeps rising on steady or improving earnings, you should continue to hold, even if your target is surpassed. However, if the stock begins to top — as indicated by a rally that stalls without reaching a new high — or some other bad news comes out (e.g., a downgraded brokerage house recommendation or a drop in earnings by 10 percent or more from projections), go ahead and sell.

In either case, always enter a stop-loss order while you are waiting for the right time to sell. And, if you're waiting to liquidate as part of an asset reallocation, keep the stop "tight" — no more than 5 to 10 percent below the market price. That way, you leave your upside potential open ended — but if bad news does strike, you won't lose too much of the profit you made by delaying your move into a different asset class.

1. If the rally appears to be sustained, with growth issues still moving higher, you liquidate 100 percent of the fund with the high percentage of financial issues — most of which have presumably already had the bulk of their upward run.

2. If the rally appears to be maturing, with growth stocks slowing and cyclical issues moving into the leadership role, you sell 50 percent of the fund weighted most heavily in financials and 50 percent of the one dominated by growth issues.

Either way, you capture a major part of the gain on the shares of the funds focused on the early rally leaders, while retaining the shares of the funds that are likely to perform best as the rally tops out. If your longer-term asset-allocation plan calls for a further shift out of equities and into debts or cash, you can then meet the reallocation requirement by selling shares in the two remaining funds, locking in the later gains scored on them.

It Works With Individual Holdings, Too

A similar approach can be followed with individual stock holdings, bonds and even bond funds (buy funds with the longest average maturity near the beginning of bond market upswings, and hold funds with the shortest average maturity as the bond rally nears a top). However, the process can be a bit more tricky with individual issues since you don't have the benefits of diversification to offset any errors in your analysis. Still, if the market is strong and your individual stock or bond is still performing well, the potential for added gain is most likely worth the modest additional risk (subject to the provisos discussed in the box above).

MANAGING YOUR TRANSACTION COSTS

Another area where having a good transition plan can prove beneficial is in managing — and, hopefully, reducing — transaction costs. With the exception of some mutual funds, you'll incur commission and other costs when you sell almost any type of asset — from stocks and bonds to real estate and collectibles. However, if you follow an orderly process and do a bit of shopping and/or negotiating, you should be able to minimize your trading expenses at this stage.

Lest you think this isn't really important enough to justify the time involved, consider just one modest example. If you can reduce your total transaction costs by just 1 percent on a $300,000 portfolio, you're talking about saving $3,000!

With that as a potential incentive, here are some guidelines we suggest individuals liquidating or reallocating their assets in anticipation of retirement:

Buy Direct From Uncle Sam and Save

If you are planning to move a sizable portion of your assets into Treasury bills, you can entirely eliminate transaction costs on your T-bill purchases by buying directly from Uncle Sam — by way of your nearest Federal Reserve Bank office. (The same applies to longer-term Treasury notes and bonds.) To get details on buying U.S. Treasury securities — or to actually purchase them — call the Federal Reserve Bank headquarters in your area and request information on the Treasury Direct program. Here are the numbers:

District 1 —	Boston	617-973-3810
District 2 —	New York,	212-720-6619
District 3 —	Philadelphia	215-574-6675
District 4 —	Cleveland	216-579-2490
District 5 —	Richmond	804-697-8372
District 6 —	Atlanta	404-521-8653
District 7 —	Chicago	312-322-5369
District 8 —	St. Louis	314-444-8703
District 9 —	Minneapolis	612-340-2075
District 10 —	Kansas City	816-881-2409
District 11 —	Dallas	214-922-6770
District 12 —	San Francisco	415-974-2330

1. Even if you've made the decision to convert every asset you own into cash in the form of T-bills or money-market funds, you don't want to liquidate all at once. Follow your transition plan and spread your sales over at least 12 to 24 months — and don't be concerned if it takes longer. As we said earlier, the economy and the markets aren't aware that you're retiring, so they may not offer you the best prices right away. Spreading out sales will also have far fewer tax consequences if you're dealing with taxable holdings.

2. Don't just hand over your entire portfolio to one broker. Just because a firm offers good rates on stocks doesn't mean it will do as well on bonds, Treasuries, mortgage-backed securities or other derivative products. Shop around to get the best rates on each component of your portfolio, and don't hesitate to tell the broker what you're doing. In other words, be aggressive. There are lots of financial people out there — most of whom would like your business — so they should be willing to compete for it.

3. If you like the broker or the firm, but they don't have the best price, feel free to negotiate. The larger your portfolio, the more power you have.

4. Point out that you're not interested in a lot of bells and whistles and won't pay for them. You aren't looking for good research or, in most cases, even good advice — just good trade execution.

Reviewing the Types of Trading Orders

Almost all investors are familiar with the basic buy, sell and stop-loss orders. However, there are a few other orders that, when used properly, can save you a lot of money:

- **Limit order** — This specifies an exact price above which you will not go when buying or below which you will not go when selling.

- **Good-till-canceled (GTC) order** — This is a limit order that stays in force until it is either filled at the desired price or you cancel it. Some brokers automatically cancel it though at 60 days.

- **Fill or kill orders** — These specify that if the order is not executed immediately, it should be canceled.

- **All or none** — Simply stated, this order demands that an entire order be filled at a limit price, or that no shares at all be bought or sold.

- **Not held order** — This order gives the floor broker the authority to use his own discretion in the execution of an order. However, if the broker chooses wrong, the investor must accept the loss.

- **Stop-buy order** — This order is used for protection when you have a short position, directing the broker to buy stock to cover your short if the price rises to a certain level. Investors who rely on technical analysis may also use stop-buy orders when they want to purchase a stock only if it "breaks out" above a certain price level.

- **Stop-sell order** — This order is similar to a stop-loss order in that it converts to a market order when the security price reaches a pre-specified level. However, unlike a stop loss, it is placed above the current security price. These orders are used by investors who are seeking a specific price objective, and hope to reach it on a sharp, but temporary upward spike.

Don't be afraid to use a specialized order if it fits your needs. While market orders ensure that you get the execution, they often fall far short of guaranteeing that you get the price you want.

5. When you do find a salesperson, stress that you aren't in a rush. You want the best possible price at the lowest possible cost — and the broker should be willing to wait for just that combination.

6. As an extension of No. 5, be aware that a discount brokerage isn't always the way to go. It frequently is — but markets are fragmented and there are different trading channels. You need someone who will search for the best price — whether it be on a domestic or a foreign exchange, over the counter or through a third-party proprietary trading system.

7. Make good use of trading orders. Avoid market orders (those that will take the first price available) and make appropriate use of limit and other specialty orders. For a review of some of the alternative order types, see the box at left.

Note: For further tips on reducing transaction expenses, see wealth-building Step 93, How to Minimize Your Costs When Liquidating, which begins on page 12.

EXAMINE YOUR CASH-FLOW SOURCES

Another important step in your transition planning is an evaluation of your future cash-flow sources. In other words, when the first of the month following your retirement date rolls around, and you don't get that regular paycheck, where is your money for the month going to come from?

All commissions are negotiable — even on smaller transactions

As you learned in the lesson titled Work, Employment and Investment, fewer and fewer people these days are covered by corporate pension plans that pay a regular monthly check — and Social Security certainly won't get you far. So, how do you make up the difference?

Do you have a sufficient flow of coupon payments from your bond holdings to meet all your income needs? Are the coupon payment dates staggered to provide regular cash flow throughout the year, or do all your payments come at the same time? Review your bond holdings in advance — and, if you need to make any adjustments, do so before you actually have to begin relying on the payments for living expenses.

Do you have enough assets in mutual funds or money-market funds that the dividend payments will support you in full or in part? Even if you do, it's likely those dividends are currently being reinvested. Those reinvestment policies will have to be changed — before you actually begin needing the money. Find out who you need to contact, what you need to do and when you need to do it and include that information in your transition plan.

Are you planning to immediately tap into your 401(k)s, Keoghs, IRAs or other tax-deferred retirement plans for either income from the earnings your assets generate or a return of some of the principal? If so, you need to contact the trustees and review the requirements and procedures. You may need to plan a roll-over — which might have to take place within a limited time period after you retire. Do you know how to do it — or what kind of investment you want to roll your assets into? Find out what to do, and decide where the money will go, as part of your transition plan.

We could likely come up with a few dozen more questions to throw at you, but you should be getting the idea by now, so we won't. We'll simply reiterate the importance of reviewing all your current holdings well in advance of your retirement date, and making (or at least planning for) all the adjustments necessary to ensure that your assets meet your needs — from the very first day those needs arise.

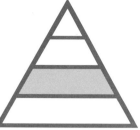

STEP 93

How To Minimize Your Costs When Liquidating

What: Make your wealth last longer — or even continue growing — by minimizing costs when you liquidate your holdings or reallocate assets.

Why: Once you've succeeded in building a substantial portfolio, transaction costs when liquidating assets can amount to thousands of dollars — meaning savings generated by reducing them can be significant.

Risk: Low. So long as you get quality executions and service, any savings you can generate by choosing the lowest-cost liquidation options will be worthwhile.

Safety: High. A greater danger would lie in paying excessive fees to liquidate your assets, thereby reducing your overall return.

Liquidity: Not applicable.

Why not: There's no reason not to seek the lowest possible transaction costs unless your focus on expenses clouds your judgment regarding the best time to dispose of certain assets.

Buy/Invest from: Not applicable.

Background: As anyone knows who has ever paid an 8 percent load to buy a mutual fund or a $160 commission to buy $2,000 worth of stock, transaction costs can dramatically impact the returns on your investments. Upfront fees lower the amount of capital you have working for you — and liquidation fees reduce the profits you've already made (or, even more painful, increase the losses you've already suffered). Thus, anything you can do to cut those costs is more than worthwhile — especially when you start unwinding your investments and reaping the rewards of your wealth-building efforts.

If you want to get started today, here's what you need to do to minimize your costs when liquidating:

Different assets require slightly different approaches, so we'll look at four different asset classes and provide guidelines for each.

For stock portfolios:

1. Avoid small transactions. Most stock brokers have minimum commissions of $35 to as much as $100. As a result, transactions in amounts of $1,500 or less will often result in exceptionally high percentage commissions. Odd-lot trades (those involving less than 100 shares of stock) are also traditionally more expensive, especially on over-the-counter or thinly traded issues. Bid/ask spreads on such trades can frequently widen to a point or more on moderately priced stocks, and up to 3 points on higher priced securities.

2. Negotiate commissions. All commissions are negotiable — even on smaller transactions — so always ask for a better deal. Of course, the larger your portfolio, the more bargaining power you will have. Regardless of size, however, the key to success when liquidating is to take an aggressive stance. You don't need a strong research department or ongoing advice; you're simply looking for the most efficient and cost-effective execution you can find. Be sure to point this out to potential brokers, and let them know up front that you'll be shopping for the best deal.

3. Consider discount brokers. Given the reasoning outlined above, discount brokers may offer the best deals on liquidations. However, you still need to make sure you are getting quality executions. The equity markets are fragmented, and there are different trading channels, so explain to any potential discount broker that you want someone who will take a little extra time to search for the best price — whether it be on a domestic or foreign exchange, over the counter or through a third-party, proprietary trading system. *Note: For more information on selecting the best broker, refer back to the lesson titled, Climbing the Pyramid: Finding the Uncommon Common Share.*

4. Make good use of trading orders. In most cases, you should be liquidating stock holdings as part of an orderly plan — not because you fear an imminent meltdown in either the market or prices for an individual issue. As such, your goal should be to get the best price, not the fastest execution. To that end, make liberal use of limit orders (those specifying the exact price you want) and use market orders (those taking the best currently available price) sparingly. If you have shares you want to hold for a bit longer, for whatever reason (e.g., because they provide high dividends), protect yourself by tightening up stop-loss levels. Likewise, if you want to hold because you think an issue has more potential, set a reasonable target and place a "sell-stop" order at that level (i.e., an order that will be triggered only when the stock price climbs to a specified level). *Note: Refer to the lesson, Timing Your Trades for more information on the types and uses of specialized trading orders.*

For mutual fund holdings:

1. Even if you "locked in" to a specific back-end load structure when you purchased your shares, feel free to negotiate for a better liquidation deal — especially if you have been a long-time shareholder or have a large account. There are now other ways of disposing of fund shares besides selling them directly back to the fund-management company (i.e., several specialized brokerage firms arrange sales directly to other investors), so you do have alternatives. Once again, be aggressive.

2. Discuss various withdrawal options. Some fund companies drop back-end load requirements if you opt for a periodic withdrawal plan rather than a cash liquidation. Others will waive back-end fees if you switch to another fund within the same family — in some cases, even a money-market fund (from which you can later withdraw funds without a charge).

3. If you have money in a fund that has diminishing back-end fees (i.e., ones that get smaller the longer you hold your shares, eventually disappearing altogether), develop a "stepped" withdrawal plan. Place partial liquidation orders, specifying that you want to sell your oldest shares first, thus incurring the lowest fees — or eliminating them entirely. *Note: Be sure to factor in the tax consequences of this approach. You will likely have the largest gains in the oldest shares, so make sure the added tax bill won't negate any commission savings.*

For bond portfolios:

1. At this stage, you may be adding to your bond holdings rather than liquidating. Nonetheless, if you do plan to sell some of your debt securities, take an approach similar to that detailed for equities — i.e., negotiate the lowest commission rate (if your broker charges a direct fee on bond trades), sell in round lots (usually 10 bonds, but sometimes 5) and specify a desired (or limit) price to avoid excessive bid/asked spreads.

2. The least expensive way to liquidate bonds is to allow them to mature or be called away by the issuer. Before selling any of your bonds, make a list of the maturities and the call dates. Then develop a liquidation plan that takes advantage of those dates — i.e., one that matches up expected cash needs with specific redemption or call dates. Sell non-maturing issues only when you have cash needs inconsistent with the schedule — or when you have capital gains on certain bonds that you feel are worth taking.

For illiquid assets:

1. Start the liquidation process early. It can take months — or even years — to dispose of some illiquid assets (e.g., real estate, stamp collections, coin collections, art portfolios) at a fair price. Be patient.

2. Make sure you have enough of a cushion in other, more liquid assets so that you can afford to ride out cyclical downturns in collectibles markets. Rare coins, stamps and Old Masters paintings all have strong long-term growth records, but all experience slumps as well. Try to avoid having to sell at market lows, when fixed commissions or agent fees will represent a much bigger percentage of your sales price.

3. Consider auctions for collectible items — but beware of high commissions or sliding scales; a fixed fee is generally best. Always make sure, however, that the auction requires a minimum bid. You don't want to agree to a fixed fee and then have to pay it on a bid only half as large as you were expecting. Be sure, as well, that you deal only with reputable firms that have a good client list (both sellers and buyers) and a strong record of promoting their sales.

Whatever you're selling (or buying), from stocks to mutual funds to real estate to collectibles, the most important rule on commissions is: Always negotiate! Brokers, dealers and agents like to pretend their rates are fixed — and they love people who believe that's the case. However, it's a rare item that can be sold by only one person — and any time you have two potential salespeople, you have a basis for negotiating on fees. ▲

Continued from p. 11

A QUICK ADDITIONAL WORD ON SOCIAL SECURITY

We'll discuss a few more of those adjustments — such as the ways to structure periodic mutual fund withdrawal plans — in just a couple of pages. First, though, a quick additional word about Social Security.

If you're like most successful wealth builders, you probably relegated any thoughts of and hopes for Social Security to the back burner long ago. Now, however, it's time to bring them back to the front. After all, over the course of your working life, you paid a tremendous amount for those meager benefits (most likely far more than they're worth), so you'll want to make sure you get them. And, because they're now taxable under certain conditions, you'll want to get them when they'll do you the most good and cost you the least.

You become eligible for Social Security when you turn 62 — but at a reduced rate. For full benefits, you have to wait until age 65 — and this age will rise in the future, as shown in the top portion of the table on the following page. Lower benefits will still be available at age 62 under the new rules, though the reduction will be bigger. There's also a "delayed retirement credit," which was 4 percent a year for workers reaching age 65 in 1995. It will gradually rise to 8 percent annually by 2008. This benefit may be accrued if you don't retire, or if you simply choose not to file for benefits. The full benefits schedule, with ages for reduced benefits and credits, is shown in the bottom part of the table.

How to Maximize Your Benefits

Given the schedules shown in the table and the current state of the tax laws relating to Social Security, there are several steps you can take to maximize your benefits:

1. Time the start of benefits to maximize overall return. If you want to get as much money back as possible, you probably should take your benefits as early as possible. If you want higher monthly payments, you should probably delay. Health is another factor — i.e., if your health is poor or longevity does not run in your family, you may want to start getting benefits as soon as you're eligible.

ELIGIBILITY AGES FOR FULL FUTURE SOCIAL SECURITY BENEFITS

Birth date	Age for full benefits	First date eligible
JAN. 1, 1938	65 YEARS, 2 MONTHS	MARCH 1, 2003
JAN. 1, 1939	65 YEARS, 4 MONTHS	MAY 1, 2004
JAN. 1, 1940	65 YEARS, 6 MONTHS	JULY 1, 2005
JAN. 1, 1941	65 YEARS, 8 MONTHS	SEPT. 1, 2006
JAN. 1, 1942	65 YEARS, 10 MONTHS	NOV. 1, 2007
JAN. 1, 1943-54	66 YEARS	JAN. 1, 2009-20
JAN. 1, 1955	66 YEARS, 2 MONTHS	MARCH 1, 2021
JAN. 1, 1956	66 YEARS, 4 MONTHS	MAY 1, 2022
JAN. 1, 1957	66 YEARS, 6 MONTHS	JULY 1, 2023
JAN. 1, 1958	66 YEARS, 8 MONTHS	SEPT. 1, 2024
JAN. 1, 1959	66 YEARS, 10 MONTHS	NOV. 1, 2025
JAN. 1, 1960	67 YEARS	JAN. 1, 2027

* The Jan. 1 birthdate is for illustration only. Individuals born on other dates in the same year would have to reach the same age listed in Column 2 in order to qualify for the full benefit.

CURRENT SOCIAL SECURITY BENEFITS STRUCTURE

Retirement Age	Monthly Benefit
62	80 PERCENT
63	85 PERCENT
65	FULL BENEFIT
68	FULL BENEFIT, PLUS 12 PERCENT
70	FULL BENEFIT, PLUS 20 PERCENT

2. Beware of earning too much early in your retirement. If you plan to continue working after retirement — say, in a hobby or as a consultant — the earnings will reduce your Social Security benefits. For example, benefits paid to people under age 65 are reduced by $1 for each $2 earned over $8,280. For those aged 65 to 69, $1 in benefits is lost for each $3 earned over $11,520. Only at age 70 and above are full benefits paid regardless of other income. In addition, if you earn too much from all sources — including your investments — a portion of your Social Security will be taxed. (The threshold for this tax is adjusted each year, so check the 1040 documents the IRS mails to you each year at tax time.) Thus, you may want to plan on using more Social Security in the first years after you retire and drawing less on your investments or post-retirement work.

3. Register for Medicare before age 65. Even though you may not plan to use the health-care coverage right away, you may face a higher premium if you fail to register by the deadline.

4. Beware of "early" retirement from your job. Regular retirement for Social Security purposes ranges from age 65 to 67, depending on your year of birth. As already noted, those who retire before that age will get reduced benefits. However, early retirement can cut your benefits in another way. Your final employment earnings weigh heavily in the calculation of your primary Social Security insurance amount. In other words, if your earnings drop sharply in the last

three or four years before you're eligible for Social Security, your benefit amount will likely be reduced accordingly.

5. Call or write the Social Security Administration to get a free estimate of your earnings and benefits. Don't wait for age 65 and risk discovering a mistake too late. Trying to verify contributions years after the fact can be impossible — and failure may cause you to forfeit some of your rightful benefits. To avoid this, call the SSA's toll-free number, 1-800-772-1213 and ask for your free "Request for Earnings and Benefits Estimate Statement."

One final note on this subject. Social Security isn't automatic — you have to file for benefits. About three months before your scheduled retirement date, call the SSA at the number above and apply. Unless there's something strange about your situation, the phone call is all it should take to get the process under way. *Note: You'll find more about actually calculating your potential Social Security benefits in the lesson titled Retirement Planning.*

SYSTEMATIC MUTUAL FUND WITHDRAWAL PLANS

If you don't have a company pension and haven't planned to rely too heavily on Social Security, it's likely the bulk of your retirement savings has been amassed in tax-deferred accounts such as IRAs or 401(k)s. And, that probably means a sizable portion is in mutual funds. Thus, it is essential that you understand the various mutual fund withdrawal options and begin making choices as part of your transition plan. (The same applies to assets accumulated in non-tax-deferred mutual fund accounts since you'll probably also be drawing on them in retirement.)

We won't make any specific recommendation about which method is best since the option selected has to reflect your particular cash-flow needs, as well as your desire for further asset growth in your later years. However, we will show a variety of examples — based on portfolios of identical size and common growth rates — to help you in making your choice (or choices). Not all mutual fund companies offer all the optional withdrawal methods but many of the major houses do. In addition to the simple lump-sum payout, the leading mutual fund withdrawal options include:

RATIO WITHDRAWAL PLAN 8% ANNUAL WITHDRAWAL, 10% GROWTH RATE		
	Value of O'Hara's holding at start of year	Amount withdrawn by O'Hara	Value of O'Hara's holdings after the withdrawal
1	$300,000	$24,000	$276,000
2	$303,600	$24,288	$279,312
3	$307,243	$24,579	$282,664
4	$310,930	$24,874	$286,056
5	$314,661	$25,173	$289,488
6	$318,437	$25,475	$292,962
7	$322,258	$25,781	$296,478
8	$326,126	$26,090	$300,036
9	$330,039	$26,403	$303,636
10	$334,000	$26,720	$307,280
11	$338,008	$27,041	$310,967
12	$342,064	$27,365	$314,699
13	$346,168	$27,693	$318,475
14	$350,322	$28,026	$322,297
15	$354,526	$28,362	$326,164

Ratio Withdrawal — With this method, you receive periodic dollar payouts with the actual amount based on a percentage of the average total asset value of the portfolio. Generally, this goal is accomplished by redeeming a specific percentage of shares each year (say, 10 percent), and having the fund management company distribute the payouts to you on a monthly or quarterly basis. *Note: You can also take the money out in one annual withdrawal, but that puts the onus of managing it on you each year, costing you the benefits of diversification and professional management.*

As an example, assume that Chuck O'Hara has a mutual fund portfolio worth $300,000. If he decides to withdraw 8 percent of his assets per year, and the fund returns 10 percent per annum on his remaining holdings, he can withdraw nearly $400,000 in a 15-year period and still have his initial principal — plus $26,164 extra (as detailed in the table on the previous page)!

RATIO WITHDRAWAL PLAN 8% ANNUAL WITHDRAWAL, 4% GROWTH RATE		
Value of O'Hara's holding at start of year	Amount withdrawn by O'Hara	Value of O'Hara's holdings after the withdrawal
1	$300,000	$24,000	$276,000
2	$287,040	$22,963	$264,077
3	$274,640	$21,971	$252,669
4	$262,775	$21,022	$241,753
5	$251,424	$20,114	$231,310
6	$240,562	$19,245	$221,317
7	$230,170	$18,414	$211,756
8	$220,226	$17,618	$202,608
9	$210,713	$16,857	$193,856
10	$201,610	$16,129	$185,481
11	$192,900	$15,432	$177,468
12	$184,567	$14,765	$169,802
13	$176,594	$14,127	$162,466
14	$168,965	$13,517	$155,448
15	$161,666	$12,933	$148,732

Note, however, that if his fund holdings fail to maintain their same high rate of return — instead falling to, say 4 percent per annum — O'Hara's does much worse. His annual withdrawals amounts steadily shrink, his total payout drops to just $269,000 and more than 50 percent of his portfolio's value has been depleted by the end of the same 15-year withdrawal period. The table at left illustrates this more dismal scenario — which clearly underscores the need to maintain an appropriate balance between growth and income during your liquidation and retirement phases.

It also emphasizes the extreme importance of carefully reviewing your fund holdings during your transitional planning period. Assume, for example, you have two fund holdings of equal value, and know that you'll want to liquidate one entirely, while making periodic withdrawals from the other. If you evaluate both during your transition, you'll likely decide your wisest course would be to close out the one with the lowest historic growth rate and retain the one with the highest (assuming, of course, there's no substantial variance in risk levels).

That way, you'll get the cash you need early in your retirement, while retaining maximum growth potential to enhance your later-life cash flow — and possibly even increase the value of your estate. The same strategy applies with any of the other periodic payout options — which, once again, include:

Fixed-Dollar Withdrawals — With this approach, you would receive a specific dollar amount each withdrawal period (e.g., $1,000 per month or $3,000 per quarter), with the fund-management company redeeming the necessary number of shares each payout period, based on the current net asset value per share. The advantage of this approach is that you know precisely how much money you'll receive in each payment. The disadvantage is that you have no way of knowing exactly how long your fund assets will last.

Fixed-Period Withdrawals — This is essentially the reverse of the fixed-dollar approach. You receive a variable dollar payout over a predetermined time period, with the fund-management company again redeeming the required number of shares each period, based on the current NAV of the shares. The exact dollar amount of the payout is determined by dividing the total value of your remaining fund holdings by the number of time periods remaining in your withdrawal schedule. Obviously, the advantage of this method is that you know exactly how long your money will last. However, short-term planning is more difficult because you never know exactly how much money you'll get each year.

Note: A more detailed discussion of both fixed-dollar and fixed-period methods — with comparative growth and payout tables — is featured in wealth-building Step 94, Two Mutual Fund Withdrawal Options, which begins on page 18.

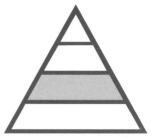

STEP 94

Two Mutual Fund Withdrawal Options

What: Devise an extended plan for the steady withdrawal of your assets from mutual funds once you retire.

Why: To ensure that your money lasts as long as you expect to need it — or, if you prefer, continues to grow even while you're making regular withdrawals. Periodic-withdrawal plans also tend to minimize tax liabilities incurred when liquidating IRAs and/or other tax-deferred accounts.

Risk: Low. A well-structured withdrawal plan, developed before you actually begin taking money out, is far less dangerous than either a piecemeal approach or a lump-sum withdrawal. Both those options expose you to irreversible asset reductions if withdrawals must be made during short-term market corrections. The potential emotional stress in trying to time withdrawals to coincide with market tops can also be quite high.

Safety: High. Virtually all mutual fund management companies have systems in place to quickly, easily and cheaply handle periodic-withdrawal plans. Although not all options may be available at all management companies.

Liquidity: High. Fund companies are required to redeem shares on demand, in any quantity. You can also change the specifics of the withdrawal plan — or drop it entirely, taking a lump-sum payout — if your circumstances change.

Why not: Given the flexibility and long-term benefits of such plans, there is really no reason not to use them unless you have a specific current need for the money in your fund account.

Sell/Liquidate through: The broker or management company that handles your fund account.

Background: Any mutual fund withdrawal plan, to be effective, must reflect your particular income and investment objectives, as well as your long-term goal for your assets — i.e., whether you plan to use them up or want to leave as large an estate as possible for your heirs. It should also be based on realistic assumptions about the expected impact of inflation and the potential for continued growth. (Note: All growth projections should be based on past performance averages over time periods comparable to the expected duration of the withdrawal plan. Be aware, however, that variability rises as the time span grows shorter. As a result, a plan designed for, say, five years should have more of a cushion built into the growth projections than one structured for a 10- or 15-year payout.)

There are a number of withdrawal options, but two of the most common are the "fixed-dollar" plan and the "fixed-period" plan. (A third alternative — the "fixed-ratio" plan — is discussed in the main text of this lesson.) With a fixed-dollar plan, you know how much you will get in each withdrawal period, but the length of the plan varies, depending on investment performance. With a fixed-period plan, you know how long the payments will last, but the exact amount varies, again based on investment performance. So you can see exactly how they work — and how investment performance impacts the payouts — we'll look at an example of each, showing the results based on two different average annual rates of return.

First, the fixed-dollar withdrawal plan. Assume Sally Sterling has $300,000 in a diversified mutual fund portfolio that averages an 8 percent annual rate of growth. She is ready to begin making withdrawals and decides she wants to take out $40,000 per year (the fixed-dollar amount). Assuming she continues to average an annual return of 8 percent on her remaining funds, the following table shows what will happen:

Step 94: *Two Mutual Fund Withdrawal Options*

Fixed-Dollar Withdrawal Plan — 8% Growth Rate

Year	Value of Sterling's holdings at start of year	Amount withdrawn by Sterling	Value of Sterling's holdings after the withdrawal
1	$300,000	$40,000	$260,000
2	$280,800	$40,000	$240,800
3	$260,064	$40,000	$220,064
4	$237,669	$40,000	$197,669
5	$213,483	$40,000	$173,483
6	$187,361	$40,000	$147,361
7	$159,150	$40,000	$119,150
8	$128,682	$40,000	$ 88,682
9	$ 95,777	$40,000	$ 55,777
10	$ 60,239	$40,000	$ 20,239
11	$ 21,858	$21,858	0

Note that, in this case, Sterling's portfolio is depleted at the middle of the eleventh year. And, had she invested more conservatively, it would have been depleted even faster. This is illustrated in the following table, which assumes the same conditions, but a growth rate of only 4 percent per year.

Fixed-Dollar Withdrawal Plan — 4% Growth Rate

Year	Value of Sterling's holdings at start of year	Amount withdrawn by Sterling	Value of Sterling's holdings after the withdrawal
1	$300,000	$40,000	$260,000
2	$270,400	$40,000	$230,400
3	$239,616	$40,000	$199,616
4	$207,601	$40,000	$167,601
5	$174,305	$40,000	$134,305
6	$139,677	$40,000	$ 99,677
7	$103,664	$40,000	$ 63,664
8	$ 66,210	$40,000	$ 26,210
9	$ 27,259	$27,259	0

In this case, Sterling's assets would have been depleted in the middle of the ninth year — meaning the reduction in her return from 8 percent to 4 percent reduced the expected lifespan of her asset base almost two full years. This underscores the need to maintain appropriate asset-allocation programs to ensure at least moderate continued growth in the wind-down and retirement stages of your investing life. It also clearly points out the necessity of making realistic assumptions about growth and tailoring your withdrawals accordingly — especially if you're planning on using the fixed-dollar approach.

Now for a look at the fixed-period approach. With this method, you determine the amount of time you want your asset base to last, and then calculate your withdrawals accordingly. For example, if you wanted your plan to cover 10 years, you would take out one-tenth of the money the first year, one-ninth the second, one-eighth the third, and so on. The exact dollar amount of the withdrawals would obviously vary, depending on how much the remaining assets in the fund earned each year. To illustrate, assume that Joe Golden has $300,000 in a diversified mutual fund portfolio that has averaged an 8 percent annual rate of growth. He's ready to begin making withdrawals and decides he wants his money to last 15 years (the fixed-period duration). Assuming he continues to average an annual return of 8 percent on his remaining funds, the following table shows what will happen:

Fixed-Period Withdrawal Plan — 8% Growth Rate

Year	Years left	Value of Sterling's holdings at start of year	Amount withdrawn by Golden	Value of Sterling's holdings after the withdrawal
1	15	$300,000	$20,000	$280,000
2	14	$302,400	$21,600	$280,800
3	13	$303,264	$23,328	$279,936
4	12	$302,331	$25,194	$277,137
5	11	$299,308	$27,210	$272,098
6	10	$293,866	$29,387	$264,479
7	9	$285,637	$31,737	$253,900
8	8	$274,212	$34,277	$239,935
9	7	$259,130	$37,019	$222,111
10	6	$239,880	$39,980	$199,900
11	5	$215,892	$43,178	$172,714
12	4	$186,531	$46,633	$139,898
13	3	$151,090	$50,363	$100,727
14	2	$108,785	$54,393	$ 54,392
15	1	$ 58,743	$58,743	0

You should be able to immediately notice some interesting differences between Golden's payout schedule and the one shown earlier for Sterling, who chose the fixed-dollar approach. For starters, Golden's portfolio actually continued to grow for two years after he began taking money out, a function of the smaller early year withdrawals. Second, the depletion rate was far slower. At the end of 10 years, Golden still had assets of $215,892 — well over two-thirds of his original total — whereas Sterling was almost broke. This can be an important factor in dealing with unexpected economic conditions or dramatic lifestyle events in later years. Finally, Golden's payout rate increased steadily over the life of his withdrawal plan, compensating for the effects of inflation (or, perhaps, for higher medical bills as he grew older).

Note, however, that we are not saying the fixed-period method is automatically better than the fixed-dollar method. You may, in fact, prefer to have a larger annual sum to spend and enjoy in the early years of your retirement and smaller amounts later as you age and become less active. The choice is obviously yours. We are merely pointing out the differences in the way the two plans unfold — as well as the value of keeping a larger sum of money at work for you (Golden's total payout on $300,000 at 8 percent was $543,042 over 15 years, whereas Sterling got just $421,858 over 10-1/2). Be aware, though, that investment performance is just as important with the fixed-period method as with the fixed-dollar approach. To illustrate, the following table assumes the same conditions for Golden as outlined above, but with an annual growth rate of just 4 percent.

Fixed-Period Withdrawal Plan — 4% Growth Rate

Year	Years left	Value of Sterling's holdings at start of year	Amount withdrawn by Golden	Value of Sterling's holdings after the withdrawal
1	15	$300,000	$20,000	$280,000
2	14	$291,200	$20,800	$270,400
3	13	$281,216	$21,632	$259,584
4	12	$269,967	$22,497	$247,470
5	11	$257,369	$23,397	$233,972
6	10	$243,331	$24,333	$218,998
7	9	$227,758	$25,306	$202,452
8	8	$210,550	$26,319	$184,231
9	7	$191,600	$27,371	$164,229
10	6	$170,798	$28,466	$142,332
11	5	$148,025	$29,605	$118,420
12	4	$123,157	$30,789	$ 92,368
13	3	$ 96,063	$32,021	$ 64,042
14	2	$ 66,604	$33,302	$ 33,302
15	1	$ 34,634	$34,634	0

You can quickly see the difference the 4 percent decline in Golden's rate of return makes. His portfolio stops growing immediately upon beginning withdrawals, and the depletion rate is much faster (more than half his original stake is gone after 10 years). In addition, while his annual payout amount climbs each year, he never gets close to the $40,000 annual income Sterling enjoyed for the life of her withdrawal plan. (However, his total payout on the $300,000 at 4 percent was still far better than Sterling's — $400,472 over 15 years, versus $347,259 over 9-1/2.)

Thus, each approach has its merits — and its drawbacks. And, it may well be that neither works as well for you as some of the other options available (such as the "ratio" method discussed in the text). That's why it's so important to carefully analyze your own situation and your personal cash-flow needs before selecting a mutual fund withdrawal plan.

▷ ▷ ▶ ▶ **If you want to get started today, here's what you need to do to begin developing a periodic-withdrawal plan for your mutual fund holdings:**

First, assess your own projected cash-flow needs, your continuing goals for growth and the time frame your withdrawal plan will likely have to cover. Make sure all estimates are realistic given your current asset base, other income sources, the outlook for the economy as a whole, the past performance of the particular fund and your life expectancy, adjusted for current health considerations. Then, contact the broker who sold you your fund shares — or the fund-management company itself — and request information on the types of withdrawal plans available, restrictions (if any) and fees (if any). Once you receive the material, review the options available to you and choose the one that best matches your projected needs and goals — or talk with the broker or fund shareholder services representative about structuring a plan specifically for you. ▲

Continued from p. 17

Life-Expectancy Withdrawals — This approach, which is considerably more complex than the three other methods, attempts to mimic the payout of an annuity policy. At the time you start your withdrawals, your remaining life expectancy is calculated based on standard actuarial tables. Your total assets are then divided by the number of payout periods in your remaining life expectancy, and that's the amount you receive. The entire process is then repeated when it comes time for the next withdrawal — i.e., your life expectancy is recalculated and your then-current asset total is divided by the number of payout periods in your revised life expectancy.

The disadvantage of this approach is that you don't know either how much you'll get each time or how long your money will last. The advantage is, if the process works perfectly, your portfolio will be totally depleted at the time you die. This makes it a good choice for people without heirs and no desire to leave an estate. However, if it turns out you live longer than average, you could wind up very old and very broke — meaning it probably shouldn't be applied to all of your resources.

THE LIFE EXPECTANCY-GROWTH DEBATE

The issue of life expectancy has prompted a considerable debate among advocates of asset allocation in recent years — and you should definitely review the arguments of both sides during your transition planning. Although we touched on this in the previous lesson, its importance bears a little expanded lip service.

The problem, from an asset-management standpoint, is that average American life expectancies have risen sharply over the past few decades. A couple of generations ago, the average 65-year-old male could be expected to live around seven more years. Now, the life expectancy for a 65-year-old man is more than double that number — and it's even longer for women of the same age. Thus, many of the traditional asset-allocation rules seem out of date.

For example, when asset allocation first came into vogue, most conservative proponents recommended an 80-20 debt-to-equity split at the time of retirement, with a gradual shift to 100-0 in later years. As should be obvious from the tables shown in wealth-building step 94, if debt securities (including cash equivalents) are returning an average of only 4 percent a year or so, even a fairly large asset base will be quickly depleted if left entirely in debt issues.

As a result, most conservative experts now suggest a 70-30 split, with a gradual narrowing to, perhaps, 85-15 — or at most, 90-10. However, a lot of more aggressive financial planners are using a formula based on the number 100, minus your age. For example, if you're 67, they would have you put 33 percent of assets (100 - 67 = 33) in equities to ensure enough continued growth to cover your extended lifespan — and only 67 percent in debt (including cash equivalents).

And, some experts are saying even that's too conservative. A recently published financial planning report recommended multiplying your age by 80 percent and putting, at most, that amount of your assets in debt securities. For example, with this formula, a 75 year old would put just 60 percent of his portfolio assets in debt issues (75 x 0.80 = 60), while leaving 40 percent in equities to promote continued growth. If life expectancies keep extending, this could well be the rule of the future.

Consider Changing Your Equity Mix

If you're concerned about the possible need for continued growth, but still want your holdings to generate more monthly income, there is an alternative to drastically changing your debt-equity mix. Instead, you can change the mix of your equity portfolio, moving away from lower-yielding growth stocks or funds and into higher-yielding income-oriented stocks or funds.

For example, if you currently have $50,000 worth of low-yielding technology issues, you might wait for the next good market rally and sell them out, capturing your gains. Then, rather than putting the proceeds into bonds or cash equivalents, you buy three or four carefully selected utility stocks or other high-dividend issues, perhaps in the banking or brokerage industries.

For example, if you currently have $50,000 worth of low-yielding technology issues, you might wait for the next good market rally and sell them out, capturing your gains. Then, rather than putting the proceeds into bonds or cash equivalents, you buy three or four carefully selected utility stocks or other high-dividend issues, perhaps in the banking or brokerage industries.

If the current yield on the new high-dividend issues averages just 5.0 percent, not at all unreasonable for the suggested sectors, you increase your annual cash flow by $2,500 (not including compounding) — and you still retain substantial potential for growth. If you doubt that, just consider these numbers:

Through till December 1995, the stocks in the Dow Jones Utilities index recorded an average price gain of 21.8 percent — and stocks in the regional bank sector (as reported by Investor's Business Daily) were up a whopping 60.8 percent!

Admittedly, 1995 was an unusually strong year in terms of market performance, so you shouldn't count on similar results in the future. However, you should be aware that a number of market studies have found that utilities and other high-dividend stocks aren't really deserving of their traditional "stodgy" image — particularly during times of only moderate market appreciation.

For example, research done by James Rea found that, from 1925 through 1975, the average annual compounded growth rate for high-dividend stocks — those with dividend yields equal to at least two-thirds the yield on AAA-rated corporate bonds — was 19.5 percent. That compared to a compounded annual return of just 7.5 percent for the Dow Industrials over the same period.

If you're not comfortable trying to pick out three or four quality individual stocks, you can follow the same approach with mutual funds — switching assets from funds in the growth category to funds in the income or balanced categories. In fact, there are several funds that actually specialize in high-dividend stocks.

You might also want to consider purchasing shares in some high-yielding closed-end funds or real estate investment trusts, both of which provide both dividend income (frequently in the 10-percent-plus range) and growth potential. *Note: Both of these investment vehicles are discussed in detail elsewhere in this course, so we won't spend additional time on them here. Refer to the lessons titled Starting Up the Pyramid: Investment Opportunities and The Equity Fund Approach if you need more information.*

Review both your needs and your options as part of your transition planning. Then you'll be fully prepared at the time you retire, rather than having to make disruptive adjustments later.

Debt Sector Adjustments Are Also Possible

If additional cash flow is of greater concern to you than growth potential, you can also consider changing the security mix within the debt segment of your portfolio. For example, you might switch from government securities into investment-grade corporate bonds, which generally offer a point or two of extra yield with only a small degree of extra risk. Likewise, you might switch a portion of your debt holdings from highly rated corporate issues to more speculative "junk" bonds (those rated BB or below by Standard & Poor's or Ba or below by Moody's).

One increasingly popular yield-improvement strategy involves structuring a split portfolio — with half your assets in AAA- or AA-rated issues and half in junk bonds. This typically produces a higher overall payout than a portfolio of medium-grade bonds (A- or BBB-rate issues), with no increase in average portfolio risk. This technique is called a "yield barbell" because the portfolio is heavily weighted at both ends of the risk spectrum, with very little in the middle.

Another option is to adjust the term structure of your debt holdings — i.e., staying within the same ratings class, but moving from short- to long-term issues to pick up a higher yield (assuming a normal yield curve).

Before you adopt any of these strategies, you should, of course, conduct a review of your personal risk tolerances. If you can't chance even a small capital loss, you probably should not use them. But, if find you can comfortably accept a slightly higher level of risk, they can improve your regular cash flow without disrupting your overall asset-allocation mix.

CAREFULLY EVALUATE ANY SPECIAL CIRCUMSTANCES

Another important aspect of your transitional planning process involves carefully reviewing any special circumstances related to your retirement. Some of these, such as the need for a second vehicle or a move to a smaller residence, are fairly simple — involving little more than ensuring the needed money is available and taking care of minor details (like address changes on investment accounts and finding storage space for excess furnishings). Others, however, can feature a host of complexities.

Just for fun, suppose you plan to buy a boat and spend the first five years of your retirement sailing the oceans of the world. Sounds terrific — a wonderful, carefree life! Well, yes, but...

Who's going to manage your investments while you're gone? Where are you going to have your Social Security and periodic mutual fund withdrawal checks sent? How will the money be passed on to you? Can you count on having it sent to your next scheduled port? If so, should it be denominated in U.S. dollars or in the local currency? What do you do if it doesn't show up? How can you be contacted in an emergency? What happens to the boat if that emergency demands your return to the United States?

We could probably string together enough of these questions to stretch a nautical mile, but you obviously get the point. All of these issues have to be considered — and dealt with — in your transition plan. You can't just buy a boat, provision it and plan to blithely set sail the morning after your retirement party.

Major Problems Arising From Moves

That's obviously an unusual example, and it probably has very little relevance to your own situation. However, even relatively common retirement plans, such as a move to another state, can be far more complicated than most people realize. For example:

- Will you face a higher state income tax burden in your new home state? All but seven states (Alaska, Florida, Nevada, South Dakota, Texas, Washington and Wyoming) impose state income taxes on residents — and some of them are quite high. The sunny beaches of Southern California may look highly appealing to someone suffering through a cold Wyoming winter, but the extra 7 to 11 percent in income taxes could make retiring there impossible.

- Even states with no income taxes can offer tax traps for retirees. For example, property taxes may be substantially higher. That could affect your ability to buy the retirement home you want — or cut into your cash flow, forcing you to accept a lower standard of living after your move.

■ Even sales taxes can be a big factor. If you move from a location with a 5 percent sales tax to one with a 9 percent levy, you face a $4 loss in purchasing power on every $100 in retirement income you plan to spend.

■ Your investment strategy can be affected. If you own a large number of tax-free municipal bonds, for example, you probably won't still get your full tax exemption in your new home state. Most states exempt only income from municipal bonds issued within their own borders, and three (Illinois, Iowa and Wisconsin) don't exempt any municipal bond income, even their own. *Tip: There is one way around this trap — municipal bonds issued by Puerto Rico, Guam and the Virgin Islands are exempt from state and local taxes in all 50 states and the District of Columbia.*

■ Your pension income could come under attack. A number of states evidently resent the fact you would live there for many years, earning money and building up a tax-deferred retirement account or corporate pension, then want to leave without paying taxes on those benefits. So, they impose taxes on pensions and nonqualified retirement account distributions paid to nonresidents from sources within the state. Currently, 13 states have laws allowing them to impose such taxes, though only 10 actually do — and only three (California, Kansas and Oregon) tax all types of nonresident retirement payouts. (California and Oregon actually apply income-tax withholding to pension payouts.) Two states — New York and Louisiana — also exempt government pension plans.

Note: Actually, tax laws in these states are written in such a way that pensions sourced outside the state can also be taxed if the benefits were earned while the recipient lived and worked within the state. Thus, you could technically be taxed on your pension by any of the 13 states in which you ever lived or worked. However, collection of such taxes is difficult, so you probably don't have to worry at this point — although that could change if the states get desperate enough for additional revenue sources. Fortunately, at least some states are on your side. Nevada has proposed a "shield" law, that would prevent any other state from taxing the income of Nevada residents, whatever the source. Nevada — along with Arizona, Colorado, New Hampshire, New Mexico, Texas and Washington — already has a law barring other states from seizing assets of newly arrived retirees.

■ You could actually face the loss of a pension. Some states limit the payment of certain government pensions only to those who maintain residences in the state. For example, Washington terminates state disability pensions for individuals who permanently move to another state.

■ Insurance costs could be dramatically different. Using the same Wyoming-to-California retiree described earlier provides a prime example: Auto insurance rates in Los Angeles are more than triple those in Laramie — for the same vehicle and driver profile.

Living Costs Also Differ

Those are just some of the specific items you must take into account in developing a transition plan that includes a move to another state. There are also numerous cost-of-living differences from area to area that must be factored in. Key spending areas that should be examined, depending on your individual situation, include transportation, food, housing, utilities, entertainment, health care and perhaps even clothing (if your new location demands a whole new wardrobe, that could represent a significant cost factor).

Some Tips on Fighting High Living Costs

Being a retiree does have some advantages with respect to high living costs, and knowing about them can both stretch your retirement dollars and improve your lifestyle. For example, many restaurants and most theaters, parks, museums, transit systems, and special events offer senior discounts, as do many airlines, hotels and other travel-industry businesses. Even some retail stores, personal services providers, repair services and mechanics offer special rates for retirees.

If you enjoy travel, cruise lines offer some of the best deals for seniors — and, if you have a special skill, talent or area of expertise developed over a lifetime of work, you may even be able to sail for free. Activities are a major feature on all ships, so the cruise lines are always on the lookout for guest lecturers and speakers (historians, anthropologists, naturalists and ornithologists are especially popular, as are financial and retirement planners). Having a Ph.D. or a master's degree in a subject, or being recog-

nized as an authority (e.g., having had articles published) can be helpful — but often your personality and enthusiasm can be more important than expertise. Retired doctors and nurses can also cruise free if they're still licensed and willing to be on call for medical emergencies.

Another advantage of being retired when it comes to costs is that you have more free time to do things like shop — and that can lead to some surprising "market" returns. The market we're talking about, of course, is the supermarket — but the return on investment can still be impressive. What you do is you watch for sales on staple items you regularly use — such as detergents, paper products, soda, canned goods, toothpaste, etc. — then buy in bulk at the lower prices. Each time you manage to get $100 worth of goods at 25 percent off, you in effect make a 33 percent return on the $75 you invest. That's better than you can do on Wall Street most of the time — and it takes far less effort.

Fortunately, there are generally a number of trade-offs in this area. For example, housing costs are higher in Los Angeles than in Laramie, but expenses for heating, winter clothes and fresh produce are far lower. Still, you need to look at the combined impact of all the pricing differences that will affect you, and factor that into your planned cash-flow needs.

Moving Overseas Has Added Complications

The analysis of and preparation for a post-retirement move is even more complicated if that move is to an overseas location rather than just to another state. This applies in particular if the move is a permanent one, but there are also some things to consider if you just plan to spend three or four months abroad each year.

For starters, you face most of the same logistical questions we detailed earlier in our example about taking off on a sailboat (e.g., who manages your money, how do you get your payouts, where do you keep your assets?). In addition, there are various potential tax consequences — this time involving the federal government rather than just a couple of states. These include:

■ An American abroad remains subject to U.S. income tax, though you do get U.S. tax credits for taxes paid to a foreign government, but only in 43 of the more leading countries. You should also check out the foreign country's tax policies — some tax U.S. Social Security income for American retirees living within their borders.

■ To qualify as a foreign resident for U.S. income tax purposes, you must live abroad for a full calendar year, or be outside the United States for 12 of 13 consecutive months. (This will also exempt you from state and local taxes here.)

■ Americans who earn income while legally residing abroad qualify for a U.S. tax exemption on the first $70,000 of earned income, plus a living allowance exclusion. This can be a real bonanza if you plan to work after retirement and the foreign country you move to doesn't impose an income tax. *Note: This is significant because — with computers, modems, faxes, satellites and overnight delivery almost everywhere in the world — it's now relatively easy for individuals living abroad to act as consultants or provide other contract services for U.S. clients.*

- Retirees may elect to keep a U.S. home as a place to stay stateside, or as a rental investment, while they live abroad. If used as a permanent home less than 183 days a year, it won't be considered a principal residence for tax purposes.

- After selling a principal residence, a person moving abroad has four years (instead of two for a move in the U.S.) to buy a home of equivalent value and qualify for tax deferral on the gain.

- A foreign home can qualify for the one-time, tax-free gain of $125,000 on the sale of a principal residence — if it has been used as your principal residence three of the last five years.

- Rules on currency restrictions and capital gains vary from country to country. However, as a general rule, it's not that easy to bring money back after a sale. Many foreign countries also have hefty estate taxes should you die while a legal resident there. For the sake of your heirs, these may be reasons to rent a home overseas, rather than buy.

Adjust Your Investments Accordingly

If you do plan to live abroad — either permanently or for a few months each year — you should probably make some major adjustments in your asset-allocation mix, greatly increasing the foreign component. *Note: Even if you plan to stay right where you are, most retirement portfolios should have at least a modest foreign component as a hedge against inflation — i.e., erosion in the purchasing power of the dollar relative to foreign-produced goods, which now make up a major portion of U.S. consumption. For some other ideas on protecting yourself against inflation, refer to wealth-building Step 95, found on page 28.*

Once you've succeeded in your wealth-building efforts and you begin liquidating, inflation is the biggest threat you face over the remainder of your life.

The extra foreign investments should be focused on the area where you plan to reside or, if possible, concentrated in the specific country. Regional or single-country closed-end funds are good choices, as are specific foreign equities that trade on U.S. exchanges either as American Depositary Receipts (ADRs) or directly through interlinked listings. Some foreign bonds can also be traded over the counter in the U.S., and there is a wide selection of Eurobonds available here.

For maximum benefit, at least some of the investments should be denominated in the currency of the country in which you plan to live. This will offset some of the exchange-rate risk you face moving funds into and out of the U.S., as well as provide additional protection against a prolonged slide in the dollar's value — which could greatly reduce the purchasing power of your retirement cash flow in your adopted country. Of course though, if you're going to live in a country with a weak currency, your money could be devalued.

If you plan to move to or spend your time in the south of France — or some other developed country with well-organized securities laws and sufficient investor protections — you may even want to open an overseas brokerage account and invest directly in the securities of your new home country. That way, you'll have local sources of income, as well as benefiting from growth in the economy to which your retirement spending is contributing.

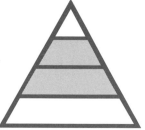

STEP 95

Three Defensive Strategies Against Inflation

What: Buy indexed annuities and floating-rate bonds — and hang on to your principal residence — as protection against inflationary erosion in your asset base when you begin coming down the pyramid.

Why: Once you've succeeded in your wealth-building efforts and you begin liquidating, inflation is the biggest threat you face over the remainder of your life. It can erode the purchasing power of your dollars, reducing the anticipated comfort of your lifestyle and wiping out the financial cushion you worked so hard to build.

Risk: Low to medium. Inflation-resistant investments tend to be conservative in nature, meaning there's little risk of actual capital loss. However, there is an opportunity risk in that returns can be limited if inflation fails to materialize.

Safety: High.

Liquidity: Medium for floating-rate bonds; low for indexed annuities and your principal residence.

Why not: The lack of liquidity reduces your flexibility, and the inflation-fighting nature of the vehicles means you won't have a firm fix on the amount of income they'll generate, which can make your planning difficult and leave you with a potentially low cash flow at times.

Buy/Invest from: Regular or discount brokers or bond dealers for floating-rate bonds; a qualified insurance agent or financial planner for indexed annuities. You should already own your residence, so no transaction will be required.

Background: Although there are many different types of inflation hedges (as you learned in the lesson How to Profit from Changing Times when we talked about inflation proofing your portfolio), all have one thing in common: When inflation picks up, reducing the purchasing power of your dollars, they either generate more income to offset the loss or increase in value by at least as much as the rise in inflation. Indexed annuities and floating-rate bonds fall into the former category, while real estate fits the latter. Here's a brief explanation of how each works:

Indexed annuities — Annuities are discussed in detail in the lesson Retirement Planning. But briefly, as you'll find in that lesson, an annuity is an investment contract usually sold by a life insurance company in which the beneficiary receives regular payments for life, or for a fixed period, in exchange for the immediate or installment deposit of a specified amount of money. You give them a large sum now and they, over time, will, at least usually, give you back more.

An indexed annuity is one in which the regular periodic payment is tied to a leading indicator of interest rates. (These are also frequently referred to as variable-rate annuities.) If interest rates rise — as they typically do during times of high inflation — your periodic payments increase as well. However, if interest rates decline, your payments will also fall. The advantage of such plans is that, so long as interest rates move in concert with changes in inflation, the amount of your annuity income will rise, thus offsetting the purchasing power loss that income suffers due to inflation. The principal drawback is that you won't know precisely what your periodic receipts from the annuity will be — which can be a significant problem if you are planning your financial future with a very specific dollar budget. As a result, we strongly recommend taking a mixed approach in the use of annuities — i.e., put 70 to 75 percent of your annuity money in fixed-rate contracts, and the remaining 25 to 30 percent in variable-rate policies. The fixed portion will provide income stability, while the smaller variable segment will increase as interest rates rise, giving you some cushion against inflation.

Step 95: *Three Defensive Strategies Against Inflation*

You'll also be able to estimate with about 90 percent accuracy (i.e., within a 10 percent range, plus or minus) what your periodic annuity income will be.

Floating-rate bonds — These are bonds that, rather than having a fixed coupon rate over the full term to maturity, have an adjustable rate that rises or falls every so often (usually at either six-month or one-year intervals) to reflect changes in the current market interest rate. As such, they provide the same type of protection as indexed annuities, with your periodic income rising when interest rates — and, presumably, inflation — are climbing and falling when rates and inflation are dropping. There are two main drawbacks:

- As with indexed annuities, your actual cash flow is uncertain, making precise budgeting more difficult.

- The selection of quality floating-rate bonds is limited.

Note: For more details on floating-rate bonds, refer to the lessons titled Wealthbuilding can be Safe, Rewarding and Fun and The Bond Alternative.

Retain your principal residence — Although prices may occasionally slump (as they did in the early 1990s), or go through long stable periods, real estate has a fairly solid long-term record of rising in value by enough to offset the impact of inflation. This makes it a viable investment choice for those concerned with preserving assets or leaving behind an estate unravaged by inflation. In the case of your principal residence, where your mortgage is either fixed or fully paid, you also benefit in that your housing costs remain constant — i.e., payable in the same number of devalued dollars that you had to lay out before high inflation struck. You also get tax benefits in that interest costs related to your principal residence are deductible, and proceeds from an eventual sale are excluded from capital gains taxes (with certain conditions and restrictions outlined elsewhere in this course). The drawbacks are the lack of liquidity and the possible impact on your desired lifestyle — e.g., you may have more house than you really need now that the children are going, or have to stay in an area you'd prefer to leave because of poor weather or lack of desired recreation activities.

▷ ▷ ▶ ▶ **If you want to get started today, here's what you need to do to implement these three defensive strategies against inflation:**

Begin by structuring a well-thought-out retirement living plan that includes a projected budget based on your primary lifestyle objectives, estimated cash-flow needs and degree of concern about inflation. Determine the amount of purchasing-power protection you feel you need and, as a result, the percentage of your assets you should devote to inflation-resistant investments. Then, begin the shopping process, carefully reviewing your alternatives and making final purchase decisions based on the criteria outlined in the sections of this course dealing with those investments. Be sure to factor any loss of liquidity into your overall retirement plan, making alternate provisions for dealing with emergencies or future changes in life conditions. ▲

Continued from p. 27

SELLING YOUR CURRENT HOME

If you are planning to move after retirement — whether across town or across an ocean — you'll probably be selling the home you have now (unless you plan to retain it as a rental property or a travel base). If so, setting up that sale should be a priority item in your transition plan.

Put your home on the market well in advance of your desired sale date, particularly if that date represents a deadline for a move to a distant locale or for the purchase of another residence.

If you're like most people, your home is one of your largest retirement assets. Unfortunately, it can also be one of the hardest and most expensive to sell — and it certainly involves the most paperwork. In today's real estate market, many homes can take six months, a year or even longer to sell — and the eventual price can be far lower than expected. As such, you should include contingencies for those possibilities in your transition plan, making your most accurate estimate of how much you think your house will really bring — and deciding how to adjust your retirement finances if it doesn't.

Put your home on the market well in advance of your desired sale date, particularly if that date represents a deadline for a move to a distant locale or for the purchase of another residence. You don't want to lose your retirement "dream home" because of your inability to sell this house, nor do you want to be dragged back from that South Seas island just to sign the closing papers for a sale that took far longer than expected.

Besides, giving yourself more time enables you to put the home on the market for a higher than expected sale price on the possibility the right buyer, in love with your home or location, will snap at it. If this doesn't happen, then you still have time to sell at the more realistic price.

This is also another area where you want to pay close attention to transaction costs. Real estate commissions are typically quoted at 6 percent of the sales price, which represents a lot of money — e.g., $12,000 on a $200,000 home sale. In addition, you will likely have $2,000 to $5,000 in additional fees and costs, depending on the value of the property.

You can't do much about some of the fees since they cover services required by law. However, you can negotiate on others — either trying to get the company involved to lower them or trying to get the buyer to pay some of them. You also can — and should — negotiate for a better rate on the sales commission. Though they heartily resist, real estate agents fairly routinely lower their commission from the standard 6 percent to 5 percent — and 4 percent is possible. That would save you $4,000 on a $200,000 sale — which is well worth the effort.

The keys to a successful home sale are twofold — be realistic about the value and terms, and allow ample time for both the sale and the closing. That way you'll have time to negotiate, or time to wait for a better offer, without coming under undue pressure. That's important because your home is far too valuable an asset to sell from a position of weakness. *Note: For further details on valuing your home and negotiating a sale, refer to the lesson titled The Profit Approach to Real Estate.*

One final planning tip on your home: If you are divorced, widowed or single and have not yet used your one-time, $125,000 capital-gains tax exclusion on the sale of your principal residence, but are planning to marry someone who has, be sure to sell your home before the wedding. Married couples are viewed as a single entity for tax purposes, and your new spouse's use of the exclusion will disqualify you from taking yours if you wait and sell after you marry.

ADJUST YOUR INSURANCE COVERAGES

Your transition plan should also include a thorough review of all your insurance coverages, as well as adjustments of some policies to reflect your retirement.

Obviously, you will still need all of the standard casualty and liability coverages, but you may still want to make some changes. For example, raising deductibles can lower your premiums and increase your annual cash flow, as can lowering coverage limits (though you must be careful to maintain full protection for your retirement assets). You may also be entitled to some premium reductions due to your new lifestyle — e.g., since you're no longer commuting, your auto rates should go down.

Health coverage will also require some study and decisions. Will you get any continued benefits from your ex-employer? Do you want to purchase your own plan or rely heavily on MediCare? Do you need or want MediCare supplements? What about long-term care or catastrophic-illness coverage? How about an HMO? Prescription plans? Answers to all of these questions will depend on your personal preferences and your personal financial situation. However, they do have to be answered — most likely before you actually retire.

As for life insurance, it's probably necessary only if there are special circumstances related to your retirement, or if it will prove beneficial from a tax standpoint for estate-planning purposes. You certainly don't need endowment policies or other types of insurance with savings provisions. They have heavy front-end costs, require long build-up periods and you can generally get better returns by investing on your own. If you decide you do need life insurance, stick to lower cost term policies. *Note: For more information on insurance and its use in estate planning, refer to the lessons dealing exclusively with those subjects.*

A Final Word You've now been given at least a brief overview of virtually all the areas you'll need to cover once you've completed your wealth-building pyramid and are ready to start coming back down. It's an extensive list, and some of the issues are complex. However, nothing is involved that you can't handle — if you allow enough time and develop a comprehensive plan.

As should now be obvious, the transition from work to retirement is one of the most significant you will ever make — and the plan for making it smoothly is just as important as either your original investment plan or your overall retirement plan. Don't neglect it when the date for your retirement draws near. ▲

Retirement planning

LESSON 31

Retirement planning

"A harvest taken too early yields a thin crop." — *American farm saying*

INTRODUCTION

Your retirement years may turn out to be golden or brass, depending on how well you have planned ahead. It's hard to pick up a financial magazine or turn to the business pages of your local newspaper without reading about another study that concludes Americans aren't saving enough for retirement. And there is hardly a shortage of articles questioning whether Social Security and Medicare will be providing adequate benefits for the duration of your retirement, especially if you are middle-aged or younger. What's more, the declining number of workers covered by corporate pension plans that make investment decisions for you and guarantee benefits, and the corresponding increase in self-directed retirement savings plans such as 401(k)s, mean that more employees than ever have the power, and responsibility, to shape their post-employment years.

Although far too many people aren't saving enough for retirement, no doubt a serious wealth builder like you is already socking away investment dollars earmarked for just such a purpose. When it comes time to make all-important asset allocation decisions for retirement, however, too many investors continue to invest too conservatively — favoring fixed income securities or failing to properly diversify. A recent study of 401(k) plans by Access Research of Windsor, CT, found that only 27% of employee's 401(k) assets were invested in stocks other than the stock of their employer, despite the higher long-term returns generated by diversified stock portfolios.

It's hard to imagine a worse mistake you could make. Academic studies have repeatedly shown that *more than 90%* of an investment portfolio's performance derives from the way the assets are allocated among stocks, bonds, cash and other investments. Your ability to select a particular stock or bond pales in importance compared to the necessity of having a significant amount of your retirement nest egg invested in growth-oriented stocks and higher yielding fixed income securities. Later in this lesson we'll underscore the importance of selecting specific categories of stocks and bonds within those broad asset classes.

You also may fail to fully appreciate the impact of inflation on your investments, even though we've touched on this subject in earlier lessons. You need a substantial equity component to provide capital appreciation potential for your retirement portfolio. Increasing longevity, increasing health costs and the corrosive effect of even modest levels of inflation on your purchasing power in retirement mean that the days of clipping fixed-income coupons as the sole source of income in your old age are long gone.

Why One Million Dollars Isn't What It Used to Be

It may be hard for you to grasp how much money you will need to retire comfortably, but surely $1 million is enough, isn't it? Let's see. Say, for instance, that you estimate your annual retirement costs in current dollars at roughly $75,000 for you and your spouse. That's more than a modest amount of income, but it hardly classifies you for a spot on *Lifestyles of the Rich and Famous*. But have you saved and invested enough to support that lifestyle? It will take more than you probably realize. A 60-year-old man today can expect to live to be 77-1/2. But if you're in good health and make it to age 70, your life expectancy jumps to 81. A woman at 60 can expect to live to be 81-1/4, and at 70 can expect to reach 83 to 84 years old. (For further details on longevity statistics, refer to the life expectancy chart in the lesson *Work, employment and investments*.)

ASSUMPTIONS FOR HOW LONG WILL $1 MILLION LAST AT RETIREMENT

STARTING ASSETS	$1,000,000
ANNUAL SPENDING	$75,000
RETURN ON INVESTMENT	10%
INFLATION RATE	4%
% SPENDING TIED TO INFLATION	75%
TAX RATE ON INCOME PERSONAL ASSETS	30%

So how long will $1 million last, yielding 10%, if you withdraw $75,000 a year, and adjust your spending to keep pace with inflation? As the chart below illustrates, your money will be gone in just 20 years, assuming 4% annual inflation and that 75% of your spending is subject to inflation. (We're ignoring for the moment any money you are entitled to receive under Social Security or other defined benefit plans.)

YEARLY USE OF $1 MILLION NEST EGG FOR RETIREMENT

Year	Starting Assets (000s)	Invest. Return	Taxes	Spend	Surplus (Deficit)	Ending Assets
1	1,000	100	(30)	(75)	(5)	995
2	995	100	(30)	(77)	(8)	987
3	987	99	(30)	(80)	(10)	977
4	977	98	(29)	(82)	(14)	963
5	963	96	(29)	(84)	(17)	946
6	946	95	(28)	(87)	(21)	926
7	926	93	(28)	(90)	(25)	901
8	901	90	(27)	(92)	(29)	872
9	872	87	(26)	(95)	(34)	838
10	838	84	(25)	(98)	(39)	799
11	799	80	(24)	(101)	(45)	754
12	754	75	(23)	(104)	(51)	703
13	703	70	(21)	(107)	(58)	645
14	645	64	(19)	(110)	(65)	580
15	580	58	(17)	(113)	(73)	507
16	507	51	(15)	(117)	(81)	426
17	426	43	(13)	(120)	(91)	335
18	335	34	(10)	(124)	(101)	235
19	235	23	(7)	(128)	(111)	123
20	123	12	(4)	(132)	(123)	GONE

Source: Bridgewater Advisors, New York.

Change a few assumptions in the example at left, and the outlook could be even bleaker. If you assume that your total investment return is 7% instead of 10%, which may be a more realistic assumption for investors who aren't heavily invested in growth stocks, then the money runs out in just 16 years. If all else remains equal and inflation averages 5% instead of 4%, then the money is gone in 15 years. The above figures do not include the possible additional taxes resulting from IRA withdrawals that exceed $150,000 a year.

Don't Panic! Our goal isn't to panic you into making bad investment decisions in order to try and boost your investment nest egg on the eve of retirement. That may be the single worst decision you could make in your investing career, as we'll discuss later in this lesson. The important figure to focus on initially isn't the rate of return on investments or the number of years until your assets are used up.

Instead, look how dramatically your retirement outlook can change if you rein-in your expected spending. If you can reduce your spending to $50,000 a year, then the $1 million will last for more than 40 years with a rate of return of 10%, 4% inflation and with 75% of your spending tied to inflation. Even if the return falls to what may be a more realistic 7%, by spending only $50,000 a year you could still make the $1 million last 26 years.

HOW MUCH MONEY WILL YOU NEED?

There are two basic ways to calculate how much money you will need to retire comfortably. The first, and simplest, is to follow one of the retirement rules of thumb: You'll need the equivalent of at least 65% to 85% of your annual after-tax income. If you are willing to drastically change your lifestyle by moving to a much smaller home or apartment in a region with a significantly lower cost of living, for instance, then you may be able to get by with a retirement income closer to the 65% end of the range.

One of the reasons we have designed these lessons, however, is so that wealth builders like yourself can take control of your financial future and fully enjoy your retirement years. You've earned it. For that reason we recommend that you plan on needing at least 85% of your income in retirement. While it may not seem so initially, this is also the more conservative approach to retirement planning. If it turns out you don't need 85% of your income to live comfortably in retirement, then you'll have some extra cash to spend as you wish or invest to offset possible unforeseen costs.

To take a more detailed approach to calculating your retirement costs, first you need to break out your current expenses and what you estimate you will need in retirement. Everyone will have an item or two to subtract or add to this list, but here are the basics. Then follow the remaining steps below to calculate how much money you will need to retire. At first glance the steps and related tables may appear daunting, but don't despair. You'll be able to scan the tables quickly and pick out the number that applies to your situation. It's easier than it looks, and well worth the effort if you want to have a firm grasp on your retirement needs.

STEP 1: Estimating Retirement Costs.

Expense	Current costs	Estimated retirement costs in current dollars	Comment
Housing (rent, mortgage payments, condo fees, utilities, property taxes, maintenance, etc.)	_____	_____	*(Expect a decline of 25% or more since most mortgages are paid off and home improvements are behind you.)*
Food	_____	_____	*(Usually about the same)*
Clothing	_____	_____	*(Expect a decline of 20% or so once you've foregone most expensive business clothing.)*
Transportation (car payments, maintenance and repair, gasoline, parking, commuting costs)	_____	_____	*(Cutting commuting costs usually reduces this item.)*
Leisure and Travel (vacations, movies, hobbies, theater and performing arts)	_____	_____	*(If travel is one of your retirement goals, increase this item by at least 25%.)*
Personal Grooming	_____	_____	*(Unless you plan on retiring to a cabin in the backwoods, don't plan on a decrease here.)*
Health - Medical	_____	_____	*(Expect nearly a 50% increase in this category — much more if you're in poor health.)*
Insurance (Life, Medical)	_____	_____	*(While most people scale back their life insurance costs in retirement by 50% or more, rising Medicare and Medigap insurance costs may more than make up for the savings on life insurance.)*
Charity	_____	_____	*(You'll be reminded that you can't take it with you. Figure on an increase.)*
Loan, debt payments	_____	_____	*(Most people aim to have home and other loans repaid by retirement.)*
Support of relatives	_____	_____	*(College costs are probably behind you, but what about helping out with the grandchildren?)*
Taxes	_____	_____	
Other	_____	_____	
Total Expenses	$_____	$_____	

STEP 2: Estimate your monthly income for your first year of retirement, in today's dollars.

To estimate your Social Security benefits, call the Social Security Administration at 1-800-772-1213 and ask for Form SSA-7004, "Request for Social Security Earnings and Benefit Statement." To estimate your company pension benefits (in today's dollars), ask your employee benefits expert. Do not include dividend and interest income from your investments. Your

Social Security benefits are indexed to keep pace with inflation, at least for the foreseeable future. Many pension plans are indexed to varying degrees, while others are not. Again, check with your company's employee benefits expert.

Estimated Monthly Income

SOCIAL SECURITY	_____
COMPANY PENSION BENEFITS	_____
EARNED INCOME	_____
BUSINESS INCOME	_____
ANNUITY	_____
RENTAL INCOME	_____
TRUST INCOME	_____
DISABILITY INCOME	_____
ALIMONY	_____
TOTAL	$_____

STEP 3: Estimate your income taxes on your estimated monthly retirement income. Multiply your estimated monthly retirement income from Step 2 (minus half of your Social Security benefit) by your combined state and federal marginal income tax rate: _____.

STEP 4: Subtract the result in Step 3 from the result in Step 2: _____.

STEP 5: Subtract your estimated after-tax retirement income (Step 4) from your estimated retirement expenses (Step 1): _____.

STEP 6: Multiply the result in Step 5 by the appropriate figure from Table 1 below. The result is the estimated gap between your retirement income and expenses, adjusted for inflation: _____.

Table 1. Inflation factors

Use this table to estimate how inflation will affect your retirement needs. For instance, if you assume that inflation will average 4 percent and that you'll retire in 15 years, the appropriate factor would be 1.80.

Years	3%	4%	5%
5	1.16	1.22	1.28
10	1.34	1.48	1.63
15	1.56	1.80	2.08
20	1,81	2,19	2,65
25	2.09	2.67	3.39
30	2.43	3.24	4.32
35	2.81	3.95	5.52
40	3.26	4.80	7.04

STEP 7: Multiply the result in Step 6 by the appropriate figure from Table 2 below to estimate how much extra money you'll need at retirement to cover the gap between your retirement income and expenses. For instance, if the gap between your monthly income and expenses is $1,000 and you estimate you'll be retired for 25 years, inflation will increase at 4%, and your after-tax rate of return on your investments will be 6 percent, you'll need $1,000 x 235.33, or $235,330. This is how much money you'll need when you retire to cover the gap between your retirement income and expenses: _____.

An important note: This calculation assumes that you'll spend both the principal and income from the principal. To live on income only, you'd need a far larger sum of money. It may be realistic for younger wealth builders to plan on living on the interest from their investments — they have decades in which the value of their investments can grow. If retirement is only 15 or 20 years away, however, it probably isn't likely you'll be living on interest only, unless you have already accumulated a substantial nest egg. And that's not such a bad thing. After all, you're the one who has worked all your life to save this money. Says Garry Pitney, president of the financial planning firm Robert J. Oberst, Sr. & Associates, Red Bank, NJ, "One of the hardest jobs we have is convincing people it's okay to spend their principal. I have to keep telling them that they've earned it!"

Table 2 After-Tax Rate of Return

Years in Retire-ment	Inflation Rate	After-tax rate of return on investments				
		5%	6%	7%	8%	9%
5	3%	56.92	55.52	54.18	52.87	51.62
	4%	58.31	56.87	55.48	54.14	52.84
	5%	59.75	58.26	56.83	55.44	54.10
10	3%	108.44	103.34	98.57	94.10	89.91
	4%	113.79	108.35	103.27	98.50	94.04
	5%	119.50	113.70	108.27	103.19	98.44
15	3%	155.07	144.52	134.95	126.24	118.32
	4%	166.57	154.96	144.42	134.86	126.17
	5%	179.25	166.44	154.85	144.33	134.78
20	3%	197.27	179.98	164.75	151.31	139.40
	4%	216.79	197.14	179.87	164.66	151.23
	5%	239.00	216.63	197.01	179.76	164.57
25	3%	235.48	210.52	189.18	170.85	155.04
	4%	264.57	235.33	210.41	189.09	170.77
	5%	298.76	264.37	235.18	210.29	188.99
30	3%	270.06	236.82	209.19	186.08	166.64
	4%	310.02	269.89	236.70	209.10	186.01
	5%	358.51	309.80	269.73	236.58	209.01

STEP 8: Estimate the net value (fair market value minus any outstanding loans) of your current investments that you're able and willing to use to pay for your retirement expenses. When in doubt, use a lower estimate.

Real estate	_____
Savings accounts	_____
Stocks and stock mutual funds	_____
Bonds and bond mutual funds	_____
Life insurance	_____
Deferred annuities	_____
Retirement plan, 401(k)s, IRAs, etc.	_____
Business	_____
TOTAL	$_____

STEP 9: Multiply the result in Step 8 by the appropriate figure from the following table to estimate what your assets will be worth when your retire if they increase in value at a certain rate of return: _____.

For instance, if you have $245,000 earmarked for retirement, it is earning a rate of return of 8 percent a year, and you'll be retiring in 10 years, find the appropriate figure in the following table (i.e., 2.16) and multiply that figure by $245,000. The result is 2.16 x $245,000, or $529,200.

Table 2 Appreciation Rates

Years till retirement	5%	6%	7%	8%	9%	10%
5	1.28	1.34	1.40	1.47	1.54	1.61
10	1.63	1.79	1.97	2.16	2.37	2.59
15	2.08	2.40	2.76	3.17	3.64	4.18
20	2.65	3.21	3.87	4.66	5.60	6.73
25	3.39	4.29	5.43	6.85	8.62	10.83
30	4.32	5.74	7.61	10.06	13.27	17.45
35	5.52	7.69	10.68	14.79	20.41	28.10
40	7.04	10.29	14.97	21.72	31.41	45.26
45	8.99	13.76	21.00	31.92	48.33	72.89

STEP 10: Estimate how much federal and state income tax you will have to pay if you sell your assets in Step 9 when you retire. Multiply the amount in Step 9 (minus your purchase price) by the sum of your federal and state marginal income tax rates: _____.

STEP 11: Subtract the result in Step 10 from the result in Step 9: _____.

STEP 12: Subtract the result in Step 11 from the result in Step 7. This is how much money you'll need when you retire. If you feel confident that you'll receive an inheritance, you can subtract the estimated amount of the inheritance from this amount: _____.

Now Take a Deep Breath

If you're like most investors, you are probably surprised at the size of the result in Step 12. That's no reason to panic. It is a reason to seriously reconsider your retirement planning goals if you want to close the gap between where you are today and where you will need to be on the eve of retirement, whether that is in 5 or 35 years. The investment options that follow in this lesson are designed to help you build a strategy that will boost the size of your retirement nest egg without exposing you to undue risk.

Before diving into investment options for retirement, let's first give you some notions of the various withdrawal options available for your retirement plans. After all, how you withdrawal may impact what cash is left over to fund all those ideas during retirement. You'll find wealth-building Step 96 starting on page 10.

INVESTMENT STRATEGIES FOR RETIREMENT

The trouble with conservative investors is that they take too many risks. That may seem like a contradictory statement to you at first blush. After all, isn't avoiding risk the essence of conservative investing? It certainly is if you are talking about market risk, or the risk that securities prices will go down. But when it comes to inflation risk, you may be rolling the dice if you are invested too conservatively — that is, if you are too heavily invested in fixed income securities. If your costs rise with inflation but the income from your portfolio of bonds remains fixed, your purchasing power quickly erodes, as we have discussed in this and earlier lessons.

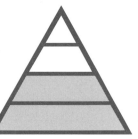

100 Steps to Wealth

How to Select the Appropriate Withdrawal Options for Your Maturing IRA's, 401(k)'s, Etc.

What: Choose the best way to take money out of your defined contribution plan or plans that meets your retirement needs in terms of maximizing your earnings and minimizing your tax bill.

Why: If you make withdrawals before, or not until, certain dates you face stiff penalties and tax consequences. Poor investment decisions made after plan contributions and earnings are withdrawn can have as dramatic an impact on your retirement savings as poor investment planning while you are building your retirement nest egg.

Risk: Low to Medium. If you plan ahead and seek professional advice if your retirement plan assets are likely to exceed roughly $1 million when you retire, then you can keep risks to a minimum. Certain strategies for reducing your tax liability are complicated and can go awry quite easily, however, if you attempt to implement them or if your advisor isn't qualified.

Safety: Medium to High. If you wait until you are close to the final starting date for plan withdrawals, you will probably be pulling assets out of relatively aggressive investment options that provided for long-term growth in your defined contribution plan and putting a greater percentage of them into safer, yield-generating assets. The earlier you begin withdrawing assets, the greater the component you need to leave in growth-oriented equity investments.

Liquidity: Medium to High. When withdrawing assets annually from a defined-contribution plan to cover expenses in retirement or for other uses it is usually wise to keep most, if not all, of the funds in short-term bond or cash equivalent investments. These can be readily converted to cash to cover unexpected costs or emergencies that aren't covered by insurance or other sources.

Why Not: If you withdraw too much money too fast from an IRA, 401(k) or other defined contribution plan, you risk depleting your assets and not leaving yourself enough to live on in later years. If too much builds up in your IRA and you make so-called excessive withdrawals, either more than $150,000 a year or a lump sum over $750,000, it will trigger a 15% tax on the withdrawal, on top of your regular federal, and possibly state, income tax. (This tax even applies on so-called excess distributions from defined contribution plans to your heirs in the event of your death.)

Buy/Invest from: If you haven't already, contact a professional investment advisor or financial planner to review your withdrawal options if the amount of money in your IRA, 401(k), etc. approaches $1 million as you near retirement. At this level you face possible additional tax penalties of 15%, mentioned above, when you start withdrawing your retirement funds. Even if your nest egg is smaller it is still usually worth the money to review your plans with a professional (the fee is probably tax-deductible) to ensure that you are executing the best possible strategy given the amount of your retirement assets, your and and your spouse's expected lifespan and for estate planning purposes, although we'll examine that subject in detail in the next lesson.

Background: Shakespeare wrote eloquently about the "seven ages of Man" that span a lifetime. By the time you approach retirement, there are five important ages you need to remember that have a direct impact on how and when you may want to withdraw assets from defined contribution plans:

- 55: If your take early retirement at 55, quit your job or are fired or laid off, known as being "separated" from your work in bureaucratese, you can receive your 401(k), Keogh or profit-sharing plan funds without paying a 10% early withdrawal penalty to the IRS. (Under certain hardship conditions, including disability, catastrophic illness and to prevent foreclosure on a home, withdrawals at any age from these plans can be made without incurring penalties.)

Step 96: *How to Select the Appropriate Withdrawal Options for Your Maturing IRA's, 401(k)'s, Etc.*

- 59 1/2: Anyone can withdraw money from an IRA, Keogh or other defined contribution plans without paying the 10% penalty. You can also receive a lump-sum pension plan distribution and use forward averaging techniques to reduce your tax bill. An often overlooked detail: You can also withdraw IRA funds prior to age 59 1/2 without penalty if you take the withdrawals in equal annual payments based on your life expectancy.

- 62: You can begin receiving 80% of your eligible Social Security benefits, but remember that if you can wait until you are 65, the monthly payments will be significantly higher. Some companies will allow you to receive full pension benefits if you retire at 62.

- 65: You are eligible for Medicare coverage and full Social Security benefits and at most companies, full pension benefits. (The official age at which full benefits kick in will slowly increase, beginning with those of you born after 1937. Refer to the chart near the middle of the lesson, Work, employment and investment.)

- 70 1/2: You have to begin making withdrawals from IRAs and other plans, the minimum amount depending on your and usually your spouse's remaining life expectancy. If you don't, you face a *50%* tax penalty.

▷ ▶ ▶ ▶ **If you want to get started today, here's what you have to do to select the appropriate withdrawal options for your maturing IRA's, 401(k)'s, etc:**

The first step in most cases is for you to have your 401(k) assets transferred directly into an IRA that you set up expressly for that purpose with an IRA custodian such as a mutual fund management company. If your employer sends the money directly to you, it may be required to withhold 20% for taxes. You can reclaim the money from the IRS when you file your yearend tax returns, but in the meantime you have to make up the 20% in the IRA with your own funds, or else it is considered a permanent taxable withdrawal and penalties may apply. You may be able to leave the money in your company's plan, or have the company transfer the funds directly to your new employer if you change jobs. If you roll the money over into a new IRA, be sure to keep the funds separate from any other IRA and don't make additional contributions to the account. If as little as $1 is added to the rollover IRA, you won't be able to move the fund's into a new employer's 401(k) plan.

Under most circumstances you will want to rollover as much of your defined contribution as possible into an IRA to continue to enjoy the benefits of tax-deferred compounding. Even if you rolled over just $50,000 at age 59 in a growth stock fund, for instance, it would be worth $129,687 by your 69th birthday if it grew at an annual rate of 10%, tax-deferred. ▲

Continued from p. 9

Even though retirement is traditionally seen as a time for you to play it safe financially, you still will need a greater equity component to your portfolio than you think. You have come back down the investing pyramid in terms of market risk, but that doesn't mean you can afford to turn your back on stocks. Of course, there is no magic equity and fixed income percentage that is going to be right for each of you, since we all have different financial requirements in retirement.

As you no doubt have learned in the process of becoming a wealth builder, investing isn't strictly an analytical process that's devoid of emotion. What kind of person you are determines the amount of investment risk you have been willing to shoulder as you accumulated your retirement nest egg. You aren't likely to suddenly become a swashbucking risk taker just because you have retired and now have more time to use your computer in analyzing a company's growth prospects. The tendency you should resist is that little voice telling you that you're getting too old to be buying growth stock or high-yield bond mutual funds.

As we said, studies have shown that more than 90% of a portfolio's performance is the result of asset allocation choices, rather than an investor's ability to pick a specific bond or stock. With that in mind we'll focus on different sectors of the bond and stock markets with an emphasis on higher-yielding, growth-oriented strategies, most using mutual funds. You've spent years working to build your nest egg, it's time to ensure that it works for you and enables you to enjoy a long and relatively worry-free retirement.

Finding the Right Portfolio Mix

Judy Shine, an Englewood, Colo. investment advisor, at first glance seems to be positively frumpy when it comes to making asset allocation recommendations. "Sixty-forty (60% in stocks, 40% in bonds) is as aggressive as I get," she says. For an investor approaching her early years of retirement, say her late 50s, Shine pulls in her horns even further, recommending an approximate 50-50 split between growth and income.

The tendency you should resist is that little voice telling you that you're getting too old to be buying growth stock or high-yield bond mutual funds.

Shine's investment strategy isn't as dull as it looks. The key to what is in fact a fairly progressive investment approach, and what may serve as an example for your retirement needs, is the choices she makes within broad stock and bond categories. Shine's strategy parallels one of the main thrusts of the lessons you have been receiving: The key to enhanced investment returns is to allocate funds to several different investment categories so that the additional risk of any one category is more than offset by the enhanced total return of the portfolio.

On the bond or yield- equivalent side, for instance, she recommends putting 5% of the portfolio in a mutual fund managed by Cohen & Steers that invests in real estate investment trusts as a substitute for owning real estate, which tends to appreciate in step with inflation, gaining when many bond funds are down. The same reasoning underlies a 5% investment in an energy fund, she says, since energy prices tend to move in step with the inflation-sensitive commodity markets. A junk bond fund, managed relatively conservatively by Northeast Investors, boosts yield without adding too much risk.

On the stock side of the equation, she recommends putting a total of 15% of the portfolio into two funds that invest in international stocks, and another 10% in aggressive and small capitalization stock funds. The argument here is that most international economies are going to be growing faster than the U.S. over the next several years, especially the so-called emerging markets in Asia and Latin America. At home, small stocks will tend to do better than larger capitalization issues, she reasons. Her remaining equity emphasis on growth and capital appreciation in US stocks is placed with Harbor Capital Appreciation Fund. Shine's recommended portfolio appears on the next page.

APPROACHING RETIREMENT: ONE MODEL PORTFOLIO

Fund	% of portfolio
COHEN & STEERS	5%
VANGUARD ENERGY	5%
FIDELITY UTILITIES	5%
LOOMIS SAYLES BOND	15%
FIDELITY CONVERTIBLES	10%
NORTHEAST INVESTORS TRUST	10%
HARBOR CAP APPRECIATION	15%
LONGLEAF PARTNERS	10%
WASATCH AGGRESSIVE EQUITY	5%
T. ROWE PRICE SMALL CAP VALUE	5%
FOUNDERS WORLDWIDE	10%
MONTGOMERY EMERGING MARKETS	5%

Source: Shine Investment Advisory Services, Inc., Englewood, CO

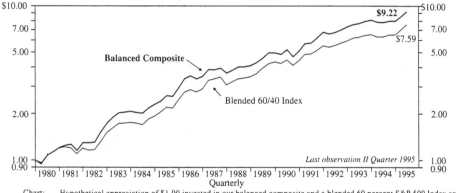

Comparative 15½-YEAR APPRECIATION of our balanced composite[1]

Chart: Hypothetical appreciation of $1.00 invested in our balanced composite and a blended 60 percent S&P 500 Index and 40 percent Salomon Broad Index over the 15½-year period ended June 30, 1995.
Sources: Salomon Brothers, Standard & Poor's, and Miller Anderson & Sherrerd, LLP.

The annualized performance of the model portfolio illustrates the importance of adding exposure to international stock markets, and the high-yield bond market, in order to boost returns.

Indeed, another investment manager, Miller Anderson & Sherrerd, Conshohocken, PA, found that a balanced portfolio including international stocks and bonds and high yield bonds easily out performed a 60-40 mix of U.S. stocks and bonds from 1980 through mid-1995. (See the graph at lower left.) The firm found that $1 invested its customized balanced portfolio of U.S. stocks and bonds, foreign stocks and bonds and high-yield bonds grew to be worth $9.22, net of management fees during the period. One dollar invested in the 60-40 mix of stocks and bonds, however, grew to just $7.59 during the same period. The 60-40 mix is based on 60% reflecting the S&P 500 and 40% the Salomon Broad Index of bond performance.

Remember, this 15 1/2 year pattern of total return (income plus appreciation) — which includes periods of negative return — illustrates the importance of maintaining a long-term investing perspective.

A Word of Caution

Shine and other money managers caution investors, especially those approaching retirement, not to embrace higher risk investment strategies in order to pump up investment returns. One of the worst mistakes an investor can make is to sharply increase the risk profile of his portfolio as a way to "reach" for higher returns, without truly understanding the risks involved. Shine may recommend a stock fund like the potentially higher returning, yet more volatile Harbor Capital Appreciation Fund, but it's worth pointing out that she only recommends putting *15%* of your portfolio in the one fund. "Active money management is not a sport that should replace golf in retirement. Being a bad golfer may be embarrassing, but being a bad money manager is lethal," she says.

Even losses that in percentage terms may seem manageable on paper can have a devastating impact in the real world. That's especially true if you are an older investor approaching retirement. A 20% loss is significant but not the end of the world for an investor in her 30s with another 30 years of active investing in front of her. But for a 60 year-old, losing $100,000 out of a $500,000 investment is an earth-shaking event that would force her to totally revamp her retirement plans. Even a 10% loss at this age can be devastating, especially if it scares you away from the very markets you need to invest in to ensure your retirement funds will continue to grow.

Equities Anonymous

Wealth builders like yourself may think you're largely immune from such concerns. After all, you're following a well thought out course designed to help you obtain financial freedom by significantly growing your investment assets. But Shine cautions that Baby Boomers especially (she is one, too) are a generation that has grown up on "equity steroids." Most boomers were too young to experience first hand the wrenching decline of the stock market in the 1973-74 bear market, when the stock market skidded more than 40% For the most part all this generation has seen is the bull market that began in the early 1980s, and the 1987 crash from which stock prices quickly recovered. The temptation, fueled by the bull market in stocks so far in 1995, is to seek ever more aggressive stock investments to enhance returns without adequately considering the risks. "We should all join Equities Anonymous," Shine says. Before turning to the equity portion of your portfolio, first you should explore different, relatively lower-risk fixed income strategies to enhance returns , she says.

Fixed Income

A key aspect of enhancing the return from the fixed income portion of your retirement portfolio is to own actively managed investments — that usually means mutual funds. For years many academics maintained that it was next to impossible to squeeze a significant amount of additional return out of most fixed income markets by actively managing a bond portfolio compared to the returns from broad-based bond indexes. But for the past decade or so, many of the top active fixed income managers in the US outperformed bond indexes by 7 to 8 percentage points, Shine notes. She hastens to add, however, that 1994, when interest rates kept rising, was a tough year for many bond managers in terms of performance return, as the net asset value of many fixed income funds fell by 6% or more.

As we've said, there is a significant difference between owning a share in a bond mutual fund and owning the bond itself. The bond holder is guaranteed a specified yield and the return of her principal (assuming the issuing company or entity doesn't default or call the bonds early) when the bond matures on a specified date. That kind of assured performance makes a core holding of bonds an important part of most investment portfolios. That assurance becomes even more important, and therefore bonds, and especially shorter-duration Treasury notes and bills, should become a larger part of your core portfolio as you enter your later retirement years — say your early 70s and up. A share in a bond mutual fund, like a share in a stock mutual fund, gives you an ownership interest in a pool of securities. Most bond funds are actively managed, so there is no guarantee that the bonds that were held by the fund managers when you bought your shares will be in the fund for any given length of time.

The best active bond managers don't always hew to a particular style. For that reason its important to ask your financial planner or broker for examples. Two cited by Shine whose investment styles cover large sectors of the fixed income markets, and who are standouts in the industry for their performance record, are Daniel Fuss, manager of the Loomis Sayles Bond Fund, and William Gross, who manages nearly $65 billion in bonds in a number of individual and institutional funds for Newport Beach, Calif. manager Pacific Investment Management Co., or PIMCO. (Many of the PIMCO funds are only available through financial planners or investment advisors.)

Fuss has been managing the $151 million Loomis Sayles Bond fund since 1991. Prior to that he was a long-time money manager for institutional clients of the Boston money management company. The fund normally invests at least 65% of its assets in investment-grade debt securities (including convertible securities), but it may invest up to 35% in below investment grade bonds, and up to 20% in preferred stocks.

Fuss's investment style is to look for special situations in the U.S. and abroad, or particular bonds that may have been overlooked by other money managers, rather than have his investment picks dictated by a broad investment theme or category. This eclectic investment approach has paid off handsomely for investors. Through the first week of September, 1995, the Loomis Sayles Bond fund was up 21.9% for the year, compared to a 13.11% gain year to date for the Merrill Lynch Corporate/Government bond index.

Spanning the globe for overlooked investment opportunities, Fuss's largest holdings in the fund range from Province of Quebec bonds yielding 9.375% and Ontario Hydro bonds with an 8.9% yield, to government bonds issued by New Zealand, Ireland, Brazil and Argentina. and US corporate debt issued by Westinghouse Electric, RJR Nabisco and Time Warner Entertainment. Fuss's investment style "continues to provide high income and substantial diversification outside of the domestic bond market," notes Morningstar Inc. analyst Kathleen Hartman.

PIMCO's Gross couldn't be more different from Fuss, except in the investment return category. The Newport Beach, CA bond manager is known for making bold calls on the direction of the bond markets, and then putting billions of his shareholders' money where his mouth is. Gross has been a raging bull on bonds, especially US Treasury bonds, for much of 1995, arguing that the yield on the 30-year US Government bond would fall to near 5.5% within a year or so as inflation worries subside.

Broaden Your Horizon to Boost Returns

Most investors approaching retirement have too many of their assets concentrated in traditional, moderate to short-term government or corporate bonds. While there's a place for those bonds in nearly every retirement portfolio at some stage of the investing cycle, they shouldn't take up too much space until relatively late in life. The way to boost returns while still retaining the yield-oriented security of bonds is to add higher yielding categories such as real estate investment trusts or Reits, convertible securities and high-yield or "junk" bonds.

Reits

Real estate investment trusts — or Reits, as we've seen before in the course — are diversified portfolios of income-producing properties which trade on exchanges like stocks. These investments give the retiree or soon to be retiree a vehicle with which to "play" the real estate market without actually owning commercial real estate. Having exposure to the real estate market allows investors to own an asset that tends to appreciate in value during inflationary periods, since land and building values, as well as rents, tend to rise in step with inflation. Some money managers argue that many retirees should dedicate a small portion of their retirement nest egg for direct investment in real estate. But the managers also concede that that may seem too risky for many investors, especially after the crash in real estate prices across much of the country in the late 1980s and early 1990s. A retiree who had to lower his asking price on his house in the Northeast or Southern California by 40% to unload it a few years ago isn't likely to be willing to take another direct plunge into the real estate market.

It may be tempting to invest in individual Reits, especially since they appear in the stock listings of newspapers with prices and trading volumes. You may be better off sticking with Reit mutual funds. Given the fact that Reits tend to concentrate on a particular type of real estate, such as self-storage units or regional shopping malls, the diversification that a Reit mutual fund can offer is more than worth the management fee. What's more, there are only slightly more than 200 Reits trading, and many of those went public just within the past year or so, and therefore don't have much of a history as a publicly traded entity. Reits also have confusing financial characteristics — a portion of property dividends are considered a return of capital, not income, so they aren't taxed — which is another reason to leave the selection to the professionals.

Funds that invest solely in Reits are a relatively new phenomenon compared to stock and bond funds. There are fewer than 30 Reit funds, according to Morningstar Inc., the Chicago, IL fund tracking service, although that number is likely to grow in coming years. One of the top performing funds over the past three years is Cohen & Steers Realty Trust.

The $580 million Cohen & Steers fund puts an equal emphasis on capital appreciation and current income by investing in the shares of US Reits, and may also put up to 10% of its assets in the shares of foreign real estate companies. This year the fund has added to its holdings in apartment Reits, based on rising occupancy rates and rents in many key markets around the country, not to mention the dearth of new construction in many regions. The fund's goal is to have between 30% and 35% of its assets in these types of Reits, says co manager Robert Steers. The fund has nearly a quarter of its assets in Reits that own regional shopping malls, based on the theory that many of them have been oversold as investors fret about anemic sales in the retail apparel stores that anchor most of the malls. Another 20% or so of the fund is invested in smaller strip mall shopping centers which tend to be anchored by grocery or drug chain stores. The fund's five largest holdings lately were Developers Diversified Realty (DDR); Rouse (ROUS); Kimco Realty (KIM); DeBartolo Realty (EJD) and Vornado Realty Trust (VNO).

Convertibles

Convertible securities tend to make good yield-boosting investments for retirees. Convertibles, as described in detail in the lesson on convertibles combine the safety or floor value of a bond, based on the future value of its interest payments, with the equity appreciation potential of the stocks into which they are convertible. Convertibles tend to perform well during periods of falling interest rates and rising stock prices. The yield from the bond component of the convertible is enhanced by potentially large returns if the underlying asset into which the bond is convertible, usually common stock, rises in value. If the conversion premium is high — that is, the price of the convertible is well above its value if it were to be exchange for stock — the convertible acts like a bond, moving with changes in interest rates. If the convertion premium (the bond's value in excess of its conversion value) is small, or low, the convertible acts like a stock, moving almost in tandem with the stock's price.

As with Reits, the best way to get a diversified portfolio of convertibles is through one of the nearly 40 convertible bond mutual funds in the US. Most convertible funds keep at least 50% of their assets in convertible securities, either bonds or preferred shares. True to their split personality, convertible funds have posted returns that place them between the returns of broad stock and bond indexes. Fidelity Management's Convertible Securities fund is one, for instance.

The fund managers study the shifting climates as do all managers. Lately the fund started shifting out of certain smaller issues to convertibles issued by larger companies in order to boost liquidity, while still maintaining a major emphasis on nonrated securities. The Fidelity management team's trading prowess was put to the test last year when two of its largest holdings, Media Vision and Regal Communications, went bankrupt, and the fund still finished in the top quartile of funds in it group based on investment returns. Earlier this year Charles Mangum replaced Andy Offit as manager of the fund.

Junk Bonds

At first blush it's hard to imagine why anyone planning for retirement would want to include high yield junk bonds in his or her investment portfolio. Junk bonds tend to be either bonds issued by formerly investment grade companies whose fortunes have soured or by smaller concerns that don't have the track record, financial soundness or other basics to warrant an investment grade rating. The bleaker the outlook for the economy, the greater the chance that junk bond issuers will default. The junk bond default rate hit bottom at about 1% of junk bonds outstanding in 1994. It is likely to peak at about 3% sometime in 1996, according to Martin Fridson, Merrill Lynch's chief high yield strategist.

The relatively high yields junk bonds offer — for the past 10 years junk bonds as a group have yielded about 2% more a year than Treasuries — are the trade-off for the higher risk that the issuers of these bonds may default on interest payments or be forced into bankruptcy. Money managers maintain that the higher yield from junk bonds is worth pursuing with a small portion of your retirement nest egg, Shine recommends no more than 10%, as long as you stick with the diversification and professional management offered by a mutual fund.

Northeast Investors Trust is considered one of the best-managed junk bond funds in the business, with a recent three-year annualized return of 13.88%. Fund manager Bruce Monrad said that the fund is balancing reduced risk short-term bonds with relatively modest yields with holdings in high-yielding emerging market debt. He bought short-term bonds issued by Argentina that yield 24% to maturity, for instance, as well as Brady bonds tied to Brazilian government debt. If stripped into the collateralized (by US government securities) and sovereign portions of the debt, the latter is yielding 22-23% to maturity. The fund is also overweighted in Atlantic City casino senior first-mortgage junk bonds, including Trump properties.

While Northeast Investors is well-managed, this fund may not be for you if you're the type of investor who has trouble sleeping nights, worrying what the net asset value of your fund is going to be tomorrow. To be sure, Monrad seeks to avoid interest-rate risk by keeping much of the fund in bonds that mature in two years or less, and therefore aren't terribly sensitive to swings in interest rates on 30-year bonds, for instance. At the same time he courts credit-quality risk by holding at times more than 40% of the fund in bonds that are rated below B or nonrated. Not the sort of thing that sweet dreams are made of if you're a risk-averse investor or already well into your retirement years.

Turbo-charge your fixed income portfolio

Mutual funds aren't the only way to get higher fixed income yields while also diversifying your holdings and tapping professional management talent. Using a financial planner or broker you can customize or turbo-charge a portion of your fixed income portfolio with the goal of enhancing your investment returns. The two model portfolios below are based on a portfolio of government guaranteed "Cats," or certificates of accrual on Treasury securities. These zero-coupon bonds don't pay any interest until they mature, and therefore are sold at a fairly steep discount. You will, however, owe taxes every year on the interest your zero-coupon bonds accrue if held in a taxable account. You'll owe nothing until after retirement if they are held in a tax-deferred account (subject of course to the usual restrictions, e.g., withdrawal after 59 1/2). The goal is to spend roughly seventy to eighty cents on the dollar face value of the bonds to buy the bonds at a discount. Since the bonds will be held to maturity, at which time they return 100 cents on the dollar, their yield is locked in. To enhance the portfolio's potential appreciation, take the remaining 20 to 30 cents on the dollar and invest most of it in equities, either in the form of mutual funds or individual stocks.

Objective: To provide a managed government portfolio with above average return. Buy a "ladder" of sequentially maturing Cats, and use the balance to buy stock mutual funds.

Assumptions:
1. Below average risk.
2. Portfolio government guaranteed
3. Projected performance to exceed 9%

Asset Allocation:

Cash	1.9%
Debt	71.7%
Equity	26.4%

Quantity	Portfolio Issue	Recent Market Value	Anticipated Income
Cash			
1,901	MONEY MKT FD	**$1,901**	$66
Debt			
10,000	TRES CPN 0% 8/15/96	$9,465	0
10,000	CAT 0% 11/15/97	$8,788	0
10,000	STRIP 0% 8/15/98	$8,416	0
10,000	CUBS 0% 8/15/99	$7,922	0
10,000	TRES CPN 0% 8/15/00	$7,395	0
10,000	CAT 0% 11/15/01	$6,788	0
10,000	REFCO 0% 10/15/02	$6,422	0
10,000	CAT 0% 11/15/03	$5,898	0
10,000	ETR 0% 11/15/04	$5,451	0
10,000	STRIP 0% 11/15/05	$5,154	0
	Cats Subtotal	**$71,699**	
Equity	**Growth Funds**		
525	STATE STREET RESEARCH CAP. B	$6,600	0
472	PUTNAM VOYAGER B	$6,600	0
Equity	**Growth & Income Funds**		
254	OPPENHEIMER MAIN ST. B	$6,600	$152
457	N. AMER. GWTH & INCOME B	$6,600	$85
	Funds Subtotal	**$26,400**	

Portfolio Value	**$100,000**
Anticipated annual income	**$303.00**
Projected annual income	**0.30%**
Projected annual accreation	**6.08%**
Projected annual growth	**4.26%**
Est. management fee	**1.00%**
Projected total return	**9.64%**

Source: Robert J. Oberst, Sr. & Associates, Red Bank, N.J.

Portfolio Objective: Boost return from deep discount Cats by buying stocks with potential high returns, and high risks.

Assumptions:

1. The portfolio principal to be government guaranteed — the Cats.
2. The equity position to seek high potential gain — the dogs.
3. Projected performance to exceed 9%
4. All fees and commissions will come out of one management fee.

Asset Allocation

Cash	1.7%
Debt	79.67%
Equity	18.63%

Proposed Managed Portfolio

Quantity	Portfolio Issue	Recent Market Value	Anticipated Income
Cash			
1,708	MONEY MKT FD	**1,708**	$60
DEBT			
100,000	LOS ANGELES 0% 4/1/01	**$79,667**	0
Equity			
400	CHIPS & TECHNOLOGY	$5,200	0
300	INSITUFORM	$4,500	0
600	ORBITAL ENGINE	$4,575	0
300	WOOLWORTH	$4,350	$45
	Equity Subtotal	**$18,625**	

Portfolio Value	**$100,000**
Anticipated annual income	$105.00
Projected annual income	0.11%
Projected annual accreation	4.48%
Projected annual growth	5.48%
Est. Management Fee	1.00
Projected total return	9.07%

Source: Robert J. Oberst, Sr. & Associates.

Equities

Too many investors don't hold enough equities in retirement portfolios to begin with. But if they do own stocks, their holdings tend to be concentrated in tried and true blue chip issues. Again, that looks like a pretty smart strategy when the 30-stock Dow Jones Industrial Average is trading in or near record territory. Longer-term, it means that you will miss out on the historically superior performance of smaller stocks, as we've said. The difference of two percentage points of return, 12% v. 10%, or roughly the historical advantage small stocks have over blue chips, doesn't sound like much. Magnified over 30 years of retirement investing, however, it can make a huge difference in the amount of money you'll have with which to enjoy your retirement. And if many international investment experts are right and foreign markets, including smaller so-called emerging markets, are likely to outpace the US market in coming years, then a blue chip strategy means you may miss out on much of the action in these markets as well.

Does that mean you should boot blue chips out of your retirement portfolio? Not at all. It does suggest, however, that, as with fixed income strategies, you should pursue a number of equity investment strategies that are intended to boost your long-term returns above what you could expect from the blue-chip averages. The Harbor Capital Appreciation Fund in Shine's model portfolio above, for instance, seeks long-term capital appreciation of stocks in companies with at least $1 billion in assets. Its recent red-hot performance is due to a nearly 30% weighting in high flying technology issues. At the opposite end of the blue chip spectrum is the following example of a manger who buys blue chips that are cheap relative to the rest of the market. Certain investors may feel more comfortable keeping a portion of their retirement equity hold-ings in a mutual fund that tracks the performance of the S&P 500 stock index. (The low-cost S&P 500 index fund offered by Vanguard Group is just one quick suggestion.)

Boosting Your Return, Stock By Stock

Most experts agree that if your are a retiree or on the brink of retirement, you should stick mainly to mutual funds as an efficient and relatively low-cost way to diversify their holdings. However, it still may be advisable to keep a portion of your retirement funds in individual stocks. This strategy allows you to take advantage of any individual stock ideas or recommen-dations you may come across. It also allows you to continue to have some fun if you wish as an active investor, especially if you built a portion of your retirement nest egg via savvy stock picking, either by following good advice or finding the stocks on your own.

A portfolio consisting mainly of individual stocks you pick on your own, combined with hold-ings in a few income-oriented mutual funds, doesn't have to be any more volatile than broad market indices. At the same time it should still being able to easily outpace the anticipated rate of inflation. The following model portfolio was constructed with the help of Robert J. Oberst, Sr. & Associates, Red Bank, N.J., and was designed for a New Jersey state resident - hence the state tax-exempt issues.

MODEL GROWTH AND INCOME PORTFOLIO

Portfolio Objective: To provide a total equity income portfolio with average risk and growth potential to beat inflation.

Assumptions:
1. Average risk.
2. High concentration of issues that have a consistent record of earnings/dividend increases.
3. Issues with Betas of 1 or less — meaning their price volatility is equal to the broader market or lower.
4. Projected performance to exceed 8%

Asset Allocation:

Cash	4.8%
Growth	24.6%
Income	70.6%

Quantity	Issue	Recent Market Value	Anticipated Income
Cash			
10,000	MONEY MARKET ACCOUNT	**$10,000**	$475
Growth & Income			
20,000	WASHINGTON MUTUAL	$20,000	$620
200	J. C. PENNEY	$9,275	$384
200	PEPSICO	$9,326	$160
200	BF GOODRICH	$12,075	$440
	Growth & income subtotal	**$50,676**	
Income			
20,000	NUVEEN NJ TAX EXEMPT	$20,000	$1,220
20,000	VKM NJ TAX EXEMPT	$20,000	$1,220
300	BELL ATLANTIC	$17,542	$840
300	FREEPORT-MCMORAN	$7,012	$500
300	DUN & BRADSTREET	$17,737	$895
1,000	OPPENHEIMER MULTI SECTOR	$9,625	$952
1,000	ACM GOV'T SECURITIES	$9,250	$989
500	UNITED DOMINION RLTY	$7,000	$450
400	NUI CORP.	$6,000	$360
400	OGDEN CORP.	$9,400	$500
300	UST INC.	$8,400	$420
300	HARTFORD STEAM BOILER	$13,800	$875
	Income subtotal	**$145,766**	

Portfolio Value	**$206,442**
Anticipated annual income	**$11,100**
Projected annual income	**5.38%**
Projected annual growth	**4.00%**
Projected total return	**9.38%**

Before examining what is the course's final investment vehicle — annuities — let's briefly wrap-up the section on planning for retirement's cash needs with wealth-building Step 97, Calculate the Timing Needs of Your Estate. You'll find it beginning on page 22.

ANNUITIES

One retirement investment option that you may want to consider are annuities. An annuity is a contract between you and, in most cases, an insurance company, although it is not life insurance. You pay a premium to the life insurance company, either in one lump payment or in several periodic payments, depending on the type of annuity, and the insurance company guarantees to pay you income in the future. Certain annuities provide for a guaranteed income stream in retirement beginning a few months after you make a lump sum payment and lasting the rest of your life. That may fit your retirement needs if you want to take your IRA, for instance, and convert it into a stream of guaranteed payments. Annuities can also be another means of having gains in your retirement account accumulate on a tax-deferred basis, without the dollar limits or excess withdrawal penalties imposed on 401(k)s, IRAs or similar vehicles.

100 Steps to Wealth

STEP 97

Calculate the Timing Needs of Your Estate and Act Early When Necessary

What: Start planning and investing now in tax-deferred plans, such as 401(k)s or IRAs, to ensure that your funds will grow to meet your retirement needs.

Why: The sooner you start, the sooner your retirement nest egg can grow, tax-deferred preferably, and enable you to enjoy your retirement years. If you start funding a defined contribution plan like a 401(k) plan in your 20s and your employer contributes, by the time you retire less than 10% of the value of the plan will be from contributions. More than 90% is from the tax-deferred compounding effect. The same effect, although with progressively less dramatic results as you get older, works for you up until you withdraw your retirement funds.

Risk: Low to Medium. By investing for retirement as soon as reasonably possible, you maximize the effect of compounding earnings, and minimize the impact of periodic market slumps that may temporarily reduce the value of your portfolio by 10% to 15%

Safety: Medium to High. Again, time is on your side. Leaving your retirement funds fully invested and in a variety of asset classes, including growth stocks, some of which will produce returns ahead of inflation, helps reduce your inflation and market risk.

Liquidity: Low to Medium. The trade-off for receiving tax-deferred compounding on your defined contribution plan is a serious penalty for withdrawing funds too early, before 59 1/2 in most cases. Many 401(k) plans allow you to borrow against your funds to fund the purchase of a house or a college education, for instance, but borrowing can cut deeply into your investment returns if the loans aren't repaid quickly.

Why Not: Lack of liquidity. Tying up much of your investment funds in tax-deferred vehicles designed to fund your retirement may not be the wisest use of your assets. Housing and college costs, among others, aren't likely to decline in coming years. Be sure you have planned ahead for these and other mid-life costs before socking away every savings dollar for retirement. You can tap funds that you have already set aside for retirement to pay for certain other needs, but it can be an expensive proposition in terms of possible IRS penalties and lost earnings power in your retirement nest egg.

Buy/Invest from: Your company benefits office will provide you with information on a 401(k) if such a plan is available. Nearly any mutual fund management company or other financial institution will help you set up an IRA. Financial planners and investment advisors will, for a fee, also help you fine-tune your investing needs depending on your financial situation and goals. There are a number of computer software financial planning packages on the market as well that allow you to perform "what if" calculations by changing assumed inflation rates and rates of return on your investment.

Background: It is all but impossible to over-emphasize the importance of benefiting from tax-free compounding of investment returns as soon as possible in your investing career. Investing relatively modest sums in your 30s and 40s in growth-oriented investments can go a long way toward financing your retirement, and help you avoid taking excessive investment risks later in life if you try to make up for lost time, and money.

By the same token, you may not fully appreciate just how drastically inflation can, and will, even at current modest rates of about 3% a year, erode your purchasing power in retirement. You can use the following table to estimate how much extra money you'll need when you retire to preserve the purchasing power of monthly payments that won't be adjusted for inflation during retirement. For example, if you estimate that your after-tax rate of return will be 6 percent, inflation will be 4 percent, and you'll be retired for 25 years, to preserve the purchasing power of a monthly $2,500 pension, you'll need $2,500 x 80.1190, or $200,297.50.

Step 97: *Calculate the Timing Needs of Your Estate and Act Early When Necessary*

**Factor to determine money needed to maintain
$2,500 in month living expenses**

Years into retirement	Inflation	After-Tax Rate of Return				
		5%	6%	7%	8%	9%
5	3%	3.9265	3.7983	3.6749	3.5561	3.4418
	4%	5.3207	5.1467	4.9791	4.8179	4.6626
	5%	6.7603	6.5387	6.3254	6.1201	5.9224
10	3%	14.1537	13.2670	12.4437	11.6788	10.9680
	4%	19.5080	18.2803	17.1405	16.0820	15.0984
	5%	25.2207	23.6261	22.1462	20.7720	19.4953
15	3%	28.6106	26.0161	23.6902	21.6030	19.7279
	4%	40.1162	36.4519	33.1687	30.2238	27.5797
	5%	52.7979	47.9398	43.5892	39.6891	36.1893
20	3%	45.7479	40.4020	35.7707	31.7510	28.2556
	4%	65.2634	57.5591	50.8911	45.1095	40.0872
	5%	87.4788	77.0454	68.0243	60.2104	53.4296
25	3%	64.4166	55.3164	47.6905	41.2812	35.8782
	4%	93.5057	80.1190	68.9189	59.5213	51.6127
	5%	127.6951	109.1656	93.6883	80.7239	69.8327

▷ ▶ ▶ ▶ **If you want to get started today, here's what you need to do to plan ahead to anticipate your retirement needs:**

If you are a relatively young wealth builder, say in your 20s or early 30s, it may be difficult to calculate your retirement costs in any detail. (If three of you are sharing a rental apartment today, how do you know what your housing costs are going to be in retirement?) Don't let that stop you from forging ahead with earmarking at least a portion of your savings for retirement. The benefits of compounding we've described here are simply too attractive to pass up. In fact, a recent study showed that starter investors in their 20s were actually saving a greater portion of their incomes for retirement than were many Baby Boomers in their 30s and 40s. So much for the sobriquet "slackers!"

Conversely, if you are in your 40s or 50s and haven't done any serious retirement savings, there also is no time like the present. You however, will be able to have a much better sense of your retirement needs than a 25-year-old. You also will have to get serious about not only putting away more money for retirement investing, but thinking about reducing your expenditures as well to shake loose even more money for your retirement nest egg. Don't, however, make the mistake of reaching for returns and making high-risk investments that could throw your account for a loss and actually leave you worse off than you started! ▲

Continued from p.21

Be forewarned. There are some serious concerns about annuities you need to consider before favoring this investment vehicle over similar alternatives:

- Those guaranteed annuity payments are fixed, while inflation is not, so your future purchasing power may be eroded.

- Annuity fees often run 1% to 2% above no-load mutual funds.

- Then there are surrender charges of 1% to 15% of the cash value of the annuity if you pull your money out before a certain period, usually 5 to 10 years.

- On top of that are the IRS penalties that are similar to the treatment of IRAs and 401(k) accounts — a 10% penalty on funds withdrawn before age 59 1/2, with all earnings treated as taxable income.

- Deffered annuities are generally only good investments for someone who is 10 years or more from retirement because of the early withdrawal penalties and related liquidation costs.

There are two basic types of annuities — immediate and deferred.

Immediate annuities. With an immediate annuity, you make a lump sum or "single" payment, with a minimum of $5,000, and start receiving income within a few months, and no later than 12 months after making the payment. The guaranteed monthly income lasts the rest of your life, and if you specify, the life of your spouse. The amount of the monthly payment is based on several factors: the amount of the payment you made to the insurer, actuarial tables on the life expectations of people your age, and interest rate expectations. Many people take the money they've saved in IRAs during their working years and buy immediate annuities so they can lock in a guaranteed source of income. If they are over 59 1/2 they can do so without incurring any early payment penalties.

The guarantee on an annuity is only as good as the insurance company issuing the annuity.

Deferred annuities. As the name implies, with a deferred annuity, earnings on your investment accumulate on a tax-deferred basis. Within this category there are two main subsets — fixed and variable.

Deferred fixed-rate annuities are somewhat similar to certificates of deposit. Typically, you will make an initial investment of $5,000 or more and receive a fixed interest rate for a certain period, say one, three or five years. The yields tend to track those of CDs with similar durations. After the end of the specified guarantee period, a new rate is set. In the meantime, the yield on the annuity doesn't fluctuate, despite changing interest rates and other events that may have an impact on fixed income securities prices.

An important difference between deferred fixed-rate annuities and CDs: Your investment in CDs, up to $100,000 per account, is insured by the Federal Deposit Insurance Corp., or FDIC, an agency of the U.S. Treasury Dept. The guarantee on an annuity is only as good as the insurance company issuing the annuity. Evaluations from insurance ratings companies including A.M. Best, Standard & Poor's, and Moody's, should be available in your local library. Look for a rating no lower than A-plus or the equivalent from two of the three. Moody's average insurance company rating is about Aa2 or Aa3. Check financial magazines such as *Money* and others for periodic updates on the health of the insurance industry and the ratings of the top companies.

Most annuities allow you to withdraw once a year up to a certain amount of money, often 10% of the total value of the annuity, without incurring any penalties. The IRS treats withdrawals from annuities first as income, which is taxable, and then as a return of your investment, which isn't taxable. For instance, if you made a lump sum payment of $75,000 into an annuity and earned $40,000 of income on the investment, the IRS will tax the first $40,000 of any withdrawal you make as income. Even if you make a withdrawal from a fixed rate annuity, the balance you leave in the account continues to earn interest at the guaranteed rate.

Deferred variable annuities are similar to a 401(k) account invested in mutual funds. You fund the investment with either a lump sum payment or periodic payments. You have the opportunity to earn higher, tax-deferred returns by assuming the higher risks associated with a number of investment options, including stocks, bonds and other securities. In fact, many insurers offer deferred variable annuities in association with a mutual fund company that actually manages the money. In most cases you can switch your assets among the investment options without incurring any charges or tax penalties.

The term variable refers to your investment returns, which will vary depending on which investment option or options you have chosen. If your annuity is heavily invested in small growth stocks and that sector of the market does well, so does your annuity. Some variable annuities offer a guaranteed minimum return on your investment, or a fixed rate account into which you can channel a portion of your funds to lock in a guaranteed return on that amount of money.

Too Many Annuities, Too Little Information

These examples hardly exhaust the annuity options available to investors. In fact, one of the major drawbacks of annuity investing is the myriad types of annuities available. With so many bells and whistles to choose from, each carrying a different fee structure, it is difficult for you to do all but the most basic comparison shopping among annuities.

The following weekly listing of variable annuities from *Barron's* gives you an idea of the kind of information that will be available for your use in tracking the performance of your annuity investment. The data includes each contract's accumulated unit value as of Wednesday, and its 4- and 52-week total returns. Performance figures reflect the effects of investment-related charges on the underlying funds, and also include insurance and other charges levied at the separate-account level. But the data, which is compiled by Lipper Analytical Services, Summit, NJ, doesn't include the potential effects of sales or redemption charges.

VARIABLE ANNUITIES

Fund Name	Unit Price	4 Week % Total Return	52 Week % Total Return
AAL CAPITAL MGMT CORP			
VARIABLE ANNUITY ACCOUNT I			
Balanced	10.293	0.64	N/A
Bond	10.046	0.76	N/A
Large Co Stock	10.466	0.51	N/A
Money Mkt	1.009	0.32	N/A
Small Co Stock	10.759	1.93	N/A
AETNA LIFE INS & ANNUITY CO			
VARIABLE ANNUITY ACCT B			
Inv Adviser NQ I	16.759	0.95	14.57
Inv Adviser NQ II	16.697	0.95	14.51
Inv Adviser NQ III	16.657	0.95	14.51
Var Encore NQ I	37.100	0.33	4.46
Var Encore NQ II	37.750	0.33	4.39
Var Encore NQ III	35.530	0.33	4.39
Income Shs NQ I	43.829	0.87	9.47
Income Shs NQ II	45.794	0.87	9.40
Income Shs NQ III	44.260	0.87	9.40
TCI Growth NQ II	13.158	2.92	26.92
Variable NQ I	156.516	0.83	16.71
Variable NQ II	110.275	0.82	16.64
Variable NQ III	105.603	0.82	16.64
AETNA LIFE INS & ANNUITY CO			
VARIABLE ANNUITY ACCT C			
Inv Advisers Q I	16.780	0.95	14.57
Inv Advisers Q III	16.718	0.95	14.51
Var Encore Q I	37.890	0.33	4.46
Var Encore Q III	37.408	0.33	4.39
Var Encore Q IV	29.603	0.35	4.65
Income Shs Q I	45.000	0.87	9.47

Fund Name	Unit Price	4 Week % Total Return	52 Week % Total Return
MUT AM All Amer	4.224	1.56	23.41
MUT AM Bond	2.549	0.94	10.46
MUT AM Composite	3.205	1.41	10.45
MUT AM Equity Indx	1.288	0.50	19.28
MUT AM M-T Bond	1.114	0.57	8.43
MUT AM Money Mkt	1.776	0.33	4.29
MUT AM S-T Bond	1.078	0.35	4.65
Scudder Bond	10.691	0.93	8.78
Scudder Cap Growth	17.783	0.82	14.79
Scudder Intl	11.594	-2.05	0.12
TCI Growth	12.109	2.93	27.16
VIP Equity Inc	17.782	1.16	N/A
VIP2 Asset Mgr	14.898	0.58	N/A
VIP2 Contra	13.464	1.79	N/A
AMERICAN REPUBLIC INS CO			
PAINEWEBBER ADVANTAGE ANNUITY			
Asset Allocation	16.806	1.79	11.18
Dividend Growth	10.861	1.36	13.00
Global Growth	13.883	-3.69	-13.07
Global Income	15.785	-0.02	8.03
Government	14.680	0.86	8.26
Growth	23.791	1.18	9.59
Money Mkt	13.353	0.29	3.60
AMERICAN SKANDIA LIFE ASSUR			
ADVISORS CHOICE			
Alger Growth	13.962	4.61	35.59
Alger Mid Cap Gro	14.854	5.24	45.71
Alger Small Cap	14.896	4.37	52.83
AST Federated HY	10.787	0.03	11.74
AST Federated Util	10.397	0.31	6.83
AST Foundrs Cap Ap	13.789	1.75	31.51
AST Henderson Intl	10.889	-0.64	-1.40
AST INVESCO Eq Inc	11.417	0.54	14.51
AST JanCap Growth	12.520	2.36	28.25
AST Lord Abbett Gl	12.206	0.29	15.94
AST Money Mkt	10.546	0.34	4.32

Straight life, or life only — Makes payments for as long as you live. There are no payments to anyone after you die. Your heirs don't receive a refund of any of the money you paid for the annuity, even if you die shortly after buying the annuity. You are gambling that your will live longer than average. The insurance company is betting that your life span will correspond with the actuarial tables for your age group and sex — that was one of the major considerations they made in setting the amount of money you receive each month. Odds may be on your side if your parents and grandparents lived into their late 80s or 90s.

Everything else being equal, single life annuities offer the highest returns, while your receipts will be reduced if you take a life policy that guarantees payments for five, 10 or 15 years. Your return will be lower still with a joint and survivor option with a guaranteed return.

Refund — Provides that payments will at least equal the amount of cash you paid in. If death occurs before all of the money is paid out, your beneficiary will receive the balance, possibly in installments.

Joint and survivor — Provides payments for as long as either you or your designated survivor lives. For a given amount of money invested the monthly payout will be lower than the straight life payout, reflecting the likely increased term of payments.

Period, or term certain — Makes payments for your lifetime with a guaranteed minimum of years, such as 10 or 20. As with the joint and survivor option, this feature reduces the size of the monthly payout compared to the straight life option.

Prepare to
Cough: Reverse
Adverse
Selection

There is a fascinating quirk in the pricing of annuities. Studies indicate quite clearly that in general people who buy life annuities are "healthier" that the average for the population. In the lingo of actuaries, these people have higher mortality rates (they live longer). This is built into the pricing structure for annuities by insurers.

There is an important implication of this so-called reverse adverse selection. If you are unhealthy, you should, by shopping around, be able to find a company willing to quote you higher rates of return than the norm since your life expectancy is lower than average.

When You Buy an Annuity, remember these four points:

- Stick with a product from one of the major insurers you're familiar with. Just because you haven't heard of a particular insurer doesn't mean that it is offering an inferior product, but it is usually wiser, especially as you near retirement, to do business with "household names" that have a good reputation in your community.

- Demand that the broker or insurance agent with whom you are dealing provide you with written explanations of all fees, up front and annual or deferred, and withdrawal or surrender penalties, that apply to the specific annuity you are considering buying.

- For deferred fixed rate annuities, beware of high "teaser" or up-front interest rates offered to attract new buyers. Ask for the company's listing of credited interest rates on deferred fixed rate annuities, and compare them to market rates available at the time.

- High rates may also indicate that the annuity will be invested in higher risk, low grade junk bonds. You may be willing to assume that risk in return for the higher rate, but you should know what you're getting into.

Now that you've read the menu of annuity options you're no doubt still wondering back to whether fixed or variable annuities are best for you. That's why we've summarized the decision factors into wealth-building Step 98, found beginning on page 28.

Shop Around   Suppose you want to take your entire $1 million retirement nest egg and put it in a single premium life annuity. What can you expect for your annual return?

There are a number of factors that will determine what you get:
1. **Your age:** Everything else being equal, the older you are, the greater the return you will be offered on an annuity. To put it another way, the older you are, the lower the price (premium) that you will pay to buy a specific monthly stream of annuity payments.

Questions to Ask About Annuities

- Are there front-end charges or annual administrative fees? How much are they and how will they affect your return?

- What is the current interest rate? How often does it change and what impact will the changes have on your future earnings?

- What is the minimum interest rate guaranteed in the contract?

- Is there a "bailout option" that permits you to cash in the annuity without withdrawal penalties (there may be tax penalties) if the interest rate drops below a specified amount?

- Are there surrender charges if you decide not to keep the contract? Do these charges gradually decrease to zero over a period of years? How much can you withdraw at any one time without paying a charge? How will your earnings be taxed if you decide to cash in early?

- What is the quality and ranking of the insurer that issued the annuity?

2. **Your Sex:** Women have higher life expectancies than men and hence, women receive lower annuity returns than males of comparable age.

3. **Your Health:** This is a somewhat macabre yet nevertheless important relationship. The annuity quotes are based on life expectancies of persons of specific ages of average or normal health. If you are very unhealthy, you can expect to receive higher annuity returns on life annuities than a healthy person. But you have to able to demonstrate this state to the insurance company.

4. **Type of Annuity:** Everything else being equal, single life annuities offer the highest returns, while your receipts will be reduced if you take a life policy that guarantees payments for five, 10 or 15 years. Your return will be lower still with a joint and survivor option with a guaranteed return.

5. **The Issuer:** While it is true that most insurance and trust companies have similar operating strategies and portfolios, no two are identical. Rates or payments offered on particular annuities at a specific time will vary widely depending on the exact composition of the asset/liability mix of each company, embedded rates on their existing assets, their expectations for future interest rates and other such factors. Some companies will not be anxious to sell annuities at a particular time and will purposely be providing "low ball" quotes. Other companies specialize in certain types of annuities (e.g., joint and survivor annuity contracts for couples aged 70 and over) and usually offer higher payments for a specific annuity purchase than competitors. These issues underscore the absolute necessity of shopping carefully for an annuity.

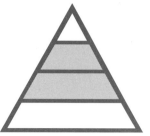

STEP 98

Choose Between Variable or Fixed Annuities

What: If you decide you want to put all or at least a portion of your retirement funds in annuities, one of the most important decisions you have to make is whether you want to receive payments that are at a fixed rate, regardless of changes in market conditions or the rate of inflation, or whether you want payments that may fluctuate, or vary, depending on the returns generated by the money you invest in the annuity.

Why: The decision you make on how to receive payments from an annuity drives all your other decisions. If you are comfortable receiving a fixed rate of return, then you may want to buy a straight life annuity, which pays a fixed rate of return to you starting within a few months and lasting the rest of your life. There are several other varieties of annuities that also are based on fixed rates, such as a deferred fixed rate annuity, which pays a fixed rate beginning on a future date and lasting for a specified period, such as 5 or 10 years. If however, you are concerned that inflation may eat away at the value of your fixed payments in retirement, and that you want to have a say in how the funds in the annuity are invested to take advantage of changing market conditions, then a variable rate annuity is for you. They also come in several different varieties.

Risk: Low to Medium. With fixed annuities, your payments are guaranteed, as long as the insurer selling you the contract remains in good financial health. Inflation may eat away at your purchasing power. With variable annuities you assume the risk that during a market downturn your investment may lose value. You also have the ability to shift funds into better performing markets without paying penalties in most cases. Many variable annuities also include a guaranteed "floor" level of return on your investment for a certain period.

Safety: Medium to High. Most insurance companies or other institutions selling fixed annuities take the money they receive from you and other customers and invest the bulk of it in investment grade securities, from fixed income bills, notes and bonds to medium and large capitalization stocks. If you buy a variable annuity, you make the choice from an investment menu, which may also include small stocks and other higher risk, potentially higher return, securities. Some insurers offering above average returns on certain types of annuities may be investing customers' funds in higher risk junk bonds. Ask where your money will be invested.

Liquidity: Low to Medium. Annuities are tax-deferred investments. As with IRAs and 401(k)s, you pay a 10% penalty in most cases — exceptions include disability and setting up a series of payments based on your life expectancy — for withdrawing funds before 59 1/2. Your insurance company may allow one withdrawal a year without adding a penalty if you withdraw funds.

Why Not: The relative lack of liquidity and penalties for withdrawals may mean that you are tying up your money in an annuity and missing out on other investment opportunities. Inflation may sharply reduce the purchasing power of a fixed life annuity, especially if you live several years beyond your predicted life expectancy. If you meet with financial difficulty or an emergency and need to cash in the annuity, insurers will charge you a surrender charge, designed to recoup their sales expenses, of as much as 15% in the first contract year.

Buy/Invest from: Insurance companies and other financial institutions such as mutual fund management companies that offer annuities in conjunction with insurers.

Background: Annuities have traditionally been fixed-rate investments, with variations on who receives the fixed payments, and when. Single straight life annuities are the simplest, paying a monthly

Step 98: *Choose Between Variable or Fixed Annuities*

income to you for the rest of your life. A common variation is the joint and survivor annuity in which you or a specified person (usually your spouse) receive the annuity payments until the second person's death. With a deferred fixed-rate annuity, you receive a fixed return on an annuity beginning at a future date, say the year you retire, and continuing for a specified period such as 5, 10 or 20 years. The growth of variable annuity offerings over the past 15 years was principally a competitive response by the insurance industry to the continuing boom in mutual fund sales, and the much higher rates of return (and higher risk) offered by many aggressive stock funds compared to traditional fixed-rate annuities.

▷ ▷ ▷ ▶ **If you want to get started today, here is what you need to do to decide whether variable or fixed annuities are the best-suited for your retirement needs:**

How comfortable are you with receiving a fixed rate of return on your investment? If you don't think inflation will be much of a problem for your expected life span, or that of your spouse, then you may want to consider a fixed rate annuity — either an immediate annuity that begins paying returns within a month or two, depending on the details of the policy, or a deferred annuity that begins payments at a future date, say the year you retire.

Let's ask the question another way. What amount of investment flexibility are you willing to give up, and what amount of inflation risk are you willing to assume, to have the investment decisions taken out of your hands when you retire or at a later date during your retirement? The lessons you have been receiving have repeatedly encouraged you to take control of your financial future and be a wealth builder. But don't underestimate the comfort you may feel at some point in shifting the decision making burden to another's (in this case an insurance company's) shoulders. If you decide that you have earned the right not to worry about what impact the stock market is going to have on your future retirement income, then you will probably want to choose a fixed annuity.

If on the other hand, you want your retirement nest egg to have a better chance of keeping pace with inflation and benefiting from future gains in the securities markets, particularly the stock market, then you should favor variable annuities. ▲

Continued from p. 27

RECENT QUOTES FROM FOUR INSURERS
Monthly Amount Payable to Annuity Holder Every Month for Life
for a Single Premium Annuity of $1 Million

Male Age	Quotes from Four Insurance Companies			
	A	B	C	D
50	$6,725	$6,130	$6,640	$7,206
55	7,141	6,555	6,960	7,655
60	7,737	7,120	7,420	8,284
65	8,638	7,930	8,100	9,208
70	9,977	9,090	9,070	10,541
75	11,965	10,660	10,480	12,471
80	15,001	12,810	NA	15,368

Quotes can change daily.
Source: Blackman Kallick Bartelstein, Chicago.

The sidebar at left shows quotes taken from four insurance companies. Each company quoted on how much monthly income they would pay if given a $1 million premium at various ages of an annuity holder. Note the wide disparity in monthly payments! At age 75 there's a variation of $1,485 a month between company A at $11,965 and company C at $10,480. This underscores the importance of shopping around.

Personal Issues: All in the Family

The next lesson deals in detail with estate planning and tax issues, so we'll just touch on some personal aspects of estate planning now and leave the details until later. If you are a successful wealth builder you most likely have not only been building a retirement nest egg, you have been accumulating an estate, as well, that will be passed on to your spouse or other heirs at your death. The most successful investors aim to live off the interest generated by their retirement investments, which leaves the bulk of their retirement assets in the form of an estate. That may not be realistic for you, but if you have planned conservatively for retirement you most likely will be leaving a portion of your savings to your heirs.

If your spouse, who is also most likely your principal beneficiary, hasn't been actively involved in the retirement planning process up to this point — it's better late than never! Make sure your spouse understands the thought process that went into the retirement decisions you have made.

If you're like most people you may not feel very comfortable talking about death, especially your own! But most experts say it is important to involve the entire family in the estate planning process if you want to help ensure that all of the time and money you've put into retirement planning doesn't come to naught as your heirs squabble over how to invest what you have left them or otherwise let your money divide them.

If you want your heirs to understand why you have chosen a particular estate planning vehicle via which to leave them your money, explain how you accumulated the wealth in the first place. Using steps similar to those included in this lesson, demonstrate to them the importance of compounding tax-deferred investment returns and anticipating the corrosive effects of inflation. That kind of background will help them understand the importance of seeking similar strategies in the future, and may even help pass the wealth building skills you've acquired on to the next generation.

If your spouse, who is also most likely your principal beneficiary, hasn't been actively involved in the retirement planning process up to this point — it's better late than never! Make sure your spouse understands the thought process that went into the retirement decisions you have made. Go over the investment results for each asset class, small stocks, convertible bonds, etc., as well as each type of retirement savings vehicle you have used — 401(k), IRA, company pension plan, etc. Introduce your spouse to any investment or estate planning professionals who advise you on important decisions in this area. Discuss how, if at all, your investments will be reconfigured upon your death for tax and estate planning reasons, and what this will mean for the income likely to be received by your spouse and other heirs. And make sure your spouse knows where all your investment and estate planning records are kept.

Wrapping It Up: Enjoy it, it's your money. With all of the number-crunching and decision making that goes into a successful retirement plan, it's easy to forget what the fuss is all about. You're making the effort now so you can enjoy your retirement years. And when we say enjoy, we mean pursue activities, such as an active travel schedule, that are going to cost you money. There's nothing wrong with spending most of your time puttering around in the garden if that's what you want to do. But if you have followed the steps in this lesson, we're confident that you will be able to afford to do much more if you so choose. ▲

Estate planning: your golden years

100 Steps to Wealth

LESSON 32

Estate planning: your golden years

"In this world nothing is certain but death and taxes."
— Benjamin Franklin

INTRODUCTION

Estate planning has undoubtedly been at the top of your to-do list for some time — ranking right up there with making that dental appointment. All teasing aside, if you're like most of us, you view estate planning as a necessary evil — necessary (unless you relish the thought of Uncle Sam becoming your biggest beneficiary), but evil in that it is both drudging and it places you face to face, however briefly, with your own mortality. Perhaps subconsciously, then, we all relegate estate planning to the bottom of our lists.

Serious wealth-builders cannot afford that luxury though. It makes little sense to work so hard, over so many years, all to let the failure to take that final planning step — establishing a properly constructed estate — to cause so much of the fruits of the effort to slip into the hands of the U.S. Treasury. After all, a little planning now can go a long way toward minimizing your future estate tax liability.

At death, which could unfortunately happen at any moment, your entire estate may be subject to taxes. Your home, your personal belongings, your checking and savings accounts, and any investments or business interests you acquired during your lifetime, may all be taxed prior to distribution to your heirs. And the tax collector does not tread lightly on such a solemn occasion. For estates valued in excess of $600,000 — not an improbable feat for serious wealth-builders who are this far into the course, especially since you must include home equity in the sum — the federal government imposes a graduated tax which begins at 37%, and slides all the way up to 55% for estates in excess of $3,000,000. For very large estates — valued at between $10,000,000 and $21,040,000 — a 5% add-on tax brings the top marginal rate up to the equivalent of 60%. Estates larger than $21,040,000 are taxed at a flat rate of 55%. These reasons, and all the others why we may need to properly establish a legal construct around our net worths, are why we've included this lesson in *100 Steps to Wealth.*

This lesson will cover nearly all the topics you'll need to know concerning estate planning. It will, among many things, adequately enable you to chose a competent estate planning professional, enable you to talk competently with her, and more easily decide which options are in your best interests. Estate planning is dry... and complicated. Although this lesson does about as good of a job as can be done explaining it in laymen's terms (while not continually saying, rely on an attorney for the details), it does not replace the necessity of retaining a certified estate planning professional. This is usually an attorney, although not necessarily. It does need to be an experienced planner, who knows the tolerances of the IRS laws, and at least uses an attorney to make any necessary legal preparations and registrations.

We'll first cover estate and gift taxes themselves then move into methods employed to avoid them including lifetime taxable transfers, split interest gifts and irrevocable trusts. All tax laws referenced, unless otherwise specified, are those in effect during the fall of 1995. Congress occasionally changes estate tax laws although less frequently than personal income tax laws. We'll also include a discussion of wills and intestacy, and the probate process itself. (Be sure to refer back to the lesson *Insuring the Now and Future Family* for our introduction to probate). We conclude with the course's final two steps: one on implementing estate freezing techniques and the other on methods for determining the proper trusts for you. First comes estate taxes!

ESTATE TAXES

As indicated earlier, personal income tax is not the only tax Uncle Sam levies on individuals. He also can take a share of your net worth upon death. And, as we saw above, it can be a severe amount. The sidebar below shows the graduated estate tax rates going from 18 percent — on the first eligible $10,000 — to 55% on all above $21,040,000.

Federal Estate and Gift Taxes

Taxable Gift or Estate		Tentative Tax	
From (1)	To (2)	Tax on (Column 1)	Rate on amount above Col. 1 (Col. 2 - Col.1)
$0	$10,000	$0	18%
$10,000	$20,000	$1,800	20%
$20,000	$40,000	$3,800	22%
$40,000	$60,000	$8,200	24%
$60,000	$80,000	$13,000	26%
$80,000	$100,000	$18,200	28%
$100,000	$150,000	$23,800	30%
$150,000	$250,000	$38,000	32%
$250,000	$500,000	$70,800	34%
$500,000	$750,000	$155,800	37%
$750,000	$1,000,000	$248,300	39%
$1,000,000	$1,250,000	$345,800	41%
$1,250,000	$1,500,000	$448,300	43%
$1,500,000	$2,000,000	$555,800	45%
$2,000,000	$2,500,000	$780,800	49%
$2,500,000	$3,000,000	$1,025,800	53%
$3,000,000	$10,000,000	$1,290,800	55%
$10,000,000	$21,040,000	$5,140,000	60%
$21,040,000+		55%	55%

Estates of $600,000 or less are spared, however. The Internal Revenue Code currently offers each taxpayer a credit — usually referred to as the Unified Credit — of $192,800, applied directly against his or her estate tax bill. This unified transfer credit, in effect, exempts up to $600,000 in assets from federal estate taxes.

Example: Suppose you have accumulated $600,000 in assets. At your death, the federal estate tax on your $600,000 estate is $192,800. However, application of your unified transfer credit leaves a federal estate tax liability of $0 (tax of $192,800 minus credit of $192,800 = $0 taxes owed).

Married couples who hold combined assets worth up to $1,200,000 may, with proper planning, eliminate their entire federal estate tax liability, through successive use of both of their unified transfer credits.

The Generation-Skipping Transfer Tax

There's more. The federal government imposes a flat, 55% "generation-skipping transfer tax" on all assets transferred to your grandchildren, or other beneficiaries younger than you by at least two generations. This tax is levied in addition to regular estate taxes. The government inflicts the generation-skipping transfer tax on what's left of your assets *after* they have *already* been diminished by federal estate taxes.

Example: Assume that, after a long and successful life, you die with an estate valued at $10,000,000. You have already used up your $1,000,000 generation-skipping transfer tax exemption (discussed below). Your will specifies that $1,000,000 in carefully selected stocks and bonds be given to your only granddaughter.

Unfortunately, your sizable estate rests squarely in the 55% estate tax bracket. Thus, the federal government's initial share of your $1,000,000 bequest to your granddaughter totals $550,000, leaving her $450,000. (55% x $1,000,000 = $550,000.)

Moreover, the federal government is very interested in the fact that the after estate tax amount of $450,000 will pass to your granddaughter. Since she qualifies as "an individual two or more generations younger than you," your bequest also triggers the generation-skipping transfer tax. Thus, a flat 55% generation-skipping transfer tax will be charged against the remaining $450,000 (55% x $450,000 = $247,500), leaving only $202,500 for your granddaughter. The federal government's total take from your $1,000,000 bequest is $797,500!

The Generation-Skipping Transfer Tax Exemption

The government does offer some relief from the generation-skipping transfer tax. Each taxpayer is entitled to a generation-skipping transfer tax exemption of $1,000,000. Therefore, you can pass a total of $1,000,000 in assets to your grandchildren, or even your great-grandchildren, without paying the generation-skipping transfer tax.

If you choose, you may apply this exemption toward specific property — gifted during life, or at death — by declaring it on a timely filed tax return. (Clearly your executor — an entity given responsibility for overseeing the distribution of assets, usually a person but occasionally a corporation or foundation — rather than you, will be filing any post-death returns.) If you allocate your exemption improperly, however — or fail to allocate it at all — your exemption will instead be applied based upon the dictates of the IRS.

The generation-skipping transfer tax exemption belongs to the donor — the one making the gift or bequest — not the donee — the one receiving the gift/bequest. Thus, you will not realize any additional tax benefits by encouraging your children to produce as many grandchildren as possible. You may pass no more than $1,000,000 in assets to the collective group of your heirs who are two or more generations younger than you, without paying generation-skipping transfer taxes. Married couples may, however, jointly use their generation-skipping transfer tax exemptions to shield a total of $2,000,000 from generation-skipping transfer taxes.

Example: After reaching the august age of 100, you die and leave an estate valued at $2,000,000 to your two grandsons. Your estate owes federal estate taxes of $363,000 (tax of $555,800 minus unified credit of $192,800 = $363,000).

After federal estate taxes, your estate is left with $1,637,000. Your $1,000,000 generation-skipping transfer tax exemption will protect $1,000,000 from generation-skipping transfer taxes, leaving $637,000 vulnerable to additional taxation. $637,000 x 55% generation-skipping transfer tax = an additional tax liability of $350,350.

$1,637,000 — the estate net after estate taxes — minus $350,350 (in generation-skipping transfer taxes) leaves an estate of $1,286,650. Thus, after the federal government has taken its slice of your $2,000,000 bequest, your grandsons will inherit $1,286,650.

State Inheritance and Estate Taxes

To perhaps add injury to insult, the federal government will not be the only entity passing a collection plate when you attempt to pass your carefully accumulated assets down to the next generation. Most states impose their own estate taxes, or inheritance taxes, or both. While more than half of the states collect a "pick-up tax," which means that the state will pick-up, or share-in, a portion of the tax already collected by the federal government — without increasing the overall amount of tax paid — the other half are authorized to levy their taxes on top of the federal estate tax paid. See the sidebars in this section.

Income In Respect of a Decedent

Finally, when contemplating tax avoidance (No, we don't mean tax evasion. Evasion is illegal; avoidance is plain smart.) through estate planning, you should consider the impact of "income in respect of a decedent," or "IRD," on your accumulated assets. First, a little background is in order.

States which Impose Inheritance Taxes and Estate Taxes

Connecticut	Kansas	Montana	North Carolina
Delaware	Kentucky	Nebraska	Pennsylvania
Indiana	Louisiana	New Hampshire	South Dakota
Iowa	Maryland	New Jersey	Tennessee

As discussed later in this chapter, gifts you choose to make during your lifetime will retain your tax basis — what you paid for an item — in the hands of the recipient. This means that any appreciated property you give away will likely be subject to income taxes, should the donee later sell it.

Example: You purchased baseball trading cards in 1945, for $1.00 and you give your trading cards to your nephew this year. Today, these cards are worth $20,000. Nonetheless, your nephew is assigned your $1.00 tax basis in the trading cards. If he later sells the cards for $20,000, he must report a taxable gain of $19,999 on his income tax return (selling price {$20,000} minus basis {$1.00} = taxable gain {$19,999}).

On the other hand, assets transferred upon the death of a transferor typically receive a "step-up" in basis to fair market value on the date of the transferor's death.

Example: In August, you buy 100 shares of AT&T stock for $55 per share. Your basis is $5,500 ($55 x 100 shares = $5,500). In September, the value of the stock rises to $67 per share. If you sell your AT&T stock in September, you must pay taxes on a gain of $1,200 ($6,700 selling price minus $5,500 basis = $1,200 gain).

States which Impose Estate Taxes which May Exceed the Federal Credit

Mississippi   Ohio   New York   Oklahoma

Instead, you hold on to your stock, until your sudden and unexpected death in November of that year. At that time, AT&T is trading at $75 per share. When your daughter finally receives the stock, her basis will be $7,500 ($75 x 100 shares = $7,500). Your original $5,500 cost basis will be stepped-up to the stock's fair market value on the date of your death, or an alternative valuation date — usually six months after death. Thus, should your daughter sell the stock in 1996 for $80 per share, she will only report a taxable gain of $500 (selling price of $8,000 minus basis of $7,500 = taxable gain of $500).

States which Impose Estate Taxes Limited to an Offset Against the Federal Credit

Alabama	Georgia	Missouri	Utah
Alaska	Hawaii	Nevada	Vermont
Arizona	Idaho	New Mexico	Virginia
Arkansas	Illinois	North Dakota	Washington
California	Maine	Oregon	West Virginia
Colorado	Massachusetts	Rhode Island	Wisconsin
DC	Michigan	South Carolina	Wyoming
Florida	Minnesota	Texas	

Note: if an asset you hold until death has decreased in value, to below what you paid for it, its basis will be "stepped-down" to fair market value on the date of death.

Now for the bad news. Any "income in respect of a decedent" does *not* receive a step-up in basis when transferred at death. Assets held by IRAs, or other qualified retirement plans, are usually characterized as IRD.

Therefore, the federal government will levy both estate taxes and income taxes when the plan owner dies — subject to certain exceptions involving spousal beneficiaries. As if that weren't enough, heavily funded qualified plans may also be subject to additional penalties in the form of excise taxes. Thus, without even considering the consequences of making a generation-skipping bequest, as little as 20% of your qualified retirement plan assets may actually pass to your heirs at your death.

The Unlimited Marital Tax Deduction

The unlimited marital tax deduction allows spouses to transfer unlimited amounts of property to each other, during life, or at death, without any federal estate tax consequences. This marital deduction effectively postpones estate tax liability until the second spouse's death.

However, overly aggressive use of the marital deduction may be counter-productive. If the first spouse to die transfers all of his/her property to the surviving spouse, no federal estate taxes will be owed at that time. Unfortunately, at the second death, the estate tax burden will likely be *greater* than if taxes had been collected at each spouse's death. If the first spouse transfers all of his/her property via the marital deduction, he/she will forfeit the right to shelter up to $600,000 in assets from federal estate taxes via the unified transfer credit. Accordingly, at the second death, only the surviving spouse's unified transfer credit will be available to shelter all of the assets accumulated by both spouses during their marriage. Let's examine the alternatives.

If the first spouse to die transfers all of his/her property to the surviving spouse, no federal estate taxes will be owed at that time. Unfortunately, at the second death, the estate tax burden will likely be greater than if taxes had been collected at each spouse's death.

Alternative Number One — you and your spouse have together accumulated $1,200,000 in assets during your marriage. Your spouse dies, leaving all of his/her assets to you via the marital deduction. The federal government collects no estate taxes at that time. You die six months later with an estate of $1,200,000. After usage of your unified transfer credit, your estate will still owe $235,000 in federal estate taxes.

Alternative Number Two — on the other hand, your spouse could have left his/her property in a trust. Although that trust would ostensibly be created for the benefit of your children, you, as surviving spouse, would have access to the trust's income, and even its principal, if necessary to maintain your standard of living. Your spouse could fund this type of trust, often referred to as a "credit shelter trust" or "B" trust, for up to $600,000, free of federal estate taxes, via the unified transfer credit.

The "B" trust assets would not be included in your estate at the time of your death. Thus, assuming no appreciation or shrinkage, you would leave behind an estate of $600,000 at your death. After application of your own unified transfer credit, your estate would owe no federal estate taxes.

Therefore, using Alternative Number Two, you and your spouse could have passed $1,200,000 to your children, free of federal estate taxes. When compared with the first alternative, your heirs would come out $235,000 ahead. (The attributes of the trust utilized by Alternative Number Two will be discussed in greater detail, later in this chapter.)

As a final note, when planning with the unlimited marital deduction, be sure to ascertain whether the state in which you reside also provides an unlimited marital deduction. While the majority of states provide a deduction similar to that offered by our federal government, Connecticut, Delaware, Maryland, and Pennsylvania offer only a limited form of marital deduction to protect surviving spouses from state estate and inheritance taxes.

GIFT TAXES

The federal government has unified its estate and gift tax systems. Unification impacts the average tax payer in several significant ways. First, under the unified approach, the applicable tax brackets are the same whether property is transferred away during life or held until death. Thus, whether you give your child $30,000 today, or leave it to him/her via your will, the federal government should collect the same amount of tax. The Table, below, sets forth the marginal rates for federal gift and estate taxes.

Second, the unified transfer credit can be utilized to shelter up to $600,000 in lifetime gifts from gift taxes. In fact, you must exhaust your unified transfer credit amount before you can begin making taxable gifts.

Third, the unified approach treats both lifetime gifts and after death transfers as part of one long transfer "continuum". While interesting in theory, the practical import of this approach becomes clear when you consider that estate and gift taxes are graduated taxes. The more you transfer away, the higher the percentage of tax levied.

Today, for purposes of assessing the size of an estate, and thus its applicable tax bracket, almost all lifetime gifts made after 1976 are added back into the calculation. Although the estate receives a credit for gift taxes paid — as long as they were paid three or more years prior to death — adding past gifts back into the estate tax calculation will effectively push the estate assets into a higher marginal tax bracket.

Calculation of Estate Tax Liability Discussed at Right

Step One: Add lifetime gifts to the value of your estate
($750,000 + $600,000 = $1,350,000)

Step Two: Calculate estate taxes on the aggregate of gifts and estate assets
(Tax on $1,350,000 = $491,300)

Step Three: Subtract unified transfer credit
($491,300 - $192,800 = $298, 500)

Step Four: Subtract tentative tax on past gifts made
($298,500 - $55,500 = $243,000)

Example: Assume that between 1976 and 1991, you gave away a total of $750,000 in gifts to your children and grandchildren. You owed no federal gift taxes on the first $600,000 in gifts, because they were sheltered by your unified transfer credit. The remaining $150,000 were taxable gifts, for which you paid gift taxes. Today, you die owning $600,000 in assets. Your estate tax liability will $243,000 as is shown at left.

Ordinarily, estate taxes on an estate of $600,000 would be $192,800 — assuming the unified credit had already been allocated. However, by grossing up the estate — by bringing back previous gifts into the calculation — the federal government will collect an additional $50,200 in estate taxes. This grossing up procedure enables the government to collect the same amount of taxes from both the taxpayer who makes lifetime gifts, and the taxpayer who waits to distribute all of his/her assets until death.

The Unified Credit

As noted above, the unified transfer credit can be used to shelter either lifetime gifts, or transfers at death, or a combination of the two, up to a current maximum of $600,000. In fact, your credit will be applied first to gifts made during your life, with any credit remaining applied at your death. As a matter of fact, you should choose to make a lifetime allocation of your credit in order to remove the growth on the gifted asset from your estate. No matter how much it appreciates, only the value of your gift, at the date it was given, should be brought back to gross up the size of your estate.

The unified transfer credit can be used to shelter either lifetime gifts, or transfers at death, or a combination of the two, up to a current maximum of $600,000.

Example: Suppose you give your son and daughter each a 50% interest in a parcel of undeveloped real estate. On the date of your gift, the property has an appraised value of $600,000. You file a gift tax return, allocate your entire unified credit, and pay no federal gift taxes.

Twenty years later, a large shopping center has been built across the street from the gifted property, and as a result, your children's property has increased in value to $5,000,000. Assume that you die in that twentieth year, owning an estate valued at $2,000,000. The federal government applies its estate tax against your assets at death ($2,000,000) plus past gifts ($600,000). Thus, federal estate taxes are calculated on an aggregate estate of $2,600,000. The tax on $2,600,000 is then diminished by the unified credit.

Although the $600,000 gift was made free of federal taxes by allocation of the unified credit at the time of the gift, the $600,000 is still brought back to gross up the size of the estate. However, the full amount of the unified credit is also brought back, and applied against total estate tax liability. This results in a wash — $600,000 in assets is still sheltered from taxes — except as to the higher marginal bracket applied to the actual estate assets.

The most significant result of making your $600,000 lifetime gift is that the $4,400,000 in the property's growth which occurred after you gave it to your children is not brought back into your estate. If you had kept the property until your death, leaving it by will to your son and daughter, your estate would have included the value of the real estate, as valued at the date of your death ($5,000,000), and that entire amount would have been subjected to estate taxes.

The Generation-Skipping Transfer Tax Exemption

Similar to the unified credit, the generation-skipping transfer tax exemption can be allocated to lifetime gifts. Once again, the value in making a lifetime allocation stems from your ability to place the future growth on up to $1,000,000 in assets outside of your estate.

Example: In 1994, you established a trust for the benefit of your grandchildren. You funded the trust with triple-tax-free municipal bonds valued at $1,000,000, paying 6% interest. You allocated both your unified credit, and your generation-skipping transfer tax exemption toward the gift, with the result that you paid $153,000 in estate taxes, and $0 in generation-skipping transfer taxes.

At your death in the year 2006, the trust assets have grown to $2,000,000, and are distributed to your grandchildren. Since you allocated your generation-skipping transfer tax exemption and your unified credit when you initially transferred assets to the trust, no additional federal taxes should be due on any part of the $2,000,000 received by your grandchildren.

The Annual Gift Tax Exclusion

The federal government offers additional relief from its gift tax, in the form of an annual, $10,000 gift tax exclusion. This exclusion allows you to give up to $10,000 in cash or property to each donee — recipient — you choose, every year, without paying gift taxes. Further, gifts made free of gift taxes via the annual gift exclusion will *not* be brought back into your estate for "gross up" purposes.

Example: Assume that every year, from 1990 through 1992, you give each of your three children $10,000. At $30,000 per year, for three years, your gifts total $90,000. You use your annual gift exclusions to shelter these gifts, and as a result you pay no federal gift taxes. If you should die in 1998, none of these gifts will be brought back to gross up the size of your estate. Couples also have the option of making joint use of their annual exclusions to give up to $20,000 per recipient.

Your annual gift exclusion can be particularly valuable, not only as a method to transfer substantial assets to your children and grandchildren, but also as a way to shrink your estate, thus minimizing your estate tax bill.

Example: Suppose you have accumulated, to date, an estate of $600,000, and you have not previously made any taxable gifts. If you die tomorrow, your estate should owe no federal estate taxes. Fortunately, you don't die tomorrow. Your $600,000 in assets — which are all liquid — generate an annual, after tax income of $32,000, and your annual living expenses are approximately $22,000.

Many have qualms about leaving large sums of money to their younger, less experienced children and grandchildren. They simply need a Crummey Trust.

Each year, that you spend only $22,000, the remaining $10,000 will be added to your taxable estate. Not surprisingly, you would prefer to keep your taxable estate at $600,000 in order to avoid future estate taxes. The solution is to give $10,000 each year to your son or daughter, tax free, via your annual exclusion. In this manner you can completely dispose of your interest income, effectively keeping your estate below the federal tax threshold.

If you are less than thrilled with the prospect of handing all of your excess income over to your children and grandchildren, you're not alone. Many potential donors hate to forego the tax advantages of the annual exclusion, but have qualms about leaving large sums of money to their younger, less experienced children and grandchildren. They can, however, have that tax advantage without the worry. They simply need a Crummey Trust.

Crummey Trusts

Only present interest gifts — those you convey the immediate right to the recipient to use, possess, or enjoy his/her gift — qualify for the annual gift tax exclusion. If, on the other hand, you make your gift now, but delay the recipient's use, possession, or enjoyment, you have made a gift of a future interest which will not qualify for the annual exclusion.

Gifts to Crummey Trusts — named after a case well known to estate planners, *Crummey v. Commissioner* — allow you to fund a trust on behalf of your children and grandchildren free of taxes, via the annual exclusion, even though your heirs may not immediately begin consuming your gifts. This unique type of irrevocable trust allows trust beneficiaries, such as the children and grandchildren, for a limited period of time, typically two weeks to one month, to withdraw a portion of the trust principal. It doesn't matter if they actually make those withdrawals. The simple fact that they had the right to make the withdrawal qualifies gifts made to a Crummey Trust as present interest gifts.

Example: Assume that you and your spouse have two children and one grandchild. Assume also that you currently have an estate of $2,000,000. You establish a Crummey Trust, naming your children and grandchild as its beneficiaries. On November 1, of each year, for ten successive years, you and your spouse fund the trust with $60,000 — $20,000 per beneficiary. These gifts qualify for your annual exclusions, and are made free of federal gift taxes.

Every November 1, your children and grandchild receive a letter from the trustee informing him/her of his/her right to withdraw $20,000 from the trust during the month of November. However, none of your heirs exercises this right. Instead, they prefer to wait while the trust's investments, e.g. stocks, bonds, and insurance, grow and appreciate.

After the tenth year, you and your spouse have contributed $600,000 to the trust, free of gift taxes. You cease making gifts. Assuming average growth of 7%, the trust assets should be worth approximately $900,000 in the tenth year. If these funds continue to compound at 7% for the next ten years, the trust should hold assets worth roughly $1,800,000. None of these assets should be subject to either gift or estate taxes at either your death, or your spouse's death.

Conversely, if you and your spouse fail to establish the trust, an additional $1,800,000 in assets will likely be included in your estate — subject to estate taxes as high as 55%.

As a final word on gift taxes, the states at left impose gift taxes above what the federal government imposes. If you live in any of these states, be sure to take into consideration their gift taxes as well.

LIFETIME TAXABLE TRANSFERS: ANY ADVANTAGE?

Yes! We've stated that estate and gift tax rates are identical. So, if you're still awake by now, you're wondering how can taxable lifetime transfers possibly have an advantage over transfers at death? In fact, you're also wondering how estate tax rates can be effectively substantially higher than gift tax rates?

The answer lies in the fact that the federal estate tax is an "inclusive" tax, while the federal gift tax is an "exclusive" tax. The IRS applies the estate tax against the entire estate, including that portion which will be paid out in estate taxes. The gift tax, on the other hand, only applies to the amount which is actually given to the donee — you don't pay a tax on the tax.

Example: Suppose you have an estate of $2,000,000, and on January 1, 1992, you give your only child a gift of $1,000,000 in cash. After allocation of your unified credit, you owe gift taxes of $153,000. Assuming that your estate enjoys no further growth, you then die a few years later with an estate of $847,000 ($2,000,000 estate less $1,000,000 gift, less $153,000 tax = estate of $847,000).

Lifetime gifts do not receive a stepped-up fair market value basis in the hands of the donee. Therefore, when determining which specific assets to give away in lifetime gifts, you should consider favoring assets which have a high basis, over those assets with a low cost basis which have experienced significant growth since you acquired them.

To calculate your estate tax, your executor adds back your gift to your estate assets, for an aggregate of $1,847,000. After also bringing back your unified credit, your estate owes federal estate taxes of $366,150 (tentative tax of $711,950 - $192,800 {unified credit} = $519,150 - $153,000 {tentative tax on gift already made} = $366,150). Total federal gift and estate taxes paid: $519,150.

On the other hand, assume that you fail to make a gift of $1,000,000 in 1992, and you die later with a $2,000,000 estate. Your estate will pay a federal estate tax of $588,000 (tentative tax of $780,800 - $192,800 {unified credit} = $588,000). Therefore, by failing to make your lifetime gift, you will have forfeited an additional $68,850 in federal taxes.

The difference here is between $519,150 and $68,850. The advantages to making lifetime gifts are obvious.

There are disadvantages to making lifetime gifts. The two most frequently voiced concerns are that the donor might have future need of the gifted funds, perhaps due to illness or injury, or that the donees may be too immature or inexperienced to handle the gift. The latter concern can be allayed by use of an irrevocable trust — discussed later in this lesson. The former is simply an issue of comfort: you should forecast your future needs, mentally setting aside funds for potential calamities, and then evaluate the size of the gift you can comfortably give.

You should also be aware of one potential tax disadvantage created by lifetime gifts. Unlike assets transferred at death, lifetime gifts do not receive a stepped-up fair market value basis in the hands of the donee. Therefore, when determining which specific assets to give away in lifetime gifts, you should consider favoring assets which have a high basis, over those assets with a low cost basis which have experienced significant growth since you acquired them.

If you make lifetime gifts of highly appreciated assets, your donees will receive your basis in the items, and will be taxed heavily, should they sell them. Nonetheless, remember that our current federal estate tax rates are quite a bit higher than federal income tax rates. Thus, if you make a tax-free lifetime gift, e.g. by use of your annual gift exclusions, of a highly appreciated asset, your donees will be subject, at most, to a 39.6% rate of income tax upon it's sale, as opposed to 55% in estate taxes if you hold the asset until death.

THE GROSS ESTATE: CALCULATING YOUR ESTATE TAX LIABILITY

Now that we've covered some of the most important estate planning basics, you can more easily estimate your own estate's future tax liability. Follow these simple steps to calculate your tentative federal estate tax.

STEP ONE: Make a list of all assets you either own outright, or have a partial interest in, and list them based upon today's fair market value — what a willing seller would pay a willing buyer on the open market. An example follows.

Assets

FAMILY HOME	$250,000
OTHER REAL ESTATE	150,000
LIMITED PARTNERSHIPS	35,000
CHECKING ACCOUNTS	2,000
SAVINGS ACCOUNTS	10,000
CASH	1,500
STOCKS	27,500
BONDS	36,000
MUTUAL FUNDS	75,000
CDS & MONEY MARKETS	8,000
RETIREMENT PLANS	350,000
ANNUITIES	65,000
LIFE INSURANCE	100,000
RECEIVABLES	27,000
COLLECTIBLES	9,000
PERSONAL PROPERTY	80,000
BUSINESS INTERESTS	200,000
MISCELLANEOUS	10,000
TOTAL	$1,436,000

Once you've done that, total all of your personal debt.

Debt (or Liabilities)

MORTGAGE	$23,000
BUSINESS DEBT	15,000
AUTOMOBILE DEBT	5,000
TOTAL	$43,000

STEP THREE: Then calculate your Adjusted Gross Estate (AGE) by simply subtracting the debt from the assets: in this case we're left with an Adjusted Gross Estate of $1,393,000 ($1,436,000 minus $43,000 = $1,393,000).

STEP FOUR: Now add your Total Taxable Gifts to your Adjusted Gross Estate — this includes gifts sheltered from gift tax through the unified transfer credit, and excludes gifts sheltered from tax via your annual gift exclusion — to arrive at an Aggregate.

Aggregate

TOTAL TAXABLE GIFTS	$200,000
A.G.E.	$1,393,000
AGGREGATE	$1,593,000

STEP FIVE: Go to the Federal Estate and Gift Tax table found on page 4 and apply the appropriate rates to the Aggregate amount — in our example $1,593,000. Our example of $1,593,000 falls in the $1,500,000 to $2,000,000 bracket, and therefore incurs the amount of $555,800 on the first $1.5 million and 45% on the balance. This forms what we might call the Unadjusted or Tentative Tax.

Calculation of Unadjusted Tax

TAX ON $1,500,000 =	$555,800
TAX ON THE EXCESS OVER $1,500,000 ($93,000)	
AT 45% =	$ 41,850
UNADJUSTED OR TENTATIVE TAX	$597,650

STEP SIX: Now to calculate your Net Federal Estate Tax, simply subtract your unified transfer credit, and any previously paid taxes on all lifetime gifts made since 1976, from your Unadjusted Tax. Our example, therefore, yields $404,850 in Net Estate Taxes.

Final Calculation of Net Estate Taxes

TENTATIVE TAX	$597,650
LESS UNIFIED CREDIT	(192,800)
LESS TAX ON PAST GIFTS	(0)
NET ESTATE TAX	$404,850

Valuation of Estate Assets

For the most part, we have assumed that your executor/trustee determines — and the IRS approves — the value of your estate assets based upon their fair market value on the date of your death. However, another option exists. Assets may also be valued on an alternative valuation date — typically six months after the date of death. Your executor or your trustee — or in the case of individuals dying without a will or trust, your administrator — can elect which valuation date to use.

Example: Suppose that you own a home in Northern California which you purchased for $50,000 in 1972. At your death, homes in your area are selling for $600,000. However, the real estate market has had its ups and downs, and right at the time of your death, the price of comparable homes is rising. In fact, on the date six months after your death, your home appraises at $750,000. Your executor has the option to use the $600,000 date of death valuation, or the $750,000 alternative valuation.

Which date the executor uses is determined by which one yields the better outcome. For example, assume that your two children do not wish to live in the home, and instead will share equally in the proceeds once they sell it. If they sell your home for anything greater than $600,000, they will have to pay income taxes on the gain, unless the property is subject to the alternative valuation date. If your executor chooses the alternative valuation, your children will not pay taxes unless they sell the home for greater than $750,000. From this point of view, the alternative valuation date has the greatest advantage, and should be utilized.

If your executor/trustee/administrator elects to use the alternative valuation date, all of your estate's assets must be valued as of that alternative date. The value on that date, not surprisingly, is the fair market value of each asset — again, what a willing buyer would pay a willing seller on the open market. However, evidence of actual sales prices — what the estate assets actually sold for — at or near the valuation date may also be admissible to determine value for estate tax purposes.

Both undervaluation and overvaluation may trigger estate tax penalties. Thus, particularly when an estate includes assets that are difficult to value — such as real estate, closely held securities, and fractional interests — professional appraisers should be used.

WILLS, TRUSTS, INTESTACY, AND THE PROBATE PROCESS

If you fail to establish either a will, or a living trust, you will relinquish control over the disposition of your property. Without a will or living trust you will die "intestate," and the laws on the books in the state where you live, or where you own real estate, will dictate a formula for the distribution of all of your assets.

Creating a will or living trust will allow you to legally express your preferences regarding the ultimate disposition of your property. Either can be altered, or revoked, at any time prior to your death. Thus, even if you have reservations about how to distribute your property, there's no legitimate reason to wait until the last minute to put pen to paper. With either a will or a living trust you always have the prerogative to change your mind.

If you don't feel comfortable leaving your assets outright to your heirs, you can also include language in your will or living trust setting forth the terms of a separate, irrevocable trust. If you would like to create a trust to manage assets for the benefit of your surviving spouse, or your minor children or grandchildren, for example, you can simply include the appropriate language within the larger will or living trust documents. You can still change your mind; even though you have included parameters for an irrevocable trust, it won't typically become operational until after probate. If you change your mind, simply alter the terms of your will or living trust prior to death, and voila! No more irrevocable trust.

Generally speaking, everyone can make a will. You simply need be 18 years old or older, and of sound mind. It's also a good idea that your will be in writing, signed, and witnessed by at least two persons.

Choosing an Executor

Most often, one of the decedent's children will act as executor of the will. You may appoint several children to act as co-executors, but from an administrative standpoint, you will have created a host of logistical problems. One expert in this area, Bill George, Esq. of Helm, Purcell and Wakeman in Westlake Village, California, recommends that you appoint only one executor, and that he/she be your child possessing either the best business sense, the most common sense, or the most responsible nature. Mr. George suggests that you only consider appointing co-executors if there is a lack of trust among your heirs, or if the appointment of only one child to act on the others' behalf would likely result in dissension.

Naming only one executor does not mean that you should refrain from appointing successor executors who will act in the event that your first choice is unwilling, or unable to fulfill the role as executor. You should name at least one successor — and preferably two — who occupies a generation below yours.

Of course, you always have the option of naming a corporate executor. Financial institutions such as trust companies, national banks, and even brokerage houses may act as your executor. The ballpark fee charged by a corporate executor tends to be one percent of estate assets.

Another alternative might be to appoint a child as executor, with a corporate co-executor. Or, you might name a financial institution as a special advisor to the executor.

Note: the above criteria for choosing an executor applies equally to your choice of successor trustees for your living trust, and even to appointment of trustees for irrevocable trusts established to benefit your children and grandchildren. Irrevocable trusts are discussed in detail, below.

Are Living Trusts More Advantageous Than Wills?

A will becomes effective only upon your death. A living trust, on the other hand, can be implemented during your lifetime. This special trust allows you — in most states — to act as the grantor, that is the trust creator, the trustee, that is the holder of title who has managerial power to invest, distribute, and dispose of trust assets, and the trust beneficiary. In states such as New York, where a unique law known as "merger of season" prevents the creator from also being the sole trustee and beneficiary, you might consider appointing a spouse or child as co-trustee.

Advantages of a living trust over a will are twofold. First, they offer administrative advantages. Although you can initially appoint yourself as trustee of your living trust, you can also designate successor trustees, who will continue to manage your assets, and distribute the income and principal — according to the terms set forth in the trust — if you should become incapacitated, or die. Conversely, if you ever lose capacity to administer your affairs, and you have not created a living trust, it is possible that no one will know your preferences for appointing a guardian, or conservator to oversee your estate, and a less capable individual may be placed in charge. The second advantage of a living trust is it can avoid aspects of probate administration and attendant probate fees.

The Probate Process

Probate is the judicially supervised process which governs final distribution of assets at death. Unless your will or living trust is contested, say by disgruntled beneficiaries, probate should, generally speaking, be nonadversarial.

Legal fees to handle the probate process are typically established by state statute, and are often based upon a percentage of the value of the assets probated. In addition to expense, the probate process can be time-consuming, and may violate your desire for privacy — matters of probate are also matters of public record. Assets owned by a living trust, unless specifically designated to revert back to the grantor's estate at death, should pass to your heirs outside of probate, without being subject to probate fees.

Post-mortem Planning

While probate fees can be somewhat expensive, Steven Sciarretta, Esq., of Sciarretta & Schner in Boca Raton, Florida, warns that post mortem planning can be far more costly. Steven reminds us that, probate or no probate, a 706 Form — the federal estate tax return — must be filed. Locating, and appraising assets for report on the 706 can be a very time consuming process. Most attorneys charge by the hour, and costs add up. To help mitigate expenses, Steven suggests establishing the living trust now. It will prove to be a valuable method to identify, and organize your assets now, rather than leaving the job to your executor, and your attorney, down the road.

Funding Your Living Trust

Creating a living trust will get you nowhere, unless you fund it. It can be funded with assets such as stocks, bonds, bank accounts, cash, personal property, business interests, and real estate. All are good candidates for ownership by your living trust.

On the other hand, note the red flag, and consult your attorney, accountant, and/or other tax specialist before you attempt to transfer tax-deferred retirement plans, life insurance, annuities, automobiles, homes, Unified Transfers To Minors (UTMA) accounts, and stock from S Corporations or Professional Corporations, to your living trust.

Tax-deferred retirement plans should not be owned by your living trust. Further, you should be exceedingly careful before naming your living trust as the beneficiary of your retirement plan. If you ultimately wish your spouse, or perhaps a charitable beneficiary, to receive the asset, having it first pass through the hands of your living trust may eliminate several important tax advantages.

Assets such as life insurance, annuities, and UTMA accounts already pass — pursuant to contract — directly to your named beneficiaries, thereby avoiding probate, and probate fees, without inclusion in your living trust. Thus, it is generally not necessary that they be owned by your trust.

Automobiles change hands so frequently that it may cause you an administrative headache to transfer them in and out of your trust.

Homes are generally quite appropriate for transfer into your living trust. However, be aware that some lending institutions are not fond of financing trust-owned property. Hence, it may be necessary to transfer your home out of the trust if you plan to sell it, or refinance.

Living trusts can hold stock in S Corporations or Professional Corporations, but only if they contain special provisions. Make sure you consult your attorney prior to any transfers.

Note: The IRS considers the grantor, or trustor, the owner of the trust property for federal income tax purposes, and any income will continue to be taxed at his/her personal income tax rate.

RESIDENCY, DOMICILE AND CITIZENSHIP

We've noted above the significance of various states' estate, inheritance, and gift taxes. As a feature of estate planning though, it's also important to consider state income taxes. The state where you reside will likely impose it's estate and/or inheritance taxes on your estate, as well as income taxes on any irrevocable trusts you create, and upon income generated by your estate until its assets are distributed to your heirs. Where you are "domiciled" should determine the cost of probating your estate.

Thus, issues of residency, and domicile, determine which state, or states, will impose its taxes on you, your trusts, and your estate.

Residency and Domicile

State statutes vary somewhat regarding their definition of a resident. Nonetheless, most states rely on a combination of the following factors to establish whether a taxpayer is also a resident:

(1) domicile in the state;
(2) presence in the state for other than a temporary or transitory purpose;
(3) presence in the state for a specified period; and
(4) maintenance of a permanent place of abode in the state.

For example, California defines a resident as "every individual who is in this state for other than a temporary or transitory purpose," and "every individual domiciled in this state who is outside the state for a temporary or transitory purpose."

New York defines a resident as someone who has "maintained a permanent place of abode in the state and spent in the aggregate more than 183 days of the taxable year within the state." Conversely, New York explicitly excludes from its definition a person "domiciled in the state who maintains no permanent place of abode in the state, maintains a permanent place of abode elsewhere, and spends not more than thirty days of the taxable year in the state."

The majority of states agree upon the definition of domicile found in Black's Law Dictionary: "That place where a man has his true, fixed, and permanent home and principal establishment, and to which whenever he is absent he has the intention of returning." A person may, therefore, have more than one residence but only one domicile.

Nonetheless, these definitions are extremely subjective, and thus difficult to interpret with any certainty. For example, what does "temporary or transitory purpose" really mean? Courts have struggled with these definitions for years, and have come up with a list of factors which can support your claim of residency or domicile in a particular state. These factors include the location of your home, your business interests, where you spend the majority of your time, where your children go to school, your ties to the community, where you vote, where you have obtained your driver's license, where your register your car, where you maintain bank accounts, where you go to see doctors, lawyers, accountants, and so forth.

Example: Suppose you retire to Florida, where you would like to take advantage of its very favorable state tax structure in your estate planning. Should you continue to own real estate in your old state, as well as your new condominium in Florida? Is it wise to spend a significant amount of time in your old state? Should you keep your old Country Club membership? What about your cars? Should you maintain your registration in your old state? Keep your old driver's license?

If you do all of these things, you may significantly complicate your attempt to assert domicile and residency in Florida. Your actions will appear ambiguous in a court of law. The worst that can happen is both the old state and your new state will impose death taxes on your estate as if you were a resident of both jurisdictions. What's more, some states have become so aggressive that even if you do make a clean break, they will still pursue your estate claiming is was amassed while a resident there.

FYI: if you have executed a will prior to moving to a new state, the general rule in effect is if a will is valid when executed, then it will be valid everywhere, regardless of state of origin. However, there are some gaps in this rule. For example, some states allow "holographic" — handwritten, or "nuncupative" — oral, wills. Unfortunately, if you move to a new state where these types of wills are not recognized, they may take on entirely new meanings. Therefore, it's a good idea to consult with an attorney practicing in your new state of residence, to determine whether you need to execute a new will.

The waters become even more muddied when interpreting residency issues for entities such as partnerships (discussed in more detail later) and trusts.

State Income Taxes

States have the power to tax their residents' personal income, regardless of its source. In fact, many more aggressive states, such as California, tax residents on their worldwide income. On the other hand, states generally cannot tax nonresidents' personal income, unless it's derived from sources within the taxing state — such as rental income from property located within the state — from property or activities deemed to receive benefits or protection from the taxing state, or if it considers certain nonresidents beneficiaries of public services provided by the state.

Taxation and Partnerships

Most states adhere to the basic federal tax structure governing taxation of partners and partnerships — they treat them as conduits, and instead directly tax the partners, themselves, on their distributive shares of income. Some exceptions: Illinois levies a "personal property replacement tax" on the net income of all business organizations, including partnerships; Michigan imposes a tax on all "persons" with business activities in the state, including partnerships; New Hampshire imposes a Business Profits Tax on partnership income, proportionate to the percentage of aggregate income attributable to resident partners; and the District of Columbia and New York City levy unincorporated business taxes on partnerships conducting business within their jurisdictions.

Limited partnerships, for most intents and purposes, are treated similarly to general partnerships. Thus, the definitive issue is whether a partnership is conducting its business within the state.

Taxation of Trusts and Estates

States tend to tax only the current income generated by trusts and estates. (Income generated by assets held by living trusts is typically taxed to the grantor, not the trust.) Resident trusts and estates are taxed on all income from whatever source derived, just as resident persons are taxed on all income, regardless of source. Nonresident trusts/estates are taxed only on income derived from sources within the taxing state.

Note: Beneficiaries who receive distributions from trusts are usually taxed by their state of residency.

Individual state law determines if your trust or estate is a resident of a particular state. For example, both California and New York will tax 100% of trust income if all trustees or all beneficiaries reside in the state. If only a portion of the trustees and beneficiaries live in the state, the state applies a complex formula.

Tax Benefits From Split Interest Gifts

For the purpose of assessing gift taxes, the value of a gift will be determined at the time that the transfer to the donee has been completed. Generally, your transfer will be deemed complete when you have relinquished dominion and control over the gifted asset(s). At that time, gift tax will be determined relative to your gift's fair market value.

Fractional ownership interests, such as family limited partnership interests, will frequently be appraised at less than a pro rata portion of the entire underlying property interest. *Note: family limited partnerships are similar to ordinary limited partnerships, except that only family members are partners.* This disparity can be accounted for by valuation discounts applied by appraisers to reflect the lack of control and lack of marketability inherent in a minority interest.

These valuation discounts are important since they can allow you to leverage your unified transfer credit to transfer more than $600,000 in assets to your children and grandchildren without tax.

Example: Assume that you own an apartment building worth $1,800,000. You establish a family limited partnership to hold your building. Initially, you own both the 1% general partnership unit — representing $18,000 in underlying assets (1% of $1,800,000) — and the 99% limited partnership units — representing $1,782,000 in underlying assets (99% of $1,800,000). However, you wish to transfer 50% in limited partnership units to your children — representing $900,000 in underlying assets.

Generally, after application of your unified credit, you would still owe $114,000 in gift taxes on a transfer of $900,000 in assets. However, you are transferring an interest in your limited partnership, not the partnership's underlying assets.

If your children receive only limited shares, they will have little or no control over management of the partnership, because managerial control is vested in the general partner. Moreover, it is unlikely that anyone outside the family would wish to purchase the children's limited shares, should they need to liquidate their percentage. Thus, no ready market for the limited shares exists.

Therefore, a qualified appraisal firm might reasonably apply a 33% discount on the value of the limited partnership interests transferred, to adequately reflect the lack of control, and lack of marketability, unique to this type of investment. Thus, a 50% limited partnership interest representing $900,000 in underlying assets might be appraised at only $600,000. The result is you can transfer the entire 50% interest to your children, free of any federal gift taxes, by using your unified credit.

Just as a small note though, unlike California, New York courts have consistently found New York to be lacking in power to tax nonresident trustees on undistributed income from resident trusts and estates.

Citizenship

The United States imposes some of the highest estate tax rates in the industrialized world. Coupled with increases in our federal income taxes over the last several years, these taxes have regenerated interest among well-heeled US citizens to seek opportunities to avoid US taxes completely through expatriation, or in other words, renunciation of United States citizenship.

If you are contemplating expatriation, you should first consider several ancillary issues. First, you should look into the living costs associated with your new country. That country may be able to collect relatively modest taxes because living expenses are quite high.

Second, you should be aware that the tests for residency under the estate and gift tax statutes are even more subjective than those employed to determine federal income tax liability. Even if you spend fewer than 122 days annually in the US, you may still be categorized as a resident alien for estate and gift tax purposes.

As a US resident alien, you will be taxed on your worldwide assets just as if you had remained a US citizen. If you truly wish to avoid resident status, you may have to minimize, or even eliminate, your contacts with the United States, and even your visits to this country. Business, social, and cultural ties should be severely limited.

Family limited partnership interests, will frequently be appraised at less than a pro rata portion of the entire underlying property interest.

Third, recognize that if you expatriate, your spouse probably should too. Otherwise, if you die leaving your estate to your surviving spouse who is a citizen of the US, your property will still be subject to federal estate taxes at the second death.

Fourth, understand that Section 2107 of the Internal Revenue Code provides that even if you have achieved non-resident, non-citizen status, but you die within ten years of expatriation, your US taxable estate will still be taxed as if you remained a resident, unless you can prove that tax avoidance was not your principal purpose behind expatriation.

Finally, be aware that any US "situs" property owned even indirectly by a former US citizen, e.g. through an offshore holding company, will likely remain subject to estate taxes upon your death.

IRREVOCABLE TRUSTS

An irrevocable trust differs from a living trust only in that it cannot be revoked. Once created, it exists as an independent entity, separate and apart from the trust creator. An irrevocable trust actually represents two forms of ownership — legal ownership, and equitable ownership. The trustee holds legal title over the property. The beneficiaries hold equitable title in the property. Therefore, while legal title — as evidenced by a grant deed, for example — will be recorded in the name of the trustee, the trustee will still have a fiduciary duty to either spend, or conserve, the trust property as will best serve the beneficiaries' interests and as spelled out in the specific terms of the trust, itself.

An irrevocable trust offers two primary benefits. First, you can remove both the value of an asset, and its future appreciation, from your estate by transferring it to an irrevocable trust. The smaller the estate, the smaller the estate tax bill. Second, through an irrevocable trust, you can transfer away excess income, or assets, from your estate, for your family's benefit, without prematurely handing over control to your children or grandchildren, who may be too inexperienced to adequately oversee your investments.

A-B Trust Provisions

Two of the most frequently employed irrevocable trusts are known simply as A-B Trusts. A-B trust provisions are usually found as part of a will or living trust, and are designed to provide a surviving spouse with access to all of your jointly accumulated wealth, while also maximizing use of both spouse's unified transfer credits.

A-B trust provisions create two trusts. The B trust will be funded with an amount equal to one spouse's unified credit equivalent — currently, $600,000 — and the A trust will hold the remaining estate assets. A trust assets will be transferred into the trust, free of estate taxes, by use of the unlimited marital tax deduction.

Ordinarily, your surviving spouse will be entitled to control the A trust, including its interest income and principal. While he or she will also have access to B trust income, this often hinges upon prior exhaustion of A trust assets. As to B trust principal, your surviving spouse's access will generally be limited by what is known as a "five and five power" — the annual, noncumulative right to withdraw the greater of 5% of the trust principal or $5,000. Your surviving spouse may also have access to the B trust principal pursuant to an "ascertainable standard," which is a clause which entitled him/her to access assets as needed for his/her health, education, maintenance and support.

Since the B trust beneficiaries are, ultimately, your children, you can fund this trust free of federal estate taxes, by allocating your unified credit. Thus, even though your surviving spouse has access to the trust income and principal, neither your initial contribution to the B trust, nor any growth or appreciation realized by the trust assets, will be included in your surviving spouse's estate for purposes of estate taxes. He/she can use his/her own unified credit to shelter any remaining assets from tax, at the second spouse's death. Thus, if executed properly, A-B provisions may entitle a married couple to shelter up to $1,200,000 from federal estate taxes.

The QTIP Trust   Pursuant to the typical terms of an "A" trust, the surviving spouse will have the right to determine who inherits the remaining assets at the second death. This may create a conflict in situations where a surviving spouse remarries, and there are children from the first marriage.

The solution is a QTIP trust. This "qualified terminable interest property" trust can either supplement, or entirely replace the A trust. And the QTIP trust specifically names the beneficiaries of the trust's assets after the death of the surviving spouse. Like the A trust, the QTIP trust allows your surviving spouse to access the trust's income, with somewhat limited access to trust principle. However, unlike an A trust, the QTIP trust can guarantee that any remaining assets left after the survivor's death will be left to whomever the trust creator designates — often those children from the first marriage.

Example: Assume that you and your spouse have an estate of $2,000,000. You have two children. You are significantly older than your spouse, and you are concerned that if your spouse remarries after you die, your children might inadvertently get left out of their inheritance. You would like your spouse to have access to all of your assets during his/her lifetime; however, you would like to be certain that your children will receive what's left, after your spouse dies.

A Creative Alternative: The WEALTH TRUST®

One of the more inventive methods for establishing a trust that we've found was pioneered by Andrew Westhem of Wealth Transfer Planning, La Jolla, California.

The trademarked Wealth Trust®, as it's called, is a third party trust and is remotely similar to irrevocable dynasty trusts formerly used by some of America's wealthiest families earlier this century.

The Wealth Trust®, actually removes assets, and their appreciation, from the taxable estate. If implemented properly, trust assets will also stay outside of the children's taxable estates, with ultimate distribution made to the grandchildren, or in some circumstances, even great-grandchildren, free of estate taxes. As a side bonus, since it is a separate, independent trust, it can effectively remove assets from the reach of creditors! — assuming no fraudulent intent on your part.

It can be funded, free of gift and estate taxes, via ones unified credit, $10,000 annual exclusion gifts — in this regard, similar to a Crummey trust — and ones generation-skipping transfer tax exemption. Typically, children and grandchildren will be the beneficiaries of the Wealth Trust®. One or more of the beneficiaries can also fill the role of trustee. When funded with life insurance, it incorporates the advantages of an irrevocable life insurance trust.

In addition it forms subtrusts — an individual trust for each children — after death. The terms of each subtrust can differ in order to fit each child's individual needs, and provide for special circumstances. It typically incorporates a special power of appointment which allows the trustee to utilize strong personal judgment over the ultimate disposition of trust assets. This special trust also includes family bank provisions that allow the trustee to treat the trust as a family bank, by authorizing him/her to loan back funds to family members (even you) for emergencies and opportunities. *Note: as is the case with many complicated, yet creative, estate constructs, the IRS may tolerate them only on a case by case basis.*

Wealth Transfer Planning works with a network of affiliated attorneys in nearly every state so, if any reader is interested — regardless of domicile — Wealth Transfer Planning may be reached at 1-800-423-4890.

Therefore, you establish a QTIP trust, and a B trust. At your death, $600,000 in assets will go to the B trust, free of taxes due to your unified credit. $400,000 will pass to the QTIP trust. During your spouse's lifetime, he/she can access both trusts. However, at his/her death, your children will receive both the B and the QTIP trusts' assets. The remaining $1,000,000 represents your spouse's interest in your total $2,000,000 estate — he/she may dispose of it at death as he/she sees fit.

Another method is to employ an "estate freezing" technique, as they are called. We've discussed these is detail in wealth-building step 99, found beginning on page 24.

Qualified Personal Residence Trusts

If you are like many people, your home is your largest single asset. Its transfer to your children — whether today, or at your death — may use up most, if not all, of your $600,000 unified credit equivalent. Fortunately, there is a way to minimize the estate tax burden on the transfer of your home, while maximizing the power of your unified credit. A qualified personal residence trust or QPRT allows you to transfer either your principal residence or vacation home, or both, to your children with little tax liability, even as you continue to reside there.

If executed properly, A-B provisions may entitle a married couple to shelter up to $1,200,000 from federal estate taxes.

As the grantor of the QPRT, you transfer your home to the trust but retain an interest in that home for a term of years. Thus, you are also known as the term holder. At expiration of the term of years the property passes to your children — the remainder beneficiaries.

The QPRT allows you to move the entire value of your home, including any future growth, outside of your estate — subject to an important caveat: you must survive the term — and thus beyond the reach of estate taxes. Nonetheless, because your children are remainder beneficiaries, the IRS calculates the value of your gift by determining the present value of that future gift, As a result, the gift to your children is only a fraction of your home's fair market value, and will require a correspondingly lower utilization of your unified credit to pass it to the next generation, free of federal estate taxes. Your annual $10,000 gift tax exclusion is inapplicable to this strategy because you are making a gift of a future interest to your children.

Charitable Trusts

You can use a charitable trust, such as a charitable remainder trust (CRT), or its relative, the charitable lead trust (CLT) to accomplish two goals: minimization of estate taxes, and philanthropy. These irrevocable, split interest trusts can provide a generous gift to your favorite charity, while also providing you and your family with significant estate, gift, and income tax benefits.

Charitable Remainder Trust, or CRT — A CRT is a split interest trust because it has two separate sets of beneficiaries. You, and your spouse, would typically be designated as its income beneficiaries, while specified qualified charities would be its remainder beneficiaries. You and/or your spouse would also likely act as trustee. The trust is designed to make payments to you over a term of years — perhaps your lifetime. At the end of the term, the trust releases its property to the charitable beneficiary.

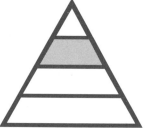

STEP 99

Implement Estate Freezing Techniques

What: A freeze partnership is a recapitalized partnership, whereby two classes of partners are created: the preferred, or frozen partner — who retains an interest similar to that of a preferred stockholder, and the common or unfrozen partners — who receive an interest similar to that enjoyed by common stockholders. The preferred partner receives a right to guaranteed annual payments, as well as a preference regarding liquidation of the partnership. The common partners have the right to share in income and distributions based upon their percentage of ownership.

Why: Since the income received by the preferred partner is fixed, if you will, the value of his/her interest is also fixed, and any future growth and appreciation on the underlying partnership assets will belong to the common partners. The common partners, interestingly enough, are your children and grandchildren.

Risk: Moderate. Risk can be minimized if knowledgeable practitioners advise you on your estate freeze, and professional appraisers are hired to value the common and preferred interests.

Safety: Again, the viability of an estate freeze hinges upon the knowledge and experience of the professionals assisting in its implementation.

Liquidity: If you establish a qualified income payment, your liquidity should be fairly high, depending upon the underlying corporate or partnership assets.

Why not: Overvaluation or undervaluation of common and preferred interests may trigger tax penalties.

Buy/Invest from: An estate freeze is more of a strategy than an investment. You should consult with an attorney who specializes in advanced estate planning techniques. Attorneys who have an accounting background, or an LL.M. — a post J.D. Masters — in taxation are highly recommended.

Background: Particularly popular during the 1970's and 1980's, sophisticated estate owners used "estate freezes" to freeze the value of property expected to appreciate, while retaining control and income from the underlying assets.

Example: Assume that in 1985, you own all of the stock in your closely held corporation, which was worth $1,000,000. You expect that by the time you die, your stock will easily be worth twice that much. Therefore, you would like to freeze the value of your stock for estate tax purposes. You attempt this freeze by recapitalizing your corporation. You surrender all of your stock in your corporation, and in return you receive 1000 shares of voting preferred stock and 100 shares of voting common stock. Your preferred stock has a par value — and a liquidation preference — of $1,000 per share, or $1,000,000 in the aggregate. The common stock has only a nominal value, e.g. $.01 per share.

Next, you give all of the common stock to your children. In this manner, you intend to give all of the company's future appreciation to them, with minimal gift taxes paid, while retaining control, as well as your current financial net worth. Further, you have "frozen" the estate tax value of your retained interest (the preferred stock) at $1,000,000, regardless of any future appreciation.

The federal government has not been terribly fond of estate freezes, and in 1988 it enacted Section 2036(c) of the Internal Revenue Code as a method to shut them down. However, Section 2036(c) was so complex that it was eventually repealed, and replaced with Chapter Fourteen of the Code. Chapter Fourteen addresses the estate tax freeze problem by creating a separate formula for valuation of a transferor's retained interest. If, under Chapter Fourteen, your retained interest were valued at $0 — returning to the above example — then the value of what you transferred to your children would have to be $1,000,000, and you would pay gift taxes accordingly.

Step 99: *Implement Estate Freezing Techniques*

The Chapter Fourteen rules apply (1) when you have control of a corporation or partnership; and (2) when you transfer an equity interest in a corporation or partnership which is (3) junior to the interest you retain, and (4) for which no publicly traded market price exists, and that transfer is made (5) to your spouse, or to any of your family who is a member of a younger generation.

If the Chapter Fourteen rules do apply, then the value of your senior, or preferred, retained interest will be determined in the following manner:

First: Determine the value of all family held interests in your partnership;

Second: Determine the value of any senior interest which is not subject to Chapter Fourteen valuation. Example: if you retained 10% of the common interest for yourself, then 10% of your preferred interest would be subject to normal valuation rules.

Third: Determine the value of the remaining preferred interest, based upon the qualified payment right. If the preferred right is nothing more than a distribution or liquidation right, and qualified payments are not established, the value of the preferred interest will likely be $0.

Fourth: Determine the value of the common interests by taking all family interests and subtracting the value of the preferred interest.

Fifth: Apply any appropriate discounts, e.g., lack of control, lack of marketability, etc.

The effect of Chapter Fourteen is that it exposes the transferred junior interest to a great deal more gift tax. In fact, if the preferred shares are valued at zero, the entire value of the partnership will be subject to gift taxes.

Estate freezes are still a viable option in the wake of Chapter Fourteen. Four situations remain where a freeze still has significant value as a device to transfer wealth to your family. First, a freeze can still be used for non-tax objectives, such as reducing their percentage interest without giving up control. Second, a freeze partnership can be useful as an initial partnership structure, if it is likely to appreciate significantly in the future — such as in the family limited partnership example, above. Third, a freeze can be valuable for businesses which generate substantial profits. As long as the older generation receives regular, qualified payments, the excess income and growth can inure to the benefit of the younger generation. Fourth, since the definition of family does not include the transferor's nieces, nephews, brothers-in-law, or sisters-in-law, a freeze can be useful in situations where the transferor does not have children of his/her own.

▷ ▷ ▷ ▶ **If you want to get started today, here's what you need to do to determine whether an estate freezing technique is right for you:**

Secure the assistance of a knowledgeable estate planner to determine whether an estate tax freeze will benefit your particular situation, and you'll require an attorney who specializes in this type of planning to create your own estate freeze. Go to your local library and ask the reference librarian for any of the directories of attorneys. Find the local listings and tele-interview those who claim experience with trusts. Ask if they're employed estate freezes and choose the one your happiest with. ▲

Continued from p. 23

If you fund your CRT with unencumbered, highly appreciated assets, they can be sold free of capital gains taxes. The entire value of the asset transferred can then be reinvested to produce income. The trust must pay you, annually, an amount no less than 5% of the value of the trust's total assets, either over your lifetime, or for a set term no longer than twenty years. In the case of reinvested assets which avoided capital gains taxes, you should receive substantially more income from the trust than if you had simply sold the assets yourself, and then reinvested the after tax amount.

Further, since the CRT's assets go straight to the charitable beneficiary at your death, they will not be included in your estate for estate tax purposes. Thus, you have effectively diminished the size of your estate tax bill. You should also receive a charitable income tax deduction based upon the present value of your gift to charity.

Example: Suppose you and your spouse have accumulated assets in excess of $5,000,000. You are both 59 years old. Out of your total estate, 3/5ths or $3,000,000 is comprised of 100,000 shares of founders stock in a booming telecommunications company. You and your spouse bought the stock for only $1 per share, but in 1994 it has a value of $30 per share. Thus, if you sell your stock, you will realize a taxable capital gain of $29 per share, or $2,900,000.

Instead, you and your spouse establish a charitable remainder unitrust, and transfer half of your stock, say, 50,000 shares to the trust. You and your spouse name yourselves as trustees of the trust, and choose an annual payout of 8% of the trust's assets — redetermined annually — for the duration of your joint lifetimes. As long as either of you remains alive, you will receive a payout. You name your favorite church or synagogue as the remainder beneficiary.

As co-trustees of your charitable remainder unitrust, you and your spouse sell the 50,000 shares of founders stock. No capital gains taxes will be owed. Instead, you can reinvest the entire $1,500,000 with several well known investment managers.

Each year you will receive annual retirement income of roughly $120,000 from your charitable remainder unitrust. You will also receive a modest charitable income tax deduction, representing the present value of the $1,500,000 in assets which will eventually go to the university.

Charitable Lead Trust, or CLT — A CLT reverses the pattern of the CRT. The charitable beneficiary receives income generated by the trust assets up front, for a set period of time, and the remainder interest typically passes to your children or grandchildren. Not only will you receive a income tax deduction for making a charitable gift, but you will also be able to leverage use of your unified credit to gift the remainder gift to your heirs. The leverage occurs because your gift or estate tax liability will be calculated against the present value of your future gift. Your grandchildren may receive $1,000,000 in twenty years, but the present value of $1,000,000 received in the year 2015 will be only a fraction of $1,000,000.

Example: Suppose that you leave your $5,000,000 estate to your grandchildren via your will. Usage of your entire unified credit will still yield an estate tax liability of approximately $2,198,000.

Moreover, usage of your entire $1,000,000 generation-skipping transfer tax exemption would leave a generation-skipping transfer tax of approximately $991,100. Therefore, out of a $5,000,000 bequest, your grandchildren will receive only $1,810,900.

On the other hand, you could leave $5,000,000 to a charitable lead unitrust for a term of 25 *years, with the remainder to your grandchildren. Based upon several assumptions — including a 7% payout to the charitable beneficiary, and anticipated growth of the assets at 7% per year — the present value of the remainder interest, that is what is left to the grandchildren, would be valued at approximately $942,450. After full utilization of your $600,000 unified credit exemption equivalent, estate taxes would total only $130,555.*

Further, usage of your $1,000,000 generation-skipping transfer tax exemption would result in the imposition of no generation-skipping transfer taxes. At the end of the term of years, approximately $4,869,445 would transfer to your grandchildren, free of taxes.

Thus, through a charitable lead trust, you could effectively leverage your unified credit and generation-skipping transfer tax exemption to shelter almost $5,000,000 from taxes.

Moreover, rather than allowing the government to take $3,189,100 from your estate in the form of estate and generation-skipping transfer taxes, you can instead leave roughly $8,750,000 (7% payout x $5,000,000 = $350,000 x 25 years = $8,750,000) to worthwhile charities.

Choosing a trust option that is right for you requires considerable reflection, as well as in-depth dialogue with a competent estate planner. Wealth-building step 100 was created to draw express attention to the need for trusts for accomplished wealth-builders. It can be found on the next page.

Conclusion   Now that you have worked your way through this lesson on estate planning, don't be too quick to pat yourself on the back. Yes, you have given estate planning some, probably, long overdue attention. However, until you actually implement some of the strategies discussed above, you won't have accomplished a thing! It's up to you to actively employ estate planning to minimize your future tax liability. The government certainly has no incentive to help you any further — for your failure to act is money in Uncle Sam's pocket. So put estate planning on the top of your to-do list, and do it; otherwise this course, and your hard work, could have largely gone for naught. ▲

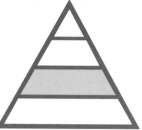

100 Steps to Wealth

STEP 100

The Method for Determining the Proper Trusts for Your Desires

What: Choose from the cornucopia of trusts available, including revocable trusts — such as living trusts — and irrevocable trusts — such as A-B trusts, QTIP trusts, The Wealth Trust®, QPRTs, and charitable trusts such as CRTs and CLTs.

Why: Revocable living trusts offer you additional control over your assets in the event of incapacity, help you lower probate costs, and provide you with an opportunity to organize your estate to minimize post mortem planning costs. Irrevocable trusts offer you the ability to remove the value of an asset, and its appreciation, from your estate, thus minimizing estate taxes for you, and even your children and grandchildren. Charitable trusts offer an additional opportunity to increase retirement income, or leverage use of your unified credit to transfer greater amounts of wealth to your family.

Risk: Low. As long as you have received good advice from a competent estate planner, and have your documents drafted by a knowledgeable attorney, your risk should be minimal.

Safety: With irrevocable trusts, in particular, even if the tax laws change, you are likely to be grand-fathered-in. In other words, there's a good chance that your pre-existing documents will continue to be interpreted according to the law at the time you executed them.

Liquidity: With a revocable, living trust, your liquidity will be as high as it was prior to the transfer. With irrevocable trusts, however, you are potentially relinquishing liquidity, because your assets, once transferred away, belong to the trust.

Why Not: It's difficult to find reasons not to execute a living trust. If you already have a will, and it adequately addresses your planning objectives, there may be no need to create a living trust. Irrevocable trusts are not recommended unless you can first retain sufficient assets for your own needs.

Buy/Invest from: You will need access to attorneys, accountants, and/or estate planners to effectuate most trust strategies.

Background: Trusts have been utilized, in one form or another, for centuries. In fact, many of the trusts utilized today are recycled versions of earlier trusts, which comply with current statutory requirements.

Creating a trust is one thing. Funding it is another. The most cleverly drafted trust in the world will have little value, if it never acquires assets. Thus, before going to the trouble and expense of creating an irrevocable trust, you should assess your own need to maintain your current standard of living, and balance it against your desire to minimize taxes, and benefit your family.

That said, irrevocable trusts are some of the most effective tools available to temper the impact of estate and gift taxes on your hard earned assets, and to provide increased retirement income for you and your family. If your home has increased significantly in value, you might consider a QPRT. If you have accumulated substantial, highly appreciated property, a CRT might be just the solution. And if you have more generalized concerns regarding protection and preservation of your estate, The Wealth Trust® mentioned on page 22 may be appropriate.

 **If you want to get started today, here's what you need to do to determine the proper trusts for your desires:**

As you can imagine, always meet with a reputable estate planner, attorney, or other professional regarding your estate. ▲

Electronic investing

LESSON 33

Electronic investing

You'll know the information highway has become part of your life when you begin to resent it if information is not available via the network.
—*Bill Gates,* The Road Ahead, *1995, Viking.*

INTRODUCTION

A decade ago only the most obsessive individual investors, those who had a lot of both time and money on their hands, used computers to try and improve their investing performance. Personal computers tended to be over-priced and under-powered, and the charting and other investment software available was expensive as well, and generally hard to use. The rest of us owe these trailblazers a debt of gratitude, however. Thanks in part to their perseverance, subsequent iterations of investment software have become vastly easier to use and more modestly priced — usually from under $100 to a few hundred dollars, depending on how sophisticated a package you want to use. Computers have also dropped in price at the same time as the features and amount of storage capacity have greatly increased. Then access to the Internet became widely available for the average computer user over the past few years, opening up new vistas of investing opportunities.

The astounding growth of the worldwide network of linked computers called the Internet, as well as on-line commercial services, is one of the most significant events of the 1990s. By 1996 as many as 20 million people, by some estimates, were logging onto the Internet and the on-line services from computers in their homes, offices or schools around the world. If you thought the Internet, or Net, and the on-line services were just for game-playing teenagers and twenty-somethings with a lot of time on their hands, think again. They have rapidly emerged as an excellent electronic tool for beginning and advanced investors alike.

In this lesson we'll cover using your computer and on-line services and the Internet for all aspects of investing, from researching stock tips and portfolio management to tracking mutual fund prices and executing trades. We'll also show you how to join the community of on-line investors, which will greatly expand your network of investment information and opinions. In fact, one of the trickiest parts of going on-line as an investor is figuring out where to find what you need, and not get swamped by the enormous amount of investment information available on-line at the click of a computer mouse. On the other hand, finding like-minded investors on-line in one of the many investing newsgroups we'll discuss later in the lesson can can be a lot of fun, and broaden your market savvy.

WHAT YOU NEED TO GET STARTED

Software There is a wide range of investment and financial planning software available to help you sharpen your money making ability as an electronic investor. Some software products — Managing Your Money for instance — are stand-alone collections of data bases and financial management tools that you use on your computer to choose investment options or find the right mix of assets for a retirement portfolio. Other software packages such as Reuters Money Network provide you with a link (via a computer modem that hooks your computer up with on-line information services using your phone line) to current stock or mutual fund quotes or other information that further enhance your investment acumen. In the following pages we've highlighted several of the best software packages available under the investment option that each product is primarily designed to serve. Morningstar Inc.'s mutual fund software, for instance, is discussed in the mutual fund section, while Intuit Inc.'s Quicken financial record keeping and planning software is included in the section on portfolio management.

Many of these software products use one or more of the major on-line commercial services as a link to stock quotes and other investment information. You can also use the on-line services directly (we'll show you how in the following pages) to further develop your electronic investing skills. And a vast and rapidly growing resource of information is also available on the Internet, which you can reach via your computer modem, either through one of the on-line services or directly by using an Internet-only service provider.

America Online, CompuServe and Prodigy are the leading on-line services (America Online's personal finance page is shown below). They offer a wide range of electronic investing services in packages that are easy to use, relatively comprehensive and economical. All three provide a basic package for about $10 a month for five hours of on-line time. Extra time researching stocks or trading is billed at about $3 an hour. Other premium-priced services are also available on CompuServe and Prodigy. (You also pay telephone connect charges for the call you make to the on-line service. For most users that will be no more than the charge for a local call.)

Software giant Microsoft has made the Internet a priority for the rest of the decade, so it's no surprise that it also has an on-line service, which debuted in 1995. The service, Microsoft Network, comes bundled with Windows 95 packages sold with IBM-compatible PCs and is expanding rapidly. Originally, Microsoft Network was planned with a full range of content to compete directly with the "big three" on-line services. The booming growth of the Internet, particularly the World Wide Web section with its astounding array of "home pages" with snazzy graphics, and even video and audio clips, led Microsoft to focus its Network squarely at the Internet.

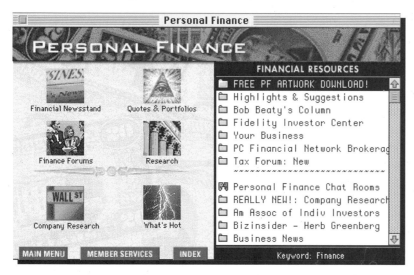

Pricing of Internet access services is likely to get even more competitive in coming months following AT&T's announcement in February, 1996 that it would offer its long-distance customers a limited amount of free Internet access for a year, and unlimited access for about $20 a month. Other corporate giants will enter the field as providers of Internet services as well (MCI to name one), which may lead to even more competition and lower prices.

If you are likely to be a heavy user of electronic investing resources you may want to consider other options. If you trade actively and are constantly looking for research materials and stock prices on companies you are targeting for investment, then a direct Internet connection may be for you. The basic monthly prices for such connections are higher than the rates charged by the big on-line services. But these are typically flat rates for 20 up to an unlimited number of hours spent on-line, so heavy users quickly come out ahead compared to the on-line services where the meter is running at about $3 an hour. Most major cities have several competing on-line service providers with basic packages starting at $20 to $30 a month for several hours longer than the five hour packages offered by the commercial services. Some of these services can be reached via 800 numbers across the country.

Getting Connected

Listed below are the major on-line services and direct Internet access providers and their contact numbers. Check with service providers for the latest prices.

Service Provider	Phone/Contact
America OnLine	800-827-6364
CompuServe	800-848-8199
Prodigy	800-776-3449

Direct Internet Connection Sampler

GNN	800-819-6112
SpryNet	http://sprynet.com
IDT	800-245-8000
Netcom	800-353-6600
PSI	800-827-7482
UUNet	800-488-6384

A number of access providers also have their software included in Internet book and software starter kits sold in bookstores and computer stores around the country. The most popular and the software considered by most experts to be most versatile is Netscape Navigator, made by Netscape Communications. Many Web sites build features that were designed specifically to be read by users of Netscape Navigator. Mosaic, the first widely used Web browsing software, is another popular option — a version of Mosaic is used in the Microsoft Network to access the Web. America Online and CompuServe have also arranged to offer both Netscape's Navigator and Microsoft Network's browser to their subscribers. Both of these products are widely available at book and computer stores. Two examples are the Internet Suite by Quarterdeck, which includes Mosaic, and Ventana's World Wide Web Kit, which comes with Netscape.

Starting with one of the on-line services may be the easiest route onto the Internet, especially for less experienced investors and computer users. But recognizing that direct access to the Internet is becoming increasingly popular, the main commercial services have recently offered or are developing direct internet services of their own that will be available to both PC and Macintosh users. The GNN service listed in the above table, for instance, is owned by America Online, and Sprynet is the Internet-only spin-off from CompuServe.

The major services are also constantly upgrading their proprietary offerings to remain competitive. They have belied predictions, so far anyway, that these services would fade as the popularity of the Internet, especially the World Wide Web, continues to grow. *Money*'s Personal Finance Center on CompuServe, for instance, offers a wealth of financial information in a well-organized package. America Online and Prodigy are also adding to their personal finance sections. AOL is known for its extensive listing of Morningstar mutual fund listings, as well as an informative and amusing section on stock investing called the Motley Fool, and also has done a better job than the other major services of integrating Internet access seamlessly into its finance offerings. We'll discuss these and other software programs used for specific investment functions, stock research, on-line trading, portfolio management, etc., in detail on the following pages as we address each of those subjects.

Hardware   In general terms, the same rules apply to electronic investing that apply to most computer uses — the bigger and faster the better. A PC powered by a Pentium chip or a Macintosh from Apple Computer with a Power PC chip will give you the biggest bang for your buck, especially when you are using on-line services or the Internet. These computers will speed-up the processing of many of the multi-media and graphics-intensive files found on the Internet in particular.

Taxing Matters

If the computer software you purchase is used exclusively for investing purposes, and your child isn't using your version of AOL to e-mail her friends every night, then it very likely is a tax-deductible expense. Monthly usage fees would probably fall into the same category, although this and all tax items should be brought to the attention of your accountant or tax adviser. In most cases tax experts recommend that the investor who doesn't buy and sell securities for a living shouldn't even consider writing off any hardware costs as investment expenses — that's a very hard sell with the Internal Revenue Service.

At a minimum your computer should have at least eight megabytes of random access memory, or 8k of RAM, to properly handle most electronic investing software programs. For instance, you need that much computer memory to easily download stock quotes or other information using one software program and have another program with a spreadsheet open that contains your historical investment information. RAM memory operates the applications you have running on your computer, which is not to be confused with the storage capacity of your computer's hard disk, which is also often referred to as memory. Some programs may say that you can get by with 4k of RAM, but don't believe them. Your machine will probably be chugging along so slowly that you'll turn it off to spare yourself the aggravation. A computer with 16k of RAM and a hard disk approaching one gigabyte (one billion bits of information) in storage capacity is rapidly becoming the norm for active users of on-line services and the Internet.

A modem that connects your computer to the Internet via your phone line and transmits data at 28.8 kilobytes a second is rapidly becoming standard Internet hardware as well. These modems are widely available starting at around $100 for off-brand PC models. The time you'll save downloading files from the Internet using a 28.8 kbs modem is well worth the money. Again, slower modems will work, but downloading large Internet files with anything less than a 14.4 kbs modem is the equivalent of watching molasses flow down a gently inclined plane.

PC or Mac?

In one sense electronic investing using the Internet is made easier by the fact that the Net is an open access system of computer networks. That means both PCs and Macs can browse at will. But as with most other types of software, the programs catering to electronic investing tend to be written first and most often for the 90+% of computer users who operate PCs. Mac users aren't shut out of the electronic investing arena, but they do often have to go the extra mile to find a program that fits their needs. If you already own a Mac, you're probably used to the inconvenience. In most cases, the Internet access software and the Internet sites we'll be referring to in the following pages are reachable using either a PC or Mac. That's true of all three major commercial on-line service providers, for instance. The investment analysis software is more heavily weighted toward PC users. On the other hand, there are easy to use and highly sophisticated Mac products out there, such as TickerWatcher by Linn Software, that can match the best Windows-based programs. When we refer in the following pages to specific programs we'll indicate whether they're written for the PC, Mac or both.

FINDING YOUR WAY AROUND CYBERSPACE

The Internet was created by the Pentagon and the defense industry in the 1960s so that the U.S. would have a decentralized communications system that could survive a nuclear attack. A similar system linking university research centers was connected several years later. The computer networks are interconnected with dedicated phone lines so that messages don't have to travel through any single site to get somewhere else. Through the late 1980s the Internet was still the domain largely of scientific researchers and university staff and students. Systems in other countries were also linked to the Net. Over the past several years the general public has slowly learned about what is available on the Net, and started to log on in rapidly increasing numbers.

Much of the Internet prior to the early 1990s consisted of individual sites where information such as research papers or government data were stored. Another section, which had started as a separate system called Usenet, consisted of newsgroups where experts in certain fields discussed particular issues of interest to them by filing electronic comments and responses to each other at a particular Internet site or address. But to connect with any of these sites you had to know the particular address for the site. When you wanted to see what was begin discussed on a related by separate site, you had to know the address of that one, log-off of the first site and log-on to the second, and so on.

Then in the early 1990s a programmer affiliated with the European scientific consortium known by its acronym CERN developed what became known as the World Wide Web. His goal was to make it easier for researchers to find Internet sites carrying information related to their studies. The Web does this by including within the body of a text file what are known as hypertext words. These words lead Internet users to other sites related to the topic of the word that appears in bold-faced hypertext. All you have to do is click with your computer mouse on the bold-faced hypertext and within seconds you are whisked around the world to another Internet site on a related topic.

Internet Roadmaps

So the Web is out there and there are plenty of linked words that will whiz you from one site to another. How do you find information on areas that interest you, say investing in stocks or economic forecasts, without spending hours browsing from one Web site to another? Programs that act as huge electronic reference libraries for the Internet have been developed to serve just such a need. They are referred to generically as search engines and have quickly become some of the most popular sites on the Web. Many of them have also developed extensive listings of investment and financial information, so they can serve as good jumping off points for your initial attempts to "surf" the Net. They are also invaluable resources for even veteran electronic investors, since the information accessible via the search engines is being constantly updated. The personal investing and finance pages of the major on-line services, most notably America Online, also offer numerous electronic road signs directing you to additional investing information.

Despite its off-the-wall name, Yahoo is a search engine that contains an excellent electronic catalog of investing and finance information (Yahoo's Business and Economy page is shown at left). Starting with broad subject areas such as business and finance and then following hypertext links to more specialized subjects such as stocks, mutual funds or electronic trading, an investor using Yahoo can quickly and rather painlessly tap into a wealth of investing information. Lycos and Webcrawler and similar search engines and also very useful. Alta Vista, a search engine site owned by the Digital Equipment Corp., has an excellent and very fast word search feature if you know specifically what you are looking for. It's less useful than the other search engines if you want to start with a general topic and then look for more specific sites containing detailed information.

SEARCH ENGINES	INTERNET ADDRESS
Yahoo	http://www.yahoo.com
Lycos	http://www.lycos.com
Webcrawler	http://www.webcrawler.com
Alta Vista	http://www.altavista.com

As you can see from the table at left, there is a standard form for addresses on the World Wide Web, the most popular section of the Internet. The addresses are known as URLs, which stands for Universal Resource Locators. You don't need to know the technical reasons they are written as they are, but you should know that typos aren't tolerated in Internet addresses. So if you type a URL with a semi-colon instead of a colon, it won't connect you to the Net. All of the above addresses are World Wide Web sites, hence the "www" in the address. That is followed by a period (which will be called a dot if someone is reading a URL to you) and then the name of the site or company that runs the site. Apple Computer's home page on the Web is reachable by substituting "apple" in one of the above addresses. The final "dot com" designation in the address tells you that this is a commercial site. By comparison, addresses for Web sites run by universities will conclude with "dot edu" for educational, and government sites will end with "dot gov."

For instance, the artificial intelligence laboratory at the Massachusetts Institute of Technology has a Web site, called MIT Stockmaster, that allows investors to call up charts showing price and volume trends in any of more than 6,000 stocks. This Web site's URL is *"http://www.ai.mit.edu/stocks/"*. The URL for the site containing SEC filings for publicly traded companies and mutual funds is *"http://www.sec.gov."* You will see this site also referred to as Edgar on other Web sites, which stands for Electronic Data Gathering, Analysis and Retrieval.

ON-LINE INVESTMENT RESEARCH

The research possibilities available on on-line services and the Internet are limited more by your imagination and time than by the amount of on-line investing resources. You can pursue in great detail fundamental analysis of a company or industry group, ferreting out projected earnings per share growth based on a new product a company has launched or the sales from each of a company's five different business units. Follow a hypertext link to another investment site and you can call up scores of screens on technical analysis of a stock or market, charting price trends and moving averages for just about any asset that's traded. Before going into detail on different sources of investment information and where to find them, let's conduct a trial on-line search to see what sort of information is quickly available even for computer neophytes and less-experienced investors. For the purposes of this beginning search we'll stick with the on-line services America Online and CompuServe.

Found in Cyberspace

Let's say you're looking for a "value" type stock that didn't run-up to stellar heights during the record-setting bull market of 1995 and early 1996. Right now you don't think it's a good idea to chase hot growth stocks that have been hitting new highs for the past few months. They might be due for a sharp correction. The type of stock you're looking for — you'd prefer the relative stability of a large capitalization stock to start out with as you test the electronic investing waters — has potential for future price appreciation, either as a result of renewed earnings growth or possibly a takeover, for instance, that hasn't been recognized by the rest of Wall Street.

It's possible to start searching for stocks without a name in mind by using computerized "screens" that, for example, will find stocks with low price-to-earnings ratios compared to the broad market. But like most serious wealth builders you have probably been keeping a few stocks in mind as potential buys based on news events or price trends that you have noticed since subscribing to the *100 Steps to Wealth* program. As an electronic investor you can quickly gather a great deal of information on nearly any exchange-traded security.

**Feeling Your
On-line Oats**

For our example we'll use Quaker Oats, a household name and a "value" investment play that trades on the New York Stock Exchange. It even has an easy stock symbol to remember: OAT. You can follow the steps below to track information gathered about Quaker, or use a symbol for a stock of your choice and gather information from the same sources.

Here's the background on Quaker, which is available from news services carried by the major on-line service providers, that would make it a candidate for a value investment. The company was widely criticized in late 1994 for paying $1.7 billion to buy soft-drink maker Snapple Beverages. The criticism appeared to be on the mark throughout 1995 as costs and charges against earnings tied to the Snapple acquisition acted as a drag on Quaker's earnings and stock price. Quaker's relatively flat stock price, especially in the face of the huge rally in large cap stocks in 1995, had made it the subject of occasional takeover rumors (Coca-Cola's name has cropped up as the leading suspect among potential acquirers). The stock has traded between the low to mid 30s for much of the past year. The issue for you the investor: does Quaker appear to have its Snapple problems behind it, and therefore are other investors looking at its past performance when they value the stock instead of the future potential? And if not, is the company a possible takeover candidate? To research the investment outlook for Quaker we'll stick with information that is available simply by using America Online and CompuServe.

America Online's personal finance section contains basic company profiles that give a snapshot of a company's financial health. The picture for Quaker wasn't very good. The company report on AOL, which you call up by clicking on the company report section and then entering the stock symbol, shows that the Chicago-based food and beverage company reported a loss of 36 cents a share for the quarter ended December 31, 1995. A news report, available by searching the business news section of AOL by entering the stock symbol, notes that the loss was the result of charges tied mainly to Snapple manufacturing changes and inventory write-offs. Not surprisingly, considering all the bad news out about the company, the AOL company report shows that Quaker's price to earnings ratio is only about 6.5 based on 1995 earnings , or only one-third the P/E ratio of the S&P 500 at the time.

The question for a value-oriented investor is has the market over-emphasized the bad news for Quaker? Switching to the Chicago Online section of AOL found on the newsstand page, an investor can search back issues of the hometown *Chicago Tribune* for news stories on the company. The *Tribune* carried a report from a food company conference in Florida that quoted Quaker chairman William Smithburg saying he was committed to boosting Snapple sales, and detailing steps the company has already taken to promote the product. The company clearly thinks that value investors are on the right track, but then most corporate officials tend to accentuate the positive when it comes to their ability to turn around a company.

What do investors who already own Quaker stock have to say about the company? AOL, as well as CompuServe and Prodigy, have lively chat groups where investors swap theories about why their stocks are or aren't going to be good investments. Many Quaker investors who had bought the stock in mid-1995 on takeover rumors were understandably sour about the fact that the stock had basically treaded water for eight months. But the prevailing opinion was summed up by one chat group contributor (in the interests of privacy we'll leave out his name) who said, "What's to lose? If they turn it around, the stock goes up. If they don't, they get acquired and the stock goes up. Only a market crash can keep this at a 6 p/e." Not a ringing endorsement, but it makes the value investment case that the risk of further loss is fairly limited compared to the potential for a future increase in the share price.

Much of the same information is available on CompuServe and Prodigy. Compuserve, via its personal finance section, also carries a service called Vestor that uses a proprietary stock evaluation system that attempts to predict a stock's potential for increasing in price. Vestor said its computer-based system rated Quaker "a major buy for long-term investors'" based on the company's earnings and recent price trends. Bingo! The value investor's case was being made for her. Vestor said Quaker is "rated in the top 20% of all companies based on fundamentals. Further, projections show that the stock could go up 33.6% within the next 12 months." The investment analysis service added that "the reward/risk ratio for Quaker Oats Co. at this time is 42/10. That is, the stock could go up 42% in a bull market and go down 10% in a bad market." (This is an extremely favorable reward/risk ratio.)

Does that mean an investor should immediately switch to an on-line brokerage service and buy Quaker shares? No amount of research, whether it's obtained in a library basement or via the Internet, can make an investment decision for you. But after spending a relatively brief amount of time on line, you were able to add significantly to your knowledge of the stock and its prospects, and even "eavesdrop" on what other investors were saying (you could have offered your two cents worth, too!). A broker who calls with a stock tip may be right about a company's prospects, but you are taking his or her word for it without having much additional information to act on. Electronic investing gives you several other sources of information to buttress your final decision.

The Yahoo Search Engine

Let's switch to Yahoo, one of the most popular Internet search engines, to get a taste of what's available for electronic investors. Once you've reached the Yahoo home page using the URL listed above, *http://www.yahoo.com*, (don't worry, fairly soon you'll be able to type "http://www." with your eyes closed) click on the bold-faced subject category "Business and Economy" (see table on next page). At any stage in a search you can save a URL and add it to a directory of Internet Web sites and other addresses. Some browsers refer to these as hotlists, others bookmarks. By doing so you can simply click on the address the next time you want to reach a particular site, rather than retyping the addresses each time. Most browser software also allows you to categorize addresses by subject matter such as investing, home business, etc.

Taking the search one step further, click on the bold-faced Markets and Investments subject category. *Note: not all browsers reproduce Web pages in exactly the same format. Yours may appear slightly different from the format in the accompanying sidebar, which was downloaded using the browser that is packaged with America Online. Web services are also constantly updating their offerings, so by the time you duplicate this search, there may be even more offerings to choose from!*

Government Sites

Going through a commercial service such as Yahoo isn't always the best way to gather Internet information, even though it is often the most convenient. (Yahoo and other commercial sites make money, or at least defray a portion of their costs, by including often-annoying ads that pop up on your screen. Feel free to ignore them.) A case in point is the Edgar hypertext link in the list at the top of page 11. Clicking on the word Edgar takes you to a number of mostly commercial sites that provide searches of corporate and mutual fund electronic filings with the SEC. But it doesn't include the SEC's Web page, which is at "*http://www.sec.gov.*" Going to that site directly gives you the list found on page 12, free of commercial search charges:

Other government sites that can be contacted directly can also be very useful for intrepid electronic investors. If a company or stock analyst bases a rosy view of the future on a certain economic projection or statistic, you might have taken their word for it in the past. Now you can make a quick trip to a government site to get confirmation.

The Commerce Dept. operates the **Economic Bulletin Board.** It has 20 file areas with current economic indicators and other economic and trades information, employment statistics and the results of U.S. Treasury auctions. This is reachable at what's known as a Gopher site (the technology was developed at the University of Minnesota, whose mascot is a gopher). Check the manual for your on-line software to see how to log-on to Gopher sites. On America Online, for instance,

Yahoo Web Search: Business and Economy: Markets and Investments

Below is the listing on Yahoo of Web sites with information likely to interest electronic investors. The number after each item in the first group indicates the number of sites that can be found in that category. There are 66 sites with mutual fund information, for instance. The second group of sites carry brief descriptions and also include hypertext links to other sites.

Group 1

- Indices (13)
- Bonds (7)
- Brokerages@
- Commercial Financial Services@
- Commercial Investment Services@
- Corporate Reports (49)
- Currency Exchange (19)
- Diamonds and Gems (1)
- Futures and Options (49)
- Magazines@
- Mutual Funds (66)
- Newsletters@
- Organizations (5)
- Real Estate@
- Regions (12)
- Stocks (121)
- Usenet (3)
- Edgar Database (9) (see next page)

Group 2

- **Info'Vest** — links to the best investment sites. summary info for sites with quotes, company research, mutual funds and more.
- **Deadman's Island** — For Investment News Worth Killing (or Dying) For!
- **Douglas Gerlach's Invest-o-Rama!** — Annotated directory of hundreds of internet resources for investors, including feature articles on growth stock investing.
- **Investec** — Stock & Commodity Trading Information
- **Investment Brokerages Guide** — A listing of many brokerages around the world, summarizing services and commissions.
- **Investment Strategies for the 21st Century** — By Frank Armstrong, from the GNN Personal Finance Center.
- **Investor Intouch** — stock charts, information, research listings, Nelson's Directory Online, unmoderated and moderated discussion groups.
- **InvestorWeb** — investment information on companies and other news.
- **Money and Investing** — diversified funds, market experiments and studies, online publications and services, price quotes and charts.
- **NAIC** — National Assoc. of Investors Corp
- **NETworth Investment Information Center**
- **Wall Street Net** — latest on what's happening in the world of corporate debt and equity financings.
- Weekly Market Summary [Gruntal & Co.]
- **FAQ** — misc.invest
- **FAQ** — misc.invest (iddis.com)

By clicking on the initial word or phrase in each bulleted item — these are bold-faced hypertext links on Yahoo — you will be switched to a site or collection of sites covering that particular site. Obviously, you need to continue narrowing your focus to find a site that meets you needs, which we'll address in the following pages.

you simply click on an icon of a gopher, and then type the address of the site into the appropriate blank field. The EEB is at: *una.hh.lob.umich.edu*. Once you're logged on, choose "ebb."

Commerce Department Statistics are also available on Stat USA, but this is a subscription service that charges for use. Reachable at *http://www.stat-usa.gov*.

The Department of Census's Housing and Household Economics Statistics Division has information on incomes and poverty, health insurance, the labor force and the wealth of households. It's Web site is: *http://www.census.gov/ftp/pub/hhes/www/. Note: Web site addresses that appear at the end of a sentence in this lesson will be followed by a period to conform with standard punctuation, but the address you type into your computer shouldn't conclude with a period.*

FinanceNet, an off-shoot of Vice President Al Gore's office of National Performance Review (remember those expensive ashtrays?) links government and financial management professionals in an effort to optimize the way government manages taxpayer resources. Its Web address is: *http://www.financenet.gov/*.

EDGAR Database of Corporate Information

- IMPORTANT INFORMATION ABOUT EDGAR (READ THIS FIRST!)
- GENERAL INFORMATION: RETRIEVING DATA
- SEARCH THE EDGAR DATABASE
- EDGAR FORM DEFINITIONS
- EDGAR DATA DOCUMENTATION
- MASTER INDICES
- SCHEDULE: PHASE IN OF REMAINING COMPANIES TO THE EDGAR SYSTEM

- CORPORATION FINANCE PHASE-IN GROUP LIST
- INVESTMENT MANAGEMENT PHASE-IN GROUP LIST
- TOOLS AND UTILITIES
- NEWS ABOUT EDGAR: INFORMATION FOR FILERS AND OTHERS INTERESTED IN THE EDGAR SYSTEM

Source: http://www.sec.gov/edgarhp.htm/

The White House has a Web sites that contains full texts of budgets and press releases (and there's no waiting in line to get in), while Congress's Web site carries the text of bills before the legislators and the Congressional Record.

White House: *http://www.white-house.gov/*
Congress: *http://thomas.loc.gov/*

Academic Sites

University sites are also rich resources of economic and other statistics, and can provide a useful reality check to commercial sources you are likely to come across using one of the main on-line service providers or a search engine to pan for investment gold. One of the most comprehensive and best-known is at the University of Michigan, which, as we noted above, is a gopher site. Other top university sources for economic information are at the University of Texas, the University of Southern Mississippi and Ohio State University's Department of Finance.

U. of Michigan: *gopher://una.hh.lib.umich.edu*

U. of Texas: *http://riskweb.bus.utexas.edu/finweb.html*

U. of S. Mississippi: *http://econwpa.wustl.edu/econfaq/econfaq.html*

Ohio State: WWW Virtual Library: Finance and Investments — *http://www.cob.ohio-state.edu/dept/fin/overview.htm.*

Ohio State: Financial Data Finder: *http://www.cob.ohio-state.edu/dept/fin/osudata.htm*

Another Web site source of economic information that deserves mention is the site operated by respected Wall Street economist Edward Yardeni: *http://www.webcom.com/~yardeni/ economic.html*

On-Line Publications

Many of the best known investment magazines, including *Money*, and newspapers can be found in whole or in part on one of the on-line services or the Net. *Money*, for instance, sponsors the personal finance site on CompuServe, and articles from the current issue as well as a daily electronic version of the magazine carrying timely features and commentary. The magazine doesn't have a "lock" on CompuServe, however. Numerous other well-known magazines, including *Forbes*, *Fortune* and *U.S. News and World Report* can be accessed using CompuServe as well. Similarly, *Business Week* is prominently displayed on the Business News page of America Online. *Money* also has a home page on the Internet that is reachable though the Pathfinder site (http://www.pathfinder.com) that was created and is maintained by the magazine's corporate parent Time-Warner. This page has several hypertext links to other investing sites on the Net, and also a constantly updated list of top investing sites on the World Wide Web that makes for informative and often times amusing reading as well.

Get Me the Newsroom!

The Newsroom — *http://www.auburn.edu/~vestmon/news.html*
This Web site offers an excellent collection of general and business news as well as links to several government information sites.

An increasing number of newspapers are setting up sites on the Web or are offered via one of the major on-line services. CompuServe has the most comprehensive listing of papers from around the country that can be searched through electronically for company names at a cost above the basic service fee. America Online raised its newsprint profile when it added "@times," the on-line version of *The New York Times*. Because of earlier contract obligations made by the *Times*, back issues aren't available here, however.

Why would you want to browse through a paper on-line? Say a friend or broker mentioned that a small but rapidly growing company based in the Twin Cities was developing a new medical device that would help reduce the length of in-hospital stays of elderly patients. The tremendous pressure on Congress to curb increases in Medicare spending combined with the aging of the population makes the product and the company sound like an interesting investment. The local brokerage firm that took the company public thinks it's a great buy, but they're hardly unbiased observers since they'll be first in line if the company makes a secondary stock offering in the future. So another source would be the local papers, the Minneapolis *Star Tribune* and its rival the *St. Paul Pioneer Press*. Both are listed on CompuServe.

The Journal for Free? Well, at Least for Now.

A better option, certainly in terms of price, is the *Journal's* Money & Investing Update site on the Web: *http://update.wsj.com*. Subscribing to the site and receiving the latest market and financial news is free — at least for now. Users are required to register, and the wording of the registration process implies that Dow Jones is likely to start charging for the service at some point in the not-too-distant future. The service would be worth a modest fee for many investors — remember that the paper itself costs 75 cents a day — since it provides a quick and reliable way to stay abreast of the market, as they say at the *Journal*.

The grand-daddy of financial papers, *The Wall Street Journal*, is available in all its voluminous detail through Dow Jones News Retrieval, owned by the paper's corporate parent Dow Jones. The service also carries stories from *The New York Times* and dozens of other publications and news services, as well as the most comprehensive listing in cyberspace of current and historical quotes for U.S. and foreign stocks. But the high monthly cost for the service, about $30 for the Private Investor Edition (formerly known as Market Monitor) software that allows eight hours of use, may be a budget-breaker for the part-time investor. The company also offers Personal Journal, an electronic version of the paper that you customize to suit your interests in particular stocks, markets or news subjects. The basic price is about $13 a month, with updates during the day costing 50 cents each.

Other Information Sources

Corporate Web Sites. An increasing number of companies have created home pages on the Web. Many are no more than Internet advertisements for themselves. Others contain a great deal of information about products and the recent earnings history of the company as well as other income statement and balance sheet data. They also almost always contain the name of a company contact, usually someone in the investor relations department, who can provide you with annual and quarterly reports and other publicly available information about the company.

Brokerage firms. Yes, they have something to sell you and would love to have you sign up as a customer. Home pages for leading firms with full or discount brokerage services, including Merrill Lynch, Charles Schwab and Fidelity Investments, also offer investment information that goes beyond product pitches and is available to non-customers.

Investor Advocacy Groups. The American Association of Individual Investors offers a variety of services and informative articles on investing through AOL. Some are taken from the group's *Computerized Investing* newsletter and critique the latest investing software packages. AOL subscribers can click on an AAII icon in the service's personal finance section. Non-subscribers can query the group via e-mail: *AAIIMEMBR@aol.com*. The National Association of Investors Corp., which caters to investment clubs, at: *http://www.better-investing.org/*.

What the Pros are Reading

Electronic investors can also tap into a vast pool of specialized investment publications that until they were made available on-line were read mainly by financial industry professionals and full-time investors. Investing newsletters cover a broad number of investment subjects and can be found on many of the more popular Web sites. Many specialized publications are also available on the major on-line services, and in many cases you can download a sample copy to see if the author's investing style and insights match your interests before paying to subscribe or buy a certain number of issues. Publications Online, for instance, is part of CompuServe's extended services that charge premiums above the normal monthly rate. The following newsletters are on Publications Online, based on information provided by CompuServe, and are followed by the per-issue surcharge unless otherwise noted. Some of the prices are steep, but if you can use the information to make money, you may consider it well worth the cost.

Beige Book Summary — offers information on the U.S. economy and local economies with snapshots of geographical regions and industry sectors derived from surveys taken by the 12 U.S. Federal Reserve Banks. Updates are released every six to seven weeks. Thomas Publishing Inc. Surcharge: $4.50.

Current Grades for Major Market Indices — lists several leading market indices with current price, grade and previous grade. Updated weekly. Trend Dynamics. $5.00.

Current Grades for S&P Industry Groups — applies the same concept to industry groups from S&P. Also updated weekly. Trend Dynamics. $5.00.

Current Grades for TIPs Equities — lists entire TIPs equities universe with current price, current grade and previous grade. Updated weekly. Trend Dynamics. $10.00.

Equity Price Projections — offers 13- and 52-week price projections for 1,000 equities highlighting the S&P 500 and the S&P Midcap 400. Updated weekly. Trend Dynamics. $2.50.

Federal Open Market Committee Minutes — offers minutes and analysis from that part of the Federal Reserve responsible for creating monetary policy. The FOMC Minutes are released every six to seven weeks, a few days after the next meeting. Thomas Publishing. $9.50.

Fitch Bond Reader — is a monthly, four-page newsletter containing research and commentary highlighting major issues of interest to bond investors, including corporate bonds, tax-exempt bonds, market risk, and strategy. Fitch Investors Service. $10.

HSL, The International Harry Schultz Letter — covers all major world stock, bond and futures markets, as well as major currencies and gold. Sections on Asia, Latin America, the United Kingdom, New Zealand, the United States, Canada and Africa are offered. Markets are technically analyzed in this chart-oriented publication, and specific recommendations for buy/sell points are given. HSL. $50.

Investing for Income — is ideal for fixed-income investors who closely follow money-market mutual funds, no-load municipal and taxable bond mutual funds, as well as the Treasury markets. providing in-depth articles about the bond-fund industry, tax tips, economic trends, and the interest rate/inflation outlook, the newsletter offers buy and sell advice for its sector strategy and features model portfolios and allocations for investors seeking total return. IBC/Donoghue Inc. $5.00.

IPO Aftermarket — tracks daily newly issued initial public offerings and makes public the managing underwriters' estimates as soon as they become available, including buy, sell and hold recommendations, as well as some stock-price target predictions. Lynch, Jones & Ryan Inc. $2.00 per IPO.

The IPO Insider — is an investment advisory newsletter published twice a month that concentrates exclusively on the IPO market. Emphasis is placed on small-cap companies with solid fundamentals and strong growth potential. Companies are rated using a proprietary system; those that score 75 or higher are given a "buy" recommendation. Capital Markets Publishing. $14.95.

IPO Maven — reviews monthly equity public offerings in the US that are larger than $10 million, including American Depository Receipts issued on foreign securities and Real Estate Investment Trusts. Each two-page company profile includes a summarized balance sheet, income and cash-flow statements, address, size of the deal, and a list of competitors and products. Also featured is information on the business environment, company strategy, product/services portfolio, and investment considerations. Each company is ranked for its potential for the long-term appreciation of 30 percent in the next three years. Otiva Inc. $5 per IPO.

MoneyBuilder — is an eight-page monthly financial advisory letter than includes information on geopolitical events impacting various markets; trends, news, and views; and the Wealth Fine-Tuner worksheet, which displays publisher Harvey Schmidt's model portfolio with predictions of how each investment will do in various financial climates. Har-v Inc. $29.00.

Moneyletter — is a mutual fund advisory newsletter for individual investors that describes, analyses and recommends no-load and low-load stock, bond and money-market mutual funds. It offers investors four risk-based portfolio strategies to follow. The newsletter also covers economic trends and personal-finance issues, such as tax strategies, insurance, retirement planning, bank products and regulations. IBC/Donoghue Inc. $5.00.

Morningstar Mutual Funds — provides coverage of more than 1,500 stock and bond funds in a one fund per page format. Each report offers over 450 key statistics and a written analysis. Also included are star ratings, investment-style boxes, tax analysis, and derivatives exposure. Morningstar. $5 per fund.

Projected Treasury Yield Curves — comprises Treasury issues ranging from the three-month T-bill to the 30-year Treasury bond. Displayed are 13-week and 52-week projected yield curves. Updated weekly. Trend Dynamics. $2.50.

The Report Card — is part of The IPO Insider and is provided as a separate report twice monthly covering all the companies reviewed in The IPO Insider. In addition to company ratings, it offers notes on company weaknesses. Capital Markets Publishing. $9.95.

S&P Industry Group Price Projections — provides 13- and 52-week price projections for selected Standard & poor's Industry Groups. Updated weekly. Trend Dynamics. $2.50.

S&P Outlook — is an advisory resource for timely, proven guidance on market activities and the forces driving them. Published weekly, it identifies the developments and trends that affect stock performance and offers recommendations on when to buy, sell and hold. Standard & Poor's. $10.

S&P Enhanced Stock Reports — is a weekly, comprehensive picture of 4,600 publicly held U.S. corporations' activities, developments, performance, and outlook. The reports include the S&P Stars, or Stock Appreciation Ranking System, which evaluates the immediate investment potential and rates the stock as buy, hold or sell. Standard & Poor's. $2 per company.

S&P Stock Reports Industry Page — offers a weekly, comprehensive investment outlook of a company's industry with the latest information on new developments and trends, as well as expert analysis of the events and forces affecting growth. A Peer Comparison ranks the company's performance against up to 15 of its nearest competitors. Also included in a comparison of the industry's stock performance compared with the S&P 500 Industry Index. S&P. $1.00.

S&P Stock Reports News Page — covers news stories S&P experts think might have an impact on the future price of a company's stock. Reported in a brief style, it is updated daily. S&P. $1 per company.

The Special Company Report — offers analysis of the companies in The IPO Insider. Capital Markets Publishing. $6.95 per IPO or company.

TIPS Newsletter — offers market commentary and review of the TIPS model portfolio. Updated monthly. Trend Dynamics. $10.

Value Line Investment Survey — provides full-page reports on about 1,700 stocks, including statistical and analytical commentary on the company and stock. Reports are revised four times a year and contain a Timeliness Rank, a Safety Rank, a three to five year price appreciation projection, analysts' commentary, up to 16 years of financial data, income statement and balance-sheet projections. While this product has long been available to the investing public, the on-line access allows you to research a company or two without paying for the entire package. Value Line Publishing Inc. $5 per company.

Value Line Mutual Fund Survey — provides full-page reports on approximately 1,500 funds. Each profile includes recent rankings, performance and risk characteristics, portfolio composition, and shareholder information, plus a performance graph and an analysts commentary. Value Line Publishing Inc. $5 per fund.

Zacks Analyst Watch — offers readers a complete overview of U.S. brokerage research as it impacts each of 5,000 stocks. Earnings estimates and stock recommendations from over 2,500 analysts at 210 brokerage firms are organized and summarized for each company. Companies are ranked within industries to identify those with the strongest broker recommendation. Zacks Investment Research. $2.50 per company.

SECURITIES AND INVESTMENTS

In each of the following sections on different investment options we'll discuss how to use the on-line services as well as the Internet to broaden your reach as an electronic investor. We've included descriptions of software packages that are tailored to each investment category e.g. stocks, currencies, etc. In some cases, a software program that is described under stocks, for instance, can also be used with ease to aid in searching for bond investment information or also for commodities.

Mutual Funds   With their broad appeal among investors, the leading on-line commercial service providers obviously consider mutual funds a priority. Information about funds is easy to find and well-organized. However, it's surprising that none of the Big Three has as extensive on-line mutual fund data banks as you might expect given the huge in-flow of investor money into mutual funds over the past few years. A number of Web sites have equaled or are close to equally what the on-line services have to offer in the mutual fund area.

America Online has an edge on its rivals with Morningstar, the best-known name in mutual fund ranking services for individual investors, as its source of mutual fund information. (As we'll see, however, some Morningstar information is also available on CompuServe.) AOL's version of Morningstar includes a data base of more than 7,000 mutual funds. Preset screens deliver Top 25 listings of funds by investment objective — aggressive growth, growth and income, etc. — for three month, one-year, three-year and five year periods. The service also provides rather bare-bones reports on each of the individual funds (see example below). AOL also carries a section on investment advice and theory, much of it concerning funds, provided by the American Association of Individual Investors.

A separate technical analysis price charting service on AOL, Decision Point Timing, also includes a number of mutual funds in its data base. It tracks several proprietary indicators that attempt to predict when a fund in the data base may be temporarily bottoming out or peaking in price.

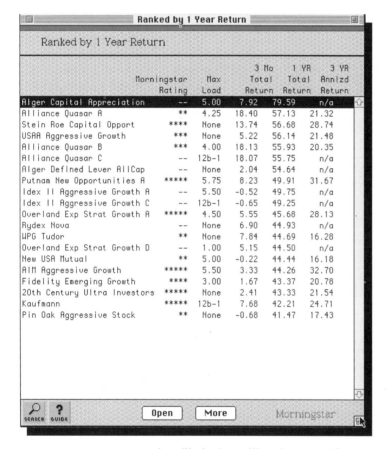

Ranked by 1 Year Return

	Morningstar Rating	Max Load	3 Mo Total Return	1 YR Total Return	3 YR Annlzd Return
Alger Capital Appreciation	--	5.00	7.92	79.59	n/a
Alliance Quasar A	**	4.25	18.40	57.13	21.32
Stein Roe Capital Opport	****	None	13.74	56.68	28.74
USAA Aggressive Growth	***	None	5.22	56.14	21.48
Alliance Quasar B	***	4.00	18.13	55.93	20.35
Alliance Quasar C	--	12b-1	18.07	55.75	n/a
Alger Defined Lever AllCap	--	None	2.04	54.64	n/a
Putnam New Opportunities A	*****	5.75	8.23	49.91	31.67
Idex II Aggressive Growth A	--	5.50	-0.52	49.75	n/a
Idex II Aggressive Growth C	--	12b-1	-0.65	49.25	n/a
Overland Exp Strat Growth A	*****	4.50	5.55	45.68	28.13
Rydex Nova	--	None	6.90	44.93	n/a
WPG Tudor	**	None	7.84	44.69	16.28
Overland Exp Strat Growth D	--	1.00	5.15	44.50	n/a
New USA Mutual	**	5.00	-0.22	44.44	16.18
AIM Aggressive Growth	*****	5.50	3.33	44.26	32.70
Fidelity Emerging Growth	****	3.00	1.67	43.37	20.78
20th Century Ultra Investors	*****	None	2.41	43.33	21.54
Kaufmann	*****	12b-1	7.68	42.21	24.71
Pin Oak Aggressive Stock	**	None	-0.68	41.47	17.43

Open   More   Morningstar

Back to Morningstar. Let's say you consider buying shares in a mutual fund whose goal is aggressive growth. You decide to request a screen of the top 25 aggressive growth funds based on one-year performance. Your search of the Morningstar database on AOL would produce the table at left.

Electronic investing is a great way to get your hands on a lot of data in a hurry, but it doesn't relieve you of analyzing the data. The above table is a case in point. Once you see the one-year data for aggressive growth funds you may realize that you aren't comfortable investing in a fund that doesn't at least have a three-year track record. The one-year performance could've been a fluke. And since you couldn't screen out funds that charge front-end sales "loads," you eliminate those that aren't no-load funds. The first three funds in the table are eliminated on one or both counts. That takes you to the fourth-ranked aggressive growth fund for the one-year period, the Stein-Roe Capital Opportunity Fund. It not only soundly beat the broad market averages last year, it did so handily in the trailing three- and five-year periods as well. Reinforcing your decision is the fact that Morningstar gives the fund a four-star ranking out of a possible five stars.

Never heard of the Stein Roe fund? Click on the fund's name and you can call up a brief report that lists the fund's investment objectives, returns relative to the S&P 500, a dated listing of Top 10 portfolio holdings, and a handful of other performance and portfolio statistics, as well as an 800 number for contacting the fund's management company. What's missing are the detailed one-page reports on funds that subscribers to Morningstar's relatively expensive CD and diskette-based fund information services receive. However, you can get one-page fund reports from Morningstar on CompuServe for $5 per report.

CompuServe allows members to screen more than 4,700 funds according to criteria such as investment objective, total return, management company, fees and expenses and others. It also includes a mutual funds information center, which includes prospectuses and promotional information from fund companies. But what sets this major on-line service apart in the individual fund reports. The one-page report on the Stein Roe fund, for instance, is jammed with fine-print information (and for this reason will seem to take forever to print out at home) on nearly every conceivable performance aspect of the fund. But it's the commentary provided by Morningstar analysts that put the performance figures in perspective and make these reports worth the added cost.

Here's an excerpt from a recent analysis of the Stein Roe Capital Opportunities fund.

> *"Prudence has lifted the Stein Roe Capital Opportunities Fund to the top of its field. When last reviewed at the beginning of the third quarter, this fund's returns looked mediocre. Since then, they have rocketed ahead of most aggressive-growth funds, and the fund has jumped to near the top of the group in one-, three- and five year trailing returns. . . Most aggressive growth peers had bigger weighting in the technology sector, where the market extracted severe penalties for disappointing earnings.*
>
> *Santella (the fund manager) had expressed concern about earnings last summer, but added that her strategy already biased her against stocks with questionable earnings. Santella looks for companies with strong and sustainable earnings growth rates. In particular, she likes companies with successful niche services or products that generate recurring revenues. In contrast, she avoids turnaround companies that require substantial cost-cutting. . . The fund won't always excel as it has in the past six months, but it's a solid growth vehicle."*

In other words, you started screening for funds on AOL in search of a good aggressive growth fund, and discovered on CompuServe that the fund you chose has achieved above average results by taking a fairly conservative approach to the aggressive growth arena. Not a bad combination.

The Internet Investor's Top 10 List

1. **PC Quote Stock Quote Service**
2. **Mutual Funds Online**
3. **Security APL Quote Server**
4. **Wall St. Journal Money & Investing Update**
5. **NETworth**
6. **Holt's Market Report**
7. **MIT Experimental Stock Market Data**
8. **Mutual Funds Home Page**
9. **The Stock Room**
10. **Quoteline**

Source: http://www.gnn.com/meta/finance

Prodigy also provides mutual fund information and screening at an added cost to the basic service of about $15 a month. Prodigy draws mutual fund data from Micropal and IDD Information Services. IDD supplies daily updates of top-performing funds for one day, week or month; three months, and one, three and five years. These daily updates are tied into monthly reports from Micropal.

Internet sites with mutual fund and stock information abound, for obvious reasons. Most of us, at least initially, think of these two categories as our primary investment vehicles. Recently the GNN Web site published a "Top Ten Personal Finance Sites" on the Web, based on the number of times investors had logged-on to the sites in a given period. The sites listed by GNN, which stands for Global Network Navigator, a Web software company that was recently purchased by America Online, clearly show the preponderance of interest in mutual funds and stocks on the Net.

As with the list from Yahoo shown earlier, the GNN list itself is a series of hypertext links. If a particular item is clicked it will lead you to that site. Of the items in the Top 10 list, numbers one and three are stock price quote services. (We'll get to those in the next section when we discuss stocks.) The second item is the home page for *Mutual Funds Magazine*, another good publication for articles about funds. We covered number four, the Journal's update site, earlier in this lesson. So let's take a look at number five, which happens to be one of the best single sources for information on mutual funds available to the electronic investor.

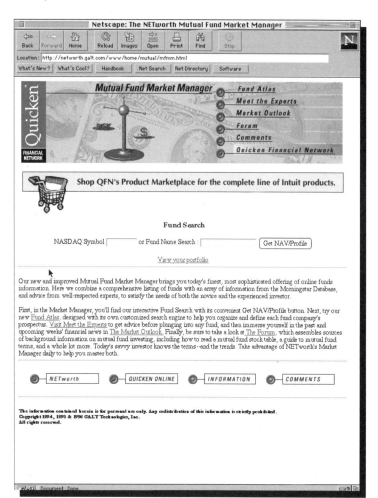

NETworth — *http://networth.galt.com*

This Web site, owned by Galt Technologies is one of the best sites on the Web for mutual fund information and for monitoring your investment portfolio (see example of on-line page at left). To get the full benefit of the site you are required to register, which is fairly painless, and free. Again, you can ignore the revenue-generating ads. Once you are a registered user you can access mutual fund screening on more than 5,000 funds using Morningstar data. Funds can be screened according to total assets, price performance over different yearly periods and other criteria. Registered users can also can set up portfolios of mutual fund and stock quotes that can be retrieved and displayed in graph form.

A color-coded series of prompts leads the user to sections of NETworth that cover mutual funds, beginning with the Mutual Fund Market Manager, stocks and other areas, including an on-line version of Quicken, the popular portfolio management software from Intuit. NETworth also includes prospectuses and other information from more than 50 mutual fund companies. The SEC ruled in 1995 that mutual funds can distribute prospectuses and other required filings electronically, which cuts costs for the fund companies and saves time for you the investor. Many mutual fund companies are expected to begin accepting electronic orders this year. Another mutual fund feature is the Ask An Expert section of NETworth. Users can pose questions to several fund managers from Montgomery Funds and the Benham Group.

Fund Company Sites

Nearly every major mutual fund company has a site on the Web. Finding them can be a problem, however. If you look for Fidelity Investments by typing *http://www.fidelity.com*, you end up at the home page of Fidelity National Financial Inc., an insurance underwriter! Fidelity Investment's home page is at: *http://www.fid-inv.com/*. Schwab and Vanguard, on the other hand, are reachable by inserting their names after the "www." in the standard Web URL address. The most efficient way to reach the fund sites is to use Yahoo or another search engine, follow the menu choices to "investments" or "markets and investments" and you'll be presented with a list of choices, many of which will be mutual fund sites.

Fund company home pages tend to reflect the personality of their creators. The Fidelity home page is a glitzy collage of color and graphics, with clearly defined sections you can pursue for fund quotes, more information on funds, retirement planning, etc. By contrast, Vanguard's home page is relatively austere, reflecting the parent company's emphasis on low-cost fund management. The Schwab home page directs you to its One Source mutual fund service, but the page, reflecting Schwab's principal business as a discount broker, is dominated by graphics highlighting e.Schwab, the on-line trading service offered by the company.

To buy and sell mutual fund shares on-line you have to open an on-line brokerage account. We'll discuss those in a later section. Several fund companies, including Fidelity, are discussing pilot programs that would offer direct trading in mutual fund shares. Security is also an issue. Fidelity general counsel Robert Pozen, writing in the *Fidelity Focus*, which is sent to

Chatting About Funds

The "chat" rooms or discussion areas on the three major on-line services contain several listings of discussions concerning mutual funds. Subjects discussed range from the mechanics of investing in funds — such as treating capital gains distributions — to which specific funds are doing well — and which ones ought to be dumped from your portfolio. The sheer volume of postings in these sections, their frequent lack of organization by topics and the number of neophyte investors asking rudimentary questions can make browsing through these sites annoyingly time-consuming.

A similar problem plagues the major Internet newsgroup devoted to mutual funds — "misc.invest.funds." Related newsgroups exist for stocks "misc.invest.stocks" and other asset classes. Just insert the name of the investment after "misc.invest." The funds newsgroup is an unregulated grouping of postings and queries about funds and, again, the questions are often elementary.

A much better organized and informative mutual fund discussion group is on the Web. It was number eight in the GNN list of most-visited investment pages: The Mutual Funds Home page (*http://www.brill.com/wwwboard/*). The site is a moderated news group, meaning that profane and defamatory comments and other personal attacks are edited out by the sites operators, known as sysops, before postings are made public. It also includes an easy to read time stamp on each filing so you can tell what's current and what's dated. You often have to decipher this information on other sites from within several lines of computerese that comprise Internet routing codes. Those posting to the site have their real names attached to their comments — no hiding behind screen names as is common practice on AOL.

fund shareholders, noted that "Fidelity continues to be concerned about the security of monetary transactions carried out on-line, given the current state of technology. Nevertheless, Fidelity may run a pilot program on making fund exchanges on the Internet. Fidelity will also closely follow developments in computer security, which in the future may provide adequate protection for on-line monetary transactions."

Mutual Fund Software

Software programs, some that download information from on-line services, others that come in CD or diskette form, also enable you to use your computer to help in finding the right mutual fund for you. We've already covered what the Big Three on-line services have to offer. Many stock analysis software programs, including several listed in the following section, also provide analysis of funds. The side bar on the next page contains a sampling of other mutual fund software programs, based on ascending order of price. Much of the information in the mini-reviews of software programs in this section as well as in the stock and portfolio management sections is drawn from The American Association of Individual Investors The *Individual Investor's Guide to Computerized Investing*. 1996 Edition, which can be obtained for $24.95 by contacting the AAII at (800)-428-2244.

Stocks The major on-line commercial providers offer a range of stock investing services, many of which are included in the basic monthly rate, others that carry a premium. They are the logical place to start to illustrate the benefits, and just as importantly the limitations, of electronic investing. The following, or a similar screen, could be performed using several on-line sites or software packages mentioned below.

CompuServe includes a stock screening service that allows the investor to choose from several general categories — high growth stocks, stocks with low P/Es, small stocks that aren't heavily owned by institutional investors, etc. For example, choosing "high growth rate" from among the options yields the following description: "Companies with high growth rate can outperform the stock market if a company's stock price is not already overvalued. This search helps identify companies that have high recent growth rates and a history of high growth. This search also filters out those companies that do not have reasonable returns on equity and long term debt to equity ratios."

You can also tailor the search according to six criteria. Immediately below is just one example of parameter settings you can choose.

CompuServe criteria	Parameters you can set
1. 15-YEAR GROWTH RATE — EARNINGS PER SHARE	MORE THAN 20%
2. 5-YEAR GROWTH RATE — SALES	MORE THAN 25%
3. PRIOR YEAR GROWTH RATE — SALES	MORE THAN 25%
4. RETURN ON EQUITY	MORE THAN 25%
5. CLOSING PRICE	MORE THAN $10
6. PRIOR YEAR QUARTER GROWTH — NET	MORE THAN 20%

Mutual Fund Analysis Software

Reuters Money Network by Reality Online Inc. — See software included with this lesson! (Windows/Win) The mutual funds module of the Reuters Money Network is one segment of a data base that covers stocks, bonds and certificates of deposit as well. The services combines a mix of on-line news and updates with a database for screening and analysis that is stored on your computer's hard drive. Month-end data can be downloaded to update your information. Novice and expert modes are available for screening. In the expert mode you can combine any of 26 criteria to create specific screens, while in the novice mode you can only specify one criterion for screening. The on-line tie-in allows for unique features such as alerts about changes in portfolio managers and one of your funds' risk ranking.

Principia for Mutual Funds by Morningstar — (800)-876-5005 $95 Yr., updated quarterly. (Win) Morningstar's mutual fund product on diskette. It lacks the depth and breadth of Morningstar's CD product (see below), but it's also less expensive. It will perform most screens of data that the average investor might demand. Graphics include total return charts for five funds or indexes at the same time. A standard deviation graph is a quick visual indicator of risk.

Mutual Fund Expert Pro Plus by Alexander Steele Systems — (800)-237-8400. $399 Yr., updated quarterly. (Win) An excellent if pricey package that covers 7,300 mutual funds. An especially useful feature allows you to compare a fund's performance against an investment category and index such as the S&P 500 over a particular period. It includes a panoply of esoteric statistics including alpha, beta, Sharpe and Treynor ratios and R-squared (a test for validity in regression analyses).

Morningstar Mutual Funds OnDisc by Morningstar — (800)-876-5005. $495 Yr., updated quarterly. (DOS) The CD version of Morningstar's printed report. It covers more than 6,500 funds and 160 information fields, and carries historical information back to 1976 — when some of today's mutual fund managers were still in grade school! OnDisc can screen funds based on portfolio statistics including average price-earnings ratio or market capitalization. The program can also scan for investment style or portfolio industry weights on portfolio cash/stock/bond composition. OnDisc even screens for funds that hold a specific stock.

The problem, of course, is that this screening doesn't enable us to compare the recent stock price with the 52-week high and low price for the issue, or some other stock price comparison. If it had, we probably would've looked for issues whose stock price was rising but not yet overvalued relative to its earnings. Our concern is that the CompuServe search doesn't reveal price plunges in stocks.

Equally disturbing is the fact that a quick search of on-line company data bases doesn't give a hint of drops in stock prices during the past year. We switched to AOL's personal finance section and clicked on Company Reports. Calling up the report on a stock known to have experienced significant swings, which was provided at no extra charge, we found nothing on the stock's price plunge, even though the report did elaborate on an executive suite fight at the company in which the chief executive left in a huff only to come back a week later. Hoover's Master List of company reports, also on AOL, also contained nothing on the stock price, nor did Hoover's or the Company Report section make any mention of the broad sell-off in that stock's industry which occurred recently. Even a search of an Earnings and Estimates report on AOL about the stock didn't turn up the price slide.

We would hope that prior to placing a buy order intrepid wealth builders would at some point check the 52-week range for a stock and catch whether its price fell off a cliff lately. But using on-line research tools certainly didn't make that fact easier to ascertain. You shouldn't be lulled into complacency by the ease and rapidity with which computerized stock screening can offer up so many investment decisions. The best computerized screen in existence is no substitute for using your stock picking judgment that you have honed by reading your *100 Steps to Wealth* lessons.

Stock Quotes

All of the major on-line service providers offer delayed stock quotes, as do several Internet sites, as you'll recall from the GNN Top Ten list of sites mentioned earlier. Choose the Personal

Finance sections on the services and then click on the stock quote icon, or graphic image, to get to the portion of the service that supplies quotes. The commercial on-line services, as well as a growing number of Web sites such as NETworth, will also allow you to list a portfolio of stock quotes and update it once a day, typically an hour or two after the close of trading on the NYSE. The MIT Stockmaster quote site mentioned earlier (*http://www.ai.mit.edu/stocks.html*) offers free detailed, multi-colored historical price and volume charts of more than 400 stocks over a two-year period and are updated daily.

Quote.com *http://www.quote.com*
PAWWS Financial Network *http://pawws.secapl.com*
These two heavily trafficked sites offer a handful of free stock or fund quotes to non-sub-scribers but also offer data screening and quote packages to subscribers for varying amounts, depending on the amount of service included in the packages. A basic subscription to Quote.com for about $9 a month offers up to 100 quotes a day and access to data banks that are similar in scope to those included in the AOL, CompuServe or Prodigy basic packages. PAWWS throws in free portfolio tracking if you use one of the discount brokers to whom it offers electronic links.

TIPnet *http://www.tipnet.com*
Subscriptions to this web site, beginning at about $10 a month, offer access to a host of stock quote, market news and stock screening and portfolio analysis tools. This is the Internet link for users of the popular Telescan stock and mutual fund software packages (see below), but subscribers to TIPnet don't have to buy the Telescan programs to use the Internet site.

Stock Talk Online

The major online services also have several stock discussion or "chat" groups that can be a good source for new investment ideas. They are also a good way to find out more about a smaller company you may have heard of but on which there isn't much readily available infor-mation in the usual spots such as news services. But anything found here should be considered a beginning for a search for additional information, not the last word on the subject. Verify everything you read here before acting on it. Many of the postings are opinions that aren't backed up with facts.

AOL's chat groups for specific stocks can be very enlightening as well as entertaining. The chat groups are reached via AOL's finance forum, which is part of its personal finance section. The relative merits of hundreds of stocks are also discussed on the message boards of the Motley Fool section of AOL. The Motley Fool, despite its name, takes investing seriously but not itself. The section was founded and is managed by David and Tom Gardner and advocates a mix of small stock investing and more conservative strategies such as buying the "dogs of the Dow." With this technique an investor buys the 10 highest yielding stocks in the Dow Jones Industrial Average from the previous year and waits for them to appreciate in price. It has tended to produce steady gains over time. The Gardners also recommend against day trad-ing, although the section provides excellent commentary on the day's trading and the stocks in their portfolio every evening. Day trading is for "wise-guys," the rest of us would do well to remember that we are "fools," says the Motley Fool.

The chat groups on AOL, CompuServe and Prodigy can have far-reaching effects on stock prices and investors. Recently, the Iomega Corp., which makes the popular Zip drives that pro-vide additional storage space for personal computers, canceled a public stock offering of 5.25 million shares because of what it called "confusion and misinformation in the marketplace" about the company and the offering. In a prospectus the company filed with the SEC for an offering of $40 million worth of convertible notes to raise cash, Iomega said the confusion resulted from comments on "electronic bulletin board postings on America Online and other similar services."

Prodigy recently settled a defamation lawsuit by Stratton Oakmont, a small brokerage firm, that had claimed it had been defamed by comments posted on Prodigy's Money Talks bulletin board. The posting said the brokerage firm, which has had a few run-ins with regulators, and its president were involved in "major criminal fraud." Despite the firm's regulatory troubles, however, criminal charges had never been brought against the firm. Prodigy apologized to end the suit and the identity of the person who posted the Stratton Oakmont note was never verified, so he or she escaped punishment.

As noted earlier, there are also numerous newsgroups on the Internet devoted to investing. The two most-followed sites are "misc.invest" and "misc.invest.stocks." The popularity of these sites and the fact that so many postings have little to do with stocks or investing can make them slow-going. The latest trend on the Net is to develop stock chat groups on major Web sites devoted to investing. Check using Yahoo or other search engines for general listings.

Stock Picking Software

There are dozens of software programs you can buy that run on your computer that analyze investments, often to a much more detailed degree than an investor can manage tapping into Web sites or using the major on-line services. These aren't stand-along products, however. Most import securities data from on-line services the Net on a daily or hourly basis, depending on the level of sophistication and frequency of price updates an investor demands.

Fundamental Analysis Software

Programs that emphasize fundamental analysis help you screen investment ideas based on the financial performance of the company. These programs, listed on the next page, allow you to screen stock universes for companies with low price/earnings ratios, capitalization, large or small, or earnings momentum and growth rates and dividend yields, to name a few areas. Fundamental analysis is most useful as a basis for making longer-term investments.

Technical Analysis Software

Technical analysis programs, on the other hand, focus on price and volume trends to predict future price performance. They are most often used to time relatively short-term purchases and sales of securities. As the example on page 25 illustrates, these programs come in a wide range of sophistication and price. They are listed in ascending order of price, but the most expensive program isn't always the best. Whenever possible, try to buy a trial version of a program before committing the full purchase price. Some vendors will allow you to deduct the trial price from the full price of the program. Also be sure to obtain the latest version of a program, since modifications and additions are always being made to the more popular offerings, and may not be reflected in the thumbnail profiles we've provided.

These programs use data downloaded from on-line Internet service providers or data service providers or CD-ROM disks. The costs shown typically don't include on-line access and usage charges.

Fixed Income Securities

Information on bonds and other fixed income securities isn't as widely available on the Net as is stock and mutual fund information, but there are still plenty of sites to check out. Once again, the major commercial online services have several discussion groups covering bonds that you can reach through their personal finance sections. A good Usenet newsgroup for information on bonds and money market funds is "clari.biz.mkt.misc."

For a macro-economic view of the outlook for interest rates and other economic trends that have an impact on bond prices, check the University of Michigan "gopher" site noted earlier in the lesson (*gopher://una.hh.lib.umich.edu:70/11/ebb*). Another good source of information on economic indicators is Briefing , which is operated by Charter Media, Inc. (*http://www.briefing.com/.*)

Fundamental Analysis Software

CoScreen by CompuServe — (800)-848-8199. Standard price of around $10 for 5 hours. (DOS; Win; Mac) CompuServe's many services include this stock screening function that allows you to search through the 11,000 publicly traded North American securities in the Disclosure database, updated daily, that is part of the service package. You can choose from up to 39 fundamental variables to comb through the data. Examples that walk you through using and modifying P/E screens are easy to follow, but the text-heavy interface still isn't as user-friendly as that of rivals America Online and Prodigy. The service also lacks industry average comparisons so you have a benchmark against which to judge the stock or stocks that pop up as a result of the screens you run on the data. Criteria for screenings also can't be saved from session to session. One of the biggest drawbacks is the fact that screens contain only a few columns of information about a company. A Disclosure report with detailed information about a company included in the screen costs $17 for each company, or nearly twice the monthly CompuServe charge. Unfortunately, such hefty add-on pricing is the norm on CompuServe when it comes to looking for most types of detailed corporate information.

Strategic Investor by Prodigy — (800)-776-3449. Standard rate of $9.95 for 5 hours, plus $14.95 a month. (DOS; Win; Mac) Over 6,000 companies can be screened according to P/E ratio, five-year earnings growth and dividend yield. The service also includes a Stock Hunter module that provides eight screening techniques such as Graham and Dodd value techniques and similar "One Up on Wall Street" techniques from Peter Lynch; low and high price-to-book value stocks; the CANSLIM system created by William O'Neil, a small-cap, neglected screen dubbed Wallflowers and screens for consistent dividends and sustainable growth. These lists are updated weekly.

Stock Investor by the American Association of Individual Investors — (312)-280-0170. $99/Yr members; $150/Yr non-members. (DOS; Win) Updated quarterly, the program contains data on more than 7,000 securities traded on U.S. exchanges. The screening function enables searches for companies meeting up to 30 criteria on over 300 variables. Comparison information on 12 sectors and 100 industry groups is included. Company data includes eight quarters of sales, earnings and dividend data, five years of sales, cash flow, earnings and dividend figures.

U.S. Equities on Floppy by Morningstar — (800)-735-0700. $145 — $995 a year. (DOS) The database covers more than 6,000 U.S. traded securities and is updated on a weekly, monthly or quarterly basis, depending on the level of service ordered. Being forced to memorize abbreviations for every field when constructing screens is a negative. But the system is considered quick to operate once that hurdle is cleared. Bar charts offer visual aids for understanding price movements.

Reuters Money Network by Reality Online Inc — $49.95 (Win) Combines investment software with on-line financial information, news and data. Information for the fundamental data base is provided by Standard and Poor's and follows the companies covered in their Stock Guide. An on-line service plan offers quotes, personalized news, stock, bond and mutual fund data, historical pricing graphs, on-line brokerage and investment alerts. The data base is updated monthly. An expert mode allows for multiple criteria used per screen.

Telescan ProSearch by Telescan, Inc. — (800)-324-4692. $295-395 plus connect fees. (DOS; Win) This on-line system is updated daily and works in concert with Telescan's technical charting program, Telescan Analyzer. ProSearch is "unique in offering a rich set of technical indicators to use for screening along with its fundamental elements," according to *The Individuals Guide to Computerized Investing*. (AAII) ProSearch allows users to search more than 8,000 U.S.-traded stocks using up to 40 of 207 fundamental, technical and forecasting criteria.

Value/Screen III by Value Line Publishing Inc. — (800)-654-0508. $325 — $1,995. (DOS; Mac) A bare bones offering of summary fundamental and technical statistics compared to the in-depth analysis included in its well-known Value Line Investment Survey publication. Data is updated weekly, monthly or quarterly depending on the level of service.

On the Web, the place to begin is with a search engine. Yahoo (*http://www.yahoo.com*) lists several additional sites with timely information on fixed income securities. The most efficient way to reach them (rather than typing in each URL address) is to go via Yahoo's business and finance section and then choose markets and investment from the menu. Another menu will offer bonds as a choice. Choose that menu and you find:

- Treasury Notes and Bond Quotes

- Fixed Income Investment Research. Provides 215 daily updated reports aimed at institutional investors.

- Pivot Market Timer. This service covers interest-rate sensitive markets with an emphasis on bonds.

- BradyNet. Quotes and analysis of emerging market debt issues.

- Daiwa Bond Index. Japanese coupon-bearing bonds.

- Usenet.

Note: most of the fundamental and technical analysis software packages mentioned earlier in the section on stocks also can incorporate fixed income securities data.

Currencies

Most of the on-line information on currencies centers around quotes and technical analysis of price and volume trends. The offerings on AOL, CompuServe and Prodigy are minimal. Using Yahoo and following the menu "tree" to markets and investments and then choosing currencies yields more than 20 sites, and many of those contain links to other sites. Several of the sites noted on Yahoo provide 24-hour currency price quotes or trading signals based on technical price trends. The Yahoo listing also includes links to news sources, including CNN Financial News.

Two popular Web sites for currency traders are:
The GNN/Koblas Currency Converter — *http://bin.gnn.com/cgi-bin/gnn/currency* This site covers 56 currencies and provides weekly updates, and can also convert any of the currencies into any other.

Olsen & Associates — *http://www.olsen.ch/foreign/websvcs.html* A Swiss company, Olsen on its site provides market analysis, models for currency trading and historical price data on currencies.

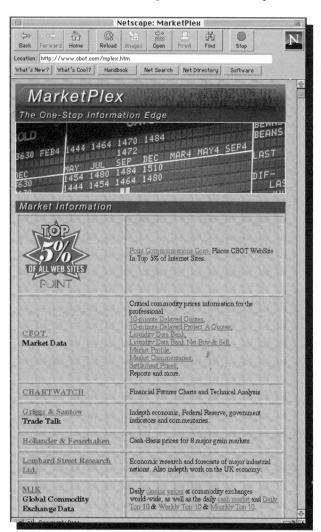

Learning How To Avoid the Trap

The two largest futures exchanges — the Chicago Board of Trade and the Chicago Mercantile Exchange — provide basic educational offerings on futures as well as statistics on financial futures contracts as well as grains and livestock. The Board of Trade also includes a selection of 15-minute delayed quotes. The exchange sites include links to news agencies and government agencies affecting the futures industry as well. (See example at left.)

Chicago Board of Trade —
http://www.cbot.com/mplex.htm
Chicago Mercantile Exchange — *http://www.cme.com*

Among the European futures exchanges, the **London International Financial Futures & Options Exchange's** Web site can be reached at — *http://www.liffe.com*

The Internet is loaded with Web sites and discussion groups hashing over the direction of prices on just about every conceivable futures contract that trades in the world. The commercial online services have separate discussion groups devoted to futures and options, and even to users of particular futures technical analysis programs. Many of the technical analysis programs mentioned earlier also analyze futures price and volume trends as well as options. Yahoo and other search engines have dozens of futures and options sites hotlinks, including links to futures-related publications and to weather services that track the expected impact of weather changes on the commodities markets.

The Investorama Web site: *http:www.investorama.com/ futures/html*, for instance, offers an extensive selection of futures sites and quote sources. The Investorama section on futures ends with a quotation from the English statesman Edmund Burke that takes on a particularly ironic meaning in the context of of an industry that is so fixated on using historical price charts to predict futures prices in a few weeks or months. "You can never plan for the future by the past."

Technical Analysis Software

MegaTech Chart System by Ret-Tech Software — (708)-382-3903. $175. (DOS) This program doesn't have all the bells and whistles of its more expensive brethren, there is no ability to back test data, but it does have some unique characteristics. Its "tech on tech" feature lets you create technical studies based on the result of previous technical studies, for instance, and it also creates alert signals for high and low price or volume moves.

Telescan Investors Platform by Telescan — (800)-324-4692. $199. (Win) This is the Windows version of Telescan's well-known DOS product and isn't strictly a technical product. It provides extensive news coverage in the areas of national and international; business; market reports, commodity and foreign, monetary and government and sports. These services and others come at added cost so bills can quickly mount depending on how long you are on-line. Telescan's data base covers more than 8,000 stocks, 2,000 mutual funds and 40,000 exchange-listed options. The program not only allows you to perform screens on 73 technical indicators but also on 134 fundamental indicators.

Windows on Wall Street Pro. — (214)-235-9594. $249. (Win) A user friendly favorite of many reviewers that's considered very flexible. Trading systems can be created by combining functions that come with the program. It also comes with an on-line research center for logging onto CompuServe or Dow Jones, and a personal assistant that can be set up to display messages, download data and other functions.

SuperCharts 3-CD by Omega Research — (800)-556-2022. $250. (Win) This program stores up to 10 years of historical data on more than 15,000 securities on CD. You store new data on your hard drive. When you display data the program merges the two sources of data. Other programs require you to switch the CD data onto your hard drive to manipulate it, which can take a big chunk out of your hard disk space. You can also perform several types of fundamental analysis on information you download. An expert analyst function makes forecasts based on the data in written form and flashes bull, bear or neutral signals.

TeleChart 2000 by Worden Brothers, Inc. — (800)-776-4940. $29 software; apppprox. $19/mth unlimited chart downloads. (DOS) A favorite of many active stock and commodity traders, TeleChart produces a broad range of charts based on widely used technical analysis tools, as well as several proprietary systems. Includes a Watch List Organizer that groups charts by performance, industry group, market averages as well as customized lists.

Market Analyzer Plus by Dow Jones & Co. — (800)-815-5100. $299. (DOS;Mac) Behind the curve in terms of eye-catching graphics, this is nonetheless a very useful tool that provides basic technical analysis and screening capabilities. The best thing about it is the link to Dow Jones' immense data base as well as historical and real-time quotes. Some of its supplemental services come at an added cost. And contrary to the trend among most software providers, the Mac version of the Dow Jones program actually has more analytical features than the DOS version, which doesn't work with a mouse.

MetaStock for Windows by Equis International — (800)-882-3040. $349. (Win) The Windows version of this popular software package is an improvement over the DOS version and easier to use. Using the explorer function you can rank, compare, filter, search and list multiple indicator values for multiple securities. It also has added a function for downloading data from one of six on-line vendors — still no on-line access for downloading fundamental information, however.

Personal Analyst by Trendsetter Software — (800)-825-1852. $395. (Mac) Despite the price tag, this the least expensive technical analysis software package from Trendsetter. Among the company's more advanced products are Personal Hotline, which makes trade recommendations, and Pro Analyst, which is a real-time system. Personal Analyst is an end-of-the-day quote tracking system. Equiview charts display two years of closing data on a security.

TickerWatcher by Linn Software — (404)-929-8802. $395-$695. (Mac) TickerWatcher comes in different versions, depending on whether you want to include real-time, 15-minute delayed or end-of-the-day quotes, fundamental analysis information from various data services or other features. A link to Microsoft's Excel spreadsheet program provides immediate updating in the Excel window as soon as data is received by TickerWatcher. TickerWatcher can monitor up to 32,000 individual security ticker symbols in up to 255 portfolios.

ON-LINE DISCOUNT BROKERS

The rapidly expanding availability of on-line trading gives you even more control over your financial well-being. The number of brokerage firms providing on-line trading is growing rapidly and is expected to continue (see following chart), according to a survey conducted by the American Association of Individual Investors. That number is expected to continue to grow, even though price competition among the on-line brokers is cutting into their profits. And while the volume of on-line trading is small compared to total stock market trading volume on any given day, it is growing. Charles Schwab officials estimate that on-line trades accounted for 15 percent of all trades by the end of last year, more than twice the 7 percent of total trading volume a year earlier.

The obvious attraction of on-line trading is the relatively cheap rates and flexibility. E*Trade, already the low-price special among discounters, shook up the industry again when it cut its per transaction rate for up to 5,000 exchange-listed securities to $14.95 from $19.95. The latter rate still applied to trades in over-the-counter stocks. Some discount brokers also offer an additional discount off their quoted rates in the table at left for on-line trading. Ceres Securities, announced a flat fee of $18 for all trades, and threw in daily comments for financial columnist Andrew Tobias at its Web site (*http://www.ceres.com/ homepage.html*).

On-line trading enables you to place orders and download quotes and other portfolio information at your convenience. No waiting for your broker to return a call. No repeating orders to a telephone sales clerk at a traditional discount broker or mutual funds company who is fresh out of school and can't tell you what information is available from his firm.

There are disadvantages to using on-line brokers. Internet technology is improving all the time, but it's still far from perfect. Regardless of

ELECTRONIC BROKERAGE SERVICES

Broker	Phone	Service Provider	100 Shrs. @ $20; 1,000 Shrs. @$20	Real-Time Quotes
AccTrade PC	800-228-3011	– –	$48; $48	$20/mth
Aufhauser & Co.	800-368-3668	http://aufhauser.com	$34; $34	$20/mth
Brown & Co.	800-822-2021	– –	$34; $34	– –
Ceres Online	800-628-6100	http://www.ceres.com/homepage.html	$34; $34	– –
Charles Schwab/ e.Schwab	800-3872-4922	software	$34; $34	50 free/mth
Schwab/Streets mart	800-435-4000	software	$55; $144 (before 10% discount)	$1.45/min. peak/$0.35 off-peak
E*Trade Securities	800-786-2575	CompuServe, AOL	$19.95; $19.95	$30/mth
Fidelity Brokerage	800-544-8666	– –	$48.60; $129.15	None
Freedom Investments	800-944-4033	– –	$25; $25	None
Howe Barnes Investments	800-638-4250	http://www.pawws.com/tni/	$38; $95	$25/mth
Jack White & Co. Investments	800-233-3411	http://www.pawws.com/jwc/jwmain.html	$36; $63	$50/mth
Lombard Institutional	800-688-3462	http://www.lombard.com/	$34; $34	– –
Max Uhle	800-223-6642	CompuServe	$35; $163	– –
Midwood Discount Brokerage	800-643-9663	software	$36.50; $36.50	None
Muriel Siebert	800-872-0711	software	$45; $75	None
National Discount Brokers	800-888-3999	http://pawws.secapl.com/ndb/	$20–$25; $20–$25	$50/mth
Pacific Brokerage Services	800-421-8395	– –	$25; $25	n/a
PC Financial Network	800-825-5723	AOL, Prodigy, Reuters	$40; $110	None
Quick & Reilly	800-672-7220	software	$37.50; $59	n/a
Royal Grimm & Davis	800-488-5195	software	$37.50; $90	n/a
T. Rowe Price	800-638-5660	– –	$46; $122	None
White Discount Securities	800-669-4483	– –	$34.50; $48	None

Source: AAII; Computer websites

what Internet service provider you use, connections for whatever reason can be suddenly severed and you will be cut off from your broker. You can usually redial and resume your trade, but the experience can be disconcerting, and potentially costly if the market is moving rapidly and you are an active day trader. During peak periods phone lines can get overloaded and you may get a repeated busy signal as you try to get through. Of course, customers doing business with your local Merrill Lynch office can jam the phones on extremely busy days, too.

It's hard to weigh price and service considerations without trying out a few brokers. Before you do, start your search is the investment newsgroups on the Net. Investors asking for tips on which discounter to use, and on-line traders airing their gripes about a company can reveal a lot about an on-line broker. Don't take what you read in an on-line newsgroup as Gospel, of course. You have no way of knowing whether the person making the on-line has an ax to grind against the broker he isn't sharing, or otherwise is a biased observer.

If you were considering signing on as an E*Trade customer you could, armed with this knowledge, ask a few more questions of the sales rep who takes your call. You should in every case ask about system reliability and recent experience with system's problems and what the broker's expansion or upgrading plans are, if any.

Comparing on-line brokers also is difficult in that no two offer exactly the same range of services. Some, including Schwab's StreetSmart service, offer discounts off the commissions quoted in the table on the previous page. Others such as Muriel Siebert, only trade Amex and NYSE-listed securities on-line. And the brokers that allow trading through Web sites, such as Lombard and those that trade through the Pawws site, are able to provide reams of data and other research at no additional cost since it is available on the Web site. Jack White, for instance, offers customers research from DTN, Griffen, Investment Alert, Barrons, Bloomberg and Value Line, all free of charge. When looking for an on-line broker it's also important to try and determine what your on-line costs will be based on how frequently you trade and what form of on-line connection you use.

What about security on the Internet?

The brokers that allow you to trade directly through a Web site, as opposed to using their proprietary software, require that you use a Netscape browser that has built-in data encryption to safeguard your financial information. In one instance Netscape's encryption was compromised, but that occurred when computer experts deployed a tremendous amount of computing power to accomplish that specific goal. It's unlikely that a computer hacker, no matter how gifted, could accomplish the same by trying to raid your individual account.

In the meantime, encryption specialists, ranging from those at Netscape to technicians at some of the largest banks and credit card companies in the world, are racing to improve the level of security on the Net so they can hasten the use of "e-cash" to carry out financial transactions on the Net. Any security gains in one aspect of Net use are likely to be rapidly applied to on-line trading.

Another trend among very small companies using the Net is to bypass stockbrokers altogether and create a forum on their Web sites where stockholders can buy and sell shares of their stock directly to each other. For example, Spring Street Brewing Co., which earlier had raised $1.6 million by selling nearly 900,000 shares over the Internet, created a trading forum on its Web site at *http://www.interport.net/witbeer*. Another company, Interactive Holdings Corp., created a similar trading set-up at its Web site: *http://www.thevine. com/ihchome.htm*.

These are both highly speculative investments. Their shares are registered with the SEC and are under the same kind of regulations as Nasdaq Bulletin Board companies, which are not required to file quarterly or annual statements to the SEC and have no minimum listing requirements. Investment professionals warn that investors assume a lot of risk trading such stocks. But Rebecca Patton, vice president of marketing and online stock brokerage at E*Trade Securities Inc., says the Web trading sites may be a sign of things to come. "The financial resources that are on the Web are growing every day and you are seeing a complete migration of financial services to the Web. People are paying way too much for investment services and that is one of the reasons you are going to see more and more people migrating to the Web."

PORTFOLIO MANAGEMENT

Putting your investments together and managing them as a single portfolio is key to successful wealth building. The practice is also greatly simplified and made much more enjoyable by several different programs that run on your home computer or also have links to the Internet, especially the fast-growing Web portion of the Net. Many of the software programs mentioned in earlier sections also include portfolio management functions.

Web Sites

Quicken Financial Network — *http://www.intuit.com/quicken* The latest versions of the popular Quicken software (Version 5 for IBM-compatible PCs and Version 6 for the Mac) is designed to tap into parent company Intuit's Quicken Financial Network site on the Web. It includes a customized version of Netscape's Navigator software for browsing on the Web and leads you directly to the Quicken Web site when you activate the program, where you can browse at no additional cost. Purchasers of the new software can also get seven free hours of Internet access a month for around $10. The Quicken site provides programs for helping you plan and management your finances and investments, much like the software package. It also supports on-line banking. There are links on the Web site as well for researching mutual fund performance, including access to the Morningstar fund data base.

NETworth — *http://networth.galt.com* Mentioned earlier, this site also has some portfolio management capabilities and also includes a hotlink to the Quicken Financial Network.

WallStreetWeb — *http://www.bulletproof.com/wallstreetweb/* This site bills itself as one of the first interactive Web sites using what's known as Java programming language to provide price quotes, graphical charts, trading stats, portfolio management and other services. It is certainly one of the most eye-catching, with a black background and brightly colored planets. To tap the full range of services you'll need a browser that incorporates Java capabilities such as the one included with Windows 95 or the Netscape 2.0 browser.

Portfolio Management Software

Managing Your Money by Meca Software — (203)-256-5000. $39.95, $49.95 CD. (DOS, Win, Mac) Basic portfolio management is included in this general purpose financial organizer. You can track multiple portfolios and use risk and return data to construct optimal portfolios, as well as produce standard charts and graphs.

Capital Gainz by Alleycat Software, Inc. — (919)-542-6117. $49 (plus $15 for graphics, $15 for quote downloader). (DOS) This program, surprisingly detailed for the price, is also available in many shareware forums on the Net. It provides an easy to understand demo version on shareware forums. The reports Capital Gainz generates also factor in time-weighted purchases, sales and distributions.When selling a security it can automatically select specific lots to minimize taxes and other objectives.

Quicken by Intuit Inc. — (800)-964-1040. $49.95/$69.95 Deluxe. (Win, Mac) Quicken is at heart a personal and small business financial organizer. It also has a fairly strong investment module that tracks a range of securities and produces graphs and reports, reports capital gains to a linked tax software package and includes an investment calculator. The latest versions of Quicken can also be put to good use tracking how you have allocated your assets among different types of investments, which, as you learned in earlier lessons, is what many experts say is the most important factor (as opposed to picking a particular stock) affecting the long-term performance of your investment portfolio. When you enter a stock into the Quicken database, for instance, skip the standardized choices of stock, bond, etc. and choose "new." Then type asset class, such as small capitalization, large cap, etc. The latest versions of the software also include links to a Quicken Web page (see above).

Fidelity On-Line Express (Fox) by Fidelity Investments — (800)-544-0246. $49.95 (DOS) For Fidelity customers only. This trading and quote retrieval software also includes basic portfolio management functions. Customers can also download check and credit card transactions.

StreetSmart by Charles Schwab & Co., Inc. — (800)-334-4455. $59 (Win, Mac) Available only to Schwab customers. Portfolio management tools are included in this investing software package from Schwab that also allows users to trade securities, get real-time quotes and use securities databases for researching investments. (See on-line trading table) Customers can download account information, review balances and positions and place and track orders. Using StreetSmart gets you a 10% off the standard Schwab discount commission.

Captool by Techserve Inc. — (800)-826-8082. $149; $299 Global Inv. (DOS) One of a number of portfolio management programs from Techserve. Powerful but complicated to use at first. Captool computes portfolio and security return on investment before and after taxes and costs, time-weighted rates of return, and an estimate of tax liability. It can produce more than 20 portfolio reports which can be customized. The global version allows for securities denominated in foreign currencies within the same portfolio as U.S. securities. Users can define up to 10 currencies from a database to denominate foreign holdings.

Portfolio Watcher by Micro Trading Software Inc. — (203)-762-7820. $149.95 (Win, Mac) This fairly basic portfolio management program can process an unlimited number of securities portfolios. The Mac version can be used in conjunction with the technical analysis programs Stock Watcher and Wall Street Watcher.

Financial Navigator by Financial Navigator International — (800)-468-3636. $249 (DOS, Win) This program takes portfolio management to the next level, justifying the price for some investors, by including financial analysis tools that can incorporate real estate or oil and gas interests, trusts, non-profit organizations, estates and self-owned businesses. The program offers cash flow planning tools, tracks multiple portfolios and can produce more than 60 different reports.

Investor's Accountant by Hamilton Software, Inc. — (800)-733-9607. $395 (DOS) A powerful program for the sophisticated investor. It handles several portfolios in a wide range of investment categories. It also converts foreign-denominated securities to local currency on reports. A demo program is included.

REGULATION

Regulation of investment related activities on the on-line services and the Internet is still in the horse and buggy era. Securities regulators at the state and federal level are starting to pay more attention to cyber-scams. But blatantly fraudulent securities offerings, including Ponzi schemes in which money from new investors is used to pay off earlier investors, are all too common on the Net. The anonymity offered by most on-line users' made-up names and nicknames also clouds issues of identity and responsibility concerning Net conversations. If you don't know who you're dealing with, you don't know how reputable his or her information is. The mask provided by your on-line name, even if it's your initials, may encourage you to spout off about a company or brokerage firm you have a beef with. But beware, on-line investors may expose themselves to libel suits for comments posted to newsgroups or other so-called "bulletin boards." You can voice an opinion about a company's stock, but you had better not say the chief executive officer is a crook unless you can back it up with hard evidence.

The SEC, despite its role as the guardian of the securities markets, hasn't taken too many steps to police the Internet, although it would like investors to think it is vigilant. "We are always keeping an eye on things," one SEC official insisted. He didn't specify how the agency, which is always fighting in Washington for a larger operating budget, was keeping an eye on the thousands of sites on the Net. State securities regulators have stepped in on occasion and filled the regulatory void with enforcement crackdowns on cyber-fraud.

In early 1995 the SEC did take action against an alleged scam involving the Internet. A U.S. District Court in Ohio granted the SEC a temporary restraining order against Pleasure Time Inc., Group Dynamics Downline and others for raising $3 million by allegedly selling unregistered securities to nearly 20,000 investors. Robert Bruson, assistant regional director of the SEC's midwest office in Chicago, cautions investors: if an on-line solicitation doesn't clearly state that the securities are registered with the SEC, stay away.

Fraudulent securities offerings and scams crop up all too frequently on the Net, despite the potential for prosecution by state or federal regulators. Network systems operators, called Sysops, try to police their own networks and remove fraudulent postings when they find them, but they often are outnumbered. To lend a hand, Net users adopt a "self-policing" approach at many sites where honest Internet users "flame" the offenders, posting vitriolic messages denouncing the scams as fraudulent and alerting the Sysops to their presence.

These "Internet posses" are fairly effective in spotting potential abuses and bringing them to the attention of other visitors to the Net site, but of course they don't have any enforcement powers. A message posted on the Internet usergroup site "misc.invest" recently that claimed readers could "get 25% to 45% on a bank deposit!" quickly unleashed a torrent of protest: "Not from a reputable bank in any country with a relatively stable world currency," chided one reader, adding "which federal agency regulates this investment. Who regulates you?" Another frequent visitor to the Net site added, "maybe the payoff was in rubles? Maybe the minimum to invest is also $500,000. I've heard of some Soviet bank bonds paying out at these rates. 'Maybe' you'll still be able to collect after their election." Others accused the author of the original 25 percent to 45 percent offer of a common mail order scam in which an upfront fee, in this case $3, is required before more information is sent. Typically in such fraudulent schemes the perpetrator pockets the up front money without following through on the offer.

The Federal Trade Commission and the U.S Postal Inspection Service are the two federal agencies who have taken the most action to alert consumers to potential fraud and sales abuses on the Internet. The Postal Inspection Service site offers examples on its Web sites of investment and insurance scams, credit card rip-offs and charity fraud, among others. The FTC's Web site notes that "the latest 'roadhazards' on the information superhighway are scams broadcast over rapidly-growing computer networks and electronic bulletin board services. The scams aren't new, just the medium. Some con artists. . . now have turned to the Internet and the online services of cyberspace as the new medium to promote their scams." Here are their on-line addresses.

The Federal Trade Commission — *http://www.ftc.gov*

The U.S. Postal Inspection Service — *http://www.usps.gov/websites/ depart/inspect/welcome.htm*

The FTC warns that fraudulent sellers use these computer services to promote familiar schemes such as bogus stock offerings, credit-repair services, and exotic or high-tech investment opportunities such as ostrich farming, gold mining, gemstones, and wireless cable television. Promotions for ineffective weight-loss and health-related products and programs also appear online. Treat all ads or would-be ads with skepticism and never make an investment or health-related purchase decision based solely on information obtained from a single source in any medium — print, broadcast or online, the FTC cautions.

We offer the following five tips for avoiding the modern day highwaymen.

- Use of hype titles and frequent use of the word "hot" to describe an investment opportunity can indicate a scam.

- Exaggerated claims of potential earnings or profit, such as "We target a return of 2 percent to 5 percent per month (up to 60 percent a year) on your protected principal. That is, YOUR PRINCIPAL IS GUARANTEED. . . no loss is possible."

- Claims of "inside" information. Such information is almost always false and, if true, trading on it is almost always illegal.

- "Pump and Dump" promotions of cheap stocks promising high returns.

- Promotions for exotic investments such as ostrich farming, gold mining, or wireless cable TV.

Resources   To find out whether an investment salesperson is licensed, or if an offered security is registered, contact the SEC's office of consumer affairs, 202-942-7040. They may also be reached via hotlinks on the SEC's Web page.

If you have a question about an apparent online consumer scam contact the National Fraud Information Center at 800-876-7060.

You can obtain FTC brochures that explain fraudulent sales practices and how to avoid them at the above Web site or by calling 202-326-2222.

Wrapping It Up   One of the most exciting things about electronic investing is that there is always something new for you to discover. First-time Internet users and veteran online traders alike are constantly being surprised by the wealth of financial and investing information available to them at the click of a mouse. Making sense of the many opportunities currently available is the purpose of this lesson. And distilling all of the opportunities into one series of recommendations is the purpose of wealth-building Bonus Step 101, found on the next page.

Part of the excitement stems from the fact that we are still in the early development years of a rapidly expanding new technology. The online community of computer users clicking from one Web site to another in the final few years of the century is in some ways where auto enthusiasts were in the first few decades of the 20th Century: There aren't enough good road maps — not to mention good roads! — and computers, like early cars, are still too difficult to use and the computers and their software are too prone to technical failure. We even use the term "crash" to describe a computer system operating failure!

If for these and other reasons such as — "I'm too old, I don't have enough time, this stuff will be easier to use and cheaper in a few years" — you've put off using a computer and the multitude of electronic investment options available. But you resolve to try and make more money and have some fun. Imagine you're standing beside a narrow country highway two generations ago and a gleaming Studs Bearcat comes roaring by. Would you rather be in the driver's seat, or waiting by the side of the road for several years until Detroit perfects automatic transmissions? ▲

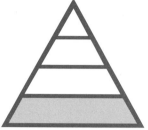

The Electronic Investor's Toolbox

WHAT: To help you get started using your computer to make money investing in the markets, we've included our suggested essential software, on-line services and Internet sites you need in your electronic 'toolbox' to join the ranks of investors on the information super-highway. Refer to the appropriate section of the lesson to get more details on each item mentioned below:

SOFTWARE

Fundamental Analysis

Reuters Money Network — The data base covers mutual funds, stocks, bonds and certificates of deposit. Money Network combines a link to on-line services for price quotes and personalized news as well as on-line brokerage with a data base for screening and analysis that is stored on your hard drive and updated monthly.

Technical Analysis

TeleChart 2000 — (800)-776-4940. A moderately priced ($29 for software, about $19/month for unlimited chart downloads, less for limited downloads) and widely used source of charts based on popular technical analysis tools. Many more expensive products include news and fundamental analysis features which you can get via Reuters Money Network. TeleChart 2000 includes a Watch List Organizer that groups charts by performance, industry group and market averages, as well as by customized lists.

ON-LINE

America Online — (800)-827-6364. Just to show we're not partial! (as you know, *Money* has the personal finance section on CompuServe), we'll mention AOL here for its ease of use and for its engaging Motley Fool investment section that offers stock picks and lively discussion groups. Prodigy comes in third, although it has a strong stock chat area.

INTERNET WEB SITES

MIT Stockmaster — *http://www.ai.mit.edu/stocks/* This site sets the Net standard for free, multi-color stock price and volume charts that can be downloaded and incorporated into many data bases and spreadsheets. Covers more than 6,000 stocks.

Yahoo — *http://www.yahoo.com* There are other search engines that also act as indexes to Web sites, but this is one of the most intuitive and easy to use.

NETworth — *http://networth.galt.com* One of the best sites on the Web for monitoring your portfolio and getting mutual fund information. Once registered you can screen Morningstar mutual fund data and set up portfolios of stock and fund holdings that can be updated and displayed in graph form.

Wallstreetweb — *http://www.bulletproof.com/wallstreetweb/* This is the Web site to check out for the latest in eye-catching electronic investing graphics and capabilities. Plenty of price quotes, charts and portfolio management services.

Money Magazine — *http://www.pathfinder.com* A good site for topical coverage of financial and investing issues, including daily commentary on events that effect your personal finances. Also a good listing of other interesting investment-related Web sites. ▲

100 Steps to Wealth

A

Accredited Investor: Term used by the Securities and Exchange Commission. An accredited investor is a person with a net worth of $1 million or more; person with an annual income of $200,000 or more; person who purchases $150,000 or more of a securities offering and this does not represent more than 20% of their net worth. A corporation selling securities to this person may not have to make as full disclosure of information as it would if it were selling to non-accredited investors.

Accrual Basis: An accounting method under which debits and credits are entered in the books of a company on the date they are incurred, rather than on the date they are paid or received.

Accrued Interest: The interest due that has accumulated since the last time interest was paid.

Acid-test Ratio: A measurement of a corporation's liquidity. It is measured by subtracting inventory from current assets then dividing the remainder by current liabilities.

Active Market: Term used to describe a marketplace that is experiencing such frequent transactions, reasonable volume and relatively narrow spreads between the bid and asked prices that transactions have only moderate price changes.

Adjustable Rate Mortgage or ARM: A mortgage in which the interest rate may be adjusted by the lender to reflect changes in the interest rate market.

Affiliated Person: A person who can influence the management decisions of a corporation and includes holders of 10% or more of the outstanding stock of a corporation, directors and elected officers.

Aftermarket: Trading activity in a security during and immediately after the period of its initial offering to the public.

Agent: A person who buys or sells on the account and risk of another. Generally, an agent takes no financial risk and charges a commission for their services.

American Depository Receipt (ADR): Negotiable receipt, registered in the name of the owner, for shares of a foreign corporation held at a foreign branch of an American bank. Foreign corporations sell their securities in the United States in the form of ADRs.

American Municipal Bond Assurance Corporation (AMBAC): A corporation that guarantees payment of principal and interest on municipal bonds. AMBAC insured bonds are generally given a superior rating.

American Stock Exchange (ASE): Located in New York City, it is the second largest of the securities exchanges in the United States.

Amortization: The process of gradually reducing the financial accounting of an asset or obligation with regular write-offs or payments.

Amortize: To gradually reduce an asset or obligation over a specified time, usually over its lifetime.

Annual Report: The yearly report made by a company to its stockholders. Federal law requires all registered corporations to file one with the SEC.

Annuitant: Designation for a party that receives benefits from an annuity.

Annuity: An investment contract usually sold by a life insurance company in which the beneficiary receives regular payments for life, or for a fixed period, in exchange for the immediate or installment deposit of a specified amount of money.

Appreciation: An increase in the value of an asset.

Arbitrage: To buy and sell the same security in different marketplaces and profit from a disparity in market prices

Arbitrageur: One who engages in arbitrage transactions.

Arbitration: A method to resolve controversies that provides a final, binding decision providing the parties to the arbitration agree to abide by the decision before the proceedings begin.

Asked Price: The lowest price at which a dealer is willing to sell a security.

Assessed Valuation: The monetary value assigned to property by a property assessor.

Assets: Anything owned that has monetary value. This may include tangible and intangible items.

Asset Financing: Any loan that uses an asset such as land, property, or plant as collateral for the loan.

Assignment: The designated ownership of a security.

Associated Person: Any person associated with a broker/dealer as a proprietor, partner, officer, director, branch office manager, investment banker, or salesperson. Persons performing clerical functions are excluded.

At The Close: Customer instruction on a market order to be executed on an exchange immediately prior to the close of that day's trading.

At The Opening: Customer instruction on a market order to be executed on an exchange immediately after the opening of that day's trading.

Audit: An examination of an organization's accounting records by an independent auditor.

Audit Report: The report prepared by an independent auditor covering the audit work.

Auditor's Statement: A letter prepared by a corporation's auditor and usually accompanying audited financial statements in which the auditor explains and certifies the methods used to produce the statements.

Authorized Shares: The maximum number of shares, either common or preferred, that a corporation may issue as stated in the corporation's charter.

Automatic Reinvestment: Feature that permits an equity owner to receive dividend distributions in the form of new shares in lieu of a cash distribution.

Average down: To buy additional shares of a security owned when the price declines, thus reducing the average cost per share.

Average up: To buy additional shares of a security owned when the price increases, thus making the cost per share higher than the original purchase.

B

Balance of Trade: Dollar difference between a country's merchandise imports and its exports.

Balance Sheet: The financial statement which discloses what an organization owns (assets), what it owes (liabilities) and its equity or net worth on a given date in accordance with generally accepted accounting principals.

Balloon Interest: Feature of a serial bond issue in which earlier years' coupons are lower than coupon interest rates for later serial maturities.

Balloon Maturity: Feature of a debt obligation in which dollar amounts of earlier payments are smaller than dollar amounts of later payments.

Banker's Acceptance: Time draft that becomes a money market instrument when payment is guaranteed to be accepted by a bank. It is used extensively in international trade.

Bankruptcy: Designates insolvency of a corporation or individual.

Barron's Confidence Index: Weekly index prepared by the publishers of Barron's that compares yields of higher grade to lower grade corporate bonds.

Base Market Value: Average value of traded securities at a specified time, used in construction of a market index. For example, the NYSE Index had an original base of 50.00 on December 31, 1965.

Basis Point: One hundredth of one point. A change in the prime rate from 8.9% to 9% represents a 100 basis point change.

Basis Price: The cost to acquire an asset. The difference between the basis and the asset's sale price is the capital gain.

Bear market: A sharply or rapidly declining market.

Bearish: Having the opinion that securities will fall in market value.

Bellwether: Something that tends to predict a movement or trend.

Beneficial Owner: The person entitled to all benefits of ownership even though another entity holds the security.

Beneficiary: Organization or person who will receive the financial benefits of an asset, subject to certain conditions.

Beta: An indicator of price volatility of a security in terms of the Standard & Poor's Index. The S&P Index is given a value of 1. Securities with a beta greater than 1 have been more volatile than the S&P; those with a beta less than 1 have been less volatile.

Bid and Asked Price: The bid is the highest price a prospective buyer will pay for a security; the asked is the lowest price at which a seller will sell a security.

Big Board: The New York Stock Exchange.

Bills: U.S. Treasury debt securities of less than one year in length sold at a discount from their face value.

Blanket Recommendation: Financial recommendation made to all customers regardless of their financial capability and investment objectives.

Block: A purchase or sale of a large number of shares or dollar value of bonds. This term is relative, however. 10,000 or more shares, or any quantity worth over $200,000, is generally considered a block.

Blue Chip: A widely known company that is a leader in its industry and has a proven record of profits and a long history of dividend payment.

Board of Directors: The group of persons, elected by vote of the stockholders, who make important management decisions and who elect the officers of a corporation.

Bond: Any debt obligation issued as a security of greater than one year in term.

Bond Rating: An assessment issued by bond rating companies of a corporation's or government's risk of default on their bond issue.

Book Value of Common Shares: The assets of a corporation less its liabilities and preferred stock obligations divided by the number of outstanding common shares.

Bridge Loan: Short term financing provided while the borrower seeks a longer term loan.

Broker: Person or firm acting as an intermediary between a buyer and seller.

Broker Loan: Short term secured loan made by a broker from a commercial bank to finance a customer's security positions.

Bull market: A market that is sharply or rapidly advancing.

Bullish: Having the opinion that prices will rise or will continue to rise.

Butterfly Spread: An option strategy. An individual sells two calls, then buys two calls, one with a strike (exercise) price higher and one with a strike price lower than short calls. The individual is consequently partially hedged in both directions and hopes to profit from both the call premium received and from the restricted movement of the underlying stock.

C

Call or Call Option Contract: An option giving the owner of the option the right to buy a stock at a specified price over a specified time.

Call Feature: With bonds, debentures or preferred stock, an option of the issuing company to repurchase or "call back" the securities at a set price over a specified time.

Call Premium: An amount paid to bond or preferred shareholders that is above and beyond the security's par value when a company calls back the securities prior to maturity.

Callable: A security which may be redeemed upon due notice by the security's issuer.

Capital Gain or Loss: The profit or loss resulting from the sale of assets such as securities or real estate. It is the difference between the selling price and the purchase price less the costs of disposition.

Capital Structure: The total dollar amount of all debt, preferred and common stock, and retained earnings of a company: also called capitalization.

Capitalizing Expenses: To place operating expenses on the balance sheet and depreciate them over time rather than expense them on an income statement when incurred.

Cash Flow: Actual cash profits or losses rather than accounting or "book" profits or losses.

Cash Surrender Value: The dollar amount an insured may receive when surrendering a life insurance policy or an annuity to the insurer.

Certificate: The document that evidences ownership of securities.

Chicago Board Options Exchange (CBOE): The largest options exchange.

Chicago Board of Trade (CBT): The largest commodities exchange.

Churning: Illegal excessive buying and selling of securities for a customer by their stockbroker primarily interested in commissions from the trades.

Closed-end Fund: An investment fund offering a fixed number of shares for sale. Shares are bought and sold on stock exchanges and over-the-counter markets.

Collateral: Something of value pledged to secure the repayment of a loan.

Commercial Paper: Short-term negotiable debt obligations issued by financially secure corporations that pay specified amounts of money at a specified time.

Commission: The fee earned by an agent for buying or selling securities on behalf of a client.

Commodity: Anything that has value and can be bought or sold.

Commodity Exchange: An exchange at which buyers and sellers of staple commodities such as wheat, corn, sugar, cotton or coffee conduct trades.

Commodity Futures Trading Commission (CFTC): The government agency that has regulatory authority over the futures market.

Common Stock: Securities which represent an ownership interest in a corporation.

Community Property: Property acquired during a marriage and held to be equally owned by husband and wife under the laws of a state providing for such ownership.

Compound Interest: Interest that is paid not only on the original principal but also on any accumulated interest.

Compounding: The continuous reinvestment of returns.

Contract (financial): A note or confirmation giving the details of a sale or purchase of a security and mailed to the client immediately after the transaction.

Conversion: The option to exchange a bond or preferred share to a common stock.

Convertible Bond or Convertible Preferred Share: A bond or preferred share that is exchangeable for a specified number of some other security usually the issuing firm's common stock.

Coupon: Refers to the rate of interest (coupon rate) paid on a bond or debenture.

Cumulative Preferred: A preferred share for which dividends accumulate if they are not paid in a given year.

Currency: Money circulated as a medium of exchange and authorized by a government.

Current Assets: Assets that are available or can be made readily available to finance current operations or to pay current liabilities.

Current Liabilities: A corporation's obligations that will come due within a year.

Current Market Price: The price of a security as it trades in the market in the present time.

Current Ratio: A company's current assets divided by its current liabilities.

Current Yield: The amount of interest or dividends received, divided by the current market price of the security.

D

Date-of-Record: The date on which ownership of a security is determined for issuing a dividend or stock right.

Day Order: An order to buy or sell a security valid only for the day the order is given.

Debenture: A long term debt obligation which, unlike a collateralized bond, gives the lender only a general claim against the borrower's assets.

Debt: A contractual obligation to pay a sum of money and interest. For investment purposes it usually means bonds and similar securities that require payment of interest until maturity and repayment of principal at maturity.

Debt Security: Any security that represents money loaned to a company or government that must be repaid. Bills, notes, bonds, debentures, commercial paper and banker's acceptances are all examples of debt securities.

Decreasing Term: A type of term insurance in which protection decreases with the insured's age.

Default: When an individual or company fails to meet its obligations.

Default Risk: The danger than an issuer will be unable to meet its financial obligations due to a decline in earnings. Default risk is sometimes referred to as financial risk.

Defined Benefit Plan: A pension plan which provides each participant with a pre-specified level of pension income at retirement.

Depreciation: The portion of the cost of a fixed asset which is charged against earnings as an expense during a particular reporting period.

Dilution: When a company issues additional common stock and as a result dilutes or reduces the percentage of ownership of the holders common stock.

Discount: The amount by which a preferred stock or bond sells below its par value. A bond with a $1,000 par value, selling for $920 is selling at an $80 discount.

Discount Broker: A broker whose primary function is processing buy and sell orders at a relatively low cost. They differ from full service brokers in that they do not provide investment advice to clients nor are supported by a research department.

Distributions: Payments made to mutual fund share or unit holders from income or profits made by the fund.

Diversification: The process of spreading one's investment portfolio over different investment vehicles, industries, companies and risk levels. This technique helps to reduce risk and usually increases long term yields.

Dividend: A payment to the registered shareholders out of the profits of a corporation in amounts proportionate to their holdings, either in cash or other valuable consideration. Dividends are declared at the discretion of the board of directors.

Dollar Cost Averaging: A practice of continually investing a fixed dollar amount at regular intervals over a period of time. The strategy is to reduce the average cost of the investment, since the investor buys more shares when the price is low and fewer shares when the price is high.

E

Earnings Per Common Share: This ratio measures the earnings after preferred dividends generated by a firm per each common share. A firm that had $5,000,000 in net income, paid $500,000 in preferred dividends and had an average of 1,000,000 common shares outstanding during the year had an earnings per share of $4.50.

Equity or Shareholders Equity: Ownership interest of common and preferred stockholders in a company. The difference between the assets and liabilities of a corporation. If there are only common shares in the company, "equity per common share" is the equity divided by the number of shares outstanding.

Estate Taxes: Taxes imposed by the federal government, and by some state governments, on the taxable estate of an individual who has died.

Exchange: A formal meeting place for traders of securities. The exchanges provide the facilities for buyers and sellers to meet and carry out trading.

Ex-dividend Date: An ex-dividend date is designated by a corporation and determines the day on which one must own a share to be eligible to receive a dividend payment. Ex-dividend is a synonym for "without dividend".

Exercise Price: The price that an option holder (writer) pays (receives) to convert a call option contract into the underlying security. It is also the price that an option holder (writer) receives (pays) to convert a put option contract. The exercise price is often called the striking price.

Extendible: A clause in a bond contract that allows the bondholder the right to extend the maturity date by a set number of years under specified conditions.

F

Face Value: The value of a security that appears on the face of the certificate unless the value is otherwise specified by the issuing company. Face value or par value is ordinarily the amount the issuing company promises to pay at maturity. Face value is normally no indication of market value.

Federal Home Loan Mortgage Corporation or Freddie Mac: A government agency that pools conventional mortgages and sells fractional participations of those mortgages on a secondary market.

Federal National Mortgage Association, FNMA or Fannie Mae: A privately owned corporation that operates a secondary market for mortgages.

Federal Savings and Loan Insurance Corporation or FSLIC: The federal government agency that insures deposits at savings and loan associations. Each account is insured up to $100,000.

Fiduciary: A person or organization in whom legal ownership of property has been vested and who has an obligation or responsibility to hold or use such property in trust for the benefit of another.

Financial Intermediary: An institution such as a trust company, bank, life insurance company, investment dealer or stockbroker which receives cash - which it invests - from suppliers of capital.

Firm Bid - Firm Offer: An undertaking to buy (firm bid) or sell (firm offer) a specified amount of securities at a specified price for a specified period of time, unless released from this obligation by the seller in the case of a "firm bid," or the buyer in the case of a "firm offer".

Fiscal Period: Any period at the end of which an organization or person determines its financial position and the results of its operations. This is often a 12-month period.

Fixed Assets: Assets of a long-term nature which are intended to continue to be held or used such as land, buildings, machinery and equipment.

Fixed Income Securities: Securities that pay their holders a set amount of income. This set amount normally does not change with changes in the financial circumstances of the company. Most bonds are fixed income securities.

Floor Trader: An employee of a brokerage firm who works on the stock exchange floor in the capacity of buyer and seller on behalf of the firm's clients.

Front End Load: Commissions or sales charges that are deducted from the initial payments into a mutual fund or trust.

Full Service Broker: Stockbroker that not only aids a customer in completing a trade but who also provides investment advice. To cover the cost of maintaining a research department, full service brokers generally charge a higher commission fee than a discount broker.

Fund Manager: A management company that for a fee, usually linked to the value of the fund's assets, looks after the business affairs of the fund.

Fundamental Analysis: The evaluation of a company and its investment attractiveness based on its financial competitiveness, earning, and growth. Analysis is carried out on historical data provided in the company's financial statements, industry reports and economic data.

Futures: Contracts to buy or sell specific quantities of a commodity or financial instruments with delivery delayed until an agreed future date.

G

Generally Accepted Accounting Principles (GAAP): Uniform minimum standards and guidelines to financial accounting and reporting. GAAP govern the form and content of the basic financial statements of a reporting entity.

Generally Accepted Auditing Standards (GAAS): Standards for the quality of auditing procedures and the objectives to be attained through their use. GAAS are concerned with the auditor's professional qualities and with the judgment exercised in the performance of an audit.

General Obligation Bonds: Bonds, the payment of which is backed by the full faith and credit of the issuing government.

General Purpose Financial Statements (GPFS): Those basic financial statements which comprise the minimum acceptable fair presentation in conformity with GAAP.

Gift Taxes: Taxes imposed by the federal government upon an individual's lifetime transfers of money or property by gift.

Government National Mortgage Association, GNMA or Ginnie Mae: The government agency that gives assistance on selected types of home mortgages. It operates within the Department of Housing and Urban Development (HUD). It sells securities that are backed by its mortgages and by the U.S. government.

Group Life Insurance: Employers or unions offer insurance to their employees or members on a group basis. This often results in lower cost premiums and no medical examination.

H

Hedging: Any transaction designed to eliminate or reduce the risk in another transaction.

High Yield Bond: A polite term for junk bond.

I

Inheritance Taxes: Taxes imposed by some states on the passing of property of a deceased person's estate to the heirs.

Income: Refers to the amount of money made by an individual or by a corporation. Strictly in terms of investing, investment income is composed of dividends on common and preferred shares and interest on bonds.

Income Bond: Bonds, issued in exchange for other bonds, that promise to pay interest only if earned or to the extent earned.

Income Statement: A specific type of statement that shows, in detail, how a company has performed financially over a specified period of time, usually one year. The statement shows sales for the period and then deducts the costs and expenses of the company to arrive at a profit or loss figure.

Income Stock: A stock with a relatively high dividend payment.

Individual Retirement Account or IRA: A tax-favored retirement plan that can be established by any individual who has earned income.

Inflation: The rate of increase in prices. It is usually measured by the Consumer Price Index (CPI), an index comprised of the prices of a variety of goods and services that consumers generally purchase ranging from gasoline to food.

Insider: All directors and senior officers of a corporation and those who may also be presumed to have access to inside information concerning a company; also anyone owning more than 10% of the voting shares in a corporation.

Insolvency: Incapable of meeting debt obligations with either assets or financing.

Institutional Investor: An organization that pools funds from smaller organizations or individuals and invests them on their behalf. Mutual funds, pension funds and insurance companies are examples of institutional investors.

Interest: The amount a borrower pays for the use of a lender's funds. Interest may be compounded on a monthly, semi-annual, annual or some other periodic basis. A bond's interest is usually paid semi-annually.

Internet, the: The global network of high speed data lines into which anyone with a minimally capable computer, telephone line, modem and access software can tap. Information sent over the Internet may or may not carry sound, graphic or video information unlike the world wide web — a subset of the Internet — which can transmit sound, graphic and video. The Internet contains a wealth of sites/addresses from where financial information can be culled to aid in investment decisions.

Investment Banker: A corporation that assists a company and sometimes individuals in securing financing. This is usually accomplished by the investment banker making the initial purchase of securities from a company and then selling the new securities on a secondary market such as the ASE. The banker makes a profit on the difference between what it paid the offering company and what it sells the securities for on the market.

Investment Vehicle: Any asset expected to yield future benefits. It may take a variety of forms: stocks, bonds, mutual funds, options, real estate, precious metals and numerous others.

Issue: Any of a company's securities or the act of distributing them.

J

Joint tenancy: A form of co-ownership which provides that each tenant has undivided interest in the whole property. When one joint tenant dies, the interest in the property passes to the surviving joint tenant or tenants. Property is not limited to real estate and may include securities.

Junk Bond: Bonds that carry a high risk and correspondingly high rate of return. They are typically issued by companies or municipalities that are highly leveraged and as a result have a relatively poor bond rating.

K

Keogh Plan: A retirement account that allows a self-employed individual to set aside a percentage of their income in a tax sheltered fund.

L

Level Premium Insurance: Type of insurance where the yearly premium is the same over the life of the policy.

Leverage (finance): The use of borrowed funds to finance working capital requirements or to purchase assets.

Leverage (investing): Using borrowed funds or special types of securities (options, warrants) to increase the potential return. While leverage can enhance returns it also increases the risk for losses.

Liabilities: Debts of a corporation, usually divided into current liabilities — generally those due and payable within one year, and long term liabilities — those payable beyond one year.

Limit order: The maximum price set by a customer at which he or she is willing to buy or sell a security.

Limited Partnership Investment: A form of business between a general partner who supplies expertise and ability to operate in a certain industry (e.g., real estate and oil and gas) and a group of limited partners who invest capital. The partnership itself pays no taxes; instead, as partners, the investors report their pro rata share of partnership profits, losses and deductions on their own tax returns.

Liquidation: The process of converting securities or other property into cash. It also refers to dissolution of a company, with cash remaining after sale of its assets and payment of all indebtedness being distributed to the shareholders.

Liquidity: The ease with which an investment can be converted into cash. It is one of the most important characteristics of an efficient market.

Listed Stock: The stock of a company which is traded on a stock exchange.

Load: A selling fee paid by investors to purchase shares or units in a load fund. Also called sales charges.

Long: Having ownership of securities rather than being "short" where one has sold securities that are not owned.

Long-Term Assets: Assets with an expected life of greater than a year.

Long-Term Liabilities: Liabilities that are not due within a year or the next operating period.

M

Management Fee: A fee paid to the fund manager for the managing of the fund's portfolio and its day to day activities. Management fees are usually a fixed percentage of the market value of assets under management.

Margin (Buying on Margin): To finance a portion of a securities purchase with borrowed funds, usually borrowed from the brokerage firm that places the order.

Margin Account: An account whereby the investor borrows money from the brokerage firm to finance a portion of a securities purchase.

Marginal Tax Rate: The rate of tax paid on the last dollar earned.

Market-maker: A brokerage firm that is active in the buying and selling of a stock trading over-the-counter.

Market Order: An order placed to buy or sell a security immediately at the best current price possible.

Material Change: A major change in the operations or in the investment objectives of a company.

Maturity: The date the principal comes due by the issuer on a debt security. Securities maturing within 3 years are conventionally called short term, those maturing within 3 - 10 years are medium term, and all others long term.

Mortgage: A lien on property created by a pledge of that property as security for repayment of a loan. It provides for the transfer of the property to the lender if the borrower defaults.

Mortgage Bond: A bond that has property pledged as security for the issue. The bondholder's representative is entitled to take possession of the property and sell it if the debt is not repaid in a timely manner. Investors are protected under the terms of the mortgage contract by a trustee, usually a trust company, who acts on behalf of all bondholders.

Municipal Bonds: The obligations of states, cities, school districts or other public authorities are referred to as municipal bonds. Interest paid on municipal bonds is generally exempt from federal taxes.

Mutual Fund: An investment company established to pool the dollars of many people or organizations and invest those dollars more productively than individuals could for themselves. Different mutual funds include:

Aggressive Growth: Seeks maximum capital gains. Current income is generally not a consideration. Fund managers may use several strategies, such as buying high-technology stocks, emerging growth stocks, or companies that have fallen on hard times or are out of favor. Some aggressive funds make use of options and futures, and/or borrow against fund's shares to buy stock. Aggressive-growth funds typically provide dramatic gains and losses for shareholders.

Balanced: Generally invests in both stocks and bonds, with the intent of providing both capital gains and income. Preservation of principal is a primary objective of balanced fund managers. These funds are for conservative investors who are looking for modest growth of capital.

Corporate Bond: Seeks to pay a high level of income to shareholders by buying corporate bonds. Some conservative bond funds buy only the debt of highly rated corporations. The yield on this kind of bond would be lower than on that of a fund buying bonds from lower-rated corporations—frequently called junk bonds or high-yield bonds. Although income, not capital gains, is the primary objective of most corporate bond shareholders, gains can be signifi-

cant if the country's general level of interest rates falls. On the other hand, losses can also be substantial if interest rates rise.

Growth: Invests in the common stock of growth companies. The primary aim is to achieve capital gains, and income is of little concern. Growth funds vary widely in the amount of risk they assume. In general they take less risk than aggressive-growth funds because the stocks they buy are those of companies with some measurable track record.

Global Bond: Invests in fixed-income securities that are generally not denominated in U.S. dollars. Such funds may purchase bonds issued by foreign corporations or by U.S. corporations in non-dollar currencies. Global bond funds also invest in bonds issued by foreign governments or their agencies. Investors in global bond funds expect a high level of current income, and capital gains, if the direction of interest rates and currency rates is favorable.

Growth and Income: Seeks to provide both capital gains and a steady stream of income by buying the shares of high-yielding, conservative stocks. Growth and income fund managers look for companies with solid records of increasing their dividend payments, as well as showing earnings gains. These funds are more conservative than pure growth funds.

Global: Invests in securities anywhere in the world. They buy stocks, bonds and money-market instruments in both the United States and in foreign countries, depending on where the fund manager sees the best opportunity for growth. Global funds' main objective is long-term capital appreciation, though they may provide some current income.

GNMA Fund: Buys Government National Mortgage Association (GNMA or Ginnie Mae) certificates, which are securities backed by home mortgages. GNMA funds are designed to provide a high level of current income to shareholders and to minimize risk to capital. These funds are subject to fluctuation because of the ups and downs of interest rates, however. They are also affected by the rate at which homeowners refinance their mortgages. When interest rates fall, more mortgages are refinanced, and therefore shareholders in GNMA funds see their yields fall. When rates rise, on the other hand, fewer mortgages are refinanced, and so the fund maintains its yield, but it does not grow very quickly. GNMA funds are designed for conservative, income-oriented investors.

High Yield Bond: Buys the debt securities issued by non-investment grade corporations and municipalities. Because these securities offer higher risks than investment-grade bonds, high-yield bonds pay higher yields. Since the companies and municipalities that issue high-yield bonds are more highly leveraged than top-quality issuers, their bonds are more subject to default, particularly if there is an economic downturn in the issuer's industry or region. Such defaults would not only cut the yield on high-yield bond funds, but also erode the capital value of the shares. Investors in high-yield bond funds, therefore, should be well aware that they are taking an extra degree of default risk in exchange for a higher level of current income than is available from more conservative bond funds.

Income: Seeks to provide a high level of current income by buying government and corporate bonds as well as high-yielding common and preferred stocks.

Income funds are not designed to provide major capital gains, but their shares do rise when interest rates fall. (Conversely, the shares fall in value when interest rates rise.) Income funds are designed for conservative, income-oriented investors.

Income Bond: Invests in a variety of bonds to produce high taxable current income for shareholders. Such funds usually invest in corporate or government bonds, but may also buy foreign bonds. They are usually managed more conservatively than bond funds that buy high-yield bonds, and therefore offer lower current yields.

Income Equity: Invests in bonds and high-yielding stocks with the objective of providing shareholders with a moderate level of current income and a moderate level of long-term capital appreciation. Income-equity funds are slightly more conservatively managed, and usually have a higher percentage of their assets in bonds than growth and income funds.

Industry: Invests in one particular industry such as bio-technology or healthcare. The fund may choose to be growth, income or balanced within its industry.

International: Invests in stocks of companies around the world as well as in bonds issued by foreign companies and governments. Some funds (also called global funds) buy American and Canadian shares in addition to those of companies in other countries, while others are restricted to buying non-North American shares. International funds provide investors with diversification among countries as well as industries. Such funds are strongly influenced by the rise and fall of foreign exchange rates — a factor important to consider before buying shares. For Americans, it would generally be beneficial to buy an international fund when the outlook is for the dollar to fall against other currencies. Conversely, international fund performance usually suffers when the dollar strengthens. International funds are for those willing to take some risks. An understanding of the effect of currency changes on holdings is essential.

Long Term Municipal Bond: Aims to provide a high level of tax-exempt income to shareholder by buying the debt obligations of cities, states and other municipal government agencies. Depending on the state in which a shareholder resides, interest earned is either totally or partially free of federal, state, and local income taxes. While such funds are designed to provide current income, their value also rises and falls inversely with the country's general level of interest rates. The municipal bonds these funds usually buy tend to mature anywhere from 10 to 20 years in the future.

Money Market: Buys short-term securities sold in the money markets to provide current income to shareholders. Because of the short-term nature of their holdings, these funds reflect changes in short-term interest rates rather quickly. The principal in money-market funds is extremely safe. Some money funds buy commercial instruments like commercial paper, banker's acceptances and repurchase agreements, while others restrict themselves to buying U.S. Treasury obligations like Treasury bills. The portfolios of some money-market funds are insured by private insurance companies. Most money funds allow checkwriting, often with a minimum check size of $250 or $500. Money market funds are

frequently included in asset management accounts offered by brokerage firms, and are used as parking places for funds while shareholders decide where the best place to invest long term might be. Otherwise, money-market funds are for extremely conservative investors, who want virtually no risk of capital loss.

Option Income: Provides high current returns by writing call options on a portfolio of dividend-paying stocks. The current return derives from dividends on stock as well as premium income earned by writing options. If the value of the stock in the portfolio declines, the net asset value of the fund will also decline, though the income earned will somewhat offset that decline. Option-income funds are designed for investors wanting high current return while being willing to risk declines in the value of their shares.

Precious Metals: Invests in the shares of gold and silver mining companies. These shares often pay high dividends, and therefore the funds often can pay high yield. As with all precious-metal investments, these funds reflect the ups and downs of investor psychology as it relates to the outlook for inflation as well as political upheaval. These funds tend to perform better when inflation is high and rising and there is considerable political turmoil in the world. Some funds invest largely in South African mines, while others restrict themselves to shares in North American mining companies.

Short-Term Municipal Bond: Buys short-term obligations of cities, states and municipal government agencies, and pass along tax-exempt income to shareholders. Since the bonds are short-term, they are less risky and usually have a lower yield than longer-term obligations. Some short-term municipal bond funds operate like tax-free money-market funds and allow checkwriting, usually with a $250 or $500 per check minimum. These funds are generally for conservative investors in income-tax brackets high enough to take advantage of tax-free income.

State Municipal Bond-Short Term: Buys the debt obligations of cities and municipal authorities in one state only. The interest from these bonds is usually tax exempt to residents of the particular state. Thus, shareholders can obtain a higher after-tax yield than if they bought the shares in an out-of-state fund on which they had to pay taxes. These funds typically buy short-term debt obligations with maturities from a few days or months to as much as five years. Therefore, they are not as subject to interest rate fluctuations as long-term funds. The funds generally allow shareholders to write checks, typically with a minimum withdrawal of $250 to $500 per check.

N

National Association of Security Dealers or NAS-DAQ: An automated information system that provides brokers and dealers with price quotations on securities that are traded OTC.

Negotiable: A certificate that is transferable by delivery and which, in the case of a registered certificate, has been endorsed and guaranteed.

Net Worth: An individual's or a corporation's assets minus liabilities.

New Issue: A security sold by a corporation for the first time. Proceeds may be used to retire outstanding securities of the company, for new plant or equipment or for additional working capital.

No-load: Mutual funds that are sold to the public with no front-end sales charges.

Nominal Yield: The annual interest rate paid on a fixed income security, also known as the coupon rate.

Note: A corporation's unsecured promise to pay.

Notes to the Financial Statements: The summary of significant accounting policies and other disclosures required for a fair presentation of the basic financial statements of a corporation in conformity with GAAP.

O

Offer: The price at which a person is ready to sell a security. The offer is in contrast to the bid which is the price at which one is willing to buy.

Option: A right to buy or sell specific securities or properties at a specified price within a specified time.

Open-end Fund: An investment company or trust, which issues and redeems shares or units on demand.

Over-the-counter (OTC): A market for securities that are not listed on an organized exchange but that are traded directly between dealers.

P

Paper Profit: Current market value of a security still owned in excess of original cost. The profit has yet to be realized by converting it into cash. Profits can be realized only when a security is sold.

Par, Discount and Premium: A $1,000 bond purchased for $1,000 is said to have been bought "at par". A bond purchased for less than par is said to have been bought "at a discount". A bond purchased for more than par is said to have been bought "at a premium".

Partnership: A form of business organization in which two or more individuals share in the financing, management, profits or losses of a business. Income from the partnership is taxed at each partner's personal tax rate.

Personal Property: Property owned by an individual other than real estate.

Points: A fee charged for initiating a loan, especially for a mortgage on real estate.

Portfolio: The composite of an individual, fund or institution's securities and/or assets.

Preferred Shares: Shares in a company that have certain preferences or rights over common shares, such as dividend payments and priority in liquidations.

Price Earnings Ratio (Multiple): It is a company's stock price divided by its annual earnings per share. The price/earnings ratio indicates how much investors are willing to pay for a dollar of earnings of a firm. If company X earns $1.50 a share and the share is selling for $18.00, the price earnings multiple is 12.

Primary Distribution: The sale of any new securities by an issuer. Primary distributions are usually made to investment banks or through private placements. Investment banks, in turn, usually issue the securities onto secondary markets such as the ASE.

Primary Market: The market through which there is an initial sale of new securities by an issuer to investors. This market should not be confused with the "secondary market" which deals with the trading of securities that are already issued and outstanding.

Prime Rate: The interest rate that banks charge to their best accounts. It is possible, although, to secure financing below prime.

Principal (investing): (i) the face value of a bond, mortgage or other fixed income security. (ii) the original amount or purchase price of an investment. (iii) an investment dealer who buys or sells securities for his own account

Principal (lending): The amount of money that is financed or borrowed.

Private Placement: A sale of securities, usually stock, made directly to a small number of investors who in turn generally do not intend to re-offer the securities on a secondary market in the near future.

Profit (Loss): Sales minus costs.

Pro Rata: In proportion to. For example, a dividend is a pro rata payment because the amount of dividend each shareholder receives is in proportion to the number of shares owned.

Probate of a Will: Literally, the process of proving that the written will of the deceased is valid.

Programmed Trading: Computer assisted trading in large blocks of securities by institutional investors. This trading usually involves complex mathematical algorithms that govern buy and sell orders.

Prospectus: A document that corporations contemplating a distribution of securities to the public must file with the Securities and Exchange Commission, in respect to the offering. This ensures that the public receives material information sufficient to judge whether they wish to buy the securities on the basis of the information in the prospectus.

Proxy: A shareholder ballot or the transfer of a right to another entity.

Purchasing Power: The ability to purchase goods and services.

Purchasing Power Risk: A risk associated with fixed income securities and fixed income funds. Persons receiving a fixed return from such securities will experience a loss of purchasing power as inflation rises.

Put or Put Option Contract: An option giving the holder of the option the right to sell stock at a specified price over a specified period. Puts are generally purchased by those who expect a decrease in the underlying stock price.

Q

Quarterly Report: A financial statement produced every three months.

Quick Ratio: Current assets divided by current liabilities. This measures a company's ability to meet short term obligations.

Quotation or Quote: The highest bid to buy and the lowest offer to sell a security at a given time.

R

Real Assets: Tangible or physical assets such as real estate and equipment as opposed to financial assets which are "paper" holdings such as debt and equity.

Real Estate Investment Trust (REIT): A company that invests exclusively in managed real estate properties or mortgages by pooling individual investor's funds. Income from REITs are taxed at the individual level not at the corporate level.

Redeemable: Bonds or preferred shares that carry the right of the issuing company to repurchase the securities at a set price over a specified period. May also be referred to as a call feature (callable).

Redemption: The procedures by which a corporation redeems (pays off) its outstanding securities by paying the holder the appropriate redemption price.

Registered Representative: A salesperson or broker employed by an investment firm that is a member of an exchange and who is qualified to serve as an account executive for that firm's clients.

Retained Earnings: The net income earned by a company that has not been distributed to shareholders as dividends.

Retirement Plans: A tax-favored employer benefit plan that defers taxation on contributions until retirement.

Retractable: A feature which may be included in a debt or preferred share issue giving the holder the right, under specific conditions, to require redemption of the security by a stated date.

Return on Investment (ROI): The ratio of net profit divided by the value of the investment employed to obtain the profit. If one buys a stock for $10 and sells it for $12, the ROI is $2/$10 or 20%.

Revenue Bonds: Bonds whose principal and interest normally are paid from the earnings of the project the bonds funded.

Right: An option allowing shareholders to acquire new shares at a specified price over a specified period.

Risk: The probability of loss on an investment.

Risk-free Rate: The yield on an investment that has virtually no risk. The risk-free rate usually refers to the T-bill rate.

Risk-return Trade-off: A tendency for more risky assets to be priced to yield higher expected returns. To compensate for the possibility of some undesirable or unexpected event, returns on risky assets must be potentially higher than for lower risk investment.

S

Secondary Market: The market for securities that have already been issued. Stock exchanges and over-the counter markets are examples of secondary markets.

Securities: The general term applied for documents issued to investors by companies, governments and quasi-government bodies that evidence ownership of capital, for-

mal loans or financial obligations. This general term covers stock certificates, bonds, debentures, notes and similar documents, all of which are normally saleable and transferable from one person to another.

Securities and Exchange Commission or SEC: The government agency that has regulatory authority over the securities industry.

Settlement Date: When a security is traded, the customer must pay for (settle) the security within a specified time period, usually five business days.

Short Sale: The sale of a security which the seller does not own. This is a transaction initiated in the hope that the price of a stock is going to fall and the seller will be able to cover the sale by buying it back later at a lower price, thereby making a profit on the operation.

Sole Proprietorship: A form of unincorporated business organization in which there is only one owner.

Speculator: One who is willing to accept a greater degree of risk in his selection of investment vehicles in pursuit of potentially higher returns. This person's risk tolerance lies between that of an investor and that of a gambler.

Split: Division of the outstanding shares of a corporation into a large number of shares. A 2-for-1 split by a company with one million shares outstanding would result in two million shares outstanding. Each holder of 100 shares before the 2-for-1 split would have 200 shares after the split and their proportionate equity in the company would remain the same.

Spread: The gap between the bid and asked prices in the quotation of a security.

Standard & Poor's Corporation: A company that rates bonds, collects and reports financial and securities data and computes market indexes.

Statement of Changes in Financial Position: The basic financial statement that presents information on the amount of the sources and uses of a company's cash or working capital during an accounting period in conformity with GAAP.

Stock Dividend: A pro-rata payment to common shareholders in the firm of additional common stock. Such payment increases the number of shares each holder owns but does not alter a shareholder's proportional ownership of the company.

Stock Index: A stock index is simply another way of saying average. Indexes can be used to analyze how a securities market is doing. The six most widely quoted indexes are described below. Each measures a different aspect of the market.

1. American Stock Exchange Index: The ASE Index, also known as the Market Value Index, takes the average of 1,000 American Stock Exchange stock prices. It is a good measure of secondary stocks' performance.

2. Dow Jones Industrial Average: The best known of the indexes, the Dow Jones is the average price of 30 large industrial companies traded on the NYSE. The prices of the 30 are totaled and the total divided by 30 to arrive at the average. Adjustments are made for stock dividends and splits. The Dow shows how large, well-established industrials are performing, but does not reflect the performance of other sectors of the market.

The Dow is not weighted by the number of shares outstanding.

3. NASDAQ Composite Index: This is the average price of about 5,000 over-the-counter issues. It, in essence, measures performance of newer, riskier stocks.

4. Nikkei Index: Japan's counterpart to the Dow, this index covers 225 large companies listed on the Tokyo Stock Exchange.

5. New York Stock Exchange Index: The NYSE Index uses every stock listed on the New York Stock Exchange to arrive at an average, which is weighted according to the number of shares outstanding (similar to the S&P 500).

6. Standard & Poor's 500 Composite Stock Price Index: This index tracks 500 companies traded on the NYSE, the ASE, and the over-the-counter market. They represent the bulk of the value of stocks traded on the NYSE. The S&P 500 is weighted as to the number of shares outstanding. The U.S. Government uses the S&P 500 as the stock market component of its leading indicator index.

Stock Option: The opportunity extended by a company for employees or underwriters to buy stock in the company at favorable prices and/or terms.

Stockbroker: One who acts as an agent in buying and selling of securities and charges a commission for their services.

Straddle: To place both a put and a call on the same stock at the same strike price.

Street Name: Securities held in the name of the broker/dealer on behalf of their customers.

Strike Price: The specified price an option holder receives or pays on a put or call option contract. It is also called the exercise price.

Switching: The practice of moving from one security to another. Switching may result in the investor paying excessive transaction costs.

Syndicated Offering: A group of investment bankers that collectively underwrite a new security offering.

Systematic Risk: Risk that simultaneously affects all investment types.

T

Tax-exempt: Income not subject to income tax. Income from many municipal bonds are often tax-exempt.

Tax-exempt Bonds: The securities of states, cities and other public authorities specified under federal law, the interest on which is either wholly or partly exempt from federal income taxes.

Tax-exempt Interest: Interest earned on securities that is not taxable. The income from municipal bonds issued within a state, for example, is often tax-exempt to residents of the state.

Technical Analysis: A method of evaluating future security and market direction based on past price and volume behavior. The analyst looks for specific patterns to predict future prices.

Tender: To surrender one's shares in response to an offer to purchase them at a given price.

Term: The life span of an obligation.

Term Insurance: Insurance that provides protection for a fixed period of time. While the policy is in force, the insured pays a set premium and if the insured dies, the beneficiary receives a specified dollar amount. A cash surrender value does not accumulate with term insurance.

Thin Market: A market in which there are few buyers or sellers.

Top Down Approach: A method of analyzing a prospective investment by examining first the economy, then the market, then the industry and then the specific company.

Trade: The sale of a security, usually facilitated for an investor by a stock broker.

Trader: One who actively buys and sells securities. This may be an investor or it may refer to a person who acts for a security firm and trades securities on the floor of the exchange (floor trader).

Trading Volume: The number of shares traded usually measured on a given day.

Transfer Agent: An agent, often a brokerage firm, a corporation or a mutual fund organization that maintains changes in the shareholder's register and provides other related services.

Treasury Bills (T-bills): Short-term government debt securities that do not pay interest directly but are issued on a discount basis and mature at a higher value. The difference between issue price and maturity price is the lender's income. Large institutional investors are the primary purchasers of T-bills.

Treasury Bonds: U.S. government long-term securities, sold to the public and having a maturity greater than five years.

Treasury Shares: Authorized but un-issued stock of a corporation or previously issued shares that have been re-acquired by the corporation held in the corporation's treasury.

Trust: A legal arrangement by which title to property is given to one party who manages it for the benefit of another, referred to as beneficiary or beneficiaries.

Trustee: An individual or corporation appointed or required by law to administer or execute a trust for the beneficiaries of the trust.

U

Underwriting: The purchase by an investment dealer or "underwriter" of a security issued by a company with the intent by the underwriter to offer the security for resale on an exchange or secondary market. The formal agreements pertaining to such a transaction are called "underwriting agreements".

Universal Life Insurance: Similar to whole life but combines protection with a savings element that accumulates tax-deferred at current interest rates. The premium amount and payment schedule are flexible and the policyowner can increase or decrease his/her coverage without purchasing a new policy.

Unlisted Security: A stock not listed on a stock exchange but traded on the over-the-counter market.

V

Variable Life Insurance: Insurance that combines protection with a savings element that can be invested in a variety of asset portfolios. Earnings on the savings element accumulate tax-deferred and the policy-owner can transfer funds among asset portfolios with varying investment objectives.

Venture Capital: Capital extended to high risk, start-up companies and small businesses in exchange for debt or equity securities. Such investments usually carry very high risk and very high returns if successful.

Volatility: Volatility is a measure of variability or the degree of fluctuation in a security's value or rate of return. The more volatile the more risky the security.

Voting Right: The stockholder's right to vote their stock in the affairs of their company. Most common shares have one vote each. Preferred stock usually has the right to vote only when its dividends are in default. The right to vote may be delegated by the stockholder to another person ("a proxy").

W

Warrant: An option that evidences the right of the holder to purchase stock in a company at a specified price over a specified period. They are usually attached to a new securities issue to increase the marketability of the issue.

Whole Life Insurance: Life insurance that has a cash value that can be borrowed, used as collateral, or withdrawn by surrendering the policy and has a lump sum benefit payable at death.

Withdrawal Plans: The various choices an investor has on liquidating their holdings. Withdrawal plans include (i) lump sum (ii) ratio (iii) fixed dollar and (iv) fixed period.

Will: The legal, written communication of a person's desire for the disposition of their property and custodial relationship of their kin after their death.

World Wide Web: The graphical portion of the Internet that allows users to display graphics, sound and video on their computer screens, no matter where they are in the world, provided they can call into it with a telephone line and a computer with access software. The world wide web contains a wealth of sites/addresses from where financial information can be culled to aid in investment decisions.

Working Capital: Short term assets minus short term liabilities.

Y

Yield or Return: The dividends or interest paid by a company on a security expressed as a percentage of that security's current price or, if you are the owner, of that security's price at purchase. The return on a stock is figured by dividing the total of dividends paid in the preceding 12 months by the current price or, if you are the owner, the original price.

Yield to Maturity (YTM): The annual return an investor would receive on a bond if they purchased a bond and held it to maturity reinvesting the coupon interest at the same rate. This calculation takes into account any premium or discount on the bond.

Z

Zero Coupon Bond: A debt security or bond that is issued at a discount, that matures at its face value and makes no interim payment of interest until its maturity.

APPENDIX

Investment industry contact information and bond ratings

Brokerage Firm Contact Information

Some of the investment activity presented in *100 Steps* may require the services of a broker. The contact information for the 91 largest full service brokerage firms and 9 discount brokers is provided as a convenience to you. Since we do not endorse any one brokerage firm, they are listed alphabetically. Please use your local directories or call the numbers below for information regarding branch offices. This information is provided as a courtesy of the brokerage industry's trade association, the Securities Industry Association, 120 Broadway, New York, NY 10271, 212-608-1501.

Full-Service Brokerage Firms

Advest, Inc.	90 State House Square, Hartford, CT 06103	203-509-1000
Alliance Capital Management L.P.	1345 Avenue of the Americas, New York, NY 10105	212-969-1000
Arnhold and S. Bleichroeder, Inc.	45 Broadway, New York, NY 10006	212-943-9200
Robert W. Baird & Co., Inc.	777 East Wisconsin Avenue, Milwaukee, WI 53202	414-765-3500
The Bank of Tokyo Trust Company	100 Broadway, New York, NY 10005	212-766-3400
The Bear Stearns Companies Inc.	245 Park Avenue, New York, NY 10167	212-272-2000
William Blair & Company	222 West Adams, Chicago, IL 60606	312-236-1600
J.C. Bradford & Co.	330 Commerce Street, Nashville, TN 37201-1809	615-748-9000
Alex. Brown & Sons Inc.	135 East Baltimore Street, Baltimore, MD 21202	401-727-1700
Brown Brothers Harriman & Co.	59 Wall Street, New York, NY 10005	212-483-1818
Cantor Fitzgerald & Co. Inc.	1840 Century Park East, 9th Floor, Los Angeles, CA 90067	310-858-5000
Chase Securities, Inc.	270 Park Avenue, 6th Floor, New York, NY 10017	212-834-3147
The Chicago Corp.	208 South LaSalle Street, Chicago, IL 60604	312-855-7600
CL Global Partners Securities Corp.	1301 Avenue of the Americas, New York, NY 10019	212-408-5700
Crowell,Weeden and Co.	624 S. Grand Avenue, Suite 2510, Los Angeles, CA 90017	213-620-1850
Dain Bosworth Inc.	60 South 6th Street, Minneapolis, MN 55402	612-371-2711
Daiwa Securities America, Inc.	Financial Square, 32 Old Slip, New York, NY 10005	212-612-7000
Dean Witter Reynolds Inc.	2 World Trade Center, New York, NY 10048	212-392-2222
Deutsche Bank Capital Corp.	31 West 52nd Street, 3rd Floor, New York, NY 10019	212-474-7000
Dillon Read & Co. Inc.	535 Madison Avenue, New York, NY 10022	212-906-7000
Dominick & Dominick Inc.	32 Old Slip, New York, NY 10005	212-558-8800
Donaldson, Lufkin & Jenrette Securities	277 Park Avenue, New York, NY 10172	212-892-3000
Dresdner Sercurities USA, Inc.	75 Wall Street, New York, NY 10005	212-429-2800
Eaton Vance Distributors, Inc.	24 Federal Street, Boston, MA 02110	617-482-8260

Full-Service Brokerage Firms (continued)

A.G. Edwards & Sons, Inc.	One North Jefferson, St. Louis, MO 63103	314-289-3000
Ernst & Co.	One Battery Park Plaza, New York, NY 10004	212-898-6200
Everen Securities	77 W. Wacker Drive, Chicago, IL 60601	312-574-6000
Federated Securities Corp.	10001 Liberty Avenue, Pittsburgh, PA 15222-3779	412-288-1900
First Boston Inc.	Park Avenue Plaza, New York, NY 10055	212-909-2000
First Manhattan Co.	437 Madison Avenue, New York, NY 10022	212-756-3100
First Southwest Co.	1700 Pacific Avenue, Suite 500, Dallas, TX 75201	214-953-4000
Furman Seiz Mager Dietz & Birney Inc.	230 Park Avenue, New York, NY 10169	212-309-8200
Gintel & Co.	Greenwich Office Park, OP-6, Greenwich, CT 06831	203-622-6400
Glickenhaus & Co.	6 East 43rd Street, New York, NY 10017	212-953-7800
Goldman Sachs & Co.	85 Broad Street, New York, NY 10004	212-902-1000
Greenwich Capital Markets, Inc.	600 Steamboat Road, Greenwich, CT 06830	203-625-2700
Gruntal & Co. Inc.	14 Wall Street, New York, NY 10005	212-267-8800
Hambrecht & Quist Inc.	One Bush Street, San Francisco, CA 94104	415-576-3300
Herzog, Heine, Geduld, Inc.	26 Broadway, New York, NY 10004	212-908-4000
J.J.B. Hilliard, W.L. Lyons Inc.	Hilliard Lyons Center, Louisville, KY 40232-2760	502-588-8400
Inter-Regional Financal Group, Inc.	Dean Bosworth Plaza, 60 S. 6th Street, Minneapolis, MN 55402	612-371-7750
Interstate/Johnson Lane Corp.	Interstate Tower, 121 W. Trade St., Ste. 1100, Charlotte, NC 28202	704-379-9000
Janney Montgomery Scott Inc.	1801 Market Street, Philadelphia, PA 19103	215-665-6000
Edward D. Jones & Co.	201 Progress Parkway, St. Louis, MO 63043	314-515-2000
Keefe, Bruyette & Woods, Inc.	Suite 8566, Two World Trade Center, New York, NY 10048	212-323-8300
Kemper Financial Services, Inc.	120 South LaSalle Street, Chicago, IL 60603	312-781-1121
Kidder Peabody & Co., Inc.	60 Broad Street, New York, NY 10004	212-510-3000
C.J. Lawrence, Morgan Grenfell Inc.	1290 Avenue of the Americas, New York, NY 10104-0101	212-468-5000
Lazard Freres & Co.	30 Rockefeller Plaza, New York, NY 10020	212-632-6000
Legg Mason, Inc.	Legg Mason Tower, 111 S. Calvert St., Baltimore, MD 21202	410-539-0000
Lehman Brothers	3 World Financial Center, New York, NY 10285	212-526-7000
Mabon Securities	One Liberty Plaza, 165 Broadway, New York, NY 10006	212-732-2820

Full-Service Brokerage Firms (continued)

Bernard L. Madoff Investment Securities	885 Third Avenue, New York, NY 10022	212-230-2424
McDonald & Company Securitries, Inc.	The McDonald Investment Center, 800 Superior Ave. Cleveland, OH 44114	216-443-2300
Merrill Lynch, Pierce, Fenner & Smith	North Tower, World Financial Center, 250 Vesey Street New York, NY 10281	212-449-1000
Mesirow Financial Holdings, Inc.	350 North Clark Street, Chicago, IL 60610	312-670-6000
Miller Tabak Hirsch & Co.	331 Madison Avenue, New York, NY 10017	212-370-0040
Montgomery Securities	600 Montgomery Street, San Francisco, CA 94111	415-627-2000
Morgan Keegan & Company, Inc.	50 Front Street, Memphis, TN 38103	901-524-4100
J. P. Morgan Securities Inc.	23 Wall Street, New York, NY 10015	212-483-2323
Morgan Stanley & Co. Inc.	1251 Avenue of the Americas, New York, NY 10020	212-703-4000
Neuberger & Bernan	522 3rd Avenue, New York, NY 10158	212-476-9000
New Japan Securities International, Inc.	One World Trade Center, Suite 9133, New York, NY 10048	212-839-0001
The Nikko Securities Co. International	200 Liberty Street, New York, NY 10281	212-416-5400
Nomura Securities International	2 World Financial Ctr., Building B, New York, NY 10281	212-667-9300
John Nuveen and Co. Inc.	333 West Wacker Drive, Chicago, IL 60606	312-917-7700
The Ohio Company	155 East Broad Street, Columbus, OH 43215	614-464-6811
Oppenheimer & Company, Inc.	Oppenheimer Tower, One World Financial Center, NY, NY 10281	212-667-7000
PaineWebber Group Inc.	1285 Avenue of the Americas, New York, NY 10019	212-713-2000
Piper, Jaffray & Hopwood Inc.	Piper Jaffray Tower, 222 S. 9th St. , Minneapolis, MN 55440	612-342-6000
Principle Financial Securities	1445 Ross Avenue, Suite 2300, Dallas, TX 75202	214-880-9000
Prudential Securities Inc.	One Seaport Plaza, 199 Water Street, New York, NY 10292	212-214-1000
Raymond James Financial	880 Carillon Parkway, St. Petersburg, FL 33733-2749	813-573-3800
Rauscher Pierce Refsnes, Inc.	2711 N. Haskell, Suite 2400, Dallas, TX 75204	214-978-0111
Robertson & Stephens Co.	555 California St., Suite 2600, San Francisco, CA 94104	415-781-9700
The Robinson-Humphrey Co., Inc.	3333 Peachtree Rd., N.E., Atlanta, GA 30326	404-266-6000
Rodman & Renshaw, Inc.	233 S. Wacker, Chicago, IL 60606	312-526-2000
Salomon Brothers Inc.	7 World Trade Center, New York, NY 10048	212-747-7000
SBCI Swiss Bank Corporation	222 Broadway, 4th Floor, New York, NY 10038	212-335-1000

Full-Service Brokerage Firms (continued)

M.A. Schapiro & Co., Inc.	One Chase Manhattan Plaza, New York, NY 10005	212-425-6600
ScotiaMcCleod (U.S.A.) Inc.	1 Liberty Plaza, 26th Floor, New York, NY 10006	212-225-6500
Securities Settlement Corporation	One Whitehall Street, New York, NY 10004	212-709-8000
Smith Barney, Inc.	388 Greenwich Street, New York, NY 10105	212-816-6000
Stern Brothers & Co.	1044 Main Street, Suite 900, Kansas City, MO 64105	816-471-6460
Tucker, Anthony Inc.	1 Beacon Street, Boston, MA 02108	617-725-2000
UBS Securities, Inc.	299 Park Avenue, New York, NY 10171	212-230-4000
Van Kampen American Capital	One Parkview Plaza, Oak Brook Terrace, IL 60181	800-856-3577
S.G. Warburg & Co. Inc.	277 Park Avenue, 3rd Floor, New York, NY 10019	212-459-7000
Weiss, Peck & Greer	One New York Plaza, New York, NY 10004	212-908-9570
Yamaichi International (America), Inc.	Two World Trade Center, New York, NY 10048	212-912-6400
The Ziegler Company, Inc.	215 North Main Street, West Bend, WI 53095	414-334-5521

Discount Brokerage Firms

Bidwell	209 S.W. Oak Street, Portland, OR 97204	800-547-6337
Burke Christensen & Lewis	303 West Madison Street, Chicago, IL 50505	800-621-0392
Fidelity Brokerage Account Assistance	161 Devonshire Street, Boston, MA 02110	800-225-1799
Fleet Brokerage Securities	2 North Riverside, Chicago, IL 60606	800-621-0662
Pacific Brokerage Services	5757 Wilshire Boulevard, Suite 3, Los Angeles, CA 90036	800-421-8395
Quick & Reilly, Inc.	26 Broadway, New York, NY 10004	800-221-5220
Charles Schwab and Co.	101 Montgomery Street, San Francisco, CA 94104	800-435-4000
Muriel Siebert and Co.	885 Third Avenue, New York, NY 10022	800-872-0711
York Securities	160 Broadway, East Building, 7th Floor, New York, NY 10038	212-349-9700

Mutual Fund Management Companies

After reading some of the investment activity presented in *100 Steps* you may want to contact major mutual fund management companies directly. These companies offer, for example, a diverse selection of mutual funds and money market investments. The contact information for the 50 largest and most diversified fund management companies is provided below as a convenience to you. Since we do not recommend any single company or any company's specific fund, the companies are listed alphabetically. This information is provided as a courtesy of The Investment Company Institute, 1401 H St. N.W., Washington, D.C., 20005, 202-326-5800. The Institute may be contacted for a variety of information about investing.

AIM Managment Group	11 Greenway Plaza, Suite 1919, Houston, TX 77046	800-347-1919
Alger Funds	75 Maiden Lane, New York, NY 10038	800-992-FUND
Alliance Capital Management	1345 Avenue of the Americas, New York, NY 10105	800-523-5695
American Capital	2800 Post Oak Boulevard, Houston TX 77056	800-421-5666
American Fund Distributors	333 South Hope Street, Los Angeles, CA 90071	800-421-0180
American Express Financial Services	IDS Tower 10, Minneapolis, MN 55440	800-328-8300
Benham Capital Management Group	1665 Charleston Road, Mt. View, CA 94043	800-321-8321
CIGNA Funds	900 Cottage Grove, Suite 210, Hartford, CT 06152	203-726-3700
Colonial Management Associates	One Financial Center, Boston, MA 02111	800-225-2365
Crabbe-Huson Funds	121 Southwest Morrison Street, Suite 1400, Portland, OR 97204	800-541-9732
Dean Witter	One World Trade Center, New York, NY 10048	800-869-FUND
Delaware Group	1818 Market Square, Philadelphia, PA 19103	800-523-4640
Dreyfus	One American Express Plaza, Providence, RI 02903	800-645-6561
Eaton Vance	24 Federal Street, Boston, MA 02110	800-225-6265
Federated Investors	Federated Investors Tower, Pittsburgh, PA 15222-3779	800-245-0242
Fidelity Investments	82 Devonshire Street, Boston, MA 02109	800-544-8888
First Investors Management Co.	95 Wall Street, New York, NY 10005	800-423-4026
Flagship	One Dayton Center, One S. Main Street, Dayton, OH 45402	800-227-4648
Franklin-Templeton Group	777 Mariners Island Blvd., San Mateo, CA 94404	800-632-2180
Invesco Funds Group	7800 East Union Avenue, Denver, CO 80237	800-525-8085
John Hancock	101 Huntington Avenue, Boston, MA 02199	800-225-5291
Jones & Babson	2440 Pershing Road, Suite G15, Kansas City, MO 64108	800-422-2766
Kemper Funds	120 South LaSalle Street, Chicago, Il 60603	800-621-1048
Keystone Investments	P.O. Box 2121, Boston, MA 02106-2121	800-343-2898

Mutual Fund Management Companies (continued)

Lazard Freres	One Rockefeller Plaza, New York, NY 10020	800-854-8525
Massachusetts Financial	500 Boylston Street, Boston, MA 02116	800-343-2829
Merrill Lynch	P.O. Box 9011, Princeton, NJ 08543-9011	800-637-3863
Midwest Group	312 Walnut Street, 21st Floor, Cincinnati, OH 45202	800-543-8721
New England Funds	399 Boylston, Boston, MA 02116	800-225-5478
Nuveen	333 West Wacker Drive, Chicago, IL 60606	800-621-7227
Oppenheimer Funds	3410 South Galena Street, Denver, CO 80231	800-525-7048
Pacific Investment Management Co.	2187 Atlantic, Stamford, CT 06902	800-628-1237
PaineWebber	1285 Avenue of the Americas, New York, NY 10019	800-647-1568
Pimco Advisors	2187 Atlanta, Stanford, CT 06902	800-628-1237
Prudential Mutual Fund Services	P.O. Box 15015, New Brunswick, NY 08906	800-225-1852
Putnam Investments	One Post Office Square, Boston, MA 02109	800-225-1581
Scudder Funds	166 Federal Street, Boston, MA 02110	800-225-2470
SEI Financial Services	680 East Swedesford Road, No. 7, Wayne, PA 19087	800-342-5734
Seligman Data Corp.	100 Park Avenue, 2nd Floor, New York, NY 10017	800-221-2450
Stephens Inc.	111 Center Street, Little Rock, AK 72201	800-643-9691
Smith Barney	388 Greenwich Street, New York, NY 10105	800-451-2010
Stein Roe Mutual Funds	1 S.Wacker, 32nd Floor, P.O. Box 804058 Chicago, IL 60680-4058	800-338-2550
Sun America	733 3rd Ave., New York, NY 10017	800-858-8850
T. Rowe Price	100 East Pratt Street, Baltimore, MD 21202	800-638-5660
Tele Vista Mutual Funds	P.O. Box 419392, Kansas City, MO 64141-6392	800-348-4782
Twentieth Century Investors	4500 Main Street, Kansas City, MO 64141	800-345-2021
Vanguard Group of Investment Companies	Vanguard Financial Ctr, P.O. Box 2600, Valley Forge, PA 19482	800-662-7447
Van Kampen American Capital	1 Park View Pl., Oak Brook, IL 60181	800-225-2222
Warburg Pincus	466 Lexington Ave, 10th Floor, New York, NY 10017-3147	800-257-5614
Wright Mutual Funds	24 Federal Street, Boston, MA 02110	800-888-9471

Regulators, Rating Agencies and References

Stock and Option Market Regulators

Securities and Exchange Commission, or SEC. Federal regulator of the securities markets, including stock options. For information on broker disciplinary histories, filing complaints and other matters: 800-SEC-0330. Office of Consumer Affairs: 202-942-7040. The SEC also has a computerized "bulletin board" listing enforcement actions, new rules and regulations and other information. It can be accessed via the Internet at "fedworld.gov."

National Association of Securities Dealers, or NASD. Brokerage industry's self-regulatory association. Hot line for a broker's disciplinary history, or for information on how and where to file a complaint against a broker or firm: 800-289-9999. NASD main number: 301-590-6500.

North American Securities Administrators Association. 202-737-0900. Umbrella group for state securities regulators, and Canadian provincial regulators. Will tell you where to seek information from or file a complaint with state regulators in your state.

New York Stock Exchange. Oldest and largest stock exchange. Main number: 212-656-3000. Department of Arbitration for handling customer-broker disputes: 212-656-2772.

American Stock Exchange. Lists stocks of mainly smaller to mid-sized companies, as well as stock options. Main number: 212-306-1000. Investor inquiries: 212-306-1381 or 212-306-1452.

Chicago Board Options Exchange. Largest options exchange. Main number: 312-786-5600. Market regulation department for customer complaints and inquiries: 312-786-7705.

Futures Market Regulators

Commodity Futures Trading Commission. Federal regulator of the futures markets. Main number: 202-418-5000.

National Futures Association. Industry self-regulatory body. Main number, and to file complaints and check broker disciplinary histories: 800-572-9400.

Chicago Board of Trade. Main number: 312-435-3500.

Chicago Mercantile Exchange. Main number: 312-930-1000.

Commodity Exchange. Main number 212-938-2000.

Rating Agencies

These companies evaluate the credit worthiness of corporate and municipal debt issuers and assign a rating to publicity traded bonds or notes, at no charge to the consumer. A table of the commonly used ratings appears at right.

Standard & Poor's. 212-208-1527.

Moody's Investors Service. 800-342-5647.

Fitch Investors Service. 800-75Fitch.

References

These companies, for a fee, provide information on and rate the performance of open- and closed-end mutual funds, as well as many debt and equity issues.

Morningstar Inc. 800-876-5005.

Value Line Inc. 212-907-1500.

POPULARLY USED BOND RATINGS

Explaination of ratings	Moody's	S&P	Fitch
HIGHEST QUALITY	Aaa	AAA	AAA
HIGH QUALITY	Aa	AA	AA
UPPER MEDIUM GRADE	A	A	A
MEDIUM GRADE	Baa	BBB	BBB
SPECULATIVE	Ba	BB	BB
SPECULATIVE, LOW GRADE	B	B	B
POOR TO DEFAULT	Caa	CCC	CCC
HIGHEST SPECULATION	Ca	CC	CC
LOWEST QUALITY	C	C	C
IN DEFAULT OR ARREARS		DDD	DDD
QUESTIONABLE VALUE		DD	DD
LOWEST RATING		D	D

INDEX

401(k), exit rules 17-17

A

Annuity
- defined G-4
- questions to ask about 31-22
- reading the tables 31-25
- two types discussed 31-24
- variable vs. fixed 31-28

Asset Allocation
- as an investment regimen 2-25
- first defined 1-5
- strategic vs. tactical 6-10
- stumbling blocks of tactical 6-10

B

Beta
- defined G-5
- role in investing 11-29

Bonds
- convertible
- first discussed 3-16
- advanced discussion 11-23
- corporate bonds 3-15
- coupon, defined 3-4
- defined G-6
- Eurobonds, discussed 3-16
- floating rate 1-18
- introduced 3-4
- municipals (see also Municipal Bonds) 3-12
- pricing 3-22
- ratings 6-13

- risks associated with 3-7
- staggering maturities 6-13
- stock index bonds 13-21
- term, defined 3-4
- understanding daily quotations 3-24
- using swaps to take a tax loss 5-21
- web sites 33-23
- yield 3-25
- yield curve 3-27
- zero coupon 3-20

Brokers
- electronic services listed 33-26
- tips on how to select 10-19
- how they make their money 10-23

C

Calls (see Puts)

Certificates of Deposit
- place in your portfolio 6-16
- variable rate 7-11

Charting
-A/D table 14-9
- bar 14-27
- full trend 14-11
- full trend example 14-28
- sources for data 14-29

Closed-end Funds
- defined G-7
- locating a discount global equity 4-27
- spotting good values 8-29

Commodity
- 4 best commodity/option combo's 27-8
- bonds, signals for buying 20-6

- defined G-7
- first discussed 22-5

Convertible Securities
- Bonds
    - first discussed 20-10
    - closed-end and convertible funds 11-26
    - when to buy. 20-28
- defined G-7
- LYONs 20-8
- preferred shares, first discussed 20-10
- super convertibles 20-26
- super convertible bond tables 20-27
- table of products and what they convert to. . . . 20-7

Currency Investing
- basic investment vehicles 24-22
- currency futures trading 24-18
- dollar, as a term. 24-4
- dollar's decline 24-10
- historically high yielding strategies 28-21
- picking the ideal
    currency denominated investments 24-11
- understanding the exchange rate tables 24-6
- web sites 33-24

D

Debt Security, defined (see bonds)

Disability Insurance (see Insurance)

Dividends
- discussed. 12-13
- DRIPs 11-27

Dollar Cost Averaging
- first discussed 2-24
- chart comparing DCA vs.
    fixed value investing 8-21

DRIPs 11-27

Economic Cycles
- 3 defensive strategies against inflation 30-28

- discussed. 29-4
- establishing alarms based on 29-21
- graphed 29-5

E

Entrepreneurism
- 10 personality traits. 18-4
- choosing the right business. 18-23
- elements of a business plan. 18-20
- important factors starting from scratch. 18-6
- tax strategy when buying a business. 19-23
- venture capital directories. 18-23

Estate Taxes
- avoiding with trusts
- living. 32-16
- irrevocable 32-21
- calculating your liability. 32-13
- discussed. 32-4
- estate freezing techniques. 32-24

Equities, (see Stocks)

F

Fixed Income Securities, (see bonds)

Foreign Currency Investments
- popular web sites for traders. 33-24
- term deposits. 7-29

Fundamental analysis
- defined G-10
- software available 33-23

Futures
- defined G-11
- discussed. 22-4
- getting started by using mini's 22-27
- how to read their prices. 22-7

- introduction to charting futures 22-22
- leading futures listed 22-6
- options on index futures 22-34
- two contained risk strategies 22-17
- using spreads 22-30

G

Gift Taxes
- annual exclusion 32-10
- defined G-11
- discussed 32-8

H

Health and Medical Insurance (see Insurance)

Historical Data
- housing prices 2-22
- returns of various investment
classes from 1925 to present 1-22

I

Indexes, Stock - most
popular ones defined G-21

Inheritance Tax
- defined G-11
- discussed & states that impose them 32-6

Income stock
- as part of the first tier of your pyramid 6-14
- defined G-12

Insurance
- disability 23-10

- health and medical
    - discussion of various plans 23-4
    - methods for trimming expenses 2-16
- financial ratings of insurance companies 23-8
- life
    - as a tax-advantaged investment 23-24
    - calculating your needs at death 23-25
    - how to evaluate 23-29
    - menu of various types 23-28
- property/residential 23-20
- vehicle 23-15

Interest rates, how determined 7-8

International investing
- best ways to sell foreign stocks 15-25
- comparative recent performances 15-13
- four major benefits to, explored 15-12
- how to identify best markets 15-7
- major exchanges and
examples of their index quotes 15-10
- using index warrant straddles 15-21

Internet
- defined G-12
- discussed as an investment tool 33-6
- sites for
    - bonds 33-23
    - currencies 33-24
    - mutual funds 33-17
    - stocks 33-21
- top sites for investors 33-17

IRA's
- defined G-12
- techniques for diversifying 17-26

L

Leverage
- how it boosts wealth-building 7-4
- use in residential real estate 9-14

LEAPs and BOUNDs 8-22

Loans
- equity loans 7-18
- hierarchy of loans 7-16
- mortgage loan considerations 9-18
- what to know when applying 7-23

Low- income Housing Tax Credits 5-13

M

Margin Buying 27-8
- advanced uses of
- defined G-13
- prevailing conventions 10-27

Marginal Tax Rates, calculating your 5-15

Money Market Funds
- international 6-21
- place in your portfolio 6-16

Mortgage Based Securities and Funds
- finding a mortgage fund 16-21
- first discussed 16-16
- Ginnie Mae Funds G-15
- mortgage securities 16-24
- mutual funds 16-17

Municipal Bonds
- defined G-14
- discussed 7-21
- tests muni's should pass 5-7

Mutual Funds
- analysis software 33-20
- defined G-14
- fitting funds into your asset allocation formula 4-24
- how to read the daily tables 4-7
- load & no-load defined 4-18
- open-end and closed-end funds 4-20
- prospectuses, what to look for 4-13

- seven-step method
  for choosing an equity fund 8-13
- sources of information 8-11
- understanding
  roller-coaster returns 4-22
- various classifications or
  investment directions defined G-14
- web sites 33-17
- withdrawal options during retirement 30-18

N

Net Worth
- calculating your personal 2-6
- defined G-17

O

Options
- 3 best option spreads 27-19
- commodity/option combo's 28-7
- covered call options 21-13
- defined G-18
- first introduced 20-18
- graph of option's time value 21-21
- on futures 21-7
- put options 21-17
- selecting an option fund 21-32
- spreads 21-27

P

Portfolio management, (also see asset allocation)
- six steps to building a diversified 12-11
- software available 33-28
- web sites relating to 33-28

Preferred Shares
- first discussed 11-4
- comparisons of their volatility with bonds . . . 11-18
- defined G-18
- how to value 11-19
- key characteristics
  and advanced discussion 11-10

PRIMEs and SCOREs.................... 11-17

Prospectus
- defined G-19
- what to look for in mutual fund 4-13

Puts, or Put Option Contracts
and Calls, or Call Option Contracts
- buying and selling puts and calls 20-19
- calls defined 26-6
- calls introduced....................... 14-32
- puts defined G-19
- puts introduced 14-32
- recommendations for
  getting started 14-33

R

Real Estate, Commercial
- commercial negotiation strategies 26-23
- national trends....................... 26-4
- recommended rate of retail space per capita. . 26-17
- returns by property type 26-14

Real Estate, Residential
- financials of being a landlord 9-22
- methods for improving
  yields on rental properties 9-25
- negotiating 9-7
- profitable home improvements............. 9-9
- research for knowing when
  to buy investment property 9-28
- three ways to buy investment
  property below market 9-33
- various tax laws concerning 5-27

Real Estate Investment Trusts (REITs)
- first discussed 6-23
- advanced discussion 16-29
- best opportunities 16-31
- defined G-20

Retirement Planning
- calculating how much you'll need 31-5
- sample portfolios during
  retirement years, beginning at 31-18
- yearly use of $1 million nest egg 31-5

Return on Investment, defined.............. G-20

Risk, Investment, 4 types defined............ 1-17

S

Securities, defined G-20

Social Security, future eligibility ages 17-23

SPDRs................................. 8-26

Standard & Poor's 500 Index
- composition of the 500 18-28
- defined G-21
- Index Funds 1-26

Stocks
- 5 step fundamental analysis 11-24
- best day and
  time of year to buy 14-8
- fundamental task in picking quoted 12-7
- historical performance vs. other asset classes
  - graph 1-22
  - select data 12-9
- how to pick growth stocks (summarized) ... 13-17
- investment characteristics................ 11-19
- finding the next hot industry
  and it's winning stocks 11-20
- on-line quote services.................. 33-20
- software for picking (see fundamental
  and technical analysis — software)

- super shares 13-25
- using filters, introduced 14-20
- using technical indicators to pick 14-7
- valuation methods 13-8
- web sites 33-21

Stock Options, (see options)

Straddle
- advanced use of 28-25
- defined G-22
- discussed, how to execute 21-30
- index warrant straddles
  in international investing 15-21

T

Tax-deferred investing 5-9

Tax-free vs. taxable investing 5-4

Technical analysis
- defined G-22
- software available 33-25

Transaction Fees
- how to reduce 10-25
- limiting when liquidating
  or reallocating assets 31-12
- using limit orders 14-22

Treasury Bills, Bonds 3-9

Total Return defined and how to calculate 1-24

Trusts, defined (also see estate taxes) G-23

V

Venture Capital
- defined G-24
- how to begin investing in 25-8
- tax advantages of investing in 25-12

W

Warrants
- defined G-24
- discussed 21-24
- dual exercise 12-30
- expiring warrant gambit 21-26
- index warrant straddles
  in international investing 15-21

World Wide Web (see Internet)
- defined G-24
- discussed as an investment tool 33-7

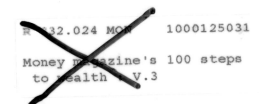